# Dictionary of Tlingit

# Dictionary of Tlingit

*Keri Edwards*

Sealaska Heritage Institute

Juneau, Alaska

ISBN: 978-0-9825786-6-7
Library of Congress Control Number: 2008939134

Sealaska Heritage Institute
One Sealaska Plaza, Suite 301
Juneau, Alaska 99801
907-463-4844
www.sealaskaheritage.org

Printing History: First Edition, December 2009
Printing: CreateSpace, Scotts Valley, CA, U.S.A.
Front cover design: Kathy Dye
Front cover artwork: Robert Hoffmann
Book design and computational lexicography: Sean M. Burke
Copy editing: Suzanne G. Fox, Red Bird Publishing, Inc., Bozeman, MT

# Dedication

To our teacher and friend, Johnny Marks.

# Contents

# Acknowledgements

This project would not have been possible without the consistent hard work of four fluent speakers who served as primary consultants to all Tlingit language information in this dictionary, listed here in alphabetical order:

Anita Lafferty

John Marks

June Pegues

Helen Sarabia

I express the deepest gratitude to these individuals whose integrity, patience, and good humor have made this project possible and a lot of fun. K̲únáx̲ gunalchéesh yeewháan!

Thanks are also due to fluent Tlingit speakers who provided example sentences and/or audio recordings for the dictionary (in addition to those named above), and are listed here in alphabetical order:

Bessie Cooley

David Katzeek

Fred White

Very special thanks is owed to Dr. Jeff Leer who served as a consultant to this project, and whose unsurpassed expertise in the Tlingit language has been critical. Dr. Leer graciously made himself available to answer questions, advise decisions, and provide support regularly throughout the compiling of this resource. It would not have been possible without him, and I cannot thank him enough. It is important to note however, that any inconsistencies or errors in this resource are my own, and should not reflect on Dr. Leer or any of the fluent speakers named above.

Information included in this resource has come from a variety of sources, including a manuscript dictionary by James Crippen as well as the following previously published dictionaries:

Leer, Jeff, Doug Hitch and John Ritter. 2001. *Interior Tlingit Noun Dictionary.* Yukon Native Language Center.

Story, Gillian L. and Constance M. Naish. 1973. *Tlingit Verb Dictionary.* Fairbanks: Alaska Native Language Center.

Twitchell, Lance. 2005. *Lingít Dictionary: Northern Dialect* 1st ed. Troubled Raven Productions.

Special thanks to James Crippen and Lance Twitchell, whose shared electronic files saved the present project much time in the area of data entry.

I thank Jessica Chester for her help in organizing the database by assigning words to appropriate semantic categories and assisting in distributing example sentences to relevant entries.

I thank Dr. Richard Dauenhauer and Nora Marks-Dauenhauer, whose mentorship and generosity have helped put me in a position to do this work, and who have provided all levels of support on this project.

Dr. Jordan Lachler and Sean Burke masterminded the database for this project. I thank them for applying their ingenuity and extreme patience in uniquely designing the program to best suit the Tlingit language.

Keri Edwards
Juneau, Alaska
November 1, 2009

# Introduction


1. Adjectives *(p14)*
2. Adverbs *(p14)*
3. Demonstratives *(p15)*
4. Interjections *(p15)*
5. Nouns *(p15)*
6. Numerals *(p17)*
7. Particles *(p17)*
8. Postpositions *(p17)*
9. Pronouns *(p18)*
10. Quantifiers *(p20)*
11. Relational Nouns *(p21)*
12. Relational Postpositions *(p21)*
13. Verbs *(p21)*
14. References *(p43)*


This is a first edition Tlingit-English dictionary compiled by Keri Edwards for the Sealaska Heritage Institute, made possible by funding from the Administration for Native Americans. This edition was also produced online and in CD-ROM format. A work in progress, this dictionary is incomplete in terms of the number of entries. The goal of this project has been to solve problems such as how to best represent Tlingit verbs, thus laying a foundation for a more comprehensive and accessible noun and verb dictionary for Tlingit. This introduction provides the information necessary to understand and use the print version of the dictionary. In the interest of saving space, the print version contains less detailed information within each word entry than do the CD-ROM and online versions. To access the CD-ROM and online versions of the dictionary, go to the SHI website at www.sealaskaheritage.org.

While some of the information in this dictionary comes directly from pre-existing resources, many important additions have been made here. This dictionary has several unique features. 1) It includes nouns and verbs as well as all the minor word categories such as adjectives, adverbs, and interjections in a single resource. 2) For each verb entry, the conjugation prefix is provided, this previously undocumented information being critical for conjugating the verb. 3) Each verb entry in the print version of the dictionary systematically gives two to three of the following verb forms, depending on the verb type: the imperfective (s/he is (verbing); s/he (verbs)); the perfective (s/he (verbed)); the repetitive imperfective (s/he (verbs) regularly); and the progressive imperfective (s/he is in the process of (verbing)). The vast majority of these verb forms have never before been documented and published. 4) The dictionary gives example sentences for most of the entries, which illustrate the word in context. 5) The online and CD-ROM versions have audio recordings of elders pronouncing individual entries and their example sentences.

The dictionary is organized into three sections: Tlingit-English, English-Tlingit, and Semantic Category. The second section, which is English-Tlingit contains minimal information, giving the English equivalent first in italics, followed by the Tlingit word. The third section of the dictionary is organized by **SEMANTIC CATEGORY**. Examples of semantic categories are “trees,” “time,” “working with wood,” and “manner of movement.” All entries are assigned to at least one semantic category. This method of organizing words is useful for locating all the words in the dictionary related to a particular topic.

The first section of the dictionary (Tlingit-English) contains the most detailed information for each entry, and is the section that this introduction focuses on. If a word is accessed first via the semantic category or English-Tlingit section, it should then be located in the Tingit-English section in order to get as much information about the word as possible. The alphabetical order of the entries in the Tlingit-English section follows the English alphabetical order as closely as possible and is as follows:

A/Aa Ch Ch’ D Dl Dz E/Ee/Ei G Gw G̲ G̲w

H I J K Kw K’ K’w K̲ K̲w K̲’ K̲’w L L’ N

Oo S S’ Sh T T’ Tl Tl’ Ts Ts’ U W

X Xw X’ X’w X̲ X̲w X̲’ X̲’w Y .

All entries in the dictionary, regardless of their word class, contain some information in common. For those entries that have alternate pronunciations, whether they be regional or individual, those pronunciations are listed as **VARIANTS**. If a variant is known to belong to a specific region, it is considered a dialectal variant, and is followed by a capital letter representing the dialect area. The four primary language consultants for this project are from Angoon, Douglas Island, and Hoonah. Of these villages, Angoon differs from the others in the pronunciation of a handful of particular words and certain verb stems. Many verbs stems containing the vowel *ei* for Hoonah and Douglas speakers are pronounced as *ee* for the Angoon speaker. Here are a few examples: *yéi awsinei* (Douglas, Hoonah) / *yéi awsinee* (Angoon) ("s/he fixed it"); *uwax̱éi* (Douglas, Hoonah) / *uwax̱ée* (Angoon) ("s/he stayed overnight"); and *áa akawdlix̱éitl'* (Douglas, Hoonah) / *áa akawdlix̱éetl'* (Angoon) ("s/he is afraid of it"). When a pronunciation particular to Angoon has been discovered, the variant is followed by (An) in the dictionary.

Any dialectal information in this dictionary pertaining to the Interior comes directly from the *Interior Tlingit Noun Dictionary* compiled by Jeff Leer, Doug Hitch, and John Ritter (Yukon Native Language Center, 2001). Entries for which Interior dialect information is known are indicated as follows:

(At) = Atlin, (C) = Carcross, (T) = Teslin

Some common variations in pronunciation pertaining to vowel tone and/or length may or may not be regional and deserve attention. Two examples are *aadéi* ("toward there") and *wéi* ("the") which have the alternate short-vowel pronunciations *aadé* and *wé*. At this point, it is not clear whether these are regional, individual, or contextual variations. While most speakers tend to consistently use one or the other pronunciation, a few speakers alternate between the two. More research is needed to determine the exact nature of this variation. The same goes for the tone on words such as *kei* and *yei* which occur before verbs, as in *áa kei uwawát* ("s/he grew up there"). For some speakers, the tone on *kei* is low and for others it is high, as in *áa kéi uwawát*. For a few speakers, the tone varies depending on the sentence. This phenomenon also requires further research. As for learners of the language, either pronunciation of these pairs is acceptable and correct: *kei/kéi, aadéi/aadé, wéi/wé*. Throughout the dictionary, there is variation as to how these are written. For the most part, vowel length has been standardized to short (*aadé, wé*), but this is not always the case in the example sentences, where you may find some written long. The tone on the preverbs *kei* and *yei* is usually written low, but may also be seen with a high tone in some places. Again, either form is considered correct. Dialect variation across the region is an understudied area of the language and further research in this area would greatly benefit the overall documentation of the language.

For many of the entries, **EXAMPLE SENTENCES** are provided. These are complete sentences containing the word, most of which were provided by fluent elders to illustrate the word in a context. At this time, some entries do not contain example sentences, but many have more than one. In some cases, the example sentences provided in the verb entries will contain verb forms which are different from the standard forms given within the entry. This is ideal in that it provides an additional verb form for the learner. The verb will always be recognizable by its stem, no matter the actual form of the verb.

Other information within the entries is particular to individual word classes. In the Tlingit-English section of the dictionary, each Tlingit word is followed by a label indicating its word class. Examples of word classes are noun, adverb, verb, adjective. Each word class will be discussed in turn below.

## 1. ADJECTIVES

An adjective is defined here as something which describes a noun. This category consists of words and one nominal suffix (a suffix which attaches to a noun). This is a very small category in Tlingit, as many words which are adjectives in other languages are expressed as verbs in Tlingit. Adjectives in Tlingit either occur before the noun: *yées shaawát* ("young woman") or after the noun: *k̲áa tlein* ("big man"). Some adjectives require a different form for modifying a plural noun. For example, consider the pairs *aas tlein* ("big tree") and *aas tlénx'* ("big trees"); and *hít kuwáat'* ("long house") and *hít kudayát'x'* ("long houses"). For adjectives that have a plural form, this form is listed as **PLURAL** in the entry. The nominal suffix included in this category is *-k'*. When attached to a noun, it gives the meaning "little" or "precious", as in *ax̲ dachx̲ánk'* ("my (precious), little grandchild").

## 2. ADVERBS

Cross-linguistically, "adverb" is a very heterogeneous and loosely defined category. For our purposes, an adverb is defined as any word which modifies the manner, direction, or time of a verb. Some examples are: *k'idéin* ("well"); *kei* ("up"); and *aag̲áa* ("then, around, after, for"). Some adverbs which denote direction have variable endings, such as *yan~* ("ashore, onto ground; to rest"). The tilde (~) following the word indicates that the ending is variable. Such adverbs have at least three variants, each taking a different postposition. The punctual *-t* postposition indicates "resting at, coming to, arriving at, or moving about." The pertingent *-x̲* indicates "prolonged contact at" or "repeatedly arriving at." The allative *-de(i)* indicates motion "toward." Note that for some adverbs, the postposition *-t* is absent in the punctual form. For example, consider *yan* ("coming to, arriving on shore") (punctual), *yax̲* ("repeatedly arriving on shore" or "in prolonged contact with shore") (pertingent), and *yánde(i)* ("toward shore") (allative). The alternate forms of variable adverbs are given in their entries. The choice of postposition is associated with the verb tense. For further discussion on this topic, see the section below titled VERB TYPES, where motion verbs are described.

### 3. DEMONSTRATIVES

Demonstratives are words that indicate which entities a speaker refers to. There are five demonstratives in Tlingit: *yá(a)*, "this" (right here); *wé(i)*, "that" (at hand); *hé(i)*, "this/that" (over here); *yú/yóo*, "that" (distant); and *tliyaa*. "farther over, way over." All but the last demonstrative can take a number of postpositions, yielding forms such as *wéit*, "that" (place), *yáadu*, "here is, here are," *héide(i)*, "over this way," and *yóot'át*. "that yonder thing." The demonstrative plus postposition combinations are given in each entry.

### 4. INTERJECTIONS

Interjections are expressions of strong feeling or sudden emotion. *Éits'k'!* ("Yum!") and *Hú!* ("Ouch!") are examples. In the English-Tlingit section of the dictionary, most interjections are listed under the heading <exclamation>.

### 5. NOUNS

Nouns can be broadly defined as words which can be possessed and/or pluralized. Nouns in Tlingit fall into three categories: proper, alienable, and inalienable. Alienable nouns have both possessed and non-possessed forms, inalienable nouns are always possessed, and proper nouns are never possessed. Proper nouns are names of people and places, like *Kaagwaantaan* (clan name) and *Sheet'ká* (Sitka). Alienable nouns include words like *x'úx'* ("book"), *kayáani* ("plant"), or *xóots* ("brown bear"), all of which you can talk about without referring to a possessor. Inalienable nouns include body parts and kinship terms such as *du jín* ("his/her hand"), and *du léelk'w* ("his/her grandparent"). It is obligatory that you use a possessive pronoun with these words in Tlingit. All inalienable nouns are listed in the dictionary either with the third person possessive pronoun *du* ("his/her") or with the non-human possessive pronoun *a* ("its") or both, depending on the noun. Note that these nouns are not alphabetized according to the possessive pronouns, but by the nouns themselves. For example, *du tláa* ("his/her mother") would be found under TL. For some inalienable nouns, especially kinship terms, the *du* exclusively refers to "his" or "her," not both. For example, *du shátx̲* means "her older sister," and cannot refer to a male's sister. This is indicated in the English translation. When possessed, alienable nouns require the possessive suffix *-(y)i/-(w)u*, as in *du x'úx'u* ("his/her book") and *du keidlí* ("his/her dog"), while inalienable nouns do not take the possessive suffix. For an explanation of when to use each of the possessive suffixes, please see *Intermediate Tlingit*, Chapter 1 (Dauenhauer & Dauenhauer, Sealaska Heritage Institute (forthcoming)). The CD-ROM and online versions of the dictionary give the **POSSESSED FORM** of alienable nouns when that information has been elicited.

Tlingit has a complex system of **CLASSIFICATORY VERBS**. These are verbs of position ("sit," "stand," "lie," "extend," etc.) and handling ("carry," "take," "give," etc.) for which importance is placed on the nature of the object being talked about. That is to say, the choice of verb is determined by the shape, size, firmness, and/or contents of the object referred to by the verb. For some of the noun entries in the dictionary, the corresponding classificatory verb is given. This information comes directly from the *Interior Tlingit Noun Dictionary* by Leer, Hitch, and Ritter (2001). The classificatory verb given for a particular noun is the position verb, which denotes that the object lies, stands, sits, extends, or whatever the English equivalent would be for that particular object. For example, consider the noun *x'óow* ("blanket"). In the entry for this noun, *áx̲* is given in the classificatory verb field. This indicates that *áx̲* is the verb that would be used to say the blanket is "lying" (someplace). Here's an example: *Wéi x'óow nadáakw kát áx̱* ("The blanket is lying on the table.") The postposition *-t* found in *kát* ("on") is always used with position verbs. See the section titled VERB TYPES below for more information on position verbs.

For some noun entries referring to flora or fauna, the **BIOLOGICAL CLASSIFICATION** is given only in the CD-ROM and online versions of the dictionary. This information comes directly from James Crippen's noun dictionary (unpublished), the electronic files for which he shared for this project.

For some nouns that can be analyzed into multiple parts, this **ANALYSIS** is provided in the analysis field of the CD-ROM and online versions of the dictionary. In some cases, this information comes from James Crippen's work, with a few minor changes made for the current resource.

## 6. NUMERALS

In Tlingit, one set of numbers is used to count things and animals (*tléix', déix̱, nás'k*, etc.) and another set is used to count people (*tléináx̱, dáx̱náx̱, nás'gináx̱*, etc.). Also included in this word class are words like *tlék'g̱aa* ("one by one") and *tleidahéen* ("once, one time"). Information in the numeral entries is self-explanatory.

## 7. PARTICLES

Particle is a catch-all category that includes sentence connectors such as *tsú* ("also") and *ch'u* ("still, even"); focus words such as *áyá* ("this right here") and *áwé* ("that" (at hand)); tag questions like *kwshé* ("Eh?, I wonder"); and conjunctions like *ḵa* ("and") as well as *ḵu.aa* ("however"). Some particles belong at the beginning of the phrase and others belong at the end of the phrase. The position that a given particle occupies is indicated in the **POSITION** field of that entry in the CD-ROM and online versions of the dictionary.

## 8. POSTPOSITIONS

Every language has a way to describe the direction of a motion. In English, this is done through prepositions such as "to," "around," and "toward," as in "I am walking to the store." In Tlingit, this is done through postpositions, or suffixes, which attach to the end of the noun describing the endpoint or direction of the motion. Examples are *-dáx̱* ("from, out of;

since"), as in: *Ḵéex̱'dáx̱ wé ḵáa* ("the man is from Kake") and *-dé(i)* ("to, toward") as in: *neildé yaa nx̱agút* ("I am walking toward home"). Often, the noun *á* ("it; that place") is used in conversation when the place has already been mentioned and the speaker and listener are already aware of where "there" or "it" is, such as in *Aadé yaa nx̱agút* ("I am going there"). Note that some nouns and relational nouns change their vowel length and tone when a postposition is added, as does the postposition itself. Also, some noun plus postposition combinations have alternate forms. Below is a table that serves to illustrate these changes and give variant forms.

Table 1. Postpositions

| | *á* "it, there" | *a ká* "its surface" | *a yá* "its face" | *a tú* "its inside" |
|---|---|---|---|---|
| *-t* "(arriving) at" | *Át* | *a kát* | *a yát* | *a tóot* |
| *-x̱* "(being) at" | *Áx̱* | *a káx̱* | *a yáx̱* | *a tóox̱* |
| *-x'* "at" | *áx'/ áa* | *a káx'/ a káa* | *a yáax'/ a yáa* | *a tóox'* |
| *-dé(i)* "to" | *aadé(i)* | *a kaadé(i)* | *a yaadé(i)* | *a tóode(i)* |
| *-dáx̱* "from" | *aax̱/ aadáx̱* | *a kaax̱/ a kaadáx̱* | *a yaax̱/ a yaadáx̱* | *a tóodáx̱/ a tóotx̱* |
| *-náx̱* "through" | *anax̱* | *a kanax̱/ a kaanáx̱* | *a yanax̱/ a yáanáx̱* | *a tóonáx̱* |
| *-u* "is/are at" | *áwu* | *a káwu* | *a yáwu* | *a tóowu* |

Note that the variants given in the table above are not regional variants, but rather are associated with position relative to the verb. The general rule for variants in the *-x'* row is that the form without *-x' (áa, a káa, a yáa)* is preferred when the word is directly before the verb, and the form with the *-x' (áx', a káx', a yáax')* is preferred elsewhere. For example, *nadáakw káa yéi yatee* ("it's on the table"). Here, *a káa* is directly before the verb *yéi yatee*, and the form without the *-x'* is preferred. On the other hand, consider *wé nadáakw káx' áwé x̱wsiteen i x'úx'u* ("I saw your book on the table"). In this case, the form with the *-x' (káx')* is used because it does not occur directly before the verb.

## 9. Pronouns

There are four categories of pronouns: subject, object, possessive, and independent. Each pronoun in the dictionary is labeled as belonging to one of these categories. The table below illustrates the pronouns in Tlingit.

Table 2. Pronouns

| | Subject | Object | Possessive | Independent |
|---|---|---|---|---|
| 1. sg. | *x̱a-* | *x̱at/ax̱* | *ax̱* | *x̱át* |
| 1. pl. | *too-/tu-* | *haa* | *haa* | *uháan* |
| 2. sg. | *ee-/i-* | *i-* | *i* | *wa.é* |
| 2. pl. | *yi-* | *yee* | *yee* | *yeewháan* |
| 3. rec. | -- | *a-/ø-* | *a* | -- |
| 3. neu. | *ø-* | *a-/ø-* | *du* | *hú* |
| 3. sal. | -- | *ash* | *ash* | -- |
| 4. hum. | *du-* | *ḵu-* | *ḵaa* | -- |
| 4. nonhum. | -- | *at* | *at* | -- |
| Reflexive | -- | *sh/ø-* | *chush* | -- |
| Reciprocal | -- | *woosh/ø-* | *woosh/wooch* | -- |
| Partitive | -- | *aa* | -- | -- |

Some information given in the table deserves explanation. The first person plural subject prefix *too-/tu-* has a long vowel *too-* when it precedes a consonant-only classifier or a zero (ø) classifier, but a short vowel *tu-* when it precedes a classifier of the shape CV (consonant + vowel). For example, compare *atoost'eix̱* ("we are trolling") with *tulatín* ("we are watching it"). In the first, the classifier is *s-* (no vowel) and the pronominal prefix has a long vowel *too-*. In the second example, the classifier is *la-* (having a vowel) and the pronominal prefix is short *tu-*. The vowel length of the second person singular subject prefix *ee-/i-* follows the same pattern. It is long when following a consonant-only or zero classifier and short when preceding a consonant plus vowel classifier. To illustrate, compare *sh tóo at eeltóow* ("you are studying") and *isa.ée* ("you are cooking it").

The only object pronouns that are written as part of the verb are the second person singular *i-* ("you"), third person *a-* ("him/her") and the fourth person human *ḵu-* ("people"). This is indicated by the hyphen following the pronominal prefix. The reason for writing these particular object pronouns as prefixes to the verbs, rather than independent words, is that they are phonologically bound to the verb. In other words, they either influence or are influenced by neighboring verbal prefixes.

Research for this project suggests that the choice of the first person object pronoun between *x̲at* and *ax̲* ("me") seems to be regional. Whereas the Hoonah and Douglas speakers use *x̲at* as in *x̲at yanéekw* ("I'm sick"), the Angoon speaker uses *ax̲* as in *ax̲ yanéekw.* More speakers would need to be consulted to confirm this analysis. This dictionary regularly uses the object pronoun *x̲at* in example sentences, as it seems to be the more common of the two, but it is important to note that for some speakers, *ax̲* is also acceptable as an object pronoun.

The third person object pronoun "him/her/it" is marked *a-* when 1) the subject is also third person; 2) there is no *-ch* (ergative marker) on the subject; and 3) the object is indefinite. Otherwise, the third person object pronoun is *ø-* (unmarked). To help clarify, compare the examples below. In example (a), the subject (the man) is third person (he, she, or it). The object (a woman– here not overtly stated, but understood) is both third person and indefinite in that no specific person has been referred to. Given these conditions, the third person object pronoun *a-* is present on the verb. In example (b), the subject (a Tsimshian) again is third person, but this time the subject has the ergative marker *-ch* and the object ("my little sister") is definite. Under these conditions, the third person object pronoun *a-* is absent. In example (c) the subject is not third person, but is second person ("you"), and therefore the third person object pronoun *a-* is absent from the verb.

(a)*Aangóondáx̲ aawasháa wé k̲áa.*
"The man married (a woman) from Angoon."

(b) *Ts'ootsxánch uwasháa ax̲ kéek'.*
"A Tsimshian married my little sister."

(c)*I k̲usax̲ánich kwé eewasháa?*
"Did you marry your sweetheart?"

## 10. Quantifiers

There are only two words categorized as quantifiers in the dictionary: *aatlein* ("much, lots of; really") and *ldakát* ("all; every"). *Aatlein* can be used either in front of nouns, in which case it means "much, lots of," or in front of verbs, in which case it means "really." For example, *aatlein kanat'á aawa.ín* means "s/he picked lots of blueberries" and *aatlein wudixwétl* means "s/he was really tired." This can also be used with the word "thank you" to emphasize one's gratitude: *aatlein gunalchéesh* means "many thanks." The word *ldakát* always comes before the noun that it quantifies.

## 11. Relational Nouns

Included in the relational nouns category in this resource are inalienable nouns which refer to parts of objects or to locations relative to an entity. Kinship terms and body parts are listed under the Noun category. Examples of relational nouns are *a ká* ("the (horizontal) surface of it"), *a tú* ("inside it"), and *a daa* ("around it"). There are many common relational noun plus postposition combinations which are given in each relational noun entry only in the CD-ROM and online versions of the dictionary. Here are a few examples: *a kát* ("on it"), *a tóode* ("into it"), and *a daadáx̲* ("from around it").

## 12. Relational Postpositions

A relational postposition is a suffix which attaches either to a possessive pronoun or a relational noun. The three examples above illustrate relational noun plus relational postposition combinations. Examples of a possessive pronoun plus relational postposition are *du yáx̲* ("like him/her") and *haa jeeyís* ("for us").

## 13. Verbs

While English verbs are listed in dictionaries in the infinitive form (meaning they are unmarked for tense and person) such as "read," "play," "speak," Tlingit verbs do not have an infinitive form, but are always marked for tense and person. This fact presents a challenge for choosing a citation form for Tlingit verbs. There are basically two options. The first is to use an actual verb form which is conjugated for person and tense, such as "I eat it," "he ate it," or "Eat it!" The second option is to use the verb theme which represents the skeleton of the verb with hyphens between the thematic prefixes, classifier, and stem, such as in *ya-x̲aa* ("eat"), this being the method used in the *Tlingit Verb Dictionary* (Naish and Story 1973).

The verbs in the print version of this dictionary are presented in up to three actual forms, conjugated for person and tense. The forms given in this dictionary are the imperfective (present tense), perfective (past tense), and repetitive imperfective (indicates a regularly occurring situation). Since motion and event verbs do not have basic imperfective forms, the progressive imperfective (indicates a situation in progress) is given in place of the imperfective for those. In the event that one of these forms does not occur for a given verb, (---) is indicated in the corresponding field. In a few cases, this may indicate that the form was not yet collected. All verbs are given in the third person. The third person refers to "he, she, or it," written as "he/she/it." In the event that a verb can only have a human subject, we write "s/he" as shorthand for "he or she," and omit "it." Verbs in the dictionary are alphabetized by verb stem and are listed under the verb stem (also called family) heading.

Let's look at some sample verb entries, after which each element will be discussed in turn. Verb entries begin with two to three actual verb forms on the first line. In the first example below, the given verb forms are the imperfective: *yak'éi*, perfective: *wook'éi*, and repetitive imperfective: *kei k'éich*. The second line gives the English translation of the verb forms. On the third line, the Leer-Edwards theme, described in detail below, is given, followed by the English translation of the theme. Note the importance of reading the theme translation in order to get the full meaning of the verb. A verb can have multiple meanings, however only one of those meanings is given as a translation below each verb form in order to save space. All the known possible meanings of the verb are given in the translation of the verb theme. For example, see the verb entry given below. The translation of the form *yak'éi* is given as "he/she/it is good". Looking at the translation of the theme however, we see that the verb can also mean "he/she/it is fine" and "he/she/it is pretty". Finally, one or two example sentences are given which show the verb in context. Most, but not all verbs have example sentences. Often times, the verbs in the example sentences are in a form other than the select few given on the first line of the verb entry. This provides students with exposure to additional verb forms, and the verb will always be recognizable by its stem.

K'EI verb root

yak'éi | wook'éi | kei k'éich
*he/she/it is good* | *he/she/it was good* | *it gets good (regularly)*
O-ø-k'éi (ga state) *For O to be good, fine, pretty.*
Yak'éi aadéi has al'eix̲ yé K̲éix̲' K̲wáan!
*How well the Kake people dance!*

The next example is a motion verb. Because motion verbs do not have imperfective forms, the first form given is the progressive imperfective, as in *aadé yaa nagút* below. Like the other verbs, this is followed by the perfective: *át uwagút* and the repetitive imperfective *áx̲ goot.*

GOOT[1] verb root

aadé yaa nagút | át uwagút | áx̲ goot
*S/he is walking there.* | *S/he arrived there (by foot).* | *S/he walks there (regularly).*
N-t~ S-ø-goot~ (ø motion) *For (singular) S to arrive at N (walking).*
Tle ash x̲ándei yaa nagúdi teen áwé yéi adaayak̲á, "Ax̲ een na.á". *As soon as he came by her, he said to her, "Come with me."*

TENSE/ASPECT

The conjugated verb forms included in the dictionary along with the example sentences will serve to clarify the necessarily abstract representations of the verbs in the verb theme. The verb forms included in the print version deserve some explanation. For more verb forms, see the CD-ROM and online versions of the dictionary, which include up to eight different conjugated forms for each verb. Along with a definition of terminology, I give a very minimal description of the Tlingit morphology associated with each form. For more information on this subject, see *The Schetic Categories of the Tlingit Verb* (Leer, 1991).

*Perfective*

The perfective form is the first form listed in a verb entry. It is roughly equivalent to the English past tense, and refers to a situation which is complete. It roughly translates as "s/he did it" or "it happened". Example perfective forms are *aawax̲áa* "s/he ate it" and *woog̲aax̲* "s/he cried". The perfective form is the most salient form found in Tlingit texts, and presumably the most frequently used form in conversation. The perfective form is included in all entries which have a perfective form. Many state verbs do not have perfective forms. For example, the state verb *tuli.aan* "s/he is kind" does not have a perfective form, as indicated by (---) in the first slot in this entry. The perfective form is characterized by the prefix *wu-,* which often contracts with neighboring prefixes, thus changing its shape.

### *Imperfective*

The imperfective form, if it exists for a given verb, occupies the second slot in the verb entries. The imperfective is roughly equivalent to the English present tense. It can usually give either of the following readings: "s/he does it" and "s/he is doing it," or "it happens" and "it is happening" and basically refers to an incomplete situation. Here is an example: *ax̲á* ("s/he is eating it"). Note that motion and event verbs do not have an imperfective form, and therefore this form is not included in those entries, but is replaced by the progressive imperfective when that form is known. See more on event and motion verbs below.

### *Progressive imperfective*

The progressive imperfective is the second choice for the second slot in a verb entry. In the event that the imperfective does not occur (motion and event verbs), then the progressive imperfective is given in that slot. If neither form has been documented for a given verb, then (---) occupies that slot. The progressive imperfective form translates as "s/he is in the process of doing it" or "it is happening (presently)." For the most part, fluent speakers don't generally use the progressive imperfective form for act and state verbs, as the present tense meaning is given by the imperfective form. Motion verbs, however, regularly use the progressive imperfective to describe a present and continuous situation. This motion verb serves as a good example: *yaa nagút* ("s/he is walking along"). The progressive imperfective requires three things. The first is a preverb (*yaa* for *ø-* and *na-* conjugation verbs, *kei* or *yaa* for *ga-* conjugation verbs, and *yei* for *g̲a-* conjugation verbs, with a few exceptions). The second requirement is the *na-* conjugation prefix (regardless of the verb's regular conjugation prefix). The third applies only to verbs ending in vowels (called open roots), and is the *-n* stem (addition of *-n* to the end of the verb and usually a long vowel in the stem). The *-n* stem can be illustrated through the verb *awsikóo* ("s/he knows it"), which in the progressive imperfective is *yaa anaskwéin* ("s/he's beginning to learn it"). Note also the vowel quality change from *oo* to *ei* in the stem. This change occurs for all verbs ending in *-oo* as well as *-aa*. For motion verbs requiring the variable *-t~* postposition (described in the postposition section), this postposition will always become *-dé(i)* in the progressive imperfective. For example, note the *-t* postposition in this perfective motion verb: *át k̲uwaháa* ("it's time for it"), and the *-dé* postposition in the progressive imperfective form: *aadé yaa k̲unahéin* ("it's getting to be time for it"). Following is an example of a verb for each conjugation prefix, given in the perfective and progressive imperfective forms:

| Conj: | Perfective: | Progressive imperfective: |
|---|---|---|
| *ø-* | *át has uwa.át*<br>"They walked there." | *aadé yaa has na.át*<br>"They're walking along there." |
| *na-* | *aag̲áa k̲oowashee*<br>"S/he searched for it." | *aag̲áa yaa k̲unashéen*<br>"S/he's going along searching for it." |
| *ga-* | *wudihaan*<br>"S/he stood up." | *kei ndahán*<br>"S/he's (in the process of) standing up." |
| *g̲a-* | *awdigaan*<br>"It's sunny." | *yei andagán*<br>"It's getting sunny." |

### *Repetitive Imperfective*

The repetitive imperfective form is the third form given in a verb entry, and roughly translates as "s/he does it regularly" or "it happens regularly." If a given verb has no repetitive imperfective form or it is not known, then (---) is given in the final slot for that entry. The repetitive imperfective form of a verb depends on the conjugation category that the verb belongs to. Depending on the conjugation prefix, some repetitive imperfective forms require a preverb (a word which occurs to the left of the verb), some specify which form of the classifier is to be used, and all require a suffix which attaches to the end of the verb. Table 3 illustrates the relationship between the conjugation prefix (CP) and the repetitive imperfective form of the verb. This table applies to non-motion verbs only. The situation for motion verbs is more complex and will be described further under VERB TYPES. For a complete description of repetitive imperfective forms for motion verbs, see Leer (1991).

Table 3. Conjugation Prefixes and Repetitive Imperfective Forms for Non-motion Verbs

| CP | Preverb | Classifier | Suffix | Example |
|---|---|---|---|---|
| ø | --- | *not specified* | *-x̱* | *as.éex̱* "he cooks it (regularly)" |
| na | *yoo* | *+I* | *-k* | *yoo ayal'únk* "he hunts it (regularly)" |
| ga | *kei* | *not specified* | *-ch* | *kei latseench* "he gets strong (regularly)" |
| g̱a | *yei* | *not specified* | *-ch* | *yei adagánch* "it gets sunny (regularly)" |

### Leer-Edwards Theme

A verb theme is an abstract representation of a verb which serves to illustrate all of its component parts. The Leer-Edwards theme was developed by Dr. Jeff Leer and adapted by Edwards for use in this dictionary. The Leer-Edwards theme presents all of the minimally required elements for each particular verb, and provides much of the information one needs to conjugate the verb. As stated elsewhere, it is important to read the theme translation in order to get the full meaning of the verb. A verb can have multiple meanings, however only one of those meanings is translated below each given verb form in order to save space. All the known possible meanings of the verb are given in the translation of the verb theme. Here is an example of a Leer-Edwards theme, using the verb *aadé aawatee* ("s/he carried it there"):

P-dé O-S-ø-tee~ (na motion)
"for S to carry, take O (general, often compact object) to P"

At first, the abstract and formulaic appearance of a verb theme can be alarming, but with a little practice, it can become a very useful tool for understanding the structure of a verb and for conjugating a verb. Each element of the Leer-Edwards theme will be described in turn, beginning with the *S* (subject).

#### *S (subject)*

Let's begin by looking at the theme for the verb *g̱áax̱* ("s/he is crying"):

S-ø-ga̱ax̱~
for (singluar) S to cry

Capital *S* represents the subject of the verb. The *S* in the theme indicates where the subject prefix goes. The subject prefixes in Tlingit are: *x̱a-* 'I', *i-/ee-* ("you"), *tu-/too-* 'we', *yi-/yee-* ("you" (plural)), or *du-* ("someone"). Note that the subject prefix for he/she/it is *ø-* (unmarked). For third person plural, use *has* ("they"), which goes to the left of the object prefix. Replacing the *S* in the theme above with actual subject prefixes renders these forms:

| | |
|---|---|
| *x̱agá̱ax̱* | "I am crying" |
| *eegá̱ax̱* | "you are crying" |
| *gá̱ax̱* | "s/he is crying" |

Because this verb only applies to a singular subject, we can't use the plural subject prefixes with it. The fact that this verb only has a subject (and no object) makes it an intransitive verb. Note the *S* in the English translation of the theme above. The *S* in the English translation "for S to cry" corresponds to the *S* in the theme. This helps the user keep track of who is doing what to whom when moving between the two languages.

***O (object)***
To discuss the object, let's look at the theme for the familiar verb *yak'éi* ("he/she/it is fine"):

O-ø-k'éi
"for O to be good, fine, pretty"

Capital *O* represents the object of the verb. This is where the object prefix or pronoun goes. Tlingit object prefixes are: *i-* ("you"), *a-/ø-* ("he/she/it"), and *ḵu-* ("someone; people"). A very important thing to note is that the third person object prefix *a-* is only present when 1) there is also a subject, 2) the subject is third person, 3) the subject does not have the *-ch* (ergative) suffix, and 4) the object is indefinite. Otherwise it is unmarked. All other object pronouns in Tlingit are not prefixes, but are independent pronouns. They are: *x̱at* ("me"), *yee* ("you" (plural)), *haa* ("us") and *has* ("them"). These occupy the same position as the object prefixes, but are written as a separate word from the verb. Note that not all Tlingit verbs require a subject. Verbs which only require an object pronoun are called "objective" verbs, and have an *O*, but no *S* in the theme. This indicates that you must use an object pronoun with this verb, not a subject prefix. For example, let's go back to the verb *yak'éi* ("he/she/it is fine"). This is an objective verb which requires the object pronoun, not a subject pronoun, as indicated in the theme above. If we were to replace the *O* in the theme with actual object pronouns, these are the forms we would get:

| | |
|---|---|
| *x̱at yak'éi* | "I am fine" |
| *iyak'éi* | "you are fine" |
| *yak'éi* | "he/she/it is fine" |
| *haa yak'éi* | "we are fine" |
| *yee yak'éi* | "you all are fine" |
| *has yak'éi* | "they are fine" |
| *ḵuyak'éi* | "people are fine" (also means "the weather is fine") |

A couple of important reminders to note in these forms are that the second person object prefix *i-* ("you") and the fourth person object prefix *ḵu-* ("people") are attached to the verb because they acts as prefixes, while all other object pronouns given are independent and are written separately from the verb. Also, the third person object prefix here is *ø-* (unmarked) for ("he/she/it") because there is no subject prefix present.

Now, let's look at a transitive verb. A transitive verb is one with both a subject *S* and an object *O*. Consider the theme for the verb *altín* ("s/he is watching him/her/it").

**O**-**S**-l-teen~
"for S to look at, gaze at, watch O"; "for S to watch, take care of, mind, look after O"

Replacing the *O* and *S* in the theme above with actual object and subject pronouns gives us these forms:

| | |
|---|---|
| *ix̱latín* | "I'm watching you" |
| *x̱alatín* | "I'm watching him/her/it" |
| *x̱at ilatín* | "you're watching me" |
| *ilatín* | "you're watching him/her/it" |
| *x̱at latín* | "he/she/it is watching me" |
| *ilatín* | "he/she/it is watching you" |

*altín* “he/she/it is watching him/her/it”
*itulatín* “we are watching you”
*has yilatín* “you (plural) are watching them”

The first thing to note about the forms above is that the third person object prefix *a-* is present in *altín* (“he/she/it is watching him/her/it”). This is because the verb has a subject AND that subject is third person *ø-* (“he/she/it”). The third person object prefix *a-* is not present in any other forms. Note also that *ilatín* can mean both “you’re watching him/her/it” and “he/she/it is watching you,” and must be determined by context. Remember that the third person subject prefix is always *ø-* (unmarked) and the third person object prefix is unmarked unless the subject is also third person. This is why these two forms are identical. In *ilatín* (“you’re watching him/her/it”), the *i-* is the second person subject prefix, and in *ilatín* (“he/she/it is watching you”), the *i-* is the second person object prefix.

### *Classifier*

Let’s begin the discussion on classifiers by looking at the theme for the verb *yat’éex’* (“it is difficult”):

ø-t’éex’
“for something to be hard (abstract), difficult”

The classifier is always located directly to the left of the stem. The classifier in the theme above is *ø-* and the stem is *-t’éex’*. Every Tlingit verb is minimally comprised of a stem and a classifier. There are sixteen classifiers in Tlingit, and they can be grouped into four sets of four, as exemplified in Table 4.

Table 4. Classifiers

| | +I | -I | +I | -I | +I | -I | +I | -I |
|---|---|---|---|---|---|---|---|---|
| -D | *si-* | *sa-* | *shi-* | *sha-* | *li-* | *la-* | *ya-* | *Ø-* |
| +D | *dzi-* | *s-* | *ji-* | *sh-* | *dli-* | *l-* | *di-* | *da-* |

The classifiers are first organized into four groups by their unifying consonant, which is most easily seen in the top row. From left to right, we have *s-, sh-, l-,* and *ø-* (no consonant). Within each group of four, the classifiers are then organized according to vowel, the left column of each group containing *i-*, the right column not containing *i-*. Note the apparent exception in the final group, which contains *ya-* in the +I column. This is in fact consistent in that *i* and *y* are phonologically very similar, as you will notice when pronouncing them in succession. The odd feature here is the *a-* following the *y*, but the *ya-* classifier indeed patterns with the other +I classifiers throughout the grammar. The other organizing feature is the presence of *d-* in many of the forms listed in the bottom row. We refer to this feature as the D component, those in the bottom row having the D component, those in the top row lacking it.

Every Tlingit verb has a classifier from one of the groups above. The actual form of the classifier (+I, -I, +D, -D) changes according to verb tense/aspect, as well as other factors. For example, affirmative perfective forms require the +I form of the classifier: *aw**si**.ée* ("s/he cooked it"), while future forms require the -I form of the classifier: *agu**x̲sa**.ée* ("s/he will cook it").

Since the actual form of a classifier changes according to the grammar, the Leer-Edwards theme always presents the classifier of a particular verb simply as the representative consonant of its group: *s-, sh-, l-,* or *ø-*(no consonant). The classifier is always given in a lowercase letter, thus the lowercase classifier *s-* is not to be confused with the subject prefix *S-*, which is given as a capital letter, as in the theme for: *awsi.ée* ("s/he cooked it"):

O-**S**-**s**-.ee~
"for S to cook O"

To summarize what we've discussed so far, given the above theme, we know that this verb uses the *s-* group of classifiers *(si-, sa-, dzi-, s-)*. Most verb forms (except for the imperfective) require a specific form of each classifier group (either +I or -I). This means that a learner can predict which member of a classifier group will be used in a given verb form for a given verb. For example, if we know that all negative perfective forms require the -I form of the classifier, and we know that the verb "cook" uses the *s-* group of classifiers, we can predict that the negative perfective form will have the *sa-* classifier, as in *tlél x̲wasa.í* ("I didn't cook it").

Regarding the ø- classifier group, the reason for including the ø- in the theme is that its alternate form *ya-* will appear in certain verb tense/aspects. By representing the classifier in the theme, this alerts the student to watch for *ya-* which sometimes contracts with a preceding syllable and is only visible as *a-*. For more information on contractions in Tlingit as well as other phonological processes, see the appendix in *Lingít X̲'éináx̲ Sá! Say It in Tlingit: A Tlingit Phrase Book* (Dauenhauer & Dauenhauer 2002; see also Leer 1991).

Verbs which use the +D forms of a classifier group exclusively are given in the Leer-Edwards theme as *d-* plus the consonant which represents the group. For example, the verb *k̲oowdzitee* ("he/she/it was born") always requires the D component of the *s-* classifier group (meaning that the classifier will either be *dz-* or *s-* throughout the paradigm), and this is represented in the theme accordingly, with *d-s-* directly before the verb stem:

O-k̲u-**d-s**-tee~
"for O to be, be in existence, live; for O to be born"

Note that when the D component of the *ø-* group is required by a verb, just the *d-* is given in the theme, and the *ø-* is omitted for simplicity. For example, see the theme for *awdigaan* ("it's sunny"):

a-**d**-gaan~
"for the sun to shine"

Given the *d-* in the theme above, we know that the classifier belongs to the *ø-* group and will always be either *di-* or *da-* in conjugated forms. For more detailed information on the use of the D component and the +I/-I feature of classifiers, see Leer (1991).

***Verb Stem and Variation***
The stem is the final element of the Tlingit verb. Verbs in the dictionary are alphabetized according to the stem. The stem of the verb *yasátk* ("he/she/it is fast") is *-sátk,* given in bold in the theme below.

O-ø-**sátk**
"for O to be fast (at doing things)"

This verb will be found under the letter S in the dictionary, alphabetized according to its stem. All verb stems are either variable or invariable. An invariable stem means that the tone and length of the vowel in the stem never changes. For example, the stem of the verb *lidzée* ("it's difficult") is *-dzée.* This verb always has a long, high vowel *(ée)* in the stem, no matter the verb tense: *wulidzée* ("it was difficult"), *kei gux̲ladzée* ("it will be difficult"), *tlél uldzée* ("it's not difficult"), and so on. Invariable stems require no special notation in the theme since they never change.

A variable stem is one in which the length and/or tone of the vowel in the stem changes with the verb tense/aspect. For example, note the changes in the stem vowel length and tone in the following forms: *aawax̲áa* ("he/she/it ate it"), *tlél awux̲á* ("he/she/it didn't eat it"), and *ag̲ax̲aa* ("let him/her/it eat it"). The stem changes from *-x̲áa* to *-x̲á* to *-x̲aa,* depending on the verb tense/aspect. A variable stem is indicated in the Leer-Edwards theme by a tilde (~) following the stem. Note the tilde (~) following the stem in the theme for *aawax̲áa.*

O-S-ø-**x̲aa~**
"for S to eat O"

Variable stems can have two variants or three variants. The capital letter "A" will be used here to represent any vowel (a, e, i, o, u). Two-variant stems have either of the following stem length and tone patterns: Á (short, high) or ÁA (long, high). Three-variant stems have any of the following stem length and tone patterns: Á (short, high), ÁA (long, high), or AA (long low). For two-variant stems, the form given in the theme is the long high form: ÁA. For three-variant stems, the form given in the theme is the long low form: AA. This way, the user will know how many variants a stem has by looking at the form given in the theme.

| | | | |
|---|---|---|---|
| Two variant stems: | Á | ÁA (form given in theme) | |
| Three variant stems: | Á | ÁA | AA (form given in theme) |

Here are some examples to clarify. The verb *aawasháat* ("s/he caught it") has a two-variant stem. The stem is always either *-sháat* or *-shát,* depending on the verb tense/aspect. The stem has a long, high vowel in the perfective form: *aawa**sháat*** ("s/he caught it") and in the future form: *kei akg̲wa**sháat*** ("s/he will catch it"), but a short high stem in the perfective habitual form: *aga**shátch*** ("s/he catches it (every time)") and in the prohibitive form: *Líl kei **ishát**jik̲!* ("Don't catch it!"). Since this is a two-variant stem, the basic stem is considered the one with a long, high vowel, *-sháat* and is given as such in the Leer-Edwards theme.

O-S-ø-**sháat~**
"for S to catch O; for S to grab, take hold of, snatch O; for S to arrest O; for S to trap O"

The tilde (~) following the stem tells the user that the stem is variable. The long, high vowel in the stem tells the user that this is a two-variant stem, always being either long and high (*-sháat*) or short and high (*-shát*). This verb never has a long, low vowel in the stem.

An example of a verb with a three-variant stem is *has woo.**aat*** ("they walked"). This verb stem has a long, low vowel in the perfective form (just given), a long high vowel in the future form: *has guga.**áat*** ("they will walk"), and a short high vowel in the perfective habitual form: *has na.**átch*** ("they walk (every time)"). The basic stem is considered that with the long, low vowel, *-.aat*, and is indicated as such in the theme:
S-ø-**.aat~**
"for (plural) S to walk, go (by walking or as a general term)"

By noting the long, low vowel in the stem followed by the tilde (~) in the theme, the user knows that this is a three-variant stem.

***P- (Postpositional Object) Plus Postposition***
All motion verbs in Tlingit require a postpositional phrase. A postpositional phrase consists of a postpositional object (usually a noun) and a postposition, and generally conveys information pertaining to the location or direction of motion described by the verb. For example, let's look at the theme for the verb *át uwagút* ("s/he arrived there").

**P-t~** S-ø-goot~
"for S to arrive at P, go to P (by walking or as general term)"

This verb cannot occur without a postpositional phrase such as *át* ("there"). The presence of the *P-t~* in the theme indicates that this is an absolutely necessary part of the verb. This particular postpositional phrase is comprised of two elements: a postpositional object (noun) *á-* ("it, there"), plus a postposition *-t~* ("at, to"). In the verb theme, the postpositional object is always represented by capital *P*. The postposition in the theme is fixed, since the particular postposition one uses changes the meaning of the verb, and sometimes the conjugation prefix, a topic we have yet to discuss. The *P* can be replaced with any noun that makes sense for the particular verb, but the postposition must match the one indicated in the theme to retain the basic meaning of the verb. Note that in the dictionary, the *P* is always replaced by the indefinite noun *á* ("it, there") in the given verb forms. This *á* can be replaced with any desired noun. To illustrate, let's replace the *P* in the theme above with a few different nouns while retaining the postposition *-t* throughout. In the first example below, we have replaced the *P* with *hoon daakahídi* ("store"), in the second example, we have *du x̲án* ("by him/her"), and in the third we have *k̲aa x̲'aká* ("meeting"), all with the postposition *-t.*

| | |
|---|---|
| *hoon daakahídit uwagút* | "s/he arrived at the store" |
| *du x̲ánt uwagút* | "s/he came to him/her" |
| *k̲aa x̲'akát uwagút* | "s/he arrived at the meeting" |

Note the tilde (~) following the postposition *-t~* in the theme above. As with its use with the variable verb stems, the tilde here represents variation. This particular postposition *-t~* ("at, to") has alternate forms that are used with different verb tense/aspects. The alternate forms are *-dé(i)* and *-x̲*. The form used in the perfective, imperative, and perfective habitual is *-t*; the form used in the future and progressive imperfective is *-dé(i)*; and the form used in the repetitive imperfective is *-x̲*, to name a few. These forms are illustrated below, all using the same verb.

***-t***

| | | |
|---|---|---|
| Perfective: | *át uwagút* | "s/he arrived there" |
| Imperative: | *Át gú!* | "Go there!" |
| Perfective Habitual: | *át ugootch* | "s/he goes there (every time)" |

***-dé(i)***

| | | |
|---|---|---|
| Progress. Imperfective: | *aadé yaa nagút* | "s/he is going there" |
| Future: | *aadé kg̲wagóot* | "s/he will go there" |

***-x̲***

| | | |
|---|---|---|
| Repetitive Imperfective: | *áx̲ goot* | "s/he goes there (regularly)" |

Most postpositions are invariable, and are therefore given in the theme without the tilde, as in the theme for *aadáx̱ woogoot* ("s/he left there"):

**P-dáx̱** S-ø-goot~
"for (singular) S to walk, go (by walking or as general term) away from P"

Here are some examples using this verb that illustrate that the postposition *-dáx̱* ("away from") does not change with verb tense/aspect:

| | |
|---|---|
| *du hídidáx̱ woogoot* | "s/he left his/her house" (perfective) |
| *aasgutúdáx̱ yaa nagút* | "s/he is walking out of the woods" (progressive) |
| *sgoondáx̱ yoo yagútk* | "s/he leaves school (regularly)" (repetitive) |

***N (Nominal object)***

Some verbs must be accompanied by a noun phrase to give their complete meaning. An example is *du tuwóo sigóo* ("s/he is happy"). The noun phrase here is *du tuwóo* ("his/her mind, feelings") and the verb is *sigóo* ("happy"). The verb is not complete without the noun phrase. The theme for this verb follows:

N toowú s-góo
"for N to be happy, glad"

The *N* in the theme represents the nominal object, which basically means that *N* is the possessor of the noun that follows. Together, the possessor *N* and the possessed noun (*toowú*) form the noun phrase which is required by the verb. *N* will always be replaced by either a possessive pronoun, a person's name, or a noun in actual spoken forms, the options for replacing *N* being restricted only by the meaning of the verb. The possessive pronouns in Tlingit are *ax̱* ("my"), *i* ("your"), *du* ("his/her"), *a* ("its"), *haa* ("our"), *yee* ("your (plural)"), and *has du* ("their"). If we replace the *N* in the theme above with actual possessive pronouns, we get these forms:

| | |
|---|---|
| *ax̱ toowú sigóo* | "I'm happy" |
| *yee toowú sigóo* | "you all are happy" |
| *has du toowú sigóo* | "they are happy" |

Sometimes noun phrases with postpositions are required by a verb. An example is *du jeet aawatée* ("s/he gave it to him/her"):

N jeet~ O-S-ø-tee~
"for S to give, take, hand O (general, esp. abstract objects) to N"

Here we have a possessor *N* followed by the noun *jee-* ("hand") with the variable postposition *-t~* ("at, to"). Here, the *N* can be replaced by a possessive pronoun or a person's name. For example:

| | |
|---|---|
| *A<u>x</u> jeet tí!* | "Give it to me!" |
| *Mary jeet aawatée* | "s/he gave it to Mary" |
| *i jeedé k<u>g</u>watée* | "s/he will give it to you" |

Here is another example of a verb that requires a noun phrase: *a yá<u>x</u> yatee* ("he/she/it is like it"), and its theme:

N yá<u>x</u> O-ø-tee~
"for O to be like, similar to N"

Here, we can replace *N* with a pronoun, a person's name, or a noun. Here are some examples.

| | |
|---|---|
| *du yá<u>x</u> yatee* | "he/she/it is like him/her" |
| *John yá<u>x</u> yatee* | "he/she/it is like John" |
| *keitl yá<u>x</u> yatee* | "he/she/it is like a dog" |

### *Adverbial Phrases*

Some verb themes in the dictionary contain *(yéi)* to the left of the verb. This indicates that an adverbial phrase is required by the verb, but it does not necessarily have to be *yéi* ("thus, so"). *Yéi* is simply there as a cover adverbial phrase to show that the verb requires one. Here is an example: *yéi yatee* ("he/she/it is that way"). The theme for this verb is:

(yéi) O-ø-tee~
"for O to be (that way)"

The definition of an adverbial phrase, for our purposes here, is any phrase that describes the time, location, number or manner of the verb. The options for replacing *yéi* in the theme above are relatively unlimited. Here are a few examples.

| | |
|---|---|
| *daax'oon yatee* | "there are four" |
| *Wáa sá iyatee?* | "How are you?" |
| *adawóotl' yatee* | "s/he is in trouble; having a hard time" |

Verbs such as this one rely on the adverbial phrase to provide the full meaning of the phrase. *Yatee* by itself just means "is", and requires the adverb to convey the rest of the meaning. Another example is *yéi yaawa<u>k</u>aa* "s/he said that". Here, *yéi* can be replaced with an adverb such as *wáa sá* as in *wáa sá yaawa<u>k</u>aa?* ("what did s/he say?"). The important thing to remember is that when a verb theme contains *(yéi)*, it means that an adverb must accompany that verb, and that *yéi* can be replaced by a different adverb, depending on the desired meaning. For verb themes with *yéi* (no parentheses), the *yéi* is always required and cannot be replaced.

***Thematic Prefixes***

Some verbs have thematic prefixes. The most common thematic prefixes are *ka-* ("surface"); *ya-* ("face"); *ji-* ("hand"); *tu-* ("inside, mind"); *<u>x</u>'a-* ("mouth"); and *<u>k</u>u-* ("weather"). The thematic prefixes occur to the left of the subject prefix *S* and to the right of the object pronoun *O*. While it is sometimes clear how the thematic prefixes relate semantically to the verb theme to which they belong, this is not always the case. An example is the verb *yéi jiné* ("s/he is working"). The theme is:

yéi **ji**-S-ø-nei~
"for S to work; for S to do"

Here it is clear that the meaning of the theme "work" relates to the thematic prefix *ji-* ("hand"). An example of a theme containing a thematic prefix that is not so clearly related to the meaning of the verb is that of the verb *akawlineek* ("s/he told the story of it"), which contains the *ka-* ("surface") prefix:

O-**ka**-S-l-neek
"for S to tell the story of O; for S to talk into O"

The thematic prefix *<u>k</u>u-* is used with verbs which describe the weather. Here is an example: *<u>k</u>uyak'éi* ("the weather is good"). Note that this form is just like *yak'éi* ("he/she/it is good"), plus the thematic prefix *<u>k</u>u-* which refers specifically to the weather. The theme for this verb is:

k̲u-ø-k'ei~
"for the weather to be good"

### *Conjugation Prefix*

Each verb belongs to one of four conjugation categories, the choices being *(ø-, na-, ga-, g̲a-)*. The exception to this statement are motion verbs, which can belong to multiple conjugation categories and are described in further detail under the section titled VERB TYPES. Knowing the conjugation prefix associated with a given verb is critical for conjugating the verb for certain tense/mode/aspects. For example, the conjugation prefix surfaces in the imperative (command) form of the verb, but not in the imperfective form of the verb. Consider the entry *al'eix̲* ("s/he is dancing"), which belongs to the *(na-)* conjugation category, as seen in the imperative form:

| | | |
|---|---|---|
| Imperative: | *Anal'eix̲!* | "Dance!" |
| Imperfective: | *al'eix̲* | "s/he dances" |

The imperative form of the verb reveals which conjugation category a verb belongs to. Compare the above example to the verb *yak'éi* ("he/she/it is good"), which belongs to the *(ga-)* conjugation category:

| | | |
|---|---|---|
| Imperative: | *Igak'éi!* | "Be good!" |
| Imperfective: | *yak'éi* | "he/she/it is good" |

Other verb forms requiring the conjugation prefix include the hortative (let him/her verb), perfective habitual (s/he verbs every time), and the potential decessive (s/he would have verbed). To summarize, it is impossible to conjugate a verb for these forms without knowing which conjugation category it belongs to. In the Leer-Edwards theme, the conjugation prefix is given in parentheses directly after the stem. Note that the information in parentheses has been omitted up until this point for the sake of simplicity. The complete theme for the verbs mentioned above *al'eix̲* ("s/he is dancing") and *yak'éi* ("he/she/it is good") are:

a-S-ø-l'eix̲~ (na act)
"for S to dance"

O-ø-k'éi (ga state)
"for O to be good, fine, pretty"

The conjugation prefix (and the verb type, which we will examine next) are given in the theme in parentheses following the stem. This information is critical for conjugating the verb. For some verbs, because they only occur in certain tense/aspects which don't require the conjugation prefix, it is impossible (and irrelevant) to know which conjugation prefix the verb takes. In these cases, we leave that information out of the Leer-Edwards theme. An example is *át la.át* ("they're lying there"). The theme for this verb is:

P-t l-.át (position)
"for several things to lie at P; for several persons or animals to lie dead, unconscious, or incapacitated at P"

Because this verb only occurs in the imperfective form, and the conjugation prefix is not required in the imperfective form, we don't know what conjugation prefix it takes. Therefore, the verb theme simply gives the verb type in parentheses, omitting the conjugation prefix. For a more detailed description of the conjugation prefixes, see the appendix of Naish and Story (1973).

### *Verb Type*

The type of each verb is given in the Leer-Edwards theme in parentheses following the conjugation prefix. There are four main types of verbs: act, state, event, and motion. Several different features distinguish these verb types from one another. Act and state verbs have basic imperfective forms while event and motion verbs do not; instead, they use progressive imperfective or repetitive imperfective forms to indicate a present continuous action. State verbs use the +I form of the classifier in the basic imperfective form, but act verbs, with a couple of minor exceptions, do not. For example, consider the state verb *lidzée* ("it is difficult"), whose imperfective form uses the +I classifier *li-*, as compared to the act verb *aklas'úk* ("s/he's frying it"), which uses the -I form of the classifier *la-* in the imperfective. Motion verbs require a direction word (either an adverb or a postpositional phrase) while no other verb types do. Table 5 outlines these differences.

Table 5. Verb Types

| | Basic Imperfective form | +I form of classifier in basic imperfective form | Require direction word |
|---|---|---|---|
| act | Yes | no | no |
| state | Yes | yes | no |
| event | No | --- | no |
| motion | No | --- | yes |

Of these four verb types, motion verbs require the most extensive explanation. As was stated earlier, each verb belongs to one of four conjugation categories: *na, ga, g̲a,* or *ø* (unmarked). Motion verbs can in fact belong to all four. The conjugation category of a motion verb is determined by the direction word that accompanies it. "Direction words" consist of adverbs such as *kei* ("up"), *yei* ("down"), and *daak* ("out to sea; out into the open"), and postpositional phrases such as *aadé* ("toward there"), *aadáx̲* ("from there"), and *a tóonáx̲* ("through it"). Each of these direction words, no matter which motion verb it accompanies, belongs to one of the four conjugation categories. Therefore, it's the direction word and not the verb itself that determines the conjugation category of a motion theme.

To illustrate this point, let's consider the postposition *-dáx̲* ("from"). This belongs to the *(na-)* conjugation category. Any motion verb accompanied by the postposition *-dáx̲* then, will take the *na-* conjugation prefix. Three examples, all given in the imperative form to show the conjugation prefix, are *Aadáx̲ nagú!* ("Leave there!"), *Aadáx̲ nax̲óot'!* ("Drag it out of there!"), and *Aadáx̲ nak̲oox̲!* ("Drive away from there!") For comparison, let's consider the (variable) postposition *-t~* ("(arriving) at, to"), which belongs to the *ø* conjugation category. Here are three examples using the same verb stems as above, but with the *-t~* postposition, all given in the imperative form: *Át gú!* ("Walk to it!"), *Át x̲út'!* ("Drag it to it!"), and *Át k̲úx̲!* ("Drive to it!") Note that the verb stem length and tone changes depending on the conjugation category. It is also important to note at this point that some postpositions of the same shape may occur under different conjugation categories, which will give different meanings from each other. An example is the *-t* postposition belonging to the *na* conjugation category and differing from the one belonging to the *ø* conjugation category in that it is not variable and it means "around, about." Here are examples, again using the same verb stems: *Át nagú!* ("Walk around!"), *Át naxóot'!* ("Drag it around!"), and *Át naḵoox̱!* ("Drive around!")

Within each of the four conjugation categories, these direction words can be further grouped according to prefixes that may be required on the verb as well as the type of repetitive imperfective form that a verb using that particular group of direction words takes. Leer has coined the term "derivational string" to describe these direction word plus conjugation prefix plus any other required verbal prefix combinations, and there are roughly sixty derivational strings which fall into nine groups. These groups of derivational strings appear in the appendix.

Let's consider Group I to illustrate how the system works. Referring to the appendix, Group I consists of about nine different direction words including *kei* ("moving up"), *daaḵ* ("moving up from beach, away from open"), and *ḵux̱* ("returning"). The defining characteristics of Group I are that: 1) they belong to the *ø* conjugation category, and 2) verbs accompanied by any of these nine direction words will have a *-ch* suffix in the repetitive imperfective form. Group I direction words have in common the general meaning of motion toward an area. Verb stem tone and length vary from group to group, but are always consistent within a group for a given tense/aspect and for a given verb. For example, if we know that the verb stem *-goot* ("to walk") has a short, high vowel in the perfective form when accompanied by *kei* as in *kei uwagút* ("s/he walked up"), then we know that the perfective form for that verb will also have a short, high stem when accompanied by any other direction word from Group I, such as in *daaḵ uwagút* ("s/he walked up from the beach") and *ḵux̱ uwagút* ("s/he walked back"). Let's consider the repetitive forms for Group I. If we know that *kei gútch* is the correct way to say "s/he walks up (regularly)," we know that *daaḵ gútch* is the correct form for "s/he walks up the beach (regularly)" and *ḵux̱ gútch* is the way to say "s/he returns (regularly)." So, given a complete motion verb paradigm using a direction word from a particular group, we can confidently replace that direction word with any other direction word from that same group and know that the verb paradigm will remain the same.

This information is extremely helpful, since if the dictionary contains a verb with a direction word from a particular group, the user can simply replace that direction word with another from the same group to change the meaning to the desired direction. While there are a wide variety of motion verb plus direction word combinations in the dictionary, four common verb stems have been systematically included using at least one direction word from each of the nine groups. These verb stems are *-goot* ("for a singular subject to go by foot"); *-.aat* ("for plural subjects to go by foot"); *-k̲oox̲* ("to go by motor vehicle"); and *-taan* ("to carry, take a container or hollow object"). Looking up these entries will help shed light on the system of motion verbs.

There is, of course, much more to say about motion verbs, but this should provide enough of a foundation to use the dictionary and understand the basic structure of motion verbs.

There is additionally one minor verb type that deserves discussion, and that is position verbs. Position verbs describe the physical position of a person or object, only occur in the imperfective form, and tend to require the postposition *-t*, although not all do. An example of a position verb is *.áa* ("s/he is sitting"). To say "s/he is sitting there," the postposition *-t* ("at") is used, as in *át .áa*. The postpositional phrase *át* ("there") is not required, and the conjugation prefix is unknown so the theme is simply:

S-ø-.aa~ (position)
"for (singlular) S to sit, be seated"

Another example of a position verb is *át tán* ("it is lying there"). In this case, the postpositional phrase is required and the theme is:

P-t ø-tán (position)
"for a container or hollow object to lie at P"

## 14. References

Dauenhauer, Nora Marks and Richard Dauenhauer. 2002. *Lingít X̲'éiná̲x̲ Sá! Say it in Tlingit: A Tlingit Phrase Book.* Sealaska Heritage Institute.

Dauenhauer, Nora Marks and Richard Dauenhauer. (forthcoming). *Intermediate Tlingit.* Sealaska Heritage Institute.

Leer, Jeff. 1991. "The Schetic Categories of the Tlingit Verb." Ph.D. diss., University of Chicago.

Story, Gillian L. and Constance M. Naish. 1973. *Tlingit Verb Dictionary.* Fairbanks: Alaska Native Language Center.

# Tlingit to English

# « A/Aa »

**a** Pronoun *its [possessive]*

**a-** Pronoun *him, her, it [object]*

**á** noun *it; that place, time, reason, fact*
·Du táayi gukshitú áwé tléik̲w áa akaawahaa. *She planted berries in the corner of her garden.*
·Áa agax̲tool'oon yé yinaadé yaa gagú! *Walk toward the place we will hunt!*

**á** particle *[puts focus on preceding phrase]*

**aa** Pronoun *one, one of [object]*
·Yées aa a kádi awliyéx̲. *He made a new spear head.*
·Tlél ushik'éiyi aa yoo x̲'atánk áwé tsá a.ax̲ji nooch . *She always only hears the bad talk.*

**áa** noun *lake*
·Áa kaadé x̲aatéen teet. *I see waves on the lake.*
·Yagéi a kaayí wé áa tlein. *The size of that big lake is immense.*

**aaá** particle *yes*

**áadaa** noun *spear (for fish and seal)*
·Yées aa áadaa aawa.oo. *He bought a new spear.*
·Áadaa du jeet awsitán. *She gave him a spear.*

**aag̲áa** Adverb *then, around, after, for*
·Náakw s'é áa yéi kk̲wa.oo ax̲ keey aag̲áa tsá wéi kashóok' gwéil. *I will put medicine on my knee first, then the heating pad.*
·Dax̲adooshú yagiyee shunaaxéex aag̲áa daak wusitani yé. *It has been raining for seven days.*

**áak'w** noun *little lake; pond*
·Áak'wde aawa.aat. *People walked to the pond.*
·Wé áak'w déint áwé át woogoot wé sheech dzísk'u tlein. *The big cow moose was walking around in the vicinity of the pond.*

**Áak'w** noun *Auke Bay*
·Áak'wde yaa nak̲úx̲. *He is driving to Auke Bay.*
·Áak'wx' uwax̲éi wé shaawát. *That woman camped at Auke Bay.*

**Áak'w K̲wáan** noun *people of Auke Bay, southern Lynn Canal, Juneau area, and northern Admiralty Island*
·Áak'w K̲wáanx̲ has sitee. *They are Auke Bay people.*
·Áak'w K̲wáan has al'eix̲. *The Auke Bay people are dancing.*

**áa ḵuyadujee yé** noun *correctional facility*

du **áali** noun *his/her grandparent*

**aan** noun *town; village; settlement; inhabited or owned land*
·Daaḵw aan sáwé? *Which town is that?*
·Ḵ'alkátsk yáxwch'ich yax̱ yawsix̱áa haa aaní kaadáx̱. *The sea otter has devoured the yellowneck clams on our land.*

**aan** postpos. *with it*
·Aan adul'eix̱ ax̱áa kaḵach'áak'wt áyá áa x̱at jikawduwaḵaa. *I have been commissioned to carve a dance paddle.*
·Aan áwé shóot ax̱wdi.ák wé kayeix̱tág̱u. *I built a fire with the wood shavings.*

**aandaat kanahík** noun *monkey*
VARIANTS: aandaat kanahígi (T), aandaat kanaheek (At), aandaat keneheek (C)
·Wé at yátx'i aandaat kanahík has awsiteen. *The children saw the monkey.*
·Wé aandaat kanahík wéix̱ yaa nashíx. *The monkey is running along there.*

**aandaayaagú** noun *rowboat*
·Tláakw ax̱áa du aandaayaagú. *He is rowing his rowboat quickly.*
·Ax̱ éek' du aandaayaagú áwé. *That is my brother's rowboat.*

**aan galaḵú** noun *flood*
VARIANTS: aan galḵú
·Aan galaḵú dei kanax̱ yaawadáa. *The flood went over the road.*
·Ch'áakw aan galaḵú yaa kandutlákw. *A flood from long ago is being researched.*

**Aangóon** noun *Angoon*
·Yaa Aangóont áyá la.áa haa hídi Aanx'aagi Hít yóo duwasáakw. *Our clan house standing in Angoon is called Aanx'aagi Hít.*
·Wé yaakw tlein Aangóonx' tleiyéi yéi wootee. *The big boat stopped in Angoon.*

**áanjís** noun *orange*
·Áanjís akawdi.oo. *She bought herself oranges.*
·At yátx'i áanjís has du tuwáa sigóo. *Children like oranges.*

**áanjís kahéeni** noun *orange juice*
·Áanjís kahéeni ḵaa ée yak'éi. *Orange juice is good for people.*
·Héen áanjís kahéeni x̱oot akawsixáa. *He poured water in with the orange juice.*

**aankadushxit át** noun *camera*
·Tsaa geení aankadushxit át teen akawshixít. *She took a picture of the seal tail flippers with a camera.*

**aank̲anáagu** noun *large-leaved avens (Geum macrophyllum) or possibly arnica species-- Arnica species, especially A. amplexicaulus, A. latifolia, A. gracilis*
NOTES: Warning: arnica increases body temperature when taken internally, externally it acts as an antiseptic
·Aankanáagu ayawsiháa. *She gathered large leafed avens.*
·Aankanáagu tín sh wudzineix̲. *She healed herself with medicine from the land.*

**aankayéx̲aa** noun *plane for scraping wood*
·Aankayéx̲aa tín akaawayéx̲. *He planed it with a plane.*
·Wé k̲áa ax̲ éesh jeedáx̲ aankayéx̲aa aawahées'. *The man borrowed a plane from my Dad.*

**Áankich** noun *Anchorage*
·Áankich yóo duwasáakw Lingít x̲'éináx̲ Anchorage. *Anchorage is called Áankich in Tlingit.*
·Shayadihéin Áankichx' k̲uwa.oowu Lingít. *There are a lot of Tlingit people living in Anchorage.*

**aan kwéiyi** noun *flag*
·Du hídi kináak áwé át wulis'ees wé aan kwéiyi. *The flag is blowing around above his house.*
·Anóoshi aan kwéiyi áwé át wududziyík̲ wé s'ísaa yaakw x̲uká. *They raised a Russian flag on the deck of that sailboat.*

**aan kwéiyi tugáas'i** noun *flagpole*
·Tlag̲anís aan kwéiyi tugáas'ix̲ has awliyéx̲. *They made a flagpole out of a sapling.*

**aank̲áawu** noun *rich man; man of wealth; chief*
·Káa tlein yíkt át yawduwax̲aa wé aank̲áawu. *The rich person is being driven around in a limosine.*
·Dáx̲náx̲ aank̲áax'u wé atyátx'i jeeyís has at wooshee. *Two chiefs sang for the children.*

**Aank̲áawu** noun *God, Lord*
·Johnch héent ayaawatée haa Aank̲áawu. *John baptised our lord.*

**aan s'aatí** noun *mayor*
·Lingít shaawát áwé haa aan s'aatí. *Our mayor is a Tlingit woman.*
·Yées aan s'aatí has du jee yéi yatee. *They have a new mayor.*

**aantk̲eení** noun *townspeople; crowd or large group of people*
·Dei káx' yéi jinéiyi x̲'eis has at gawdzi.ée wé aantk̲eení. *The townspeople cooked food for the people working on the road.*
·Wé aantk̲eení woosh ji.een gán has aawaxásh. *The townspeople cut wood together.*

**aan x̲'ayee** noun *in a town, on the streets of a town*
·Aan x̲'ayeedé (ha)s woo.aat du káani teen. *She and her sister-in-law*

*went downtown.*
·Aan x̲'ayeex' awduwal'eix̲. *People danced in the streets of town.*

**aanyádi** noun *high class person, aristocrat*
VARIANTS: aanyédi (C)
·Aanyádi áwé wé shaatk'. *The young girl is an aristocrat*
·Aanyátx'i áwé wéide iyatéen. *Those are high class people you see there.*

**aan yaduxas' át** noun *razor*
VARIANTS: aan yatxas' át
·Tlagu aan yaduxas' át aawat'ei. *He found an old-time razor.*
·Aan yaduxas' át du jeewú wé k̲áa shaan. *The old man has a razor.*

**aas** noun *tree (esp. conifer)*
·Aax̲ xásh wé aas x'áni! *Cut the outer limbs of the tree off!*
·Yóo tliyaa aasdéi ksaxát wéi kaxées' ax̲ at shí k̲óok gúgu yís! *Attach the wire to that tree over there for my radio antenna!*

**aasdaag̲áadli** noun *bracket fungus*
·Aasdaag̲áadli ayatéen. *She sees the tree fungus.*
·Aasdaag̲áadli aax̲ aawas'úw. *He chopped off the tree fungus.*

**aasdaak'óox̲'u** noun *tree pitch*
·Aasdaak'óox̲'u náakw sákw yéi awsinei. *She gathered tree pitch for medicine.*
·Náakwx̲ awliyéx̲ aasdaak'óox̲'u. *She made medicine out of pitch.*

**aasdaax'ées'i** noun *tumor in a tree, with branches growing from it*
·Aasdaax'ées'i tléil aas ée uk'é. *A tree tumor is not good for the tree.*
·Aasdaax'ées'i yakoogé ayatéen. *He sees lots of tree tumors.*

**aasgutú** noun *forest; timbered area*
VARIANTS: aasgatú (T), aasgetú (C)
·Kalag̲éi nooch aasgutú yeist k̲uwuhaayí. *The forest is brilliant when fall comes.*
·Aasgutóot wugoodí, dzísk'w x̲'us.eetí awsiteen. *He saw moose tracks when he was walking in the woods.*

**aas jiseiyí** noun *the shelter of a tree*
VARIANTS: aas seiyí (At)
·Aas seiyí áa wdlisáa. *He rested in the shelter of the tree.*
·Wé aas seiyít wujixíx séew tóodáx̲. *She ran to the shelter of the tree to get out of the rain.*

**aas yádi** noun *sapling*
VARIANTS: asyádi

**aashát** noun *steelhead trout*
·Aashát tlein awdzit'eix̲. *She hooked a big steelhead trout.*
·A káx̲ akg̲wast'éix̲ aashát yaa yanahéini. *He will fish for steelhead trout when they run upriver.*

**du aat** noun *his/her paternal aunt*
·Yak'éiyi x̲'ayeit áwé du jeewú ax̲ aat. *My paternal aunt has nice dishes.*
·Wé hoon s'aatí een yóo x̲'ali.átk ax̲ aat. *My paternal aunt is talking with the storekeeper.*

**aatlein** Quantifier *much, lots of, really*
·Aatlein dáxw aawa.ín. *She picked lots of lowbush cranberries.*
·Aatlein shaax̲ kanéegwál' yéi x̲wsinei. *I made a lot of gray currant berry sauce.*

**Áa Tlein** noun *Atlin*
·Áa Tlein káa kawduwayél'. *It is calm on Atlin Lake.*

**Áa Tlein K̲wáan** noun *people of Atlin*
·Áa Tlein K̲wáan áwé yáax' haat has uwa.át. *Atlin Lake people came here.*
·Áa Tlein K̲wáan áwé has aawal'eix̲. *The Atlin people danced.*

**áa yax̲** Adverb *turning over*

**ách at dusx̲a át** noun *fork*
VARIANTS: ách at yadusx̲a át
NOTES: The variant listed here contains the ya- prefix and is the form used by one of the fluent speakers consulted for this project.
·Haandé wé ách at dusx̲a át! *Hand me the fork!*
·Ách at dusx̲a át tlein aawa.oo. *She bought a big fork.*

**ach kooshx̲'íl'aa yeit** noun *sled (for recreational sledding)*
VARIANTS: ech koolx̲'íl'aa yeit (C)

**adátx'i** noun *children*
VARIANTS: atyátx'i, atyétx'i (T), adétx'i (T), edétx'i (C)
·Wéi Sheet'kaadáx̲ adátx'i at gutóox' áwé has du ée at dultóow. *The kids from Sitka are taught out in the wilderness.*

**adawóotl** noun *war; trouble; rush, hurry*
·Adawóotl yáx̲ at woonei du aaníx'. *There was trouble in her town.*
·Wé éil' héen diyáanax̲.á adawóotl yáx̲ áa at yatee. *There is a war going on across the ocean.*

**Aganáa!** interj. *Oh no!; Yikes!*

**ágé** particle *[focus + interrogative]*

**áhé** particle *this/that (over here), the other [focus]*

**akahéix̲i** noun *farmer*
·Wé akahéix̲i jeedáx̲ k'únts' has aawa.oo. *They bought potatoes from the farmer.*
·Wasóos wé akahéix̲i jee shayadihéin. *The farmer has lots of cows.*

**akoolx̱éitl’** noun *fear*
VARIANTS: akoolx̱éetl’ (AnAT), ekoolx̱éitl’ (C)

**ákyá** particle *this (right here) [interrogative]*

**ákyú** particle *that (distant), yonder [interrogative]*

**ák.hé** particle *this/that (over here), the other [interrogative]*

**ák.wé** particle *that (at hand) [interrogative]*
·Héen táatx̱ ák.wé du.een wéi kantáḵw? *Is the lupine picked from the water?*
·Ch’as héen ák.wé a kaadéi yóo yadudzixéik yá kat’ákx̱i? *Is water all that was put on these dried berries?*

**aldaawáa** noun *checkers; games played using string in the hands*

**alḵáa** noun *gambling; game of chance*

**al’eix̱** noun *dance*
·Ax̱ al’eix̱ k’oodás’i ch’áagu kawóot áwé a daawú á. *There are old beads on my dance shirt.*

**al’óon** noun *hunt*
·Al’óon wugoodí ux̱ganḵáas’ du g̱altóode ayaawa.oo. *When he was going hunting, he put matches in his pocket.*
·Wé al’óon tlél wáa sá wootee. *The hunt went alright.*

**al’óoni** noun *hunter*
·Al’óoni wé wanadóo ítx̱ kei nagút. *The hunter is following the sheep that is going uphill.*
·Éil’ héeni diyáanax̱.á áa yéi yatee wé al’óoni. *The hunter lives across the ocean.*

**Anáaski** noun *Alaska*

**anahoo** noun *rutabaga; turnip*
·Anahoo s’ín teen wudustaayí yak’éi. *Turnip boiled with carrots is good.*
·Anahoo has akanahéijin. *They used to plant turnips.*

**Ana.óot** noun *Aleut*
·Ana.óot ḵu.oo haa x̱ánt has uwa.át. *Aleut people came to see us.*
·Ana.óot x̱oox’ uwawát wé ḵáa. *That man grew up among the Aleut people.*

**ánk’w** noun *person who cries easily*
·Ḵúnáx̱ ánk’w áwé wé shaatk’átsk’u. *The young girl is a real crybaby.*
·Ánk’w áwé kéi has anaswát wéit lingítch. *Those people are raising a crybaby.*

**Anóoshi** noun *Russian*
·Yáa ax̱ éesh yinaanáx̱ ḵu.aa áyá Anóoshix̱ wusitee, Héenx̱ Ḵuwala.aadíx̱ wusitee. *My father's side was Russian, he was a baptizer.*

·Anóoshi aan kwéiyi áwé át wududziyík̲ wé s'ísaa yaakw x̲uká. *They raised a Russian flag on the deck of that sailboat.*

**Anóoshi aaní** noun *Russia*

·Anóoshi Aanídáx̲ áyá yaa San Fransiscot has wuligás'. *They had moved to San Fransisco from Russia.*

·Ch'a yóo Anóoshi Aaníx' yaa German shaawát áyá du x̲ánx' yéi wootee. *While in Russia he was with a German woman.*

**asgutuyiksháa** noun *spider*

**asg̲eiwú** noun *seine fisherman; seine boat*

·Yaakw k̲a g̲eiwú asg̲eiwú jishagóonx̲ sitee. *A boat and a net are a seine fisherman's tools.*

·Asg̲eiwú s'aatíx̲ sitee ax̲ wóo. *My father-in-law is a master seiner.*

**ast'eix̲í** noun *fisherman (troller)*

**asx'aan sháach'i** noun *green bird (sparrow or finch)*

**ashalx̲óot'i** noun *sport fisherman*

**át** noun *thing*

·At géit wudzigít wé k̲áa átx'i aawutáawu. *He went against the law when he stole the man's belongings.*

·L át yáx̲ k̲oonook. *He doesn't act normal.*

**átk' aheen** noun *faith*

VARIANTS: étk' eheen (C), átx' aheen (T)

**átk' aheení** noun *believer*

VARIANTS: étk' eheení (C), átx' aheení (T)

**atk'átsk'u** noun *child*

·Yá atk'átsk'u li.oos ch'ak'yéis' yáx̲. *This child is as playful as a young eagle.*

·Ch'a tlákw áwé yéi nateech ax̲ x̲úx̲, ch'u atk'átsk'ux̲ sateeyídáx̲. *My husband is like this often, and has been even since he was a child.*

**át k̲ukawu.aag̲ú** noun *director, planner; commander*

VARIANTS: át at kawu.aag̲ú, ét et kawu.aag̲ú (C), ét k̲ukawu.aag̲ú (C)

**atxaayí** noun *centipede*

·Héen kát jinaskwanchi át áwé wé atxaayí. *The centipede swims on top of the water.*

·Lushik'éiyi át ákwé atxaayí? *Is the centipede poisonous?*

**atx'aan hídi** noun *smokehouse*

VARIANTS: etx'aan hídi (C)

·Ax̲ atx'aan hídi tleidooshú k̲aa x̲'oos k̲a daax'oonx̲ sitee. *My smoke house is six feet by four feet.*

·Jikak̲áas' káx̲ ashayaawatée wé g̲aat atx'aan hídi yeex'. *She hung the sockeye salmon on the stick in the smokehouse.*

**atx̲á** noun *food, a meal*
·Costcodáx̲ aawa.óow atx̲á. *He bought food from Costco.*
·Cháanwaan atx̲aayíg̲aa awóo! *Order some Chinese food!*

**atx̲a át** noun *moth*
·Atx̲a átch áwé uwax̲áa ax̲ kinaak.ádi. *A moth ate my coat.*
·Atx̲a át náagu a x̲oo yan yéi ksané! *Put some moth balls among it!*

**atx̲á daakahídi** noun *restaurant; tavern*
·Atx̲á daakahídix' gishoo taayí k̲a k'wát' awdzig̲áax̲. *She ordered bacon and eggs at the restaurant.*
·Tle a tuwán áwé atx̲á daakahídi áa wdudliyéx̲. *They built a restaurant next to it.*

**atx̲á jishagóon** noun *kitchen utensil*

**atyátx'i** noun *children*
VARIANTS: atyétx'i (T), adétx'i (T), edétx'i (C), adátx'i
·Sgóonwaan atyátx'i has shayadihéin Yaakwdáatx'. *There are a lot of school children in Yakutat.*
·Dáx̲náx̲ aank̲áax'u wé atyátx'i jeeyís has at wooshee. *Two chiefs sang for the children.*

**atyátx'i latíni** noun *babysitter*
·Keil atyátx'i latínix̲ nax̲satee yá xáanaa. *Let Keil be the babysitter this evening.*
·Atoosg̲eiwú atyátx'i latíni x̲ánx̲ has g̲ak̲éech ax̲ yátx'i. *When we are gillnetting my children stay with a babysitter.*

**átl'áni** noun *slime (inside clamshell)*

**Atskanée!** interj. *Yikes!; Scary!*

**áwé** particle *that (at hand) [focus]*
·Ch'as a gooshí áwé duteen nooch kéet. *All that can be seen of a killerwhale is the dorsal fin.*
·Tl'aadéin áwé át tán wé k̲óok. *The box is sitting sideways.*

**áx' k̲aa ée at dultóow yé** noun *school*
·Áx' k̲aa ée at dultóow yé áa yéi x̲at gug̲watée seig̲án. *I will be in school tomorrow.*

**ax̲** Pronoun *my [possessive]*
·Giyak̲w K̲wáanx̲ sitee ax̲ x̲ooní, Russell. *My friend Russell is Alutiq.*
·Wáang̲aneensx' yanax̲ kei shak'íx̲'ch ax̲ yoo x̲'atángi. *Sometimes my words get hung up.*

**ax̲áa** noun *paddle*
·Daax'oon yatee ax̲ ax̲áayi yaakw yíx'. *There are four paddles in my skiff.*
·Aan adul'eix̲ ax̲áa kak̲ach'áak'wt áyá áa x̲at jikawduwak̲aa. *I have been commissioned to carve a dance paddle.*

**áyá** particle *this (right here) [focus]*
·K̲únáx̲ k'eeljáa yéi ayagux̲datée ách áyá haa yaagú dák̲de tusax̲út'x'. *It's going to get stormy so we are dragging our boats up.*
·L'ook kaháagu áyá yak'éi kanat'á kanéegwál' sákw. *Coho salmon eggs are good for blueberry sauce.*

**ayaheeyáa** noun *curlew*

**ayáx̲** particle *thus, that's how*

**áyú** particle *that (distant), yonder [focus]*

# « Ch »

**-ch** postpos. *because of; by means of*
NOTES: Indicates agent of transitive verb with definite object.
·Jidukéei at wuskóowux sateeyéech. *He is paid because he is a knowledgeable person.*
·Sheendé! Táach ikgwasháa. *Get up! You're going to oversleep. (Lit: Sleep will marry you.)*

CHAA verb root

• **akawlicháa | aklachéix | aklachéix**
*s/he strained it | s/he is straining it | s/he strains it (regularly).*
THEME: O-ka-S-l-chaa~ (ø act)
*for S to strain, filter, drain off O*
·Akawsitaayi tléikw kagádaa tóonáx akawlicháa. *He strained the boiled berries through cheesecloth.*

CHAAK verb root

• **akaawachák | akacháak | akachákx**
*s/he packed it | s/he's packing it | s/he packs it (regularly).*
THEME: O-ka-S-ø-cháak~ (ø act)
*for S to pile, stack away neatly, pack O (food, clothing, firewood, etc.)*
·Cháash a kaadéi kawtuwachák wé wutuwa.uni dzísk'w. *We packed branches on the moose that we shot.*
·A k'óol'de kaychák! *You all pack it in the stern!*

du **chaan** noun *his/her mother-in-law*

CHAAN verb root

• **wulichán | lichán | kei lachánch**
*he/she/it stank | he/she/it stinks | he/she/it stinks (regularly).*
THEME: O-l-chán (ga state)
*for O to stink, have unpleasant odor, smell bad; for O to smell strongly*
·Wé xéel' wuls'eexí lichán. *When the slime rots it stinks.*

**Cháanwaan** noun *Chinese*
·Cháanwaanch áwé wuliyéx yá xáat daakahídi. *The Chinese built this cannery.*
·Cháanwaan atxaayígaa awóo! *Order some Chinese food!*

**cháas'** noun *pink salmon; humpy, humpback salmon*
·Cháas' yak'éi s'eikx sateeyí. *Pink salmon is good smoked.*
·A wanáax' yakoojél wé cháas'! *Put the Humpback salmon separate from them!*

**cháash** noun *bough, branch with needles on it, especially of spruce*
·Cháash a kaadéi kawtuwachák wé wutuwa.uni dzísk'w. *We packed branches on the moose that we shot.*
·K'idéin kachák wé cháash! *Pack the branches well!*

**cháatl** noun *halibut*
·Cháatl tíx'i yaa (ha)s a shuká naḵúx̱. *They're setting halibut gear.*
·Tséek éen has awsi.ée wé cháatl. *They barbecued the halibut.*

**cháatl ast'eix̱í** noun *halibut fisherman*

**cháax̱** noun *horned grebe or red-necked grebe*
·Cháax̱ héen táade awjit'ákw. *The grebe dove into the water.*

**cháayoo** noun *tea*
·Wé shaatk' gúx'aa kát cháayoo ax̱ jeet awsi.ín. *The young girl gave me tea in a cup.*
·Gúx'aa kat'óott kaawadáa wé cháayoo. *The cup is filled part way up with tea.*

**chál** noun *platform cache; house cache; shed*
VARIANTS: chíl
·É! Shahíkx̱ haa cháli ḵaatáa yéi daatooneiyí. *Check it out! When we are out trapping, our storehouse is full.*
·Wé héen x̱'ayaax̱ chál wutuliyéx̱. *We built a storehouse on the edge of the river.*

**cheech** noun *porpoise*
·Dax̱yeekaadéi cheech áwé yaa éil' kaadéi xwsiteen. *I have seen two kinds of porpoise in this ocean.*
·Chichuwaa cheech yáx̱ kaax̱át. *Dolphins look like porpoise.*

**chéx̱'i (C)** noun *shade, shadow(s) cast by landforms, etc.*
VARIANTS: chíx̱'i (T), chéex̱'i (At), chéex̱'aa (At), chéix̱'aa (C)
·Wé aas chéx̱'i tayeet áwé tooḵéen. *We are sitting in the shade of the tree.*
·Awdlisín chéx̱'i tóox'. *He is hiding in the shadows.*

**chichuyaa** noun *shark (porpoise-like)*
VARIANTS: chichuwaa
·Chichuwaa cheech yáx̱ kaax̱át. *Dolphins look like porpoise.*

**chíl xook** noun *fish air-dried in cold weather and allowed to freeze*
VARIANTS: chál xook
·Ḵúnáx̱ yasixúkk chíl xook. *That salmon smoked after freezing dries very easily.*
·Yéi x̱a.áx̱jin yáa chíl xook Jilḵáatx' áwé yéi daadunéiyin. *I used to hear of smoked salmon being prepared on the Chilkat.*

**chookán** noun *grass*
VARIANTS: chookén (C), chookwán (T)

**Chookaneidí** noun *Chookaneidí; a clan of the Eagle moiety whose principal crests are the Porpoise and Brown Bear*

**CHOON** verb root

- **awlichún | --- | alchúnx̱**
  *s/he injured it | --- | s/he injures it (regularly).*
  THEME: O-S-l-choon~ (ø event)
  *for S to wound, injure, bruise O*
  ·Du goosh awlichún. *He hurt his thumb.*
  ·Du ḵatlyá awlichún. *He hurt his side.*
- **wudichún | --- | dachúnx̱**
  *he/she/it is injured | --- | s/he gets injured (regularly).*
  THEME: O-d-choon~ (ø event)
  *for O to be wounded, injured, bruised; for O to be hurt (emotionally)*
  NOTES: The most common use of this verb is in the perfective form. Note that it can also refer to a mental state, as in: ḵúnáx̱ haa wdichún "we're really hurting (emotionally)" (after the loss of a family member, e.g.).
  ·Ḵaa dzísk'w gwéinli wudichún. *The hoof of the bull moose is injured.*

**chooneit** noun *arrow*
·Chooneitx̱ áwé dulyéix̱ wé ch'áal'. *Willow is made into arrows.*
·Téix' gwáa wégé átx̱ dulyeix̱ín chooneit sákw. *Little stones must have been used to make arrows.*

**CHOOX** verb root

- **akaawachúx | akachóox | akachóoxx̱**
  *s/he kneaded it | s/he kneads it; s/he is kneading it | s/he kneads it (regularly).*
  THEME: O-ka-S-ø-choox~ (ø act)
  *for S to knead, press, pat O with palm of hand*

**chudéi** noun *tomcod*
·A eex̱í geix̱ yá chudéi dus.eeyí. *There is a lot of oil in the tom cod when it's cooked.*
·Chudéi áwé a ḵ'anoox̱ú áwu. *Tom cod have a beard.*

# « Ch' »

**ch'a** particle *the very, just*
·Ch'a áa yan awli.át wé gán láx̱'i. *He just left the wet outer part of firewood there.*
·Yáa ḵutaanx' aadé ḵugax̱tootéen ixkée ch'a g̱aax̱tusatéen wé sháa. *This summer we are going to travel down south just to see the girls.*

**ch'a aadóo sá** noun *anyone, anybody; whoever*
VARIANTS: ch'a aa sá

**ch'a aan** particle *although, even though, however, nonetheless, yet*
·Wusi.áax'w du yoo x̱'atángi, ch'a aan áwé du x̱'éide ḵuwdudzi.aax̱. *His words were biting, yet people listened to him.*

**ch'a aa sá** noun *anyone, anybody; whoever*
VARIANTS: ch'a aadóo sá

**ch'áagu** adj. *old*
·Ax̱ al'eix̱ k'oodás'i ch'áagu kawóot áwé a daawú á. *There are old beads on my dance shirt.*
·Dei ch'áagu at sheeyí ḵúnáx̱ du tuwáa sagóo nuch. *S/he always likes old time songs.*

**ch'áakw** Adverb *long ago; back then; in the old days*
VARIANTS: ch'ákw
·Ch'áakw x̱'eint'áax'aa shaawát x̱'é yéi ndu.eich. *Long ago women would wear a labret.*
·Tléi ch'áakw x̱á wé aatx̱ kéi haa wsidáḵ. *It was a long time ago that we migrated from there.*

**ch'áak'** noun *bald eagle*
·Ch'áak' naax̱ x̱at sitee. *I am of the eagle moiety.*
·Ch'áak' lú yóo katán. *A bald eagle's beak is curved.*

**ch'áak' loowú** noun *dark yellow; eagle's beak*
·Ch'áak' loowú yáx̱ néegwál' x̱waa.oo. *I bought some dark yellow paint.*
·Ch'áak' loowú yáx̱ néegwál' teen x̱waanéegwál' kax̱ach'áagu kootéeyaa. *I painted my totem carving with dark yellow paint.*

**CH'AAK'W** verb root

- **akaawach'ák'w | akach'áak'w | akach'ák'wx̱**
*s/he carved it | s/he is carving it | s/he carves it (regularly).*
THEME: O-ka-S-ø-ch'áak'w~ (ø act)
*for S to carve O (usually smaller, detailed work) using a knife*
·Xíxch' a yáax' kax̱waach'ák'w. *I carved a frog on it's face.*

·At xáshdi téel sákw áwé kanágaa akaawach'ák'w ax̱ jeeyís. *He carved a form for making moccasins for me.*

**ch'áal'** noun *willow*
·Chooneitx̱ áwé dulyéix̱ wé ch'áal'. *Willow is made into arrows.*
·Du jinák̲ daak wulihásh wé ch'áal'. *The willow drifted out away from him.*

du **ch'áatwu** noun *his/her skin (surface)*

**CH'ÁCH'X̱** verb root

• **--- | kadlich'ách'x̱ | ---**
--- | *it's spotted* | ---.
THEME: ka-d-l-ch'ách'x̱ (state)
*for a natural object (wood, rock, etc.) to be spotted*
NOTES: This verb only occurs in the imperfective.

**ch'a daa sá** noun *anything; whatever*

**ch'a goot'á sá** noun *anywhere, anyplace; wherever*
VARIANTS: ch'a goot'é sá (C)

**ch'a gwátgeen sá** noun *any time (in the future); whenever (in the future)*

**ch'a g̱ég̱aa** Adverb *in vain; for nothing; without success*
·Ch'a g̱ég̱aa x̱ax̱oox̱. *I call him (but he won't come).*
·Ch'a g̱ég̱aa aax̱ kei dahánch. *He tries to stand up from there (but is unable to).*

**ch'a g̱óot** particle *different, other*
·Ch'a g̱óot k̲áa at óowu, tléil áx̱ ooshee. *You don't touch another person's possessions.*
·Hú k̲u.aa áyá ch'a g̱óot yéide yan kawdiyáa ax̱ tláa, du éeshch áyá du yát saa uwatí Shaaxeidi Tláa. *But with my mother it happened differently, because her father named her Shaaxeidi Tláa.*

**Ch'a keetáanáx̱!** interj. *Cool it!; Calm down!*

**ch'a koogéiyi** Adverb *however, any which way*

**ch'ákw** Adverb *long ago; back then; in the old days*
VARIANTS: ch'áakw

**ch'a k'ikát** particle *at least, once in a while*
VARIANTS: ch'a k'át, ch'a k'eekát (AtT)
·Ch'a k'ikát du jeeyís at na.oo! *At least buy him something!*
·Tsaa Éix̱' kaadáx̱ áwé yawtuwadlaak̲ ch'a k'ikát wé kaneilts'ákw. *We finally managed to get some swamp currants from Seal Slough.*

**ch'ak'yéis'** noun *immature eagle*
·Ch'akyéis' áwé yéi has kaaxát atx̱á g̱aa. *Young eagles are after food.*

·Yá atk'átsk'u li.oos ch'ak'yéis' yáx̲. *This child is as playful as a young eagle.*

**ch'a ldakát át** noun *everything*

**ch'a ldakát k̲áa** noun *everyone, everybody*

**ch'a ldakát yé** noun *everywhere*
VARIANTS: ldakát yé

**ch'as** particle *only, just*
·Ch'as a gooshí áwé duteen nooch kéet. *All that can be seen of a killerwhale is the dorsal fin.*
·Ch'as k'éets'an áyá yáag̲aa wootee. *There's nothing but false azalea around here.*

**ch'a tlákw** particle *always, all the time, constantly*
·Ch'a tlákw áwé yéi nateech ax̲ x̲úx̲, ch'u atk'átsk'ux̲ sateeyídáx̲. *My husband is like this often, and has been even since he was a child.*

**ch'a yák'w** particle *suddenly, immediately, right away*
VARIANTS: ch'a yáak'w, ch'a yóok'

**ch'a yéi** particle *ordinary, usual*

**ch'a yóok'** particle *suddenly, immediately, right away*
VARIANTS: ch'a yák'w, ch'a yáak'w

**ch'éen** noun *ribbon*
·X̲'aan ch'éen i shax̲aawú káx' kei kg̲wak'éi. *A red ribbon in your hair would be good.*
·Wooch g̲unayáadei ch'éen i dlaak' jeewú. *Your sister has different kinds of ribbons.*

**ch'eet** noun *auklet or murrelet*
·Ch'eet sheishóox̲ áwé akaawach'ák'w. *She carved a murrelet rattle.*

**ch'éetg̲aa** noun *skate (ocean creature related to the shark and the ray)*
·Ch'éetg̲aa kéi awdzit'éx̲. *He pulled up a skate.*

**ch'eex̲'** noun *thimbleberry*
VARIANTS: ch'eix̲'
·K̲uk'éet' gax̲too.áat ch'eex̲'g̲aa. *We are going to pick thimbleberries.*
·Ch'eex̲' yagéi yóo dei yaax̲. *There are plenty of thimbleberries along the road.*

du **ch'éex̲'i** noun *his/her first finger*

**CH'EIX̲'W** verb root

- **awlich'éx̲'w | yaa analch'éx̲'w | alch'éx̲'wx̲**
  *s/he got it dirty | s/he's getting it dirty | s/he gets it dirty (regularly).*
  THEME: O-S-l-ch'éix̲'w~ (ø event)
  *for S to dirty, soil O (esp. clothing or person)*

• **wulich'éx̲'w | yaa nalch'éx̲'w | ---**
*he/she/it is dirty | he/she/it is getting dirty | ---.*
THEME: O-l-ch'éix̲'w~ (ø event)
*for O to be dirty*
·I jín wulich'éx̲'w. *Your hands are dirty.*
·K̲únáx̲ wulich'éx̲'w yoo x̲'atánk áwé átx̲ ilayéix̲. *You are using very dirty language.*

**ch'éix̲'w** noun *dirt, dust*
·K'idéin aax̲ na.óos' ch'éix̲'w! *Wash the dirt off good!*
·A yaadéi gé ch'éix̲'w iyatéen? *Do you see dirt on the face of it?*

**ch'iyáash** noun *sea otter hunting canoe with an angular prow for breaking the waves*
·Nas'gadooshú ch'iyáash kax̲waach'ák'w hun yayís. *I carved eight sea otter hunting canoes to sell.*

**ch'u** particle *still, even*
VARIANTS: ch'oo
·Ch'a tlákw áwé yéi nateech ax̲ x̲úx̲, ch'u atk'átsk'ux̲ sateeyídáx̲. *My husband is like this often, and has been even since he was a child.*
·X̲'aan yakawlikís'. Wé kél't' k̲u.aa, ch'u uwat'áa. *The fire has gone out but the ashes are still warm.*

**ch'u déix̲** Numeral *both*

**ch'u shóogu** particle *the same*
·Ch'u shóogu aan wududliyex̲i túk̲l' áwé a kax̲yee wéi ANB hall. *Those are the original young spruce they used to build the ceiling of the ANB hall.*

**ch'u tlei** particle *when, while*

**ch'u tleix̲** particle *forever*

# « D »

a **daa** RelationalNoun *around it; about it; concerning it*
·Wé x'akaskéin daax' áwé yéi jiné. *She is working on the unfinished basket.*
·I tuk̲'atáali i daax̲ yei jeekanaxíx. *Your pants are falling down.*

DAA[1] verb root

- **anax̲ yaawadáa | anax̲ yaa nadéin | ---**
*it flowed through it | it is flowing through it | ---.*
THEME: P-náx̲ ya-ø-daa~ (ø motion)
*for water, the tide to flow through P; for water, the tide to flood P*
·Aan galak̲ú dei kanax̲ yaawadáa. *The flood went over the road.*
- **át kaawadáa | --- | ---**
*the (water) level rose to there | --- | ---.*
THEME: P-t~ ka-ø-daa~ (ø motion)
*for water to flow, rise to P*
·Gúx'aa kat'óott kaawadáa wé cháayoo. *The cup is filled part way up with tea.*
- **át uwadáa | aadé yaa nadéin | áx̲ daa**
*it flowed to it | it's flowing to it | it flows to it (regularly).*
THEME: P-t~ ø-daa~ (ø motion)
*for water to flow to P*
·X̲'ahéeni du x̲'éit uwadáa. *He is drooling.*
- **áx̲ kaawadaa | áx̲ kanaadaa | ---**
*it flowed along it | it's flowing along it | ---.*
THEME: P-x̲ ka-ø-daa~ (na motion)
*for water, blood to flow, run along P*
·Du tl'átgi dagiygé áwé héenák'w áx̲ kanaadaa. *A small stream flows in the middle of her land.*
·G̲íl' yáx̲ kanaadaa wé héen. *The water is flowing down the face of the rock cliff.*
- **daak̲ uwadáa | daak̲ nadéin | ---**
*the tide is in | the tide is coming in | ---.*
THEME: daak̲ ø-daa~ (ø motion)
*for the tide to rise, come in*
·Daak̲ uwadáa. *The tide is in.*
- **kaawadaa | --- | ---**
*it flowed; it's flowing | --- | ---.*
THEME: ka-ø-daa~ (na motion)
*for water, blood to flow; for a nose to run*
·Du x̲'ahéeni kaawadaa. *His saliva is flowing.*
- **kei uwadáa | kei nadéin | ---**
*the water level rose | the water level is rising | ---.*

THEME: kei ø-daa~ (ø motion)
*for water level, tide to rise*
·Haat kei wudaayí tléil ux̲satínch. *He has not seen the tide rise yet.*

DAA² verb root

• **du x̲'éix̲ woodaa | du x̲'éix̲ yaa nadéin | du x̲'éix̲ yoo yadéik**
*s/he got used to (the flavor, pronunciation of) it | s/he is getting used to (the flavor, pronunciation of) it | s/he gets used to (the flavor, pronunciation of) it (regularly).*
THEME: N x̲'éix̲ ø-daa~ (na event)
*for N to become used to, accustomed to it (of manner of speech or flavor of food)*
·Ax̲ x̲'éix̲ woodaa. *I got used to (the pronunciation, flavor of) it.*

**dáa** noun *weasel*

du **daadleeyí** noun *his/her flesh*

**dáadzi** noun *firestone; iron pyrite*

**dáag̲i** Adverb *out of the water onto the beach, shore*

**daak** Adverb *out to sea; out into the open; (falling) down*
·Watsíx áa káa daak has awlikél' wé g̲ooch. *The wolves chased the caribou out onto the lake.*
·Has du yáa daak uwagút wé xóots tlein kanat'á has a.éeni. *While they were picking blueberries, the brown bear came face to face with them.*

a **daaká** RelationalNoun *around the outside surface of it*
·K'idéin layéx̲ yá k̲'anáax̲án wé gishoo daaká yís! *Build this fence well around those pigs!*

du **daakanóox'u** noun *his/her grandparent (term of respect)*
·Aangóondáx̲ áwé ax̲ káani du daakanóox'u. *My sister-in-law's ancestors are from Angoon.*

du **daakashú** noun *his/her fate*

**daakeit** noun *container for it*
·Wé náakw daakeidí áyá. *This is a container for that medicine.*
·Kóox daakeit káa yéi du.úx̲x'. *Rice is put into a container.*

**daak̲** Adverb *up in the woods; inland; back (away from the open, away from the water's edge, inside)*
·Daak̲ uwadáa. *The tide is in.*

DAAK̲² verb root

• **kei wsidák̲ | --- | ---**
*s/he migrated | --- | ---.*
THEME: kei O-s-daak̲~ (ø motion)
*for O to move household (permanently), migrate*

·Tléi ch'áakw x̲á wé aatx̲ kéi haa wsidák̲. *It was a long time ago that we migrated from there.*

**daak̲w.aa sá** noun *which (one); some (certain one)*
·Daak̲w aan sáwé? *Which town is that?*
·Tléil x̲wasakú daak̲w.aa x̲áat sá a k̲'anoox̲ú k̲usteeyí. *I don't know which fish have beards.*

DAAL verb root

- **woodál | yadál | kei dálch**
*it got heavy | it's heavy | it gets heavy (regularly).*
THEME: O-ø-dál (ga state)
*for O to be heavy (usually of inanimate things); (fig.) to be weighty, important (of abstracts)*
·Yadál wé tináa. *The copper shield is heavy.*
·A kat'óott shalatl'ít', tlél kei kg̲wadál! *Fill it halfway, then it won't be heavy!*

a **daaleilí** noun *its wrinkled, baggy skin, hide*

a **dáali** noun *its rumen, main stomach (of ruminant)*
·Dzísk'u tl'óog̲u k̲a a dáali ax̲ x̲'é yak'éi. *I like to eat moose liver and its tripe.*
·Watsíx dáali agawdzi.ée. *She cooked caribou tripe for herself.*

DAAL' verb root

- **akawlidál' | akladáal' | akladál'x̲**
*s/he typed it | s/he is typing it | s/he types it (regularly).*
THEME: O-ka-S-l-dáal'~ (Ø act)
*for S to type O*

**dáanaa** noun *silver*

**dáanaa** noun *money, coin, dollar*
·Ax̲ dáanayi a wanáa yéi aa na.oo! *Put my money separate from the others!*
·Du jintáax' yéi yatee du dáanayi. *His money is in his grip.*

**dáanaa kat'éex̲'i** noun *silversmith*

**dáanaa s'aatí** noun *rich man*

**dáanaa shoowú** noun *half dollar; fifty cents*

**dáanaa t'éex̲'i** noun *silversmith*

DAAS' verb root

- **awdlidás' | --- | aldás'x̲**
*s/he snared it | --- | s/he snares it (regularly).*
THEME: O-S-d-l-dáas'~ (ø event)

*for S to snare O*
·G̱áx̱ awdlidás'. *She snared a rabbit.*

**dáas'aa** noun *snare*

du **daashagóon** noun *his/her body parts*
VARIANTS: du daashegóon

a **daat** noun *(telling) about it*
·Yáa a daat x'úx' yáx̱ áwé a daax' yéi jix̱waanei. *I worked on it according to the book.*
·Tlél kei gux̱lats'áa i daat sh kalneek. *Gossip about you is not going to smell good.*

**daaw** noun *seaweed, kelp on which herring spawn*

**daax'oon** Numeral *four*
·Ax̱ atx'aan hídi tleidooshú ḵaa x̱'oos ḵa daax'oonx̱ sitee. *My smoke house is six feet by four feet.*
·Daax'oon ḵaa x̱'oos a kaayí wé nadáakw. *That table measures four feet.*

**daax'oondahéen** Numeral *four times*
VARIANTS: daax'oondehéen (C)

**daax'ooníná̱x̱** Numeral *four (people)*
NOTES: This is used for counting people only.
·Daax'ooníná̱x̱ ḵáa shaa shakéede al'óon has woo.aat. *Four men went up on the mountain hunting.*

**dáax̱** noun *canoe under construction*

a **daax̱ yaa dulsheech át** noun *banister; railing*

a **daayí** noun *its bark*

at **daayí** noun *birch*
VARIANTS: et daayí (C)

at **daayí ḵákw** noun *birch bark basket*

du **daa.eit x̱'áak** noun *his/her joints*

du **daa.it** noun *his/her/its body*

**daa.ittunéekw** noun *arthritis*
VARIANTS: daa.ittunóok (T)

du **daa.itwéis'i** noun *his/her gland*

a **dachóon** RelationalNoun *straight towards it; directly towards it*
·Dzísk'w awusteení tle a dachóon kéi uwagút. *When he saw the moose he turned to walk straight towards it.*

du **dachx̱án** noun *his/her grandchild*
·G̱uwakaan at xáshdi téel ax̱ dachx̱ánk' jeeyís ax̱ tuwáa sigóo. *I would like deer skin moccasins for my grandchild.*
·Teiḵweidí dachx̱án áyá x̱át. *I am a grandchild of the Teiḵweidí.*

**dágáa** particle *indeed, for sure*
VARIANTS: sdágáa

**dagatgiyáa** noun *hummingbird*
VARIANTS: degwatgeeyáa (C), dagwatgiyáa (AtT)
·Dagwatgiyáa lú yayát' ḵa yéi kwlisáa. *A hummingbird's beak is long and skinny.*

a **dagiygé** RelationalNoun *middle of it*
VARIANTS: a dagikyé, a dagiyigé
·Wé áak'w ḵúnáx̱ a dagiygé áwé watsíx át hán. *A caribou is standing right in the middle of the pond.*
·Du tl'átgi dagiygé áwé héenák'w áx̱ kanaadaa. *A small stream flows in the middle of her land.*

**dag̱a-** Other *[pluralizer]*
VARIANTS: dax̱-, daḵ-
NOTES: The distributive prefix "dag̱a-" attaches to the verb and indicates plurality of the referent, and refers only to inanimate or recessive animate participants, while the pluralizer "has" refers to animate (non-recessive) participants. The distributive prefix is only used to refer to the absolutive argument (the subject of an intransitive verb or the object of a transitive or objective verb).
·Yú sg̱óon tl'átgi tlein, a g̱óonnáx̱ dax̱yanaagóo wé káa. *The cars are traveling on the isthmus of the big school yard.*
·G̱unakadeit daat tlaagú dax̱ḵudzitee. *There are legends about sea monsters.*

**dag̱anḵú** noun *afterlife, "happy hunting ground"*
·Dag̱anḵúde woogoot. *He left us (died).*

**dag̱asaa** noun *squid*
VARIANTS: daḵsaa

**dahooní** noun *salesman; clerk; storekeeper*

**dákde át** noun *thing heading offshore, esp. wind*
·Dákde át xóon áwé ayawditee. *An offshore east wind is blowing.*

**dákdesak'aak** noun *mackerel*
VARIANTS: dákdesax'aak

**dákwtasi** noun *cracklings of rendered fat, grease unfit for consumption*
·Dákwtasi átx̱ dulyéix̱ táay yíx'. *Rendered fat is used in the garden.*

**dáḵde** Adverb *toward the inland, interior; up to the woods; back (away from the open)*

VARIANTS: dáḵdei
·Dáḵde ḵákw aawayaa i léelk'w. *Your grandmother died. (Lit: Your grandmother took her basket into the woods).*
·Ḵúnáx̱ k'eeljáa yéi ayagux̱datée ách áyá haa yaagú dáḵde tusax̱út'x'. *It's going to get stormy so we are dragging our boats up.*

**daḵéis'** noun *sewing*
·X̱alak'ách' x̱aawú daḵéis' teen átx̱ dulyéix̱. *Porcupine quills are used in sewing.*
·Du jiyeex' yan awli.át du daḵéis'i. *She placed her sewing nearby for her.*

**daḵḵá** noun *up in the woods; inland; back (away from the open, away from the water's edge, inside); inland; interior*
·Daḵḵá yoo aawa.át. *People walked into the interior.*
·Tléil yá daḵḵáx' yéi utí wé g̱anook. *Here in the Inland we don't have any petrels.*

**Daḵl'aweidí** noun *Daḵl'aweidí, locally called "Killer Whale"; a clan of the Eagle moiety whose principal crest is the Killer Whale*

**daleiyí** noun *lake trout*
·Tléil a ḵ'anoox̱ú ḵoostí daleiyí. *Lake trout do not have beards.*

at **danáayi** noun *drunk; drunkard*

**daneit** noun *large box for storing grease, oil*

**daséikw** noun *life; breath*
·Yées daséikwg̱aa woogoot. *He went to get fresh air.*

**dáxw** noun *lowbush cranberry, bog cranberry*
·Aatlein dáxw aawa.ín. *She picked lots of lowbush cranberries.*
·Sháchgi káa ka.éix̱ dáxw. *Lowbush cranberries grow in the meadow.*

**-dáx̱** postpos. *from, out of; since*
VARIANTS: -tx̱
NOTES: Note that when -dáx̱ attaches to a noun ending in a vowel, -dáx̱ optionally loses its vowel, becoming -tx̱. For example, either of the following are acceptable for "from around the house": wé hít daadáx̱ / wé hít daatx̱. These nouns and relational nouns have alternate forms when combined with -dáx̱:
á "it, there"+ dáx̱ = aadáx̱ / aax̱ "from it; from there"
a ká "surface" + -dáx̱ = a kaadáx̱ / a kaax̱ "from its surface"
a yá "its face" + -dáx̱ = a yaadáx̱ / a yaax̱ "from its face"
a tú "its inside" + -dáx̱ = a tóodáx̱ / a tóox̱ "from its inside"
·Ax̱ éek' si.áat'i héen goondáx̱ ayáayin. *My brother used to pack cold water from a spring.*
·Ḵunáagu jeedáx̱ jika.át yéi aya.óo. *He is wearing a wrist guard from the doctor.*

**dax̱áchx'i** noun *tugboat*
·Dax̱áchx'i yaakw tlénx' át has anax̱áchch.. *Tugboats tow large vessels.*

**dax̱adooshóonáx̱** Numeral *seven (people)*

**dax̱adooshú** Numeral *seven*

·Dax̱adooshú kaay yéi kunaaléi wé aan, héen sháakdáx̱. *The town is seven miles from the head of the river.*

·Dax̱adooshú yagiyee shunaaxéex aag̱áa daak wusitani yé. *It has been raining for seven days.*

**dax̱dahéen** Numeral *twice, two times*

VARIANTS: déix̱ dahéen

·Dax̱dahéen yan yaawagás'. *He fell on his face twice.*

**dáx̱g̱aa** Numeral *two at a time, two by two*

·Dáx̱g̱aa a yíkde has woo.aat wé yaakw. *They boarded the boat two by two.*

**dáx̱g̱aanáx̱** Numeral *two (people) at a time*

·Dáx̱g̱aanáx̱ yaa has anal'éx̱. *They're dancing two by two.*

**dáx̱náx̱** Numeral *two (people)*

NOTES: This is used for counting people only.

·Dáx̱náx̱ naa sháadi náḵx'i wé at yátx'i has du jeeyís has at wooshee. *Two chiefs sang for the children.*

·Dáx̱náx̱ ḵáa ya.áak áwé. *It's wide enough for two people.*

**dax̱yeekaadé** Adverb *two different kinds, types; two different ways, directions*

VARIANTS: dax̱yeekaadéi

·Dax̱yeekaadéi cheech áwé yaa éil' kaadéi x̱wsiteen. *I have seen two kinds of porpoise in this ocean.*

a **dayéen** RelationalNoun *facing it*

·Wé shaa dayéen áayáx̱ uwahán. *He turned around to face the mountain.*

·Ax̱ dayéen hán xóon niyaa. *He is standing facing me, shielding me from the North Wind.*

**de** particle *already, (by) now*

VARIANTS: dei

·S'eek de has du ḵoowú tóode has woo.aat. *Black bears have already gone into their dens.*

·Dei át has woo.aat wéi yées kéidladi. *The young seagulls are already walking around.*

**deegáa** noun *dipnet (for eulachon)*

·Yawóol yá deegáa. *This 'dipnet has holes in it.*

**DEES** verb root

- **awdlidées | --- | yei aldéesch**

  *the moon is shining | --- | the moon shines (regularly).*

  THEME: a-d-l-dées~ (g̱a event)

  *for the moon to shine*

·Wé kag̱ít tóox̱ yaa ntoo.ádi awdlidées. *As we walked along in the darkness, the moon shined bright.*

**DEEX’** verb root

• **ax̱’eiwadíx’ | --- | ax̱’adíx’x̱**
*s/he corked it up | --- | s/he corks it up (regularly).*
THEME: O-x̱’e-S-ø-déex’~ (ø event)
*for S to cork up O (bottle); for S to shut, cover mouth of O*
·Ḵ’ateil tóodei yanasxá k’idéin x̱’adíx’! *Pour it in the jug and cork it up!*

**dei** noun *path, trail; road, street*
·Dei káx’ yéi jinéiyi x̱’eis has at gawdzi.ée wé aantḵeení. *The townspeople cooked food for the people working on the road.*
·Téil dei yaax̱t la.át. *Scraps of pitchwood are lying along the road.*

**déi** particle *now, this time*
·Tlél déi x̱wateen ax̱ kawóot ka.íshaa. *I can't see my needle anymore.*
·S’íx’ x̱oot ilt’ách déi! *Wash up the dishes now! (Lit: Slap (up) the dishes now).*

**Déi áwé!** interj. *Stop it!; That's enough!*

**-dé(i) ~ -de(i)** postpos. *to, toward; until; in the manner of*
NOTES: The tone on the postposition -dei is the opposite of that on the final syllable of the noun which it attaches to. This postposition can be pronounced long or short (-dei or -de), depending on speaker dialect.
Some nouns and relational nouns undergo changes in vowel length and/or tone when combined with -dé(i):
á "it, there" + -dé(i) = aadé(i) "toward it; toward there"
a ká "its surface" + -dé(i) = a kaadé(i) "toward (the surface of) it"
a yá "its face" + -dé(i) = a yaadé(i) "toward (the face of) it"
a tú "its inside" + -dé(i) = a tóode(i) "toward (the inside of) it"
·G̱ítg̱aa ayax̱saháa yóode woogoot. *She went over there to gather spruce needles.*
·Dleeyg̱áa áwé aadéi aawa.aat. *People went there for meat.*

**Deikeenaa** noun *Haida*
·Deikeenaa ḵa Ts’ootsxán áa shayadihéin Kichx̱áan. *There are a lot of Haida and Tsimshian people in Ketchikan.*
·Deikeenaa tóode haa kdlixwás’. *Our roots stem from the Haida*

**déili** noun *shelter (from wind or weather), harbor*
·Déili áa has shawdziyaa. *They anchored in a harbor.*
·G̱eey tá déilit awsiḵúx̱ du yaagú. *She drove her boat to the head of the bay.*

a **déin** RelationalNoun *(in) the area of it or around it, (in) its vicinity*
·Wé áak’w déint áwé át woogoot wé sheech dzísk’u tlein. *The big cow moose was walking around in the vicinity of the pond.*
·Wé shaa a déinde áa yaa nagút. *He is walking in the direction of the mountain.*

**a déinde aa** RelationalNoun *the rest of it*
·A déinde aa du naa.ádi aax̱ awli.aat. *She picked up the rest of her clothes.*
·A déinde aa wé gán yax̱ ayakawlixút'. *He chopped up the rest of the wood.*

**Deisleen** noun *Teslin*
·Deisleenx' keijín has yatee ḵaa sháade náḵx'i. *In Teslin there are five leaders.*
·Deisleen jáaji k'idéin wududzikóo. *Teslin snowshoes are well-known.*

**Deisleen Ḵwáan** noun *Teslin Lake people*

**Deisheetaan** noun *Deisheetaan, locally called "Beaver"; a clan of the Raven moiety whose principal crest is the Beaver*
·S'igeidí Deisheetaan ḵaa at oohéini áwé. *The Beaver is the property of the Deisheetaan Clan.*

**Deishú** noun *Haines*
·Ts'ak'áawásh Deishúdáx̱ has aawa.oo. *They bought dried fish strips from Haines.*
·Deishúx' awsiteen wé g̱anook. *She saw a petrel in Haines.*

**déix̱** Numeral *two*
·Déix̱ x̱áat haa jeex' ajeewanáḵ. *He left two salmon for us.*
·Tlei déix̱ ḵ'ateil yáx̱ áwé wutusineix̱ shákw kahéeni. *We just saved two gallons of the strawberry juice.*

**dei yaax̱** noun *side of the path, trail, road, street*
·Ch'eex̱' yagéi yóo dei yaax̱. *There are plenty of thimbleberries along the road.*

**dei yík** noun *on the path, trail, road; bed of the path, trail, road*

**digitgiyáa** noun *hummingbird*
·Ax̱ tl'eiḵ káa wjiḵaaḵ digitgiyáa. *A hummingbird landed on my finger.*

**Dikáanḵáawu** noun *God*
VARIANTS: Dikée aanḵáawu

**Dikée aanḵáawu** noun *God*
VARIANTS: Dikáanḵáawu
·Dikée aanḵáawu du éek' atuwaheen. *We believe in God.*
·Dikée aanḵáawu du yéet ítx̱ na.aadí has du een sh káa x̱'awdigáx'. *Jesus prayed with his disciples.*

**dís** noun *month*
·Yées dís áwé haadé yaa nagút. *A new month is coming.*

**dís** noun *moon*
·Wé dís kagáni káax' yéi jiné. *He works by moonlight.*

**dís wooxéiyi** noun *calendar*

**dís x'usyee** noun *moonbeam*

·Dís x'usyee kawdli.ít'ch wé dleit káx. *Moonbeams are sparkling on the snow.*

du **díx'** noun *his/her back*

·Du díx' néekw nooch. *His back always hurts.*

**diyáanax.á** noun *area across, on the other side (especially of body of water)*

·Wé éil' héen diyáanax.á adawóotl yáx áa at yatee. *There is a war going on across the ocean.*

·Yóo diyáanax.aadáx áwé haat yaxwaaxáa wéi kax'ás'ti haa hídi sákw. *I hauled the lumber from across the other side for our house.*

**Diyée aankáawu** noun *Satan*

·Diyée aankáawu jeet wudzigít. *He fell into satan's hands.*

**Doó!** interj. *See how you are!; Look what you did!*

a **doogú** noun *its skin (of animal); hide*

·X'alitseen wé xalt'ooch' naagas'éi doogú. *The skin of a black fox is expensive.*

·Téil yéi aya.óo at doogú aklas'ékxi yís. *She is using dry wood for smoking that hide.*

du **dook** noun *his/her skin, complexion*

·Du dook yak'éi. *Her complexion is good.*

**dóol** noun *sandhill crane*

du **doonyaa** noun *under or inside his/her clothes; next to his/her skin*

**doonyaax k'oodás'** noun *undershirt*

·Du doonyaax k'oodás'i áx gaashóo. *His undershirt is hanging out.*

**doonyaaxl'aak** noun *petticoat; slip*

·Doonyaaxl'aak yéi aya.óo. *She's wearing a slip.*

**dóosh** noun *cat*

·Wé dóosh kadagáax. *The cat is crying.*

·Wé dóosh jín dleit kaax kínde alshát. *The cat is holding its paw up off the snow.*

**dóosh yádi** noun *kitten*

·Dóosh yádi een áwé ash koolyát wé atk'átsk'u. *The boy is playing with a kitten.*

DOOX' verb root

- **akaawadúx' | akadóox' | akadúx'x**

*s/he tied it | s/he's tying it | s/he ties it (regularly).*
THEME: O-ka-S-ø-dóox'~ (ø act)

*for S to tie O in a knot*
·Du téel x̱'adzaasí akaawadúx'. *She tied her shoelaces.*

**du** Pronoun *his/her [possessive]*
·Du keidlí du jináḵ ḵut wujixeex. *His dog ran away from him.*
·Wé ḵáa du jishagóoni ḵut kaawasóos. *The man's tools are lost.*

**dúḵ** noun *cottonwood*
·Dúḵ een dulyéix̱ seet yaakw. *The canoe is made out of cottonwood.*

**dúḵ** noun *canoe made of cottonwood*

**dúḵl'** noun *young spruce or hemlock*

**dús'** noun *soot*
·Dús' áa yagéi wé x̱'aan eetí. *There's soot where the fire was.*

**dúsh** noun *tadpole; polliwog*

# « Dl »

du **dlaak’** noun *his sister*

·Wooch g̱unayáadei ch’éen i dlaak’ jeewú. *Your sister has different kinds of ribbons.*

·Ax̱ dlaak’ tín Xunaadé ḵugax̱tootéen kanat’á ḵuk’éet’ yís. *We are going to travel to Hoonah to pick blueberries with my sister.*

**DLAAḴ** verb root

• **ayaawadlaaḵ | --- | yoo ayaadláḵk**

*s/he won it | --- | s/he wins it (regularly).*

THEME: O-ya-S-ø-dlaaḵ~ (na event)

*for S to win, gain, get, obtain, acquire O; for S to succeed, accomplish O; for S to defeat, beat O*

NOTES: The prohibitive forms "Don’t win it!" require context in order to make sense. An example would be this statement, said jokingly: Líl yoo yeedláḵgiḵ - yakḵwadláaḵ! "Don’t win it - I’m going to win it!"

·Xákw ká ayaawadlaaḵ. *He made it to the sand bar.*

·Tsaa Éix̱’ kaadáx̱ áwé yawtuwadlaaḵ ch’a k’ikát wé kaneilts’ákw. *We finally managed to get some swamp currants from Seal Slough.*

**DLAAN** verb root

• **woodlaan | g̱aadlaan | yei dlánch**

*it became deep | it's deep | it gets deep (regularly).*

THEME: ø-dlaan~ (g̱a state)

*for water to be deep; for snow to be piled thickly*

NOTES: This verb is one of a very small set of dimensional verbs with extensional imperfective forms (Leer, 1991). It is distinguished by an imperfective form which requires the g̱a-conjugation prefix.

·Kaldaag̱éináx̱ yaa gax̱tooḵóox̱, tlél g̱wadlaan yá éix̱’ yík. *We will travel along slowly, it's not deep in this slough.*

• **yan kaawadlán | yánde yaa kanadlán | ---**

*it's piled up | it's beginning to pile up | ---.*

THEME: yan~ ka-ø-dlaan~ (ø motion)

*for grain-like objects, pine needles, snow to be deep, thick, pile up*

• **yéi kaawadláan | yéi kg̱waadláan | ---**

*it got that deep | it's that deep | ---.*

THEME: yéi ka-u-ø-dláan (g̱a state)

*for a body of water to be so deep*

·Tleiḵáa waat yéi kg̱waadláan. *It's twenty fathoms deep.*

**DLAAX̱'W** verb root

- **yax̱ woodláax̱'w | --- | yax̱ kei dláx̱'wch**
  *it got stuck on the beach | --- | it gets stuck on the beach (regularly).*
  THEME: yax̱ ø-dláax̱'w~ (ga event)
  *for a boat, sea mammal to get stuck (on beach), be beached*
  ·Wé yáay yax̱ woodláax̱'w. *The whale is stuck on the beach.*
  ·Yax̱ kei kg̱wadláax̱'w wé yaakw. *The boat will get stuck on the beach.*

**dlagwáa** noun *fish spear; harpoon for spearing salmon*

**dlágwaa** noun *peavy*
·Yées aa dlágwaa áwé. *That is a new peavey.*
·Dlágwaa tín yéi jiné. *He is working with a peavey.*

**dleey** noun *meat, flesh*
·Wé g̱uwakaan dleeyí at x̱'ax̱éedli k'idéin aax̱ xásh, téix̱ sákw! *Cut the trimming off the deer meat well for the broth!*
·Wé dleey yat'éex'. *The meat is tough.*

**dleit** noun *snow*
·Dís x̱'usyee kawdli.ít'ch wé dleit káx̱. *Moonbeams are sparkling on the snow.*
·Héen sákw wé dleitdáx̱ kalóox̱jaa tayeex' yan tán! *Set that below the snow drip for our water!*

**dleit** noun *white*
·Wé g̱áx̱ dleit yáx̱ x̱asitee. *The rabbit is white.*
·Gúḵl' dleit yáx̱ dag̱aatee. *Swans are white.*

**dleit g̱éedi** noun *snowstorm, snow shower*

**dleit kakétsk** noun *dry snow*

**dleit ḵáa** noun *White, European, Caucasian (man or person)*
·Dleit ḵáach áwé awliyéx̱ wé x̱'éi shadagutx̱i lítaa. *The white man invented the pocket knife.*

**dleit ḵaadí** noun *snowslide; snow avalanche*

**dleit tléig̱u** noun *snowberry*

**DLÉNX̱AA** verb root

- **akaawadlénx̱aa | akoodlénx̱aa | yoo akayadlénx̱aa**
  *he/she/it tempted him/her | he/she/it is tempting him/her | he/she/it tempts him/her (regularly).*
  THEME: O-ka-u-S-ø-dlénx̱aa (na act)
  *for S to tempt, try out, test O*
  ·Dáanaa tín has akoodlénx̱aa. *They tempted him with money.*
  ·Wáa yateeyi aa shaax'wsáani sá ash koodlénx̱aa? *What kind of girls does he find tempting?*

# « Dz »

**dzaas** noun *babiche, string, leather thonging*
·Du jáaji a dzaasí yei nasháash. *The thongs of his snowshoes are wearing thin.*
·Dzaas áwé yéi akg̲wa.oo g̲eeg̲ách' akawusneiyí. *She will use string when she crochets a hammock.*

**dzánti** noun *flounder*
·Cháatl yátx'i oowayáa dzánti. *Flounders look like little halibut.*
·Dzánti áwé cháatl k̲ín k̲udligéi. *Flounders are smaller than halibut.*

**Dzántik'i Héeni** noun *Juneau; Gold Creek (in Juneau)*
·Dzántik'i Héenix' áwé x̲at k̲oowdzitee. *I was born in Juneau.*
·K'idéin has jiduk̲éi katíx̲'aa s'aatí Dzántik'i Héenix'. *Jailers are paid well in Juneau.*

**DZEE** verb root

• **wulidzée | lidzée | kei ladzéech**
*it was difficult | it's difficult | it gets difficult (regularly).*
THEME: O-l-dzée (ga state)
*for O to be difficult, frustrating*
·Yaaw xídlaa yéi wdu.oowú, tlél uldzée nooch. *Using a herring rake is not difficult.*
·Lidzée kayaaní a kaadéi kawuls'éesi wé laak̲'ásk. *It's frustrating when leaves are blown onto the black seaweed.*

**dzéex'w** noun *baby clams*

**dzeit** noun *ladder; stairs*
·Dzeit áx̲ kei wlishóo. *The ladder extends up there.*

**dzeit** noun *dock, pier*

**dzeit shuyee** noun *at the landing of a dock*
·Dzeit shuyeet uwak̲úx̲ wé yaakw. *The boat motored to the landing.*

**dzísk'w** noun *moose*
·Dzísk'u g̲ádzi yaa anayéin. *He is packing a moose hindquarter.*
·Kat'íshaa JoAnne Fabricsdáx̲ x̲waa.oo dzísk'u doogú yís. *I bought a leather needle from JoAnne Fabrics for (sewing) moose hide.*

**dzísk'w (AtT)** noun *owl; great horned owl*

**dziyáagin** Adverb *after a while; later on*
·Ch'a tle dziyáaginx' tsá g̲unéi gax̲too.áat. *Pretty soon we're going to start walking.*

**dziyáak** Adverb *just now; a while ago, earlier*
·Dziyáak áwé woogoot. *He left a while ago.*
·Ch'u dziyáak áwé ishuwtusitee. *We were expecting you a while ago*

**dzóox'** noun *tiny clams (too small to eat)*
·Éekx' yéi teex dzóox'. *Small clams are found on the beach.*

du **dzúk** noun *at his/her back; right behind him/her*

# « E/Ee/Ei »

**É!** interj. *Check it out!; Wow!*
NOTES: This is an exclamation of pride, achievement, or wonder.
·É! Shahíkx̲ haa cháli g̲aatáa yéi daatooneiyí. *Check it out! When we are out trapping, our storehouse is full.*

du **ee~** Pronoun *him, her*
NOTES: This is a pronominal base which postpositions are added to, resulting in the following forms:
du éet
du éex̲
du eedé(i) / du éede(i)
·Háas' du éet yéi uwanéi yá yagiyee. *He has been vomiting today.*

**Ée!** interj. *Yuck!; Eeeew!*

**eech** noun *reef; large rock or boulder lying on the ocean floor*
·Eech kát uwak̲úx̲ wé yaakw. *The boat ran over a reef.*

**eech kakwéiyi** noun *fixed buoy*
·Tlákw s'eenáa a káa yéi nateech eech kakwéiyi. *There's always a light on a fixed buoy.*
·Point Retreat eech kakwéiyi áwé *Point Retreat is a fixed buoy.*

**eech kwéiyi** noun *floating buoy*

**éech'** noun *something compact and very heavy*
·Éech' akaawanóot' Yéil. *Raven swallowed a stone.*

**éedaa** noun *phosphorescence (sparks of light in ocean water); luminescence (on rotten wood)*
·Kadli.ít'ch éedaa xáanax'. *The phosphoresence glows at night.*

a **eeg̲áa** noun *waiting for it*
·Wé sakwnéin éewu yan g̲a.eet eeg̲áa áwé x̲a.áa. *I am sitting, waiting for the bread to finish cooking.*

a **eeg̲ayáak** RelationalNoun *the beach, shore below it (a town)*
·Kóoshdaa haa eeg̲ayáaknáx̲ yan uwahín. *The land otter swam through our beachfront.*
·Aan eeg̲ayáax' shóot awdi.ák. *He made fire for himself below the town.*

**éeg̲i** Adverb *from the woods onto the beach, shore*

du **éek'** noun *her brother, cousin*
·Ax̲ éek' du aandaayaagú áwé. *That is my brother's rowboat.*
·Tsú yáa ax̲ tláa k̲u.aa Sheet'káx' áyá k̲oowdzitee. K̲a du éek' tsú

áa ḵoowdzitee. *My mother was born in Sitka. And her brother was also born there.*

**eeḵ** noun *copper*

**éeḵ** noun *beach; waterside; down on the beach, shore*
VARIANTS: éiḵ
·X̱'al'daayéeji éeḵt wujixeex. *The sandpiper is running around the beach.*
·Éeḵx' yéi teex̱ dzóox'. *Small clams are found on the beach.*

**eeḵ háatl'i** noun *verdigris*

**éeḵ lukaḵées'i** noun *low tide (point at which the tide will begin coming in)*

**een** postpos. *(along) with, by means of; as soon as*
VARIANTS: tin, tín, teen, téen
·Ax̱ éek' ḵa ax̱ sáni al'óoni een át has na.átjin. *My brother and my paternal uncle used to accompany hunters.*
·Góon dáanaa een áwé kawduwat'íx̱' ax̱ jeeyís yá kées. *This bracelet was pounded out of a gold coin for me.*

du **een aa** noun *his/her kinsman, moiety mate*

**éenaa** noun *scraper, as for scraping off bark from roots*

du **éenee** noun *his/her armpit*
VARIANTS: du éenyee, du éeni (C)

du **éenee x̱aawú** noun *his/her armpit hair*
VARIANTS: du éenyee x̱aawú, du éeni x̱aawú (C)

**éenwu** noun *food taken home from a feast or dinner to which one was invited*
VARIANTS: éenu (TC)

du **éesh** noun *his/her father*
·Ch'a yá Lingít yinaanáx̱ ḵu.aa áyá tléil ḵaa éeshch áyú ḵaa yádi saa a yáx̱ uteeyín. *In our Tlingit culture, a father never names the children.*
·Yá ḵut'aayg̱áa gági ugootch yee éesh. *During the warm season your father would come out.*

**Eesháan!** interj. *Poor thing!*
·Eesháank' kaltéelḵ áwé haat wujixíx ax̱ dachx̱ánk'. *Poor thing, my grandchild ran over here shoeless.*
·Eeshandéin tuwatee. *He's feeling sad.*

**eet** noun *room*
·Haat has ḵuwuteení yís áyá yan x̱wasinéi yáa eet ká. *I have reserved this room for when they arrive.*

a **eetéenáx̱** Adverb *lacking it; without it*
·Éil' eetéenáx̱ yatee wé tax̱héeni. *The broth needs salt.*
·Kooxéedaa eetéenáx̱ yatee wé shaatk'. *The young girl needs a pencil.*

**a eetí** RelationalNoun *(in) place of it; place where it was; its imprint or aftermath*
·Xein nageich k̲utaan eetíx'. *After the summer there are a lot of spawned-out salmon.*
·Laaxw eetí wé k̲aa jeedáx̲ atx̲á has du g̲aneix̲íx̲ wusitee. *After the famine, the food given to them became their salvation.*

**du eetí ká** noun *(in) his/her room, bedroom*
VARIANTS: du eetí
·Du eetí a kax̲yeet akawlis'íx'w k̲aa yahaayí wé shaatk'átsk'u. *The young girl pasted a photo on the ceiling of her room.*

**éetkatlóox̲u** noun *bullhead*

**éex** Adverb *downstream; south*

**eex̲** noun *oil, grease*
VARIANTS: eix̲ (C)
·A eex̲í geix̲ yá chudéi dus.eeyí. *There is a lot of oil in the tom cod when it's cooked.*
·Tsaa eex̲í teen yak'éi at x̲'éeshi. *Seal oil is good with dryfish.*

**eex̲ kát sakwnein** noun *fry bread, bannock*
·Ax̲ tláa jiyáx̲ eex̲ kát sakwnéin x̲asa.ée. *I cook fry bread like my mom does.*

**eey** noun *bay*

**éil'** noun *salt*
·Éil' eetéenáx̲ yatee wé tax̲héeni. *The broth needs salt.*
·Éil' a kaadéi kanasxá wéi a kát yadu.us'ku át! *Pour salt in the wash basin!*

**éil'** noun *ocean; salt water*
VARIANTS: éil' héen, éil' héeni
·Wé éil' héen diyáanax̲.á adawóotl yáx̲ áa at yatee. *There is a war going on across the ocean.*
·Éil' kaadáx̲ x̲áat k'idéin aax̲ yixás' a kajeig̲í! *You all scrape the scales off the fish from the salt water well!*

**éil' kahéeni** noun *saltwater brine*
·Éil' kahéeni káa yéi na.oo wé kaháakw. *Put the fish eggs in the saltwater brine.*

**Éits'k'!** interj. *Yum!*

**eix̲ (C)** noun *oil, grease*
VARIANTS: eex̲
·Tsaa eix̲í teen áwé yak'éi t'á at x̲'éeshi. *Dry fish king salmon is good with seal oil.*
·Tsaa eix̲í du daagú ágé a yanáax̲ yei at dutánch? *Is a cover put on when rendering seal oil?*

**éix̲'** noun *slough*

·Kaldaag̲éinán̲x̲ yaa gax̲tooḵóox̲, tlél g̲wadlaan yá éix̲' yík. *We will travel along slowly, it's not deep in this slough.*

# « G »

GAA verb root

- **yan akawligáa | yánde yaa akanalgéin | yax̱ aklagáa**
  *s/he put up food | s/he is putting up food | s/he puts up food (regularly).*
  THEME: yan~ O-ka-S-l-gáa~ (ø motion)
  *for S to put up, store up, accumulate O (esp. food for winter); for S to finish distributing things (esp. at party)*

**gáal'** noun *cataract*
VARIANTS: wak̲gáal'

**gáal'** noun *clam*
·Gáal' has akaháa. *They are digging clams.*

**gaan** noun *smokehole*

GAAN[1] verb root

- **át akaawagán | --- | áx̱ akagaan**
  *it's lit | --- | it lights (regularly).*
  THEME: P-t~ a-ka-ø-gaan~ (ø motion)
  *for P (light) to be on; for P (fire) to burn, catch alight*
  ·S'eenáat akaawagán. *The light is on.*
- **át akawligán | --- | áx̱ aklagaan**
  *s/he lit it | --- | s/he lights it (regularly).*
  THEME: P-t~ a-ka-S-l-gaan~ (ø motion)
  *for S to light, set fire to, cause P to shine; for S to turn on P (light)*
  ·Toow s'eenáa át has akawligán. *They lit a candle.*
  ·Ux̱gank̲áas' tin áx̱ akdulgaan. *It is lit with a match.*
- **awdigaan | yei andagán | yei adagánch**
  *it's sunny | it's getting sunny | it's sunny (regularly).*
  THEME: a-d-gaan~ (g̲a event)
  *for the sun to shine*
  ·Awdagaaních áwé, dleit kaax̱ kalóox̱jaa koolx'áasch hít kaadáx̱. *Because the sun is shining, the snow drips fast off the house.*
  ·Yei andagán. *The sun is beginning to shine.*
- **a kát kawdigán | --- | a káx̱ kadagaan**
  *it's shining on it | --- | it shines on it (regularly).*
  THEME: P-t~ ka-d-gaan~ (ø event)
  *for a light to shine on P*
  ·Hít kageidí át kawdigán wé s'eenáa. *The light is shining on the side of the house.*
  ·K̲únáx̱ áwé k̲'asigóo i shax̱aawú, a kát akawdagaaní. *Your hair is really beautiful when the sun shines on it.*

- **kawdigán | --- | kadagánx̱**
  *it's bright | --- | it brightens (regularly).*
  THEME: ka-d-gaan~ (ø event)
  *for something to shine, produce light by burning*
- **kei awsigán | kei anasgán | kei asgánch**
  *s/he burned it up | s/he is burning it up | s/he burns it up (regularly).*
  THEME: kei O-S-s-gaan~ (ø motion)
  *for S to burn O up*
  NOTES: A common use of this verb is in discussing the traditional practice of burning the clothes one was wearing when s/he passed away, as indicated in the example sentence.
  ·K̲aa naa.ádi kei dusgánch. *They burn the person's clothes up.*

**gáan** noun *outdoors; outside*
·Gáande yaa nay.ádi wooch yáx̱ x'wán anayl'eix̱! *Be sure to all dance alike when you walk out!*
·Aawa.óos'i jig̲wéinaa gáanx̱ ashayaawatée. *She hung the towel that she washed outside.*

**gáan** noun *menstrual discharge; period*
NOTES: Gáan aawa.oo "she had her period".

**gaan ká** noun *smokehole*

**gaan woolí** noun *opening of smokehole*
·Gaan woolí a kaháadi áa kei aawatée. *He put the cover for the smoke hole up there.*

**gaan x̱'aháadi** noun *smokehole cover*

**GAAS'** verb root

- **aadé wligáas' | --- | aadé yoo ligás'k**
  *s/he moved there | --- | s/he moves there (regularly).*
  THEME: P-dé O-l-gáas'~ (na motion)
  *for O to move household (with future plans unspecified) to P*
- **át wuligás' | --- | áx̱ lagáas'**
  *s/he moved there | --- | s/he moves there (regularly).*
  THEME: P-t~ O-l-gáas'~ (ø motion)
  *for O to move household (with future plans unspecified) to P*
  ·Anóoshi Aanídáx̱ áyá yaa San Fransiscot has wuligás'. *They had moved to San Fransisco from Russia.*
- **a kát sh wudligás' | --- | a káx̱ sh ilgáas'**
  *he/she/it leapt on it | --- | he/she/it leaps on it (regularly).*
  THEME: P-t~ sh S-d-l-gáas'~ (ø motion)
  *for S to leap, pounce on P*
  ·Yóot sh wudligás' a k̲oowúdáx̱. *It charged out of its den.*
  ·A wándáx̱ áwé a yíkt sh wudligás' wé yéil. *The raven leapt into it from the edge.*

- **yan yaawagás' | --- | yax̲ yagáas'**
  *s/he fell on his/her face | --- | s/he is nodding off, falling asleep while sitting.*
  THEME: yan~ O-ya-ø-gáas'~ (ø motion)
  *for O to fall on face; for O to nod off, fall asleep while sitting up*
  ·Dax̲dahéen yan yaawagás'. *He fell on his face twice.*

**gáas'** noun *house post*

**gaaw** noun *bell*
·Wé x̲'agáax' daakahídi gaawú ik̲náach' teen wududliyéx̲ *The church bell is made of brass.*

**gaaw** noun *time*
·Yat'éex'i gaaw a tóonáx̲ yiyagût. *You walked through that period of hard time.*
·X'oon gaawx' sá? *At what time?*

**gaaw** noun *drum*

**gaaw** noun *clock*

**GAAW** verb root

- **sawligaaw | saligaaw | kei salagaawch**
  *he/she/it was loud-voiced | he/she/it is loud-voiced | he/she/it gets loud-voiced (regularly).*
  THEME: O-sa-l-gaaw (ga state)
  *for O to be loud-voiced, noisy in speech*
  NOTES: Note a related verb with a similar meaning: x̲'aligaaw "s/he has a loud, powerful voice."
  ·Aank̲áawu G̲eeyx' áwé has saligaaw k̲únáx̲ wé kag̲eet. *The loons are really loud in Ankau Bay.*

**gaawák̲** noun *serviceberry; saskatoonberry*

**gaaw ítx'** noun *late; after the appointed time*
VARIANTS: gaaw ít (C)

**Gaawt'ak̲.aan** noun *Hoonah*

**gaaw x̲'áak** noun *hour*

**gaaw yáx̲** noun *on time; in time*
VARIANTS: gaaw yéx̲ (T)

**gáaxw** noun *duck*
·Héen wát át has wusikwaan wé gáaxw. *The ducks are swimming around at the mouth of the river.*
·Du séek' yageeyí kayís áwé gáaxw awsi.ée. *She cooked a duck for her daughter's birthday.*

**GAAX'** verb root

- **sh káa x̱'awdigáx' | sh káa x̱'adagáax' | sh káa x̱'adagáx'x̱**

*s/he prayed | s/he prays; s/he is praying | s/he prays (regularly).*

THEME: sh káa x̱'e-S-d-gáax'~ (ø act)

*for S to pray*

·G̱aneix̱ káx̱ sh káa x̱'awdigáx'. *She prayed for his salvation.*

·Dikée aank̲áawu du yéet ítx̱ na.aadí has du een sh káa x̱'awdigáx'. *Jesus prayed with his disciples.*

**gági** Adverb *from hiding into open*

·Yá k̲ut'aayg̱áa gági ugootch yee éesh. *During the warm season your father would come out.*

**gán** noun *firewood*

·Xáshaa yéi ndu.eich gán yéi daaduneiyí. *A saw is used to work on wood.*

·Wé aantk̲eení woosh ji.een gán has aawaxásh. *The townspeople cut wood together.*

**ganaltáak** noun *in the fire*

·Ganyal'óot' ganaltáakdáx̱ kéi wjitúk. *The flame shot up out of the fire.*

**ganaswáan** noun *worker; crew*

**gandaa** noun *around the fire*

VARIANTS: gaan daa

·Gandaax' té áa has akaawachák. *They piled rock around the fire.*

·Gandaat has k̲éen. *They are sitting around the fire.*

**gandaadagóogu** noun *woodpecker*

·Gandaadagóogu wéit wudik̲een. *A woodpecker is flying around there.*

·Gandaadagóogu kayéik x̱aa.áx̱ch. *I can hear the sound of a woodpecker.*

**gandaas'aají** noun *bee; wasp*

·Gandaas'aají k̲'eikaxwéin x̱oot kawdliyeech. *Bees are flying around among the flowers.*

·A kúdi daat wudik̲een wé gandaas'aají. *There is a bee flying around the nest.*

**gandaas'aají háatl'i (T)** noun *honey*

VARIANTS: gendaas'aají háatl'i (C)

**gandaas'aají kúdi** noun *bee's nest*

·Wé s'eek gandaas'aají kúdi aawat'ei. *The black bear found a bee's nest.*

**gánde nagoodí** noun *feces*

·Tléik̲w x'aakeidí áwé ts'ítskw gánde nagoodí tóox' yéi nateech. *Berry seeds are found in bird poop.*

**gan eetí** noun *ashes*
·Gan eetí kél't' k̲ugáas' yáx̲ yatee. *Ashes from the fireplace are gray.*

**gangook** noun *fireside; by the fire, facing the fire*
·Áat' jiyeet, gangookt k̲ukawdik'ít'. *People crowded close around the fire because of the cold weather.*
·Wé k̲áa dzísk'u shaayí gangooknáx̲ as.eeyín. *He used to cook moose head next to the campfire.*

**gangukg̲áx̲i** noun *fish heads cooked on ground around fire*
·Gangukg̲áx̲i k̲únáx̲ has du x̲'é yak'éi. *The fish heads cooked around the fire are very tasty to them.*
·Gangukg̲áx̲i has du sitgawsáan atx̲aayí áwé. *The fish heads cooked around the fire are their lunch.*

**ganigeidí** noun *smoke spreaders (board suspended horizontally above smokehouse fire)*

**gán kak̲ás'ti** noun *kindling*
·Gán kak̲ás'ti akawlix̲óot' wé x̲'aan yís. *He chopped kindling for the fire.*
·Gán kak̲ás'ti k̲óok tóox' neil awsi.ín. *He brought the kindling inside in a box.*

**gán láx̲'i** noun *dead wood that's wet on the outside*
·Yat'éex' át akawdusgaaní gán láx̲'i. *It is hard to burn the wet outer part of firewood.*
·Ch'a áa yan awli.át wé gán láx̲'i. *He just left the wet outer part of firewood there.*

**gántiyaakw** noun *steamboat; riverboat*
VARIANTS: gántinyaakw
·Gántiyaakw kaadé yís gán has aawaxaash. *They cut wood to put on the steamboat.*
·Has aawanéegwál' wé gántiyaakw. *They painted the steamboat.*

**Gántiyaakw Séedi** noun *Petersburg*
·Gántiyaakw Séedidáx̲ Lingít áwé. *That is a Tlingit from Petersburg.*
·Gántiyaakw Séedix' yaakw tlein yíx̲ aawa.aat. *People boarded the big boat at Petersburg.*

**gantutl'úk'x̲u** noun *woodworm*
VARIANTS: gentutl'úk'x̲u (C)
·Gantutl'úk'x̲u tléil daa.usx̲áaw. *Woodworms are not furry.*

**gantuxoogú** noun *dry inner part of firewood*

**gán tl'áak'** noun *wet firewood*

**ganyal'óot'** noun *flame*
·Wé ganyal'óot' s'oow yáx̲ yatee. *That flame is green.*
·Ganyal'óot' ganaltáakdáx̲ kéi wjitúk. *The flame shot up out of the fire.*

**gán yátx'i** noun *small pieces of firewood; kindling*

**gawdáan** noun *horse*
·Du gawdáani aadé woo.aadi yé, a niyaadé g̲unéi wjixíx. *He started running in the direction his horses went.*
·Wé k̲áa du dachx̲ánk'i yís gawdáan aawa.oo. *The man bought his grandchild a horse.*

**gawdáan yádi** noun *colt*
·Wé gawdáan yádi át wujik'éin. *That colt is jumping around.*

**gé** particle *[interrogative marks yes-no questions]*
·Dux̲á gé g̲eey kanax̲ k̲utées'? *Are ratfish edible?*
·Yaa indashán óosh gé! *If only you were getting old!*

a **géek** noun *stern (of a boat)*
VARIANTS: a gík
·Yées washéen a géekt satéen wé yaakw. *A new motor sits at the stern of that boat.*
·A géekde yadál wé yaakw. *The boat is stern heavy.*

a **geení** noun *its tail flippers*
·Tsaa geení aankadushxit át teen akawshixít. *She took a picture of the seal tail flippers with a camera.*
·Aax̲ awlixaash a geení wé tsaa. *He cut the tail flippers off of the seal.*

**geesh** noun *kelp*
·Geesh x̲oot wootlóox' wé yáxwch'. *The sea otter is rolling around in the kelp.*
·Geesh toot uwak̲úx̲ wé yaakw. *The boat drove in among the kelp.*

GEET[1] verb root

- **aadé wdzigeet | --- | aadé yoo dzigítk**
*he/she/it fell there | --- | s/he falls there (regularly).*
THEME: P-dé O-d-s-geet~ (na motion)
*for O (live creature) to fall into P*
·Té x̲'áakde wdzigeet. *He fell in the crevice.*

- **anax̲ yei wdzigít | --- | ---**
*s/he fell over it | --- | ---.*
THEME: P-náx̲ yei O-d-s-geet~ (ø motion)
*for O (live creature) to fall down, trip over P*
·X'éedadi kaanáx̲ yéi ax̲ wudzigít at gutóox'. *I fell over a stump in the woods.*

- **át wudzigít | --- | ---**
*he/she/it fell against it | --- | ---.*
THEME: P-t~ O-d-s-geet~ (ø motion)
*for O (live creature) to fall into, against P*
·Diyée aank̲áawu jeet wudzigít. *He fell into satan's hands.*

- **daak wudzigít | --- | daak isgítch**
  *he/she/it fell | --- | s/he falls (regularly).*
  THEME: daak O-d-s-geet~ (ø motion)
  *for O to fall (of live creature)(esp. off of something)*
  ·T'óok' x̲oodé daak ax̲ wudzigít. *I fell into the stinging nettles.*
  ·Yaa ntoo.ádi áwé, daak wudzigít yax̲ akaawax̲ích wutuwa.ini kaneilts'ákw. *When we were walking along, she fell down and spilled all the swamp currants we picked.*
- **kei awsigít | --- | kei asgítch**
  *s/he woke him/her up | --- | s/he wakes him/her up (regularly).*
  THEME: kei O-S-s-geet~ (ø motion)
  *for S to wake O up, rouse O from sleep*
- **kei wdzigít | --- | ---**
  *s/he woke up | --- | ---.*
  THEME: kei O-s-geet~ (ø motion)
  *for O to wake up*
  ·Ts'ootaat kei ax̲ wudzigít. *I woke up in the morning.*
- **k̲ut wudzigeet | --- | k̲ut kei isgítch**
  *s/he got lost | --- | s/he gets lost (regularly).*
  THEME: k̲ut O-d-s-geet~ (ga motion)
  *for O to lose oneself, be lost, usure of one's location*
  ·Wé wanadóo yádi k̲ut wudzigeet. *The lamb got lost.*

GEET[2] verb root

- **at géit wudzigít | at géide yaa nasgít | ---**
  *s/he did something wrong | s/he is doing something wrong | ---.*
  THEME: at géit~ S-d-s-geet~ (ø event)
  *for S to violate, break (law or custom), do something wrong*
  ·At géit wudzigít wé k̲áa átx'i aawutáawu. *He went against the law when he stole the man's belongings.*

**géewaa** noun *beer*

GEI[1] verb root

- **--- | digéix' | ---**
  *--- | they're big | ---.*
  THEME: d-géix' (ga state)
  *for (plural) objects to be big*
  ·Haadaag̲ooji a oox̲ú dak̲digéix'. *Lion teeth are large.*
- **--- | kadigéix' | ---**
  *--- | they're big | ---.*
  THEME: ka-d-géix' (ga state)
  *for plural, usually spherical objects to be big*
  ·Dak̲kadigéix' du guk.ádi. *Her earrings are big.*
- **--- | kayagéi | ---**
  *--- | it's big | ---.*
  THEME: ka-ø-gei~ (na state)

*for a singular, usually round, spherical object to be big*
·Nás'k a doogú x'óow áwé du káa kakg̱wagéi k'oodás' sákw, wé ḵáa tlein. *It will take three leather blankets for the big man's shirt.*

• **--- | ligéi | ---**
--- | *he/she/it is big* | ---.
THEME: O-l-gei~ (na state)
*for O (esp. live creature or building) to be big, tall*

• **woogéi | yagéi | ---**
*it was big; there were many* | *there are many* | ---.
THEME: ø-gei~ (na state)
*for a solid mass or abstracts to be big (in quantity), be lots, many, plenty*
·X̱aatl' áwé yagéi Jilḵáatx'. *There is a lot of algae in the Chilkat.*
·Héen x̱'ayaax̱ yagéi kaxwéix̱. *There are a lot of highbush cranberries along the river.*

• **yéi kaawagéi | yéi koogéi | ---**
*it got this big; there were this many* | *it's this big; there are this many* | ---.
THEME: (yéi) k-u-ya-gei~ (na state)
*for a thing to be (so) big; for things to be (so) many*
·Wáa sá koogéi wé k'wát'? *How many eggs are there?*
·A ḵín ax̱ jee koogéi wé k'oodás' yeidí. *I have less than the price of that shirt.*

• **--- | yéi kwdigéi | ---**
--- | *they're that big* | ---.
THEME: (yéi) + ka-u-d-gei~ (na state)
*for (plural) objects to be (so) big*
·Woosh g̱uwanyáade kwdigéi túlx'u. *Drill bits come in different sizes.*

• **--- | yéi kwdzigéi | ---**
--- | *they're small* | ---.
THEME: (yéi) ka-u-d-s-gei~ (ga state)
*for grain-like objects to be small*
·Yéi kwdzigeiyi aa ḵákwx' áwé akooshtánin yéi daané ax̱ léelk'w. *My grandmother loved to make those little baskets.*

GEI[2] verb root

• **du daa yaa ḵushuwsigéi | du daa yaa ḵushusigéi | du daa kei yaa ḵushusagéich**
*s/he understood* | *s/he understands* | *s/he understands (regularly).*
THEME: N daa yaa ḵu-shu-s-géi (ga state)
*for N to understand, comprehend*
·Ax̱ x̱ooní Lingít tlél du daa yaa ḵushusgé. *My friend doesn't understand Tlingit.*

a **géit~** Adverb *against it; wrongly, improperly*
·Haat kanadaayí géide kei naḵúx̱. *She is going against the current.*
·Té géit kaawagwátl wé kooch'éit'aa. *The ball rolled against a rock.*

**géxtl’** noun *aluminum*
·Du k̲’wádli géxtl’ix̲ sitee. *Her pots are made of aluminum.*
·Géxtl’ tléil udál. *Aluminum is not heavy.*

**gí** particle *perhaps; I guess, it would seem*

**gijook** noun *kind of hawk*
VARIANTS: kijook
·Gijook wéit kawdliyeech. *Hawks are flying around there.*
·Dak̲káx’ "Golden Eagle" gijook yóo tuwasáakw. *In the Inland, we call the Golden Eagle "gijook".*

**Ginjichwáan** noun *Canadian, British*
VARIANTS: Ginjoochwáan
·Ginjichwáan k’isáani áwé, wéix’ has at shí. *The young British men are singing there.*
·Ginjichwáan aanídáx̲ áwé wé shaatk’. *That young woman is from Canada.*

**Ginjoochwáan** noun *Canadian, British*
VARIANTS: Ginjichwáan

**gis’óok̲** noun *northern lights; aurora borealis*
·K̲únáx̲ woo.aat gis’óok̲ yá xáanaa. *The Northern Lights are really moving about this evening.*
·X̲’aan yáx̲ teeyí gis’óok̲, tlél dultínx̲ *When the northern lights are red, they aren't to be looked at.*

**gishoo** noun *pig*
·Gishoo a kígi ax̲ jeet wududzitáa. *I was given half of a pig.*
·K’idéin layéx̲ yá k̲’anáax̲án wé gishoo daaká yís! *Build this fence well around those pigs!*

**gishoo taayí** noun *bacon*
·Atx̲á daakahídix’ gishoo taayí k̲a k’wát’ awdzig̲áax̲. *She ordered bacon and eggs at the restaurant.*
·Gishoo taayí k̲a dleey wóosh teen akawlis’úk. *She fried the meat with bacon.*

**Giyak̲w** noun *Aleut*
·Giyak̲w K̲wáan yoo x̲’atángi k̲óox’ altóow. *He is teaching people the Alutiq language.*
·Giyak̲w K̲wáanx̲ sitee ax̲ x̲ooní, Russell. *My friend Russell is Alutiq.*

GOO[1] verb root

• **k̲’awsigóo | k̲’asigóo | ---**
*it was fun | it's fun | ---.*
THEME: k̲’a-s-góo (ga state)
*for something to be enjoyable, fun, make one happy (esp. of speeches or songs at party); for something to be appealing to the eye*
·K̲únáx̲ áwé k̲’asigóo i shax̲aawú, a kát akawdagaaní. *Your hair is*

*really beautiful when the sun shines on it.*
·Ḵ'asigóo kaltéelḵ l'éiw kát át wusheex. *It's fun running around barefoot in the sand.*

- **du toowú wsigóo | du toowú sigóo | ---**
  *s/he was happy | s/he is happy | ---.*
  THEME: N toowú s-góo (ga state)
  *for N to be happy, glad*
- **du tuwáa wsigóo | du tuwáa sigóo | ---**
  *s/he wanted it | s/he wants it | ---.*
  THEME: N tuwáa S-s-góo (ga state)
  *for N to want, like, desire S; for S to be pleasing to N*
  ·G̱uwakaan at xáshdi téel ax̱ dachx̱ánk' jeeyís ax̱ tuwáa sigóo. *I would like deer skin moccasins for my grandchild.*
  ·Áx̱ akawdudlis'eig̱i ishḵeen du tuwáa sagóowun ax̱ éesh. *My dad used to like smoked black cod.*

GOO[2] verb root

- **anax̱ has yaawagóo | anax̱ yaa (ha)s yanagwéin | anax̱ yoo (ha)s yaagwéik**
  *they traveled through it | they are traveling through it | they travel through it (regularly).*
  THEME: P-náx̱ ya-S-ø-goo~ (na motion)
  *for S (a group of cars, fleet of boats) to travel through P together (by motor); for a school of sea mammals to swim through P together*
  ·Yú sgóon tl'átgi tlein, a góonnáx̱ dax̱yanaagóo wé káa. *The cars are traveling on the isthmus of the big school yard.*
- **át has yaawagoo | --- | ---**
  *they are traveling around; they traveled around | --- | ---.*
  THEME: P-t ya-ø-goo~ (na motion)
  *for S (a group of cars, fleet of boats) to travel around at P (by motor); for a school of sea mammals to swim around at P*
  ·Yaakwdáatx' áwé yakwyádi kát át ḵuyaawagoowún héen kát. *People used to travel around in flat-bottomed canoes in the rivers in Yakutat.*
- **át yawsigóo | --- | áx̱ yasagoo**
  *they swam to it | --- | they swim to it (regularly).*
  THEME: P-t~ ya-s-goo~ (ø motion)
  *for sea mammals to swim in a school to P*
  ·Áa atoosg̱eiwú yé áwé kéet haa daat yawsigóo. *The killer whales came around where we were gillnetting.*

**gooch** noun *small hill; mound, knoll*
·Gooch shakéex' wutusiteen wé sheech dzísk'w. *We saw the cow moose on top of the hill.*
·Gooch litká aadé duwatéen wé g̱ooch. *The wolf on the ridge of the hill is visible.*

GOOK verb root

- **awshigóok | ashigóok | ---**

  *s/he learned how to do it | s/he knows how to do it | ---.*
  THEME: O-S-sh-góok (ga state)
  *for S to know, learn how to do O*
  ·K'idéin ashigóok kakúxaa layeix̱. *He knows how to build bailers really well.*
  ·Náakw yís kayaaní ashigóok, áx' ḵu.aa akwdlix̱éitl' ḵaa x̱'éix̱ aa wuteeyí. *He knows medicinal plants but he is afraid to give them to anyone.*

GOOḴ verb root

- **aadé (ha)s loowagooḵ | aadé yaa (ha)s lunagúḵ | aadé yoo (ha)s luwagúḵk**

  *they ran there | they are running there | they run there (regularly).*
  THEME: P-dé O-lu-ø-gooḵ~ (na motion)
  *for (plural) O to run toward P*
  ·Yóode loowagoog̱u dzísk'w a ítde akḵwal'óon. *I will go hunting those moose that ran over that way.*

- **át has luwagúḵ | aadé yaa (ha)s lunagúḵ | áx̱ has loogook**

  *they ran to it | they are running to it | they run to it (regularly).*
  THEME: P-t~ O-lu-ø-gooḵ~ (ø motion)
  *for (plural) O to run to P*
  ·Kéi daḵinji s'áaxw tlein a tayeet ḵaa luwagúḵ séew tóodáx̱. *People ran under the big umbrella out of the rain.*

- **has loowagooḵ | yaa has lunagúḵ | yoo has luwagúḵk**

  *they ran | they are running | they run (regularly).*
  THEME: O-lu-ø-gooḵ~ (na motion)
  *for (plural) O to run*
  ·Jáaji kát yaa has lunagúḵ. *They are running on snowshoes.*
  ·Yaa ḵaa lunagúg̱u a kayéik has aawa.áx̱. *They heard the sound of people running.*

- **a ítx̱ has loowagooḵ | a ítx̱ yaa (ha)s lunagúḵ | a ítx̱ yoo (ha)s luwagúḵk**

  *they ran after it | they are running after it | they run after it (regularly).*
  THEME: N ítx̱ O-lu-ø-gooḵ~ (na motion)
  *for (plural) O to run after N*
  ·Watsíx ítx̱ yaa lunagúḵ wé g̱ooch. *The wolves are chasing after the caribou.*

**goon** noun *spring (of water)*
·Ax̱ éek' si.áat'i héen goondáx̱ ayáayin. *My brother used to pack cold water from a spring.*

**góon** noun *gold*
·Wé ḵáa góon awsiteen héenák'w táade. *The man saw gold at the bottom of the creek.*

·Góon dáanaa een áwé kawduwat'íx̱' ax̱ jeeyís yá kées. *This bracelet was pounded out of a gold coin for me.*

a **góon** noun *portage, passage across it; its isthmus*

du **góos** noun *privates (of female); vulva; vagina*

**góos'** noun *cloud cover; sky, cloudy sky*
·Góos' tóonáx̱ ayatéen. *She sees it through the clouds.*
·Tlél góos' ḵuwustee tatgé. *There weren't clouds yesterday.*

GÓOS' verb root

• **ḵoowligóos' | ḵuligóos' | kei ḵulagóos'ch**
*it was cloudy | it's cloudy | it gets cloudy (regularly).*
THEME: ḵu-l-góos' (ga state)
*for the sky to be cloudy*

**goos' shú** noun *horizon*
VARIANTS: gus'shú
·Gus'shóode duwatéen wé g̱agaan. *The sun is visible on the horizon.*
·Gus'shóode x̱aatéen wé watsíx. *I see the caribou on the horizon.*

du **goosh** noun *his/her thumb*
·Du goosh awlichún. *He hurt his thumb.*
·Wudix'ís' du goosh. *His thumb is swollen.*

a **gooshí** noun *its dorsal fin (of killerwhale)*
·Ch'as a gooshí duwatéen wé kéet. *Only the dorsal fin of the killerwhale is visible.*
·Jinkaat kéet gooshí ayatéen wé ḵáa shaan. *The old man sees ten killerwhale dorsal fins.*

**gooshúg̱unáx̱** Numeral *nine (people)*
VARIANTS: gooshúḵnáx̱

**gooshúḵ** Numeral *nine*
·Gooshúḵ dáanaa yéi x̱'alitseen wé x'úx'. *The book costs nine dollars.*
·Gooshúḵ yatee du keidlx'í. *He has nine dogs.*

GOOT[1] verb root

• **aadáx̱ woogoot | aadáx̱ yaa nagút | aadáx̱ yoo yagútk**
*he/she/it left there | he/she/it is leaving there | he/she/it leaves there (regularly).*
THEME: P-dáx̱ S-ø-goot~ (na motion)
*for (singular) S to walk, go (by walking or as general term) away from P*
·Ḵaa yat'éináx̱ hít yeedáx̱ woogoot. *He left the house when no one was looking.*

• **aadé woogoot | aadé yaa nagút | aadé yoo yagútk**
*he/she/it went there | he/she/it is going there | he/she/it goes there (regularly).*
THEME: P-dé S-ø-goot~ (na motion)
*for (singular) S to walk, go (by walking or as general term) toward P*
·Hoon daakahídidéi nagú káaxweig̱áa! *Go to the store for some coffee!*

·Hinyaa Ḵwáan x̱ánde woogoot wé shaawát. *The woman went to visit the Klawock people.*

• **aag̱áa woogoot | aag̱áa yaa nagút | aag̱áa yoo yagútk**
*s/he went to get it | s/he is going to get it | s/he goes to get it (regularly).*
THEME: P-g̱aa S-ø-goot~ (na motion)
*for (singular) S to go after P, go seeking P (on foot)*
NOTES: Note that -g̱aa takes the opposite tone of the final syllable of the noun that it attaches to. Hence: kanat'ág̱aa "(going) after blueberries", but shaawg̱áa "(going) after gumboots".
·Was'x'aan tléig̱ug̱áa woogoot ax̱ tláa. *My mom walked to get salmonberries.*

• **anax̱ yaawagút | anax̱ yaa wunagút | anax̱ yaa gútch**
*he/she/it walked through it | he/she/it is walking through it | he/she/it walks through it (regularly).*
THEME: P-náx̱ ya-u-S-ø-goot~ (ø motion)
*for (singular) S to walk, go (by walking or as general term) through P*
NOTES: This verb can be used metaphorically to indicate that someone has pulled through an illness: A tóonáx̱ yaawagút "s/he got through it (an illness, eg.)".
·Yat'éex'i gaaw a tóonáx̱ yiyagút. *You walked through that period of hard time.*

• **át uwagút | aadé yaa nagút | áx̱ goot**
*he/she/it arrived there | he/she/it is going there | he/she/it goes there (regularly).*
THEME: P-t~ S-ø-goot~ (ø motion)
*for (singular) S to arrive at P, go to P (by walking or as general term)*
·Nukshiyáan g̱aatáa x̱'éit ugootch. *The mink walks into the mouth of the trap every time.*
·Du séek' du x̱ánt uwagút. *Her daughter came to her.*

• **át woogoot | --- | át yoo yagútk**
*he/she/it is walking around there; he/she/it walked around there | --- | he/she/it walks around there (regularly).*
THEME: P-t S-ø-goot~ (na motion)
*for (singular) S to walk, go (by walking or as general term) around at P*
·X'at'daayéejayi héenák'w át nagútch. *The black turnstone walks around in shallow water.*
·Héen wantóot woogoot wé gus'yadóoli. *The sandpiper is walking around the riverbank.*

• **áx̱ woogoot | áx̱ yaa nagút | áx̱ yoo yagútk**
*he/she/it walked along it | he/she/it is walking along it | he/she/it walks along it (regularly).*
THEME: P-x̱ S-ø-goot~ (na motion)
*for (singular) S to walk, go (by walking or as general term) along P*
·Yá neechx̱ yaa neegúdi yei kg̱isatéen yá katóok. *As you walk along this shoreline you will see this cave.*
·Yeedát ḵuyak'éi g̱aatáa yéi daané yís yá kaxwaan káx̱ yaa nagúdi. *Today the weather is good for walking out on the frost to check the traps.*

• **ayawdigút | yaa ayandagút | awudagútx̲**
*s/he turned back | s/he is turning back | s/he turns back (regularly).*
THEME: a-ya-u-S-d-goot~ (ø motion)
*for (singular) S to turn back, go back (by walking or as general term)*

• **daak uwagút | daak yaa nagút | daak gútch**
*he/she/it walked into the open | he/she/it is walking into the open | he/she/it walks into the open (regularly).*
THEME: daak S-ø-goot~ (ø motion)
*for (singular) S to walk, go (by walking or as general term) into the open*
·Wé k̲aa sháade háni k̲aa x̲áni daak uwagút. *The leader came out to the people.*
·Has du yáa daak uwagút wé xóots tlein kanat'á has a.éeni. *While they were picking blueberries, the brown bear came face to face with them.*

• **gági uwagút | gági yaa nagút | gági gútx̲**
*he/she/it emerged | he/she/it is emerging | he/she/it emerges (regularly).*
THEME: gági S-ø-goot~ (ø motion)
*for (singular) S to emerge, walk out into the open*
·Yá k̲ut'aayg̲áa gági ugootch yee éesh. *During the warm season your father would come out.*

• **héide yaawagút | héide yaa wunagút | héide yaa gútch**
*s/he moved over that way | s/he is moving over that way | s/he moves over that way (regularly).*
THEME: héide ya-u-S-ø-goot~ (ø motion)
*for (singular) S to move over (away from speaker)*

• **a ítx̲ woogoot | a ítx̲ yaa nagút | ---**
*he/she/it followed it | he/she/it is following it | ---.*
THEME: N ítx̲ yaa S-ø-goot~ (ga motion)
*for (singular) S to follow N (on foot)*
NOTES: Note that the preverb yaa does not occur in the perfective form.
·Wéix̲ yaa na.ádi watsíx, xóots a ítx̲ yaa nagút. *A grizzly bear is walking behind the herd of caribou going that way.*
·Wé yées k̲áa du húnx̲w ítx̲ yaa nagút. *The young man's older brother is walking along behind him.*

• **k̲ut woogoot | k̲ut kei nagút | k̲ut kei gútch**
*s/he got lost | s/he is getting lost | s/he gets lost (regularly).*
THEME: k̲ut S-ø-goot~ (ga motion)
*for (singular) S to get lost (on foot)*

• **a nák̲ woogoot | a nák̲ yaa nagút | a nák̲ yoo yagútk**
*s/he left it behind | s/he is leaving it behind | s/he leaves it behind (regularly).*
THEME: P-nák̲ S-ø-goot~ (na motion)
*for (singular) S to leave P behind, walk away from P*
·G̲alsaayít áwé du yéi jineiyí a nák̲ woogoot. *She went away from her work so that she could rest.*

·A nák yaa nagúdi yaa shukanashéen. *She is singing as she is leaving it behind.*

• **--- | yaa nagút | ---**

*--- | s/he is walking along | ---.*

THEME: yaa S-ø-gút (ga motion)

*for (singular) S to be walking along, going along (by walking or as a general term)*

NOTES: This is an example of a progressive epiaspectual paradigm (Leer, 91), which basically means that all forms are based on the progressive aspect. The progressive epiaspect is characterized by: 1)having the yaa preverb in all forms, 2)having no perfective form, and 3)denotes semantically a continuous transition from one location or state to another.

·Áa agaxtool'oon yé yinaadé yaa gagú! *Walk toward the place we will hunt!*

·A wánx áwé yaa gagútch wé kaxéel' teen. *He walks on the edge of trouble.*

• **yaax woogoot | --- | yaax yei gútch**

*s/he went aboard | --- | s/he goes aboard (regularly).*

THEME: yaax S-ø-goot~ (ga motion)

*for (singular) S to go aboard (a boat)*

**gootl** noun *bump, lump, hump, mound*

·Gootl kát áa wé gáx. *The rabbit is sitting on a mound.*

·Gootl kanax yawjik'én wé naagas'éi. *The red fox jumped over a mound.*

a **goowú** noun *its stump, butt end (of tree or other plant)*

·Wé aas goowú káa woonook. *She sat on that tree stump.*

·Wé aas goowú aax aawas'úw. *He chopped off that tree stump.*

**goox** noun *slave*

·Goox kaa jeex' yéi téeyin. *People used to have slaves.*

·Ch'áakw goox shayadahéinin. *There were lots of slaves long ago.*

a **gúgu** noun *its antenna (of radio)*

·Yóo tliyaa aasdéi ksaxát wéi kaxées' ax at shí kóok gúgu yís! *Attach the wire to that tree over there for my radio antenna!*

du **gúk** noun *his/her ear*

·Kínaa teen aawaták du gúk. *She pierced her ear with a quill.*

·Du gúkx' tsú yéi aa wduwa.oo wéi s'aak k'anoox. *They put the small bone labret in his ear too.*

**guk kajaash** noun *earring*

·A k'ishataaganí yéi ndu.eich guk kajaashí yís. *Its quills are used for earrings.*

·Guk kajaash yéi aya.óo. *She is wearing earrings.*

**gukkudayáat'** noun *donkey*

·Yaa at nayáan wé gukkudayáat'. *The donkey is packing things.*

a **gukshatú** RelationalNoun *(in) the corner of it*
VARIANTS: a gukshitú (An)

**gúkshi** noun *corner*
·Gúkshi yan sa.ín wé kaḵáshx̱i a káa yéi tuwa.oowu káast! *Put the barrel we put the steamed berries in in the corner!*

a **gukshitú (An)** RelationalNoun *(in) the corner of it*
VARIANTS: a gukshatú
·Du hídi gukshitú niyaadé áwé aas anax̱ akaawahaa. *He planted the tree toward the corner of his house.*
·Wé hít gukshitúdáx̱ kasixát wé kaxées'. *The wire runs from the corner of that house.*

**guk tl'éinx̱w** noun *earring; yarn dangling from the ears that sways during dancing*

du **gukyikk'óox̱'u** noun *his/her earwax*

**guk.át** noun *earring*
VARIANTS: guk.édi (C)
·Du guk.ádi yaayí ḵut akaawaǥéex'. *She lost one of her earrings.*
·Ax̱ léelk'w jeeyís áyá kax̱waa.oo yá kanéist guk.át. *I bought these cross earrings for my grandmother.*

**gúḵl'** noun *swan*
VARIANTS: gáḵl'
·Gúḵl' wéit wusikwaan. *Swans are swimming around there.*
·Gúḵl' dleit yáx̱ daǥaatee. *Swans are white.*

**Gunalchéesh!** interj. *Thank you!*
·Gunalchéesh ax̱ x̱'éit yeeysa.aax̱í. *Thank you all for listening to me.*
·Wé haa sháade háni "gunalchéesh" haa jeeyís yéi yanaḵéich. *Our leader says "thank you" for us.*

**gúnl'** noun *growth on the trunk of a tree, burl*
·Gúnl' aax̱ aawaxaash. *He cut the burl off.*
·Gúnl' yéi aawa.oo nadáakw ax̱layeix̱ít. *He used a burl to make a table.*

**gunx̱aa** noun *abalone*
·Gunx̱aa yaka.óot' aawa.oo. *She bought abalone buttons.*
·Gunx̱aa yaka.óot' du l.uljíni kát akaawaḵáa. *She sewed the abalone buttons on her vest.*

**gus'k'iḵwáan l'oowú** noun *oak*
·Gus'k'iḵwáan l'oowú teen wududliyéx̱ wé nadáakw. *The table is made of oak.*

**Gus'k'iyee ḵwáan** noun *White, European, Caucasian (man or person)*
VARIANTS: Gus'k'eeḵwáan

**gus'yadóoli** noun *sandpiper*
·Gus'yadóoli taakw.eetíx' haax̱ kalyeech. *Sandpipers fly here in the early summer.*
·Héen wantóot woogoot wé gus'yadóoli. *The sandpiper is walking around the riverbank.*

**gus'yé kindachooneidí** noun *pigeon or dove*
·Tusconx' áwé aa sax̱waa.áx̱ gus'yé kindachooneidí. *I heard some doves in Tuscon.*

**gút** noun *dime*
·Tléix' gút akaawahées'. *He borrowed one dime.*
·Gút akawdit'ei. *She found herself a dime.*

**Gutéix̱'** noun *Chugach Eskimo*

at **gutú** noun *woods; bush; brush, underbrush*
VARIANTS: at gatú (T), et getú (C)
·Wé g̱aatáa yéi daanéiyi at gutóodáx̱ daak uwagút. *The trapper came out of the bush.*
·Wéi Sheet'kaadáx̱ adátx'i at gutóox' áwé has du ée at dultóow. *The kids from Sitka are taught out in the wilderness.*

at **gutu.ádi** noun *thing of the woods*
·Wáa yateeyi yéix' at gutu.ádi g̱alsháatadix̱ dulyéx̱ch. *Sometimes wild animals are held captive.*

**gútl** noun *blunt arrow for stunning*
·Yées aa gútl du jeet wududzitán. *He was given a new blunt arrow.*
·Gútl teen al'óon woogoot. *He went hunting with a blunt arrow.*

**guwáatl'** adj. *short*

**gúx'aa** noun *cup; can*
VARIANTS: gúx'waa
·Wé shaatk' gúx'aa kát cháayoo ax̱ jeet awsi.ín. *The young girl gave me tea in a cup.*
·Gúx'aa kat'óott kaawadáa wé cháayoo. *The cup is filled part way up with tea.*

**gu.aal** particle *I hope; would that*
·Gu.aal kwshé iwulx̱éidlik̲. *Bless you. (Lit: I hope you get lucky.)*

# « Gw »

**gwáa** particle *[expression of strong surprise]*
VARIANTS: gu.áa

**GWAAL** verb root

- **aawagwaal | agwáal | ---**
  *s/he beat it | s/he beats it; s/he is beating it | ---.*
  THEME: O-S-ø-gwaal~ (ga act)
  *for S to beat O (esp. drum); for S to ring O (bell); for S to stab O*
  ·Ch'a hú du woowká aawagwál. *He pounded his own chest.*
  ·Du x̱'ás' aawagwál wé ḵáa. *That man socked him on the jaw.*
- **ayaawagwál | --- | ayagwálx̱**
  *s/he hit him/her in the face | --- | s/he hits him/her in the face (regularly).*
  THEME: O-ya-S-ø-gwaal~ (ø event)
  *for S to hit O in the face (with fist), punch O*
- **sh wudigwál | sh dagwáal | sh dagwálx̱**
  *it rang | it's ringing | it rings (regularly).*
  THEME: sh da-gwaal~ (ø act)
  *for a telephone or bell to ring*

**GWAAS'** verb root

- **ḵoowdigwás' | yaa ḵundagwás' | ḵudagwás'x̱**
  *it's foggy; it was foggy | it's getting foggy | it gets foggy (regularly).*
  THEME: ḵu-d-gwáas'~ (ø event)
  *for the weather to be foggy*

**GWAATL** verb root

- **át kaawagwátl | aadé yaa kanagwátl | áx̱ kagwaatl**
  *it rolled to it | it's rolling to it | it rolls to it (regularly).*
  THEME: P-t~ ka-ø-gwáatl~ (ø motion)
  *for a spherical object to roll to P*
  ·Té géit kaawagwátl wé kooch'éit'aa. *The ball rolled against a rock.*

**gwál** particle *perhaps*
·Gwál tleiḵáa x̱'oos áwé a kax̱yeedé. *It must be twenty feet to the ceiling.*

**gwálaa** noun *dagger; machete, long knife*
·Yées aa gwálaa aawax̱oox̱. *He asked for a new dagger.*
·Gwálaa teen ch'áal' aawas'úw ḵaa x̱'oos deiyí kaax̱. *He chopped willows off the foot trail with a machete.*

**gwéil** noun *bag; sack*
·Nadáakw kát téen wé x'úx' gwéil. *The paper bag is lying on the table.*
·Du jeeg̱áa koodáal du gwéili. *He can handle the weight of his backpack.*

a **gwéinli** noun *its hoof*
·T'ooch' yáx̲ yatee a gwéinli wé dzísk'w. *The moose's hoof is black.*
·S'igeidí g̲eiwú yís a gwéinli aax̲ awlixaash, wé watsíx. *He cut the hooves off the caribou for a beaver net.*

# « G̱ »

**g̱aa** Adverb *enough, acceptably*

**-g̱aa** postpos. *(distributed) in the area of; (going) after, (waiting) for; about the time of*
VARIANTS: -g̱áa
NOTES: The tone on the postposition -g̱aa is the opposite of that on the final syllable of the noun which it attaches to.
·X̱'aan yáx̱ kakéing̱aa neelhoon! *Go buy me some red yarn!*
·Ḵuk'éet' áwé gax̱too.áat kalchaneit tléig̱ug̱áa. *We are going to pick mountain ash berries.*

**g̱áach** noun *mat, doormat; rug*
·Wé du tuwáa sigóowu g̱áach aawa.oo. *She bought the rug she wanted.*
·X̱'aan yáx̱ kawdiyés' wé g̱áach. *The rug is colored red.*

**g̱aaḵ** noun *lynx*

**G̱aanax̱teidí** noun *G̱aanax̱teidí, locally called "Frog"; a clan of the Raven moiety whose principal crest is the Frog*

**G̱AAS'** verb root

• **--- | kadlig̱áas' | ---**
--- | *it's striped* | ---.
THEME: ka-d-l-g̱áas' (state)
*for something to be striped*
NOTES: This verb only occurs in the imperfective.
·Haadaadóoshi kadlig̱áas'. *Tigers are striped.*

**g̱aat** noun *sockeye salmon; red salmon*
·Ḵúnáx̱ yak'éi wé g̱aat. *The sockeye salmon is really good.*
·Jikaḵáas' káx̱ ashayaawatée wé g̱aat atx'aan hídi yeex'. *She hung the sockeye salmon on the stick in the smokehouse.*

**g̱aatáa** noun *trap (esp. steel trap)*
·Nukshiyáan g̱aatáa x̱'éit ugootch. *The mink walks into the mouth of the trap every time.*
·Yeedát ḵuyak'éi g̱aatáa yéi daané yís yá kaxwaan káx̱ yaa nagúdi. *Today the weather is good for walking out on the frost to check the traps.*

**g̱aatáa yéi daanéiyi** noun *trapper*
·Ax̱ éesh g̱aatáa yéi daanéiyix̱ satéeyin. *My dad was a trapper.*
·Wé g̱aatáa yéi daanéiyi at gutóodáx̱ daak uwagút. *The trapper came out of the bush.*

**g̱áatl** noun *pilot bread*

·Wé g̱áatl ax̱ tuwáa sigóo. *I want the pilot bread*

·G̱áatl aawak'ít'. *He finished the pilot bread.*

**g̱áax'w** noun *herring eggs*

·Wé s'íx' g̱áax'w a káa yéi yatee. *There are herring eggs on that plate.*

·Haaw héende awli.aat g̱áax'w káx̱. *She put branches in the water for herring eggs.*

**g̱aax̱** noun *crying, weeping*

·g̱aax̱ shí teen áwé yaawaxeex wé ḵu.éex'. *A cry song took place at the potlatch.*

**G̱AAX̱** verb root

- **awdzig̱áax̱ | asg̱áax̱ | yei asg̱áax̱ch**

  *s/he asked for it | s/he is asking for it | s/he asks for it (regularly).*

  THEME: O-S-d-s-g̱áax̱ (g̱a act)

  *for S to cry for, ask for O*

  ·Atx̱á daakahídix' gishoo taayí ḵa k'wát' awdzig̱áax̱. *She ordered bacon and eggs at the restaurant.*

- **kawdig̱aax̱ | kadag̱áax̱ | ---**

  *he/she/it cried out | he/she/it is crying out | ---.*

  THEME: ka-S-d-g̱aax̱~ (ga act)

  *for S to cry loudly (of child, or person in great pain), to cry out or scream (in fear or pain)*

  ·Wé dóosh kadag̱áax̱. *The cat is crying.*

- **woog̱aax̱ | g̱áax̱ | kei g̱áx̱ch**

  *s/he cried | s/he cries; s/he is crying | s/he cries (regularly).*

  THEME: S-ø-g̱aax̱~ (ga act)

  *for (singluar) S to cry*

a **g̱ádzi** noun *its hindquarters; thigh*

·Dzísk'u g̱ádzi yaa anayéin. *He is packing a moose hindquarter.*

·Watsíx g̱ádzi yei akanaxásh. *She is cutting up a caribou hindquarter.*

**g̱agaan** noun *sun*

·Wé g̱agaan kei yaséich wé ḵeix̱'ét ḵuwuhaayí. *The sun lifts its face when dawn breaks.*

·G̱agaan daak uwaxíx wé séew ítdáx̱. *The sun came out after the rain.*

**g̱agaan kas'úkwx̱u** noun *sun-dried*

**g̱agaan x̱'usyee** noun *sunbeam; ray of sunlight*

·Wé ts'ats'ée g̱agaan x̱'usyeet .áa. *That song bird is sitting in the ray of sunlight.*

·Wé shaa shakéede duwatéen wé g̱agaan x̱'usyee. *The ray of sunlight can be seen on the mountain top.*

**g̲ákw** noun *dried and hard; stiff (as canvas, dry fish)*
·Wé x̲áat g̲ákw yáx̲ uwaxúk. *That fish is dried stiff.*
·Wé yées xwaasdáa g̲ákw yáx̲ yatee. *The new tent is stiff.*

**g̲alg̲aak̲u** noun *wilderness; the bush*
VARIANTS: katk̲aak̲ú, g̲walg̲ak̲ú (At), kalg̲ak̲ú (T)

**g̲alsháatadi** noun *captive*
VARIANTS: g̲alsháatedi (C)
·Wé k̲áa neech káx' áwé g̲alsháatadix̲ wududliyéx̲. *The man was made captive for nothing.*
·Wáa yateeyi yéix' at gutu.ádi g̲alsháatadix̲ dulyéx̲ch. *Sometimes wild animals are held captive.*

**g̲altú** noun *pocket*
·Al'óon wugoodí ux̲gank̲áas' du g̲altóode ayaawa.oo. *When he was going hunting, he put matches in his pocket.*

**g̲altulítaa** noun *pocket knife*
VARIANTS: k̲atltulítaa (AtT), galtulítaa (C)
·Yées aa g̲altulítaa du léelk'w jeeyís aawa.oo. *He bought his grandpa a new pocketknife.*
·Yalik'áts' du g̲altulítayi. *His pocketknife is sharp.*

**G̲alyáx̲ K̲wáan** noun *people of Kaliakh River (Cape Yakataga to Controller Bay)*
·G̲alyáx̲ K̲wáan áwé Yaakwdáat k̲wáan x̲oox' yéi s yatee. *The Kaliakh River people live among the Yakutat people.*
·G̲alyáx̲ K̲wáan áwé G̲alyáx̲ Kaagwaantaanx̲ has sitee. *The Kaliakh River people are the Kaliakh River Kaagwaantaan.*

**g̲ánch** noun *tobacco*
·Hoon daakahídidáx̲ g̲ánch has aawa.oo. *They bought tobacco from the store.*
·G̲ánch áwé aan yéi daaduné wéi kat'éx̲'aa yeit. *He uses the mortar for pounding his tobacco.*

**g̲aneix̲** noun *recovery; salvation*
·Lingít x̲'éináx̲ yoo x̲'atánk a.áx̲ji g̲aneix̲ yáx̲ áwé du ée yatee. *Hearing the Tlingit language is like salvation to her.*
·Laaxw eetí wé k̲aa jeedáx̲ atx̲á has du g̲aneix̲íx̲ wusitee. *After the famine, the food given to them became their salvation.*

**g̲anook** noun *petrel*
·Wé g̲anook has du déint wudik̲een. *The petrel is flying around near them.*
·Tléil yá dak̲káx' yéi utí wé g̲anook. *Here in the Inland we don't have any petrels.*

**du g̲áts** noun *his/her buttocks, thighs*
·Du g̲áts kalshúk'x̲. *His thighs cramp regularly.*
·Du g̲átsig̲áa wootee yá kawáat. *There are tumors all over her thigh.*

du **g̲atsx̲'áak** noun *his/her crotch; between his/her legs*

**g̲áx̲** noun *rabbit*
·Wé g̲áx̲ dleit yáx̲ x̲asitee. *The rabbit is white.*
·Xáanaa atx̲aayí yís g̲áx̲ akawlis'úk. *She fried rabbit for dinner.*

**g̲ayéis'** noun *iron, tin*
VARIANTS: g̲iyéis', ik̲yéis'
·Kaduch'áak'w lítaa sákw yak'éiyi aa g̲ayéis' neil tí! *Bring home a good piece of iron for a carving knife!*
·G̲ayéis' k̲'wátl dak̲yadál. *Iron pots are heavy.*

**g̲ayéis' háatl'i** noun *rust*
·G̲ayéis' a háatl'ix̲ yóo siteek. *Iron rusts.*

**g̲ayéis' hít** noun *jail*
VARIANTS: g̲iyéis' hít
·Ch'áakw yéi kdunéek g̲ayéis' hítdáx̲ áwé haa x̲oot yawduwax̲áa Anóoshi. *It is told that long ago, Russians were brought among us from jail.*
·G̲ayéis' hítde kawduwanáa. *He was sent to jail.*

**g̲ayéis' layeix̲í** noun *blacksmith*
VARIANTS: g̲iyéis' layeix̲í, g̲iyéis' leyeix̲í (C)
·G̲ayéis' layeix̲í jeedé x̲'awditaan du éet g̲adasheet. *She telephoned the blacksmith to help her.*
·G̲ayéis' layeix̲íx̲ nax̲sateeyít sgóoni yoo uwagút. *He went to school to become an engineer.*

**g̲ayéis' tíx'** noun *cable*
VARIANTS: g̲iyéis' tíx'
·Wé g̲ayéis' tíx' áwé du jín táakt yawdig̲ích. *The steel cable poked him in the hand.*
·G̲unayéide kwditlawu g̲ayéis' tíx' du jeewú. *He has steel cables of different sizes.*

**g̲ayéis' t'éix̲'i** noun *blacksmith*
·G̲ayéis' t'éix̲'i sháade háni haat k̲uwatín tatgé. *The chief blacksmith traveled here yesterday.*
·G̲ayéis' t'éix̲'ix̲ nax̲sateet áwé. *She is becoming a blacksmith.*

G̲EECH verb root

- **aadé yawdig̲eech | --- | aadé yoo yadig̲íchk**
*it pierced it | --- | it pierces it (regularly).*
THEME: P-dé ya-d-g̲eech~ (na motion)
*for a sharp object to pierce, enter, prick P; for an animal to bite P*
·Táax'ál' x'aan áwé ax̲ tl'eik̲ tóode yawdig̲eech. *The needle point poked my finger.*

- **át yawdig̲ích | --- | áx̲ yadag̲eech**
*it pierced it | --- | it pierces it (regularly).*
THEME: P-t~ ya-d-g̲eech~ (ø motion)

*for a sharp object to pierce, enter, prick P; for an animal to bite P*
·Wé g̱ayéis' tíx' áwé du jín táakt yawdig̱ích. *The steel cable poked him in the hand.*
·Du tl'eiḵt yawdig̱iji sheey kaḵáas'i áx' wudliḵít'. *It got infected where the splinter poked her finger.*

- **át yawdlig̱ích | --- | áx̱ yalg̱eech**
*they peirced it | --- | they pierce it (regularly).*
THEME: P-t~ ya-d-l-g̱eech~ (ø motion)
*for (plural) sharp objects to pierce, enter, prick P*
·Wé x̱alak'ách' x̱aawú ax̱ keidlí x̱'éit yawdlig̱ích. *The porcupine quills stuck in my dogs mouth.*

**g̱éechadi** noun *windfall; tree lying in the woods*
·Dei kát la.ádi g̱éechadi aax̱ yéi awsinei. *He removed the windfall lying in the road.*
·Gán yís akaawaxaash wé g̱éechadi. *She cut up the dead trees for firewood.*

**g̱eeg̱ách'** noun *swing; hammock*
·Tíx' ḵa x'óow tin g̱eeg̱ách' awliyéx̱ t'ukanéiyi jeeyís. *She made a hammock for the baby with rope and a blanket.*
·Dzaas áwé yéi akg̱wa.oo g̱eeg̱ách' akawusneiyí. *She will use string when she crochets a hammock.*

**g̱éejadi** noun *windfall; dead tree(s) or brush that has fallen*
VARIANTS: g̱éejedi (C)

G̱EEL verb root

- **yaawdig̱íl | yaa yandag̱íl | yadag̱ílx̱**
*it's dull | it's getting dull | it gets dull (regularly).*
THEME: ya-d-g̱eel~ (ø event)
*for an edge to be blunt, dull*
·Yaawdig̱íl du túlayi. *His drill became dull.*

G̱EEL' verb root

- **ayaawag̱íl' | ayag̱éel' | ayag̱íl'x̱**
*s/he sharpened it | s/he is sharpening it | s/he sharpens it (regularly).*
THEME: O-ya-S-ø-g̱éel'~ (ø act)
*for S to sharpen O (with a grindstone)*
·Du t'eix̱í ayaawag̱íl'. *He sharpened his fish hooks.*

G̱EET verb root

- **aawag̱éet | --- | yóo ayag̱éetk**
*it's pouring rain; it poured rain | --- | it pours rain (regularly).*
THEME: a-ø-g̱éet (na event)
*for rain, hail, snow to fall (often hard, in dark rainstorm)*
·Ḵúnáx̱ x̱at wuditl'ák', kaklahéen áyá aawag̱éet. *I'm so wet - wet snow is coming down hard.*

- **k̲ukawjig̲ít | yaa k̲ukanashg̲ít | k̲ukashg̲ítx̲**
  *it's dark | it's getting dark | it gets dark (regularly).*
  THEME: k̲u-ka-j-g̲éet~ (ø event)
  *for the sky to be dark*
  NOTES: The k̲u- prefix refers to weather or the sky in general. Without the k̲u- prefix, this verb can also refer to darkness of a room. For example: kawjig̲ít "it's dark".
  ·Wé kóok̲ a yee kawjig̲ít. *It is dark inside the cellar.*

**G̲EEX'** verb root

- **akaawag̲éex' | --- | yoo akayag̲ix'k**
  *s/he donated it | --- | s/he donates it (regularly).*
  THEME: O-ka-S-ø-g̲éex' (na event)
  *for S to donate O (esp. money); for S to load O (gun), put bullet in; for S to shoot O (basketball)*
  NOTES: To include the recipient of the donation in the sentence, you would use: du jeet "to him/her", as in: Du jeet akaawag̲éex'. "S/he donated it to him/her." If the recipient is an organization, you would use: a kagéi yís "to it", replacing the a with the name of the organization. For example, Wé Salvation Army kagéi yís akaawag̲éex'. "S/he donated it to the Salvation Army."
- **át kawdig̲íx' | --- | áx̲ kadag̲éex'**
  *s/he contributed to it | --- | s/he contributes to it (regularly).*
  THEME: P-t~ ka-S-d-g̲éex'~ (ø motion)
  *for S to donate, contribute, add to P*
  ·A x̲oonéet kax̲wdig̲íx'. *I added to it.*
- **kawdig̲éex' | yaa kandag̲íx' | yoo kdig̲íx'k**
  *s/he contributed | s/he is contributing | s/he contributes (regularly).*
  THEME: ka-S-d-g̲éex'~ (na event)
  *for S to donate, contribute*
- **kei akaawag̲íx' | --- | kei akag̲íx'ch**
  *s/he threw it | --- | s/he throws it (regularly).*
  THEME: kei O-ka-S-ø-g̲éex'~ (ø motion)
  *for S to throw O (esp. ball) up in the air*
  ·Kei kawduwag̲ix'i té du káak't kaawaxíx. *The rock that was thrown hit him on the forehead.*
- **k̲ut aawag̲éex' | k̲ut kei anag̲íx' | k̲ut kei ag̲íx'ch**
  *s/he lost it | s/he is losing it | s/he loses it (regularly).*
  THEME: k̲ut O-S-ø-g̲éex'~ (ga motion)
  *for S to lose O*
- **k̲ut akaawag̲éex' | --- | k̲ut kei akag̲íx'ch**
  *s/he lost it | --- | s/he loses it (regularly).*
  THEME: k̲ut O-ka-S-ø-g̲éex'~ (ga motion)
  *for S to lose O (round, spherical object)*
  ·T'áa kát k̲ushí ax̲ jeeyís - k̲ut kax̲waag̲éex' ax̲ kawóot ka.íshayi!

*Look on the floor for me - I lost my needle!*
·Du guk.ádi yaayí ḵut akaawaG̱éex'. *She lost one of her earrings.*

**g̱eey** noun *bay*
VARIANTS: g̱eiy (TC)
·Aanḵáawu G̱eeyx' áwé has saligaaw ḵúnáx̱ wé kaG̱eet. *The loons are really loud in Ankau Bay.*

**g̱eey kanax̱ ḵutées'** noun *ratfish*
·Tléil x̱wasakú g̱eey kanax̱ ḵutées' yóo duwasáagu x̱áat. *I don't know the fish called ratfish.*
·Dux̱á gé g̱eey kanax̱ ḵutées'? *Are ratfish edible?*

**g̱eey tá** noun *head of the bay*
·G̱eey tá héen yaa nalt'íx'. *The water at the head of the bay is freezing.*
·G̱eey tá déilit awsiḵúx̱ du yaagú. *She drove her boat to the head of the bay.*

**a g̱ei** RelationalNoun *enclosed within (the folds of) it, between the folds, covers, walls of it*
·X'aa g̱eiyí niyaadé kei ayawli.át. *He steered (his boat) toward the inside of the point.*
·Wé x'aa g̱ei xóon tléil aan utí. *The North Wind does not bother the shelter of the point.*

**G̱EI** verb root

- **kawlig̱éi | kalig̱éi | kei klag̱éich**
  *he/she/it was fancy | he/she/it is fancy | he/she/it gets fancy (regularly).*
  THEME: O-ka-l-g̱éi (g̱a state)
  *for O to be fancy, prominent (esp. in appearance), conspicuous, attracting attention*
  ·Kalag̱éi nooch aasgutú yeist ḵuwuhaayí. *The forest is brilliant when fall comes.*
- **--- | shaklig̱éi | ---**
  --- | *she is pretty* | ---.
  THEME: O-sha-ka-l-g̱éi (ga state)
  *for O to be pretty, cute*
  NOTES: This verb is used to describe a beautiful woman or something cute such as a puppy or kitten. It isn't generally used to describe pretty objects such as beadwork.
- **--- | sh tukdlig̱éi | ---**
  --- | *s/he is proud* | ---.
  THEME: sh tu-ka-S-d-l-g̱éi (ga state)
  *for S to be proud (esp. of oneself), conceited; for S to be particular, picky, snooty*
  NOTES: This verb only occurs in the imperfective. Note that it can have a negative connotation, meaning "to be conceited." It can also be used to indicate that one is proud of something or someone by inserting N kaax̱ "of N" into the sentence. Usually the N represents something or someone that the individual has a

personal stake in. For example: A kaax̲ sh tukdlig̲éi du dachx̲ánx'iyán. "She is proud of her grandchildren." Otherwise, another verb is used: Du toowú klig̲éi du kaadáx̲. "She is proud of him."

·A kaax̲ sh tukdlig̲éi du tsaa doogú at xáshdi téel. *She is proud of her seal skin moccasins.*

• **du toowú kawlig̲éi | du toowú klig̲éi | du toowú kei klag̲éich**

*s/he became proud | s/he is proud | s/he gets proud (regularly).*

THEME: N toowú ka-l-g̲éi (ga state)

*for N to be proud of, highly pleased with*

NOTES: To add who one is proud of in the sentence, use: N kaadáx̲ "of N". For example: Mary toowú klig̲éi John kaadáx̲. "Mary is proud of John."

**g̲eig̲ách'** noun *swing, hammock*

VARIANTS: g̲eeg̲ách' (T)

**G̲EIN** verb root

• **aadé awdlig̲ein | --- | ---**

*he/she/it looked there | --- | ---.*

THEME: P-dé a-S-d-l-g̲ein~ (na motion)

*for S to look in the direction of P*

VARIANTS: -g̲een~ (An)

·Gáandei aneelg̲ein g̲ayéis'g̲aa! *Look outside for some iron!*

·I léelk'u keekándei aneelg̲ein - x̲áat yéi adaané! *Go check on your grandpa - he's working on fish!*

**g̲eitl'** noun *thick mucus, phlegm*

**G̲EIWOO** verb root

• **awdzig̲eiwú | asg̲eiwú | ---**

*s/he seined | s/he is seining | ---.*

THEME: a-S-s-g̲eiwú (na act)

*for S to fish with net, seine*

·Atoosg̲eiwú atyátx'i latíni x̲ánx̲ has g̲ak̲éech ax̲ yátx'i. *When we are gillnetting my children stay with a babysitter.*

·Áa atoosg̲eiwú yé áwé kéet haa daat yawsigóo. *The killer whales came around where we were gillnetting.*

**g̲eiwú** noun *fish net; seine net*

VARIANTS: g̲eiwóo (C)

·Kawdis'éil' ax̲ g̲eiwú. *My net is all torn up.*

·G̲eiwú wooch yáx̲ awsinei tle daak ashakaawak̲úx̲. *She straightened the net out and then she set it.*

a **g̲eiwú** noun *its web (of spider)*

**a g̲eiyí** noun *its edible part (of clam)*
·Gáal' g̲eiyí dux̲á. *Someone is eating clam muscles.*
·Wé gáal' g̲eiyí aan nagú i léelk'w x̲ánde! *Go with the clams to your grandparent!*

**g̲eiy (TC)** noun *bay*
VARIANTS: g̲eey

**g̲ík̲s** noun *fish hung over the fire to cook*
·X̲áat yádi g̲ík̲s yís akaawaxaash. *She cut the whitefish to barbeque over the fire.*
·Yées t'á g̲ík̲si sitgawsáanx' has aawax̲áa. *They ate fresh king salmon barbequed over the fire at noon.*

**g̲ík̲saa (T)** noun *fish roasted whole, strung up by its tail over the fire and twirled periodically*
VARIANTS: g̲ík̲si (AtT)

**g̲íl'** noun *cliff*
·G̲íl' yáx̲ kanaadaa wé héen. *The water is flowing down the face of the rock cliff.*
·G̲íl' yáx̲ kei naltl'ét' wé yadák'w. *The young boy is climbing the cliff face.*

**g̲íl'aa** noun *grindstone*
·K'wát' yáx̲ kaaxát du g̲íl'ayi. *His grindstone is shaped like an egg.*
·Du gwéili tóode aawatee wé g̲íl'aa. *He put the grindstone in his bag.*

**g̲ítg̲aa** noun *pine needles, spruce needles*
·G̲ítg̲aa ayax̲saháa yóode woogoot. *She went over there to gather spruce needles.*
·Náakw yís awsitáa wé g̲ítg̲aa. *He boiled the pine needles for medicine.*

**g̲íx̲'jaa k̲óok** noun *organ, piano*
·Sh tóo awdlitóow g̲íx̲'jaa k̲óok al.áx̲ji. *He taught himself to play the piano.*
·X̲'agáax' daakahídix' ali.áx̲ch wé g̲íx̲'jaa k̲óok. *He plays the organ at the Church.*

**G̲OO** verb root

- **awlig̲oo | alg̲éikw | yei alg̲wéich**
  *s/he wiped it | s/he wipes it; s/he's wiping it | s/he wipes it (regularly).*
  THEME: O-S-l-g̲oo~ (g̲a act)
  *for S to wipe, mop, clean O by wiping*
  ·Wé x̲éel' du jíndáx̲ awlig̲oo. *She wiped the slime off her hands.*
  ·Aax̲ gatí wéi kaxíl'aa kadushxeet t'áa yá g̲alg̲ú! *Pick up the eraser and clean the chalkboard!*

**g̲ooch** noun *wolf*
·Watsíx áa káa daak has awlikél' wé g̲ooch. *The wolves chased the caribou out onto the lake.*

·Gooch litká aadé duwatéen wé g̱ooch. *The wolf on the ridge of the hill is visible.*

**a g̱óot** RelationalPostposition *without it; lacking it*

·A g̱óot woogoot du s'áaxu. *He went without his hat.*

·Tléiḵw g̱óot awsi.ée du sakwnéini. *She cooked her bannock without berries.*

**G̱OOTL** verb root

• **akaawag̱útl | akag̱óotl | akag̱útlx̱**

*s/he mashed it | s/he is mashing it | s/he mashes it (regularly).*

THEME: O-ka-S-ø-g̱ootl~ (ø act)

*for S to mash O by squeezing in the hand; for S to squeeze O tightly*

·Du jintáak teen akag̱útlx̱ wé tléiḵw. *She mashes the berries with the palm of her hand.*

**G̱unaax̱oo Ḵwáan** noun *people of Dry Bay*

·Yaakwdáatx' yéi has yatee yeedát G̱unaax̱oo Ḵwáan. *The Dry Bay people now live in Yakutat.*

·G̱unaax̱oo Ḵwáanx̱ has sitee wé lingít. *Those people are Dry Bay people.*

**g̱unakadeit** noun *legendary sea monster*

·G̱unakadeit daat tlaagú dax̱ḵudzitee. *There are legends about sea monsters.*

·Tléil yáax' yéi aa utí g̱unakadeit. *There are no sea monsters here.*

**G̱unanaa** noun *Athabaskan (Indian)*

·X̱aldleit kinaa.át yéi aya.óo wé G̱unanaa ḵáa. *That Athabaskan man is wearing a white fox overcoat.*

·A x̱oo aa Lingít G̱unanaa has du x̱oo ḵuya.óo. *Some Tlingits live among the Athabascans.*

**g̱unanaa tetl** noun *punk wood, decayed dry wood*

**a g̱unayáade** Adverb *differently from it*

VARIANTS: a g̱unayáadei, a g̱uwanyáade (An), a g̱unáade (C)

·Aadéi keenik yé g̱unayáade x̱aatéen. *I see it differently from the way you tell it.*

·Wé naakéedáx̱ lingít g̱unayáade yóo has x̱'ali.átk. *The people from the north speak differently.*

**g̱unayéi** Adverb *beginning*

VARIANTS: g̱unéi

·Ḵukawduyéil'i áwé Galyéx̱dei g̱unayéi uḵoox̱ch wéi yaakw tlein. *The big boat would start traveling to the Kahliyet River when the weather was calm.*

**g̱unayéide** Adverb *different*

VARIANTS: g̱unayéidei

·G̱unayéide kwditlawu g̱ayéis' tíx' du jeewú. *He has steel cables of*

*different sizes.*
·G̲unayéide a daat sh tudinook yeedát. *He feels differently about it now.*

**g̲unéi** Adverb *start, begin*
·Taan áa awsiteeni yé a niyaadé g̲unéi uwak̲úx̲. *He started motoring in the direction he had seen the sea lion.*
·K̲ee.á shukát áwé g̲unéi gax̲took̲óox̲. *We will start traveling before dawn.*

du **g̲ushká** noun *(on) his/her lap*
·Wé shaawát du g̲ushkáa yan awsi.ín du s'íx'i. *The woman put her plate on her lap.*
·Du dachx̲ánk' du g̲ushkáa kei awsinúk. *He lifted his grandchild up onto his lap.*

**g̲uwakaan** noun *deer*
VARIANTS: k̲uwakaan (TC), k̲uyakaan (At)
·G̲uwakaan at xáshdi téel ax̲ dachx̲ánk' jeeyís ax̲ tuwáa sigóo. *I would like deer skin moccasins for my grandchild.*
·G̲uwakaan taayí kas'úkx̲u yís akaawaxaash. *She cut up deer fat for frying.*

**g̲uwakaan yádi** noun *fawn*
·G̲uwakaan yádi kajikáx'x̲. *A fawn is spotted.*
·Wé g̲uwakaan yádi a tláa teen yóode yaa nashíx. *The fawn is running over that way with its mother.*

a **g̲uwanyáade (An)** noun *differently from it*
VARIANTS: a g̲unayáade, a g̲unáade (C)
·A g̲uwanyáadé ágé iyatéen? *Do you see the difference?*

# « G̲w »

**g̲wáal’** noun *fart*

**G̲WAAT’**[1] verb root

- **át wudig̲wáat’ | --- | át yoo dig̲wát’k**
  *s/he is crawling around there; s/he crawled around there | --- | s/he crawls around there (regularly).*
  THEME: P-t S-d-g̲wáat’~ (na motion)
  *for S (esp. child) to crawl around on hands and knees at P*
  ·I yádi ax̲ x̲’usyeet wudig̲wáat’. *Your child is crawling around under my feet.*
- **daak̲ wudig̲wát’ | --- | daak̲ dag̲wát’ch**
  *s/he crawled away (from the open) | --- | s/he crawls away (from the open) (regularly).*
  THEME: daak̲ S-d-g̲wáat’~ (ø motion)
  *for S (esp. child) to crawl up (from beach), away (from open) on hands and knees*
  ·Tléi a x’aant áwé daak̲ wudig̲wát’ wé yadák’w. *The young boy crawled out the limb.*

# « H »

**haa** Pronoun *our [possessive]*
·Haa tláa hás k̲útl'gig̲áa has na.átch has du k̲'eikaxwéini yís. *Our mothers send us for soil for their flowers.*
·Haa kagéide yaa ana.át. *People are coming toward us.*

**haa** Pronoun *us [object]*
·Tle yeedát yáatx̲ haa kagux̲dayáa. *We need to leave from here right now.*

HAA verb root

- **akaawahaa | akahéix̲ | yoo akayaheix̲k**
*s/he planted it | s/he is planting it | s/he plants it (regularly).*
THEME: O-ka-S-ø-haa~ (na act)
*for S to plant O*
·Du hídi gukshitú áa akaawahaa wé k̲'eikaxwéin. *She planted the flowers at the corner of her house.*
·Anahoo has akanahéijin. *They used to plant turnips.*
- **akaawahaa | akahéix̲ | yoo akayaheix̲k**
*s/he gardened | s/he is gardening | s/he gardens (regularly).*
THEME: a-ka-S-ø-haa~ (na act)
*for S to garden, dig*
- **akaawaháa | akaháa | ---**
*s/he dug it | s/he is digging it | ---.*
THEME: O-ka-S-ø-háa~ (ø act)
*for S to dig O*
·Gáal' has akaháa. *They are digging clams.*
- **át has yawdiháa | --- | áx̲ has yadahaa**
*they crowded the place | --- | they crowd the place (regularly).*
THEME: P-t~ O-ya-d-haa~ (ø motion)
*for O (large numbers, esp. people, birds) to move in, come around to P*
·K'isáani át yawdiháa. *There's a crowd of young men there.*
·Ldakát wooch x̲oot has yawdiháa. *Everybody came together.*
- **át k̲uwaháa | aadé yaa k̲unahéin | áx̲ k̲oohaa**
*it's time for it | it's getting to be time for it | the time comes for it (regularly).*
THEME: P-t~ k̲u-ø-haa~ (ø motion)
*for the time to come for P*
·Xáats'de yaa k̲unahéin. *It is becoming twilight.*
·Shayadihéin tl'áxch' táakwde yaa k̲unahéini. *There are a lot of dead branches when it becomes winter.*
- **ayawsiháa | ayasahéix̲ | ---**
*s/he gathered it | s/he's gathering it | ---.*
THEME: O-ya-S-s-haa~ (ø act)

*for S to gather up, pick up, take up O*
·G̱ítg̱aa ayax̱saháa yóode woogoot. *She went over there to gather spruce needles.*
·Ḵ'áach' ayawsiháa. *She gathered ribbon seaweed.*

- **du éet ḵuwaháa | du eedé yaa ḵunahéin | du éex̱ koohaa**
  *it's his/her turn | his/her turn is coming up | s/he gets a turn (regularly).*
  THEME: N éet~ ḵu-ø-haa~ (ø motion)
  *for N to have a turn*

- **du éet yaan uwaháa | --- | du éex̱ yaan haa**
  *s/he is hungry | --- | s/he gets hungry (regularly).*
  THEME: N éet~ yaan ø-haa~ (ø event)
  *for N to be hungry*

- **kei akaawaháa | kei akanahéin | ---**
  *s/he dug it up | s/he is digging it up | ---.*
  THEME: kei O-ka-S-ø-haa~ (ø motion)
  *for S to dig O up*
  ·Tle hít tuwán áwé kóoḵ áa kei has akaawaháa. *Right next to the house they dug a pit.*
  ·Kei akaawahaayi góon, aawahoon. *He sold the gold that he mined.*

- **shayawdihaa | shayadihéin | ---**
  *there got to be a lot | there are a lot | ---.*
  THEME: O-sha-ya-d-haa~ (na state)
  *for O to be many, plenty, lots*
  ·Sgóonwaan atyátx'i has shayadihéin Yaakwdáatx'. *There are a lot of school children in Yakutat.*
  ·Wasóos wé akahéix̱i jee shayadihéin. *The farmer has lots of cows.*

- **--- | tlél goohá | ---**
  *--- | it's obvious | ---.*
  THEME: tlél ga-u-ø-háa (ga state)
  *for something to be obvious, clearly visible*
  NOTES: Note that this verb is unique in that it requires the conjugation prefix (ga-) in all modes and only occurs in the negative. The negative imperfective tlél goohá "it's obvious" is the most common form, although the negative future has also been documented.
  ·Tlél goohá aadéi k'idéin daḵéis'i yé. *It's obvious how well she sews.*

**haadaadóoshi** noun *man-eating feline; mountain lion; tiger, leopard*
·Haadaadóoshi teen yéi jiné wé ḵáa. *That man is working with tigers.*
·Haadaadóoshi kadlig̱áas'. *Tigers are striped.*

**haadaag̱oojí** noun *man-eating animal; lion; tiger; man-eating wolf*
·Haadaag̱oojí éil' héen diyáanax̱.áx' dul'óon. *People hunt lions across the ocean.*
·Haadaag̱oojí a oox̱ú daḵdigéix'. *Lion teeth are large.*

**HAAN**[1] verb root

- **--- | hán | ---**

  --- | *s/he is standing* | ---.
  THEME: S-ø-hán (position)
  *for (singular) S to be standing*
  NOTES: This verb only occurs in the imperfective. Note that a noun phrase with (-t) postposition is used to indicate where one is standing, but this noun phrase is not required by the verb. For example, one could say: hán "s/he is standing", or: át hán "s/he is standing there."
  ·A x̱'anaa áwé át eehán. *You are standing in its way.*
  ·Du waḵkas'óox' áwé át eehán. *You're blocking his view.*

- **wudihaan | kei ndahán | kei dahánch**

  *s/he stood up* | *s/he is standing up* | *s/he stands up (regularly).*
  THEME: S-d-haan~ (ga event)
  *for (singular) S to stand up, rise*
  ·Ch'a g̱ég̱aa aax̱ kei dahánch. *He tries to stand up from there (but is unable to).*
  ·Gunalchéesh yéi yanḵaḵaat áyá x̱wdihaan. *I stood up to say thank you.*

- **yan uwahán | --- | yax̱ haan**

  *s/he remained standing* | --- | *s/he keeps standing (regularly).*
  THEME: yan~ S-ø-haan~ (ø motion)
  *for (singular) S to keep standing*
  ·I yoo x̱'atángi káa yan hán! *Stand on your words!*
  ·A yaadéi nagú a tuwánx' yan hán! *Walk to the face of it and stand beside it!*

**haandé** Adverb *hand it here, bring it here*
VARIANTS: haandéi
NOTES: Although it has the postposition -dé and therefore looks like an adverb, this word is unique in that it functions syntactically as a predicate, replacing a verb in the sentence.
·Haandé wé ách at dusx̱a át! *Hand me the fork!*

**HAAS'** verb root

- **uwahás' | --- | yahás'kw**

  *s/he is vomiting; s/he vomited* | --- | *s/he vomits (regularly).*
  THEME: O-ø-háas'~ (ø event)
  *for O to vomit*

**háas'** noun *vomit; urge to vomit*
·Háas' yáx̱ sh tudinook. *He feels like vomiting.*
·Háas' du éet yéi uwanéi yá yagiyee. *He has been vomiting today.*

**HAASH** verb root

- **át wulihaash | --- | át yoo liháshk**

  *it's floating around; it floated around* | --- | *he/she/it floats around (regularly).*
  THEME: P-t O-l-haash~ (na motion)

*for O to float, drift around at P*
·Héen shóot wulihaash wé kayaaní. *The leaf floated around the edge of the water.*

• **át wulihásh | aadé yaa nalhásh | áx̲ lahaash**
*he/she/it drifted to it | he/she/it is drifting to it | he/she/it drifts to it (regularly).*
THEME: P-t~ O-l-haash~ (ø motion)
*for O to float, drift to P*
·Heentu.eejí kát wulihásh du yaagú. *Her boat drifted onto a reef.*
·Tleidahéen áwé Yaakwdáatt aa wlihásh wé kanóox'. *One time a turtle floated to Yakutat.*

• **daak wulihásh | --- | ---**
*he/she/it drifted out to sea; he/she/it is drifting out to sea | --- | ---.*
THEME: daak O-l-haash~ (ø motion)
*for O to float, drift out to sea*
·Du jinák̲ daak wulihásh wé ch'áal'. *The willow drifted out away from him.*

**haat~** Adverb *hither, toward speaker*
·Gus'yadóoli taakw.eetíx' haax̲ kalyeech. *Sandpipers fly here in the early summer.*
·Eesháank' kaltéelk̲ áwé haat wujixíx ax̲ dachx̲ánk'. *Poor thing, my grandchild ran over here shoeless.*

**haat** noun *current, tide*
·Haat kei wudaayí tléil ux̲satínch. *He has not seen the tide rise yet.*
·Haat kanadaayí géide kei nak̲úx̲. *She is going against the current.*

**haat kool** noun *whirlpool*
·Haat kool héen yíkde duteen nooch. *Whirlpools are visible in rivers.*
·Éil' héenx' yéi dag̲aateeyi haat kool dak̲digéix'. *Whirlpools in the ocean are large.*

**háatl'** noun *feces; dung*

**haaw** noun *bough, branch with needles on it, especially of hemlock*
·Haaw héende awli.aat g̲áax'w káx̲. *She put branches in the water for herring eggs.*
·Haaw yan awli.át a káa ng̲ataayít. *He put branches down so he could sleep on them.*

**Haa yátx'u ée!** interj. *Poor baby!*
NOTES: This exclamation is used when a child hurts himself/herself or when a child is upset.

**Hadláa!** interj. *Good grief!*
NOTES: This exclamation is used in association with things exaggerated or overdone, including an overdressed person, too much food on a plate, or an exaggerated story.

**has** Pronoun *they [subject]*
VARIANTS: s (optionally, after a vowel)
·Watsíx áa káa daak has awlikél' wé g̱ooch. *The wolves chased the caribou out onto the lake.*
·Nás'k yagiyee a kaanáx̱ has yaawa.át. *They walked for three days.*

**has** Pronoun *them [object]*
VARIANTS: s (optionally, after a vowel)
·K'idéin has jiduḵéi katíx̱'aa s'aatí Dzántik'i Héenix'. *Jailers are paid well in Juneau.*
·Gáanu hás, i yeeg̱áax̱ has sitee. *They are outside waiting for you.*

**hás** adj. *[plural marker for kinship terms]*
NOTES: This word is categorized as an adjective in that it modifies a noun. Hás is the plural marker for kinship terms.
·Haa tláa hás ḵútl'gig̱áa has na.átch has du ḵ'eikaxwéini yís. *Our mothers send us for soil for their flowers.*
·Hoon daakahídidé has woo.aat ax̱ séek' hás. *My daughters have gone to the store.*

**hás** Pronoun *they [independent]*
·Gáanu hás, i yeeg̱áax̱ has sitee. *They are outside waiting for you.*

**has du** Pronoun *their [possessive]*
·Haa tláa hás ḵútl'gig̱áa has na.átch has du ḵ'eikaxwéini yís. *Our mothers send us for soil for their flowers.*
·Yeeytéen has du téix̱' tóotx̱ áyá toodé has yee uwaxích haa ḵu.éex'i. *You all can see that our hosts thank you from their hearts.*

**Ha.é!** interj. *[exclamation toward someone who is putting on airs in order to impress others]*

**hé** Demonstrative *this/that (over here), the other*
VARIANTS: héi

HEEK verb root

- **ashawlihík | yaa ashanalhík | ashalahíkx̱**
*s/he filled it | s/he is filling it | s/he fills it (regularly).*
THEME: O-sha-S-l-heek~ (ø event)
*for S to fill O (with solids or abstracts)*
·Tláakw ashawlihík wé kadádzaa yeit. *She filled the berry basket quickly.*
·X̱áat teen áwé shawdudlihík wé kaxwénaa. *The brailer bag was filled with salmon.*
- **shaawahík | yaa shanahík | shahíkx̱**
*he/she/it is full | he/she/it is getting full | he/she/it gets full (regularly).*
THEME: O-sha-ø-heek~ (ø event)
*for O to be filled, be full (general and abstract)*
·Haa a tóox' at dult'ix' át shaawahík dzísk'u dleeyí teen. *Our freezer is full of moose meat.*

·É! Shahíkx̲ haa cháli g̲aatáa yéi daatooneiyí. *Check it out! When we are out trapping, our storehouse is full.*

- **yan ashawlihík | --- | ---**

*s/he finished it | --- | ---.*
THEME: yan~ O-sha-S-l-heek~ (ø motion)
*for S to finish, complete O*
·Yan ashawlihík yá haa tláach. *This mother of ours has completed everything.*
·K̲aa oox̲ yéi daanéiyi yís sgóon yan ashawlihík *She finished dentistry school.*

HEEN[1] verb root

- **du éek' aawaheen | du éek' ayaheen | ---**

*s/he believed him/her | s/he believes him/her | ---.*
THEME: N éek' a-S-ø-heen~ (ga state)
*for S to believe, trust, believe in N*
·Dikée aank̲áawu du éek' atuwaheen. *We believe in God.*

HEEN[2] verb root

- **yan uwahín | yánde yaa nahín | yax̲ heen**

*it swam ashore | it's swimming to shore | it swims ashore (regularly).*
THEME: yan~ ø-heen~ (ø motion)
*for sea animal to swim ashore*
·Kóoshdaa haa eeg̲ayáaknáx̲ yan uwahín. *The land otter swam through our beachfront.*

**héen** noun *water*
·Ax̲ éek' si.áat'i héen goondáx̲ ayáayin. *My brother used to pack cold water from a spring.*
·Ch'as héen ák.wé a kaadéi yóo yadudzixéik yá kat'ákx̲i? *Is water all that was put on these dried berries?*

**héen** noun *river, stream, creek*
·Héen kát jinaskwanchi át áwé wé atxaayí. *The centipede swims on top of the water.*
·Héent wushix̲'íl'. *He slipped into the water.*

**héenák'w** noun *creek; small stream*
·X'at'daayéejayi héenák'w át nagútch. *The black turnstone walks around in shallow water.*
·Wé k̲áa góon awsiteen héenák'w táade. *The man saw gold at the bottom of the creek.*

**héen gúx'aa** noun *water dipper; ladle*

**héeni** Adverb *into water*

**héen kanadaayí** noun *current; tidal action*
·Héen yík héen kanadaayí wáa yateeyi yéix' kulix̲éitl'shán nooch. *Sometimes currents in a river are dangerous.*

**héen sháak** noun *head of river, stream*
·Wé héen sháakx' áwé atx'aan hídi áa awliyéx̱. *He built a smokehouse at the head of the river.*
·Dax̱adooshú kaay yéi kunaaléi wé aan, héen sháakdáx̱. *The town is seven miles from the head of the river.*

**héen shú** noun *edge of body of water*
VARIANTS: hinshú (At)
·Héen shú át hán wé dzísk'w. *That moose is standing at the edge of the water.*
·Héen shóot wulihaash wé kayaaní. *The leaf floated around the edge of the water.*

**héen táak** noun *in the water; in the river*
·Té tlénx' héen táakde duwatéen. *Big rocks are visible on the bottom of the river.*
·Héen táatx̱ ák.wé du.een wéi kantáḵw? *Is the lupine picked from the water?*

**héen wantú** noun *edge of river channel*
·Lingít kóoxu aax̱ du.eenín héen wantú. *Wild rice used to be picked along the riverbank.*
·Héen wantóot woogoot wé gus'yadóoli. *The sandpiper is walking around the riverbank.*

**héen wát** noun *mouth of river, stream*
·Héen wát át has wusikwaan wé gáaxw. *The ducks are swimming around at the mouth of the river.*
·Héen wátt uwax'ák wé t'ási. *The grayling swam to the mouth of the river.*

**héenx̱** Adverb *into water*

**héen x̱'aká** noun *on (top of) the water, river*
·Óoxjaa héen x̱'akát uwaxíx. *Wind has hit the surface of the water.*

**héen x̱'ayaax̱** noun *riverside*
·Wé héen x̱'ayaax̱ chál wutuliyéx̱. *We built a storehouse on the edge of the river.*
·Héen x̱'ayaax̱ yagéi kaxwéix̱. *There are a lot of highbush cranberries along the river.*

**héen yík** noun *(in the) river valley*
·Héen yíkde wooḵoox̱ wé yaakw. *The boat went up the river.*
·Héen yíkde aawa.aat al'óon. *People went up the river hunting.*

**HEES'** verb root

• **aawahées' | ahées' | kei ahées'ch**
*s/he borrowed it | s/he is borrowing it | s/he borrows it (regularly).*
THEME: O-S-ø-hées' (ga act)
*for S to borrow O*
·Wé ḵáa ax̱ éesh jeedáx̱ aankayéx̱aa aawahées'. *The man borrowed a*

*plane from my Dad.*
·Aawahées' du káani yaagú. *He borrowed a boat from his brother-in-law.*

- **akaawahées' | akahées' | kei akahées'ch**
  *s/he borrowed it | s/he is borrowing it | s/he borrows it (regularly).*
  THEME: O-ka-S-ø-hées' (ga act)
  *for S to borrow O (esp. round, spherical object)*
  ·Tléix' gút akaawahées'. *He borrowed one dime.*

- **du éet aawahís' | --- | du éex̱ ahées'**
  *s/he lent it to him/her | --- | s/he lends it to him/her (regularly).*
  THEME: P-t~ O-S-ø-hées'~ (ø motion)
  *for S to lend O to P*
  ·Tleik̲áa dáanaa ax̱ éet hís'! *Lend me twenty dollars!*

HEIN verb root

- **aawahéin | ayahéin | ---**
  *s/he claimed it | s/he claims it | ---.*
  THEME: O-S-ø-héin (ga state)
  *for S to own, claim O (esp. clan property)*
  ·Yaa L'úx yinaanáx̱ yá saa áyá yaa L'úx áyá has aawahéin. *They claimed the name Mt. Edgecumbe as their crest.*
  ·Xíxch' at óowu woosh jeedé duhéin nooch. *The frog crest is claimed by more than one clan.*

**héix̱waa** noun *sympathetic magic, charm*
·Héix̱waa yéi daadunéiyin ch'áakw. *People used to use magic long ago.*

HÉIX̱WAA verb root

- **aawahéix̱waa | ahéix̱waa | ---**
  *s/he performed rites | s/he is performing rites | ---.*
  THEME: S-ø-héix̱waa (na act)
  *for S to make magic, perform rites to bring desirable results in nature or give youngsters power and confidence*
  ·Al'óon kaadé aawahéix̱waa du keidlí. *He used magic on his dog for hunting.*

**hinshú (At)** noun *end of body of standing water*
VARIANTS: héen shú

**hintaak xóodzi** noun *polar bear*
VARIANTS: hintakxóodzi
·Hintaak xóodzi akawshixít. *She photographed a polar bear.*
·Hintaak xóodzi has aawal'óon. *They hunted polar bears.*

**hintaak x'óosi** noun *coral*
VARIANTS: hintakx'óosi
·Hintaak x'óosi tléil yáax' yéi aa utí. *There is no coral here.*
·Hintakx'óosi nóox'u kayat'éex' *Coral shells are hard.*

**hintakx'úxi** noun *coral*

**hintakx'wás'g̱i** noun *bufflehead (duck)*

**hintu.eejí** noun *underwater reef; large rock or boulder lying under the water*
VARIANTS: heentu.eejí
·Heentu.eejí kát wulihásh du yaagú. *Her boat drifted onto a reef.*
·Héen kawulkuxú duteen nooch wé hintu.eejí. *When the water level drops, the reef can always be seen.*

**hinx̱uká** noun *on (top of) the water, river*
VARIANTS: héen x̱uká

**Hinyaa Ḵwáan** noun *people of Klawock*
·Hinyaa Ḵwáan x̱ánde woogoot wé shaawát. *The woman went to visit the Klawock people.*
·Hinyaa Ḵwáan Celebrationx' has aawal'eix̱. *The Klawock people danced at Celebration.*

**hinyikgáaxu** noun *kind of duck*
·Hinyikgáaxu kúdi awsiteen. *She saw a golden eye duck's nest.*
·Hinyikgáaxu kindachooneit x̱oot wusikwaan. *Golden eye ducks are swimming around among the Mallard ducks.*

**hinyikl'eix̱í** noun *dipper; water ouzel*

**hít** noun *house; building*
·Yaa Aangóont áyá la.áa haa hídi Aanx'aagi Hít yóo duwasáakw. *Our clan house standing in Angoon is called Aanx'aagi Hít.*
·Héen t'iká át la.áa du hídi. *His house sits beside the river.*

**hít da.ideidí** noun *house timbers*

**hít ká** noun *roof*
·Wé hít ká áa yéi jiduné. *Someone is working on that roof.*
·G̱ayéis' du hídi kát akawsix'óo. *He nailed tin on his roof.*

**hít kagaadí** noun *rafters (modern)*

**hít kaságu** noun *rafters (large roof beams)*
·Yan uwaneiyi hít kaságug̱áa kawduwaḵaa. *He was sent for ready-made rafters.*
·Hít kaságu yaa anasxát'. *He is dragging rafters along.*

**hít kat'áayi** noun *shingle(s)*
·Hít kat'áayi yóox' dulyéix̱. *They manufacture shingles over there.*
·Hít kat'áayi yátx'i wé sée hídi káa yéi awa.oo. *He put the small shingles on that doll house.*

**hít kax'úx'u** noun *bark roofing material; tarpaper*
VARIANTS: hít kex'úx'u (C)
·T'ooch' yáx̱ yatee wé hít kax'úx'u. *That roofing is black.*

**hít s'aatí** noun *head of a clan house; master of the house*
·Ax̱ éesh haa hít s'aatíx̱ satéeyin. *My dad was the head of our house.*
·Wé hít s'aatí John yóo duwasáakw. *That house leader's name is John.*

**hít shantú** noun *upstairs; attic*
·Hít shantóode akaawajeil wé x'óow. *She took the blankets upstairs.*
·Hít shantú k'idéin awsinei. *She cleaned upstairs.*

**hít tayeegáas'i** noun *piling, foundation post; floor joist*
VARIANTS: hít teyeegáas'i (C)
·Hít tayeegáas'i yís aas aawas'úw. *He chopped down trees for pilings.*
·Hít tayeegáas'i káa awliyéx̱ du hídi. *He built his house on pilings.*

HOO verb root

- **yan uwahóo | yánde yaa nahú | yax̱ hoo**
*he/she/it waded ashore | he/she/it is wading ashore | he/she/it wades ashore (regularly).*
THEME: yan~ S-ø-hoo~ (ø motion)
*for (singular) S to wade ashore*
·Wé áa kaanáx̱ yan uwahóowu watsíx a ítnáx̱ yan uwak̲úx̱ wé yaakw. *The boat followed behind the caribou that swam the lake.*

**Hóoch!** interj. *That's all!; All gone!; No more!; All done!*
VARIANTS: Hóochk'!

**hoon** noun *sale*
VARIANTS: hun
·Nas'gadooshú ch'iyáash kax̱waach'ák'w hun yayís. *I carved eight sea otter hunting canoes to sell.*
·Hoon yís aswáat gishoo. *He raises pigs to sell.*

HOON verb root

- **aawahoon | ahóon | yoo ayahúnk**
*s/he sold it | s/he is selling it | s/he sells it (regularly).*
THEME: O-S-ø-hoon~ (na act)
*for S to sell O*
·Kei akaawahaayi góon, aawahoon. *He sold the gold that he mined.*
·K̲aa ji.eetí wéix' duhóon. *They are selling handmade crafts there.*
- **awlihóon | yaa analhún | ---**
*s/he went peddling it | s/he is peddling it | ---.*
THEME: O-S-l-hoon~ (na event)
*for S to go selling, peddle, hawk O*
- **wudlihoon | yaa nalhún | yoo dlihúnk**
*s/he went shopping | s/he is shopping | s/he goes shopping (regularly).*
THEME: S-d-l-hoon~ (na event)
*for S to go spending, go shopping*
·Ace Hardwaredé neelhoon kas'éet katíx̱'aag̱áa! *Go to Ace Hardware and buy a screwdriver!*

·Lowesdéi neelhoon a káa dul.us'ku átg̲aa! *Go to Lowes and buy a washboard!*

**hoon daakahídi** noun *store*

·Hoon daakahídidé has woo.aat ax̲ séek' hás. *My daughters have gone to the store.*
·I dlaak' kajúxaa kát kanaljoox hoon daakahídidé. *Take your sister to the store in the wheel barrow.*

**hoon s'aatí** noun *merchant; seller*

·Wé hoon s'aatí een yóo x̲'ali.átk ax̲ aat. *My paternal aunt is talking with the storekeeper.*
·Wé hoon s'aatí jeeyís yéi jiné wé shaatk'. *The young girl is working for that storekeeper.*

**hú** Pronoun *he, she [independent]*

·Hú áwé ax̲ éet wudishée. *It is he who helped me.*
·Hú áwé x̲'ak̲g̲eewóos'. *It is he that you will ask.*

**Hú!** interj. *Ouch!*

du **húnx̲w** noun *his older brother, cousin*

·Ax̲ húnx̲w ya.áakdáx̲ woonú! *Make room for my older brother!*
·Wé yées k̲áa du húnx̲w ítx̲ yaa nagút. *The young man's older brother is walking along behind him.*

**Húsh!** interj. *Shame on you! [reprimand]*

# « I »

**i** Pronoun *your (singular) [possessive]*
·I léelk'u keekándei aneelg̱ein - x̱áat yéi adaané! *Go check on your grandpa - he's working on fish!*
·I tuḵ'atáali i daax̱ yei jeekanaxíx. *Your pants are falling down.*

**i-** Pronoun *you (singular) [subject]*
VARIANTS: ee-

**i-** Pronoun *you (singular) [object]*
·Ikawdzitíx̱'. *You're crooked (wicked).*

**du iḵká** noun *top of his/her foot*

**Iḵkaa** noun *Ahtna, Copper River Athabascan*
·Wé shaawát Iḵkaa aa lingítx̱ sitee. *That woman is a Copper River Athabascan person.*

**iḵnáach'** noun *brass*
·Wé x̱'agáax' daakahídi gaawú iḵnáach' teen wududliyéx̱ *The church bell is made of brass.*
·Iḵnáach'x̱ sitee wé lítaa sákwti. *The handle of that knife is brass.*

**iḵyéis'** noun *iron, tin*
VARIANTS: g̱ayéis'

**Ilí!** interj. *Don't!; Stop it!*
VARIANTS: Lí!, Ihí!

**Ilí s'é!** interj. *Wait!*
VARIANTS: Ilí s'á!

**ín** noun *flint*
·Ín tléil du jee yéi aa utí. *He doesn't have any flint.*
·Íng̱aa ḵushée. *He is looking for flint.*

**ín x'eesháa** noun *bottle; jug*
·Wé at x'aakeidí ín x'eesháa tóox' yéi na.oo! *Put the seeds in a bottle!*
·Yaawat'aayi káaxwei ín x'eesháa tóot haat awsi.ín. *She brought hot coffee in a bottle.*

**ísh** noun *fishing hole; hole in stream, river, creek*
·Ísh yíkde x̱áat ayatéen. *She sees salmon in the deep hole in the creek.*
·Ísh yíkde shalx̱óot'. *She is casting into the deep water hole.*

**ishḵeen** noun *black cod*
·Áx̱ akawdudlis'eig̱i ishḵeen du tuwáa sagóowun ax̱ éesh. *My dad used to like smoked black cod.*

·Áx̱ akawdudlis'eig̱i ishk̲een aa x̱waa.oo. *I bought some smoked black cod.*

**a ít** RelationalNoun *after it*
·X̱'éishx'w áwé nageich k̲utaan ítdáx̱. *After the summer is over there are a lot of bluejays*
·S'íx' kawtoo.óos'i ítnáx̱ agax̱toolk̲áa. *After we have washed the dishes we will play cards.*

**du ít** RelationalNoun *(following) him, her, it*
·Wé yées k̲áa du húnx̱w ítx̱ yaa nagút. *The young man's older brother is walking along behind him.*

**a ít aa** noun *the next one, the following one*

**du ítx̱ nagoodí** noun *his/her follower, disciple*
·Dikée aank̲áawu du yéet ítx̱ nagoodí Peter yóo duwasáakw. *Peter is the name of Jesus' disciple.*

**du ítx̱ na.aadí** noun *his/her followers, disciples*
VARIANTS: du ítx̱ na.aatx'í, du ítx̱ ne.aatx'í (C)
·Jinkaat k̲a déix̱ yatee Dikée aank̲áawu du yéet ítx̱ na.aadí. *There are twelve disciples of Jesus.*
·Dikée aank̲áawu du yéet ítx̱ na.aadí has du een sh káa x̱'awdigáx'. *Jesus prayed with his disciples.*

**ít'ch** noun *glass (the substance)*
·Ít'chi s'íx' k̲'áatl' du jeewú. *She has a glass plate.*
·Ít'ch s'íx' du jeet x̱waatán. *I gave her a glass dish.*

**íxde** Adverb *(toward) downstream*
VARIANTS: íxdei
·Dliwkát sh eeltín íxde yaa neek̲úx̱u yáa kanaadaayi héen káx'. *Watch yourselves going down this river.*

**ixkée** noun *downstream; south; lower 48 states, (locally: down south)*
·Yáa k̲utaanx' aadé k̲ugax̱tootéen ixkée ch'a g̱aax̱tusatéen wé sháa. *This summer we are going to travel down south just to see the girls.*
·Ax̱ sée du kacháwli áwé ixkéex' yéi yatee. *My daughter's sweetheart lives down south.*

**íx̱t'** noun *shaman; medicine man*
·Yanéegu lingít x̱ánde wuduwax̱oox̱ wé íx̱t'. *The medicine man was called to the sick person.*
·Wé íx̱t'ch du een akaawaneek wáa sá at gug̱waneiyí. *The medicine man told him what was going to happen.*

# « J »

JAA verb root

- **ashukaawajáa | ashukoojeis’ | ashukajeix̱**

  *s/he instructed him/her | s/he is instructing him/her | s/he instructs him/her (regularly).*

  THEME: O-shu-ka-S-ø-jaa~ (ø act)

  *for S to instruct, show O (by word); for S to advise, give advice to, counsel O*

  ·Ax̱ tláak’wch áa x̱at shukaawajáa, aadé yéi daadunei yé. *My maternal aunt taught me how to make it.*

**jáa** interj. *honey!*

**jáaji** noun *snowshoe*

·Du jáaji a dzaasí yei nasháash. *The thongs of his snowshoes are wearing thin.*

·Jáaji kát yaa has lunagúḵ. *They are running on snowshoes.*

JAAḴ verb root

- **aawajáḵ | yaa anajáḵ | ajáḵx**

  *s/he killed him/her/it | s/he is (in the process of) killing it | s/he kills it (regularly).*

  THEME: O-S-ø-jaaḵ~ (ø event)

  *for S to kill (singular) O; (fig.) for S to let go of O without expecting any return (at party)*

  ·Táach x̱at gug̱ajáaḵ. *I'm going to fall asleep. (Lit: Sleep is going to kill me.)*

  ·Wé ḵáa watsíx aawajáḵ. *That man killed a caribou.*

**jaaḵúx̱** noun *canoe of caribou skins*

JAAḴW[1] verb root

- **aawajáaḵw | ajáaḵw | yoo ayajáaḵwk**

  *s/he beat him/her up | s/he's beating him/her up | s/he beats him/her up (regularly).*

  THEME: O-S-ø-jáaḵw (na act)

  *for S to beat up, assault, violently attack O*

**jánwu** noun *mountain goat*

VARIANTS: jénu (C), ján (T), jánu (T)

·Du x̱ikshá káx̱ yaa anayéin wé jánwu. *He is carrying the moutain goat on his shoulder.*

·Jánwu dleeyí aatlein yak’éi, gwál wé a s’óog̱u. *Mountain goat meat is really good, especially the ribs.*

**du jee** noun *in his/her possession*

·Diyée aanḵáawu jeet wudzigít. *He fell into satan's hands.*

·Laaxw eetí wé k̲aa jeedáx̲ atx̲á has du g̲aneix̲íx̲ wusitee. *After the famine, the food given to them became their salvation.*

JEE[1] verb root

• **yoo akaawajeek | yoo akaajeek | yoo akayajeek**

*s/he wondered about it | s/he is wondering about it | s/he wonders about it (regularly).*

THEME: O-ka-S-ø-jeek (na act)

*for S to wonder, be curious, anxious about O*

·Yoo akaajeek a kaayí wé a káx̲ yaa nagudi dei. *He is wondering about the measure of the road he's walking on.*

JEE[2] verb root

• **kawlijée | kalijée / kulijée | ---**

*it looked terrible | it looks terrible | ---.*

THEME: O-ka-(u)-l-jée (ga state)

*for O to be awful, terrible, eerie (in appearance), unattractive*

NOTES: Note that in classical Tlingit, this verb had a thematic prefix (u-) which is slowly falling out of modern day speech. This is indicated in the Leer-Edwards theme as (u)-. Either imperfective form given here is acceptable: kalijée / kulijée.

·Du shax'ées'i kulijée. *His matted hair is unattractive.*

du **jeeg̲áa** noun *(big) enough for him/her to have or use; adequate for him/her*

·Du jeeg̲áa yatee du yéi jineiyí. *He is capable of handling his work.*

·Du jeeg̲áa koodáal du gwéili. *He can handle the weight of his backpack.*

du **jeeyís** RelationalPostposition *for him/her*

VARIANTS: du jis

·Yéil x'óow aawak̲áa du x̲án aa jeeyís. *She sewed a Raven blanket for her husband.*

·Wé haa sháade háni "gunalchéesh" haa jeeyís yéi yanak̲éich. *Our leader says "thank you" for us.*

a **jeig̲í** noun *its scale (of fish)*

·Wé x̲áat a jeig̲í teen yax̲ ayawlixásh. *She cut up the fish with the scales on.*

·Wé x̲áat a jeig̲í wé s'íx' kaax̲ aawa.óos'. *She washed the scales of her fish off the plate.*

JEIL verb root

• **aadé akaawajeil | aadé yaa akanajél | aadé yóo akayajélk**

*s/he carried it all there | s/he is carrying it all there | s/he carries it all there (regularly).*

THEME: P-dé O-ka-S-ø-jeil~ (na motion)

*for S to carry, take O to P (esp. to one place, making several trips)*

·Hít shantóode akaawajeil wé x'óow. *She took the blankets upstairs.*

- **aadé at kaawajeil | aadé yaa at kanajél | aadé yoo at kayajélk**
  *s/he carried stuff there | s/he is carrying stuff there | s/he carries stuff there (regularly).*
  THEME: P-dé at ka-S-ø-jeil~ (na motion)
  *for S to carry, take things to P (esp. to one place, making several trips)*
  ·Haadéi at kaga<u>x</u>dujéil, a ya.áak x'wán yéi nasné! *Make sure you make room, they will be bringing it all!*
- **ana<u>x</u> yaawajél | --- | ---**
  *s/he reached his/her hand through it | --- | ---.*
  THEME: P-ná<u>x</u> ya-u-S-ø-jeil~ (ø motion)
  *for S to reach a hand through P*
  ·Du kasánná<u>x</u> áwé yaawajél, <u>g</u>unéi has aawal'é<u>x</u>. *He put his hand around her waist and they began dancing.*

du **jigúnl'i** noun *his/her wrist*
·Du jigúnl'i akaawas'ít. *He bandaged his wrist.*

du **ji<u>g</u>ei** noun *crook of his/her arm; in his/her embrace*
·Du tláa ji<u>g</u>eix' táach uwajá<u>k</u> wé t'ukanéiyi. *The baby fell asleep in his mother's arms.*
·Du ji<u>g</u>ei<u>x</u> yaa anasnúk du séek'. *He is carrying his daughter in his arms.*

**ji<u>g</u>ei.át** noun *wrist guard*
VARIANTS: ji<u>g</u>ei.ét (C), jika.át

**ji<u>g</u>wéinaa** noun *towel, hand towel*
·Yées ji<u>g</u>wéinaa du léelk'u jeet yéi awsinei. *He gave his grandmother new towels.*
·Aawa.óos'i ji<u>g</u>wéinaa gáan<u>x</u> ashayaawatée. *She hung the towel that she washed outside.*

du **jiká** noun *back of his/her wrist*
·Du jiká awlichún, ách áwé jika.át yéi aya.óo. *She hurt her wrist. That's why she's wearing a wrist guard.*

**jika<u>k</u>áas'** noun *long smokehouse pole(s)*
·Jika<u>k</u>áas' ká<u>x</u> ashayaawatée wé <u>g</u>aat atx'aan hídi yeex'. *She hung the sockeye salmon on the stick in the smokehouse.*

**jikawáach** noun *wristwatch*

**jika.át** noun *wrist guard*
VARIANTS: ji<u>g</u>ei.át, ji<u>g</u>ei.ét (C)
·Du jiká awlichún, ách áwé jika.át yéi aya.óo. *She hurt her wrist. That's why she's wearing a wrist guard.*
·<u>K</u>unáagu jeedá<u>x</u> jika.át yéi aya.óo. *He is wearing a wrist guard from the doctor.*

du **jiklix'ées'** noun *his/her wrist*

**du jikóol** noun *back of his/her hand*
·Du jikóol wudix̲'íx̲'. *The back of his hand was burned.*
·Du jikóol kawdiyés' *The back of her hand is bruised.*

**du jín** noun *his/her hand*
·Wé x̲éel' du jíndáx̲ awlig̲oo. *She wiped the slime off her hands.*
·I jín wulich'éx̲'w. *Your hands are dirty.*

**jinaháa** noun *fate; bad luck*
VARIANTS: jineháa (C)
·Tléil áyáx̲ at wuneiyí, jinaháa áwé yóo kdulneek. *When something bad happens they say it's bad luck.*
·"Tliyéix', jinaháa haa kát g̲waaxeex," yóo x̲'ayak̲á du tláa. *Her mother says, "Behave, bad luck might befall us!"*

**du jinák̲** noun *away from it, leaving it behind (taking something away from him/her)*
·Du keidlí du jinák̲ k̲ut wujixeex. *His dog ran away from him.*
·Ax̲ jinák̲ k̲ut wujixeex. *He ran away from me.*

**a jíni** noun *its paw*
VARIANTS: a jín
·Wé dóosh du jín dleit kaax̲ kínde alshát. *That cat is holding its paw up off the snow.*
·Wé dóosh jín dleit kaax̲ kínde alshát. *The cat is holding its paw up off the snow.*

**a jíni** noun *it's sleeve (of shirt, coat)*

**jinkaadináx̲** Numeral *ten (people)*
VARIANTS: jinkaatnáx̲

**jinkaat** Numeral *ten*
·Jinkaat dáanaa yéi x̲'alitseen wé x'óow. *That blanket costs ten dollars.*
·Jinkaat g̲anook has ayatéen. *They see ten petrels.*

**jinkaat k̲a tléináx̲** Numeral *eleven (people)*

**jinkaat k̲a tléix'** Numeral *eleven*
·Jinkaat k̲a tléix' du katáagu wé shaatk'. *That girl is eleven years old.*

**du jintáak** noun *his/her palm (of hand)*
·Du jintáak teen akag̲útlx̲ wé tléik̲w. *She mashes the berries with the palm of her hand.*
·Du jintáax' jiwduwanák̲. *He was put in charge of it. (Lit: It was left in his hands).*

**du jintakyádi** noun *his/her palm (center)*

**du jintú** noun *his/her grip*
·Du jintóox̲ kasixát wé tíx'. *The rope is in his grip.*

**du jís** noun *for him/her*
VARIANTS: du jeeyís

**a jiseiyí** RelationalNoun *shelter of it (especially a tree)*
·Wé x'aa jiseiyínáx̱ yan uwaḵúx̱ wé yaakw. *The boat moored in the shelter of the point.*
·A jiseiyít aḵéen aas tlénx'. *People are sitting in the shelter of the big trees.*

**jishagóon** noun *tool, tools*
VARIANTS: jishegóon (C)
·Yaakw ḵa g̱eiwú asg̱eiwú jishagóonx̱ sitee. *A boat and a net are a seine fisherman's tools.*
·Wé ḵáa du jishagóoni ḵut kaawasóos. *The man's tools are lost.*

**du jiwán** noun *outer edge of his/her hand*
·Du jiwán aawaḵ'ék'w. *He cut the outside edge of his hand.*
·Du jiwán wudix̱'íx̱'. *The outside edge of her hand was burned.*

**du jix̱án** noun *near him/her, by him/her (at hand, for him/her to work with)*
·Du jix̱ánx' yan satán wé shunax̱wáayi! *Leave the axe near him!*
·Du jix̱áni yan tí wé lítaa, dleey aan akg̱waxáash! *Leave the knife near her, she will cut meat with it!*

**du jiyagéix̱** noun *against it, wrong (so as to foul up what s/he had done)*

**du jiyáx̱** noun *according to the way s/he does it*
·Ax̱ tláa jiyáx̱ eex̱ kát sakwnéin x̱asa.ée. *I cook fry bread like my mom does.*
·Wé shaatk' du léelk'w jiyáx̱ daḵéis'. *That young girl sews the way her grandmother does.*

**du jiyee** noun *ready, waiting for him/her to use*
NOTES: The postposition -x' has an alternate form -ø (unmarked), which explains the discrepancy between the forms: du jiyee and du jiyeex' in the examples given. Either form is acceptable in either sentence.
·Du jiyeex' yan awsitée du gwéili. *He placed her bag within her reach.*
·Du jiyee yan aawatée wé atóowu x'úx'. *She placed the book he was reading near him.*

**a jiyeet** RelationalNoun *under the burden, weight of it; belabored or suffering from it (a burden, hardship)*
·Toowú néekw jiyeet g̱áax̱ wé shaawát. *The woman is crying under the burden of sadness.*
·Áat' jiyeet, gangookt ḵukawdik'ít'. *People crowded close around the fire because of the cold weather.*

**du ji.een** noun *working with him/her; helping him/her work or do something*
·Wé aantḵeení woosh ji.een gán has aawaxásh. *The townspeople cut wood together.*

·Wé aantk̲eení woosh ji.een gán has aawaxásh. *The townspeople cut wood together.*

du **ji.eetí** noun *his/her handiwork, artifact*
·Ax̲ ji.eetíg̲aa áyá k̲ux̲ashée. *I'm looking for my handiwork.*

JOOX verb root

- **aadé akawlijoox | --- | aadé yoo aklijúxk**
*s/he wheeled it there | --- | s/he wheels it there (regularly).*
THEME: P-dé O-ka-S-l-joox~ (na motion)
*for S to wheel O to P*
·I dlaak' kajúxaa kát kanaljoox hoon daakahídidé. *Take your sister to the store in the wheel barrow.*
- **át akawlijúx | --- | áx̲ aklajoox**
*s/he wheeled it to it | --- | s/he wheels it to it (regularly).*
THEME: P-t~ O-ka-S-l-joox~ (ø motion)
*for S to wheel O to P*
·Haat kalajúx wé t'ooch'! *Wheel the coal over here!*
- **kaawajóox | yaa kanajúx | kei kajúxch / kei kajooxch**
*it's running; it ran | it's running | it runs for a while (and then quits).*
THEME: ka-ø-joox~ (ga event)
*for a wheel to roll, spin; for an engine to start, run*
NOTES: A noun derived from this verb is: kayajuxti át "thing that starts right away, runs well". Note that both repetitive imperfective forms given here are acceptable to speakers: kei kajúxch and kei kajooxch both mean "it runs for a while (and then quits)".
·Yaa kanajúx wé toolch'án. *The top is spinning.*

**júx̲'aa** noun *sling*
VARIANTS: jóox̲'aa (At)
·Júx̲'aa awliyéx̲. *She made a sling.*
·Júx̲'aa tóot astán du jín. *He has his arm in a sling.*

# « K »

a **ká** RelationalNoun *the (horizontal) surface of it; on it; on top of it; in it ( a dish; a path)*
·Laak̲'ásk gé ax̲ oox̲ káwu? *Do I have seaweed on my teeth?*
·Wé x'ees du kaanáx̲ yatee. *The boil is too much for him.*

KAA[1] verb root

- **--- | oodzikaa | ---**
--- | *s/he is lazy* | ---.
THEME: a-u-S-d-s-kaa (ga state)
*for S to be lazy, slow*
·Oodzikaayi k̲áa áyá táakwx' gug̲waláaxw. *A lazy man will starve in the winter.*

**káa** noun *car, automobile*
·Héen yáx̲ kawdiyés' has du káayi. *Their car is dark blue-gray in color.*
·Wéide wook̲oox̲u káa a ítde kk̲wagóot. *I will go after that car that went that way.*

a **káa dul.us'ku át** noun *washboard*
VARIANTS: kát dul.us'ku át
·Ax̲ jeet satán a káa dul.us'ku át! *Hand me the washboard!*
·Lowesdéi neelhoon a káa dul.us'ku átg̲aa! *Go to Lowes and buy a washboard!*

**Kaagwaantaan** noun *Kaagwaantaan, locally called "Wolf"; a clan of the Eagle moiety whose principal crest is the Wolf*
·G̲alyáx̲ K̲wáan áwé G̲alyáx̲ Kaagwaantaanx̲ has sitee. *The Kaliakh River people are the Kaliakh River Kaagwaantaan.*

KAAK verb root

- **wusikaak | sikaak | kei sakaakx̲**
*it became thick* | *it's thick* | *it gets thick (regularly).*
THEME: s-kaak (ga state)
*for something to be thick (cloth, board, food, etc.)*
- **yéi kawsikaak | yéi kwsikaak | yéi kwsakákx̲**
*it got that thick; it thickened* | *it's that thick* | *it gets that thick (regularly).*
THEME: (yéi) ka-u-s-kaak~ (na state)
*for a board, cloth, etc. to be (so) thick*
·K̲áa dzísk'w a doogú yéi kwsikaak. *The hide of a bull moose is this thick.*

du **káak** noun *his/her maternal uncle*
·Has du x̲'áakt wuhaan du káak. *His maternal uncle stood between them.*
·Du káak du ée at latóow. *His maternal uncle is teaching him.*

du **káak’** noun *his/her forehead*
·Kei kawduwag̲ix’i té du káak’t kaawaxíx. *The rock that was thrown hit him on the forehead.*
·Du káak’ wudix’ís’ k̲a kawdiyés’. *His forehead is swollen and bruised.*

a **káa k̲ududziteeyi yoo x̲’atánk** noun *law, words one lives by*
·Tléil oowaa wé aan káa k̲ududziteeyi yoo x̲’atánk géide k̲udunoogú. *It is wrong to act against the law of the land.*

du **káalk’w** noun *her fraternal niece, nephew, cousin*
·Du káalk’w gán du jeeyís aawaxásh. *Her nephew cut wood for her.*

du **káani** noun *his/her brother-in-law, sister-in-law*
·Aangóondáx̲ áwé ax̲ káani du daakanóox’u. *My sister-in-law's ancestors are from Angoon.*
·Du káani ji.een xáanaa atx̲aayí awsi.ée. *She cooked the evening meal with her sister-in-law.*

**káast** noun *barrel*
·Wé káast kaadéi lít wé a x’éix’u! *Throw the gills in the barrel!*
·Gúkshi yan sa.ín wé kak̲áshx̲i a káa yéi tuwa.oowu káast! *Put the barrel we put the steamed berries in in the corner!*

**káas’** noun *ocean algae*
·Káas’ léin káa yéi nateech. *There is always algae on the riverbank.*

**kaat** noun *long, flat loosely woven basket for pressing out herring oil*

**káat’** noun *sharpened stick (for digging up clams, roots, etc.); gardening fork*

at **kaawaxûkw** noun *dried thing, esp. food*

**káaxwei** noun *coffee*
VARIANTS: káxwei
·Hoon daakahídidéi nagú káaxweig̲áa! *Go to the store for some coffee!*

**káax’** noun *spruce grouse, spruce hen; chicken*
·Dunák̲ kawdliyeech wé káax’. *The grouse flew away from him.*
·Káax’ akawlis’úk. *She fried chicken.*

**káa x̲ex̲x’u yeit** noun *bed*
·Káa x̲ex̲x’u yeit káa yan awsinúk du séek’. *She put her daughter down on the bed.*
·Shayeit a kát satéen káa x̲ex̲x’u yeit . *The pillow is lying on the bed.*

**kaay** noun *measuring stick*
·Tleidooshú k̲aa x̲’oos yéi kwliyáat’ wé kaay. *That measuring stick is six feet long.*

**kaay** noun *measure; mile*
·Dax̲adooshú kaay yéi kunaaléi wé aan, héen sháakdáx̲. *The town is seven miles from the head of the river.*

·Du hídidáx̲ kaay shoowú yéi kunaaléi hoon daakahídi. *The store is a half mile from her house.*

**káayag̲ijeit** noun *chair*
VARIANTS: káayak̲ijeit, k̲áakejeit (C)
·Wé káayag̲ijeit káa g̲anú! *Sit on that chair!*
·Káayag̲ijeit anéegwál'. *He is painting the chair.*

at **kaayí** noun *cord (of wood)*
VARIANTS: et kaayí (C)

a **kaayí** noun *pattern, model, template for it; measure of it; measurement for it*
·Daax'oon k̲aa x̲'oos a kaayí wé nadáakw. *That table measures four feet.*
·Yoo akaajeek a kaayí wé a káx̲ yaa nagudi dei. *He is wondering about the measure of the road he's walking on.*

du **kacháwli** noun *his/her sweetheart*
·Ax̲ sée du kacháwli áwé ixkéex' yéi yatee. *My daughter's sweetheart lives down south.*

at **kach'áak'u** noun *carver*
VARIANTS: kadach'áak'u

**kach'ák'waa** noun *rounded carving chisel*
·Kach'ák'waa teen akaawach'ák'w wé kootéeyaa. *He carved a totem pole with a chisel.*
·Yées aa kach'ák'waa aawa.oo. *He bought himself a new chisel.*

**kadádzaa yeit** noun *basket or pan used to collect berries by knocking them off the bush*
·Kadádzaa yeit teen woogoot yóode. *She went over there with a berry basket.*
·Tláakw ashawlihík wé kadádzaa yeit. *She filled the berry basket quickly.*

**kadánjaa** noun *dust; pollen*
·Wás' kadánjaa áwé tláakw k̲uya.óo. *People are overcome by the pollen.*

**kadás'** noun *hail*
·Kadás' daak wusitán. *It is hailing.*
·Wáa yateeyi yéix' kadás' kakandagéix'ch. *Sometimes hail stones are big.*

**kadéix'** noun *shame, embarrassment*
VARIANTS: kedéix' (C)
·Kadéix' du yát uwaxíx tatgé. *Shame fell on him yesterday.*
·Yéi daayaduk̲á, "Tlél kadéix' haa káx̲ sheeteek̲!" *He is told "Don't bring shame on us!"*

a **kádi** noun *its head (of spear)*
·A kádi yalik'áts'. *The spear head is sharp.*
·Yées aa a kádi awliyéx̲. *He made a new spear head.*

a **kadíx'i** noun *its stem (of plant); pith (of tree)*

**kadooheix̱.aa** noun *currants*

**kadúkli** noun *fish smoked for a short time with the backbone taken out*
·Kadúkli atx'aan hídidé yéi awsinei. *She put the fish in the smokehouse.*
·Aawsi.ée wé kadúkli atx'aan hídi yeedáx̱. *She cooked some of the fish from the smokehouse.*

**kadulg̱óok s'eenáa** noun *flashlight*
VARIANTS: kadulg̱úkx̱ s'eenáa
·Kadulg̱óok s'eenáa teen áx̱ yaa nagút. *He is walking along with a flashlight.*
·Haayí wé kadulg̱óok s'eenáa! *Hand over that flashlight!*

**kadulg̱úkx̱ s'eenáa** noun *flashlight*
VARIANTS: kadulg̱óok s'eenáa

**kadushxit t'aa yá** noun *blackboard, chalkboard*
VARIANTS: kadushxeet t'aa yá
·Aax̱ gatí wéi kaxíl'aa kadushxeet t'áa yá g̱alg̱ú! *Pick up the eraser and clean the chalkboard!*

**kadútlx̱i** noun *fish cleaned and hung to dry*

**kadu.uxx̱u át** noun *balloon*
·Du jintáak teen at'ácht wé kadu.uxx̱u át. *She is slapping the balloon with the palm of her hand.*

**kagán** noun *light*
·Wé dís kagáni káax' yéi jiné. *He works by moonlight.*
·Kagán shaa kát uwaxíx. *Light fell on the mountain.*

du **kagé** noun *meeting, encountering, intercepting it; (arriving) at the same place or time as it*
·Haa kagéide yaa ana.át. *People are coming toward us.*

a **kageidí** noun *side of it (house, building, animal); slab of meat covering its ribcage*
·Hít kageidí át kawdigán wé s'eenáa. *The light is shining on the side of the house.*
·A kageidéex' áwé x̱waa.ún wé g̱uwakaan tlein. *I shot the big deer in its side*

**kag̱áak** noun *mouse, deer mouse; vole*
VARIANTS: kag̱ák

**kag̱ádaa** noun *cheesecloth, loose-woven cloth; netting, screen*
·Kag̱ádaa hoon daakahídidáx̱ aawa.oo. *He bought cheesecloth from the store.*
·Akawsitaayi tléik̲w kag̱ádaa tóonáx̱ akawlicháa. *He strained the boiled berries through cheesecloth.*

**kag̱ák** noun *mouse*
·Kag̱ák wududziteen. *Someone saw a mouse.*

**kag̱akl'eedí** noun *yarrow; (locally) rat's tail*
·Kag̱akl'eedí ldakát yéix' kanas.éich. *Yarrow grows all over.*
·Kag̱akl'eedí náakwx̱ dulyéix̱. *Yarrow is used for medicine.*

**kag̱eet** noun *common loon*
·Aanḵáawu G̱eeyx' áwé has saligaaw ḵúnáx̱ wé kag̱eet. *The loons are really loud in Ankau Bay.*
·X̱áat yís áwé has akawliník Yéilch, wé kéidladi ḵa kag̱eet. *Raven talked the seagull and loon out of the salmon.*

**kag̱ít** noun *darkness*
·Wé kag̱ít tóox̱ yaa ntoo.ádi awdlidées. *As we walked along in the darkness, the moon shined bright.*
·Áa akwdlix̱éitl' wé kag̱ít tú. *He is afraid of the dark.*

**kag̱útlx̱i** noun *mashed berries*

a **kaháadi** noun *its covering; cover (over a large opening or something without an opening)*
·Du gáni a kaháadi yís áwé xwaasdáa aawa.oo. *He bought a tarp to cover his firewood.*
·Wé té tlein a kaháadi káa yan tán! *Put that large rock on top of its cover!*

**kaháakw** noun *roe, eggs (of fish)*
·Kaháakw daax' yéi jiduneiyí, xén tlél ushk'é. *Using plastic to prepare salmon eggs is not good.*
·L'ook kaháagu áyá yak'éi kanat'á kanéegwál' sákw. *Coho salmon eggs are good for blueberry sauce.*

at **kahéeni** noun *juice*
·Tlei déix̱ ḵ'ateil yáx̱ áwé wutusineix̱ shákw kahéeni. *We just saved two gallons of the strawberry juice.*

a **kajeig̱í** noun *its scales (of fish)*
VARIANTS: a kajeeg̱í (T)
·Wé x̱áat a kajeig̱í aax̱ yéi awsinei. *She took the scales off the fish.*
·X̱'áakw hél a kajeig̱í ḵoostí. *The freshwater sockeye doesn't have any scales.*

**kajúxaa** noun *flywheel; wheelbarrow; wagon; hand truck*
·I dlaak' kajúxaa kát kanaljoox hoon daakahídidé. *Take your sister to the store in the wheel barrow.*

**kakatáx'aa** noun *pliers*
·Aadéi dutlákw yé áyá, kakatáx'aa teen yawduwadlaaḵ. *As the story goes, he was defeated by a pair of pliers.*
·Kakatáx'aa ax̱ jeet tí, Chx̱ánk'! *Hand me the pliers, Grandson!*

**kakéin** noun *yarn; wool*
·Ax̱ léelk'w jeedáx̱ kakéin l'ée x'wán áyá ax̱ tuwáa sigóo. *I like the yarn socks from my grandmother.*
·X̱'áan kakéin haat yéi x̱wsiné kasné yís. *I brought some red yarn for knitting.*

**kakéin k'oodás'** noun *sweater*
·Xeitl kakéin k'oodás' ax̱ yageeyí kaadéi áa ḵaa jikaawaḵaa ax̱ léelk'wch. *My grandmother commissioned a Thunderbird sweater for my birthday.*
·Ḵusi.áat' gáan - kakéin k'oodás' yéi na.oo! *It's cold out - wear a sweater!*

**kaklahéen** noun *wet snow; slush*
VARIANTS: kuklahéen
·Ḵúnáx̱ x̱at wuditl'ák', kaklahéen áyá aawag̱éet. *I'm so wet - wet snow is coming down hard.*
·Tláakw áyá haa ḵg̱watée wult'éex'i yá kaklahéen. *We will be in tough shape if this wet snow freezes.*

**kakúxaa** noun *bailer*
·K'idéin ashigóok kakúxaa layeix̱. *He knows how to build bailers really well.*
·Tlél a káx̱ yiseix'aag̱úḵ wé yaakw kakúxaa! *Don't you all forget the bailer for the boat!*

**kak'dakwéiy s'aatí** noun *captain; person in charge*
·Ax̱ éesh kak'dakwéiy s'aatíx̱ sitee, x'úx' awux̱áax'un. *As a captain, my father used to haul mail.*
·Ax̱ éesh kak'dakwéiy s'aatíx̱ wusitee s'ísaa yaakw káx'. *My father became the captain of the sailboat.*

**kak'kakwéiy s'aatí (At)** noun *captain (in the navy)*
VARIANTS: kak'kwéiy s'aatí (TC)

du **kak'x̱aawú** noun *his/her bangs*
VARIANTS: du kek'x̱aawú (C)

**kaḵáshx̱i** noun *steamed berries put up in soft grease*
·Gúkshi yan sa.ín wé kaḵáshx̱i a káa yéi tuwa.oowu káast! *Put the barrel we put the steamed berries in in the corner!*
·Ḵu.éex'dei nasx̱óot' yá kaḵáshx̱i! *Pack the steamed berries to the potlatch!*

**kalchaneit** noun *mountain ash*
·Tlél kalchaneit áa koo.éix̱ Yaakwdáat. *Mountain ash doesn't grow in Yakutat.*

**kalchaneit tléig̱u** noun *mountain ash berry*
·Ḵuk'éet' áwé gax̱too.áat kalchaneit tléig̱ug̱áa. *We are going to pick mountain ash berries.*

**kaldaag̲ákw** noun *bare; naked*

**kaldaag̲éinák̲x̲** Adverb *slowly*
·Shux'áanáx̲ kaldaag̲éináx̲ áwé dugwáal yá shí. *The drumming starts out slow in this song.*
·Kaldaag̲éináx̲ yaa gax̲took̲óox̲, tlél g̲wadlaan yá éix̲' yík. *We will travel along slowly, it's not deep in this slough.*

**kaldáal'i** noun *typist*
VARIANTS: kaldáal'
·Wéix' yéi jix̲aneiyí kaldáal'ix̲ áwé x̲at satéeyin. *I was a typist when I worked there.*
·Yasátk aadéi ashigóogu yé wé kaldáal'. *The typist knows how to type fast.*

**kaldáanaak̲** noun *broke; penniless; without money*
·Kaldáanaak̲ áwé yaakwt wujixíx. *He jumped aboard the ship without money.*
·At toox̲'áan áyá táakwni yís, kaldáanaak̲x̲ haa nasteech. *We are smoking fish for the winter because we are usually without money.*

**kalóox'jaa** noun *fast drip, leak*
VARIANTS: kalóox̲jaa

du **kalóox'shani** noun *his/her bladder*
·Du kalóox'sháni néegooch áwé du daa yawdudzi.aa. *He is being examined because of his bladder pain.*
·Náakw du x̲'éix̲ wuduwatee du kalóox'sháni néegooch. *She was given medicine for her bladder pain.*

**kalóox̲jaa** noun *fast drip, leak*
VARIANTS: kalóox'jaa
·Awdagaaních áwé, dleit kaax̲ kalóox̲jaa koolx'áasch hít kaadáx̲. *Because the sun is shining, the snow drips fast off the house.*
·Héen sákw wé dleitdáx̲ kalóox̲jaa tayeex' yan tán! *Set that below the snow drip for our water!*

**kals'éesjaa** noun *dust cloud; snow cloud*
·Kals'éesjaa wéix̲ yaa nals'ís. *Dust is blowing along there.*
·Táakwx' dleit kals'éesjaa duteen nooch. *You can see blowing snow in the winter time.*

**kals'áak (T)** noun *squirrel*
VARIANTS: kanals'áak
·Sakwnéin áwé du x̲'éix̲ x̲ateex̲ wé kals'áak. *I feed bread to the squirrel.*
·Ch'áakw dux̲áa noojín wé kals'áak. *They used to eat squirrels long ago.*

**kaltásk** noun *berrying basket*
VARIANTS: kaltálk
·K̲uk'éet' yís áwé yéi daaduné wé kaltálk. *The berrying basket is made for picking berries.*

**kaltéelk̲** noun *barefoot; shoeless*
·Eesháank' kaltéelk̲ áwé haat wujixíx ax̲ dachx̲ánk'. *Poor thing, my grandchild ran over here shoeless.*
·K̲'asigóo kaltéelk̲ l'éiw kát át wusheex. *It's fun running around barefoot in the sand.*

**kanaadaayi héen** noun *river; stream; creek*
·Dliwkát sh eeltín íxde yaa neek̲úx̲u yáa kanaadaayi héen káx'. *Watch yourselves going down this river.*

**kanágaa** noun *stretcher, form for shaping*
·At xáshdi téel sákw áwé kanágaa akaawach'ák'w ax̲ jeeyís. *He carved a form for making moccasins for me.*
·K̲únáx̲ dugóogun kanágaa layeix̲. *People really used to know how to make a moccasin-shaping form..*

**kanals'áak** noun *red squirrel*
VARIANTS: kals'áak (T)

**kanálx̲i** noun *steamed berries*

**kanas.aadí** noun *crawling insect; spider*

**kanashú** noun *drunkenness; inebriation; giddiness*

**kanat'á** noun *blueberry; huckleberry*
·Kanat'á a x̲oo yéi nateech kaxwéix̲. *Blueberries are usually in the midst of cranberries.*
·L'ook kaháagu áyá yak'éi kanat'á kanéegwál' sákw. *Coho salmon eggs are good for blueberry sauce.*

**kanat'á kahéeni** noun *blueberry juice; purple*
·Wé x̲aat kanat'á kahéeni káa yéi gax̲too.oo. *We will put the roots in the blueberry juice.*
·Du oox̲ kanat'á kahéeni yáx̲ kawdisék̲'w. *Her teeth are the color of blueberry juice.*

**kanéegwál'** noun *dish made with berries and salmon eggs*
·Shaax̲ a.éen haa hídi daatx̲ kanéegwál' sákw. *She is picking gray currants from around our house for a berry and salmon egg dish.*
·L'ook kaháagu áyá yak'éi kanat'á kanéegwál' sákw. *Coho salmon eggs are good for blueberry sauce.*

**kaneilts'ákw** noun *black currants or swamp currants*
VARIANTS: kanalts'ákw (T), kaneilts'íkw (At), kaneilts'ook (T)
·Yaa ntoo.ádi áwé, daak wudzigít yax̲ akaawax̲ích wutuwa.ini kaneilts'ákw. *When we were walking along, she fell down and spilled all the swamp currants we picked.*
·Tsaa Éix̲' kaadáx̲ áwé yawtuwadlaak̲ ch'a k'ikát wé kaneilts'ákw. *We finally managed to get some swamp currants from Seal Slough.*

**kaneilts'íkw (At)** noun *black currants or swamp currants*
VARIANTS: kaneilts'ákw, kanalts'ákw (T), kaneilts'ook (T)

**kanéist** noun *cross*
·Ax̱ léelk'w jeeyís áyá kax̱waa.oo yá kanéist guk.át. *I bought these cross earrings for my grandmother.*
·X̱áay een áwé x̱waliyéx̱ wé kanéist. *I built that cross out of yellow cedar.*

**kanóox'** noun *turtle*
VARIANTS: tadanóox', tanóox', tadanóox'u (At)
·Tleidahéen áwé Yaakwdáatt aa wlihásh wé kanóox'. *One time a turtle floated to Yakutat.*
·Kanóox' áwé kéi anasx̱ít. *He is breeding turtles.*

**kantáḵw** noun *lupine*
VARIANTS: kentáḵw
NOTES: Warning: some lupine species contain toxic alkaloids, be certain of species before use.
·Héen táatx̱ ák.wé du.een wéi kantáḵw? *Is the lupine picked from the water?*

du **kasán** noun *his/her waist*
·Du kasánnáx̱ áwé yaawajél, g̱unéi has aawal'éx̱. *He put his hand around her waist and they began dancing.*
·Ḵaa kasán tayeet shukatáni áwé yak'éi wéi s'él' kinaak.át. *A raincoat that hangs below the waist is the best.*

**kasanka.át** noun *corset*

a **kaséiḵ'u** noun *its color*
·A kaséiḵ'u x̱'éishx'w kayaax̱ sitee. *The color is in the likeness of a bluejay.*

**kaséiḵ'w** noun *neck cord worn for dance*

**kaséḵ'x̱u** noun *dye*
·Yán aas daadáx̱ kayeix̱ áwé átx̱ gag̱ilayéix̱ s'agwáat kaséḵ'x̱u sákw. *Shavings from a hemlock tree is what you will use for the brown dye.*

**kasg̱aax̱** noun *mourning, wailing, loud weeping or crying; wail, groan, moan*

**kasiyaayi héen** noun *liquor; booze; alcoholic beverage*

**kasiyéiyi s'eiḵ** noun *marijuana*
VARIANTS: kasiyéiyi s'eeḵ

**kasné** noun *knitting, crocheting*
·X̱'aan kakéin haat yéi x̱wsiné kasné yís. *I brought some red yarn for knitting.*

**kast'áat'** noun *cotton; cotton blanket, quilt*
·Ḵóok yígu ax̱ kast'áat'i - ax̱ jeet .áx̱. *My quilt is in the box - give it to me.*

·Kast'áat' tlein áwé wóoshde ak̲éis' ax̲ yádi jeeyís. *She is sewing together a big quilt for my child.*

**kast'áat' x'óow** noun *quilt; cotton blanket*

**kas'éet** noun *screw*
·Wéi yaakw yax̲ak'áaw kas'éet áa yéi du.oowú, k'idéin yéi agux̲lasháat. *If a screw is put in the thwart of the boat, it will hold pretty well.*

**kas'éet kagwádlaa** noun *wrench*
VARIANTS: kas'éet kag̲úkwaa; kas'éet kakéigwaa
·Craftsman kas'éet kagwádlaa áwé Sears Roebuckdáx̲ x̲waa.oo. *I bought a Craftsman wrench from Sears Roebuck.*
·Yaakw yíx' yan tí wéi kas'éet kagwádlaa. *Leave the wrench in the boat.*

**kas'éet kag̲úkwaa** noun *wrench*
VARIANTS: kas'éet kagwádlaa, kas'éet kakéigwaa

**kas'éet katíx̲'aa** noun *screwdriver*
VARIANTS: kas'éet katéx̲'aa (C)
·Kas'éet katíx̲'aa tlein áyá yaakwt kax̲atéen. *I have a big screwdriver lying in the boat.*
·Ace Hardwaredé neelhoon kas'éet katíx̲'aag̲áa! *Go to Ace Hardware and buy a screwdriver!*

**kas'ígwaa yeit (A)** noun *frying pan, skillet*
VARIANTS: kas'úgwaa yeit (TC)

a **kas'úkx̲u** noun *fried food*
·G̲uwakaan taayí kas'úkx̲u yís akaawaxaash. *She cut up deer fat for frying.*

**kas'úwaa** noun *chopper*
·Yá kas'úwaa teen a yíkdáx̲ x̲út'! *Chip the inside out with this chopper!*
·Yax'át yá kas'úwaa ax̲ jeeyís! *Sharpen this chopper for me!*

**kashéek'w gwéil** noun *heating pad*

**kashéex̲'** noun *praise, glorification*
·X̲'agáax' daakahídix' áwé at kashéex̲' shí áa dushí. *Songs of praise are sung in church.*

**kashóok'** noun *electricity*

**kashóok' gwéil** noun *heating pad*
·Wéi kashóok' gwéil ax̲ x̲eek káa yan satí! *Set the heating pad on my upper arm!*
·Náakw s'é áa yéi kk̲wa.oo ax̲ keey aag̲áa tsá wéi kashóok' gwéil. *I will put medicine on my knee first, then the heating pad.*

**kashóok' yoo x̲'atánk** noun *email*

**kashxeedí** noun *writer; scribe; secretary*
·Kashxeedíx̱ sitee haa yéet. *Our son is a scribe.*

du **katáagu** noun *his/her age*
·Tleiḵáa ḵa tléix' áwé du katáagu. *He is twenty-one years old.*
·Jinkaat ḵa tléix' du katáagu wé shaatk'. *That girl is eleven years old.*

at **katáx'aa** noun *pliers*

**kát dul.us'ku át** noun *washboard*
VARIANTS: a káa dul.us'ku át

at **katé** noun *bullet*
·Du kwéiyi ḵínt kaawaxíx wé at katé. *The bullet fell short of his mark.*

**katéix̱** noun *soup, porridge*
·X̱alak'ách' katéix̱i ax̱ x̱'é yak'éi. *Porcupine soup is delightful to my mouth.*

**katíx̱'aa** noun *key*
VARIANTS: katéx̱'aa (C)
·A kát tsé iseix'áaḵw haa hít katíx̱'aayi! *Don't forget our house key!*
·Tléix' dáanaa yéi x̱'alitseen katíx̱'aa x'úx' daakahídix'. *A key costs one dollar at the post office.*

**katíx̱'aa s'aatí** noun *keeper of the key; jailer; night watchman*
·Katíx̱'aa s'aatíx̱ x̱at gux̱satée yá keijín yagiyeedáx̱. *After Friday I will be the jailer.*
·K'idéin has jiduḵéi katíx̱'aa s'aatí Dzántik'i Héenix'. *Jailers are paid well in Juneau.*

**katḵaaḵú** noun *wilderness; the bush*
VARIANTS: galg̱aaḵu, g̱walg̱aḵú (At), kalg̱aḵú (T)

**katóok** noun *cave*
·A daat shkalneek ḵudzitee yá katóok. *There is a story about this cave.*
·Yá neechx̱ yaa neegúdi yei ḵg̱isatéen yá katóok. *As you walk along this shoreline you will see this cave.*

a **kát sh kadultsex̱t át** noun *bicycle*

**kát yadu.us'ku át** noun *wash basin*
·Yat'aayi héen a káa yéi nay.oo wéi a kát yadu.us'ku át! *You all put hot water in the wash basin!*
·Éil' a kaadéi kanasxá wéi a kát yadu.us'ku át! *Pour salt in the wash basin!*

**kat'ákx̱i** noun *half-dried, compressed food, esp. berries or seaweed*
·Aatlein shákw áwé wutuwa.ín kat'ákx̱i yéi nax̱tusaneit. *We picked a lot of strawberries so we can make dried berry patties.*
·Ch'as héen ák.wé a kaadéi yóo yadudzixéik yá kat'ákx̱i? *Is water all that was put on these dried berries?*

**kat'éex'** noun *(plug of) chewing tobacco*
·Wé shaawát g̱ánch kat'éex' du jeet wuduwatée. *The woman was given a plug of tobacco.*

**kat'éx̱'aa** noun *pounder (for meat or grease)*

**kat'éx̱'aa yeit** noun *mortar for pounding*
·G̱ánch áwé aan yéi daaduné wéi kat'éx̱'aa yeit. *He uses the mortar for pounding his tobacco.*

**kat'íshaa** noun *three-cornered needle for sewing skin or leather*
·Yá kat'íshaa at xáshdi téel aan x̱aḵéis'. *I sew moccasins with this leather needle.*
·Kat'íshaa JoAnne Fabricsdáx̱ x̱waa.oo dzísk'u doogú yís. *I bought a leather needle from JoAnne Fabrics for (sewing) moose hide.*

a **kat'óot** noun *partway up it; halfway up it (the inside of a vessel or container)*
·Gúx'aa kat'óott kaawadáa wé cháayoo. *The cup is filled part way up with tea.*
·A kat'óott shalatl'ít', tlél kei kg̱wadál! *Fill it halfway, then it won't be heavy!*

**katl'áak'** noun *mica*

**katl'áak'** noun *gold-rust; flecked with gold or rust*

**katl'úḵjaa** noun *drip, leak with dripping*
·Taat kanax̱ x̱at wusix̱éḵ wé katl'úḵjaa. *All night I was kept awake by that slow drip.*

**káts** noun *pounded shell powder*
·Wé káts táay káa yéi na.oo! *Put the pounded shell powder on the garden!*

**katsóowaa** noun *planting stick*
·Ax̱ jeet tán wéi katsóowaa! *Hand me the planting stick!*

**kawáat** noun *lump in the flesh; tumor*
·Du g̱átsig̱áa wootee yá kawáat. *There are tumors all over her thigh.*

**kawóot** noun *bead*
·Ax̱ al'eix̱ k'oodás'i ch'áagu kawóot áwé a daawú á. *There are old beads on my dance shirt.*
·Kawóot teen ḵ'eikaxwéin a káa kaḵá! *Embroider a flower on it with beads!*

**kawóot ka.íshaa** noun *fine needle for stringing beads*
·Tlél déi x̱wateen ax̱ kawóot ka.íshaa. *I can't see my needle anymore.*
·T'áa kát ḵushí ax̱ jeeyís - ḵut kax̱waag̱éex' ax̱ kawóot ka.íshayi! *Look on the floor for me - I lost my needle!*

**kaxágwaa yeit** noun *mortar for grinding*
·Aẖ jeet tán wé kaxágwaa yeit, yáa s'áxt' aan yéi nḵasaneiyít! *Hand me the mortar so I can use it on this devil's club!*

**kaxéel'** noun *trouble; conflict*
·A wánẖ áwé yaa gagútch wé kaxéel' teen. *He walks on the edge of trouble.*
·Kaxéel' sháade hániẖ sitee wé shaatk'. *The young girl is a troublemaker.*

**kaxées'** noun *wire*
·Wé hít gukshitúdáẖ kasixát wé kaxées'. *The wire runs from the corner of that house.*
·Kaxées' teen wóoshdei kdudzixát du ẖ'ás'. *His jaw is held together with a wire.*

**kaxíl'aa** noun *scrubber*
·Aẖ yéi jineiyí áwé kaxíl'aa k'idéin daané. *My job is to clean erasers.*
·Aaẖ gatí wéi kaxíl'aa kadushxeet t'áa yá g̱alg̱ú! *Pick up the eraser and clean the chalkboard!*

**kaxwaan** noun *frost*
·Yeedát ḵuyak'éi g̱aatáa yéi daané yís yá kaxwaan káẖ yaa nagúdi. *Today the weather is good for walking out on the frost to check the traps.*
·Tlél tlaẖ kooshẖ'íl'k yá kaxwaan. *It's not very slippery with this frost.*

**kaxweitl** noun *itch; rash*
·Yak'éiyi náakw áwé yéi awsinei yá kaxweitl káa yéi aawa.oo. *He made some good medicine and put it on the rash.*

**kaxwéiẖ** noun *high bush cranberry*
·Kanat'á a ẖoo yéi nateech kaxwéiẖ. *Blueberries are usually in the midst of cranberries.*
·Kanéegwál' yís yéi daaduné kaxwéiẖ. *Highbush cranberries are used for the berry and salmon egg dish.*

**kaxwénaa** noun *dipper, scoop, ladle; brailer bag*
·H̱áat teen áwé shawdudlihík wé kaxwénaa. *The brailer bag was filled with salmon.*
·Kaxwénaa yee yís áwé ẖwliyéẖ aẖ yaagú yíkx'. *I built space for the brailer bags in my boat.*

**kax'áasjaa** noun *trickle of water; steady drip or leak*
·Tlei ult'íx'ch taatx' wéi hít daadáẖ kax'áasjaa. *The water dripping from the house freezes at night.*

**kax'ás'aa** noun *rip saw; double-handled saw for sawing lumber*
·Kax'ás'aa teen áwé kg̱eexáash ldakát wéi t'áa! *You will cut all those boards with a rip saw!*
·Kax'ás'aa yax'áat áwé ashigóok. *He really knows how to sharpen the rip saw.*

**kax'ás'ti** noun *lumber*
·Wé kóok̲ kax'ás'ti a yanáa yan aawatán. *He put plywood over the pit in the ground.*
·Yóo diyáanax̲.aadáx̲ áwé haat yax̲waax̲áa wéi kax'ás'ti haa hídi sákw. *I hauled the lumber from across the other side for our house.*

**kax'ás'ti daakahídi** noun *sawmill*
·Kax'ás'ti daakahídi x̲ánt hán. *He is standing next to the sawmill.*

**KÁX'X̲** verb root

• **--- | kajikáx'x̲ | ---**
--- | *it's spotted* | ---.
THEME: ka-j-káx'x̲ (ga state)
*for something to be spotted, have polka-dots*
VARIANTS: -gáx'x̲
NOTES: This verb only occurs in the imperfective.
·G̲uwakaan yádi kajikáx'x̲. *A fawn is spotted.*

at **káx̲ adéli** noun *guard, watchman*

**kax̲gáani yeit** noun *frying pan, skillet*

a **káx̲i** noun *its sap, phloem*

a **kax̲yee** RelationalNoun *its ceiling*
·Dleit yáx̲ wuduwanéegwál' wé kax̲yee. *The ceiling was painted white.*
·Gwál tleik̲áa x̲'oos áwé a kax̲yeedé. *It must be twenty feet to the ceiling.*

**kax̲'át'** noun *green, unripe berry*

**kax̲'ees** noun *strong urine smell*
VARIANTS: kex̲'ees (C)

**kax̲'íl'aa** noun *iron (for ironing)*
·Ch'áagu aa kax̲'íl'aa stoox káx' áwé yan dutéeych yag̲at'aayít. *The irons of long ago were set on the stove to heat up.*

a **kayaa** noun *something sort of like it; something not measuring up to it; where one expects it to be*
·A kaséik̲'u x̲'éishx'w kayaax̲ sitee. *The color is in the likeness of a bluejay.*

**kayaaní** noun *leaf, leaves; vegetation, plants, herbs, herbiage*
·Héen shóot wulihaash wé kayaaní. *The leaf floated around the edge of the water.*
·G̲uwakaan x̲ax̲oox̲ nooch k̲'eikaxétl'k kayaaní teen. *I always use a bunchberry leaf to call deer.*

**kayáash** noun *platform; porch*
·Yéi áwé wduwasáa Kayáash Hít L'uknax̲.ádich. *The Coho Salmon tribe has named it Platform House.*

du **kayádi** noun *her fetus, unborn child*
VARIANTS: du keyédi (C)

a **kayéik** noun *sound, noise of it*
·Washéen kayéik aawa.áx̱. *She heard the sound of the machine.*
·Gandaadagóogu kayéik x̱aa.áx̱ch. *I can hear the sound of a woodpecker.*

**kayéil'** noun *peace, calm*

**kayeix̱** noun *wood shavings*
·Yán aas daadáx̱ kayeix̱ áwé átx̱ gag̱ilayéix̱ s'agwáat kasék̲'x̱u sákw. *Shavings from a hemlock tree is what you will use for the brown dye.*

**kayeix̱tág̱u (C)** noun *wood chips; wood shavings*
VARIANTS: kayeix̱tag̱ú (AtT)
·Aan áwé shóot ax̱wdi.ák wé kayeix̱tág̱u. *I built a fire with the wood shavings.*
·X̱áay kayeix̱tág̱u a takáx' yéi na.oo! *Put yellow cedar shavings in the bottom of it!*

a **kayís** Adverb *for it (a day, week; a dish)*
·Du séek' yageeyí kayís áwé gáaxw awsi.ée. *She cooked a duck for her daughter's birthday.*
·Woosh gax̱dusháa a kayís áwé yées l'aak aawak̲áa. *She sewed a new dress for the wedding that was to take place.*

a **ka.aasí** noun *its mast (of boat)*

du **keekán** noun *coming to see him/her*
·I léelk'u keekándei aneelg̱ein - x̱áat yéi adaané! *Go check on your grandpa - he's working on fish!*

du **kéek'** noun *her younger sister; his younger brother; cousin*
·Ts'ootsxánch uwasháa ax̱ kéek'. *A Tsimshian married my little sister.*
·Du kéek' teen áwé k̲uk'éet' has woo.aat. *She went berry picking with her younger sister.*

**kéel** noun *auklet or murrelet*
·Sheishóox̱ áwé akaawach'ák'w, kéel a káa yéi aawa.oo. *He carved a rattle and put a murrelet on it.*

**kées** noun *bracelet*
·Góon dáanaa een áwé kawduwat'íx̱' ax̱ jeeyís yá kées. *This bracelet was pounded out of a gold coin for me.*
·Xeitl a káa kawduwach'ák'w yá kées. *A Thunderbird is carved on this bracelet.*

**KEES'** verb root

• **ayakawlikís' | --- | ayaklakís'x̱**
*s/he put it out* | --- | *s/he puts it out (regularly).*

THEME: O-ya-ka-S-l-kées'~ (ø event)
*for S to put out, extinguish O (fire); for S to turn off O (light)*

- **yakawlikís' | yaa yakanalkís' | yaklakísx̱**
  *it went out | it's starting to go out | it goes out (regularly).*
  THEME: ya-ka-l-kées'~ (ø event)
  *for a fire, light to go out*
  ·X̱'aan yakawlikís'. Wé kél't' ḵu.aa, ch'u uwat'áa. *The fire has gone out but the ashes are still warm.*

**kéet** noun *killerwhale*
·Ch'as a gooshí duwatéen wé kéet. *Only the dorsal fin of the killerwhale is visible.*
·Áa atoosg̱eiwú yé áwé kéet haa daat yawsigóo. *The killer whales came around where we were gillnetting.*

du **keey** noun *his/her knee*
·Náakw s'é áa yéi kḵwa.oo ax̱ keey aag̱áa tsá wéi kashóok' gwéil. *I will put medicine on my knee first, then the heating pad.*
·Du keey áwé wuduwaxaash. *They cut into his knee.*

du **keey shakanóox'u** noun *his/her kneecap*
VARIANTS: du kiyshakanóox'u, du kiyshakunóox'u (At), du kiyshekenóox'u (C)
·Du keey shakanóox'u áwé tlei át nashx̱'íl'ch. *His kneecap slides around.*

**kei** Adverb *up*
VARIANTS: kéi
·Haat kei wudaayi tleil ux̱satinch. *He has not seen the tide rise yet.*
·Ánk'w áwé kéi has anaswát wéit lingítch. *Those people are raising a crybaby.*

KEI verb root

- **akawsikei | aksakéikw | yei aksakéich**
  *s/he untangled it | s/he is untangling it | s/he untangles it (regularly).*
  THEME: O-ka-S-s-kei~ (g̱a act)
  *for S to trail, follow tracks of O; for S to untangle O; for S to rip back, undo O (sewing, knitting)*
  ·Kax̱saké a kóon wé kinaak.át! *Unravel the hem on the coat!*

**kéi daḵinji s'áaxw** noun *umbrella*
·Kéi daḵinji s'áaxw tlein a tayeet ḵaa luwagúḵ séew tóodáx̱. *People ran under the big umbrella out of the rain.*
·Áa akwdlix̱éitl' wéi kéi daḵinji s'áaxw. *He is afraid of the umbrella.*

**kéidladi** noun *gull, seagull*
·X̱áat yís áwé has akawliník Yéilch, wé kéidladi ḵa kag̱eet. *Raven talked the seagull and loon out of the salmon.*
·Dei át has woo.aat wéi yées kéidladi. *The young seagulls are already walking around.*

du **keigú** noun *his/her lungs*
·Du keigú tóox' áwé kawáat aawasháat. *He got lung cancer.*

**keijín** Numeral *five*
·Deisleenx' keijín has yatee ḵaa sháade náḵx'i. *In Teslin there are five leaders.*
·Keijín ax̱ yaadéi kei jisataan! *Give me five!*

**keijíninááx̱** Numeral *five (people)*

**keijín yagiyee** noun *Friday*
·Katíx̱'aa s'aatíx̱ x̱at guxsatée yá keijín yagiyeedáx̱. *After Friday I will be the jailer.*

KEIL verb root

- **akawlikél | yaa akanalkél | aklakélx̱**
  *s/he soaked it | s/he is soaking it | s/he soaks it (regularly).*
  THEME: O-ka-S-l-keil~ (Ø event)
  *for S to soak O*

du **kéilk'** noun *his sororal niece, nephew*
VARIANTS: du kéilk'w
·Asix̱án áwé du kéilk'. *He loves his nephew.*
·Du kéilk' du x̱'eis at wusi.ée. *His niece cooked for him.*

KEIL'[1] verb root

- **daak awlikél' | daak analkél' | daak alkél'ch**
  *he/she/it chased it into the open | he/she/it is chasing it into the open | he/she/it chases it into the open (regularly).*
  THEME: daak O-l-keil'~ (ø motion)
  *for S to chase O into the open, out to sea*
  NOTES: This verb is often used to describe the practice used by net fishermen of running the boat along the net to chase fish into it.
  ·Watsíx áa káa daak has awlikél' wé g̱ooch. *The wolves chased the caribou out onto the lake.*

**keishísh** noun *alnus alder (beach or mountain alder)*
·Keishísh áwé lats'áa nooch ḵutaanx'. *Alder always smells good in the summer.*

**kéit'u** noun *pick, pickaxe*
·Jishagóon áwé kéit'u. *A pick is a tool.*

**keitl** noun *dog*
·Wé x̱alak'ách' x̱aawú ax̱ keidlí x̱'éit yawdlig̱ích. *The porcupine quills stuck in my dogs mouth.*
·Igayeiḵ tsá wé keitl! *Don't let the dog bite you!*

**kélaa** noun *dish; platter*
VARIANTS: kílaa
·Kílaa yáx̱ i yá kaaxát. *Your face is shaped like a platter.*

**kél't'** noun *ash; ashes*
·Kél't' tuwaakúx̲ dulyéix̲. *They make tobacco out of wood ashes.*
·X̲'aan yakawlikís'. Wé kél't' k̲u.aa, ch'u uwat'áa. *The fire has gone out but the ashes are still warm.*

**Kenasnoow** noun *Killisnoo*
·Kenasnoow áa k̲oowdzitee wé k̲áa. *That man was born in Killisnoo.*

**ketllóox'u** noun *yellow*
·Ketllóox'u yáx̲ yatee wé k̲'eikaxwéin. *The flower is light yellow.*

**Kichx̲áan** noun *Ketchikan*
·Deikeenaa k̲a Ts'ootsxán áa shayadihéin Kichx̲áan. *There are a lot of Haida and Tsimshian people in Ketchikan.*

**kichx̲.anagaat** noun *rainbow*
·Kichx̲.anagaat daat shkalneek tlél wuduskú. *There aren't any stories known about rainbows.*

**kichyát** noun *tern*
·Kichyaat ilk'wát'x̲ sít' yáx'. *Terns lay eggs by glaciers.*

a **kígi** noun *half of it (something cut or broken in half); one side of it (a symmetrical object)*
·Gishoo a kígi ax̲ jeet wududzitáa. *I was given half of a pig.*

a **kíji** noun *its wing*
·Du kíji áwé wool'éex' wé ts'ítskw, ách áwé tlél át wudak̲een. *The songbird's wing broke, that's why it doesn't fly around.*

**kijook** noun *kind of hawk*
VARIANTS: gijook
·Kijook s'áaxw k̲udzitee. *There is a hawk hat.*

du **kík** noun *one side of his/her torso*
·Ch'a du kíkt uwagút. *He walked by his side.*
·Du kíkt hán wé du yéet. *His son is standing beside him.*

a **kík** noun *alongside it; catching up with it*

a **kíknáx̲** noun *in addition to it; along with it; to the side of it; besides that*
·Du kíknáx̲ kei x̲'anatán. *He is talking while someone else is talking.*

**Kiks.ádi** noun *Kiks.ádi, locally called "Frog"; a clan of the Raven moiety whose principal crest is the Frog*

du **kikyádi** noun *his/her twin*
VARIANTS: du kikyédi (C)
·Déix̲ wooch kikyátx'i ax̲ jeewú. *I have two sets of twins.*

**kík'i aa** noun *younger one*
·Xóots x̲'us.eetí áwé awsiteen wé kík'i aa. *The younger one saw the bear tracks.*

**kílaa** noun *dish; platter*
VARIANTS: kélaa
·Kílaa ax̱ jeewú, tlél ḵu.aa átx̱ ux̱layeix̱ *I have a platter but I don't use it.*
·Tlé kílaa kát áwé ḵaa x̱'éix̱ has at wootee. *They fed the people from platters.*

a **kináak** RelationalNoun *above it*
·Shaa kináakdei yaa nagút. *He is walking to the top of the mountain.*
·Du hídi kináak áwé át wulis'ees wé aan kwéiyi. *The flag is blowing around above his house.*

**kinaak.át** noun *coat, overcoat*
VARIANTS: kinaa.át, kinaa.ét (C)
·Atx̱a átch áwé uwax̱áa ax̱ kinaak.ádi. *A moth ate my coat.*
·Ḵaa kasán tayeet shukatáni áwé yak'éi wéi s'él' kinaak.át. *A raincoat that hangs below the waist is the best.*

**kinaa.át** noun *coat, overcoat*
VARIANTS: kinaak.át, kinaa.ét (C)
·X̱aldleit kinaa.át yéi aya.óo wé G̱unanaa ḵáa. *That Athabaskan man is wearing a white fox overcoat.*

**kindachooneit** noun *mallard duck*
·Kindachooneit kuḵa.óon xáanaa atx̱aayí yís. *I will shoot a mallard duck for dinner.*
·Hinyikgáaxu kindachooneit x̱oot wusikwaan. *Golden eye ducks are swimming around among the Mallard ducks.*

**kíndei** Adverb *upward*
VARIANTS: kínde, dikíndei, dikínde
·K̲'anashgidéi ḵáa áwé kíndei alshát du shá. *The poor man is holding his head high.*
·Wé dóosh du jín dleit kaax̱ kínde alshát. *That cat is holding its paw up off the snow.*

**kinguchwáan x'óowu** noun *Hudson Bay blanket*
·Kinguchwáan x'óowu du káx̱ kawduwayaa. *He was covered with a Hudson Bay blanket.*

**kít'aa** noun *pry; stick or tool for prying; crowbar*
·Kít'aa áwé átx̱ has alyeix̱ín haa léelk'u hás. *Our grandparents used to use a peavey.*

du **kiyshá** noun *end of his/her knee*

du **kiyshakanóox'u** noun *his/her kneecap*
VARIANTS: du keey shakanóox'u, du kiyshakunóox'u (At), du kiyshekenóox'u (C)

KOO$^{2}$ verb root

- **awsikóo | yaa anaskwéin | askweix̲**

  *s/he knows it | s/he's beginning to learn it | s/he realizes it (regularly).*

  THEME: O-S-s-koo~ (ø event)

  *for S to know, be acquainted with, make known O (esp. people, facts); for S to learn O (esp. facts)*

  ·Has g̲aduskóot áwé koogéinaa yéi s aya.óo. *They are recognizable by the sash that they wear.*

  ·Tléil x̲wasakú g̲eey kanax̲ k̲utées' yóo duwasáagu x̲áat. *I don't know the fish called ratfish.*

**kóoch'** noun *noiseless fart*

**kooch'éit'aa** noun *ball*

VARIANTS: kooch'éet'aa

·Kooch'éit'aa áwé aan has ash koolyát wé atyátx'i. *The children are playing with a ball.*

·Té géit kaawagwátl wé kooch'éit'aa. *The ball rolled against a rock.*

**koogéinaa** noun *sash (worn over shoulder)*

VARIANTS: koogwéinaa

·Has g̲aduskóot áwé koogéinaa yéi s aya.óo. *They are recognizable by the sash that they wear.*

**koojúxaa (TC)** noun *wheelbarrow; hand truck, dolly*

VARIANTS: koojúxwaa (An), koojíxwaa (At)

·Koojúxaa káx' áwé has akaawachák wé gán. *They hauled the firewood in the wheel barrel.*

**koojúxwaa (An)** noun *wheelbarrow; hand truck, dolly*

VARIANTS: koojúxaa (TC), koojíxwaa (At)

at **kookeidí** noun *parable*

**kookíts'aa** noun *seesaw*

VARIANTS: kookéets'aa (At)

·Ldakát school áwé kookíts'aa áa yéi duwa.óo *A seesaw is put at every school.*

**kook'énaa** noun *sandhopper*

·Át wujik'éin wé kook'énaa. *The sandhopper is hopping around.*

**kóok̲** noun *pit; hole dug in the ground; cellar*

·Tle hít tuwán áwé kóok̲ áa kei has akaawaháa. *Right next to the house they dug a pit.*

·Wé kóok̲ a yee kawjig̲ít. *It is dark inside the cellar.*

**kook̲énaa** noun *messenger; angel*

·Kook̲énaach áwé has du een kaawaneek yá aag̲áa k̲oowdziteeyí yé haa Dikée aank̲áawu. *The messenger told them when our Lord was born.*

·Du kook̲énayi k̲ut wujixeex. *His messenger ran away.*

du **kool** noun *his/her navel, bellybutton*
·Du kool áwé kawlixwétl. *His navel itches.*

**kooléix̲'waa** noun *walrus*
·Kooléix̲'waa dleey gé dux̲á? *Is walrus meat eaten?*

du **kóon** noun *hem of his/her coat, shirt, dress*

**kóon** noun *northern flicker*
·Kóon t'aawú yéi ndu.eich al'eix̲ yís. *Flicker feathers are used in dancing.*

a **kóon** noun *its hem, bottom edge (of coat, dress, shirt); rim (of hat)*
·Kax̲saké a kóon wé kinaak.át! *Unravel the hem on the coat!*

**kóoshdaa** noun *land otter; river otter*
·Kóoshdaa haa eeg̲ayáaknáx̲ yan uwahín. *The land otter swam through our beachfront.*
·Aas t'éik áwé áa awdlisín wé kóoshdaa. *The land otter hid behind a tree.*

**kóoshdaa náagu** noun *liniment*

**kootéeyaa** noun *totem pole*
·Du x̲'ayáx̲ awliyéx̲ wé kootéeyaa. *He made the totem according to his instructions.*
·Kootéeyaa gax̲dulyeix̲í x̲áay yéi ndu.eich. *When a totem is made it is yellow cedar that is used.*

**koot'áax'aa** noun *marble*
·Koot'áax'aa ash katoolyát noojín. *We always used to play with marbles.*

**kootl'éit'aa** noun *tern*

**koow** noun *slippers (shell creature)*

a **koowú** noun *its tail (of bird or fish)*
·Ch'u tle a koowú teen x̲waax̲áa. *I ate the tail and all.*

KOOX verb root

- **kawlikoox | yaa kanalkúx | yoo klikúxk**
  *it drained out | it's draining out | it drains out (regularly).*
  THEME: ka-l-koox~ (na event)
  *for a kettle, container etc. to drain out, go dry*
  ·Héen kawulkuxú duteen nooch wé hintu.eejí. *When the water level drops, the reef can always be seen.*
- **shaawakúx | --- | shakúxx̲**
  *s/he is thirsty | --- | s/he gets thirsty (regularly).*
  THEME: O-sha-ø-koox~ (ø event)
  *for O to be thirsty; for O to be dry*

**kóox** noun *rice; Kamchatka lily root*
·Kóox een dus.ée tl'aak̲'wách'. *Wild rice is cooked with wild rhubarb.*
·Kóox daakeit káa yéi du.úx̲x'. *Rice is put into a container.*

**kooxéedaa** noun *pencil; pen; brush*
·Kooxéedaa eetéenáx̲ yatee wé shaatk'. *The young girl needs a pencil.*
·Wéit tin x'úx' áwé a káa yan kaysatán i kooxéedayi! *Put your pencil on top of that book laying there!*

**kooxídaa (At)** noun *fish spear with a long pole and detachable gaff hook*

**Kooya K̲wáan** noun *Kuiu Island people*

a **kúdi** noun *nest (of animal)*
·Hinyikgáaxu kúdi awsiteen. *She saw a golden eye duck's nest.*

**kuhaankée** noun *orphan*

**kúk̲dlaa** noun *bubbles, esp. from whale*
VARIANTS: gúk̲dlaa

**kúk̲jaa** noun *fast drip with bubbles*

**kunag̲eey** noun *cove; bight*
VARIANTS: kunag̲eiy

**kusakaak** adj. *thick*

**kút** noun *nest*
·A kúdi daat wudik̲een wé gandaas'aají. *There is a bee flying around the nest.*

**kutlá** adj. *stout*

**kuts'een** noun *mouse; rat*

**kuwáat'** adj. *long*

**kux** Adverb *aground, into shallow water*

## « Kw »

**kwaan** noun *smallpox*

**KWAAN** verb root
- **át has wusikwaan | --- | ---**
*they are swimming around there; they swam around there | --- | ---.*
THEME: P-t s-kwaan~ (na motion)
*for birds to swim around on surface of water at P*
·Héen wát át has wusikwaan wé gáaxw. *The ducks are swimming around at the mouth of the river.*
·Gúḵl' wéit wusikwaan. *Swans are swimming around there.*
- **át jiwsikwaan | --- | ---**
*it is swimming around there; it swam around there | --- | ---.*
THEME: P-t ji-s-kwaan~ (na motion)
*for a bird or insect to swim around on surface of water at P (esp. aimlessly or in circles)*
·Héen kát jinaskwanchi át áwé wé atxaayí. *The centipede swims on top of the water.*

**Kwaashk'i Ḵwáan** noun *Kwaashk'i Ḵwáan, locally called "Humpback Salmon"; a clan of the Raven moiety whose principal crest is the Humpback Salmon*

**kwéiy** noun *marker; mark, sign*
·Du kwéiyi ḵínt kaawaxíx wé at katé. *The bullet fell short of his mark.*

**kwshé** particle *Eh?; I wonder*
VARIANTS: kwshéi, kushé, kushéi
·Gu.aal kwshé iwulx̲éidliḵ. *Bless you. (Lit: I hope you get lucky.)*

**kwshéi** interj. *maybe; I'm not sure; [expression of uncertainly]*
VARIANTS: kwshé, gushéi, gushé

**-k'** adj. *little; precious; [diminutive suffix]*
NOTES: Adding -k' to the end of a noun indicates small size. When added to a kin term, it serves as a term of endearment.
·Eesháank' kaltéelḵ áwé haat wujixíx ax̲ dachx̲ánk'. *Poor thing, my grandchild ran over here shoeless.*

# « K' »

**k'aagán** noun *stickleback*

K'AAN verb root

- **awshik'aan | ashik'áan | ---**
  *s/he hated him/her/it | s/he hates him/her/it | ---.*
  THEME: O-S-sh-k'aan~ (ga state)
  *for S to hate O*
  NOTES: This is the only known stative verb with ga- conjugation prefix and a variable stem. All other stative verbs with ga- conjugation prefix have invariable stems.

**k'ákw** noun *owl without ear tufts*
·Tlél aa k͟wasatínch wé k'ákw yóo duwasáagu aa tsísk'w. *I have never seen the bird they call the owl without ear tufts.*
·Taatx' áwé has al'óon wé k'ákw. *Owls hunt at night.*

K'ÁTS' verb root

- **yawlik'áts' | yalik'áts' | kei yalak'áts'ch**
  *it got sharp | it's sharp | it gets sharp (regularly).*
  THEME: ya-l-k'aats'~ (ga state)
  *for an edge to be sharp*
  ·Nóosk x͟aagú k͟únáx͟ yalik'áts'. *Wolverine claws are really sharp.*
  ·Yalik'áts' du g͟altulítayi. *His pocketknife is sharp.*

**k'eeljáa** noun *chinook wind; south wind*
VARIANTS: k'eiljáa
·K'eeljáa tóonáx͟ yaa nak͟úx͟. *He is driving through a storm.*
·K'eeljáa teen áyá séew haat ayawditée. *Rain came with the storm.*

K'EET' verb root

- **aadé (ha)s kawdik'éet' | aadé yaa (ha)s kandak'ít' | aadé yoo (ha)s kadak'ít'k**
  *the group went there | the group is going there (in stages) | the group goes there (regularly).*
  THEME: P-dé O-ka-di-k'éet'~ (na motion)
  *for O (group of people) to all go or come to P*
  ·Aan kaadé k͟ukawdik'éet'. *Everyone went uptown.*
- **át has kawdik'ít' | aadé yaa (ha)s kandak'ít' | áx͟ has kadak'éet'**
  *the group went to it | the group is going to it (in stages) | the group goes to it (regularly).*
  THEME: P-t~ O-ka-d-k'éet'~ (ø motion)
  *for O (group of people) to all leave, go or come to P*

·Áat' jiyeet, gangookt ḵukawdik'ít'. *People crowded close around the fire because of the cold weather.*

- **ḵoowak'ít' | ḵuk'éet' | ḵuk'ít'x̱**

  *s/he picked berries | s/he is picking berries | s/he picks berries (regularly).*
  THEME: ḵu-S-ø-k'éet'~ (ø act)
  *for S to pick berries (esp. pick in quantity to take home)*
  ·Ḵuk'éet' gax̱too.áat ch'eex̱'g̱aa. *We are going to pick thimbleberries.*
  ·Ax̱ dlaak' tín Xunaadé ḵugax̱tootéen kanat'á ḵuk'éet' yís. *We are going to travel to Hoonah to pick blueberries with my sister.*

**k'éets'an** noun *false azalea (fruitless bush)*
·Ch'as k'éets'an áyá yáag̱aa wootee. *There's nothing but false azalea around here.*

**K'EEX̱'** verb root

- **yanax̱ wushik'éex̱' | --- | yanax̱ kei shak'íx̱'ch**

  *he/she/it got hung up | --- | he/she/it gets hung up (regularly).*
  THEME: P-náx̱ O-sh-k'éex̱'~ (ga motion)
  *for O to get delayed, stuck, hung up at P*
  VARIANTS: -k'éix̱'
  ·Wáang̱aneensx' yanax̱ kei shak'íx̱'ch ax̱ yoo x̱'atángi. *Sometimes my words get hung up.*

a **k'eeyí** noun *its base (of tree or other plant); the lower part of its trunk or stem*
·Aas k'eeyéet ash aawatán du óonayi. *He leaned his rifle against the tree trunk.*

**K'EI** verb root

- **awlik'éi | kei analk'éin | kei alk'éich**

  *s/he improved it | s/he is improving it | s/he improves it (regularly).*
  THEME: O-S-l-k'éi~ (ga event)
  *for S to improve O; for S to make peace, make up with O (after quarrel)*

- **ḵoowak'ei | ḵuwak'éi | yei ḵuk'éich**

  *the weather became good | the weather is good | the weather becomes good (regularly).*
  THEME: ḵu-ø-k'ei~ (g̱a state)
  *for the weather to be good*
  ·Yeedát ḵuyak'éi g̱aatáa yéi daané yís yá kaxwaan káx̱ yaa nagúdi. *Today the weather is good for walking out on the frost to check the traps.*

- **du toowú wook'éi | du toowú yak'éi | du toowú kei k'éich**

  *s/he was happy | s/he is happy | s/he gets happy (regularly).*
  THEME: N toowú ø-k'éi (ga state imperf. -k'éi/-k'é)
  *for N to be glad, happy, feel fine*
  ·Ḵúnáx̱ wé yee woo.éex'i aa tsú yee x̱oo yéi kg̱watée toowú k'é teen. *Your hostess will welcome you all as well. (Lit: Your hostess will be among you all with good feelings.)*
  ·Ḵa x̱át tsú ax̱ toowú yak'éi yaa a káa yéi x̱at gug̱wateeyí yaa

Lingítx̲ x̲at sateeyí. *And I too am thankful that I'm part of this being that I'm Lingít.*

- **tlél wushk'é | tlél ushk'é | tlél kei ushk'éich**

  *he/she/it was bad | he/she/it is bad | he/she/it gets bad (regularly).*

  THEME: tlél O-sh-k'éi~ (ga state)

  *for O to be bad, evil, no good*

  NOTES: Some fluent speakers consider this a taboo word to use in reference to another person, while others find it acceptable. For speakers who find it acceptable, here is an example: Tlél ushik'éiyi k̲áa áwé. "That man is no good."

  ·Lushik'éiyi át ákwé atxaayí? *Is the centipede poisonous?*

  ·Tlél ushik'éiyi aa yoo x̲'atánk áwé tsá a.ax̲ji nooch . *She always only hears the bad talk.*

- **wook'éi | yak'éi | kei k'éich**

  *he/she/it was good; he/she/it got better | he/she/it is good | he/she/it gets better (regularly).*

  THEME: O-ø-k'éi (ga state)

  *for O to be good, fine, pretty*

  ·L'ook at x̲'éeshi áwé yak'éi. *Coho salmon dryfish is good.*

  ·L'ook kaháagu áyá yak'éi kanat'á kanéegwál' sákw. *Coho salmon eggs are good for blueberry sauce.*

- **du x̲'é wook'éi | du x̲'é yak'éi | ---**

  *s/he liked the taste of it | s/he likes the taste of it | ---.*

  THEME: N x̲'é ø-k'éi (ga state)

  *for N to like the taste of something*

  ·G̲áx̲ dleeyí gé i x̲'é yak'éi? *Does rabbit meat taste good to you?*

  ·Gangukg̲áx̲i k̲únáx̲ has du x̲'é yak'éi. *The fish heads cooked around the fire are very tasty to them.*

**k'eiljáa** noun *chinook wind; south wind*

VARIANTS: k'eeljáa

**K'EIN** verb root

- **át wujik'éin | --- | ---**

  *he/she/it is jumping around; he/she/it jumped around | --- | ---.*

  THEME: P-t S-j-k'éin~ (na motion)

  *for (singular) S to jump around at P*

  ·Át wujik'éin wé kook'énaa. *The sandhopper is hopping around.*

  ·Wé gawdáan yádi át wujik'éin. *That colt is jumping around.*

- **kei has kawduwak'én | kei (ha)s kanduk'én | kei (ha)s kaduk'énx̲**

  *they jumped | they're getting ready to jump | they jump (regularly).*

  THEME: kei O-ka-du-ø-k'éin~ (ø motion)

  *for (plural) O to jump*

  ·Tlákw kaduk'énx' wé cheech. *The porpoise always jump.*

**k'eit** noun *young salmonberry bush shoots (edible)*
·K'eit dux̱áayin. *Young salmonberry bush shoots used to be eaten.*

**K'EIX̱'** verb root

- **ashaawak'éx̱' | --- | ashak'éx̱'x̱**
  *s/he hooked it in the head | --- | s/he hooks it in the head (regularly).*
  THEME: O-sha-S-ø-k'éix̱'~ (ø event)
  *for S to hook O (fish) in the head*
  VARIANTS: -k'éex̱'~ (An)

du **k'í** noun *his/her rump; the flesh around his/her hips*
·Ch'a tlákw .áa áwé yanéekw du k'í. *His rump hurts from sitting all the time.*
·Ax̱ k'í wulix'wás'k̲. *My rump is numb.*

a **k'í** RelationalNoun *the base or foot of it (a standing object)*

du **k'idaaká** noun *next door to him/her/it*
·Yee k'idaaká k̲u.óowu gaysax̱án! *Love your neighbor!*

**k'idaaká aa** noun *neighbor*
·Haa k'idaaká k̲u.óowu taat kanax̱ has at wooshee. *Our neighbors sang all night long.*

**k'idaak̲wáani** noun *neighbors*

**k'idéin** Adverb *well*
·K'idéin aax̱ xásh wé t'áa at x̱'ax̱éedli! *Cut the trimming off the board good!*
·K'idéin gé sh eeltín? *Are you taking good care of yourself?*

du **k'ik̲l'án** noun *his/her palate*
VARIANTS: du k'ik̲l'én (C)

**k'inashóo** noun *pneumonia*
·K'inashóo néekw áyá aawasháat. *She caught pneumonia.*

**k'inchéiyi** noun *rose*
·K'inchéiyi áwé ax̱ tláa jeeyís x̱waa.oo. *I bought a rose for my mother.*

**k'inchéiyi tléig̲u** noun *rosehip*
·K'inchéiyi tléig̲u teen wududzi.ée yóo kanat'á. *Those blueberries were cooked with rosehips.*

**k'ínk'** noun *aged fish head*
·Yak'éi k'ínk' x̱oox' x̱áat yik.ádi. *The fish guts are good in fermenting stink heads.*
·K'ínk'i tséegi k̲únáx̱ yak'éi. *Barbecued fermented salmon heads are very good.*

**k'isáani** noun *boys, young men*
·K'isáani át yawdiháa. *There's a crowd of young men there.*

·K'isáanich gán du jeeyís has aawaxásh. *The young men cut wood for him.*

a **k'ishataaga̱ní** noun *quills on rear end of it (porcupine)*
VARIANTS: a k'ishetaaga̱ní (C)
·A k'ishataaga̱ní yéi ndu.eich guk kajaashí yís. *Its quills are used for earrings.*

**k'íx̱'aa** noun *gaff hook; grappling hook*
VARIANTS: k'éx̱'aa

a **k'iyee** RelationalNoun *near the base of it; at the foot of it; the back, rear or it (house); behind it (house); under the shelter of it (a standing object or structure)*
·Wé aas k'iyeet áwé has ḵéen. *They're sitting beneath the tree.*

**k'oodás'** noun *shirt*
VARIANTS: goodás', k'oodés' (C)
·Nás'k a doogú x'óow áwé du káa kakg̱wagéi k'oodás' sákw, wé ḵáa tlein. *It will take three leather blankets for the big man's shirt.*
·Ax̱ al'eix̱ k'oodás'i ch'áagu kawóot áwé a daawú á. *There are old beads on my dance shirt.*

a **k'óol'** noun *its back end; stern (of boat)*
VARIANTS: a k'óol'i
·A k'óol'de kaychák! *You all pack it in the stern!*
·A k'óol'i has g̱aag̱aḵee wé at yátx'i. *Let the children sit in the stern.*

du **k'óol'** noun *his/her tailbone; bottom of his/her spine*

**K'OOTS** verb root

- **awlik'oots | --- | yoo alik'útsk**
  *s/he broke it | --- | s/he breaks it (regularly).*
  THEME: O-S-l-k'oots~ (na event)
  *for S to break O (esp. rope-like objects)*
  ·A x'éix'u áwé yoo dudlik'útsk wé x̱áat. *One breaks the gills of the fish.*

**k'óox** noun *marten*
·K'óoxg̱aa al'óon áwé has woo.aat. *They went hunting for marten.*

**k'óox dísi** noun *Venus*

**k'óox̱'** noun *gum; lead*
·Gút yéi x̱'alatseenín k'óox̱'. *Gum used to cost a dime.*

**k'óox̱' létl'k** noun *soft lead*

**k'óox̱' tíx'i** noun *leadline (of net)*

**k'ul'kaskéxkw** noun *beetle*

**k'únts'** noun *potato*
·Wé akahéix̱i jeedáx̱ k'únts' has aawa.oo. *They bought potatoes from the farmer.*

**a k’únts’i** noun *its testicles (of moose, caribou)*

**k’uwaaní** noun *deer cabbage, lily-of-the-valley*

# « K'w »

**k'wálx̲** noun *fiddlehead fern (with edible rhizome)*

**k'wát'** noun *egg (of bird)*

·Wáa sá koogéi wé k'wát'? *How many eggs are there?*

·K'wát' X'áadidé gax̲took̲óox̲ kéidladi k'wádig̲áa. *We are going to Egg Island for seagull eggs.*

du **k'wát'** noun *his testicles*

K'WÁT' verb root

- **awdlik'wát' | --- | alk'wát'x̲**

  *it laid an egg | --- | it lays eggs (regularly).*

  THEME: a-d-l-k'waat'~ (ø event)

  *for birds to lay eggs, nest*

  NOTES: Note that the verb in the example sentence here: ilk'wát'x̲ is the intransitive repetitive form, while the repetitive form given above: alk'wát'x̲ is transitive. The difference is that the transitive form focuses more on the object (in this case, the egg). For example, alk'wát'x̲ could be translated as "it lays eggs" while ilk'wát'x̲ could be translated as "it reproduces (in the form of an egg)".

  ·Kichyaat ilk'wát'x̲ sít' yáx'. *Terns lay eggs by glaciers.*

# « K̲ »

**k̲a** particle *and*

·S'igeidí l'eedí yawúx̲' k̲a k̲'áatl' yáx̲ yatee. *A beaver's tail is wide and flat.*

·T'ooch' k̲a tl'áatl' yáx̲ dag̲aatée gandaas'aají. *Bees are black and yellow.*

**K̲AA**[1] verb root

• **áa ajikaawak̲aa | --- | áa yoo ajikaayak̲éik**

*s/he gave him/her orders* | --- | *s/he gives him/her orders (regularly).*

THEME: áa O-ji-ka-(u)-S-ø-k̲aa~ (na event)

*for S to instruct, give O orders (to do)*

NOTES: Note that in classical Tlingit, this verb had a thematic prefix (u-) which is slowly falling out of modern day speech. This is indicated in the Leer-Edwards theme as (u)-. Alternate forms given online show one form with the thematic (u)- and one without, both of which are acceptable in modern speech.

·Aan adul'eix̲ ax̲áa kak̲ach'áak'wt áyá áa x̲at jikawduwak̲aa. *I have been commissioned to carve a dance paddle.*

·Xeitl kakéin k'oodás' ax̲ yageeyí kaadéi áa k̲aa jikaawak̲aa ax̲ léelk'wch. *My grandmother commissioned a Thunderbird sweater for my birthday.*

• **akaawak̲aa | --- | yoo akayak̲éik / yoo akuwak̲éik**

*s/he sent him/her on an errand* | --- | *s/he sends him/her on an errand (regularly).*

THEME: O-ka-(u)-S-ø-k̲aa~ (na event)

*for S to send O (esp. on a mission or errand, or to deliver a message)*

NOTES: Note that in classical Tlingit, this verb had a thematic prefix (u-) which is slowly falling out of modern day speech. This is indicated in the Leer-Edwards theme as (u)-. Alternate forms given above show one form with the thematic (u)- and one without, both of which are acceptable in modern speech.

·Yan uwaneiyi hít kaságug̲áa kawduwak̲aa. *He was sent for ready-made rafters.*

• **--- | yéi adaayak̲á | ---**

--- | *s/he tells him/her that* | ---.

THEME: (yéi) O-daa-ya-S-ø-k̲á (act)

*for S to tell O (that)*

NOTES: This verb only occurs in the imperfective.

·Yéi daayaduk̲á, "Tlél kadéix' haa káx̲ sheeteek̲!" *He is told "Don't bring shame on us!"*

• **yéi yaawak̲aa | yéi x̲'ayak̲á | yoo x̲'ayak̲eik**

*s/he said that* | *s/he is saying that* | *s/he says that (regularly).*

THEME: (yéi) (x̲'a)-ya-S-ø-k̲aa~ (na act)

*for S to say (a certain thing); for S to confess, acknowledge, declare (a certain thing)*

NOTES: Note that the imperfective forms and prohibitive forms require the thematic prefix x̲'a- which refers to the mouth. Also note that some speakers use yóo instead of yéi, as in: yóo yaawak̲aa "s/he said that".

·X̲'agáax' áwé litseen yéi yaawak̲aa ax̲ léelk'w. *My grandparent said that prayer is powerful.*

·"Tliyéix', jinaháa haa kát g̲waaxeex," yóo x̲'ayak̲á du tláa. *Her mother says, "Behave, bad luck might befall us!"*

- **yoo ayawsik̲aa | yoo ayanask̲á | yoo ayasik̲éik**

  *s/he told him/her that | s/he is telling him/her that | s/he tells him/her (regularly).*

  THEME: (yoo) O-ya-S-s-k̲aa~ (na event)

  *for S to tell, say (that) to O; for S to ask O to do (that)*

  ·"Ix̲six̲án," yoo ayawsik̲aa du yadák'u. *She told her boyfriend, "I love you."*

  ·At géide ayawsik̲aa du kéek' tatgé. *She spoke wrongly against her younger sister yesterday.*

**K̲AA**[2] verb root

- **aawak̲áa | ak̲éis' | ---**

  *s/he sewed it | s/he is sewing it | ---.*

  THEME: O-S-ø-k̲aa~ (ø act)

  *for S to sew O*

  ·Yá ax̲ l'eix̲ k'oodás' a wán shóot at k̲á! *Sew something to the edge of my dance shirt!*

  ·Yá kat'íshaa at xáshdi téel aan x̲ak̲éis'. *I sew moccasins with this leather needle.*

- **a káa akaawak̲áa | a káa akak̲éis' | a káa akak̲éix̲**

  *s/he embroidered it on it | s/he's embroidering it on it | s/he embroiders it on it (regularly).*

  THEME: O-ka-S-ø-k̲aa~ (ø act)

  *for S to sew beads, embroider O*

  NOTES: To indicate what the design was embroidered onto, use: N káa "on N". For example: Yéil du luljíni káa akaawak̲áa. "S/he embroidered a raven on his/her vest." This is not required with this verb, however, and therefore is not given in the Leer-Edwards theme. This sentence is also acceptable: Yéil akaawak̲áa. "S/he embroidered a raven."

  ·Gunx̲aa yaka.óot' du l.uljíni kát akaawak̲áa. *She sewed the abalone buttons on her vest.*

  ·Kawóot teen k̲'eikaxwéin a káa kak̲á! *Embroider a flower on it with beads!*

- **a kát akawlik̲áa | a kaadé yaa akanalk̲éin | a káx̲ aklak̲éix̲**

  *s/he sewed it on it | s/he is sewing it on it | s/he sews it on it (regularly).*

  THEME: P-t~ O-ka-S-l-k̲aa~ (ø motion)

  *for S to sew O on P*

• **wudik̲áa | dak̲éis' | ---**
*s/he sewed | s/he sews; s/he is sewing | ---.*
THEME: S-d-k̲aa~ (ø act)
*for S to sew*
·Tl'ik̲naa.át een duk̲éis'. *A thimble is used for sewing.*
·Tlél gooháa aadéi k'idéin dak̲éis'i yé. *It's obvious how well she sews.*

K̲AA$^{3}$ verb root

• **awdlik̲áa | alk̲áa | ---**
*s/he gambled | s/he is gambling | ---.*
THEME: a-S-d-l-k̲áa (na act)
*for S to gamble (by means of gambling sticks, dice, etc.); for S to play cards*
·S'íx' kawtoo.óos'i ítnáx̲ agax̲toolk̲áa. *After we have washed the dishes we will play cards.*

**k̲áa** noun *man; male; person, people*
·Nás'k a doogú x'óow áwé du káa kakg̲wagéi k'oodás' sákw, wé k̲áa tlein. *It will take three leather blankets for the big man's shirt.*
·Sagú yáx̲ k̲aa yayík du.ax̲ji nooch héendei yaa ana.ádi. *Men's voices would always sound happy when they went to the sea.*

**k̲aa at oohéini** noun *possession; that which is claimed*
·G̲ooch Yanyeidí k̲aa at oohéini áwé. *The Wolf crest is the property of the Yanyeidí Clan.*
·S'igeidí Deisheetaan k̲aa at oohéini áwé. *The Beaver is the property of the Deisheetaan Clan.*

**k̲aa at óowu** noun *possession(s); that which is owned (by them)*
VARIANTS: k̲aa et óowu (C)
·X'átgu áwé Shangukeidí has du at óowux̲ sitee. *The dogfish is an artifact of the Thunderbiird people.*
·Shayadihéini at óow wéide yaa ndusxát'. *They are hauling lots of someone's possessions over that way.*

**K̲aachx̲ana.áak'w** noun *Wrangell*
·K̲aachx̲ana.áak'wde daak uwak̲úx̲ wé yaakw. *The boat set out for Wrangell.*
·K̲aachx̲ana.áak'wdáx̲ haat aawa.át. *People walked here from Wrangell.*

**K̲aach.ádi** noun *K̲aach.ádi, locally called "Sockeye"; a clan of the Raven moiety whose principal crest is the Sockeye*

**k̲aa daakeidí** noun *coffin; casket*
·K̲aa daakeidí wududliyéx̲. *Someone built a casket.*

**k̲aadaaxaashí** noun *surgeon*
·K̲aadaaxaashí x̲ánde kawduwanáa. *He was sent to the surgeon.*
·Dr. Smith yóo duwasáakw wé k̲aadaaxaashí. *The surgeon's name is Dr. Smith.*

**k̲aa daa yaséix̲i** noun *doctor*

**ḵaa ji.eetí** noun *handiwork, handmade crafts*
·Ḵaa ji.eetí wéix' duhóon. *They are selling handmade crafts there.*
·Ḵúnáx̱ yak'éi áyá ḵaa ji.eetí. *This is really good handiwork.*

**ḵaa kanax̱ḵáa** noun *snob; person who considers himself/herself better than others*
VARIANTS: ḵaa kenax̱ḵáa (C)

**ḵáakwt~** Adverb *accidentally, wrongly*
·Áa ḵúx̱ teedataan wé ḵáakwt iwuneiyí! *Think back to the time when you got hurt!*

**ḴAAḴ** verb root

- **wujiḵaaḵ | --- | yei ishḵáḵch**

*he/she/it squatted | --- | he/she/it squats (reguarly).*
THEME: S-j-ḵaaḵ~ (g̱a event)
*for (singular) S to squat, sit down low; for (singular) S to sit down quickly, squat down; for (singular) S to land (of waterfowl, plane)*
·Ax̱ tl'eiḵ káa wjiḵaaḵ digitgiyáa. *A hummingbird landed on my finger.*

**ḵaaḵx̱wdaagané (A)** noun *accident; unfortunate mistake or mishap*
VARIANTS: ḵaaḵx̱wdaganée (T)

**ḵaanaawú tl'átgi** noun *graveyard*
·Ḵaanaawú tl'átgi kaadéi yakḵwax̱áa ḵ'eikaxwéin. *I will transport flowers to the graveyard.*

**ḵaankak.eetx' (T)** noun *in public; at a potlatch, feast*
VARIANTS: ḵaankag̱eetx' (T), ḵaank'eg̱eex' (C)
·Ḵaankak.eetx' yoo x̱'eiwatán. *He spoke in public.*
·Ḵaankak.eetx' has at wooshee ḵa (ha)s aawal'eix̱. *They sang and danced in public.*

**ḵaa oox̱ layeix̱í** noun *dentist*
VARIANTS: ḵaa oox̱ leyeix̱í (C)

**ḵaa oox̱ yei daanéiyi** noun *dentist*
·Du yéet ḵaa oox̱ yéi daanéiyix̱ sitee. *His son is a dentist.*
·Du ée yan at wududlitóow ḵaa oox̱ yéi daanéiyi yís. *She completed dentistry school.*

**ḵáas'** noun *match; stick*
·A x̱'éináx̱ áwé kadul.eesh wé ḵáas' kaadéi wé saak. *Those hooligan are strung through the mouth on the stick.*
·Al'óon wugoodí ux̱ganḵáas' du g̱altóode ayaawa.oo. *When he was going hunting, he put matches in his pocket.*

**ḵaa s'aatí** noun *boss*
·Wuduwax̱oox̱ yóode wé ḵaa s'aatí. *The boss was called to go over there.*

du **ḵáash** noun *his/her pelvis, hip*

**k̲aa sháade háni** noun *leader*
VARIANTS: k̲aa sháade héni (C)
·Wé k̲aa sháade háni k̲aa x̲áni daak uwagút. *The leader came out to the people.*
·Wé haa sháade háni "gunalchéesh" haa jeeyís yéi yanak̲éich. *Our leader says "thank you" for us.*

**k̲aa sháade nák̲x'i** noun *leaders*
·Deisleenx' keijín has yatee k̲aa sháade nák̲x'i. *In Teslin there are five leaders.*
·Nás'giná̲x̲ has yatee wé Yéil naa sháade nák̲x'i. *There are three Raven Clan leaders.*

**k̲áa shaan** noun *old man*
·Wé gán aan nagú wé k̲áa shaan du shóot ag̲ida.aagít! *Go with the wood to build a fire for the elderly man!*
·Jinkaat kéet gooshí ayatéen wé k̲áa shaan. *The old man sees ten killerwhale dorsal fins.*

**k̲aa shaksayéigu** noun *comb*

**k̲aa shaksayík̲s'i** noun *hair pendant*

**k̲aashashx̲áaw** noun *dragonfly*
·K̲aashashx̲áaw taakw.eetíx' haax̲ kalyeech. *The dragonflies come in the summer time.*
·K̲aashashx̲áaw tláakw át nadak̲ínch. *The dragonfly flies around fast.*

**k̲aashaxáshaa** noun *scissors*
·K̲aashaxáshaa ax̲ jeet katí! *Hand me the scissors!*
·Wé k̲aashaxáshaa yalik'áts' *The scissors are sharp.*

**k̲aatoowú** noun *chickadee*
VARIANTS: k̲aatook'ú (C)
·K̲aatoowú yáax' shayadihéin k̲ukawult'éex'i. *There are lots of chickadees here when it's still icy.*
·Wáa yateeyi yéix' yáax' yéi aa nateech táakw kanax̲ wé k̲aatoowú. *Sometimes some chickadees stay here through the winter.*

**k̲aa toowú lat'aa** noun *comfort*
VARIANTS: k̲aa toowú let'aa (C)
·K̲aa toowú lat'aa yáx̲ du ée yatee wé kinaak.át k̲usa.áat' tóox'. *The coat is a comfort to him in the cold.*
·K̲aa toowú lat'aa áwé x̲'aan. *The fire is a comfort.*

du **k̲aatl** noun *his/her flank, side of his/her belly*

du **k̲áawu** noun *his/her husband's clan brother; his/her man, boyfriend, husband*
·Yat'aayi héen du k̲áawu x̲'éit awsi.ín. *She gave her husband's clan brother coffee.*

**k̲áax'w** noun *men*
·Nás'giná̲x k̲áax'w áwé hít káa yéi jiné. *There are three men working on that house.*

**k̲aax̲** noun *merganser*
·K̲aax̲ haax̲ kalyeech. *Mergansers migrate here.*
·K̲aax̲ aawa.ún. *He shot a merganser.*

**k̲aa x̲'a.eetí** noun *leftovers, food scraps*
·K̲aa x̲'a.eetí awsit'áa. *She warmed up the leftovers.*
·K̲aa x̲'a.eetí keitl x̲'éix̲ aawatee. *He fed the scraps to the dog.*

**k̲aa x̲'éidáx̲ kashxeedí** noun *secretary (stenographer)*
VARIANTS: k̲aa x̲'éitx̲ kashxeedí
·K̲aa x̲'éidáx̲ kashxeedí yáx̲ yéi jiné. *She works as a secretary.*
·Ax̲ x̲ooní k̲aa x̲'éidáx̲ kashxeedí áwé. *My friend is a secretary.*

**k̲aa x̲'oos** noun *foot (measurement)*
·Tléix' k̲aa x̲'oos yéi kwliyáat' wé tíx'. *That rope is one foot long.*
·Gwál tleik̲áa x̲'oos áwé a kax̲yeedé. *It must be twenty feet to the ceiling.*

**k̲aa x̲'oos deiyí** noun *foot path*
VARIANTS: k̲aa x̲'usdeiyí
·Gwálaa teen ch'áal' aawas'úw k̲aa x̲'oos deiyí kaax̲. *He chopped willows off the foot trail with a machete.*
·Shaanáx̲ yaawashóo wé k̲aa x̲'oos deiyí. *The foot trail extends through the valley.*

**k̲aa yakg̲wahéiyagu** noun *spirit*
·X̲'agáax' tóonáx̲ k̲aa yakg̲wahéiyagu litseen. *Through prayer, a person's spirit is strong.*
·Du yakg̲wahéiyágu tléil ultseen. *His spirit is weak.*

**k̲aayaku.óot'i (At)** noun *button*
VARIANTS: k̲aayuka.óot'i (T)

**k̲aa yat'éináx̲** noun *in secret (where nobody can see); away from people's view*
·K̲aa yat'éináx̲ hít yeedáx̲ woogoot. *He left the house when no one was looking.*
·K̲aa yat'éináx̲ x'wán daasa.áx̲w wé k̲óok! *Wrap that box when no one is looking now!*

**k̲aayuka.óot'i x'óow (T)** noun *button blanket*
VARIANTS: yuka.óot' x'óow, k̲aayaku.óot'i x'óow (At), k̲aakóot'i x'óow (T), kaakóot'i x'óow (C)

**k̲achoo** particle *actually; in fact; contrary to what was thought*
VARIANTS: x̲achoo

**k̲ákw** noun *basket*
·K̲ákw yéi daané yís áwé yéi daax̲ané yá sháak. *I am collecting this*

*timothy grass for making baskets.*
·Dáḵde ḵákw aawayaa i léelk'w. *Your grandmother died. (Lit: Your grandmother took her basket into the woods).*

**ḵashde** particle *I thought*
VARIANTS: ḵashdei

du **ḵatlyá** noun *his/her flank, side of his/her body between the ribs and the hip*
·Ax̱ ḵatlyát wujix̱ín wé x̱áaw tlein. *That big log fell on my side.*
·Du ḵatlyá awlichún. *He hurt his side.*

**ḴEE** verb root

• **--- | has ḵéen | ---**
--- | *they are sitting* | ---.
THEME: S-ø-ḵee~ (position)
*for (plural) S to be seated*
NOTES: This verb only occurs in the imperfective. Note that a noun phrase with (-t) postposition is used to indicate where one is sitting, but this noun phrase is not required by the verb. For example, one could say: has ḵéen "they are sitting", or: át has ḵéen "they are sitting there".
·Wé aas chéx̱'i tayeet áwé tooḵéen. *We are sitting in the shade of the tree.*
·Dáx̱náx̱ a géekt aḵéen wé yaakw. *There are two people sitting at the stern of the boat.*

• **has wooḵee | yei (ha)s naḵéen | yei has ḵéech**
*they sat down* | *they are sitting down* | *they sit down (regularly).*
THEME: S-ø-ḵee~ (g̱a event)
*for S to sit down*
·Atoosg̱eiwú atyátx'i latíni x̱ánx̱ has g̱aḵéech ax̱ yátx'i. *When we are gillnetting my children stay with a babysitter.*
·A k'óol'i has g̱aag̱aḵee wé at yátx'i. *Let the children sit in the stern.*

**ḵéech'** noun *scab*

**ḴEEN** verb root

• **át wudiḵeen | --- | át yoo diḵéenk**
*he/she/it is flying around; he/she/it flew around* | --- | *he/she/it flies around (regularly).*
THEME: P-t S-d-ḵeen~ (na motion)
*for (singular) S (bird, or persons in a plane) to fly around at P*
·Du kíji áwé wool'éex' wé ts'ítskw, ách áwé tlél át wudaḵeen. *The songbird's wing broke, that's why it doesn't fly around.*
·Gandaadagóogu wéit wudiḵeen. *A woodpecker is flying around there.*

**ḵées'** noun *flood; tide*

**ḵées' shuwee** noun *high tide line*
VARIANTS: ḵées' shuyee

**K̲EET’** verb root

- **wudlik̲ít’ | yaa nalk̲ít’ | ilk̲ít’x̲**

  *it's infected | it's getting infected | it gets infected (regularly).*

  THEME: d-l-k̲éet’~ (ø event)

  *for a wound to be infected, have pus*

  NOTES: Note that both forms given in the perfective habitual are acceptable to all speakers consulted for this project.

  ·Du tl’eik̲t yawdig̲iji sheey kak̲áas’i áx’ wudlik̲ít’. *It got infected where the splinter poked her finger.*

**k̲éet’** noun *pus; discharge (from a sore, wound); sore, wound that discharges pus*

·A daa át kas’ít déi wéi k̲éet’! *Wrap something around the pus now!*

**K̲éex̲’** noun *Kake*

VARIANTS: K̲éix̲’

**k̲eex̲’é** noun *dawn, daybreak*

VARIANTS: k̲ee.ax̲’é, k̲ei.x̲’é (An), k̲ee.á, k̲ei.á

·K̲eex̲’é shukát áwé shoodanookch ax̲ léelk’w. *My grandfather wakes up before dawn.*

**K̲éex̲’ K̲wáan** noun *people of Kake*

**k̲ee.á** noun *dawn, daybreak*

VARIANTS: k̲ei.á, k̲eex̲’é, k̲eix̲’é (An), k̲ee.ax̲’é

·K̲ee.á shukát áwé g̲unéi gax̲took̲óox̲. *We will start traveling before dawn.*

**K̲EI[1]** verb root

- **ajeewak̲éi | ajik̲éi | yóo ajiyak̲éik**

  *s/he paid him/her | s/he pays him/her; s/he is paying him/her | s/he pays him/her (regularly).*

  THEME: O-ji-S-ø-k̲éi (na act)

  *for S to pay O (esp. a person, for work done); for S to pay for O*

  ·Jiduk̲éi at wuskóowux̲ sateeyéech. *He is paid because he is a knowledgeable person.*

  ·K’idéin has jiduk̲éi katíx̲’aa s’aatí Dzántik’i Héenix’. *Jailers are paid well in Juneau.*

**k̲éich’ál’** noun *seam*

**K̲éix̲’** noun *Kake*

VARIANTS: Kéex̲’

·Du daat shkalneek k̲udzitee K̲éix̲’dáx̲ k̲’atx̲áan. *There is a story about the coward from Kake.*

·K̲éix̲’dei nax̲took̲oox̲ shaawg̲áa. *Let's travel to Kake for some gumboots.*

**k̲eix̲’é (An)** noun *dawn, daybreak*

VARIANTS: k̲ee.ax̲’é, k̲eex̲’é, k̲ei.á, k̲ee.á

·Wé g̲agaan kei yaséich wé k̲eix̲’ét k̲uwuhaayí. *The sun lifts its face when dawn breaks.*

**ḵei.á** noun *dawn, daybreak*
VARIANTS: ḵee.á, ḵee.ax̱'é, ḵeex̱'é, ḵeix̱'é (An)

**ḵénaa** noun *long feather; quill (of bird)*
VARIANTS: ḵínaa

**ḵín** noun *brant (small goose)*

**a ḵín** RelationalPostposition *less than it; (reaching, falling) short of it; not (big or far) enough for it*
·A ḵín kaawagei. *There wasn't enough.*
·A ḵín ax̱ jee koogéi wé k'oodás' yeidí. *I have less than the price of that shirt.*

**ḵínaa** noun *long feather; quill (of bird)*
VARIANTS: ḵénaa
·Ḵínaa teen aawatáḵ du gúk. *She pierced her ear with a quill.*

**ḴOO** verb root

- **wudliḵoo | ilḵú | yoo iliḵúk**
  *s/he vomited | s/he vomits; s/he is vomiting | s/he vomits (regularly).*
  THEME: S-d-l-ḵoo~ (na act)
  *for S to vomit, throw up*

**ḵóo at latóowu (T)** noun *teacher*
VARIANTS: ḵóo at latéewu (At), ḵóo et letóowu (C)
·Ḵóo at latóowu yís áwé du ée at wududlitóow. *He was taught to be a teacher.*

**ḵóok** noun *box*
·Ḵóok shutú aawatséx̱. *She died. (Lit: S/he kicked the edge of the box.)*
·Tl'aadéin áwé át tán wé ḵóok. *The box is sitting sideways.*

**ḵoon sh kalneegí** noun *storyteller; preacher*
·Haa ḵoon sh kalneegí áwé ḵúnáx̱ tuli.aan. *Our preacher is very kind.*

**ḴOOTL'** verb root

- **kawshiḵútl' | kashiḵútl'k | kashaḵútl'x̱**
  *it got muddy | it's muddy | it gets muddy (regularly).*
  THEME: ka-sh-ḵóotl'~ (ø state)
  *for a road, etc. to be muddy*
  ·Kashiḵútl'k wé héen táak. *The bottom of that river is muddy.*

**ḵoowajag̱i aa** noun *murderer*
·Wé ḵoowajag̱i aa du daach kalneek x'úx' káa yéi yatee. *There is a story about the murderer in the paper.*

**a ḵoowú** noun *its den, lair (of animal, undergound)*
·Yóot sh wudligás' a ḵoowúdáx̱. *It charged out of its den.*
·Tléil awuskú xóots ḵoowú káx̱ wugoodí. *He did not know that he had walked over a grizzly bear den.*

a ḵóox' Relationalnoun *in the midst of it (a crowd, an activity or event involving several people); in the hubbub*
·Yaa ḵu.éex' ḵóox' ḵu.aa áyá aḵ yaawdudlit'áa yá saa Ḵaajaaḵwtí. *Though during potlatches they call me this name, Ñaajaañwtí.*

**ḴOOX¹** verb root

- **aadé awsiḵooḵ | aadé yaa anasḵúx̱ | aadé yoo asiḵúx̱k**
  *s/he drove it there | s/he is driving it there | s/he drives it there (regularly).*
  THEME: P-dé O-S-s-ḵooḵ~ (na motion)
  *for S to drive O (boat, car) to P*

- **aadé wooḵooḵ | aadé yaa naḵúx̱ | aadé yoo yaḵúx̱k**
  *s/he drove there | s/he is driving there | s/he drives there (regularly).*
  THEME: P-dé S-ø-ḵooḵ~ (na motion)
  *for S to travel, go toward P (in a boat, car)*
  ·Héen yíkde wooḵooḵ. *He went up the river (by boat).*
  ·A kayéikgaa áwé ḵuntoos.áx̱ch shtéen káa haadé yaa naḵúx̱u. *We always listen for the sound of the steam engine when it's coming.*

- **át awsiḵúx̱ | aadé yaa anasḵúx̱ | áx̱ asḵooḵ**
  *s/he drove it to it | s/he is driving it to it | s/he drives it to it (regularly).*
  THEME: P-t~ O-S-s-ḵooḵ~ (ø motion)
  *for S to drive O (boat, car) to P*
  ·Geey tá déilit awsiḵúx̱ du yaagú. *She drove her boat to the head of the bay.*

- **át uwaḵúx̱ | aadé yaa naḵúx̱ | áx̱ ḵooḵ**
  *s/he drove to it | s/he is driving to it | s/he drives to it (regularly).*
  THEME: P-t~ S-ø-ḵooḵ~ (ø motion)
  *for S to travel, go to P (by boat, car)*
  ·Dzeit shuyeet uwaḵúx̱ wé yaakw. *The boat motored to the landing.*
  ·Geesh tóot uwaḵúx̱ wé yaakw. *The boat drove in among the kelp.*

- **át wooḵooḵ | --- | át yoo yaḵúx̱k**
  *s/he is driving around; s/he drove around | --- | s/he drives around (regularly).*
  THEME: P-t S-ø-ḵooḵ~ (na motion)
  *for S to travel, go around at P (by boat, car)*
  ·Yaakw áa kát wooḵooḵ. *A boat is cruising around on the lake.*
  ·Ḵutx̱.ayanahá káax' át has naḵúx̱ch. *They navigate by the stars.*

- **awsiḵooḵ | yaa anasḵúx̱ | yoo asiḵúx̱k**
  *s/he drove it | s/he is driving it | s/he drives it (regularly).*
  THEME: O-S-s-ḵooḵ~ (na motion)
  *for S to drive O (car); for S to skipper O (boat)*
  ·Wé ḵáa a géeknáx̱ áwé yaa anasḵúx̱ du yaagú. *The man is driving his boat from the stern.*

- **ayawdiḵúx̱ | --- | awudaḵúx̱x̱**
  *s/he turned back | --- | s/he turns back (regularly).*
  THEME: a-ya-u-S-d-ḵooḵ~ (ø motion)
  *for S to turn back, return (by boat, car)*

- **daak uwak̲úx̲ | daak nak̲úx̲ | daak k̲úx̲ch**
  *s/he went out to sea | s/he is going out to sea | s/he goes out to sea (regularly).*
  THEME: daak S-ø-k̲oox̲~ (ø motion)
  *for S to go out to sea (in a boat); for S to move into the open (in a boat, car)*
  ·K̲aachx̲ana.áak'wde daak uwak̲úx̲ wé yaakw. *The boat set out for Wrangell.*
- **a daax̲ yaawak̲úx̲ | a daax̲ yaa nak̲úx̲ | a daax̲ yaa k̲úx̲ch**
  *s/he drove around it | s/he is driving around it | s/he drives around it (regularly).*
  THEME: N daax̲ ya-u-S-ø-k̲oox̲~ (ø motion)
  *for S to circle, drive around N (by boat, car)*
  ·X'aa daax̲ yaawak̲úx̲ wé yaakw. *The boat motored around the point.*
- **g̲unéi uwak̲úx̲ | --- | g̲unéi k̲oox̲x̲**
  *s/he started driving | --- | s/he starts driving (regularly).*
  THEME: g̲unéi S-ø-k̲oox̲~ (ø motion)
  *for S to begin traveling, going (by boat, car)*
  ·Taan áa awsiteeni yé a niyaadé g̲unéi uwak̲úx̲. *He started motoring in the direction he had seen the sea lion.*
  ·K̲ee.á shukát áwé g̲unéi gax̲took̲óox̲. *We will start traveling before dawn.*
- **k̲ut wook̲oox̲ | k̲ut kei nak̲úx̲ | k̲ut kei k̲úx̲ch**
  *s/he got lost | s/he is getting lost | s/he gets lost (regularly).*
  THEME: k̲ut S-ø-k̲oox̲~ (ga motion)
  *for S to get lost (going by motorized vehicle)*
- **a tóonáx̲ yaawak̲úx̲ | a tóonáx̲ yaa nak̲úx̲ | a tóonáx̲ yaa k̲úx̲ch**
  *s/he drove through it | s/he is driving through it | s/he drives through it (regularly).*
  THEME: P-náx̲ ya-u-S-ø-k̲oox̲~ (ø motion)
  *for S to travel, go through P (by boat, car)*
  ·K'eeljáa tóonáx̲ yaa nak̲úx̲. *He is driving through a storm.*
- **wook̲oox̲ | yaa nak̲úx̲ | yoo yak̲úx̲k**
  *s/he went (by motorized vehicle) | s/he is going (by motorized vehicle) | s/he goes (by motorized vehicle) (regularly).*
  THEME: S-ø-k̲oox̲~ (na motion)
  *for S to travel, go (by boat, car)*
  ·Yaa nak̲úx̲ stéen káa x̲'anaat áwé hán wé dzísk'w tlein. *The big moose was standing in the way of the steam train.*
- **--- | yaa nak̲úx̲ | ---**
  *--- | s/he is going along (by boat, car) | ---.*
  THEME: yaa S-ø-k̲oox̲~ (ga motion)
  *for S to be going, traveling along (by boat, car)*
  NOTES: This is an example of a progressive epiaspectual paradigm (Leer, 91), which basically means that all forms are based on the progressive aspect. The progressive epiaspect is characterized by: 1)having the yaa preverb in all forms, 2)having no perfective form,

and 3)denotes semantically a continuous transition from one location or state to another.
·Kaldaag̲éinák̲ yaa gax̲took̲óox̲, tlél g̲wadlaan yá éix̲' yík. *We will travel along slowly, it's not deep in this slough.*

- **yan uwak̲úx̲ | yánde yaa nak̲úx̲ | yax̲ k̲oox̲**
  *s/he went ashore | s/he is going ashore | s/he goes ashore (regularly).*
  THEME: yan~ S-ø-k̲oox̲~ (ø motion)
  *for S to go ashore (in a boat); for S to come to a rest, stop (in a boat, car)*
  ·Wé áa kaanáx̲ yan uwahóowu watsíx a ítnáx̲ yan uwak̲úx̲ wé yaakw. *The boat followed behind the caribou that swam the lake.*
  ·Aan eeg̲ayáaknáx̲ yan uwak̲úx̲ wé yaakw. *The boat landed below the town.*

**k̲ugáas'** noun *gray; fog*
VARIANTS: k̲ugwáas'
·Gan eetí kél't' k̲ugáas' yáx̲ yatee. *Ashes from the fireplace are gray.*

**k̲ugóos'** noun *cloud(s)*

**k̲ukadlénx̲aa** noun *temptation, trial*

**k̲ukahín** noun *crankiness; irritation; petulance*
NOTES: K̲ukahínt uwanúk "s/he's acting irritated, cranky".

**k̲ukalt'éex' ká** noun *spring (AT)*

**k̲ulagaaw** noun *fighting; war, conflict*
VARIANTS: k̲ulegaaw (C)
·K̲ulagaaw yinaa.át yéi aya.óo. *He is wearing war clothes.*

**k̲úlk** noun *very rotton wood*

**k̲unáagu** noun *healer; doctor; nurse*
·K̲unáagu jeedáx̲ jika.át yéi aya.óo. *He is wearing a wrist guard from the doctor.*

**k̲únáx̲** Adverb *very*
·Nóosk x̲aagú k̲únáx̲ yalik'áts'. *Wolverine claws are really sharp.*
·K̲únáx̲ wé yee woo.éex'i aa tsú yee x̲oo yéi kg̲watée toowú k'é teen. *Your hostess will welcome you all as well. (Lit: Your hostess will be among you all with good feelings.)*

**k̲usax̲ak̲wáan** noun *tribe of cannibals, man-eaters*

**k̲usax̲án** noun *love (of people)*
·X'éig̲aa átx̲ sitee k̲usax̲án. *Love is true.*

**k̲usa.áat'** noun *cold weather*
VARIANTS: k̲use.áat' (C)
·K̲aa toowú lat'aa yáx̲ du ée yatee wé kinaak.át k̲usa.áat' tóox'. *The coat is a comfort to him in the cold.*

**k̲usa.áat' néekw** noun *chest cold*

**k̲ustí** noun *life; way of living*

**k̲us.ook'** noun *plaything*

**k̲ut** Adverb *astray, getting lost*
·Ax̲ jinák̲ k̲ut wujixeex. *He ran away from me.*
·Wé k̲'wátl yana.áat'ani k̲ut x̲waataan. *I misplaced the lid for the pot.*

**k̲utaan** noun *summer*
·Xéen áwé woogéi yá k̲utaan. *There were a lot of blue bottle flies this summer.*
·Yáa k̲utaanx' aadé k̲ugax̲tootéen ixkée ch'a g̲aax̲tusatéen wé sháa. *This summer we are going to travel down south just to see the girls.*

**k̲utí** noun *weather*

**k̲útx̲** Adverb *too much*

**k̲utx̲.ayanahá** noun *star*
VARIANTS: k̲utx̲.anaháa (AtT), k̲utx̲'anaháa (T)
·K̲utx̲.ayanahá káax' át has nak̲úx̲ch. *They navigate by the stars.*

**k̲utl'ídaa** noun *shovel*

**k̲útl'kw** noun *mud*
·Haa tláa hás k̲útl'gig̲áa has na.átch has du k̲'eikaxwéini yís. *Our mothers send us for soil for their flowers.*
·L'éx̲'kw, k̲útl'kw nasteech séew daak wustaaní *Soil turns to mud when it rains.*

**k̲uwakaan (TC)** noun *deer*
VARIANTS: g̲uwakaan

**k̲uxaak** noun *dry weather; clear day*

**k̲ux̲** Adverb *(returning) back*

**k̲ux̲ dak'óol'een** Adverb *backwards*
·K̲ux̲ dak'óol'een áwé kát adatéen du k'oodás'i. *He's wearing his shirt backwards.*
·Ldakát át áwé k̲ux̲ dak'óol'in x̲waasáakw. *I said everything backwards.*

**k̲u.aa** particle *however*
VARIANTS: k̲u.a
·X̲'aan yakawlikís'. Wé kél't' k̲u.aa, ch'u uwat'áa. *The fire has gone out but the ashes are still warm.*
·Náakw yís kayaaní ashigóok, áx' k̲u.aa akwdlix̲éitl' k̲aa x̲'éix̲ aa wuteeyí. *He knows medicinal plants but he is afraid to give them to anyone.*

**k̲u.áx̲ch** noun *hearing*

**k̲u.áx̲ji** noun *hearing aid*

**k̲u.eení** noun *murderer*

**k̲u.éex'** noun *feast, potlatch; party*
·G̲aax̲ shí teen áwé yaawaxeex wé k̲u.éex'. *A cry song took place at the potlatch.*
·Atx̲á tlein áyá k̲u.éex'de yakk̲wax̲áa. *I am going to haul a lot of food to the potlatch.*

**k̲u.oo** noun *people; community*
·Ana.óot k̲u.oo haa x̲ánt has uwa.át. *Aleut people came to see us.*
·A x̲oo aa k̲u.oo woolnáx̲ wooshk̲ák̲ has al'óon. *Some people hunt the wren.*

# « K̲w »

**k̲waak̲x̲ daak̲** Adverb *by mistake, wrongly*

a **k̲wáan** noun *person or people from that place*

·Ch'a a k̲wáanch áwé yéi uwasáa Deishú. *The local people gave Haines its name.*

·Deishú k̲wáan has at shí k̲a has al'eix̲. *The Haines People are singing and dancing.*

# « K̲' »

**k̲'áach'** noun *ribbon seaweed*
·K̲'áach' du tuwáa sigóo. *She wants ribbon seaweed.*
·K̲'áach' ayawsiháa. *She gathered ribbon seaweed.*

**k̲'aakanéi** noun *large rectangular tub for soaking skins while tanning them*

**k̲'aan** noun *dolphin*
·K̲'aan du tuwáa sigóo aatlein ax̲ dachx̲ánk'. *My granddaughter really likes dolphins.*
·K̲'aan yahaax'ú wutuwa.oo du jeeyís. *We bought her pictures of dolphins.*

**k̲'áatl'** adj. *thin (flat object)*
·S'igeidí l'eedí yawúx̲' k̲a k̲'áatl' yáx̲ yatee. *A beaver's tail is wide and flat.*

**k̲'alkátsk** noun *razor clam*
·K̲'alkátsk yáxwch'ich yax̲ yawsix̲áa haa aaní kaadáx̲. *The sea otter has devoured the yellowneck clams on our land.*
·K̲'alkátsk kahaa yís léinde gax̲too.áat yá xáanaa. *This evening we are going yellowneck clam digging.*

**k̲'anáax̲án** noun *fence*
·Yanshukáx' áwé k'idéin wutuliyéx̲ ya k̲'anáax̲án. *We built the fence really well out here in the wilderness.*
·K'idéin layéx̲ yá k̲'anáax̲án wé gishoo daaká yís! *Build this fence well around those pigs!*

**k̲'anashgidéi k̲áa** noun *poor man*
·K̲'anashgidéi k̲áa áwé kíndei alshát du shá. *The poor man is holding his head high.*
·K̲'anashgidéi k̲áax̲ satéeyin. *He used to be a poor man.*

**k̲'anoox̲** noun *labret, small lip plug*
·Du gúkx' tsú yéi aa wduwa.oo wéi s'aak̲ k̲'anoox̲. *They put the small bone labret in his ear too.*
·S'aak̲ áwé shux'áanáx̲ átx̲ wududliyéx̲ ax̲ léelk'w du k̲'anoox̲ú yís. *My grandmother's first labret was made out of bone.*

**k̲'anoox̲ eetí** noun *labret hole*

a **k̲'anoox̲ú** noun *its whiskers, beard (of fish)*
·Tléil a k̲'anoox̲ú k̲oostí daleiyí. *Lake trout do not have beards.*
·Chudéi áwé a k̲'anoox̲ú áwu. *Tom cod have a beard.*

**k̲'ateil** noun *pitcher; jug*

·Wé k̲'ateil xákwti ax̲ jeet tán!. *Hand me the empty pitcher!*

·K̲'ateil tóodei yanasxá k'idéin x̲'adíx'! *Pour it in the jug and cork it up!*

**k̲'atx̲áan** noun *coward*

·Du daat shkalneek k̲udzitee K̲éix̲'dáx̲ k̲'atx̲áan. *There is a story about the coward from Kake.*

·Ch'a g̲óot yéidei yéi jiné has du jeex̲ dutee wéi k̲'atx̲áan. *Cowards are given different jobs to perform.*

**k̲'eikaxétl'k** noun *bunchberry*

·G̲uwakaan x̲ax̲oox̲ nooch k̲'eikaxétl'k kayaaní teen. *I always use a bunchberry leaf to call deer.*

**k̲'eikaxwéin** noun *flower; blossom*

·Ketllóox'u yáx̲ yatee wé k̲'eikaxwéin. *The flower is light yellow.*

·Kawóot teen k̲'eikaxwéin a káa kak̲á! *Embroider a flower on it with beads!*

K̲'EIK'W[1] verb root

- **aawak̲'ék'w | --- | ak̲'ék'wx̲**
  *s/he cut it* | --- | *s/he cuts it (regularly).*
  THEME: O-S-ø-k̲'éik'w~ (ø event)
  *for S to cut O (human body), usually accidentally; for S to wound O with a sharp instrument*
  ·Du jiwán aawak̲'ék'w. *He cut the outside edge of his hand.*
- **sh wudik̲'ék'w | --- | sh dak̲'ék'wx̲**
  *s/he cut himself/herself* | --- | *s/he cuts himself/herself (regularly).*
  THEME: sh S-d-k̲'éik'w~ (ø event)
  *for S to cut himself/herself, usually accidentally; for S to wound himself/herself with a sharp instrument*

**k̲'eik̲'w** noun *tern*

·Ha yéi áwé has duwasáakw K̲'eik̲'w Sháa Xunaadáx̲. *They are called the Sea Pigeon gals from Hoonah.*

**k̲'éik̲'w** noun *cut; knife wound*

**k̲'eildaháak'u** noun *pretending; make-believe*

**k̲'eishkaháagu** noun *bog cranberry; low bush cranberry*

·Tl'átgi káa yéi nateech k̲'eishkaháagu. *Low bush cranberries are on the ground.*

# « K̲'w »

**k̲'wátl** noun *pot, cooking pot*

·K̲'wátl kaadé yéi adaané wé gáal'. *She is putting clams into the cooking pot.*

·Wé k̲'wátl yana.áat'ani k̲ut x̲waataan. *I misplaced the lid for the pot.*

# « L »

**LAA**[1] verb root

- **áx̱ woolaa | áx̱ yei naléin | ---**
  *the tide went out from under it | the tide is going out from under it | ---.*
  THEME: P-x̱ ø-laa~ (g̱a motion)
  *for the tide to ebb, go out from under P*
  ·Du yaagú yeix̱ woolaa. *The tide went out from under his boat.*
- **wuliláa | yaa nalléin | laléix̱**
  *it melted | it's melting | it melts (regularly).*
  THEME: l-laa~ (ø event)
  *for something to melt, dissolve, thaw*
- **yan uwaláa | yánde yaa naléin | yax̱ laa**
  *the tide is low | the tide is going out | the tide goes out (regularly).*
  THEME: yan~ ø-laa~ (ø motion)
  *for the tide to go out, be low*

**laaḵ'ásk** noun *dulse (type of seaweed)*
·Laaḵ'ásk gé ax̱ oox̱ káwu? *Do I have seaweed on my teeth?*
·Lidzée kayaaní a kaadéi kawuls'éesi wé laaḵ'ásk. *It's frustrating when leaves are blown onto the black seaweed.*

du **láaw** noun *privates (of male); penis and testicles*

**laaxw** noun *famine; starvation*
·Laaxw eetí wé ḵaa jeedáx̱ atx̱á has du g̱aneix̱íx̱ wusitee. *After the famine, the food given to them became their salvation.*

**LAAXW** verb root

- **uwaláxw | yaa naláxw | ---**
  *he/she/it starved | he/she/it is starving | ---.*
  THEME: O-ø-laaxw~ (ø event)
  *for O to be starving, starved*
  ·Oodzikaayi ḵáa áyá táakwx' gug̱waláaxw. *A lazy man will starve in the winter.*

**laax̱** noun *red cedar*
·Laax̱ teen áwé has awliyéx̱ wé hít kat'áayi. *They made those shingles out of cedar.*

**láax̱** noun *dead dry tree, still standing*

du **laayig̱águ** noun *his/her ring finger*

**lagaaw** noun *noise*

**lag̱wán** noun *bow (ribbon tied into a bow)*

du **laká** noun *inside of his/her mouth*

du **lak'éech'** noun *his/her occiput; nape of neck; back of head*

du **lak'eech'kóog̱u** noun *pit at base of his/her skull*

**lak'eech'wú** noun *scooter duck*

**láḵt** noun *bentwood box*

**lanáalx̱** noun *wealth; prosperity; riches*

**latseen** noun *strength, power*
·S'eiḵ x̱áat xáas'i áwé yak'éi g̱altóot idateení latseen sákw at eel'óoni. *When you're out hunting a piece of smoked fish skin in your pocket is good for energy.*

**Lawáak** noun *Klawock*

**lawúx̱** noun *young seagull*

**lawúx̱** noun *gray*

**láx̱'** noun *heron; Canada crane*

a **láx̱'i** noun *its sapwood; its sappy inner bark (of a tree)*

**láx̱' loowú** noun *swamp blueberry*
NOTES: The name derives from the similar gray-bluish color of the heron's beak.

at **layeix̱ s'aatí** noun *carpenter*
VARIANTS: et leyeix̱ s'aatí (C)

at **la.át** noun *baggage, luggage; things, stuff packed up for carrying*
VARIANTS: et le.ét (C)

**ldakát** Quantifier *all; every*
·Kax'ás'aa teen áwé kg̱eexáash ldakát wéi t'áa! *You will cut all those boards with a rip saw!*
·Ldakát wooch x̱oot has yawdiháa. *Everybody came together.*

**ldakát át** noun *everything*
·Awdagaaní yáa yagiyee, ldakát át kaadáx̱ kagux̱lax'áas. *When it sunshines today everything will be dripping off.*
·Ldakát át áwé ḵux̱ dak'óol'in x̱waasáakw. *I said everything backwards.*

**ldakát yé** noun *everywhere*
VARIANTS: ch'a ldakát yé
·Kag̱akl'eedí ldakát yéix' kanas.éich. *Yarrow grows all over.*

du **léelk'w** noun *his/her grandparent*
·Yaa ax̱ léelk'w ax̱ tláa yinaanáx̱ Ḵéin yóo dusáagun yaa

Xutsnoowúdáx̲. *My grandmother on my mother's side was called Ñéin, from Angoon.*
·I léelk'u keekándei aneelg̲ein - x̲áat yéi adaané! *Go check on your grandpa - he's working on fish!*

**Léelk'w!** noun *Grandmother!; Grandfather!*
NOTES: This is the form used to address one's grandparent.

LEET verb root

**• át aawalít | --- | áx̲ aleet**
*s/he threw it to it | --- | s/he throws it to it (regularly).*
THEME: P-t~ O-S-leet~ (ø motion)
*for S to throw O (usually with force so that object scatters) to P*
NOTES: Note that in the example sentence below, the postposition -dé (káast kaadé "in the barrel") occurs with the imperative form: lít "throw it", where we would expect the postposition -t (as in káast kát). Both forms are acceptable, this being a peculiarity of this particular verb.
·Wé káast kaadéi lít wé a x'éix'u! *Throw the gills in the barrel!*

**léet'** noun *roots or vines used in basket decoration*

LEI verb root

**• yéi kaawalei | yéi kunaaléi | ---**
*it became that far | it's that far | ---.*
THEME: (yéi) ka-u-ø-lei~ (na state)
*for something to be (so) far, distant (in time or space)*
VARIANTS: -lee~
NOTES: The perfective form: yéi kaawalei "it was that far" is commonly used in situations where one just fell short of making it to a destination. In other words, "I almost made it, it was just that far away".
·Dax̲adooshú kaay yéi kunaaléi wé aan, héen sháakdáx̲. *The town is seven miles from the head of the river.*
·Du hídidáx̲ kaay shoowú yéi kunaaléi hoon daakahídi. *The store is a half mile from her house.*

du **leikachóox̲'u** noun *his/her windpipe; pharynx*
VARIANTS: du leikechóox̲'u (C)

**léikwaa** noun *Easter bread; communion bread*

**léik̲'w** noun *red rockfish; red snapper*

**léin** noun *tide flats*
·K̲'alkátsk kahaa yís léinde gax̲too.áat yá xáanaa. *This evening we are going yellowneck clam digging.*
·Káas' léin káa yéi nateech. *There is always algae on the riverbank.*

**leineit shál** noun *sheep or goat horn spoon*

du **leitóox̱** noun *his/her throat*

**léix̱'w** noun *crimson red; face paint*

**leiyís** noun *fir*

**lékwaa** noun *fighting spirit*

du **lidíx̱'** noun *back of his/her neck*
VARIANTS: du ludíx̱'
·Xéesh áwé du lidíx̱' yéi yatee. *He has a rash on his neck.*

**lingít** noun *person*
·X̱'éidei kakg̱ilatix̱' yé ch'a yeisú lingít áwu. *There are still people in the place you are locking.*
·Wáa yateeyi lingít sáwé wa.é? *What kind of person are you?*

**Lingít** noun *Tlingit*
·Ḵa x̱át tsú ax̱ toowú yak'éi yaa a káa yéi x̱at gug̱wateeyí yaa Lingítx̱ x̱at sateeyí. *And I too am thankful that I'm part of this being that I'm Lingít.*
·Lingít x̱'éináx̱ kashxeet áwé ashigóok. *He knows how to write in the Tlingit language.*

**lingít aaní** noun *world*

**lingít k'únts'i** noun *water hemlock*

**lingít shákw** noun *wild strawberry*
NOTES: used in comparison to the commercial strawberry, "shákw"

**lingít x'áax'i** noun *crabapple*

**lítaa** noun *knife*
·K'idéin yax'át wé lítaa x'aan! *Sharpen the tip of the knife good!*
·X̱áat jeig̱í du lítayi kaax̱ aawa.óos'. *She washed fish scales off her knife.*

**lítaa eetí** noun *knife wound*

a **litká** RelationalNoun *(on) the back of it (fish); on the crest, ridge, backbone of it (hill, ridge, point)*
·Gooch litká aadé duwatéen wé g̱ooch. *The wolf on the ridge of the hill is visible.*
·Shaa litká aadé dax̱duwatéen wé watsíx. *The caribou are visible on the mountain ridge.*

**lit.isdúk** noun *black bass*

**l ḵool.áx̱ji** noun *deaf person*

**l ḵooshtéeni** noun *blind person*

**lḵ'ayáak'w x̱'us.eetí** noun *Milky Way*

**lookanáa** noun *person who acts crazy or possesssed*

**lóol** noun *fireweed*

**lóol** noun *pink*

**loon** noun *dry woody outer bark*

**lóot'** noun *eel*

a **loowú** noun *its beak*
·Ch'áak' lú yóo katán. *A bald eagle's beak is curved.*
·Dagwatgiyáa lú yayát' k̲a yéi kwlisáa. *A hummingbird's beak is long and skinny.*

du **lóox'u** noun *his/her urine*

l **s'aatí shaawát** noun *widow*

**Ltu.aa** noun *Lituya Bay*

a **lú** noun *its point (of a long thin pointed object)*
·Wé tséek a lú yalik'áts'. *The point of the barbeque stick is sharp.*
·Du tséegi a lú akaawayéx̲. *He sharpened the point of his barbecue stick.*

du **lú** noun *his/her nose*
·Ax̲ lú tukawlixwétl. *My nose tickled (inside).*

du **ludíx̲'** noun *back of his/her neck*
VARIANTS: du lidíx̲'

**lugán** noun *tufted puffin*
VARIANTS: lugén (C)

du **lugóoch'** noun *lobe of his/her nostril*

**lug̲eitl'** noun *snot*

**lug̲wéinaa** noun *handkerchief*

a **lukatíx'i** noun *its bowstay*

**lukat'íshaa** noun *leather needle*

**lukshiyáan** noun *mink*
VARIANTS: nukshiyáan

l **ulitoogu K̲aa Yakg̲wahéiyagu** noun *Holy Spirit*

**lunás** noun *nose ring*

l **ushk'é** noun *evil, sin*

du **lutú** noun *inside of his/her nose*

a **lututúḵl'i** noun *his/her nose cartilage*
·Wé dzísk'w a lututúḵl'i a kaax̱ kéi akaawas'él'. *She tore (the membrane) off the soft bone in the moose nose.*
·Watsíx a lututúḵl'i tléil tlax̱ ugé. *The soft bone in a caribou nose is not very big.*

du **lut'aaḵ** noun *side of his/her nose*

**l uwaxwachgi néekw** noun *paralysis; polio*

a **lux'aa** noun *its tip, point*

at **lux'aaḵáawu** noun *troublemaker*
VARIANTS: et lux'aaḵáawu (C)
·At lux'aaḵáawu áwé yéi yatee wé shaatk'. *That young girl is a troublemaker.*

**l yaa ḵooshgé** noun *foolishness; recklessness*

**l yoo ḵ'eishtángi** noun *mute; person who cannot speak*
VARIANTS: l yoo ḵ'eishténgi (C)

**l.uljíni** noun *vest; sleeveless top*
·Gunx̱aa yaka.óot' du l.uljíni kát akaawaḵáa. *She sewed the abalone buttons on her vest.*

# « L' »

**du l'aa** noun *his/her breast*

**l'aak** noun *dress*
·Woosh gax̲dusháa a kayís áwé yées l'aak aawak̲áa. *She sewed a new dress for the wedding that was to take place.*

**l'áak̲w** noun *old, worn-out boat*

**l'áax̲'** noun *grayish; blond (hair)*

**l'ag̲akáx̲** noun *west wind*

**l'ákwti** noun *fallen tree*

**l'át'aa** noun *tongs*

**l'ax̲keit** noun *dance regalia*
VARIANTS: l'ex̲keit

**l'ée** noun *wool blanket (used as potlatch gift or for dancing)*

a **l'eedí** noun *its tail (of animal)*
·S'igeidí l'eedí yawúx̲' k̲a k̲'áatl' yáx̲ yatee. *A beaver's tail is wide and flat.*
·S'eek l'eedí tléil ulyát'. *A black bear's tail is short.*

**L'eeneidí** noun *L'eeneidí, locally called "Dog Salmon"; a clan of the Raven moiety whose principal crest is the Dog Salmon*
·Tsu tsá yá naax̲ satí k̲u.aa áyá yaa téel' áyá haa shukáx̲ sitee, L'eeneidí. *Also the dog salmon is our clan crest, L'eeneidí.*

**L'EEX'** verb root

- **aawal'éex' | --- | yoo ayal'íx'k**
*s/he broke it | --- | s/he breaks it (regularly).*
THEME: O-S-ø-l'éex'~ (na event)
*for S to break O (general, solid object)*
NOTES: This verb would be used to talk about breaking such things as a tooth, leg, board, or a stick.
- **awlil'éex' | --- | yoo alil'íx'k**
*s/he broke it | --- | s/he breaks it (regularly).*
THEME: O-S-l-l'éex'~ (na event)
*for S to break O (often by bending) (usually long objects)*
·Du woosáani awlil'éex'. *He broke his spear.*
- **wool'éex' | --- | yoo yal'íx'k**
*it broke | --- | it breaks (regularly).*

THEME: ø-l'éex'~ (na event)
*for a general, solid object to break*
·Du x̱eek áwé wool'éex'. *His upper arm is broken.*
·Du kíji áwé wool'éex' wé ts'ítskw, ách áwé tlél át wudaḵeen. *The songbird's wing broke, that's why it doesn't fly around.*

- **wulil'éex' | --- | yoo lil'íx'k**
*it broke | --- | it breaks (regularly).*
THEME: l-l'éex'~ (na event)
*for a long object to break*
·Aatx̱ wulil'éex' wé nadáakw x̱'oosí. *The table leg broke off.*

**l'ée x'wán** noun *sock(s)*
·Du jeeyís l'ée x'wán kax̱wsinei. *I knitted socks for her.*
·Ax̱ léelk'w jeedáx̱ kakéin l'ée x'wán áyá ax̱ tuwáa sigóo. *I like the yarn socks from my grandmother.*

**l'éiw** noun *sand; gravel*
·Du x̱aakw eetí áwé wé l'éiw káwu. *His fingernail markings are in the sand.*
·Ḵ'asigóo kaltéelḵ l'éiw kát át wusheex. *It's fun running around barefoot in the sand.*

**l'eiwú** noun *wood, piece of wood; wood chip*

**l'éiw x'aayí** noun *sand point*

**l'éiw yátx'i** noun *fine sand or gravel*

**L'EIX̱** verb root

- **aawal'eix̱ | al'eix̱ | yoo ayal'éx̱k**
*s/he danced | s/he dances; s/he is dancing | s/he dances (regularly).*
THEME: a-S-ø-l'eix̱~ (na act)
*for S to dance*
·Has ang̱al'eix̱ ḵaa shukát wé atyátx'i. *Let the children dance before everyone.*
·Jilḵoot Ḵwáan has al'eix̱. *The Chilkoot people are dancing.*

- **daak aawal'éx̱ | daak anal'éx̱ | daak al'éx̱ch**
*s/he danced out | s/he is dancing out | s/he dances out (regularly).*
THEME: daak S-ø-l'eix̱~ (ø motion)
*for S to dance out into the open*
·Tlék'g̱aa áwé anax̱ daak has aawal'éx̱. *One by one they danced out.*

- **g̱unéi aawal'éx̱ | --- | g̱unéi al'éx̱x̱**
*s/he started dancing | --- | s/he starts dancing (regularly).*
THEME: g̱unéi S-ø-l'eix̱~ (ø motion)
*for S to begin dancing*
·Du kasánnáx̱ áwé yaawajél, g̱unéi has aawal'éx̱. *He put his hand around her waist and they began dancing.*

**l'éx̱'kw** noun *soil; dirt*

·L'éx̱'kw, ḵútl'kw nasteech séew daak wustaaní *Soil turns to mud when it rains.*

**du l'íli** noun *his penis*

**l'ook** noun *coho salmon; silver salmon*

·L'ook at x̱'éeshi áwé yak'éi. *Coho salmon dryfish is good.*

·L'ook kaháagu áyá yak'éi kanat'á kanéegwál' sákw. *Coho salmon eggs are good for blueberry sauce.*

**L'OON** verb root

- **aawal'óon | al'óon | yoo ayal'únk**

  *s/he hunted it | s/he hunts it; s/he is hunting it | s/he hunts it (regularly).*

  THEME: O-S-ø-l'óon~ (na act)

  *for S to hunt O (wild game)*

  ·A x̱oo aa ḵu.oo woolnáx̱ wooshḵáḵ has al'óon. *Some people hunt the wren.*

  ·Yóode loowagoog̱u dzísk'w a ítde akḵwal'óon. *I will go hunting those moose that ran over that way.*

- **aawal'óon | al'óon | yoo ayal'únk**

  *s/he hunted | s/he is hunting | s/he hunts (regularly).*

  THEME: a-S-ø-l'óon~ (na act)

  *for S to hunt*

  ·Áa agax̱tool'oon yé yinaadé yaa gagú! *Walk toward the place we will hunt!*

  ·Taatx' áwé has al'óon wé k'ákw. *Owls hunt at night.*

**du l'óot'** noun *his/her tongue*

**l'oowú** noun *wood, piece of wood; wood chip*

**l'oowú táḵl** noun *mallet, wooden hammer*

**l'óox̱** noun *silty, murky water*

**L'ukaax̱.ádi** noun *L'ukaax̱.ádi, locally called "Sockeye"; a clan of the Raven moiety whose principal crest is the Sockeye*

**L'uknax̱.ádi** noun *L'uknax̱.ádi, locally called "Coho"; a clan of the Raven moiety whose principal crest is the Coho*

·Yéi áwé wduwasáa Kayáash Hít L'uknax̱.ádich. *The Coho Salmon tribe has named it Platform House.*

**l'ut'tláaḵ** noun *snake*

# « N »

**naa** noun *nation; moiety; clan; band of people*

·Yaa uháan haa naax̱ sitee, Yéil áyá haa shukáx̱ sitee. *For our clan, Raven is our main crest.*

·Xeitl naax̱ has sitee Shangukeidí. *The Shangukeidí are Thunderbird.*

NAA[2] verb root

- **awdináa | adaná | adanáax̱**

  *s/he drank it | s/he drinks it; s/he is drinking it | s/he drinks it (regularly).*

  THEME: O-S-d-naa~ (ø act)

  *for S to drink O*

  ·Tléik̲w kahéeni awdináa. *He drank berry juice.*

- **at wudináa | at daná | ---**

  *s/he drank | s/he drinks, is drinking | ---.*

  THEME: at S-d-naa~ (ø act)

  *for S to drink*

NAA[3] verb root

- **aadé akaawanáa | aadé akoonáa | aadé yoo akayanáakw**

  *s/he sent him/her there | s/he is sending him/her there | s/he sends him/her there (regularly).*

  THEME: O-ka-u-S-ø-náa~ (na act)

  *for S to order (esp. to go), send, command O; (fig.) for S to give O (esp. in accordance with clan relationship)*

  ·K̲aadaaxaashí x̱ánde kawduwanáa. *He was sent to the surgeon.*

  ·G̲ayéis' hítde kawduwanáa. *He was sent to jail.*

a **náa** RelationalNoun *(draped) over it, covering it*

**naadaayi héen** noun *river; stream; creek*

·Tláakw naadaayi héen kulix̱éitl'shán. *A fast river is dangerous.*

**naag̲as'éi** noun *fox; red fox*

·Du k̲oowú tóode wujixéex wé naag̲as'éi. *The red fox ran into his den.*

·Gootl kanax̱ yawjik'én wé naag̲as'éi. *The red fox jumped over a mound.*

**naa káani** noun *master of ceremonies, elder of the opposite clan consulted conducting a ceremony*

**naakée** Adverb *upstream; north*

·Wé naakéedáx̱ lingít g̲unayáade yóo has x̱'ali.átk. *The people from the north speak differently.*

·K̲ukawduwayél' áyá - naakéede nax̱took̲oox̱. *It's calm out - let's go up the bay.*

**náakw** noun *medicine*

·Náakwx̱ awliyéx̱ aasdaak'óox̱'u. *She made medicine out of pitch.*
·Kag̱akl'eedí náakwx̱ dulyéix̱. *Yarrow is used for medicine.*

**NAAḴ**[1] verb root

• **--- | has náḵ | ---**
--- | *they are standing* | ---.
THEME: S-ø-náḵ (position)
*for (plural) S to be standing*
NOTES: This verb only occurs in the imperfective. Note that a noun phrase with (-t) postposition is used to indicate where one is standing, but this noun phrase is not required by the verb. For example, one could say: has náḵ "they are standing", or: át has náḵ "they are standing there".

• **yan has uwanáḵ | --- | yax̱ has naaḵ**
*they kept standing; they stood* | --- | *they stay standing (regularly).*
THEME: yan S-ø-naaḵ~ (ø motion)
*for (plural) S to stand, stay standing*
·A yáa yan yináḵ! *You all stand in front of it!*

**NAAḴ**[2] verb root

• **ajeewanáḵ | --- | ajináḵx**
*s/he let it go* | --- | *s/he lets it go (regularly).*
THEME: O-ji-S-ø-naaḵ~ (ø event)
*for S to let go, release, relinquish O; for S to leave, desert O; for S to hand over, deliver up O*
·Déix̱ x̱áat haa jeex' ajeewanáḵ. *He left two salmon for us.*
·Du jintáax' jiwduwanáḵ. *He was put in charge of it. (Lit: It was left in his hands).*

**naaḵw** noun *rotten wood*

**NAAḴW**[1] verb root

• **yawdináḵw | yadanáḵws' | yadanáḵwx̱**
*s/he baited hooks* | *s/he is baiting hooks* | *s/he baits hooks (regularly).*
THEME: ya-S-d-naaḵw~ (ø act)
*for S to bait hooks, put bait on fish hooks*
·Yadanáḵws' cháatlg̱aa. *He is baiting hooks for halibut.*

**náaḵw** noun *octopus; devilfish*

·Shayadihéin has du tl'eeg̱í wé náaḵw. *Octopus have a lot of tentacles.*

**NÁALX̱** verb root

• **wulináalx̱ | lináalx̱ | ---**
*s/he got rich* | *s/he's rich* | ---.
THEME: O-l-náalx̱ (ga state)
*for O to be rich, wealthy, profitable*

·Yéi át a<u>x</u>wdishée iwulnáal<u>x</u>i. *I wish you wealth.*
·Ast'ei<u>x</u> tlél ulnáal<u>x</u>in. *Trolling didn't used to be profitable.*

**naanyaa kanat'aayí** noun *huckleberry; blueberry*

**naasa.áa** noun *large cannister*

du **naasí** noun *his/her intestines, guts*

**naa shukla<u>g</u>eeyí** noun *the life of the party*

**náaw** noun *liquor; booze; alcoholic beverage*

**náaw éesh** noun *alcoholic*

**náaw s'aatí** noun *drunk; drunkard*

**naaxein** noun *Chilkat blanket*
·Teey woodí naaxein<u>x</u> dulyéi<u>x</u>. *Yellow cedar bark is used to make a chilkat robe.*

**náayadi** noun *half-dried salmon (smoked)*
·A xáas'i teen áwé duxáash náayadi sákw. *Half smoked fish is cut with the fish skin intact.*

**naa.át** noun *clothes, clothing; garment*
VARIANTS: naa.ét (C)
·A déinde aa du naa.ádi aa<u>x</u> awli.aat. *She picked up the rest of her clothes.*
·Yak'éiyi naa.át aa<u>x</u> du.óow wé hoon daakahídi. *Good clothing can be bought from that store.*

**naa.át kaxít'aa** noun *clothes brush*
VARIANTS: naa.ét kexít'aa (C)

**nadáakw** noun *table*
·Nadáakw káx' yéi na.oo! *Put it on the table!*
·Wéidu <u>g</u>ánch gwéili nadáakw káa yan satí! *Put that bag of tobacco on the table!*

**nakwnéit** noun *priest; pastor; minister*

**nakws'aatí** noun *witch*

a **ná<u>k</u>** RelationalPostposition *(going, taking something) away from it*
·<u>G</u>alsaayít áwé du yéi jineiyí a ná<u>k</u> woogoot. *She went away from her work so that she could rest.*
·A ná<u>k</u> yaa nagúdi yaa shukanashéen. *She is singing as she is leaving it behind.*

**nalháashadi** noun *driftwood*

**naná** noun *death*

**nas'gadooshóonáx** Numeral *eight (people)*

**nas'gadooshú** Numeral *eight*
·Nas'gadooshú ch'iyáash kaxwaach'ák'w hun yayís. *I carved eight sea otter hunting canoes to sell.*

**nas'gidahéen** Numeral *three times*
VARIANTS: nás'k dahéen

**nás'gigáa** Numeral *three at a time, three by three*

**nás'gináx** Numeral *three (people)*
·Nás'gináx has yatee wé Yéil naa sháade nákx'i. *There are three Raven Clan leaders.*

**nás'k** Numeral *three*
·Nás'k a doogú x'óow áwé du káa kakgwagéi k'oodás' sákw, wé káa tlein. *It will take three leather blankets for the big man's shirt.*
·Nás'k yagiyee a kaanáx has yaawa.át. *They walked for three days.*

**nás'k jinkaat** Numeral *thirty*

**nás'k jinkaat ka tléix'** Numeral *thirty one*

**náxw** noun *halibut hook (made of wood)*

**-náx** postpos. *along, via; including the time of*
NOTES: Some nouns and relational nouns undergo changes in vowel length and/or tone when combined with -náx:
á "it, there" + -náx = anax "through it; through there"
a ká "its surface" + -náx = a kanáx / a kaanáx "through (the surface of) it; throughout it"
a yá "its face" + -náx = a yanax / a yáanáx "through (the face of) it"
a tú "its inside" + -náx = a tóonáx "through (the inside of) it"
·Yat'éex'i gaaw a tóonáx yiyagút. *You walked through that period of hard time.*
·Nás'k yagiyee a kaanáx has yaawa.át. *They walked for three days.*

**né** noun *hairy grass, seaweed on which herring spawn*

**neech** noun *shoreline; beach*
·Xeil neech káa yéi nateech xóon wudunoogú. *Foam is on the beach when the north wind blows.*
·Yá neechx yaa neegúdi yei kgisatéen yá katóok. *As you walk along this shoreline you will see this cave.*

**neechkayádi** noun *fatherless child; bastard*
VARIANTS: nichkayádi (An)

**néegwál'** noun *paint*
·A yáanáx áwé kaylisék'w yá néegwál'. *You tinted this paint too much.*
·Ch'áak' loowú yáx néegwál' xwaa.oo. *I bought some dark yellow paint.*

**NÉEGWÁL'** verb root

- **aawanéegwál' | anéegwál' | yoo ayanéegwál'k**

  *s/he painted it | s/he is painting it | s/he paints it (regularly).*
  THEME: O-S-ø-néegwál' (na act)
  *for S to paint O*
  ·X̲'aan yáx̲ wutuwanéegwál' a yá. *We painted the side of it red.*
  ·Has aawanéegwál' wé gántiyaakw. *They painted the steamboat.*

**neek** noun *news; gossip, rumor*
·Neek ash atláx'w yaa k̲udzigéiyi ts'ats'ée. *Pigeons carry messages.*

**NEEK** verb root

- **akaawaneek | akanéek | yóo akaaníkk**

  *s/he told about it | s/he tells about it; s/he is telling about it | s/he tells about it (regularly).*
  THEME: O-ka-S-ø-neek~ (na act)
  *for S to tell about, report about, give facts about O; for S to witness to, tell about, testify about O*
  NOTES: To indicate who the listener is, use: N een. For example, Mary een akaawaneek. "S/he told Mary about it." This is not required with this verb however, and is therefore not included in the Leer-Edwards theme.
  ·Aadéi keenik yé g̲unayáade x̲aatéen. *I see it differently from the way you tell it.*
  ·Wé íx̲t'ch du een akaawaneek wáa sá at gug̲waneiyí. *The medicine man told him what was going to happen.*

- **akawlineek | aklaneek | yoo akliníkk**

  *s/he told the story of it | s/he tells the story of it; s/he is telling the story of it | s/he tells the story of it (regularly).*
  THEME: O-ka-S-l-neek (na act)
  *for S to tell the story of O; for S to talk into O*
  ·Tléil áyáx̲ at wuneiyí, jinaháa áwé yóo kdulneek. *When something bad happens they say it's bad luck.*

- **a káx̲ akawliník | --- | ---**

  *s/he talked him/her out if it | --- | ---.*
  THEME: N káx̲ O-ka-S-l-neek~ (ø event)
  *for S to defraud, talk O out of N*
  ·X̲áat yís áwé has akawliník Yéilch, wé kéidladi k̲a kag̲eet. *Raven talked the seagull and loon out of the salmon.*

- **sh kawdlineek | sh kalneek | ---**

  *s/he told a story | s/he is telling a story | ---.*
  THEME: sh ka-S-d-l-neek (na act)
  *for S to preach, narrate, tell a story*
  NOTES: To include in the sentence what the story is about, use: N daat "about N". To include who the story is being told to, use: N een "to N". For example: Mary áwé John een sh kawdlineek wé naaxein daat. "Mary told John a story about the Chilkat robe."

·Yéi sh kadulneek a yahaayí kudzitee dáanaa. *They say money has a spirit.*
·Ha wáa sás sh kadulneek? *What's the latest news?*

**neek s'aatí (T)** noun *gossip; rumormonger*
VARIANTS: niks'aatí

**neek shatl'éḵx'u** noun *gossip; rumormonger*
VARIANTS: neek shetl'éḵx'u (C)

NEEKW verb root

- **woonéekw | yanéekw | kei néekwch**
*s/he got sick | s/he's sick | s/he gets sick (regularly).*
THEME: O-ø-néekw (ga state)
*for O to be sick; for O to hurt, be in pain*
·Du díx̲' néekw nooch. *His back always hurts.*
·Du g̲áts dag̲aanéekw. *His thighs are sore.*

**néekw** noun *sickness; illness; disease*
VARIANTS: nóokw
·Néekwch at ash yaawa.aat. *Sickness is trying to get him.*
·Náakw du x̲'éix̲ wuduwatee du kalóox'shání néegooch. *She was given medicine for her bladder pain.*

**nées'** noun *sea urchin*

NEEX' verb root

- **awsiníx' / awdziníx' | asinéex' | asníx'x̲**
*s/he smelled it | s/he smells it | s/he smells it (regularly).*
THEME: O-S-(d)-s-néex'~ (ø act)
*for S to smell O*
·Wé xóots awusnéex'i a yinaadé wjixeex haa keidlí. *Our dog is running toward the brown bear it smelled.*

**néex̲'** noun *marble*
VARIANTS: néix̲'

NEI verb root

- **aax̲ yéi awsinei | --- | aax̲ kei yéi asneich**
*s/he picked them up off of it | --- | s/he picks them up off of it (regularly).*
THEME: P-dáx̲ yéi O-S-s-nei~ (ga motion)
*for S to pick up, lift up, take (plural) O (objects) up off of P*
VARIANTS: -nee~ (An)
·Atx̲á aax̲ yéi awusneiyi yé, dáanaa a eetíx' yan akaawatée. *She put money in place of the food she picked up.*
·Dei kát la.ádi g̲éechadi aax̲ yéi awsinei. *He removed the windfall lying in the road.*
- **akawsinei | aksané | ---**
*s/he knitted it | s/he is knitting it | ---.*
THEME: O-ka-S-s-nei~ (na act)

*for S to make O (cloth of any kind) (by weaving, knitting, or crocheting); for S to make or mend O (net)*
·Du jeeyís l'ée x'wán kax̱wsinei. *I knitted socks for her.*
·Dzaas áwé yéi akg̱wa.oo g̱eeg̱ách' akawusneiyí. *She will use string when she crochets a hammock.*

- **du jeet yéi awsinei | --- | du jeex̱ yéi asnei**
*s/he gave them to him/her | --- | s/he gives them to him/her (regularly).*
THEME: N jeet~ yéi O-S-s-nei~ (ø motion)
*for S to give, take, hand (plural) O to N*
VARIANTS: -nee~ (An)
·Yées jig̱wéinaa du léelk'u jeet yéi awsinei. *He gave his grandmother new towels.*

- **kawdzinéi | kasné | ---**
*s/he knitted | s/he is knitting; s/he knits | ---.*
THEME: ka-S-d-s-néi~ (ø act)
*for S to knit, weave, or crochet*

- **ḵáakwt uwanéi | --- | ḵáakwx̱ nei**
*s/he had an accident | --- | s/he has accidents (regularly).*
THEME: ḵáakwt~ O-ø-nei~ (ø motion)
*for O to have an accident, get hurt; for something bad to happen to O*
VARIANTS: -nee~ (An)
·Áa ḵúx̱ teedataan wé ḵáakwt iwuneiyí! *Think back to the time when you got hurt!*

- **du waḵshiyeex' yéi awsinei | --- | ḵaa waḵshiyeex' yoo asineik**
*s/he demonstrated it to him/her | --- | s/he demonstrates it to people (regularly).*
THEME: N waḵshiyeex' yéi O-S-s-nei~ (na event)
*for S to demonstrate, perform publicly, show N how to do O by action*
VARIANTS: -nee~ (An)
·Ax̱ waḵshiyeex' yéi nasné! *Show me how it's done!*

- **wooch yáx̱ awsinei | wooch yáx̱ yaa anasnéin | ---**
*s/he straightened it out | s/he is straightening it out | ---.*
THEME: wooch yáx̱ O-S-s-nei~ (na event)
*for S to straighten out O, smooth O over (literal or abstract)*
VARIANTS: -nee~ (An)
·G̱eiwú wooch yáx̱ awsinei tle daak ashakaawaḵúx̱. *She straightened the net out and then she set it.*

- **du yáa ayaawanéi / du yáa awuwanéi | du yáa kei ayananéin | ---**
*s/he respects him/her | s/he is beginning to respect him/her | ---.*
THEME: N yáa a-ya-u-S-ø-néi (ga act)
*for S to respect, regard highly, think highly of N*

- **yan awsinéi | yánde yaa anasnein | yax̱ asnei**
*s/he finished it | s/he is finishing it | s/he finishes it (regularly).*
THEME: yan~ O-S-s-nei~ (ø motion)

*for S to finish, complete O*
VARIANTS: -nee~ (An)
·Yan awsinéi du s'ís'aa hídi eetí. *He fixed up the place for his tent.*

- **yan sh wudzinéi | yánde yaa sh nasnein | ya<u>x</u> sh isnei**

*s/he is dressed up | s/he's getting dressed up | s/he gets dressed up (regularly).*
THEME: yan~ sh S-d-s-nei~ (ø event)
*for S to dress up*
VARIANTS: -nee~ (An)
·Yan sh wudzinéi. *She's all dressed up.*

- **yan uwanéi | yánde yaa nanein | ya<u>x</u> nei**

*he/she/it is ready | he/she/it is getting ready | he/she/it is always ready.*
THEME: yan~ O-ø-nei~ (ø motion)
*for O to be permanent, happen for good; for O to be finished, complete, ready; for O to be prepared, ready*
VARIANTS: -nee~ (An)
·Yan uwanéi ágé wé tléix' aa yá<u>x</u>? *Is it ready like the other one?*
·Yan uwaneiyi hít kaságu<u>g</u>áa kawduwa<u>k</u>aa. *He was sent for ready-made rafters.*

- **yan yéi akawsinéi | --- | ya<u>x</u> yéi aksanei**

*s/he put them down | --- | s/he puts them down (regularly).*
THEME: yan~ yéi O-ka-S-s-nei~ (ø motion)
*for S to put down, leave O (plural round objects)*
VARIANTS: -nee~ (An)
·At<u>x</u>a át náagu a <u>x</u>oo yan yéi ksané! *Put some moth balls among it!*

- **--- | yéi adaanéi | ---**

*--- | s/he does it; s/he is doing it | ---.*
THEME: (yéi) O-daa-S-ø-nei~ (na act)
*for S to do, perform O (a particular action); for S to work on O*
·A<u>x</u> tláak'wch áa <u>x</u>at shukaawajáa, aadé yéi daadunei yé. *My maternal aunt taught me how to make it.*
·A<u>x</u> yéi jineiyí áwé kaxíl'aa k'idéin daané. *My job is to clean erasers.*

- **yéi at woonei | --- | yéi at yaneik**

*that's what happened | --- | that's what happens (regularly).*
THEME: (yéi) at ø-nei (na event)
*for something to happen*
VARIANTS: -nee~ (An)
·Tleidahéen, yéi at woonei. *Once upon a time, this happened.*
·Tléil áyá<u>x</u> at wuneiyí, jinaháa áwé yóo kdulneek. *When something bad happens they say it's bad luck.*

- **yéi awsinei | yéi yaa anasnéin | yéi yoo asineik**

*s/he fixed it | s/he is fixing it | s/he fixes it (regularly).*
THEME: (yéi) O-S-s-nei~ (na event)
*for S to do (that) to O; for S to fix, cause (that) to happen to O*
VARIANTS: -nee~ (An)
·K'idéin nasné wé nadáakw! *Clear and clean the table!*
·Hít shantú k'idéin awsinei. *She cleaned upstairs.*

- **yéi jeewanei | yéi jiné | yéi yoo jiyaneik**
  *s/he worked | s/he works; s/he is working | s/he works (regularly).*
  THEME: yéi ji-S-ø-nei~ (na act)
  *for S to work; for S to do*
  ·Seig̲án gé i tuwáa sigóo ax̲ een yéi jiyineiyí? *Do you want to work with me tomorrow?*
  ·Yan yéi jiwtooneiyí a ítnáx̲ tsá gax̲too.áat. *After we have finished work, then we will go.*
- **yéi woonei | yéi yaa nanein | yéi yoo yaneik**
  *that happened to him/her/it | that's happening to him/her/it | that happens to him/her/it (regularly).*
  THEME: (yéi) O-ø-nei (na event)
  *for (that) to happen, occur to O*
  VARIANTS: -nee (An)

**neigóon** noun *nagoonberry, lagoonberry, dwarf nagoonberry*

**neil~** Adverb *inside, into the house, home*
·Kaduch'áak'w lítaa sákw yak'éiyi aa g̲ayéis' neil tí! *Bring home a good piece of iron for a carving knife!*
·Gán kak̲ás'ti k̲óok tóox' neil awsi.ín. *He brought the kindling inside in a box.*

**neil** noun *home*
·Xít'aa een du neilí axít'gi nooch. *He always sweeps his house with a broom.*
·L s'eik̲x̲ usiteeyi neil áyá. *This is a smoke-free home.*

**neil ycc táax'ayi** noun *housefly*

**neilyeetéeli** noun *slipper(s); house shoe(s)*

**néil'** noun *basket of woven red cedar bark*

**neis'** noun *oil, grease (for coating skin or rubbing); lotion; liniment*

du **néix'i** noun *his/her inheritance; possessions of deceased given to him/her at a feast*

**NEIX̲** verb root

- **awsineix̲ | --- | yei asneix̲ch**
  *s/he saved him/her/it | --- | s/he saves him/her/it (regularly).*
  THEME: O-S-s-neix̲ (g̲a event)
  *for S to save O; for S to heal, cure O*
  ·Aankanáagu tín sh wudzineix̲. *She healed herself with medicine from the land.*
  ·Tlei déix̲ k̲'ateil yáx̲ áwé wutusineix̲ shákw kahéeni. *We just saved two gallons of the strawberry juice.*
- **wooneix̲ | yei nanéx̲ | yei néx̲ch**
  *s/he recovered | s/he is beginning to recover | s/he recovers (regularly).*

THEME: O-ø-neix̲~ (g̲a event)
*for O to be saved; for O to be healed, cured, recover; for O to be satisfied*
·Wuwtunéekw jeedáx̲ áwé wooneix̲. *She was saved from tuberculosis.*

**néx̲'w** noun *yellow cloudberry*

**niks'aatí** noun *gossip, rumormonger*
VARIANTS: neek s'aatí (T)

**nisdaat** noun *last night*

a **niyaa** RelationalNoun *in its way; keeping it away; protecting, shielding, screening from it; blocking it*
·Ax̲ dayéen hán xóon niyaa. *He is standing facing me, shielding me from the North Wind.*

a **niyaadé** Adverb *in the direction or general area of it; (headed) toward it*
VARIANTS: a niyaadéi, a yinaadé, a yinaadéi
·Áa niyaadé yaa nagút. *He is walking toward the lake.*
·A niyaadé yaa nagút. *He is walking toward it.*

**niyaháat** noun *body armor, breastplate*

**nooch** Other *always; [auxiliary]*
VARIANTS: nuch
NOTES: The auxiliary nooch follows a verb and is used in the imperfective habitual aspect, giving the verb a habitual meaning "always".
·K̲aa tuk'éi nooch g̲agaan duteení. *People are always happy when they see the sun.*
·Tlél ushik'éiyi aa yoo x̲'atánk áwé tsá a.ax̲ji nooch . *She always only hears the bad talk.*

NOOK[1] verb root

• **áa wdinook | --- | ---**
*the building was situated there (suddenly as if overnight) | --- | ---.*
THEME: d-nook~ (g̲a event)
*for a building to be situated*

• **át awsinook | --- | át yoo asinúkk**
*s/he is carrying him/her/it around; s/he carried him/her/it around | --- | s/he carries him/her/it around (regularly).*
THEME: P-t O-S-s-nook~ (na motion)
*for S to carry, take O (live creature) around at P*

• **awsinook | --- | yei asnúkch**
*s/he seated him/her | --- | s/he seats him/her (regularly).*
THEME: O-S-s-nook~ (g̲a event)
*for S to seat O*

• **awsinook | yaa anasnúk | yoo asinúkk**
*s/he carried him/her/it | s/he is carrying him/her/it | s/he carries him/her/it (regularly).*

THEME: O-S-s-nook~ (na motion)
*for S to carry, take O (live creature)*
·Du ji<u>g</u>ei<u>x</u> yaa anasnúk du séek'. *He is carrying his daughter in his arms.*

- **kei awsinúk | --- | kei asnúkch**
*s/he lifted him/her/it up | --- | s/he lifts him/her/it up (regularly).*
THEME: kei O-S-s-nook~ (ø motion)
*for S to lift up O (live creature)*
·Du dachxánk' du <u>g</u>ushkáa kei awsinúk. *He lifted his grandchild up onto his lap.*

- **shawdinúk | --- | shadanúkx̱**
*s/he got up | --- | s/he gets up (regularly).*
THEME: sha-S-d-nook~ (ø event)
*for (singular) S to get up, rise*
·Ts'ootaat shax̱wdinúk. *I got up in the morning.*
·<u>K</u>eex̱'é shukát áwé shoodanookch ax̱ léelk'w. *My grandfather wakes up before dawn.*

- **woonook | --- | yei núkch**
*s/he sat down | --- | s/he sits down (regularly).*
THEME: S-ø-nook~ (<u>g</u>a event)
*for (singular) S to sit, sit down (esp. act of sitting)*
·At x̱éidi yax'aat a shóox' <u>g</u>anú! *Sit down and do some arrow-head sharpening!*
·Wé aas goowú káa woonook. *She sat on that tree stump.*

- **yan awsinúk | --- | yax̱ asnook**
*s/he put him/her/it down | --- | s/he puts him/her/it down (regularly).*
THEME: yan~ O-S-s-nook~ (ø motion)
*for S to put down O (live creature)*
·Káa x̱ex̱x'u yeit káa yan awsinúk du séek'. *She put her daughter down on the bed.*

NOOK² verb root

- **jée awdinúk | jée adinook | jée adanúkx̱**
*s/he felt it | s/he's feeling it | s/he feels it (regularly).*
THEME: jée O-S-d-nook~ (ø state)
*for S to feel, touch O (esp. with hands)*
NOTES: This verb is commonly used in reference to labor pains. For example: Jée gé idinook? "Are you feeling it (contractions)?"

- **wuduwanúk | yaa ndunúk | dunúkx̱**
*it blew; it's blowing | it's starting to blow | it blows (regularly).*
THEME: du-ø-nook~ (ø event)
*for the wind to blow, be felt (esp. a breeze, light wind)*
·Xóon wuduwanúk. *A north wind is blowing.*
·X̱eil neech káa yéi nateech xóon wudunoogú. *Foam is on the beach when the north wind blows.*

- **x'áant uwanúk | x'áande yaa nanúk | x'áanx̱ nook**
  *s/he's angry | s/he's getting angry | s/he gets angry (regularly).*
  THEME: x'áan-t~ S-ø-nook~ (ø motion)
  *for S to be angry*
- **x̱'éi awdinúk | x̱'éi adinook | x'éi adanúkx̱**
  *s/he tasted it | s/he tastes it | s/he tastes it (regularly).*
  THEME: x̱'éi O-S-d-nook~ (ø state)
  *for S to taste, sample O*
- **yéi ḵoowanook | yéi ḵuwanóok | ---**
  *s/he did it | s/he is doing it | ---.*
  THEME: (yéi) ḵu-S-ø-nook~ (na act)
  *for S to behave, do, act (in a certain way)*
  VARIANTS: -neekw
  ·Tléil oowaa wé aan káa ḵududziteeyi yoo x̱'atánk géide ḵudunoogú. *It is wrong to act against the law of the land.*
  ·L át yáx̱ ḵoonook. *He doesn't act normal.*
- **yéi sh tuwdinook | yéi sh tudinook | ---**
  *s/he felt that way | s/he feels that way | ---.*
  THEME: (yéi) sh tu-S-d-nook~ (na act)
  *for S to feel (that way) (esp. physical sensation)*
  ·Háas' yáx̱ sh tudinook. *He feels like vomiting.*
  ·G̱unayéide a daat sh tudinook yeedát. *He feels differently about it now.*

**nóosk** noun *wolverine*
VARIANTS: nóoskw
·Nóosk káx̱ g̱aatáa yan awli.át. *He set traps for wolverine.*
·Nóosk x̱aagú ḵúnáx̱ yalik'áts'. *Wolverine claws are really sharp.*

**nóoskw** noun *wolverine*
VARIANTS: nóosk

**nóosh** noun *dead salmon (after spawning)*

NOOT' verb root

- **akaawanóot' | --- | yoo akayanút'k**
  *s/he swallowed it | --- | s/he swallows it (regularly).*
  THEME: O-ka-S-ø-nóot'~ (na event)
  *for S to swallow O (pill, etc.)*
  ·Éech' akaawanóot' Yéil. *Raven swallowed a stone.*

NOOTS[1] verb root

- **at kaawanúts | at kanútst | ---**
  *s/he is grinning; s/he grinned | s/he is trying to grin | ---.*
  THEME: at ka-S-ø-nóots~ (ø act)
  *for S to smile at something (often knowingly or sarcastically), grin*
  ·At kadunuts nuch ax̱ saayí g̱adu.áx̱ín. T'aaw Chán. *They always grin when they hear my name, T'aaw Chán.*

**noow** noun *fort*

**noow** noun *flat-topped island with steep sides; low flat island or hill*

**noow g̲ei** noun *in a fort, shelter, cove*

**nóox'** noun *shell; shell-like chip or flake; china; carapace*
·Nóox' tóodáx̲ aawaxás' wé x̲éel'. *He scraped the slime out of the shell.*
·Hintakx'óosi nóox'u kayat'éex' *Coral shells are hard.*

**nóox'** noun *eggshell*

**nukshiyáan** noun *mink*
VARIANTS: lukshiyáan

**núkt** noun *blue grouse*

**NÚKTS** verb root
• **wulinúkts | linúkts | ---**
*it was sweet | he/she/it is sweet | ---.*
THEME: O-l-núkts (ga state)
*for O to be sweet*

# « Oo »

**oolxéis’** noun *wish; prayer*

**óonaa** noun *gun, rifle*
·Aas k’eeyéet ash aawatán du óonayi. *He leaned his rifle against the tree trunk.*

**óonaa eetí** noun *gunshot wound*

**óos’i** noun *laundry*

**Óos’k’!** interj. *Cute!*
VARIANTS: Óots’k’!
NOTES: This exclamation is used in association with little, cute things such as babies, puppies, or small objects.

**óosh** particle *as if; if only; even if*
·Yaa indashán óosh gé! *If only you were getting old!*

**óot’** noun *rock pile fish trap*

a **óot’i** noun *its sucker (devilfish)*

**óoxjaa** noun *wind*
·Aan kwéiyi óoxjaa tóot wulis’ees. *A flag is blowing in the wind.*
·Wé litseeni óoxjaa géide áwé yaa has na.át. *They are walking against the strong wind.*

a **óoxu** noun *spray of air exhaled through its blowhole (of sea mammal)*

du **óox’u** noun *his/her shoulderblade; scapula*

du **oox̱** noun *his/her tooth*
·Laaḵ’ásk gé ax̱ oox̱ káwu? *Do I have seaweed on my teeth?*
·Du oox̱ kanat’á kahéeni yáx̱ kawdiséḵ’w. *Her teeth are the color of blueberry juice.*

**oox̱ katság̱aa** noun *toothpick*

du **oox̱k’i.eetí** noun *his/her missing tooth*

a **oox̱ú** noun *its tooth*
·Haadaag̱ooji a oox̱ú daḵdigéix’. *Lion teeth are large.*

# « S »

**sá** particle *[interrogative - marks WH-questions]*
·Wáa yateeyi lingít sáwé wa.é? *What kind of person are you?*
·X'oon gaawx' sá? *At what time?*

**saa** noun *name*
·A<u>x</u> tláa saayí <u>k</u>u.aa áyá Shaaxeidí Tláa yóo áwé wduwasáa. *My mother's name was Shaaxeidi Tláa.*
·<u>X</u>'aháat kináak áwé át akawsix'óo, du saayí. *He nailed his name above the door.*

**SAA**[1] verb root

• **--- | yéi kwlisáa | ---**
--- | *it's narrow* | ---.
THEME: yéi ka-u-l-saa~ (state)
*for something (esp. container) to be narrow*
NOTES: This verb occurs in the imperfective only.
·Dagwatgiyáa lú yayát' <u>k</u>a yéi kwlisáa. *A hummingbird's beak is long and skinny.*

**SAA**[2] verb root

• **yéi aawasáa | --- | ---**
*s/he named him/her/it that* | --- | ---.
THEME. O-S-ø-saa~ (ø event)
*for S to name O; for S to nominate O*
NOTES: The difference between: yéi aawasáa "s/he named him/her/it that" and yéi aawasáakw "s/he called him/her/it that" is one of repetition. The former denotes a one-time event in which someone or something was given a name, while the latter depicts repeatedly calling someone or something by a name. Note that the latter form: yéi aawasáakw has the iterative suffix (-kw), which generally denotes a repeated action.
·A<u>x</u> tláa saayí <u>k</u>u.aa áyá Shaaxeidí Tláa yóo áwé wduwasáa. *My mother's name was Shaaxeidi Tláa.*
·Yéi áwé wduwasáa Kayáash Hít L'ukna<u>x</u>.ádich. *The Coho Salmon tribe has named it Platform House.*

• **yéi aawasáakw | yéi ayasáakw | ---**
*s/he called him/her/it that* | *s/he calls him/her/it that* | ---.
THEME: O-S-ø-sáakw (na state)
*for S to call O by a certain name*
NOTES: The difference between: yéi aawasáa "s/he named him/her/it that" and yéi aawasáakw "s/he called him/her/it that" is one of repetition. The former denotes a one-time event in which someone or something was given a name, while the latter depicts

repeatedly calling someone or something by a name. Note that the latter form: yéi aawasáakw has the iterative suffix (-kw), which generally denotes a repeated action.
·Yaa a<u>x</u> léelk'w a<u>x</u> tláa yinaaná<u>x</u> <u>K</u>éin yóo dusáagun yaa Xutsnoowúdá<u>x</u>. *My grandmother on my mother's side was called Ñéin, from Angoon.*
·Ldakát át áwé <u>k</u>u<u>x</u> dak'óol'in <u>x</u>waasáakw. *I said everything backwards.*

**SAA**[3] verb root

- **wudlisáa | (tlákw) yaa nalséin | ulséi<u>x</u>**
  *s/he rested; s/he's resting | s/he is (always) resting | s/he rests (regularly).*
  THEME: S-d-l-saa~ (ø event)
  *for S to rest*
  ·Aas seiyí áa wdlisáa. *He rested in the shelter of the tree.*
  ·<u>G</u>alsaayít áwé du yéi jineiyí a ná<u>k</u> woogoot. *She went away from her work so that she could rest.*

**saak** noun *eulachon; candlefish; hooligan*
·A <u>x</u>'éiná<u>x</u> áwé kadul.eesh wé <u>k</u>áas' kaadéi wé saak. *Those hooligan are strung through the mouth on the stick.*

**saak ee<u>x</u>í** noun *hooligan oil*

**sáaná<u>x</u>** noun *wind (blowing) from the south*

du **saayee** noun *underside of his/her knee; (inside of) his/her lower leg*

du **saayí** noun *his/her name; his/her namesake*

**sadaat'aay** noun *neck scarf; kerchief*
·Du gúk ká<u>x</u> ayaawayeesh du sadaat'aayí. *She pulled her scarf down over her ears.*

**sagú** noun *joy; happiness*
·Sagú yá<u>x</u> <u>k</u>aa yayík du.a<u>x</u>ji nooch héendei yaa ana.ádi. *Men's voices would always sound happy when they went to the sea.*

at **sa<u>g</u>ahaayí** noun *will; wish(es)*
VARIANTS: et se<u>g</u>ahaayí (C)

**saka.át** noun *necktie*

**sákw** adj. *future (noun), (noun) to be, for (noun)*
·Nás'k a doogú x'óow áwé du káa kak<u>g</u>wagéi k'oodás' sákw, wé <u>k</u>áa tlein. *It will take three leather blankets for the big man's shirt.*
·L'ook kaháagu áyá yak'éi kanat'á kanéegwál' sákw. *Coho salmon eggs are good for blueberry sauce.*

**sakwnéin** noun *flour; bread*
·Tléi<u>k</u>w <u>g</u>óot awsi.ée du sakwnéini. *She cooked her bannock without berries.*
·Sakwnéin áwé du <u>x</u>'éi<u>x</u> <u>x</u>atee<u>x</u> wé kals'áak. *I feed bread to the squirrel.*

**sakwnéin éewu** noun *(loaf of) bread*
·Wé sakwnéin éewu yan g̲a.eet eeg̲áa áwé x̲a.áa. *I am sitting, waiting for the bread to finish cooking.*

**sakwnéin katéix̲i** noun *porridge*

**sakwnéin kax̲'eiltí** noun *bread crumbs*

a **sákwti** noun *its handle (stick-like); its shaft (of spear, etc.)*
VARIANTS: a sáxwdi, a síxwdi (AtT), a súxdi (T), a súxti (TC)
·Ik̲náach'x̲ sitee wé lítaa sákwti. *The handle of that knife is brass.*

**sák̲s** noun *bow*

du **sáni** noun *his/her paternal uncle, cousin*
·Ax̲ éek' k̲a ax̲ sáni al'óoni een át has na.átjin. *My brother and my paternal uncle used to accompany hunters.*

**sankeit** noun *armor made of tough hide or wooden rods*

**Sanyaa K̲wáan** noun *people of Cape Fox, Saxman*

SÁTK verb root

- **woosátk | yasátk | kei sátkch**
*he/she/it was fast | he/she/it is fast | he/she/it gets fast (regularly).*
THEME: O-ø-sátk (ga state)
*for O to be fast (at doing things)*
·Yasátk aadéi ashigóogu yé wé kaldáal'. *The typist knows how to type fast.*

du **satú** noun *his/her voice*

a **sáxwdi** noun *its handle (stick-like); its shaft (of spear, etc.)*
VARIANTS: a síxwdi (AtT), a súxdi (T), a súxti (TC)

**sáx'** noun *cambium, sap scraped from inner bark*

at **sax̲án** noun *love (of things, of everything)*

du **sé** noun *his/her voice*

**sée** noun *doll*
·Hít kat'áayi yátx'i wé sée hídi káa yéi awa.oo. *He put the small shingles on that doll house.*

du **sée** noun *his/her daughter, cousin*
·Yóo áyú aawasáa du sée ax̲ tláa. *That's what my mother named her daughter.*
·Du séek' du x̲ánt uwagút. *Her daughter came to her.*

SEEK[1] verb root

- **yaawasík | --- | woosíkx̲**
*s/he is delayed | --- | s/he gets delayed (regularly).*

THEME: O-ya-ø-seek~ (ø event)
*for O to be delayed, prevented, held back from plans (often due to inclement weather)*

**séek** noun *belt*

**SEEN** verb root

- **awdlisín | --- | ---**
  *he/she/it hid; s/he's hiding | --- | ---.*
  THEME: a-S-d-l-seen~ (ø event)
  *for S to hide oneself, remain out of sight*
  ·Awdlisín chéx̲'i tóox'. *He is hiding in the shadows.*
  ·X'éedadi tóox' awdlisín. *She hid in a tree stump.*
- **awlisín | --- | alsínx̲**
  *s/he hid it; s/he's hiding it | --- | s/he hides it (regularly).*
  THEME: O-S-l-seen~ (ø event)
  *for S to hide, conceal, put O out of sight*

**seet** noun *dug-out canoe designed to go through shallow waters*
·Dúk̲ een dulyéix̲ seet yaakw. *The canoe is made out of cottonwood.*

**séet** noun *draw, gully, box canyon*

**séew** noun *rain*
VARIANTS: sóow (C)
·Wé aas seiyít wujixíx séew tóodáx̲. *She ran to the shelter of the tree to get out of the rain.*
·X̲at wulixwétl wé séew. *I'm tired of the rain.*

**séew kooshdaneit** noun *swallow*

**seig̲án** noun *tomorrow*
VARIANTS: seig̲ánin
·Seig̲án gé i tuwáa sigóo ax̲ een yéi jiyineiyí? *Do you want to work with me tomorrow?*
·Áx' k̲aa ée at dultóow yé áa yéi x̲at gug̲watée seig̲án. *I will be in school tomorrow.*

**seig̲ánin** noun *tomorrow*
VARIANTS: seig̲án

**seig̲atáanaa** noun *berrying basket or can hung around the neck, resting on the chest*

**SEIK̲'W** verb root

- **akawlisék̲'w | aklasék̲'w | aklasék̲'wx̲**
  *s/he dyed it | s/he is dying it | s/he dyes it (regularly).*
  THEME: O-ka-S-l-séik̲'w~ (ø act)
  *for S to stain, dye, color the surface of O*
  ·A yáanáx̲ áwé kaylisék̲'w yá néegwál'. *You tinted this paint too much.*

·Tléik̲w kahéeni áwé átx̲ dulyéix̲ kalsék̲'x̲u yís. *Berry juices are used for dyeing.*

- **kawdisék̲'w | --- | kadasék̲'wx̲**
  *it's dyed | --- | it's dyed (regluarly).*
  THEME: O-ka-d-séik̲'w~ (ø event)
  *for O to be stained, dyed*
  ·Du oox̲ kanat'á kahéeni yáx̲ kawdisék̲'w. *Her teeth are the color of blueberry juice.*

**séik̲'w** noun *the quick (the flesh under the outer skin)*

**seit** noun *necklace*

a **seiyí** RelationalNoun *the shelter of it; the lee of it; the (beach) area below it (a mountain, hill, etc.)*

**sgóon** noun *school*
·G̲ayéis' layeix̲íx̲ nax̲sateeyít sgóoni yoo uwagút. *He went to school to become an engineer.*
·Yú sgóon tl'átgi tlein, a góonnáx̲ dax̲yanaagóo wé káa. *The cars are traveling on the isthmus of the big school yard.*

**sgóonwaan** noun *student; pupil; scholar*
·Sgóonwaan atyátx'i has shayadihéin Yaakwdáatx'. *There are a lot of school children in Yakutat.*

**sitgawsáan** noun *noon*
·Gangukg̲áx̲i has du sitgawsáan atx̲aayí áwé. *The fish heads cooked around the fire are their lunch.*
·Yées t'á g̲ík̲si sitgawsáanx' has aawax̲áa. *They ate fresh king salmon barbequed over the fire at noon.*

**sít'** noun *glacier*
·Kichyaat ilk'wát'x̲ sít' yáx'. *Terns lay eggs by glaciers.*

**sít' tuxóodzi** noun *glacier bear*

**si.áat'i héen** noun *cold water*
·Ax̲ éek' si.áat'i héen goondáx̲ ayáayin. *My brother used to pack cold water from a spring.*
·Si.áat'i héen ín x'eesháa tóode akawsixaa. *She poured cold water into the bottle jug.*

**si.áax'u át** noun *pepper*

**sook̲** noun *peat moss*

**soos**[1] verb root

- **k̲ut akaawlisóos | --- | k̲ut kéi aklasóosch**
  *s/he lost them | --- | s/he loses them (regularly).*
  THEME: k̲ut O-ka-S-l-sóos (ga motion)
  *for S to lose (plural) O*

• **k̲ut has kaawasóos | --- | k̲ut kei has kasóosch**
*they are lost; they got lost | --- | they get lost (regularly).*
THEME: k̲ut O-ka-ø-sóos (ga event)
*for (plural) O (objects, people) to be lost*
·Wé k̲áa du jishagóoni k̲ut kaawasóos. *The man's tools are lost.*

**sóow (C)** noun *rain*
VARIANTS: séew

**stoox** noun *stove*
·X̲'aan yeenayát'ch wé yées stoox tóox'. *The fire lasts in the new stove.*
·Stoox káa yan sa.ín wé at téix̲i! *Set the broth on top of the stove!*

**sú** noun *bull kelp*

**Suk̲teeneidí** noun *Suk̲teeneidí, locally called "Dog Salmon"; a clan of the Raven moiety whose principal crest is the Dog Salmon*

**suk̲téitl'** noun *goose tongue*

# « S’ »

**s’aach** noun *shield fern*

**s’aag̲itunéekw (AtT)** noun *rheumatism*
VARIANTS: s’aag̲itunóok (TC)

**s’aak̲** noun *bone*
·Du gúkx’ tsú yéi aa wduwa.oo wéi s’aak̲ k̲’anoox̲. *They put the small bone labret in his ear too.*
·S’aak̲ áwé shux’áanáx̲ átx̲ wududliyéx̲ ax̲ léelk’w du k̲’anoox̲ú yís. *My grandmother's first labret was made out of bone.*

at **s’aan.ax̲w dzáas** noun *spear which binds rope around seal*

**s’áas’** noun *goldfinch, canary*

du **s’aatí** noun *his/her boss, master*
·Yées k̲áa áwé has du s’aatí. *Their boss is a young man.*

**s’áaw** noun *dungeness crab*
·Goosú á yana.áat’ani wé s’áaw a kát isa.eeyi k̲’wátl? *Where is the cover for the pot you're cooking the crab in?*

**s’áaxw** noun *hat*
·Kijook s’áaxw k̲udzitee. *There is a hawk hat.*
·A g̲óot woogoot du s’áaxu. *He went without his hat.*

**s’aax̲** noun *hoary marmot; groundhog, whistler*

**s’áax̲’** noun *ling cod*

**s’agwáat** noun *brown*
·Yán aas daadáx̲ kayeix̲ áwé átx̲ gag̲ilayéix̲ s’agwáat kasék̲’x̲u sákw. *Shavings from a hemlock tree is what you will use for the brown dye.*

**s’agwáat** noun *flaky surface of the outer bark of conifers, especially hemlock*

a **s’ak̲shutúk̲l’i** noun *cartilage, gristle at the end of its bones*

**s’ak̲tu.eex̲í** noun *his/her bone marrow*
VARIANTS: s’ak̲tu.eix̲í (C)

a **s’ak̲tu.eex̲í** noun *its bone marrow*
VARIANTS: a s’ak̲tu.eix̲í (C)

a **s’ak̲x̲’áak túk̲l’i** noun *cartilage, gristle between its bones*

**s’áx** noun *starfish*

**s'áxt'** noun *devil's club*

·Ax̱ jeet tán wé kaxágwaa yeit, yáa s'áxt' aan yéi nḵasaneiyít! *Hand me the mortar so I can use it on this devil's club!*

**s'é** noun *clay; alluvial silt*

**s'é** particle *first*

·Náakw s'é áa yéi kḵwa.oo ax̱ keey aag̱áa tsá wéi kashóok' gwéil. *I will put medicine on my knee first, then the heating pad.*

du **s'ee** noun *his/her eyebrow*

VARIANTS: du s'ei

**s'eek** noun *black bear*

·S'eek l'eedí tléil ulyát'. *A black bear's tail is short.*

·Wé s'eek gandaas'aají kúdi aawat'ei. *The black bear found a bee's nest.*

**s'eeḵ** noun *smoke*

VARIANTS: s'eiḵ

**s'eeḵ kawóot** noun *light bluish-gray trade bead(s)*

**s'eenáa** noun *lamp*

·Ux̱ganhéen s'eenáa káax' has daḵéis'in. *They used to sew by kerosene lamp.*

·S'eenáat akaawagán. *The light is on.*

**s'eenáa yaakw** noun *gas-powered boat*

S'EES verb root

- **aadé kawdlis'ées | aadé yaa kanals'ís | ---**

  *it's blowing in the wind there | it's blowing in the wind there | ---.*

  THEME: P-dé ka-l-s'ées~ (na motion)

  *for an object to be blown in the wind to P*

  ·Lidzée kayaaní a kaadéi kawuls'éesi wé laaḵ'ásk. *It's frustrating when leaves are blown onto the black seaweed.*

- **át wulis'ees | --- | ---**

  *it's blowing around; it blew around | --- | ---.*

  THEME: P-t O-l-s'ees~ (na motion)

  *for O to be blown around at P (by wind), to sail*

  ·Aan kwéiyi óoxjaa tóot wulis'ees. *A flag is blowing in the wind.*

  ·Du hídi kináak áwé át wulis'ees wé aan kwéiyi. *The flag is blowing around above his house.*

S'EET verb root

- **akaawas'ít | akas'éet | akas'ítx̱**

  *s/he bandaged it | s/he is bandaging it | s/he bandages it (regularly).*

  THEME: O-ka-S-ø-s'eet~ (ø act)

  *for S to bind up, wrap around, bandage O*

·Du keitl jíni akaawas'ít. *He bandaged his dog's paw.*
·Du jigúnl'i akaawas'ít. *He bandaged his wrist.*

**s'eex** noun *dirt; scrap(s); rubbish, trash, clutter; lint*

**S'EEX** verb root

- **wulis'íx | yaa nals'íx | las'íxx̱**
  *it aged | it's aging | it ages (regularly).*
  THEME: l-s'eex~ (ø event)
  *for animal matter to age, spoil to stage where still firm, but smelly*
  ·Wé x̱éel' wuls'eexí lichán. *When the slime rots it stinks.*

**s'éex'át** noun *shrimp*

**S'EEX'W** verb root

- **át akawlis'íx'w | --- | áx̱ aklas'éex'w**
  *s/he stuck it to it | --- | s/he sticks it to it (regularly).*
  THEME: P-t~ O-ka-S-l-s'éex'w~ (ø motion)
  *for S to stick O (esp. paper) to P*
  ·Du eetí a kax̱yeet akawlis'íx'w ḵaa yahaayí wé shaatk'átsk'u. *The young girl pasted a photo on the ceiling of her room.*

du **s'ei** noun *his/her eyebrow*
VARIANTS: du s'ee

**s'eiḵ** noun *smoke*
VARIANTS: s'eeḵ
·S'eiḵ x̱áat xáas'i áwé yak'éi g̱altóot idateení latseen sákw at eel'óoni. *When you're out hunting a piece of smoked fish skin in your pocket is good for energy.*
·L s'eiḵx usiteeyi neil áyá. *This is a smoke-free home.*

**S'EIḴ** verb root

- **áx̱ akawlis'eiḵ | --- | áx̱ aklas'éḵx**
  *s/he tanned it | --- | s/he tans it (regularly).*
  THEME: áx̱ a-ka-S-l-s'eiḵ~ (na event)
  *for S to tan, smoke, cure something by placing in smoke*
  VARIANTS: -s'eeḵ~ (An)
  ·Áx̱ akawdudlis'eig̱i ishḵeen du tuwáa sagóowun ax̱ éesh. *My dad used to like smoked black cod.*
  ·Téil yéi aya.óo at doogú aklas'éḵxi yís. *She is using dry wood for smoking that hide.*
- **sh x̱'awdis'eiḵ | sh x̱'adas'eiḵ | yoo sh x̱'adis'eiḵk**
  *s/he smoked | s/he's smoking | s/he smokes (regularly).*
  THEME: sh x̱'a-S-d-s'eiḵ (na act)
  *for S to smoke (cigarettes, etc.)*
  ·Sh x̱'áx̱das'eiḵ. *I smoke.*

**s'eiḵ daakahídi** noun *smokehouse (with smoke piped in from outside)*
VARIANTS: s'eiḵ hídi, s'eiḵ daakéedi (C)

·Awdziǥeiwu ǥaat s'eiḵ hídi yeex̱ ash ayaawatée. *She hung the sockeye salmon that she netted in the smokehouse.*

**s'eiḵdaakeit** noun *pipe (for tobacco)*

**S'EIL'** verb root

- **aawas'éil' | yaa anas'él' | yoo ayas'él'k**
  *s/he tore it | s/he's tearing it | s/he tears it (regularly).*
  THEME: O-S-ø-s'éil' (na event)
  *for S to tear O*
- **akaawas'éil' | akas'él't | yei akas'éil'ch**
  *s/he tore it | s/he is tearing it | s/he tears it (regularly).*
  THEME: O-ka-S-ø-s'éil' (ǥa act)
  *for S to tear, tear up, rip off O; for S to peel off O (bark from a tree)*
- **ax̱'eiwas'él' | ax̱'as'él'x̱ | ---**
  *s/he held it open | s/he is holding it open | ---.*
  THEME: O-x̱'a-S-ø-s'éil'~ (ø act)
  *for S to tear O away (from hook); for S to stretch or hold O (opening) open*
  NOTES: With this verb, it is best to name the thing being held open. For example: gwéil ax̱'eiwas'él' "s/he held the bag open". Otherwise, it sounds like someone is holding their mouth open with their hands.
  ·A x̱'é áwé aawasháat wé ḵáa tlein, tle ax̱'éiwas'él'. *The big man grabbed its mouth and tore it apart.*
- **kawdis'éil' | --- | yei kdas'él'ch**
  *it's torn | --- | it gets torn (regularly).*
  THEME: ka-d-s'éil' (ǥa event)
  *for something to be torn up*
  ·Kawdis'éil' ax̱ ǥeiwú. *My net is all torn up.*
- **x̱aat awlis'él' | x̱aat als'éil' | x̱aat als'éil'x̱**
  *s/he pulled up spruce roots | s/he pulls up spruce roots; s/he is pulling up spruce roots | s/he pulls up spruce roots (regularly).*
  THEME: O-S-l-s'éil'~ (ø act)
  *for S to tear up, pull up O (roots)*
  ·X̱aat áyá gax̱tulas'éil'. *We're going to dig spruce roots.*

**s'éil'** noun *wound*

**s'éil' tsáax'** noun *rubber gloves*

**s'éix̱wani** noun *lichen that hangs down from trees*

**s'éix̱wani** noun *yellow*

**s'élasheesh** noun *flathead duck*

**s'él'** noun *rubber*

·Ḵaa kasán tayeet shukatáni áwé yak'éi wéi s'él' kinaak.át. *A raincoat that hangs below the waist is the best.*

**s'éx̱** noun *swamp hemlock*

**s'igeek̲áawu yaagí** noun *red mussel*

**s'igeidí** noun *beaver*
VARIANTS: s'ikyeidí
·S'igeidí k̲a yáay a káa kashaxít wé at doogú x'óow! *Draw a Beaver and whale design on the leather blanket!*
·S'igeidí káx̱ g̲aatáa héen táakde awsitee. *He set a trap underwater for beaver.*

**s'igeidí áayi** noun *beaver dam*

**s'igeidí x̱aayí** noun *beaver's den*

**s'ig̲eek̲áawu** noun *ghost*
VARIANTS: s'igeek̲áawu (T)

**s'ig̲eek̲áawu tléig̲u** noun *various odd looking, tasteless, or otherwise undesirable berries, some poisonous; meaning varies locally, incl. twistedstalk (Streptopus species), snowberry (Symphoricarpos albus), fool's huckleberry (Menziesia ferruginea), etc.*

**s'íksh** noun *false hellebore*
NOTES: Warning: extremely poisonous

**s'ikshaldéen** noun *Hudson Bay tea*
NOTES: Warning: the similar bog-rosemary (Andromeda polifolia), and bog-laurel (Kalmia microphylla subspecies occidentalis) are toxic, they lack brown rusty hairs under the leaves and have pink flowers)

**s'ik̲daakeit** noun *tobacco pipe*
VARIANTS: s'eik̲daakeit

**s'ín** noun *carrot*
·Anahoo s'ín teen wudustaayí yak'éi. *Turnip boiled with carrots is good.*

**s'ísaa** noun *cloth; sailcloth*
·S'ísaa gwéil tóox' duhoonín kóox. *Rice used to be sold in cloth bags.*
·S'ísaa k̲áas' hoon daakahídidáx̱ aawa.oo. *She bought a yard of fabric from the store.*

**s'ísaa hít** noun *tent*
·Yan awsinéi du s'ís'aa hídi eetí. *He fixed up the place for his tent.*

**s'ísaa yaakw** noun *sailboat*
·Ax̱ éesh kak'dakwéiy s'aatíx̱ wusitee s'ísaa yaakw káx'. *My father became the captain of the sailboat.*
·Anóoshi aan kwéiyi áwé át wududziyík̲ wé s'ísaa yaakw x̱uká. *They raised a Russian flag on the deck of that sailboat.*

**s'íx'** noun *dish; plate*

·Wé s'íx' g̱áax'w a káa yéi yatee. *There are herring eggs on that plate.*
·S'íx' x̱oot ilt'ách déi! *Wash up the dishes now! (Lit: Slap (up) the dishes now).*

**s'íx'g̱aa** noun *moss*

**s'íx' ḵ'áatl'** noun *plate*

VARIANTS: s'íx' t'áal' (C)
·Ít'chi s'íx' ḵ'áatl' du jeewú. *She has a glass plate.*

du **s'óog̱u** noun *his/her rib*

·Jánwu dleeyí aatlein yak'éi, gwál wé a s'óog̱u. *Mountain goat meat is really good, especially the ribs.*

**s'ook** noun *barnacle*

S'OOK verb root

- **akawlis'úk | aklas'úk | aklas'úkx̱**

*s/he fried it | s/he's frying it | s/he fries it (regularly).*
THEME: O-ka-S-l-s'ook~ (ø act)
*for S to toast O (bread); for S to fry O (usually till crisp)*
VARIANTS: O-ka-S-l-s'éekw~ (ø act)
·Gishoo taayí ḵa dleey wóosh teen akawlis'úk. *She fried the meat with bacon.*
·Xáanaa atx̱aayí yís g̱áx̱ akawlis'úk. *She fried rabbit for dinner.*

**s'óos'** noun *pole(s) on which fish are hung for drying in smokehouse*

**s'óos'ani** noun *pine cone, spruce cone*

VARIANTS: s'óos'eni (C)

**s'oow** noun *greenstone*

**s'oow** noun *green, light blue*

·Wé ganyal'óot' s'oow yáx̱ yatee. *That flame is green.*

S'OOW verb root

- **aawas'úw | as'úw | ---**

*s/he chopped it | s/he's chopping it; s/he chops it | ---.*
THEME: O-S-ø-s'óow~ (na act)
*for S to chop O (esp. chopping down trees, chopping off branches)*
NOTES: Can also be used metaphorically to mean to terminate something.
·Aasdaag̱áadli aax̱ aawas'úw. *He chopped off the tree fungus.*
·Hít tayeegáas'i yís aas aawas'úw. *He chopped down trees for pilings.*

**s'oow x̱út'aa** noun *stone adze*

**s'uḵkasdúk** noun *solid-ribbed brown bear*

**s’ús’** noun *harlequin duck*

**s’úwaa** noun *awl; chopping block*

# « Sh »

du **shá** noun *his/her head*
VARIANTS: du shán
·K̲'anashgidéi k̲áa áwé kíndei alshát du shá. *The poor man is holding his head high.*

a **shá** noun *its head*
·Wé k̲áa dzísk'u shaayí gangooknáx̲ as.eeyín. *He used to cook moose head next to the campfire.*

**shaa** noun *mountain*
·Wé shaa dayéen áayáx̲ uwahán. *He turned around to face the mountain.*
·Shaa litká aadé dax̲duwatéen wé watsíx. *The caribou are visible on the mountain ridge.*

SHAA[1] verb root

- **aawasháa | --- | ---**
*s/he married him/her; s/he is married | --- | ---.*
THEME: O-S-ø-shaa~ (ø event)
*for S to marry O*
·Sheet'kaadé k̲u.aa áyá wdusháayin Teik̲weidéech áyá. *She was married to a man from Sitka from Teik̲weidí clan.*
·Sheendé! Táach ikg̲washáa. *Get up! You're going to oversleep. (Lit: Sleep will marry you.)*

- **wooch has wudisháa | --- | ---**
*they married each other | --- | ---.*
THEME: wooch S-d-shaa~ (ø event)
*for S (two people) to marry each other*
NOTES: Either wooch or woosh can be used with this verb.

- **wuduwasháa | --- | ---**
*s/he got married | --- | ---.*
THEME: O-du-ø-shaa~ (ø event)
*for O to get married*

**sháa** noun *women*
·Yáa k̲utaanx' aadé k̲ugax̲tootéen ixkée ch'a g̲aax̲tusatéen wé sháa. *This summer we are going to travel down south just to see the girls.*
·Ha yéi áwé has duwasáakw K̲'eik̲'w Sháa Xunaadáx̲. *They are called the Sea Pigeon gals from Hoonah.*

**sháach'** noun *young herring*

a **shaadí** noun *its sprouts, fleshy leaves growing toward the top of the stem (e.g. of bear root)*

**sháak** noun *timothy grass (used for basket decoration)*
·K̲ákw yéi daané yís áwé yéi daax̲ané yá sháak. *I am collecting this timothy grass for making baskets.*

**shaak̲** noun *snag; driftlog, driftwood*

**sháal** noun *fish trap*

**shaan** noun *old age*

**shaan** noun *old person*

SHAAN verb root

• **wudishán | yaa ndashán | ---**
*s/he is old | s/he's getting old | ---.*
THEME: O-d-shaan~ (ø event)
*for O to show signs of old age (esp. grey hair), for O to become old, age*
·Yaa indashán óosh gé! *If only you were getting old!*

**shaanák'w** noun *(little) old person*

**shaanáx̲** noun *mountain valley; valley*
·Shaanáx̲ yaawashóo wé k̲aa x̲'oos deiyí. *The foot trail extends through the valley.*

**shaa seiyí** noun *the shelter of a mountain, area on the beach below a mountain*

SHAASH verb root

• **woosháash | yei nasháash | yei sháashch**
*it wore out | it's wearing out | it wears out (regularly).*
THEME: ø-sháash (g̲a event)
*for something to wear out by continuous friction*
·Yá washéen katág̲ayi woosháash. *This connecting rod wore out.*
·Du jáaji a dzaasí yei nasháash. *The thongs of his snowshoes are wearing thin.*

**shaa shakée** noun *mountaintop; on top of the mountain*
VARIANTS: shaa shekée (C)
·Wé shaa shakéede duwatéen wé g̲agaan x̲'usyee. *The ray of sunlight can be seen on the mountain top.*

SHAAT verb root

• **aawasháat | --- | kei ashátch**
*s/he caught it | --- | s/he catches it (regularly).*
THEME: O-S-ø-sháat~ (ga event)
*for S to catch O; for S to grab, take hold of, snatch O; for S to arrest O; for S to trap O*
·S'eik̲ ash daa dleeyí aawasháat. *S/he's addicted to smoking. (Lit: Smoke took hold of his/her body.)*
·K̲únáx̲ haa téix̲' aawasháat. *It really caught our hearts.*

- **át ayawashát | aadé yaa ayanashát | ---**
  *the wind hit it in gusts | the wind is hitting it in gusts | ---.*
  THEME: P-t~ a-ya-ø-shát (ø motion)
  *for the wind, weather to move in gusts to P*
  ·Haa kát ayawashát wé xóon. *The north wind hit us in gusts.*
- **awlisháat | alshát | yei alshátch**
  *s/he held it | s/he is holding it | s/he holds it (regularly).*
  THEME: O-S-l-sháat~ (g̱a act)
  *for S to hold, retain O in one's grasp; for S to capture, hold O captive*
  ·Wé dóosh du jín dleit kaa̱x̱ kínde alshát. *That cat is holding its paw up off the snow.*
  ·Wéi yaakw yax̱ak'áaw kas'éet áa yéi du.oowú, k'idéin yéi agux̱lasháat. *If a screw is put in the thwart of the boat, it will hold pretty well.*

**shaatk'** noun *young woman (not married)*
·Ginjichwáan aanídáx̱ áwé wé shaatk'. *That young woman is from Canada.*
·Kaxéel' sháade hánix̱ sitee wé shaatk'. *The young girl is a troublemaker.*

**shaatk'átsk'u** noun *girl*
VARIANTS: shaatk'iyátsk'u, shaatk'iyétsk'u (C)
·Shaatk'átsk'ux̱ x̱at siteeyí ax̱ x̱'é k'éiyin wé tl'aadéin.aa. *When I was a little girl, I used to love turnips.*
·K̲únáx̱ ánk'w áwé wé shaatk'átsk'u. *The young girl is a real crybaby.*

du **shaatk'í** noun *his/her girlfriend*
·Wé yées shaawát du shaatk'íx̱ sitee. *That young woman is his girlfriend.*

**shaatk'iyátsk'u** noun *girl*
VARIANTS: shaatk'iyétsk'u (C), shaatk'átsk'u

**shaaw** noun *gumboots; chiton*
·K̲éix̱'dei nax̱took̲oox̱ shaawg̱áa. *Let's travel to Kake for some gumboots.*

du **shaawádi** noun *his old lady (wife)*
VARIANTS: du shaawadí (TC)

**shaawát** noun *woman*
·Ch'a yóo Anóoshi Aaníx' yaa German shaawát áyá du x̱ánx' yéi wootee. *While in Russia he was with a German woman.*
·Wé yées shaawát du shaatk'íx̱ sitee. *That young woman is his girlfriend.*

du **sháawu** noun *his/her clan sister*

**shaax'wsáani** noun *girls, young women*
·Wáa yateeyi aa shaax'wsáani sá ash koodlénx̱aa? *What kind of girls does he find tempting?*

**shaax̱** noun *gray currant, stink currant*
·Shaax̱ a.éen haa hídi daatx̱ kanéegwál' sákw. *She is picking gray currants from around our house for a berry and salmon egg dish.*

·Aatlein shaax̲ kanéegwál' yéi x̲wsinei. *I made a lot of gray currant berry sauce.*

**shaayáal** noun *kind of hawk*

**shaa yadaa** noun *mountainside; around the mountain*

**sháchgi tléig̲u** noun *swamp berries*
·A yee.ádi gataan sháchgi tléig̲u yís! *Carry a container for swamp berries!*

**sháchk** noun *swamp*
·Sháchgi káa ka.éix̲ dáxw. *Lowbush cranberries grow in the meadow.*

**sháchk kax̲'wáal'i** noun *cottongrass, Alaska cotton, swamp cotton*

**sháchk ka.aasí** noun *stunted tree in swamp; jackpine, swamp spruce*

**shach'éen** noun *hair ribbon*

a **shadaa** RelationalNoun *around the top of it (object with rounded top)*

du **shadaadoogú** noun *his/her scalp*

**shadaa.át** noun *headscarf, kerchief covering the head*

**shadakóox̲'** noun *ceremonial woven root hat with a stack of basket-like cylinders on top*

a **shagóon** noun *its what it is (to be) made of; its parts, components, materials*

du **shagóon** noun *ancestor(s) of his/her clan or nation; his/her background, heredity*

du **shakakóoch'i** noun *his/her curly hair*
VARIANTS: du shekekóoch'i (C)

**shákdéi** particle *perhaps, probably*

a **shakée** RelationalNoun *top of it (something with a rounded top, as a mountain); above it; (elevated) over it*
·Gooch shakéex' wutusiteen wé sheech dzísk'w. *We saw the cow moose on top of the hill.*
·Daax'oonínáx̲ k̲áa shaa shakéede al'óon has woo.aat. *Four men went up on the mountain hunting.*

**shakee.át** noun *headdress, dance hat*
·A x̲'adaadzaayí áwé átx̲ dulyéix̲ shakee.át daax'. *Its whiskers are used for a headdress.*

**shakéil'** noun *dandruff*
·Dleit yáx̲ yatee i shakéil'i. *Your dandruff is white.*

**shákw** noun *strawberry*
VARIANTS: shíkw
·Aatlein shákw áwé wutuwa.ín kat'ákx̲i yéi nax̲tusaneit. *We picked a*

*lot of strawberries so we can make dried berry patties.*
·Tlei déix̱ ḵ'ateil yáx̱ áwé wutusineix̱ shákw kahéeni. *We just saved two gallons of the strawberry juice.*

**shak'áts'** noun *double-ended dagger*

**shak'únts'** noun *deer sprouting horns*

**shál** noun *spoon*

**shalas'áaw** noun *deer with full-grown antlers*

du **shaláx̱'** noun *back of his/her head at the base*

**shals'áaw** noun *deer or other ruminant with full-grown horns*
VARIANTS: shalas'áaw

**shaltláax̱** noun *nucleus of emerging river island; reef above high tide level*

du **shanáa** noun *over his/her head; covering his/her head*

**shanax̱wáayi** noun *axe*
VARIANTS: shanx̱wáayi

**shanax̱wáayi yádi** noun *hatchet*

**Shangukeidí** noun *Shangukeidí, locally known as "Thunderbird"; a clan of the Eagle moiety whose principal crest is the Thunderbird*
·X'átgu áwé Shangukeidí has du at óowux̱ sitee. *The dogfish is an artifact of the Thunderbiird people.*
·Xeitl naax̱ has sitee Shangukeidí. *The Shangukeidí are Thunderbird.*

du **shashaaní** noun *gray hair*
VARIANTS: du sheshaaní (C)

du **shát** noun *his wife*

**shataag̱áa** noun *deer or other ruminant having a horn with only one point*

du **shátx̱** noun *her older sister, cousin*

du **shax̱aawú** noun *his/her hair*
·X̱'aan ch'éen i shax̱aawú káx' kei kg̱wak'éi. *A red ribbon in your hair would be good.*
·Ḵúnáx̱ áwé ḵ'asigóo i shax̱aawú, a kát akawdagaaní. *Your hair is really beautiful when the sun shines on it.*

**shax̱dáḵw** noun *man-eating shark (legendary)*
VARIANTS: shux̱dáḵw, shax̱dáḵ (At)

**shax̱'ée x'wál'** noun *hair pin*

at **shax̱ishdi dzáas** noun *spear for clubbing*

**shax̱'út'aa** noun *fishing rod*

**shax̲'wáas' (T)** noun *bald spot; bald head*

**shayéen** noun *nail*

**shayéinaa** noun *anchor*

**shayeit** noun *pillow*
·Shayeit a kát satéen káa x̲ex̲x̲'u yeit . *The pillow is lying on the bed.*

**sh daxash washéen** noun *chainsaw*

**shé** noun *blood*
VARIANTS: shí
·Shí anax̲ naadaa wé taan geení. *There is blood coming from the sea lion's tail flippers.*
·Shé a x̲oodé ayatéen du x̲'astóox̲u. *He sees blood in his sputum.*

**shé** particle *[expression of mild surprise]*
VARIANTS: shéi

SHEE[1] verb root

- **aag̲áa k̲oowashee | aag̲áa k̲ushée | aag̲áa yoo k̲uyasheek**
*s/he looked for it | s/he is looking for it | s/he looks for it (regularly).*
THEME: P-g̲áa k̲u-S-ø-shee~ (na act)
*for S to search for, look for, hunt for, seek P*
·Ax̲ ji.eetíg̲aa áyá k̲ux̲ashée. *I'm looking for my handiwork.*
·Íng̲aa k̲ushée. *He is looking for flint.*
- **át awdishée | --- | ---**
*s/he hopes for it | --- | ---.*
THEME: át a-S-d-shee~ (ø event)
*for S to hope, desire and expect something*
·Yéi át ax̲wdishée iwulnáalx̲i. *I wish you wealth.*
- **át k̲uwashée | át k̲ushée | ---**
*s/he searched there | s/he is searching there | ---.*
THEME: P-t k̲u-S-ø-shee~ (ø act)
*for S to search at P*
·T'áa kát k̲ushí ax̲ jeeyís - k̲ut kax̲waag̲éex' ax̲ kawóot ka.íshayi! *Look on the floor for me - I lost my needle!*
- **át uwashée | --- | áx̲ shee**
*s/he touched it | --- | s/he touches it (regularly).*
THEME: át~ S-ø-shee~ (ø motion)
*for S to touch, take, pick up*
·Ch'a g̲óot k̲áa at óowu, tléil áx̲ ooshee. *You don't touch another person's possessions.*
- **ax̲ éet wudishée | ax̲ eedé yaa ndashéen | ax̲ éex̲ dashee**
*he/she/it is helping me; s/he helped me | he/she/it is beginning to help me |*

*he/she/it helps me (regularly).*
THEME: N éet~ S-d-shee~ (ø event)
*for S (person, medicine, etc.) to help, give help to, assist N*
·Hú áwé ax̱ éet wudishée. *It is he who helped me.*
·G̱ayéis' layeix̱í jeedé x̱'awditaan du éet g̱adasheet. *She telephoned the blacksmith to help her.*

**SHEE**[2] verb root

- **aawashee | ashí | ---**
  *s/he sang it | s/he sings it; s/he is singing it | ---.*
  THEME: O-S-ø-shee~ (ga act)
  *for S to sing O*
  ·X̱'agáax' daakahídix' áwé at kashéex̱' shí áa dushí. *Songs of praise are sung in church.*
- **at wooshee | at shí | ---**
  *s/he sang | s/he sings; s/he is singing | ---.*
  THEME: at S-ø-shee~ (ga act)
  *for S to sing*
  ·Dáx̱náx̱ naa sháadi nák̲x'i wé at yátx'i has du jeeyís has at wooshee. *Two chiefs sang for the children.*
  ·Jilk̲áat K̲wáan has at shí. *The Chilkat people are singing.*

**Shee At'iká K̲wáan** noun *people of Sitka*
VARIANTS: Sheet'ká K̲wáan

**sheech** adj. *female (animal)*
VARIANTS: shich
·Gooch shakéex' wutusiteen wé sheech dzísk'w. *We saw the cow moose on top of the hill.*
·Wé áak'w déint áwé át woogoot wé sheech dzísk'u tlein. *The big cow moose was walking around in the vicinity of the pond.*

**Sh eelk'átl'!** interj. *Shut up!; Be quiet!*

**sheen** noun *wooden bailer (for boat)*

**shéen** noun *large wooden spoon*

**sheen x̱'ayee** noun *dipper (for dipping water)*

**Sheet'ká** noun *Sitka*
·Sheet'kaadé k̲u.aa áyá wdusháayin Teik̲weidéech áyá. *She was married to a man from Sitka from Teik̲weidí clan.*
·Wéi Sheet'kaadáx̱ adátx'i at gutóox' áwé has du ée at dultóow. *The kids from Sitka are taught out in the wilderness.*

**sheexw** noun *close quarter bow and arrow*

at **shéex'i** noun *singers, choir*
VARIANTS: et shéex'i (C)

**sheey** noun *stick*
VARIANTS: sheey ka<u>k</u>áas'i

**sheey** noun *limb, primary branch; limb knot*

at **shéeyi** noun *singer*
VARIANTS: et shéeyi (C)

**sheey ka<u>k</u>áas'i** noun *splinter, sliver*
·Sheey ka<u>k</u>áas'i du jíndá<u>x</u> kei aawayísh. *She pulled a splinter out of her hand.*
·Du tl'ei<u>k</u>t yawdi<u>g</u>iji sheey ka<u>k</u>áas'i áx' wudli<u>k</u>ít'. *It got infected where the splinter poked her finger.*

**sheey tukagoodlí** noun *limb knot*

**sheey woolí** noun *knot hole*

a **sheidí** noun *its horn*

**sheishóo<u>x</u>** noun *rattle (of shaman)*
·Ch'eet sheishóo<u>x</u> áwé akaawach'ák'w. *She carved a murrelet rattle.*
·Sheishóo<u>x</u> áwé akaawach'ák'w, kéel a káa yéi aawa.oo. *He carved a rattle and put a murrelet on it.*

**sheixw** noun *close quarter bow and arrow*
VARIANTS: sheexw

SHEI<u>X</u>' verb root

- **akaawashé<u>x</u>' | akashéi<u>x</u>' | ---**
*s/he praised him/her | s/he is praising him/her | ---.*
THEME: O-ka-S-ø-shéi<u>x</u>' (ø act)
*for S to praise, glorify O; for S to approve, commend O; for S to comment on O*
VARIANTS: -shée<u>x</u>' (An)
·Kawduwashí<u>x</u>' haa sháade háni. *Our leader was really praised.*

**shéi<u>x</u>'w** noun *red alder*

**shéi<u>x</u>'w** noun *orange (in color)*

**shéiyi** noun *Sitka spruce*

**she<u>x</u>'wtáax'i** noun *bright red or orange*

**Sh<u>g</u>agwei** noun *Skagway*

at **shí** noun *music, singing, song*
VARIANTS: et shí (C)
·Ginjichwáan k'isáani áwé, wéix' has at shí. *The young British men are singing there.*
·A ná<u>k</u> yaa nagúdi yaa shukanashéen. *She is singing as she is leaving it behind.*

**shí** noun *song*

·Shí áwé shukḵwalax̱óox̱. *I'm going to compose a song.*
·X̱'agáax' daakahídix' áwé at kashéex̱' shí áa dushí. *Songs of praise are sung in church.*

**shich** adj. *female (animal)*

VARIANTS: sheech

at **shí ḵóok** noun *radio, phonograph, stereo, music box, ipod; any device that plays music*

·Yóo tliyaa aasdéi ksaxát wéi kaxées' ax̱ at shí ḵóok gúgu yís! *Attach the wire to that tree over there for my radio antenna!*
·Anóoshi x̱'asheeyí at shí ḵóok tóode too.áx̱jin. *We used to hear Russian songs on the radio.*

a **shís'ḵ** noun *its green wood (of tree)*

a **shís'ḵ** noun *its raw (flesh or meat); rare (meat)*

**sh kadax'áshti hít** noun *sawmill*

**sh kahaadí** adj. *crazy; insane; disturbed; mentally unbalanced*

**sh kalneegí** noun *preacher*

**shkalneek** noun *story*

·X̱éet' a daat shkalneek ḵudzitee. *There is a story about a giant clam.*
·Tlél kei gux̱lats'áa i daat sh kalneek. *Gossip about you is not going to smell good.*

**sh kalyéiyi** noun *prostitute*

SHOO[1] verb root

- **--- | áx̱ g̱aashóo | ---**

  --- | *it's hanging there* | ---.
  THEME: P-x̱ ø-shoo~ (g̱a motion)
  *for a bulky item to hang, extend down along P*
  NOTES: This verb is one of a small set of motion verbs with extensional imperfective forms (Leer, 1991). It is distinguished by an imperfective form which requires the conjugation prefix, in this case g̱a-.
  ·Du doonyaax̱ k'oodás'i áx̱ g̱aashóo. *His undershirt is hanging out.*

- **áx̱ kei wlishóo | --- | ---**

  *it extends up there* | --- | ---.
  THEME: P-x̱ kei l-shóo~ (ø motion)
  *for a complex object (esp. road) to extend up to P*
  ·Dzeit áx̱ kei wlishóo. *The ladder extends up there.*

- **áx̱ yaawashóo | --- | ---**

  *it extends around it* | --- | ---.
  THEME: P-x̱ ya-u-ø-shoo~ (ø motion)

*for a slender item (esp. road) to extend around, along P*
·Héen t'ikáx̱ yaawashóo ḵaa x̱'oos deiyí. *The foot trail goes beside the river.*
·Shaanáx̱ yaawashóo wé ḵaa x̱'oos deiyí. *The foot trail extends through the valley.*

SHOOCH verb root

• **wudishúch | dashóoch | dashúchx̱**
*s/he bathed | s/he is bathing | s/he bathes (regularly).*
THEME: S-d-shooch~ (ø act)
*for S to take a bath*
·Ús'aa een daa dushóoch *People bathe with soap.*

**shóogunáx̱** Adverb *(at) first; originally; in the beginning*

SHOOK' verb root

• **kawdlishúk' | --- | kalshúk'x̱**
*it cramped; it's cramping | --- | it cramps (regularly).*
THEME: O-ka-d-l-shóok'~ (ø event)
*for O to have cramps; for O to get shocked (by electricity)*
·Ax̱ x̱'oos kawdlishúk'. *My foot got a cramp.*
·Du g̱áts kalshúk'x̱. *His thighs cramp regularly.*

at **shooḵ** noun *laughter*

SHOOḴ verb root

• **at wooshooḵ | at shooḵ | ---**
*s/he laughed | s/he laughs; s/he is laughing | ---.*
THEME: at S-ø-shooḵ (na act)
*for S to laugh; for S to smile (often with laughter)*

a **shoowú** RelationalNoun *part of it; half of it*
·Du hídidáx̱ kaay shoowú yéi kunaaléi hoon daakahídi. *The store is a half mile from her house.*

**shoox̱'** noun *robin-like bird*

**shóo yax̱** Adverb *turning over endwise*

**Shtax'héen** noun *Stikine River*

**shtéen káa** noun *steam engine, train*
·A kayéikg̱aa áwé ḵuntoos.áx̱ch shtéen káa haadé yaa naḵúx̱u. *We always listen for the sound of the steam engine when it's coming.*

**sh tuwáa kasyéiyi** noun *tourist*

a **shú** RelationalNoun *the end of it*
·Yá ax̱ l'eix̱ k'oodás' a wán shóot at ḵá! *Sew something to the edge of my dance shirt!*

du **shuká** noun *in front of him/her; his/her geneology, history; his/her ancestors*

a **shuká** RelationalNoun *front of it; ahead of it*
·Cháatl tíx'i yaa (ha)s a shuká nak̲úx̲. *They're setting halibut gear.*
·K̲eex̲'é shukát áwé shoodanookch ax̲ léelk'w. *My grandfather wakes up before dawn.*

**shukalx̲aají** noun *troller*
VARIANTS: shukelx̲aají (C)

**shunax̲wáayi** noun *axe*
·Du jix̲ánx' yan satán wé shunax̲wáayi! *Leave the axe near him!*

du **shutóox̲'** noun *outer side of his/her foot up to the anklebone*

a **shutú** RelationalNoun *(in) the corner, (on or along) the edge, end of it*
·K̲óok shutú aawatséx̲. *She died. (Lit: S/he kicked the edge of the box.)*

a **shuwadaa** RelationalNoun *around it (bypassing it, avoiding it); around the end of it*

a **shuwee** RelationalNoun *the foot of it; below it (raised place); flat area at the end of it (lake); down from the crest of it (slope); the end of it (dock)*
VARIANTS: a shuyee

**shux'áanáx̲** Adverb *(at) first, originally*
·Shux'áanáx̲ kaldaag̲éináx̲ áwé dugwáal yá shí. *The drumming starts out slow in this song.*
·S'aak̲ áwé shux'áanáx̲ átx̲ wududliyéx̲ ax̲ léelk'w du k̲'anoox̲ú yís. *My grandmother's first labret was made out of bone.*

a **shuyee** RelationalNoun *the foot of it; below it (raised place); flat area at the end of it (lake); down from the crest of it (slope); the end of it (dock)*
VARIANTS: a shuwee

**sh yáa awudanéiyi** noun *respected person; gentleman; lady*

# « T »

**-t** postpos. *(resting) at; coming to, arriving at; moving about*

NOTES: -t has different meanings depending on what verb it occurs with. With "sit" or "stand" it means "at"; with (ø-) conjugation motion verbs it means "coming to, arriving at"; with na-conjugation motion verbs it means "moving around, about".

·Gootl kát áa wé g̱áx̱. *The rabbit is sitting on a mound.*

·Háas' du éet yéi uwanéi yá yagiyee. *He has been vomiting today.*

**tá** noun *sleep*

·Du taayí yoo x̱'ayatánk. *She talks in her sleep.*

·Sheendé! Táach ikg̱washáa. *Get up! You're going to oversleep. (Lit: Sleep will marry you.)*

TAA[1] verb root

- **wootaa | tá | teix̱**

  *s/he slept | s/he is sleeping | s/he sleeps (regularly).*

  THEME: S-ø-taa~ (na act)

  *for (singular) S to sleep, sleep alone*

  ·Haaw yan awli.át a káa ng̱ataayít. *He put branches down so he could sleep on them.*

- **a yáanáx̱ yaawatáa | --- | ---**

  *s/he overslept | --- | ---.*

  THEME: a yáanáx̱ ya-u-S-ø-táa~ (ø motion)

  *for S to oversleep*

  ·A yáanáx̱ yaawatáa. *She slept in.*

TAA[3] verb root

- **awsitáa | asteix̱ | asteix̱**

  *s/he steamed it | s/he is steaming it | s/he steams it (regularly).*

  THEME: O-S-s-taa~ (ø act)

  *for S to boil, steam O (food, esp. meat)*

  ·Teey woodí dustéix̱. *Yellow cedar bark is boiled.*

  ·Anahoo s'ín teen wudustaayí yak'éi. *Turnip boiled with carrots is good.*

a **táak** RelationalNoun *the bottom of it (a cavity)*

·Wé g̱ayéis' tíx' áwé du jín táakt yawdig̱ích. *The steel cable poked him in the hand.*

**táakw** noun *winter; year*

·Shayadihéin tl'áxch' táakwde yaa ḵunahéini. *There are a lot of dead branches when it becomes winter.*

·Oodzikaayi ḵáa áyá táakwx' gug̱waláaxw. *A lazy man will starve in the winter.*

**taakw aanási** noun *jellyfish*

**táakw niyís** noun *(in preparation) for winter*
·At toox̱'áan áyá táakwni yís, kaldáanaaḵx̱ haa nasteech. *We are smoking fish for the winter because we are usually without money.*
·Táakw niyís kinaa.át áwé x̱waa.oo. *I bought a coat for winter.*

**taakw.eetí** noun *summer; early summer*
·Gus'yadóoli taakw.eetíx' haax̱ kalyeech. *Sandpipers fly here in the early summer.*
·Ḵaashashx̱áaw taakw.eetíx' haax̱ kalyeech. *The dragonflies come in the summer time.*

TAAḴ[1] verb root

- **aawatáḵ | --- | atáḵx̱**
  *s/he poked it | --- | s/he pokes it (regularly).*
  THEME: O-S-ø-taaḵ~ (ø event)
  *for S to spear, prod, poke, jab at O*
  ·Ḵínaa teen aawatáḵ du gúk. *She pierced her ear with a quill.*
- **yaakw daak ayawlitáḵ | yaakw daak ayanaltáḵ | ---**
  *s/he pushed the boat out (with a pole) | s/he's pushing the boat out (with a pole) | ---.*
  THEME: daak O-ya-S-l-taaḵ~ (ø motion)
  *for S to pole, push O (canoe, boat) out away from the shore with a pole*
  ·Tság̱aa een yaakw daak has ayawlitáḵ. *They pushed the boat offshore with a pole.*

**táal** noun *flat open basket woven from wide strips of bark (for carrying fish, etc.); large platter*

**taan** noun *sea lion*
·Shí anax̱ naadaa wé taan geení. *There is blood coming from the sea lion's tail flippers.*
·Taan áa awsiteeni yé a niyaadé g̱unéi uwaḵúx̱. *He started motoring in the direction he had seen the sea lion.*

TAAN verb root

- **aawataan | yaa anatán | kei atánch**
  *s/he carried it | s/he's carrying it | s/he carries it (regularly).*
  THEME: O-S-ø-taan~ (ga motion)
  *for S to carry, take O (usually a container or hollow object)*
  ·A yee.ádi gataan sháchgi tléig̱u yís! *Carry a container for swamp berries!*
  ·X'eesháa yaa anatán. *She is carrying a bucket.*
- **áa yan shukaawatán | --- | ---**
  *it ended there | --- | ---.*
  THEME: yan shu-ka-ø-taan~ (ø event)
  *for something to end*

- **áa yax̱ aawatán | --- | áa yax̱ atánx̱**
  *s/he turned it over | --- | s/he turns it over (regularly).*
  THEME: áa yax̱ O-S-ø-taan~ (ø motion)
  *for S to turn O (usually container, hollow object) over
- **akaawataan | yaa akanatán | yoo akayatánk**
  *s/he bent it | s/he is bending it | s/he bends it (regularly).*
  THEME: O-ka-S-taan~ (na event)
  *for S to bend O (usually long, simple object) over*
- **--- | akwshitán | ---**
  *--- | s/he's in the habit of doing it | ---.*
  THEME: O-ka-u-S-sh-tán (ga state)
  *for S to be in habit of doing O; for S to do O frequently because S enjoys doing it*
  NOTES: In addition to hobbies, this verb can be used to describe habits with a negative connotation. For example: K̲aa yat'éi yoo x̱'atánk akwshitán "S/he likes to talk behind people's backs" or: Akwshitán k̲aa yáx̱ kei x̱'adatánch "S/he likes to argue". In the negative, this verb is used to indicate that someone doesn't like to do something, and therefore doesn't do it often. For example: Tlél akooshtán dak̲éis' "S/he doesn't like to sew (and therefore doesn't do it often)".
  ·Yéi kwdzigeiyi aa k̲ákwx' áwé akooshtánin yéi daané ax̱ léelk'w.
  *My grandmother loved to make those little baskets.*
- **át aawataan | --- | át yoo ayatánk**
  *s/he is carrying it around; s/he carries it around | --- | s/he carries it around (regularly).*
  THEME: P-t O-S-ø-taan~ (na motion)
  *for O to carry O (usually container or hollow object) around at P*
- **át aawatán | aadé yaa anatán | áx̱ ataan**
  *s/he carried it there | s/he's carrying it there | s/he carries it there (regularly).*
  THEME: P-t~ O-S-ø-taan~ (ø motion)
  *for S to carry, take O (usually a container or hollow object) to P*
  ·Aas k'eeyéet ash aawatán du óonayi. *He leaned his rifle against the tree trunk.*
- **--- | át astán | ---**
  *--- | s/he has it lying there | ---.*
  THEME: P-t O-S-s-taan (position)
  *for S to have O (usually long, complex object) lying at P*
  ·Júx̱'aa tóot astán du jín. *He has his arm in a sling.*
- **--- | át shukatán | ---**
  *--- | it extends to it | ---.*
  THEME: P-t shu-ka-ø-tán (position)
  *for something to extend to, end at P*
  NOTES: This verb only occurs in the imperfective.
  ·K̲aa kasán tayeet shukatáni áwé yak'éi wéi s'él' kinaak.át. *A raincoat that hangs below the waist is the best.*

• **--- | át tán | ---**

*--- | it's sitting there | ---.*

THEME: P-t ø-tán (position)

*for a container or hollow object to sit at P*

NOTES: This verb only occurs in the imperfective.

·Tl'aadéin áwé át tán wé k̲óok. *The box is sitting sideways.*

• **a daa toowditaan | --- | ---**

*s/he made a decision about it | --- | ---.*

THEME: (yéi) tu-S-d-taan~ (na event)

*for (singular) S to decide, make up one's mind (that way)*

• **a daa yoo toowatán | a daa yoo tuwatánk | a daa yoo tuwatánk**

*s/he thought about it | s/he thinks about it; s/he is thinking about it | s/he thinks about it (regularly).*

THEME: N daa yoo tu-S-ø-taan~ (ø act)

*for (singular) S to think over, consider, make up one's mind about N*

• **du éet x̲'eiwatán | --- | du éex̲ x̲'ataan**

*s/he spoke to him/her | --- | s/he speaks to him/her (regularly).*

THEME: N éet~ x̲'a-S-ø-taan~ (ø motion)

*for S to speak, talk to N*

·Tula.aan een du éet x̲'eiwatán. *He spoke to her with kindness.*

• **du jeedé x̲'awditaan | --- | du jeedé yoo x̲'aditánk**

*s/he called him/her on the phone | --- | s/he calls him/her on the phone (regularly).*

THEME: N jeedé x̲'a-S-d-taan~ (na motion)

*for S to call N on telephone*

·G̲ayéis' layeix̲í jeedé x̲'awditaan du éet g̲adasheet. *She telephoned the blacksmith to help her.*

• **du jeet aawatán | du jeedé yaa anatán | du jeex̲ ataan**

*s/he gave it to him/her | s/he is giving it to him/her | s/he gives it to him/her (regularly).*

THEME: N jeet~ O-S-ø-taan~ (ø motion)

*for S to give, take, hand O (usually container or hollow object) to N*

·Wé k̲'ateil xákwti ax̲ jeet tán!. *Hand me the empty pitcher!*

·Ax̲ jeet tán wé kaxágwaa yeit, yáa s'áxt' aan yéi nk̲asaneiyít! *Hand me the mortar so I can use it on this devil's club!*

• **du jeet awsitán | --- | du jeex astaan**

*s/he gave it to him/her | --- | s/he gives it to him/her (regularly).*

THEME: N jeet~ O-S-s-taan~ (ø motion)

*for S to give, take, hand O (usually long, complex object) to N*

·Yées aa gútl du jeet wududzitán. *He was given a new blunt arrow.*

·Ax̲ jeet satán a káa dul.us'ku át! *Hand me the washboard!*

• **du jeet x̲'awditán | --- | du jeex̲ x̲'adataan**

*s/he called him/her on the phone | --- | s/he calls him/her (regularly).*

THEME: N jeet~ x̲'a-S-d-taan~ (ø motion)
*for S to call N on telephone*

- **du jikaadáx̲ ayaawatán | --- | du jikaadáx̲ yaa atánch**
*s/he moved it out of his/her way | --- | s/he moves it out of his/her way (regularly).*
THEME: N jikaadáx̲ O-ya-u-S-ø-taan~ (ø motion)
*for S to move O (usually container or hollow object) out of N's way*

- **jiwsitaan | yaa jinastán | kei jisatánch**
*it's rough | it's getting rough | it gets rough (regularly).*
THEME: ji-s-taan~ (na event)
*for the ocean to be rough*

- **a kanax̲ jiyawsitán | a kanax̲ yaa jiyanastán | ---**
*waves washed over it | waves are washing over it | ---.*
THEME: N kanax̲ ji-ya-s-taan~ (ø motion)
*for waves to wash over N*
·Has du yaagú kaanáx̲ jiyawsitán. *Waves washed over their boat.*

- **kei awsitán | --- | kei astánch**
*s/he brought it out | --- | s/he brings it out (regularly).*
THEME: kei O-S-s-taan~ (ø motion)
*for S to bring out, unearth O (usually long, complex object)(esp. from a box or other container or place which O is kept); for S to pick up, lift up O*
·Du jín kei awsitán. *She raised her hand.*

- **kei jiwsitán | --- | ---**
*s/he raised his/her hand | --- | ---.*
THEME: kei ji-S-s-taan~ (ø motion)
*for S to raise a hand*
·K̲aa yáx̲ kei jisatánch wáadishgaa. *The priest blesses people.*
·Keijín ax̲ yaadéi kei jisataan! *Give me five!*

- **k̲ut aawataan | --- | k̲ut kei atánch**
*s/he lost it | --- | s/he loses it (regularly).*
THEME: k̲ut O-S-ø-taan~ (ga motion)
*for S to lose, misplace O (usually a container or hollow object)*
·Ax̲ k̲'wádli yanáak aa tsé k̲ut gaytáan! *Don't misplace my pot cover!*
·Wé k̲'wátl yana.áat'ani k̲ut x̲waataan. *I misplaced the lid for the pot.*

- **k̲ux̲ aawatán | --- | k̲ux̲ atánch**
*s/he returned it | --- | s/he returns it (regularly).*
THEME: k̲ux̲ O-S-ø-taan~ (ø motion)
*for S to return O (usually a container or hollow object)*

- **séew daak wusitán | séew daak nastán | séew daak satánx̲**
*it's raining | it's starting to rain | it rains (regularly).*
THEME: daak s-taan~ (ø event)
*for rain, snow to fall*
·L'éx̲'kw, k̲útl'kw nasteech séew daak wustaaní *Soil turns to mud when it rains.*

·Kaklahéen daak gux̲sataaní yáx̲ k̲uwatee. *The weather looks like it will snow (wet snow).*

- **x̲'awditaan | yaa x̲'andatán | yoo x̲'aditánk**
  *s/he spoke | s/he is speaking | s/he speaks (regularly).*
  THEME: x̲'a-S-d-taan~ (na event)
  *for S to speak, talk, make a speech*
  ·A yáanáx̲ tsé x̲'anidataan! *Don't say too much now!*
- **yaax̲ aawataan | --- | yaax̲ yei atánch**
  *s/he carried it aboard | --- | s/he carries it aboard (regularly).*
  THEME: yaax̲ O-S-ø-taan~ (g̲a motion)
  *for S to carry O (usually container or hollow object) aboard (a boat)*
- **yan aawatán | yánde yaa anatán | yax̲ ataan**
  *s/he put it down | s/he is putting it down | s/he puts it down (regularly).*
  THEME: yan~ O-S-ø-taan~ (ø motion)
  *for S to put down, lay down, leave, place O (usually container or hollow object)*
  ·Wé té tlein a kaháadi káa yan tán! *Put that large rock on top of its cover!*
  ·Wé kóok̲ kax'ás'ti a yanáa yan aawatán. *He put plywood over the pit in the ground.*
- **a yanáax̲ at wootaan | --- | a yanáax̲ yei at tánch**
  *s/he covered it | --- | s/he covers it (regularly).*
  THEME: at S-ø-taan~ (g̲a event)
  *for S to cover (esp. pot) with something*
  ·Tsaa eix̲í du daagú ágé a yanáax̲ yei at dutánch? *Is a cover put on when rendering seal oil?*
- **yan akawsitán | --- | ---**
  *s/he put it down | --- | ---.*
  THEME: yan~ O-ka-S-s-taan~ (ø motion)
  *for S to put down, lay down, leave, place O (usually quite small, stick-like object)*
  ·Wéit tin x'úx' áwé a káa yan kaysatán i kooxéedayi! *Put your pencil on top of that book laying there!*
- **yan awsitán | --- | ---**
  *s/he put it down | --- | ---.*
  THEME: yan~ O-S-s-taan~ (ø motion)
  *for S to put down, lay down, leave, place O (usually long, complex object)*
  ·Du jix̲ánx' yan satán wé shunax̲wáayi! *Leave the axe near him!*
- **yan jiwsitán | --- | ---**
  *s/he put his/her hand down | --- | ---.*
  THEME: yan~ ji-S-s-taan~ (ø motion)
  *for S to lower a hand*
- **yan jiwsitán | --- | ---**
  *waves reached the beach | --- | ---.*
  THEME: yan~ ji-s-taan~ (ø motion)
  *for waves to reach the beach*

- **--- | yóo katán | ---**
  --- | *it's bent* | ---.
  THEME: yóo ka-ø-tán (position)
  *for something to be bent*
  NOTES: This verb only occurs in the imperfective.
  ·Yóo katán wé tuháayi. *The nail is bent.*
  ·Ch'áak' lú yóo katán. *A bald eagle's beak is curved.*
- **yoo x̱'eiwatán | yoo x̱'ayatánk | yoo x̱'ayatánk**
  *s/he talked* | *s/he is talking* | *s/he talks (regularly).*
  THEME: yoo x̱'a-S-ø-taan~ (ø act)
  *for S to talk, speak*
  ·K̲aankak.eetx' yoo x̱'eiwatán. *He spoke in public.*
  ·A géide yoo x̱'ayatánk wé aadé át kadu.aak̲w yé. *He is speaking out against the proposed decision.*

**táanaa** noun *spear (for devilfish)*

du **taaní (TC)** noun *his/her umbilical cord*
VARIANTS: du taanú (AtT)

du **taanú (AtT)** noun *his/her umbilical cord*
VARIANTS: du taaní (TC)

**taan x̱'adaadzaayí** noun *horsetail*

**taashuká** noun *river flats; tidelands; mudflats*

**taat** noun *night*
·Haa k'idaaká k̲u.óowu taat kanax̱ has at wooshee. *Our neighbors sang all night long.*
·Taat kanax̱ oonk̲al'eix̱ín. *I would have danced all night.*

**taat aayí adéli** noun *night watchman*

**taat sitgawsáani** noun *midnight*

**taat yeen** noun *during the night; in the middle of the night*

TAAW verb root

- **aawatáw | atáaw | atáawx̱**
  *s/he stole it* | *s/he steals it* | *s/he steals it (regularly).*
  THEME: O-S-ø-táaw~ (ø act)
  *for S to steal O*
  ·At géit wudzigít wé k̲áa átx'i aawutáawu. *He went against the law when he stole the man's belongings.*

**táaw s'aatí** noun *thief*

TAAX' verb root

- **ash wusitáax' | --- | kei ash satáx'ch**
  *it bit him/her/it* | --- | *it bites him/her/it (regularly).*

THEME: O-s-taax'~ (ga event)
*for an insect to bite O*
NOTES: Note that ash wusitáax' and awsitáax' both have basically the same meaning "it bit him/her/it". The difference is that the object pronoun ash "him/her/it" is used when the referent is prominent in the conversation.
·Xeitl táax'aa x̲at wusitáax'. *A horsefly bit me.*
·Wanatíxch wusitáax' du wankach'eek̲. *The ant bit his little finger.*

**táax'aa** noun *mosquito*

**táax'aa x̲'uskudayáat'** noun *daddy long legs; mosquito eater*

**táax'ál'** noun *needle*
·Táax'ál' x'aan áwé ax̲ tl'eik̲ tóode yawdig̲eech. *The needle point poked my finger.*

**táax̲'** noun *slug, snail*

TAAX̲'W verb root

• **wootáax̲'w | yei natáx̲'w | yoo yatáx̲'w**
*it sank | it's sinking | it sinks (regularly).*
THEME: ø-táax̲'w (na event)
*for something to sink*

**taay** noun *fat; blubber*
·G̲uwakaan a taayí teen awsi.ée. *She cooked deer with the fat on.*
·G̲uwakaan taayí kas'úkx̲u yís akaawaxaash. *She cut up deer fat for frying.*

**táay** noun *garden; field*
·Dákwtasi átx̲ dulyéix̲ táay yíx'. *Rendered fat is used in the garden.*
·Wé káts táay káa yéi na.oo! *Put the pounded shell powder on the garden!*

**táay kahéix̲i** noun *gardener*

**tadanóox'** noun *turtle*
VARIANTS: kanóox', tanóox', tadanóox'u (At)

**tág̲aa** noun *lancet*

**tag̲anís** noun *sapling; pole made from sapling*

a **taká** RelationalNoun *the inside surface of its bottom (of container, vessel)*
·X̲áay kayeix̲tág̲u a takáx' yéi na.oo! *Put yellow cedar shavings in the bottom of it!*

**tak̲aadí** noun *rockslide*
VARIANTS: tek̲aadí (C)

**ták̲l** noun *hammer*

**tás** noun *thread; sinew*

**a tási** noun *its sinew*

**tatgé** noun *yesterday*
·G̲ayéis' t'éix̲'i sháade háni haat k̲uwatín tatgé. *The chief blacksmith traveled here yesterday.*
·At géide ayawsik̲aa du kéek' tatgé. *She spoke wrongly against her younger sister yesterday.*

**tatóok** noun *cave*

**tawéi** noun *mountain sheep, bighorn sheep*

**tax'aayí** noun *rock point*

**tax̲héeni** noun *soup broth; soup*
·Éil' eetéenáx̲ yatee wé tax̲héeni. *The broth needs salt.*

**Tax̲héeni** noun *Takhini hot springs (north of Whitehorse, Yukon Territory)*

**tayashagoo** noun *small red sea anemone*

**tayataayí** noun *sea anemone*

**a tayee** RelationalNoun *underneath it; beneath it; below it*
·Wé aas chéx̲'i tayeet áwé took̲éen. *We are sitting in the shade of the tree.*
·Kéi dak̲inji s'áaxw tlein a tayeet k̲aa luwagúk̲ séew tóodáx̲. *People ran under the big umbrella out of the rain.*

**tayees** noun *stone axe*

**tayeidí** noun *bladder rack; rock weed; yellow seaweed*

**té** noun *stone; rock*
·Téix' gwáa wégé átx̲ dulyeix̲ín chooneit sákw. *Little stones must have been used to make arrows.*
·Wé té tlein a kaháadi káa yan tán! *Put that large rock on top of its cover!*

**TEE**[1] verb root

- **a eetéenáx̲ wootee | a eetéenáx̲ yatee | a eetéenáx̲ yoo yateek**
  *he/she/it needed it | he/she/it needs it | he/she/it needs it (regularly).*
  THEME: N eetéenáx̲ O-ø-tee~ (na state)
  *for O to need, lack, require N*
  ·Yées túlaa eetéenáx̲ x̲at yatee. *I need a new drill.*
  ·Kooxéedaa eetéenáx̲ yatee wé shaatk'. *The young girl needs a pencil.*
- **k̲oowdzitee | k̲udzitee | ---**
  *it existed; s/he was born | it exists; s/he is alive | ---.*
  THEME: O-k̲u-d-s-tee~ (g̲a state)
  *for O to be, be in existence, live; for O to be born*
  ·Tsú yáa ax̲ tláa k̲u.aa Sheet'káx' áyá k̲oowdzitee. K̲a du éek' tsú áa k̲oowdzitee. *My mother was born in Sitka. And her brother was also born there.*

·Tléil x̲wasakú daak̲w.aa x̲áat sá a k̲'anoox̲ú k̲usteeyí. *I don't know which fish have beards.*

- **(noun)-x̲ wusitee | (noun)-x̲ sitee | ---**

*s/he became a (noun) | s/he is a (noun) | ---.*
THEME: P-x̲ O-s-tee~ (na state)
*for O to be P (a member of a group); for O to become P*
NOTES: This verb requires that the preceding noun phrase have the -x̲ postposition. In the forms given here, (noun) can be replaced by any noun which makes sense. An example is the name of a profession such as: asg̲eiwú "seiner" as in: asg̲eiwúx̲ wusitee "s/he became a seiner". Another example is the name of a moiety such as: ch'áak' naa "eagle moiety" in the common phrase: Ch'áak' naax̲ x̲at sitee "I am of the Eagle moiety". Please see the example sentences for more options.
·K̲a x̲át tsú ax̲ toowú yak'éi yaa a káa yéi x̲at gug̲wateeyí yaa Lingítx̲ x̲at sateeyí. *And I too am thankful that I'm part of this being that I'm Lingít.*
·L s'eik̲x̲ usiteeyi neil áyá. *This is a smoke-free home.*

- **sh tóog̲áa wditee | sh tóog̲áa ditee | sh tóog̲áa yoo diteek**

*s/he was grateful | s/he is grateful | s/he is grateful (regularly).*
THEME: sh tóog̲áa O-d-tee~ (na state)
*for O to be grateful, thankful, satisfied*
·Sh tóog̲áa wditee ax̲ yoowú. *My stomach was satisfied.*

- **tleiyéi yéi wootee | tleiyéi yéi yatee | tleiyéi yéi teex̲**

*he/she/it became still | s/he is still | he/she/it is still (regularly).*
THEME: tleiyéi yéi O-ø-tee~ (na state)
*for O to be still, quiet; for O to stop (car, clock, e.g.)*
·Wé yaakw tlein Aangóonx' tleiyéi yéi wootee. *The big boat stopped in Angoon.*

- **du wak̲shiyeex' yéi wootee | du wak̲shiyeex' yéi yatee | du wak̲shiyeex' yéi teex̲**

*he/she/it appeared before him/her | he/she/it is in front of his/her eyes | he/she/it appears before him/her (regularly).*
THEME: N wak̲shiyeex' yéi O-ø-tee~ (na state)
*for O to appear to N; for O to be apparent to N*
·I wak̲shiyeex' yéi yatee. *It's in front of your eyes.*

- **du x̲ánx' yéi wootee | du x̲ánx' yéi yatee | du x̲ánx' yéi teex̲**

*s/he was with him/her | s/he is with him/her | s/he stays with him/her (regularly).*
THEME: P-x' yéi O-ø-tee~ (na state)
*for O to be, stay, remain at P; for O to dwell, live at P*
·Ch'a yóo Anóoshi Aaníx' yaa German shaawát áyá du x̲ánx' yéi wootee. *While in Russia he was with a German woman.*
·Ax̲ sée du kacháwli áwé ixkéex' yéi yatee. *My daughter's sweetheart lives down south.*

• **a yáx̱ wootee | a yáx̱ yatee | ---**
*he/she/it was like it | he/she/it is like it | ---.*
THEME: N yáx̱ O-ø-tee~ (na state)
*for O to be like, similar to N*
·Wé yées xwaasdáa g̱ákw yáx̱ yatee. *The new tent is stiff.*
·Gan eetí kél't' ḵugáas' yáx̱ yatee. *Ashes from the fireplace are gray.*

• **yéi ḵoowatee | yéi ḵuwatee | yéi yoo ḵuyateek**
*the weather was that way | the weather is that way | the weather is that way (regularly).*
THEME: (yéi) ḵu-ø-tee~ (na state)
*for the weather to be (that way)*
NOTES: To specify how the weather is, replace yéi with a weather term + yáx̱. For example: séew yáx̱ ḵuwatee "it looks like rain". In the negative, one can say: tlél áyáx̱ ḵootí "the weather looks bad".
·Kaklahéen daak gux̱sataaní yáx̱ ḵuwatee. *The weather looks like it will snow (wet snow).*

• **--- | yéi tuwatee | ---**
*--- | s/he feels that way | ---.*
THEME: (yéi) O-tu-ø-tee~ (na state)
*for O to want to do, feel like doing (that); for O to feel a certain way*
·Eeshandéin tuwatee. *He's feeling sad.*

• **yéi wootee | yéi yatee | yóo yateek**
*he/she/it was that way | he/she/it is that way | he/she/it is that way (regularly).*
THEME: (yéi) O-ø-tee~ (na state)
*for O to be (that way)*
·Ḵa x̱át tsú ax̱ toowú yak'éi yaa a káa yéi x̱at gug̱wateeyí yaa Lingítx̱ x̱at sateeyí. *And I too am thankful that I'm part of this being that I'm Lingít.*
·Wé al'óon tlél wáa sá wootee. *The hunt went alright.*

TEE[2] verb root

• **aadé aawatee | aadé yaa anatéen | aadé yoo ayateek**
*s/he carried it there | s/he is carrying it there | s/he carries it there (regularly).*
THEME: P-dé O-S-ø-tee~ (na motion)
*for S to carry, take O (general, often compact object) to P*
·Du gwéili tóode aawatee wé g̱íl'aa. *He put the grindstone in his bag.*

• **aadé awsitee | aadé yaa anastéen | aadé yoo asiteek**
*s/he carried it there | s/he is carrying it there | s/he carries it there (regularly).*
THEME: P-dé O-S-s-tee~ (na motion)
*for S to carry, take O (solid, often complex object) to P*
·S'igeidí káx̱ g̱aatáa héen táakde awsitee. *He set a trap underwater for beaver.*

• **aax̱ aawatée | --- | aax̱ kei ateech**
*s/he picked it up off of it | --- | s/he picks it up off of it (regularly).*
THEME: P-dáx̱ O-S-ø-tee~ (ga motion)
*for S to pick O (general, compact object) up off of P*

·Aax̲ gatí wéi kaxíl'aa kadushxeet t'áa yá g̲alg̲ú! *Pick up the eraser and clean the chalkboard!*

• **ashoowsitee | ashusitee | yoo ashusiteek**

*s/he expected him/her/it | s/he's expecting him/her/it | s/he expects him/her/it (regularly).*

THEME: O-shu-S-s-tee~ (na state)

*for S to anticipate, foresee O; for S to expect, consider O likely to happen or arrive*

·Ch'u dziyáak áwé ishuwtusitee. *We were expecting you a while ago*

·Ch'u tliyaatgé áwé shux̲wsitee. *I was expecting it the other day.*

• **--- | át akatéen | ---**

*--- | s/he has it lying there | ---.*

THEME: P-t O-ka-S-téen (positional)

*for S to have (round, spherical) O lying at P*

·Kas'éet katíx̲'aa tlein áyá yaakwt kax̲atéen. *I have a big screwdriver lying in the boat.*

• **--- | át satéen | ---**

*--- | it's sitting there | ---.*

THEME: P-t s-téen (position)

*for a solid, often complex object to sit at P*

NOTES: This verb only occurs in the imperfective.

·Yées washéen a géekt satéen wé yaakw. *A new motor sits at the stern of that boat.*

• **awsitee | yaa anastéen | kei asteech**

*s/he carried it | s/he is carrying it | s/he carries it (regularly).*

THEME: O-S-s-tee~ (ga motion)

*for S to carry, take O (solid, often complex object)*

• **áx̲ aawatee | --- | ---**

*s/he put it there | --- | ---.*

THEME: P-x̲ O-S-ø-tee~ (g̲a motion)

*for S to install, hang, place O at P*

• **áx̲ ashayaawatée | --- | áx̲ ashayateex̲**

*s/he hung it there | --- | s/he hangs it there (regularly).*

THEME: P-x̲ O-sha-ya-S-ø-tee~ (ø motion)

*for S to hang up O at P (esp. to dry)*

·Wé atx'aan hídi yee áwé áx̲ ashayaawatée wé x̲áat. *She hung the fish inside the smokehouse.*

·Jikak̲áas' káx̲ ashayaawatée wé g̲aat atx'aan hídi yeex'. *She hung the sockeye salmon on the stick in the smokehouse.*

• **ayawditee | yei ayandatéen | yei ayadateech**

*it's stormy | it's getting stormy | it gets stormy (regularly).*

THEME: a-ya-d-tee~ (g̲a event)

*for the weather to be stormy, rough*

·Dákde át xóon áwé ayawditee. *An offshore east wind is blowing.*

·K̲únáx̲ k'eeljáa yéi ayagux̲datée ách áyá haa yaagú dák̲de tusax̲út'x'. *It's going to get stormy so we are dragging our boats up.*

- **héent ayaawatée | --- | héenx̲ ayatee**

*s/he baptized him/her | --- | s/he baptizes him/her (regularly).*
THEME: héent~ O-ya-S-ø-tee~ (ø motion)
*for S to baptize, immerse (singular) O in water or pour water upon O as a religious rite*
·Johnch héent ayaawatée haa Aank̲áawu. *John baptised our lord.*

- **du jeet aawatée | --- | du jeex̲ atee**

*s/he gave it to him/her | --- | s/he gives it to him/her (regularly).*
THEME: N jeet~ O-S-ø-tee~ (ø motion)
*for S to give, take, hand O (general, esp. abstract object) to N*
·Du gúk yís náakw du jeet wuduwatée. *He was given medicine for his ear.*
·Ch'a g̲óot yéidei yéi jiné has du jeex̲ dutee wéi k̲'atx̲áan. *Cowards are given different jobs to perform.*

- **du jeet akaawatée | du jeedé yaa akanatéen | du jeex̲ akatee**

*s/he gave it to him/her | s/he's giving it to him/her | s/he gives it to him/her (regularly).*
THEME: N jeet~ O-ka-S-tee~ (ø motion)
*for S to give, take, hand O (round object) to N*
·Haa léelk'u hás tuwáadáx̲ áwé gútk haa jeet kawduwatée. *If it wasn't for our elders, we wouldn't be here. (Lit: Because of our elders, we were given a dime.)*
·K̲aashaxáshaa ax̲ jeet katí! *Hand me the scissors!*

- **--- | kát adatéen | ---**

*--- | s/he is wearing it | ---.*
THEME: kát O-S-d-tee~ (position)
*for S to wear O*
NOTES: This verb only occurs in the imperfective. For all other modes, speakers use the verb: yéi aawa.oo 's/he wore it'.
·K̲ux̲ dak'óol'een áwé kát adatéen du k'oodás'i. *He's wearing his shirt backwards.*

- **du kát ashuwatée | --- | du káx̲ ashutee**

*s/he blamed it on him/her | --- | s/he blames it on him/her (regularly).*
THEME: P-t~ O-shu-S-ø-tée~ (ø motion)
*for S to bring O (abstract, esp. shame, blame, joy) onto P*
NOTES: This verb can be used with nouns such as joy, shame, but note that when no noun is explicitly given, the meaning is "blame" for this verb. N éet~ can replace N kát~ to give the same meaning. For example, du éet ashuwatée "s/he blamed it on him/her". To blame someone for eating something, use N x̲'éit~, as in: du x̲'éit shux̲waatée "I blamed him for eating it". To blame someone for doing something with the hands, use N jeet~, as in: du jeet shux̲waatée "I blamed him for doing it".
·Yéi daayaduk̲á, "Tlél kadéix' haa káx̲ sheeteek̲!" *He is told "Don't bring shame on us!"*

- **káx̱ awditee | --- | káx̱ yéi adateech**
*s/he put it on | --- | s/he puts it on (regularly).*
THEME: káx̱ O-S-d-tee~ (g̱a event)
*for S to put on O (shirt, dress, etc.)*

- **kei aawatée | --- | kei ateech**
*s/he brought it out | --- | s/he brings it out (regularly).*
THEME: kei O-S-ø-tee~ (ø motion)
*or S to bring out, unearth O (general, often compact object)(esp. from a box or other container or place which O is kept); for S to pick up, lift up O*
·Gaan woolí a kaháadi áa kei aawatée. *He put the cover for the smoke hole up there.*

- **neil aawatée | --- | neilx̱ atee**
*s/he brought it inside | --- | s/he brings it inside (regularly).*
THEME: neil O-S-ø-tee~ (ø motion)
*for S to carry, take O (general, often compact object) home, inside*
·Kaduch'áak'w lítaa sákw yak'éiyi aa g̱ayéis' neil tí! *Bring home a good piece of iron for a carving knife!*

- **du x̱'éix̱ aawatee | --- | du x̱'éix̱ ateex̱**
*s/he fed it to him/her/it | --- | s/he feeds it to him/her/it (regularly).*
THEME: N x̱'éix̱ O-S-ø-tee~ (na event)
*for S to feed O to N; for S to give O to N to eat*
·Náakw du x̱'éix̱ wuduwatee du kalóox'sháni néegooch. *She was given medicine for her bladder pain.*
·Náakw yís kayaaní ashigóok, áx' ḵu.aa akwdlix̱éitl' ḵaa x̱'éix̱ aa wuteeyí. *He knows medicinal plants but he is afraid to give them to anyone.*

- **du x̱'éix̱ at wootee | du x̱'éix̱ yaa at natéen | du x̱'éix̱ at teex̱**
*s/he fed him/her/it | s/he is feeding him/her/it | s/he feeds him/her/it (regularly).*
THEME: N x̱'éix̱ at S-ø-tee~ (na event)
*for S to feed N, give food to N (for immediate consumption)*
·Tlé kílaa kát áwé ḵaa x̱'éix̱ has at wootee. *They fed the people from platters.*

- **yan aawatée | --- | yax̱ atee**
*s/he put it down | --- | s/he puts it down (regularly).*
THEME: yan~ O-S-ø-tee~ (ø motion)
*for S to put down, lay down, leave, place O (general, often compact object)*
·Du jix̱áni yan tí wé lítaa, dleey aan akg̱waxáash! *Leave the knife near her, she will cut meat with it!*
·Ch'áagu aa kax̱'íl'aa stoox káx' áwé yan dutéeych yag̱at'aayít. *The irons of long ago were set on the stove to heat up.*

- **yan akaawatée | --- | yax̱ akatee**
*s/he put it down | --- | s/he puts it down (regularly).*
THEME: yan~ O-ka-S-ø-tee~ (ø motion)
*for S to put down, lay down, leave, place O (round, spherical object)*
·Du jintáak káa yan akaawatée du tl'iḵkakéesi. *He put his ring in the center of his palm.*

·Atx̱á aax̱ yéi awusneiyi yé, dáanaa a eetíx' yan akaawatée. *She put money in place of the food she picked up.*

- **yan awsitée | --- | yax̱ astee**
  *s/he put it down* | --- | *s/he puts it down (regularly).*
  THEME: yan~ O-S-s-tee~ (ø motion)
  *for S to put down, lay down, leave, place O (solid, often complex object)*
  ·Wéi kashóok' gwéil ax̱ x̱eek káa yan satí! *Set the heating pad on my upper arm!*
  ·Wéidu g̱ánch gwéili nadáakw káa yan satí! *Put that bag of tobacco on the table!*

**TEE**[3] verb root

- **ax̱'eiwatee | ax̱'atee | yoo ax̱'ayateek**
  *s/he imitated him/her* | *s/he's imitating him/her* | *s/he imitates him/her (regularly).*
  THEME: O-x̱'a-S-ø-tee (na act)
  *for S to imitate O; for S to mimic O's speech; for S to quote O*

**teel** noun *scar*

**téel** noun *shoe(s)*
·I téeli yee.át x̱'usyeex' yéi na.oo! *Put your shoes at the foot of the bed!*
·Wooshdakádin x̱'oosdé awdiyiḵ du téeli. *He put his shoes on the wrong feet.*

**téel daakeyéis'i (C)** noun *shoe polish*

**téel iḵkeidí** noun *moccasin top*

**téel layeix̱í** noun *shoemaker, cobbler*

**téel tukanágaa** noun *wooden form for shaping/stretching moccasins*
VARIANTS: téel kanágaa

**téel x̱'adzaasí** noun *shoelace(s)*
VARIANTS: téel x̱'akadzaasí, téel x̱'agudzaasí
·Du téel x̱'adzaasí akaawadúx'. *She tied her shoelaces.*

**téel x̱'agudzaasí** noun *shoelace(s)*
VARIANTS: téel x̱'adzaasí; téel x̱'akadzaasí

**téel x̱'akadzaazí** noun *shoelace(s)*
VARIANTS: téel x̱'adzaasí, téel x̱'agudzaasí

**téel'** noun *dog salmon; chum salmon*
·Tsu tsá yá naax̱ satí ḵu.aa áyá yaa téel' áyá haa shukáx̱ sitee, L'eeneidí. *Also the dog salmon is our clan crest, L'eeneidí.*

**teen** postpos. *(along) with, by means of; as soon as*
VARIANTS: téen, tin, tín, een
·Tsaa eix̱í teen áwé yak'éi t'á at x̱'éeshi. *Dry fish king salmon is good with seal oil.*

·Du jintáak teen at'ácht wé kadu.uxx̲u át. *She is slapping the balloon with the palm of her hand.*

**TEEN** verb root

- **aadé k̲oowateen | aadé yaa k̲unatín | aadé yoo k̲uyateenk**
  *s/he traveled there | s/he is traveling there | s/he travels there (regularly).*
  THEME: P-dé k̲u-S-ø-teen~ (na motion)
  *for S to travel, go on a trip to P*
  ·Haadé yaa s k̲unatín Waashdan K̲wáan. *The Americans are traveling here.*
  ·Yáa k̲utaanx' aadé k̲ugax̲tootéen ixkée ch'a g̲aax̲tusatéen wé sháa. *This summer we are going to travel down south just to see the girls.*
- **át k̲uwatín | --- | áx̲ k̲uteen**
  *s/he traveled there | --- | s/he travels there (regularly).*
  THEME: P-t~ k̲u-S-ø-teen~ (ø motion)
  *for S to travel, go on a trip to P*
  ·G̲ayéis' t'éix̲'i sháade háni haat k̲uwatín tatgé. *The chief blacksmith traveled here yesterday.*
  ·Yáa k̲utaanx' aadé k̲ugax̲tootéen ixkée ch'a g̲aax̲tusatéen wé sháa. *This summer we are going to travel down south just to see the girls.*
- **awlitín | altín | altínx̲**
  *s/he watched him/her/it | s/he is watching him/her/it | s/he watches him/her/it (regularly).*
  THEME: O-S-l-teen~ (ø act)
  *for S to look at, gaze at, watch O; for S to watch, take care of, mind, look after O*
  ·X̲'aan yáx̲ teeyí gis'óok̲, tlél dultínx̲ *When the northern lights are red, they aren't to be looked at.*
  ·K'idéin gé sh eeltín? *Are you taking good care of yourself?*
- **awsiteen | --- | ---**
  *s/he sees it; s/he saw it | --- | ---.*
  THEME: O-S-s-teen~ (g̲a event)
  *for S to see, behold O (usually specific)*
  ·Dzísk'w awusteení tle a dachóon kéi uwagút. *When he saw the moose he turned to walk straight towards it.*
  ·Aag̲áa tsá x̲wsiteeni yé. *It's about time I saw it; I finally saw it.*
- **--- | ayatéen | ---**
  *--- | s/he can see it | ---.*
  THEME: O-S-ø-teen~ (ga state)
  *for S to see, perceive O (often abstract)*
  NOTES: This verb only occurs in the imperfective.
  ·A g̲uwanyáadé ágé iyatéen? *Do you see the difference?*
  ·Yeeytéen has du téix̲' tóotx̲ áyá toodé has yee uwaxích haa k̲u.éex'i. *You all can see that our hosts thank you from their hearts.*
- **--- | k̲uwatéen / k̲uyatéen | k̲uwatínx̲**
  *--- | s/he has sight | s/he recognizes people (regularly).*

THEME: ḵu-S-ø-téen (ga state)
*for S to have sight (see people)*
NOTES: Note that this verb has the prefix ḵu-, which often refers to "people." The only form in which this specific meaning seems to arise however, is the repetitive imperfective form, which translates as "recognizes people." This verb is often used with the adverb k'idéin, as in: tlél k'idéin ḵooxateen "I don't see well."

- **--- | tlél ḵooshtéen | ---**
  --- | *s/he is blind* | ---.
  THEME: tlél ḵu-S-sh-téen (ga state)
  *for S to be blind*

**TÉES'SHÁN** verb root

- **kawlitées'shán | kulitées'shán | ---**
  *it was a sight to behold* | *it's a sight to behold* | ---.
  THEME: ka-u-l-tées'shán (ga state)
  *for something to be fascinating to watch, to be a wonderful sight*
  ·X̱'eis'awáa l'eix̱í kulitées'shan nooch. *The dance of the ptarmigan is always a wonder to behold.*

**teet** noun *wave; swell*
·Áa kaadé x̱aatéen teet. *I see waves on the lake.*

**teet x̱'achálx̱i** noun *foam (on waves); sponge*

**téet'** noun *vein; tendon (inside body)*

**TEEX̱'** verb root

- **kawdzitíx̱' | --- | kastíx̱'x̱**
  *it's crooked; s/he is crooked, wicked* | --- | *it gets crooked (regularly).*
  THEME: O-ka-d-s-téex̱'~ (ø event)
  *for O to be crooked, wicked*
  VARIANTS: -teix̱'
  ·Tléi kawdzitíx̱' a yá shawtoot'éex̱'i. *It's face twisted when we clubbed it.*
  ·Du toowú kawdzitíx̱' *His inner thoughts are crooked.*

**téey** noun *patch*

du **téey** noun *his/her chin*

**téeyí** noun *soaked dried fish*

**teey woodí** noun *yellow cedar bark (for weaving)*
VARIANTS: teey hoodí (T)
·Teey woodí naaxeinx̱ dulyéix̱. *Yellow cedar bark is used to make a chilkat robe.*
·Teey woodí dustéix̱. *Yellow cedar bark is boiled.*

**teiḵ** noun *shawl; cape; poncho*

**Teiḵweidí** noun *Teiḵweidí, locally called "Brown Bear"; a clan of the Eagle moiety whose principal crest is the Brown Bear*
·Sheet'kaadé ḵu.aa áyá wdusháayin Teiḵweidéech áyá. *She was married to a man from Sitka from Teiḵweidí clan.*
·Teiḵweidí dachx̱án áyá x̱át. *I am a grandchild of the Teiḵweidí.*

**téil** noun *pitch scab (where bark has been removed); pitchwood*
·X̱'aan aan dulyéix̱ téil. *Pitchwood is used to make fire.*
·Téil dei yaax̱t la.át. *Scraps of pitchwood are lying along the road.*

**téix̱** noun *boiled food; broth*
VARIANTS: at téix̱i, a téix̱i
·Wé g̱uwakaan dleeyí at x̱'ax̱éedli k'idéin aax̱ xásh, téix̱ sákw! *Cut the trimming off the deer meat well for the broth!*

a **téix̱i** noun *boiled food; broth*
VARIANTS: at téix̱i, téix̱
·Stoox káa yan sa.ín wé at téix̱i! *Set the broth on top of the stove!*

**TEIX̱'** verb root

- **át akawlitíx̱' | aadé yaa akanaltíx̱' | áx̱ aklatéex̱'**
  *s/he screwed it on it | s/he's screwing it on it | s/he screws it on it (reguarly).*
  THEME: P-t~ O-ka-S-l-téex̱'~ (ø event)
  *for S to screw O into P*
  VARIANTS: -téix̱'~
  ·A x̱'oosí k'idéin át kalatéx̱'! *Screw the leg on it good!*
- **x̱'éit akawlitíx̱' | x̱'éide yaa akanaltíx̱' | x̱'éix̱ aklatéex̱'**
  *s/he locked it | s/he's locking it | s/he locks it (regularly).*
  THEME: x̱'éi-t~ O-ka-S-l-teex̱'~ (ø event)
  *for S to lock O*
  VARIANTS: -téix̱'~
  ·X̱'éidei kakg̱ilatix̱' yé ch'a yeisú lingít áwu. *There are still people in the place you are locking.*

du **téix̱'** noun *his/her heart*
·Yeeytéen has du téix̱' tóotx̱ áyá toodé has yee uwaxích haa ḵu.éex'i. *You all can see that our hosts thank you from their hearts.*
·Wé ḵáa watsíx téix̱'i akawlis'úk. *The man fried caribou heart.*

du **teiyí** noun *his/her bile*

**té kas'úgwaa yeit (T)** noun *cast-iron skillet*

**té ḵáas'** noun *rock crevice; fissure in rock*

**té ḵ'áatl'** noun *wide, flat stone (used for cooking)*

**té shanax̱wáayi** noun *sledgehammer*

**té tayee tlóox̱u** noun *little bullhead (found under beach rocks)*

**té xóow** noun *cairn; rock pile*

**tin** postpos. *(along) with, by means of; as soon as*
VARIANTS: tín, teen, téen, een
·Dáanaa tín has akoodlénx̱aa. *They tempted him with money.*
·Ax̱ dlaak' tín Xunaadé ḵugax̱tootéen kanat'á ḵuk'éet' yís. *We are going to travel to Hoonah to pick blueberries with my sister.*

**tináa** noun *copper shield*
·Yadál wé tináa. *The copper shield is heavy.*

**tínx** noun *alpine bearberry, kinnikinnick*
·Tínx kaxwéix̱ oowayáa tl'átgi káx' ḵu.aa ka.éix̱. *Bearberries look like cranberries but they grow on the ground.*

**tíx** noun *flea*
·Líl tíx eewustáax'iḵ! *Don't let the bedbugs bite! (Lit: Don't let the fleas bite you!)*
·Eesháan, haa keidlí awsitáax' wé tíx. *Our poor dog was bit by a flea.*

**tíxwjaa (At)** noun *sound of stamping, pounding fists, clapping; sound of running quickly*
VARIANTS: túxjaa (TC)

**tíx'** noun *rope*
·Cháatl tíx'i yaa (ha)s a shuká naḵúx̱. *They're setting halibut gear.*
·Tíx' ḵa x'óow tin g̱eeg̱ách' awliyéx̱ t'ukanéiyi jeeyís. *She made a hammock for the baby with rope and a blanket.*

**tíx' yádi** noun *string*

**tíyaa** noun *chisel*

**too-** Pronoun *we [subject]*
VARIANTS: tu-
·Tuháayi teen áwé át kawtusix'óo. *We nailed it on it with a nail.*

a **tóo at dult'ix'x̱i át** noun *freezer*
VARIANTS: a tóo at dult'ix' át, a tóox' at dult'ix' át
·Haa a tóox' at dult'ix' át shaawahík dzísk'u dleeyí teen. *Our freezer is full of moose meat.*

TOOK[2] verb root

• **kei wjitúk | --- | kei ishtúkx̱**
*it exploded | --- | it explodes (regularly).*
THEME: kei sh-tóok~ (ø event)
*for something to explode, blow up*
·Ganyal'óot' ganaltáakdáx̱ kéi wjitúk. *The flame shot up out of the fire.*

**tooḵ** noun *needlefish*

du **tóoḵ** noun *his/her buttocks, butt*

**toolch'án** noun *top (spinning toy)*
VARIANTS: toolch'én (T), toolch'ánaa (At)
·Yaa kanajúx wé toolch'án. *The top is spinning.*

a **tóonáx kadus'ii̲ks' át** noun *straw (for drinking)*

**tóonáx̲ ka̲ateen** noun *mirror*
·Wé tóonáx̲ ka̲ateen kaadé awsiteen du yahaayí. *He saw his image in the mirror.*

**tóos'** noun *shark*
·Tóos' hítdáx̲ áwé du x̲úx̲. *Her husband is from the Shark house.*

**toow** noun *tallow, hard fat*

TOOW verb root

- **aawatóow | atóow | yoo ayatóowk**
*s/he read it | s/he reads it; s/he is reading it | s/he reads it (regularly).*
THEME: O-S-ø-tóow (na act)
*for S to read O*
VARIANTS: -teew (An)
·Du jiyee yan aawatée wé atóowu x'úx'. *She placed the book he was reading near him.*

- **du éex' at wulitóow | du éex' at latóow | ---**
*s/he taught him/her | s/he's teaching him/her | ---.*
THEME: P-x' at S-l-tóow (ø act)
*for S to teach P*
NOTES: With the noun phrase du ée "to him/her; in his/her company", the postposition -x' has a variant form -ø (unmarked). Therefore, you will notice that in some examples, the postposition -x' is present, as in: du éex' at wulitóow "s/he taught him/her" and in others it is not, as in: du ée at wulitóow "s/he taught him/her". Both forms are acceptable and have the same meaning.
·Du káak du ée at latóow. *His maternal uncle is teaching him.*
·Du ée yan at wududlitóow ka̲a oox̲ yéi daanéiyi yís. *She completed dentistry school.*

- **du éex' awlitóow | du éex' altóow | ---**
*s/he taught it to him/her | s/he is teaching it to him/her | ---.*
THEME: P-x' O-S-l-tóow (ø act)
*for S to teach O to P*
NOTES: With the noun phrase du ée "to him/her; in his/her company", the postposition -x' has a variant form -ø (unmarked). Therefore, you will notice that in some examples, the postposition -x' is present, as in: du éex' awlitóow "s/he taught him/her" and in others it is not, as in: du ée awlitóow "s/he taught him/her". Both forms are acceptable and have the same meaning.
·Giyak̲w K̲wáan yoo x̲'atángi k̲óox' altóow. *He is teaching people the Alutiq language.*

- **sh tóo at wudlitóow | sh tóo at iltóow | sh tóo at iltóowx̱**
  *s/he studied | s/he studies; s/he is studying | s/he studies (regularly).*
  THEME: sh tóo at S-d-l-tóow (ø act)
  *for S to study, teach oneself*
- **sh tóo awdlitóow | sh tóo altóow | sh tóo altóowx̱**
  *s/he studied it | s/he is studying it | s/he studies it (regularly).*
  THEME: sh tóo O-S-d-l-tóow (ø act)
  *for S to study, learn O; for S to practice, rehearse O*
  ·Sh tóo awdlitóow g̱íx̱'jaa ḵóok al.áx̱ji. *He taught himself to play the piano.*
- **wuditóow | datóow | yoo ditóowk**
  *s/he read | s/he reads; s/he is reading | s/he reads (regularly).*
  THEME: S-d-tóow (na act)
  *for S to read*
  VARIANTS: -téew (An)

**toow s'eenáa** noun *candle*
·Toow s'eenáa át has akawligán. *They lit a candle.*

du **toowú** noun *his/her inner being; mind; soul; feelings; intention*
·I toowúch a yáx̱ ákwé? *Is it like you think?*
·K'wáax̱' yáx̱ ax̱ toowú yatee. *I feel blah.*

**toowú klag̱é** noun *pride; self-esteem, feeling good about oneself*
·Ḵútx̱ toowú klag̱é tlél áyáx̱ utí. *Too much pride is not good.*

**toowú k'é** noun *good thoughts; felicity; happiness*
VARIANTS: tuk'é

**toowú latseen** noun *strength of mind or heart; courage; resolve*

**toowú néekw** noun *sorrow; sadness*
VARIANTS: toowú nóok
·Toowú néekw jiyeet g̱áax̱ wé shaawát. *The woman is crying under the burden of sadness.*
·Toowú néekw ḵaa káa yéi teeyí, tlél oodul'eix̱. *When there is sorrow, there's no dancing.*

**toowú nóok** noun *sorrow; sadness*
VARIANTS: toowú néekw

**TOOX̱** verb root

- **yóot ḵ'awdzitúx̱ | --- | yóox̱ ḵ'astoox̱**
  *s/he spat | --- | s/he spits (regularly).*
  THEME: yóot~ ḵ'a-S-d-s-toox̱~ (ø motion)
  *for S to spit, spit out*

**TOOX̲’** verb root

- **--- | du x̲’óol’ kastóox̲’ | ---**
  --- | *his/her stomach is growling* | ---.
  THEME: ka-s-tóox̲’ (ø act)
  *for the stomach to growl, gurgle*
  NOTES: This verb only occurs in the imperfective.
- **du x̲’óol’ kawditóox̲’ | du x̲’óol’ kadatóox̲’ | ---**
  *his/her stomach growled* | *his/her stomach is growling* | ---.
  THEME: ka-d-tóox̲’ (ø act)
  *for the stomach to growl, gurgle*
  ·Du x̲’óol’ kadatóox̲’. *His stomach is growling.*

a **tú** RelationalNoun *inside it*
·X̲’áal’ tóox’ wutusi.ée. *We cooked it in skunk cabbage.*
·Yeeytéen has du téix̲’ tóotx̲ áyá toodé has yee uwaxích haa k̲u.éex’i. *You all can see that our hosts thank you from their hearts.*

**tudaxákw** noun *basket with a rattle in the lid*
VARIANTS: tuk̲daadaxákw

at **tugáni** noun *gunpowder*
VARIANTS: et tugáni (C)

**tuháayi** noun *nail*
·Tuháayi teen áwé át kawtusix’óo. *We nailed it on it with a nail.*
·Yóo katán wé tuháayi. *The nail is bent.*

a **tukayátx’i** noun *its seeds (inside it, as inside a berry)*
·Xéel’i kútx̲ a tukayátx’i yagéi. *Mossberries have too many seeds.*

a **tuk̲daa** RelationalNoun *(around) the bottom of it*
·Wuditláx̲ a tuk̲daa. *The bottom of it is moldy.*

**tuk̲daadaxákw** noun *basket with rattle in the lid*
VARIANTS: tudaxákw

**tuk̲daa.át** noun *diaper*
·Tlél dé tuk̲daa.át du.ús’k. *Diapers aren't washed anymore.*

**túk̲l’** noun *young spruce or hemlock*
·Ch’u shóogu aan wududliyex̲i túk̲l’ áwé a kax̲yee wéi ANB hall. *Those are the original young spruce they used to build the ceiling of the ANB hall.*

a **túk̲l’i** noun *cartilage, gristle*

du **tuk̲.woolí** noun *his/her anus*
VARIANTS: du toox̲’é (T)

**tuḵ'atáal** noun *pants, trousers*
·Tuḵ'atáal x̱'oosdé awdiyíḵ. *He put on his pants.*
·I tuḵ'atáali i daax̱ yei jeekanaxíx. *Your pants are falling down.*

**túlaa** noun *drill*
·Yées túlaa eetéenáx̱ x̱at yatee. *I need a new drill.*
·Yaawdiǥíl du túlayi. *His drill became dull.*

**tula.aan** noun *kindness; generosity of heart*
VARIANTS: tule.aan (C)
·Tula.aan een du éet x̱'eiwatán. *He spoke to her with kindness.*

**túlx'u** noun *drill bit*
·Woosh ǥuwanyáade kwdigéi túlx'u. *Drill bits come in different sizes.*

**tunax̱hinnadaa** noun *pipe (for carrying water)*

**tundatáan** noun *thought*
VARIANTS: tundetáan (C)
·I tundatáani kakǥinéek. *You will tell your thoughts.*

**tután** noun *hope; intention; focus of hopes or thoughts*

**tuteesh** noun *loneliness; boredom*

a **tuwáadáx̱** Adverb *because of it; due to it; by virtue of it; on the strength of it; encouraged by it*
·Haa léelk'u hás tuwáadáx̱ áwé gútk haa jeet kawduwatée. *If it wasn't for our elders, we wouldn't be here. (Lit: Because of our elders, we were given a dime.)*

**tuwaakú** noun *tobacco*
·Kél't' tuwaakúx̱ dulyéix̱. *They make tobacco out of wood ashes.*

a **tuwán** RelationalNoun *beside it, next to it*
·Tle hít tuwán áwé kóoḵ áa kei has akaawaháa. *Right next to the house they dug a pit.*
·Tle a tuwán áwé atx̱á daakahídi áa wdudliyéx̱. *They built a restaurant next to it.*

du **tuwáx'** noun *in his/her opinion; to his/her way of thinking, feeling*
·I tuwáx' yeewooyáat' yóo ḵu.éex'. *You thought the potlach was long.*

**túxjaa** noun *sound of stamping, pounding fists, clapping; sound of running quickly*
VARIANTS: tíxwjaa (At)
·Wé ḵu.éex' túxjaa duwa.áx̱ch aadé. *Stamping and clapping was heard at the potlach.*

**tux'andaxeech** noun *anxiety; wracked nerves; preoccupation; something weighing on one's mind*
VARIANTS: tux'endexeech (C)

du **tux̱'ax'aayí** noun *crack of his/her buttocks; his/her butt crack*

at **tux̱'wáns'i** noun *buckshot; moccasin lining*

**tux̱'wáns'i náakw** noun *pepper*
VARIANTS: tux̱'wáns'i náagu
·Tux̱'wáns'i náagu átx̱ dulyeix̱ín ch'áakw. *Long ago they made medicine out of pepper.*

# « T’ »

**t’á** noun *king salmon; chinook salmon; spring salmon*

·Tsaa eix̱í teen áwé yak’éi t’á at x̱’éeshi. *Dry fish king salmon is good with seal oil.*

·Yées t’á g̱íḵsi sitgawsáanx’ has aawax̱áa. *They ate fresh king salmon barbequed over the fire at noon.*

**T’AA** verb root

- **awsit’áa | ast’eix̱ | ast’eix̱**

  *s/he warmed it up | s/he is warming it up | s/he warms it up (regularly).*

  THEME: O-S-s-t’aa~ (ø act)

  *for S to warm O (water, etc.)*

  NOTES: The form: ast’eix̱ gives both a basic imperfective meaning "s/he is warming it up" and a repetitive imperfective meaning "s/he warms it up (regularly)".

  ·Ḵaa x̱’a.eetí awsit’áa. *She warmed up the leftovers.*

- **ḵoowat’áa | ḵuwat’áa / ḵuyat’áa | ---**

  *the weather got hot | the weather is hot | ---.*

  THEME: ḵu-ø-t’aa~ (ø state)

  *for the weather to be warm, hot*

  NOTES: This may be the only stative verb with a ø- conjugation prefix.

- **du toowú awlit’áa | du toowú alt’eix̱ | du toowú alt’eix̱**

  *he/she/it comforted him/her | he/she/it is comforting him/her | he/she/it comforts him/her (regularly).*

  THEME: N toowú S-l-t’aa~ (ø act)

  *for S to comfort N*

  NOTES: The form: du toowú alt’eix̱ gives both a basic imperfective meaning "he/she/it is comforting him/her" and a repetitive imperfective meaning "he/she/it comforts him/her (regularly)".

- **uwat’áa | yaa nat’éin | ---**

  *it's hot | it's getting hot | ---.*

  THEME: ø-t’aa~ (ø event)

  *for something to be warm, hot*

  ·Wé áak’w héeni uwat’áa. *The pond water is warm.*

  ·X̱’aan yakawlikís’. Wé kél’t’ ḵu.aa, ch’u uwat’áa. *The fire has gone out but the ashes are still warm.*

- **yaawat’áa | yaa yanat’éin | yat’éix̱**

  *it's hot | it's getting hot | it gets hot (regularly).*

  THEME: ya-ø-t’aa~ (ø event)

  *for something to be hot, heated*

  ·Wé yaawat’aayi héeng̱aa woogoot. *He went to get some heated water.*

·Ch'áagu aa kax̱'íl'aa stoox káx' áwé yan dutéeych yag̱at'aayít. *The irons of long ago were set on the stove to heat up.*

**t'áa** noun *board*

·K'idéin aax̱ xásh wé t'áa at x̱'ax̱éedli! *Cut the trimming off the board good!*

·Kax'ás'aa teen áwé kg̱eexáash ldakát wéi t'áa! *You will cut all those boards with a rip saw!*

**T'AACH** verb root

- **aawat'ách | at'ácht | at'áchx̱**

*s/he slapped him/her/it | s/he is slapping him/her/it | s/he slaps him/her/it (regularly).*

THEME: O-S-t'aach~ (ø act)

*for S to slap O; for S to tag O (as in game of tag)*

·Du jintáak teen at'ácht wé kadu.uxx̱u át. *She is slapping the balloon with the palm of her hand.*

du **t'aag̱í** noun *his/her clan brother or sister, distant relative, comrade*

**t'áa jáaji** noun *ski(s)*

**t'áa jáaji wootsaag̱ayí** noun *ski pole(s)*

du **t'áak** noun *behind him/her; back of him/her; at his/her back*

·K̲aa t'áak áwé áa awliyéx̱ du hídi. *He built his house behind the village.*

·K̲aa t'áak áwé áa uwax̱ée. *She camped behind everyone.*

a **t'áak** RelationalNoun *behind it; back inland from it; on the landward side of it (something on the water)*

**t'áa ká** noun *floor*

·T'áa kát k̲ushí ax̱ jeeyís - k̲ut kax̱waag̱éex' ax̱ kawóot ka.íshayi! *Look on the floor for me - I lost my needle!*

**t'áa kayéx̱aa** noun *plane for scraping wood*

VARIANTS: t'áa keyéx̱aa (C)

**T'AAKW** verb root

- **héende awjit'ákw | --- | héende asht'ákwx̱**

*it dove into the water | --- | it dives into the water (regularly).*

THEME: a-j-t'aakw~ (ø event)

*for something to dive into the water; for something to slap tail down hard as going down in water (esp. of killerwhale and beaver)*

·Cháax̱ héen táade awjit'ákw. *The grebe dove into the water.*

a **t'aak̲** RelationalNoun *beside it, at its side*

**T'aak̲ú** noun *Taku*

**t'áa shukaayí** noun *square (for marking boards)*

**t'áa shuxáshaa** noun *narrow saw used to cut corners off lumber; bevel saw*

**t'aaw** noun *feather*
·Kóon t'aawú yéi ndu.eich al'eix̲ yís. *Flicker feathers are used in dancing.*

**t'aawák̲** noun *Canada goose*
·Yei googénk'i at x̲éidi teen áwé x̲waat'úk wé t'aawák̲. *I shot the Canada goose with a small arrow.*

**t'aawák̲ x'eesháa** noun *tea kettle (originally with long curved spout)*

**T'aawyáat** noun *American Indian*

T'AAX̲' verb root
- **wusit'áax̲' | --- | sat'áax̲'x̲**
*it's burning hot | --- | it burns hot (regularly).*
THEME: s-t'áax̲' (ø event)
*for a fire, etc. to be hot, radiate, throw out heat*
·X̲'aan wusit'áax̲'. *The fire is burning hot.*

**t'áax̲'w** noun *wart*

**t'aay** noun *hot springs*

**t'áa yá** noun *wall*

**t'aa yátx'i** noun *shingles*

**t'aay néekw (AtT)** noun *fever*
VARIANTS: t'aay nóok (TC)

**T'ak̲deintaan** noun *T'ak̲deintaan, locally called "Seagull"; a clan of the Raven moiety whose principal crest is the Seagull*

a **t'ak̲ká** RelationalNoun *beside, alongside, next to it*
·Wildflower Court wé hospital t'ak̲káa yéi yatee. *Wildflower Court is next to the hospital.*

du **t'ak̲ká** RelationalNoun *beside, alongside, next to him/her*

a **t'áni** noun *its secondary branch*

**t'ási** noun *grayling*
·Héen wátt uwax'ák wé t'ási. *The grayling swam to the mouth of the river.*

**t'áx'x̲i** noun *dentalia shells*

**t'éesh** noun *tanning frame; frame for stretching skin*

**t'éesh kaayí** noun *square*

T'EEX' verb root
- **kaawat'íx' | kayat'éex' | kat'íx'x̲**
*it hardened | it's hard | it hardens (regularly).*

THEME: ka-ø-t'éex'~ (ga state)
*for something to harden, cake up*
·Hintakx'óosi nóox'u kayat'éex' *Coral shells are hard.*

• **--- | kasit'éex' | ---**
*--- | it's hard | ---.*
THEME: ka-s-t'éex'~ (ga state)
*for something to be hard (esp. of round object)*

• **woot'éex' | yat'éex' | kei t'íx'ch**
*it was difficult | it's difficult | it gets difficult (regularly).*
THEME: ø-t'éex' (ga state)
*for something to be hard (abstract), difficult*
·Yat'éex'i gaaw a tóonáx̱ yiyagút. *You walked through that period of hard time.*
·Wé dleey yat'éex'. *The meat is tough.*

• **wudlit'íx' | yaa nalt'íx' | ult'íx'x̱**
*it's frozen; it froze | it's freezing | it freezes (regularly).*
THEME: d-l-t'éex'~ (ø event)
*for something to harden, solidify; for something to freeze*
·G̱eey tá héen yaa nalt'íx'. *The water at the head of the bay is freezing.*
·Tlei ult'íx'ch taatx' wéi hít daadáx̱ kax'áasjaa. *The water dripping from the house freezes at night.*

**t'éex'** noun *ice*

**T'EEX̱'** verb root

• **akaawat'éx̱' | akat'éix̱' | akat'éx̱'x̱**
*s/he pounded it | s/he is pounding it | s/he pounds it (regularly).*
THEME: O-ka-S-ø-t'éix̱'~ (ø act)
*for S to smash O up by pounding; for S to mash O by pounding with something heavy; for S to pound, hammer on O*
VARIANTS: t'éex̱'~ (An)
·Góon dáanaa een áwé kawduwat'íx̱' ax̱ jeeyís yá kées. *This bracelet was pounded out of a gold coin for me.*

du **t'eey** noun *his/her elbow*

**T'EI**[1] verb root

• **aawat'ei | --- | kei at'eich**
*s/he found it | --- | s/he finds it (regularly).*
THEME: O-S-ø-t'ei (ga event)
*for S to find O (usually as the result of searching)*
·Tlagu aan yaduxas' át aawat'ei. *He found an old-time razor.*
·Wé s'eek gandaas'aají kúdi aawat'ei. *The black bear found a bee's nest.*

• **akaawat'ei | --- | kei akat'eich**
*s/he found it | --- | s/he finds it (regularly).*
THEME: O-ka-S-ø-t'ei (ga event)
*for S to find O (usually round, spherical object)*

a **t'éik** RelationalNoun *behind it*
·Aas t'éik áwé áa awdlisín wé kóoshdaa. *The land otter hid behind a tree.*

a **t'einyaa** noun *the inside of it (clothing, bedding); lining it*
VARIANTS: a t'einaa (C)

a **t'einyaakawoowú (At)** noun *its lining*
VARIANTS: a t'einyaakayoowú (T), a t'einyaakewoowú (C)

**t'eix̱** noun *fish hook*
·Du t'eix̱í ayaawag̱íl'. *He sharpened his fish hooks.*

**T'EIX̱** verb root

- **awdzit'eix̱ | ast'eix̱ | yoo adzit'eix̱k**
  *s/he fished (with a hook) | s/he is fishing (with a hook) | s/he fishes (with a hook) (regularly).*
  THEME: a-S-d-s-t'eix̱~ (na act)
  *for S to fish with hooks, catch on a hook, troll*
  ·Aashát tlein awdzit'eix̱. *She hooked a big steelhead trout.*
  ·Ast'eix̱ tlél ulnáalx̱in. *Trolling didn't used to be profitable.*

**t'eix̱áa (T)** noun *fish hook*
·T'eix̱áa een áwé cháatl has aawasháat. *They caught halibut with hooks.*

a **t'iká** RelationalNoun *beside it; out past it; out away from it; (on) the outskirts of it (town)*
·Héen t'ikáx̱ yaawashóo ḵaa x̱'oos deiyí. *The foot trail goes beside the river.*
·Héen t'iká át la.áa du hídi. *His house sits beside the river.*

du **t'iyshú** noun *tip of his/her elbow*

**t'ooch'** noun *charcoal*
·T'ooch' aa yéi nateech wé x̱'aan eetí. *There's charcoal where the fire was.*
·Haat kalajúx wé t'ooch'! *Wheel the coal over here!*

**t'ooch'** noun *black*
·T'ooch' yáx̱ shasitee. *She has black hair.*
·T'ooch' ḵa tl'áatl' yáx̱ dag̱aatée gandaas'aají. *Bees are black and yellow.*

**t'ooch' eex̱í** noun *petroleum, oil*

**t'ooch'ineit** noun *bottle; jug*

**t'ooch' ḵáa** noun *Black (man or person); African-American*
·Tléináx̱ t'ooch' ḵáa haa x̱oo yéi yatee. *There's only one black man among us.*

**t'ooch' té** noun *coal*

**t'ook** noun *cradleboard; papoose carrier*
·T'ook kát as.áa du yádi. *He has his child seated on the papoose board.*

## T'OOK verb root

- **aawat'úk | --- | at'úkx̲**

  *s/he shot it | --- | s/he shoots it (regularly).*

  THEME: O-S-ø-t'óok~ (ø event)

  *for S to shoot O (with bow and arrow); for S to choose O (in gambling with sticks)*

  ·Yei googénk'i at x̲éidi teen áwé x̲waat'úk wé t'aawák̲. *I shot the Canada goose with a small arrow.*

  ·Wé yadak'wátsk'u chooneit tín áwé aawat'úk wé ts'ítskw. *The young boy shot the bird with a barbed arrow.*

**t'óok'** noun *nettle*

NOTES: Warning: stinging hairs contain formic acid which causes rash and edema

·T'óok' x̲oodé daak ax̲ wudzigít. *I fell into the stinging nettles.*

**t'ukanéiyi** noun *baby*

VARIANTS: t'ookanéiyi (T)

·Goox' sáwé yéi has gax̲dusk̲éi wé t'ukanéiyi? *Where will they seat the babies?*

·Tíx' k̲a x'óow tin g̲eeg̲ách' awliyéx̲ t'ukanéiyi jeeyís. *She made a hammock for the baby with rope and a blanket.*

# « Tl »

TLAA verb root

- **--- | yéi kwditláa | ---**

  --- | *it's that big around* | ---.
  THEME: (yéi) ka-u-d-tlaa~ (na state)
  *for something to be (so) big around, in girth*
  ·G̲unayéide kwditlawu g̲ayéis' tíx' du jeewú. *He has steel cables of different sizes.*

**du tláa** noun *his/her mother*
·Yaa ax̲ léelk'w ax̲ tláa yinaanáx̲ K̲éin yóo dusáagun yaa Xutsnoowúdáx̲. *My grandmother on my mother's side was called Ñéin, from Angoon.*
·Yan ashawlihík yá haa tláach. *This mother of ours has completed everything.*

**tlaagú** noun *myth; legend; children's tale*
·G̲unakadeit daat tlaagú dax̲k̲udzitee. *There are legends about sea monsters.*

TLAAKW verb root

- **akaawatlaakw | yaa akanatlákw | yoo akayatlákwk**

  *s/he's investigating it; s/he investigated it* | *s/he's (in the process of) investigating it* | *s/he investigates it (regularly).*
  THEME: O-ka-S-ø-tlaakw~ (na event)
  *for S to investigate, make inquiry into, research O*
  ·Ch'áakw aan galak̲ú yaa kandutlákw. *A flood from long ago is being researched.*

- **k̲oon aawatlákw | k̲oon atláakw | ---**

  *s/he told people a legend* | *s/he is telling people a legend* | ---.
  THEME: O-S-ø-tlaakw~ (ø act)
  *for S to tell, recount, narrate O (legend, myth, fairy tale, etc.)*
  ·Aadéi dutlákw yé áyá, kakatáx'aa teen yawduwadlaak̲. *As the story goes, he was defeated by a pair of pliers.*

**tláakw** Adverb *fast*
·Tláakw ax̲áa du aandaayaagú. *He is rowing his rowboat quickly.*
·Tláakw naadaayi héen kulix̲éitl'shán. *A fast river is dangerous.*

**du tláak'w** noun *his/her maternal aunt*
·Ax̲ tláak'wch áa x̲at shukaawajáa, aadé yéi daadunei yé. *My maternal aunt taught me how to make it.*

**tláak̲** noun *sharp arrow for killing*
·Tláak̲ du eedé ksixát. *The arrow is stuck in his body.*

**tlaax̱** noun *mold*
·Tlaax̱ áa yaa kana.éin. *Mold is growing there.*

**TLAAX̱** verb root
• **wuditláx̱ | yaa ndatláx̱ | ditláx̱kw**
*it's moldy; it got moldy | it's getting moldy | it molds (easily, regularly).*
THEME: d-tlaax̱~ (ø event)
*for something to be moldy*
·Wuditláx̱ a tuḵdaa. *The bottom of it is moldy.*

du **tlagooḵwansaayí** noun *his/her namesake*
VARIANTS: du tlegooḵwansaayí (C)
·Du léelk'w du tlagooḵwansaayíx̱ sitee. *His grandparent is his namesake.*

**tlagu** adj. *old; from the past*
·Aanḵáawuch áwé woo.oo, wé tlagu hít tlein. *A rich person bought the big old house.*
·Wé tlagu hídi gáannáx̱ wuduwanéegwál'. *Someone painted the outside of the old house.*

**tlagu ḵwáanx'i** noun *people of long ago*

**tlagu ts'ats'éeyee** noun *grey singing bird (sparrow or finch)*

**tlag̱anís** noun *pole; sapling*
·Tlag̱anís aan kwéiyi tugáas'ix̱ has awliyéx̱. *They made a flagpole out of a sapling.*

du **tlag̱eiyí** noun *his/her brain*
VARIANTS: du tleg̱eiyí (C)
·Átx̱ layéx̱ dé i tlag̱eiyí! *Use your brain now!*

**tlákw** particle *always, all the time, constantly*
·Tlákw kaduk'énx' wé cheech. *The porpoise always jump.*
·Tlákw s'eenáa a káa yéi nateech eech kakwéiyi. *There's always a light on a fixed buoy.*

**Tlákw Aan** noun *Klukwan*
·Tlákw Aandáx̱ haa shoow sitee. *Our roots stem from Klukwan.*
·Jilḵáat Ḵwáan Tlákw Aanx' has ḵuya.óo. *The Chilkat people live in Klukwan.*

**Tláp!** interj. *Oops!*

**tlax̱** particle *very*
·Watsíx a lututúḵl'i tléil tlax̱ ugé. *The soft bone in a caribou nose is not very big.*
·Tlél tlax̱ kooshx̱'íl'k yá kaxwaan. *It's not very slippery with this frost.*

**tlax̱aneis'** noun *kingfisher*

**tle** particle *just, simply; just then*
VARIANTS: tlei
·Tlei déix̱ ḵ’ateil yáx̱ áwé wutusineix̱ shákw kahéeni. *We just saved two gallons of the strawberry juice.*
·G̱eiwú wooch yáx̱ awsinei tle daak ashakaawaḵúx̱. *She straightened the net out and then she set it.*

**tleidahéen** noun *once, one time*
VARIANTS: tlex’dahéen, tleidehéen (C)
·Tleidahéen, yéi at woonei. *Once upon a time, this happened.*
·Tleidahéen áwé Yaakwdáatt aa wlihásh wé kanóox’. *One time a turtle floated to Yakutat.*

**tleidooshóonáx̱** Numeral *six (people)*

**tleidooshú** Numeral *six*
·Ax̱ atx’aan hídi tleidooshú ḵaa x̱’oos ḵa daax’oonx̱ sitee. *My smoke house is six feet by four feet.*
·Tleidooshú ḵaa x̱’oos yéi kwliyáat’ wé kaay. *That measuring stick is six feet long.*

**tleikatánk** noun *red huckleberry*
·Tleikatánk kanat’á een yak’éi. *Red huckleberries are good with blueberries.*
·Tleikatánk áwé kanat’áx̱ x̱oo yéi nateech. *Red huckleberries are always among blueberries.*

**tléik’** particle *no*
VARIANTS: tlåyk’

**tleiḵáa** Numeral *twenty*
·Tleiḵáa dáanaa ax̱ éet hís’! *Lend me twenty dollars!*
·Gwál tleiḵáa x̱’oos áwé a kax̱yeedé. *It must be twenty feet to the ceiling.*

**tleiḵáa ḵa tléináx̱** Numeral *twenty one (people)*

**tleiḵáa ḵa tléix’** Numeral *twenty one*
·Tleiḵáa ḵa tléix’ áwé du katáagu. *He is twenty-one years old.*

**tleiḵáanáx̱** Numeral *twenty (people)*

**tléiḵw** noun *berry, berries*
·Wé tléiḵw daakeidí yís áyá. *This is a container for the berries.*
·Yeisú kadlix̱’át’ wé tléiḵw. *The berries are still green.*

**tléiḵw kahéeni** noun *berry juice*
·Tléiḵw kahéeni awdináa. *He drank berry juice.*
·Ax̱ x̱’éit aa kax̱ích tléiḵw kahéeni! *Give me some juice! (Lit: Throw some juice at my mouth!)*

**tleiḵw kahínti** noun *watermelon berry, twisted stalk, wild cucumber*

**tléiḵw wás'i** noun *berry bush*
VARIANTS: tléḵw wás'i
·Tléiḵw wás'i áa kaawa.aa. *Berry bushes are growing there.*

**tléil** particle *no, none, not*
VARIANTS: tlél, l, hél
·Du tl'eḵtlein áwé tlél á. *His middle finger is missing.*
·Kaldaag̱éináx̱ yaa gax̱tooḵóox̱, tlél g̱wadlaan yá éix̱' yík. *We will travel along slowly, it's not deep in this slough.*

**tlein** adj. *big*
·Ax̱ léelk'u hás jeeyís áwé wududliyéx̱ wé atx'aan hídi tlein. *That big smoke house was built for my grandparents.*
·Ḵukawduyéil'i áwé Galyéx̱dei g̱unayéi uḵoox̱ch wéi yaakw tlein. *The big boat would start traveling to the Kahliyet River when the weather was calm.*

**tléináx̱** Numeral *one (person)*
·Tléináx̱ t'ooch' ḵáa haa x̱oo yéi yatee. *There's only one black man among us.*
·Tléináx̱ ḵáa áx̱ yaa nagút. *One person is walking along there.*

**tléix'** Numeral *one*
·Yan uwanéi ágé wé tléix' aa yáx̱? *Is it ready like the other one?*
·Tléix' ḵ'ateil yáx̱ áwé liyék wéi xén. *That plastic container can hold one gallon.*

**tléix' hándit** Numeral *one hundred*

**tleiyán** noun *shoreline*

**tleiyeekaadé** Adverb *one kind, type; one way, direction*
VARIANTS: tleiyeekaadéi

**tlék'g̱aa** Numeral *one at a time, one by one*
·Tlék'g̱aa áwé anax̱ daak has aawal'éx̱. *One by one they danced out.*

**tlék'g̱aanáx̱** Numeral *one (person) at a time*
·Tlék'g̱aanáx̱ áwé has wuduwax̱oox̱. *They called them one by one.*

**tléḵw yádi** noun *raspberry*
VARIANTS: tléiḵw yádi
·Tléiḵw yádi has aawa.ín. *They picked raspberries.*

**tlél daa sá** noun *nothing*
VARIANTS: tléil daa sá, hél daa sá

**tlex'dahéen** Numeral *once, one time*
VARIANTS: tleidahéen, tleidehéen (C)
·Ch'a tlex'dahéen du een kananeek! *Just tell him once!*

**tl'ik̲kakées** noun *ring*

·Du jintáak káa yan akaawatée du tl'ik̲kakéesi. *He put his ring in the center of his palm.*

**tliyaa** Demonstrative *farther over; way over*

·Tliyaa aani k̲wáani haa x̲ánt has uwa.át. *The people from that town have come to visit us.*

·Yóo tliyaa aasdéi ksaxát wéi kaxées' ax̲ at shí k̲óok gúgu yís! *Attach the wire to that tree over there for my radio antenna!*

**tliyaatgé** noun *the other day; a few days ago*

VARIANTS: tliyaatatgé (At)

·Ch'u tliyaatgé áwé shux̲wsitee. *I was expecting it the other day.*

TLOOX' verb root

- **aadé wootlóox' | --- | aadé yoo yatlúx'k**

  *he/she/it crawled there on his/her/it's belly | --- | he/she/it crawls there on his/her/its belly (regularly).*

  THEME: P-dé S-ø-tloox'~ (na motion)

  *for S to creep, crawl on hands and toes with body close to ground (usually when stalking game) toward P*

- **át wootlóox' | --- | ---**

  *he/she/it is crawling around on his/her/its belly; he/she/it crawled around on his/her/its belly | --- | ---.*

  THEME: P-t S-ø-tloox'~ (na motion)

  *for S to creep, crawl around on hands and toes with body close to ground (usually when stalking game) at P; for S to squirm around on the ground at P*

  ·Geesh x̲oot wootlóox' wé yáxwch'. *The sea otter is rolling around in the kelp.*

**tlóox̲** noun *mud bullhead*

·Tlóox̲ tlél toox̲á. *We don't eat bullhead.*

# « Tl' »

**tl'aadéin** Adverb *sideways*
·Tl'aadéin áwé át tán wé k̲óok. *The box is sitting sideways.*

**tl'aadéin.aa** noun *turnip*
·Shaatk'átsk'ux̲ x̲at siteeyí ax̲ x̲'é k'éiyin wé tl'aadéin.aa. *When I was a little girl, I used to love turnips.*

TL'AAK' verb root

- **wuditl'ák' | yaa ndatl'ák' | datl'ák'x̲**
*he/she/it is wet | he/she/it is getting wet | he/she/it gets wet (regularly).*
THEME: O-d-tl'aak'~ (ø event)
*for O to be wet (may be thoroughly wet, but not by actual immersion)*
·K̲únáx̲ x̲at wuditl'ák', kaklahéen áyá aawag̲éet. *I'm so wet - wet snow is coming down hard.*

**tl'áak'** noun *pale; pastel*
·Tl'átgi káa yagéi wé tl'áak'. *There are a lot of dead leaves on the ground.*

**tl'aak̲'wách'** noun *sourdock; wild rhubarb*
NOTES: Warning: leaves contain oxalic acid, possibly harmful in large quantities
·Tl'aak̲'wách' een áwé awsi.ée wé kaxwéix̲. *She cooked wild rhubarb with cranberries.*
·Kóox een dus.ée tl'aak̲'wách'. *Wild rice is cooked with wild rhubarb.*

**tl'áatl'** noun *yellow*
·Tl'áatl' aas yít wudik̲een. *The small bird flew into the tree.*
·T'ooch' k̲a tl'áatl' yáx̲ dag̲aatée gandaas'aají. *Bees are black and yellow.*

**tl'ag̲áa** Adverb *enough; adequate*
·De tl'ag̲áa áwé yakoogéi. *There is enough.*

**tl'átk** noun *earth; land, country; soil*
VARIANTS: tl'átgi, tl'étk (C)
·Tl'átgi káa yéi nateech k̲'eishkaháagu. *Low bush cranberries are on the ground.*
·Yú sgóon tl'átgi tlein, a góonnáx̲ dax̲yanaagóo wé káa. *The cars are traveling on the isthmus of the big school yard.*

**tl'áxch'** noun *old, dead branch*
·Shayadihéin tl'áxch' táakwde yaa k̲unahéini. *There are a lot of dead branches when it becomes winter.*

a **tl'eegí** noun *its tentacle (of octopus)*
VARIANTS: a tl'eigí (C)
·Shayadihéin has du tl'eegí wé náakw. *Octopus have a lot of tentacles.*

**tl'éek'at** noun *sticks woven through the fish lengthwise after it has been filleted for barbecuing*

du **tl'eek** noun *his/her finger*
VARIANTS: du tl'eik
·Du tl'eek áwé ax yáa ash akaawliyén. *He's shaking his finger at me.*

TL'EET' verb root

- **ashawlitl'ít' | yaa ashanaltl'ít' | ashalatl'ít'x**
*s/he filled it | s/he is filling it | s/he fills it (regularly).*
THEME: O-sha-S-l-tl'éet'~ (ø event)
*for S to fill O (with liquid)*
·A kat'óott shalatl'ít', tlél kei kgwadál! *Fill it halfway, then it won't be heavy!*

**tl'eex** noun *filth, mess; trash, rubbish, garbage*
·Gáande wé tl'eex! *Put the dirt outside!*

a **tl'eigí (C)** noun *its tentacle (of octopus)*
VARIANTS: a tl'eegí

du **tl'eik** noun *his/her finger*
VARIANTS: du tl'eek
·Táax'ál' x'aan áwé ax tl'eik tóode yawdigeech. *The needle point poked my finger.*
·Ax tl'eik káa wjikaak digitgiyáa. *A hummingbird landed on my finger.*

a **tl'éili** noun *its semen; its milt (of fish)*

TL'EIT' verb root

- **a daax kei wdlitl'ét' | a daax kei naltl'ét' | a daax kei iltl'ét'ch**
*he/she/it climbed up it | he/she/it is climbing up it | he/she/it climbs up it (regularly).*
THEME: N daax kei S-d-l-tl'eit'~ (ø motion)
*for S to climb up along N (tree, rope, etc.) by holding on tightly*
·Aas daax kei wdlitl'ét'. *He climbed up the tree.*

- **a yáx wudlitl'éit' | a yáx kei naltl'ét' | a yáx kei iltl'ét'ch**
*he/she/it climbed the face of it | he/she/it is climbing the face of it | s/he climbs the face of it (regularly).*
THEME: N yáx S-d-l-tl'éit'~ (ga motion)
*for S to climb up along the face of N (mountain, cliff, fence, etc.)*
·Gíl' yáx kei naltl'ét' wé yadák'w. *The young boy is climbing the cliff face.*

**tl'éitl'** noun *moonfish, suckerfish, blowfish*
VARIANTS: tl'étl'

du **tl'ek̲shá** noun *his/her fingertip*
VARIANTS: du tl'ik̲shá
·Du tl'ek̲shá áwé awlix̲'éx̲' wé stoox káx'. *He burned his fingertip on the stove.*

du **tl'ek̲tlein** noun *his/her middle finger*
VARIANTS: du tl'ik̲tlein
·Du tl'ek̲tlein áwé tlél á. *His middle finger is missing.*

du **tl'ek̲x̲'áak** noun *between his/her fingers*

**tl'ik̲naa.át** noun *thimble*
·Tl'ik̲naa.át een duk̲éis'. *A thimble is used for sewing.*

du **tl'ik̲shá** noun *his/her fingertip*
VARIANTS: du tl'ek̲shá

du **tl'ik̲tlein** noun *his/her middle finger*
VARIANTS: du tl'ek̲tlein

**tl'ildaaskeit** noun *littleneck clams*

du **tl'óog̲u** noun *his/her liver*
·Dzísk'u tl'óog̲u k̲a a dáali ax̲ x̲'é yak'éi. *I like to eat moose liver and its tripe.*
·Du tl'óog̲u áwé ash kaawaxíl'. *Her liver is bothering her.*

**tl'ook̲** noun *rotting sore; gangrene; cancer*
·Tl'ook̲ du jín daa yéi yatee. *There are sores on his hand.*

**tl'úk'x̲** noun *worm; larva; grub; caterpillar; snake*
·Tl'úk'x̲ awsiwadi shaawát daatx̲ shkalneek k̲udzitee. *There's a story about the woman who raised the worm.*

# « Ts »

**tsá** particle *only then*

·Náakw s'é áa yéi kk̲wa.oo ax̲ keey aag̲áa tsá wéi kashóok' gwéil. *I will put medicine on my knee first, then the heating pad.*

·Tlél ushik'éiyi aa yoo x̲'atánk áwé tsá a.ax̲ji nooch . *She always only hears the bad talk.*

**tsaa** noun *hair seal*

·A kaax̲ sh tukdlig̲éi du tsaa doogú at xáshdi téel. *She is proud of her seal skin moccasins.*

·Aax̲ awlixaash a geení wé tsaa. *He cut the tail flippers off of the seal.*

**Tsaagweidí** noun *Tsaagweidí; a clan of the Eagle moiety whose principal crests are the Seal and Killerwhale*

**tsaag̲ál'** noun *spear*

·Tsaag̲ál' átx̲ dulyeix̲ín ch'áakw. *Spears were used long ago.*

**TSAAK̲** verb root

• **kei jiwlitsák̲ | --- | kei jilatsák̲x̲**

*s/he raised a hand* | --- | *s/he raises a hand (regularly).*

THEME: kei ji-S-l-tsaak̲~ (ø event)

*for (singular) S to raise the hand (in voting, etc.)*

**tsáats** noun *bear root, Indian potato*

**tság̲aa** noun *pole (for boating, for pushing skin toboggan)*

·Tság̲aa een yaakw daak has ayawliták̲. *They pushed the boat offshore with a pole.*

**tsálk** noun *arctic ground squirrel*

**tsé** particle *be sure not to*

NOTES: This particle is used with the admonitive verb form, which gives the meaning "be sure not to (verb)"; "see that you don't (verb)".

**TSEEK** verb root

• **awlitsík | altséek | altsíkx̲**

*s/he barbecued it* | *s/he's barbecueing it* | *s/he barbecues it (regularly).*

THEME: O-S-l-tseek~ (ø act)

*for S to broil O slowly, cook O directly over live coals, barbecue*

**tséek** noun *spit, skewer, roasting stick, barbecue stick*

·Tséek één has awsi.ée wé cháatl. *They barbecued the halibut.*

·K'ínk'i tséegi k̲únáx̲ yak'éi. *Barbecued fermented salmon heads are very good.*

**TSEEN** verb root

- **tlél wultseen | tléil ultseen | tlél kei ultseench**
  *he/she/it was weak | he/she/it is weak | s/he doesn't get stronger.*
  THEME: tlél O-l-tseen (ga state)
  *for O to be weak; for O to be mild (of weather); for O to be anemic*
  VARIANTS: -cheen
  ·Du yakg̲wahéiyágu tléil ultseen. *His spirit is weak.*
- **wulitseen | litseen | kei latseench**
  *he/she/it became strong | he/she/it is strong | he/she/it gets strong (regularly).*
  THEME: O-l-tseen (ga state)
  *for O to be strong, powerful*
  ·Wóoshnáx̲ x̲'akakéix̲i tíx' yáanáx̲ litseen. *Chain is stronger than rope.*
  ·Xunaa K̲áawu áwé k̲únáx̲ has litseen. *Hoonah people are very strong.*
- **x̲'awlitseen | x̲'alitseen | kei x̲'alatseench**
  *it was expensive | it's expensive | it gets expensive (regularly).*
  THEME: x̲'a-l-tseen (ga state)
  *for something to be expensive, high-priced; for something to be precious, of great value*
  ·T'á k̲únáx̲ x̲'alitseen Dzantik'i Héenix'. *King salmon is very expensive in Juneau.*
  ·Tléix' dáanaa yéi x̲'alitseen katíx̲'aa x'úx' daakahídix'. *A key costs one dollar at the post office.*

**tseeneidi shál** noun *handmade ladle*

**tseenx̲'é** noun *lizard, newt*

**TSEIX̲** verb root

- **aawatséx̲ | atséx̲t | atséx̲t**
  *s/he kicked it | s/he's kicking it | s/he kicks it (regularly).*
  THEME: O-S-ø-tseix̲~ (ø act)
  *for S to kick O; for S to stamp O, put foot down on O violently*
  NOTES: The form: atséx̲t gives both a basic imperfective meaning "s/he is kicking it" and a repetitive imperfective meaning: "s/he kicks it (regularly)".
  ·K̲óok shutú aawatséx̲. *She died. (Lit: S/he kicked the edge of the box.)*

**du tseiyí** noun *his/her sweetheart*

**tsín** noun *muskrat*

**tsísk'w** noun *owl with ear tufts*
·Xáanaax' áwé du.ax̲ji nooch tsísk'w. *Owls are heard at night.*
·Tlél aa k̲wasatínch wé k'ákw yóo duwasáagu aa tsísk'w. *I have never seen the bird they call the owl without ear tufts.*

**TSOOW** verb root

- **g̲agaan át x̲'oos uwatsóow | --- | ---**

  *sun rays are shining on it* | --- | ---.

  THEME: g̲agaan P-t~ x̲'oos ø-tsóow (ø event)

  *for the sun rays to shine on P*

  ·G̲agaan át x̲'oos uwatsóow. *Sun rays are shining on it. (Lit: The sun is poking its feet out.)*

**tsu** particle *again; still; some more*

VARIANTS: tsoo

·Tsu yéi wunak̲á! *You can say that again!*

**tsú** particle *also, too, as well*

·Du gúkx' tsú yéi aa wduwa.oo wéi s'aak̲ k̲'anoox̲. *They put the small bone labret in his ear too.*

·K̲únáx̲ wé yee woo.éex'i aa tsú yee x̲oo yéi kg̲watée toowú k'é teen. *Your hostess will welcome you all as well. (Lit: Your hostess will be among you all with good feelings.)*

# « Ts' »

**TS'AA** verb root

- **wulits'áa | lits'áa | kei lats'áaych**

  *he/she/it was fragrant | he/she/it is fragrant | he/she/it becomes fragrant (reguarly).*

  THEME: O-l-ts'áa (ga state)

  *for O to be fragrant, sweet-smelling*

  ·Keishísh áwé lats'áa nooch k̲utaanx'. *Alder always smells good in the summer.*

  ·Tlél kei gux̲lats'áa i daat sh kalneek. *Gossip about you is not going to smell good.*

**ts'ak'áawásh** noun *dried fish strips, dried necktie style*
·Ts'ak'áawásh Deishúdáx̲ has aawa.oo. *They bought dried fish strips from Haines.*

**ts'ák̲l** noun *black with dirt, filth, stain*

**ts'anéi** noun *round basket made of split red cedar branches*

**ts'ats'ée** noun *songbird; bird*
VARIANTS: ts'ets'ée (C)
·Ts'ats'ée áwé x̲waa.áx̲ tatgé ts'ootaat. *I heard a songbird yesterday morning.*
·Wé ts'ats'ée g̲agaan x̲'usyeet .áa. *That song bird is sitting in the ray of sunlight.*

**ts'axweil** noun *crow*
·Ts'axweil át kawdliyeech. *Crows are flying around.*

**ts'eeg̲éeni** noun *magpie*
VARIANTS: ts'eig̲éeni (T)

**ts'éekáx̲k'w** noun *alpine blueberry*
·Ts'éekáx̲k'w has aawa.ín. *They picked alpine blueberries.*

a **ts'éek'u** noun *its muscles (of shell creature)*

**ts'eig̲éeni (T)** noun *magpie*
VARIANTS: ts'eeg̲éeni

**ts'ésx̲'w** noun *snail with shell*

at **ts'ík'wti** noun *muscles of a shell creature; pincher; thing that pinches*

**ts'ítskw** noun *songbird; bird*
·Du kíji áwé wool'éex' wé ts'ítskw, ách áwé tlél át wudaḵeen. *The songbird's wing broke, that's why it doesn't fly around.*

**ts'ootaat** noun *morning*
·Ts'ats'ée áwé x̱waa.áx̱ tatgé ts'ootaat. *I heard a songbird yesterday morning.*
·Ts'ootaat shax̱wdinúk. *I got up in the morning.*

**Ts'ootsxán** noun *Tsimshian*
VARIANTS: Ts'ootsxén
·Deikeenaa ḵa Ts'ootsxán áa shayadihéin Kichx̱áan. *There are a lot of Haida and Tsimshian people in Ketchikan.*
·Ts'ootsxánch uwasháa ax̱ kéek'. *A Tsimshian married my little sister.*

# « U »

**-u** postpos. *is/are at*
·Chudéi áwé a k̲'anoox̲ú áwu. *Tom cod have a beard.*
·Gáanu hás, i yeeg̲áax̲ has sitee. *They are outside waiting for you.*

**uháan** Pronoun *we [independent]*
·Ldakát uháan haa wduwa.éex'. *All of us were invited.*

**ús'aa** noun *soap*
·Ús'aa een daa dushóoch *People bathe with soap.*

**útlx̲i** noun *boiled fish*
·X̲'áakw útlx̲i awsi.ée. *She cooked freshwater sockeye soup.*
·X̲'áax'w útlx̲i áwé yak'éi. *Boiled ling cod is good.*

**ux̲ganhéen** noun *kerosene; coal oil*
·Ux̲ganhéen s'eenáa káax' has dak̲éis'in. *They used to sew by kerosene lamp.*

**ux̲gank̲áas'** noun *match*
·Ux̲gank̲áas' tin áx̲ akdulgaan. *It is lit with a match.*
·Al'óon wugoodí ux̲gank̲áas' du g̲altóode ayaawa.oo. *When he was going hunting, he put matches in his pocket.*

**ux̲ kei** Adverb *out of control; blindly*

du **ux̲k'idleeyí** noun *his/her gums*

# « W »

**wáachwaan** noun *policeman; policewoman*

**wáadishgaa** noun *priest*
·K̲aa yáx̲ kei jisatánch wáadishgaa. *The priest blesses people.*

du **waak̲** noun *his/her eye*
·Du waak̲náx̲ kaawaxeex. *He's staring at it. (Lit: It fell through his eye.)*

**wáang̲aneens** Adverb *sometimes, once in a while*
·Wáang̲aneensx' yanax̲ kei shak'íx̲'ch ax̲ yoo x̲'atángi. *Sometimes my words get hung up.*

**wáa sá** Adverb *how*
·Wé íx̲t'ch du een akaawaneek wáa sá at gug̲waneiyí. *The medicine man told him what was going to happen.*
·Wáa yateeyi lingít sáwé wa.é? *What kind of person are you?*

**Waashdan K̲wáan** noun *American*
·Haadé yaa s k̲unatín Waashdan K̲wáan. *The Americans are traveling here.*

**waat** noun *armspan; fathom*
·Tleik̲áa waat yéi kg̲waadláan. *It's twenty fathoms deep.*

WAAT verb root

- **awsiwát | aswáat | aswátx̲**
  *s/he raised him/her/it | s/he raises him/her/it; s/he is raising him/her/it | s/he raises him/her/it (regularly).*
  THEME: O-S-s-wáat~ (ø act)
  *for S to raise O (child, animal); for S to grow O (plant)*
  ·Tl'úk'x̲ awsiwadi shaawát daatx̲ shkalneek k̲udzitee. *There's a story about the woman who raised the worm.*
  ·Ánk'w áwé kéi has anaswát wéit lingítch. *Those people are raising a crybaby.*
- **kei uwawát | kei nawát | ---**
  *s/he grew up | he/she/it is growing up | ---.*
  THEME: O-ø-wáat~ (ø event)
  *for O to grow up (size and maturity) (esp. of human and animal)*
  NOTES: Note that the kei in: kei uwawát "he/she/it grew up" is optional, and therefore is not given in the Leer-Edwards theme. However, speakers generally prefer to use the verb with kei.
  ·Ana.óot x̲oox' uwawát wé k̲áa. *That man grew up among the Aleut people.*
  ·A tóodáx̲ kei uwawát. *He grew out of it.*

**wáa yateeyi yéix'** Adverb *sometimes*
·Wáa yateeyi yéix' yáax' yéi aa nateech táakw kanax̱ wé ḵaatoowú. *Sometimes some chickadees stay here through the winter.*
·Wáa yateeyi yéix' at gutu.ádi g̱alsháatadix̱ dulyéx̱ch. *Sometimes wild animals are held captive.*

**waḵdáanaa** noun *eyeglasses*
·Waḵdáanaa waaḵt akal.át. *She has eyeglasses on. (Lit: She has glasses lying on her eyes.)*

**waḵdlóoḵ** noun *sleep in his/her eyes*
·Wé i waḵdlóog̱u aax̱ na.óos'! *Clean the sleep from your eyes!*

du **waḵḵá** noun *blocking his/her view; in his/her way (so that he/she can't see)*
VARIANTS: du waḵḵas'óox'

du **waḵḵadoogú** noun *his/her eyelid*
VARIANTS: du waḵḵedoogú (C)

**waḵḵadóox'** noun *blindfold*
·Waḵḵadóox' du yáa yéi duwa.óo. *He was blindfolded.*

**waḵḵals'oox̱' gáaxw** noun *scooter duck*
·Gáaxw áwé yéi duwasáakw waḵḵals'oox̱' gáaxw. *That duck is called a scooter duck.*

du **waḵḵas'óox'** noun *blocking his/her view; in his/her way (so that he/she can't see)*
VARIANTS: du waḵḵá
·Du waḵḵas'óox' áwé át eehán. *You're blocking his view.*

du **waḵlatáak** noun *inside of his/her eye*
VARIANTS: du waḵltáak

du **waḵltáak** noun *inside of his/her eye*
VARIANTS: du waḵlatáak
·Du waḵltáaknáx̱ át wooxeex. *Something fell in her eye.*

du **waḵshiyee** noun *before his/her eyes; where he/she can see (it)*
VARIANTS: du waḵshee (C)
·Ax̱ waḵshiyeex' yéi nasné! *Show me how it's done!*
·I waḵshiyeex' yéi yatee. *It's in front of your eyes.*

du **waḵshú** noun *corner of his/her eye*

a **wán** RelationalNoun *edge of it; (to the) side of it*
·Yá ax̱ l'eix̱ k'oodás' a wán shóot at ḵá! *Sew something to the edge of my dance shirt!*
·A wándáx̱ áwé a yíkt sh wudligás' wé yéil. *The raven leapt into it from the edge.*

a **wanáak** RelationalNoun *separate from it; on the edge, side of it; missing its mark*
VARIANTS: a wanyáak
·A wanáax' yakoojél wé cháas'! *Put the Humpback salmon separate from them!*
·A wanáax' yéi inatí wé kaxéel'! *Separate yourself from trouble!*

**wanadóo** noun *sheep*
VARIANTS: wanedóo (C)
·Shaa yá daat na.átch wanadóo. *Sheep walk the mountainsides.*
·Al'óoni wé wanadóo ítx̲ kei nagút. *The hunter is following the sheep that is going uphill.*

**wanadóo latíni** noun *shepherd*
VARIANTS: wanedóo letíni (C)
·Wé wanadóo latíni táach uwaják̲. *The shepherd fell asleep.*

**wanadóo yádi** noun *lamb*
VARIANTS: wanedóo yédi (C)
·Wé wanadóo yádi k̲ut wudzigeet. *The lamb got lost.*

**wanatíx** noun *ant*
·Ash wusitáax' wé wanatíx. *The ant bit him.*
·Wanatíxch wusitáax' du wankach'eek̲. *The ant bit his little finger.*

**wanatóox** noun *ant*
VARIANTS: wanatíx (T)

a **wanká** RelationalNoun *on the edge, side of it (as a trail); on the shoulder of it*
·A wankát has k̲éen wé yéil. *The ravens are sitting on the edge of it.*

du **wankach'eek̲** noun *his/her little finger*
VARIANTS: du wankech'eek̲ (C)
·Wanatíxch wusitáax' du wankach'eek̲. *The ant bit his little finger.*

**wankashxéet** noun *starry flounder*
·Dux̲á wankashxéet. *Starry flounders are eaten.*

**wasóos** noun *cow*
·Wasóos áwé a dleeyí yak'éi. *Cow meat is good.*
·Wasóos wé akahéix̲i jee shayadihéin. *The farmer has lots of cows.*

**wasóos l'aayí** noun *cow's milk*
·Wasóos l'aayí yak'éi wásh een. *Cow milk is good with mush.*

**wás'** noun *bush*
·Wás' kadánjaa áwé tláakw k̲uya.óo. *People are overcome by the pollen.*

**Was'eeneidí** noun *Was'eeneidí; a clan of the Eagle moiety whose principal crests are the Wolf and Auklet*

**was'x'aan tléig̱u** noun *salmonberry*
·Was'x'aan tléig̱ug̱áa woogoot ax̱ tláa. *My mom walked to get salmonberries.*

du **wásh** noun *his/her cheek*

**wásh** noun *mush, oatmeal, porridge*

**washéen** noun *engine, motor*
·Yées washéen a géekt satéen wé yaakw. *A new motor sits at the stern of that boat.*
·Washéen kayéik aawa.áx̱. *She heard the sound of the machine.*

**washéen katág̱ayi** noun *engine cylinder connecting rod*
·Yá washéen katág̱ayi woosháash. *This connecting rod wore out.*

du **washká** noun *(outside of) his/her cheek*
·X̱'aan yáx̱ yatee du washká. *His cheek is red.*

du **washtú** noun *inside of his/her cheek*
·Du washtú áwé yanéekw. *The inside of his cheek hurts.*

a **wát** RelationalNoun *mouth of it (a river, creek)*
·Xóow héen wátx' yéi wdudzinei. *They put a memorial pile of rocks at the mouth of the water.*

**watsíx** noun *caribou*
·Watsíx dleeyí áwé x̱waax̱áa. *I ate caribou meat.*
·Watsíx a lututúḵl'i tléil tlax̱ ugé. *The soft bone in a caribou nose is not very big.*

du **wax̱'ahéeni** noun *his/her tears*
VARIANTS: du waḵhéeni
·Du wax̱'ahéeni wulilóox̱. *His tears flowed.*

du **wax̱'ax̱éix̱'u** noun *his/her eyelash*
VARIANTS: du waḵx̱'ax̱éix̱'u (C)
·Dliyát'x' du wax̱'ax̱éix̱'u. *Her eyelashes are long.*

**wa.é** Pronoun *you (singular) [independent]*
·Wáa yateeyi lingít sáwé wa.é? *What kind of person are you?*

**wé** Demonstrative *that (at hand)*
VARIANTS: wéi
·Ánk'w áwé kéi has anaswát wéit lingítch. *Those people are raising a crybaby.*
·Tl'aadéin áwé át tán wé ḵóok. *The box is sitting sideways.*

**wéiksh** noun *woman's curved knife*

**wéis'** noun *louse, lice*
·Wéis' du shaktóot uwa.át. *She got lice in her hair.*

**wéix̲’** noun *bullhead, sculpin*
·Wéix̲’ tlein aawasháat. *She caught a big sculpin.*

WOO[1] verb root

• **aag̲áa aawawóo | --- | aag̲áa awéix̲**
*s/he ordered it | --- | s/he orders it (regularly).*
THEME: P-g̲áa a-S-ø-wóo~ (ø event)
*for S to send for, order P (usually from a catalog)*
·Cháanwaan atx̲aayíg̲aa awóo! *Order some Chinese food!*

du **wóo** noun *his/her father-in-law*
·Asg̲eiwú s’aatíx̲ sitee ax̲ wóo. *My father-in-law is a master seiner.*

**wooch** Pronoun *together [object]*
VARIANTS: woosh
·Wooch x̲oot wuduwa.át. *People came together.*
·Ldakát wooch x̲oot has yawdiháa. *Everybody came together.*

**wooch yáx̲ yaa datóowch** noun *math*

**wool** noun *hole*

WOOL verb root

• **--- | yawóol | ---**
--- | *it has a hole in it* | ---.
THEME: ø-wóol (ga state)
*for something to have a hole, outlet*
·Yawóol yá deegáa. *This 'dipnet has holes in it.*

**woolnáx̲ wooshk̲ák̲** noun *wren*
VARIANTS: woolnáx̲ wooshk̲áx̲
·A x̲oo aa k̲u.oo woolnáx̲ wooshk̲ák̲ has al’óon. *Some people hunt the wren.*

**woon** noun *maggot*

**woosáani** noun *spear for hunting*
·Du woosáani awlil’éex’. *He broke his spear.*

WOOS’[1] verb root

• **ax̲’eiwawóos’ | ax̲’awóos’ | yoo ax̲’ayawóos’k**
*s/he asked him/her | s/he's asking him/her | s/he asks him/her (regularly).*
THEME: O-x̲’a-S-ø-wóos’ (na act)
*for S to ask, question O*
·Hú áwé x̲’ak̲g̲eewóos’. *It is he that you will ask.*

**woosh** Pronoun *together [object]*
VARIANTS: wooch
·Wé aank̲áax’u wéix’ woosh x̲oot has wudi.át. *The chiefs gathered there.*
·Kaxées’ teen wóoshdei kdudzixát du x̲’ás’. *His jaw is held together with a wire.*

**wooshdakádin** Adverb *different directions*
·Wooshdakádin x̲'oosdé awdiyik̲ du téeli. *He put his shoes on the wrong feet.*

**woosh g̲unayáade** Adverb *differently*
VARIANTS: woosh g̲uwanáade, woosh g̲uwanyáade

**woosh g̲unayáade aa** noun *different ones; variety*
·Woosh g̲unayáade téel x̲aatéen. *I see a variety of different shoes.*

**woosh g̲uwanyáade** Adverb *differently*
VARIANTS: woosh g̲unayáade, woosh g̲uwanáade
·Woosh g̲uwanyáade kwdigéi túlx'u. *Drill bits come in different sizes.*

**wóoshnáx̲ x̲'akakéix̲i** noun *chain*
·Wóoshnáx̲ x̲'akakéix̲i tíx' yáanáx̲ litseen. *Chain is stronger than rope.*

**woosh yaayí** noun *pair*
·Woosh yaayí hél du jee. *He doesn't have a pair.*

**wootsaag̲áa** noun *cane; walking stick; staff*
VARIANTS: yootsaag̲áa (C)

du **wóow** noun *his/her chest*
·Du wóow áwé káast yáx̲ koogéi. *His chest is as large as a barrel.*

**wóow** noun *food, lunch, provisions taken along (on a trip, to work or school)*
·Wóow yéi awsinei. *He made lunch.*

**wóow daakeit** noun *container for traveling provisions; lunch basket, lunch container*
·Shaklig̲éiyi wóow daakeit áwé. *That is a pretty lunch basket.*

du **woowká** noun *(on) his/her chest*
·Ch'a hú du woowká aawagwál. *He pounded his own chest.*

**woox̲'** verb root

• --- | **yawúx̲'** | ---
--- | *it's wide* | ---.
THEME: ø-wúx̲' (ga state)
*for something to be wide, broad*
NOTES: This verb only occurs in the imperfective.
·S'igeidí l'eedí yawúx̲' k̲a k̲'áatl' yáx̲ yatee. *A beaver's tail is wide and flat.*

at **wuskóowu** noun *knowledgeable person*
·Du léelk'w áwé at wuskóowux̲ wusitee . *His grandfather was a knowledgeable man.*
·Jiduk̲éi at wuskóowux̲ sateeyéech. *He is paid because he is a knowledgeable person.*

at **wuskú daakahídi** noun *school*

**wuwtunéekw** noun *chest pain; tuberculosis*

·Wuwtunéekw jeedá<u>x</u> áwé wooneи<u>x</u>. *She was saved from tuberculosis.*

# « X »

**XAA** verb root

- **aadé akawsixaa | --- | aadé yoo aksixeik**
  *s/he poured it out there | --- | s/he pours it out there (regularly).*
  THEME: P-dé O-ka-S-ø-xaa~ (na motion)
  *for S to pour O into P, pour O out at P; for S to dump, empty O in one mass (by turning over container) at P*
  ·Naaliyéidei kanasxá wé x̱áat yik.ádi! *Dump the fish guts far away!*
  ·Éil' a kaadéi kanasxá wéi a kát yadu.us'ku át! *Pour salt in the wash basin!*
- **át akawsixáa | --- | áx̱ aksaxaa**
  *s/he poured it there | --- | s/he pours it there (regularly).*
  THEME: P-t~ O-ka-S-s-xaa~ (ø motion)
  *for S to pour, dump, empty O at P*
  ·Héen áanjís kahéeni x̱oot akawsixáa. *He poured water in with the orange juice.*
- **a kaadé ayawsixaa | a kaadé yaa ayanasxéin | a kaadé yoo ayasixéik**
  *s/he poured it on there | s/he is pouring it on there | s/he pours it on there (regularly).*
  THEME: P-dé O-ya-S-s-xaa~ (na motion)
  *for S to pour O on/in P*
  ·Ch'as héen ák.wé a kaadéi yóo yadudzixéik yá kat'ákx̱i? *Is water all that was put on these dried berries?*
  ·Ḵ'ateil tóodei yanasxá k'idéin x̱'adíx'! *Pour it in the jug and cork it up!*

du **xaagú** noun *his/her skeleton, bare bones*
VARIANTS: du xaagí
·Ch'as du xaagú áwé wuduwat'ei. *Only his skeleton was found.*

**xáak** noun *empty bivalve shell*
·Xáak hél daa sá a tú. *There is nothing in the bivalve shell.*

**xáanaa** noun *evening*
·Keil atyátx'i latínix̱ nax̱satee yá xáanaa. *Let Keil be the babysitter this evening.*
·Ḵ'alkátsk kahaa yís léinde gax̱too.áat yá xáanaa. *This evening we are going yellowneck clam digging.*

**xaas** noun *bison, buffalo; ox, muskox; cow; horse*
·Xaas al'óon woogoot. *She went hunting for muskox.*

XAAS' verb root

- **aawaxás' | axáas' | axás'x̲**

*s/he scraped it | s/he is scraping it; s/he scrapes it | s/he scrapes it (regularly).*
THEME: O-S-ø-xáas'~ (ø act)
*for S to scrape O*
·Nóox' tóodáx̲ aawaxás' wé x̲éel'. *He scraped the slime out of the shell.*
·Éil' kaadáx̲ x̲áat k'idéin aax̲ yixás' a kajeig̲í! *You all scrape the scales off the fish from the salt water well!*

a **xáas'i** noun *its skin (of fish)*
·S'eik̲ x̲áat xáas'i áwé yak'éi g̲altóot idateení latseen sákw at eel'óoni. *When you're out hunting a piece of smoked fish skin in your pocket is good for energy.*
·A xáas'i teen áwé duxáash náayadi sákw. *Half smoked fish is cut with the fish skin intact.*

XAASH verb root

- **aawaxaash | axáash | yoo ayaxáshk**

*s/he cut it | s/he cuts it; s/he is cutting it | s/he cuts it (regularly).*
THEME: O-S-ø-xaash~ (na act)
*for S to cut O with knife; for S to saw O*
·A xáas'i teen áwé duxáash náayadi sákw. *Half smoked fish is cut with the fish skin intact.*
·Du keey áwé wuduwaxaash. *They cut into his knee.*

- **aax̲ aawaxásh | aax̲ axáash | aax̲ axásht**

*s/he cut it off | s/he's cutting it off | s/he cuts if off (regularly).*
THEME: O-S-ø-xaash~ (ø act)
*for S to cut, saw O (esp. cutting something off or cutting wood)*
·K'idéin aax̲ xásh wé t'áa at x̲'ax̲éedli! *Cut the trimming off the board good!*
·K'isáanich gán du jeeyís has aawaxásh. *The young men cut wood for him.*

- **akaawaxaash | yei akanaxásh | yei akaxáshch**

*s/he cut it up | s/he is cutting it up | s/he cuts it up (regularly).*
THEME: O-ka-S-ø-xaash~ (g̲a event)
*for S to cut O in several pieces; for S to carve O (on surface); for S to slice O (e.g., bread)*
·Watsíx g̲ádzi yei akanaxásh. *She is cutting up a caribou hindquarter.*
·G̲uwakaan taayí kas'úkx̲u yís akaawaxaash. *She cut up deer fat for frying.*

- **awlixaash | alxáash | yoo alixáshk**

*s/he cut it | s/he's cutting it | s/he cuts it (regularly).*
THEME: O-S-l-xaash~ (na act)
*for S to cut O (esp. rope-like object)*
·S'igeidí g̲eiwú yís a gwéinli aax̲ awlixaash, wé watsíx. *He cut the hooves off the caribou for a beaver net.*
·Aax̲ awlixaash a geení wé tsaa. *He cut the tail flippers off of the seal.*

- **wudixaash | daxáash | yoo dixáshk**

  *s/he cut | s/he cuts; s/he is cutting | s/he cuts (regularly).*
  THEME: S-d-xaash~ (na act)
  *for S to cut*

XAAT[1] verb root

- **aadé akawsixát | --- | aadé aksaxátx̲**

  *s/he connected it there | --- | s/he connects it there (regularly).*
  THEME: P-dé O-ka-S-s-xaat~ (ø event)
  *for S to connect, attach O to P*
  ·Yóo tliyaa aasdéi ksaxát wéi kaxées' ax̲ at shí k̲óok gúgu yís!
  *Attach the wire to that tree over there for my radio antenna!*
  ·Kaxées' teen wóoshdei kdudzixát du x̲'ás'. *His jaw is held together with a wire.*

- **--- | aadé ksixát | ---**

  *--- | it's connected there | ---.*
  THEME: P-(dé) ka-s-xáat~ (ø state)
  *for something to be connected, attached, tied (to) P*
  NOTES: This verb requires a postpositional phrase which describes where or what something is connected to. This is not a motion verb however, and the conjugation prefix does not change when different postpositions are used. In the Leer-Edwards theme, the P-(dé) indicates that P (object of a postposition) is required, as is a postposition, but it can be something other than -dé, as indicated by the example sentences.
  ·Wé hít gukshitúdáx̲ kasixát wé kaxées'. *The wire runs from the corner of that house.*
  ·Tláak̲ du eedé ksixát. *The arrow is stuck in his body.*

- **k'idéin akawsixát | --- | k'idéin aksaxátx̲**

  *s/he pulled it tight | --- | s/he pulls it tight (regularly).*
  THEME: O-ka-S-s-xaat'~ (ø event)
  *for S to tighten, pull on O (something fastened at the other end)*
  NOTES: This verb can be used in a metaphorical sense: Du jeeyís akawsixát. "S/he is pulling for him/her." This could be used in reference to someone running for office, or a competitor in a race of any kind.

XAAT[2] verb root

- **--- | a yáx̲ kaaxát | ---**

  *--- | it looks like it | ---.*
  THEME: N yáx̲ ka-ø-xaat~ (ø state)
  *for something to resemble N (esp. in shape)*
  NOTES: This verb can also refer to one's behavior. For example: Tlél a yáx̲ kooxát wéit'aa. "That one doesn't act normal, right."
  ·Chichuwaa cheech yáx̲ kaaxát. *Dolphins look like porpoise.*
  ·K'wát' yáx̲ kaaxát du g̲íl'ayi. *His grindstone is shaped like an egg.*

XAAT' verb root

- **aadáx̲ awsixáat' | aadáx̲ yaa anasxát' | aadáx̲ yoo asixát'k**
  *s/he dragged it away | s/he is dragging it away | s/he drags it away (regularly).*
  THEME: P-dáx̲ O-S-s-xaat'~ (na motion)
  *for S to drag, pull O (esp. heavy object or limp object such as dead animal) away from P; for S to haul, transport O (by non-motor power) away from P*
  ·Aasgutúdáx̲ gán yaa anasxát'. *He is hauling firewood out of the woods.*
- **aadé awsixáat' | aadé yaa anasxát' | aadé yoo asixát'k**
  *s/he dragged it there | s/he is dragging it there | s/he drags it there (regularly).*
  THEME: P-dé O-S-s-xaat'~ (na motion)
  *for S to drag, pull O (esp. heavy object or limp object such as dead animal) toward P; for S to haul, transport O (by non-motor power) toward P*
  ·Shayadihéini at óow wéide yaa ndusxát'. *They are hauling lots of someone's possessions over that way.*
- **awsixáat' | yaa anasxát' | yoo asixát'k**
  *s/he drug it | s/he is dragging it along | s/he drags it (regularly).*
  THEME: O-S-s-xaat'~ (na motion)
  *for S to drag, pull O (esp. heavy object or limp object such as dead animal); for S to haul, transport O (by non-motor power)*
  ·Héen yaa anasxát'. *He is hauling water.*
  ·Hít kaságu yaa anasxát'. *He is dragging rafters along.*

**xáatl** noun *iceberg*
·Xáatl kát uwak̲úx̲ wé yaakw. *That boat ran into an iceberg.*

**xáatl kaltság̲aa** noun *poles used to push aside ice (from a boat)*

**xáatl'ákw** noun *mouth ulcer; soreness of the mouth (as of a baby teething)*

**xáats'** noun *clear sky, blue sky*
·Xáats'de yaa k̲unahéin. *It is becoming twilight.*

**xáats'** noun *sky blue*

**xákw** noun *sandbar; gravel bar; sand beach; gravel beach*
·Xákw ká ayaawadlaak̲. *He made it to the sand bar.*

**xákwl'i** noun *soapberry*
·Xákwl'i yak'éi yéi wdusneiyí. *Soapberries are good when they're prepared.*

a **xákwti** noun *its empty shell (of house); empty container*
·Wé k̲'ateil xákwti ax̲ jeet tán!. *Hand me the empty pitcher!*

**xáshaa** noun *saw*
·Xáshaa yéi ndu.eich gán yéi daaduneiyí. *A saw is used to work on wood.*

at **xáshdi téel** noun *moccasins*
VARIANTS: et xáshdi téel (C)

·A kaa<u>x</u> sh tukdli<u>g</u>éi du tsaa doogú at xáshdi téel. *She is proud of her seal skin moccasins.*
·At xáshdi téel sákw áwé kanágaa akaawach'ák'w a<u>x</u> jeeyís. *He carved a form for making moccasins for me.*

at **xáshdi x'óow** noun *blanket sewn from scraps of hide*

**xát'aa** noun *sled*
VARIANTS: xét'aa (C)

**XEECH** verb root

• **aawaxích | --- | axích<u>x</u>**
*s/he exerted his/her full strength on it; s/he is exerting his/her full strength on it | --- | s/he exerts his/her full strength on it (regularly).*
THEME: O-S-ø-xeech~ (ø event)
*for S to exert one's full strength on, strive for O; for S to concentrate on, put effort into O*
·Yeeytéen has du téi<u>x</u>' tóot<u>x</u> áyá toodé has yee uwaxích haa <u>k</u>u.éex'i. *You all can see that our hosts thank you from their hearts.*

**XEEL'** verb root

• **akaawaxíl' | yaa akanaxíl' | akaxíl'<u>x</u>**
*he/she/it bothered him/her; he/she/it is bothering him/her | he/she/it is starting to bother him/her | he/she/it bothers him/her (regularly).*
THEME: O-ka-S-ø-xéel'~ (ø event)
*for S to bother, trouble, cause trouble or anxiety for O*
·Du tl'óo<u>g</u>u áwé ash kaawaxíl'. *Her liver is bothering her.*

**xéel'i** noun *mossberry*
·Xéel'i kút<u>x</u> a tukayátx'i yagéi. *Mossberries have too many seeds.*

**xéen** noun *housefly; bluebottle fly*
·Xéen áwé woogéi yá <u>k</u>utaan. *There were a lot of blue bottle flies this summer.*

du **xées' (C)** noun *his/her shin*
VARIANTS: du xées'i
·Du xées' <u>k</u>úná<u>x</u> wudlix'ís'. *His shin is really swelling.*

a **xées'i** RelationalNoun *its cutwater; the curved part of a bow or stern (of boat)*
·A xées'i ágé tsú yéi duwasáakw a ya<u>x</u>ak'áaw? *Is the bow of a boat also called the yaÿak'áaw?*
·A xées'i s'é yánde .á<u>x</u>w! *Tie the bow of the boat first!*

**xéesh** noun *rash*
·Xéesh áwé du lidí<u>x</u>' yéi yatee. *He has a rash on his neck.*

**XEET** verb root

• **akawshixít | akshaxeet | akshaxít<u>x</u>**
*s/he wrote it | s/he writes it; s/he is writing it | s/he writes it (regularly).*
THEME: O-ka-S-sh-xeet~ (ø act)

*for S to write, draw, or paint a picture of O; for S to print O by hand; for S to photograph, take pictures, X-rays of O*
·S'igeidí k̲a yáay a káa kashaxít wé at doogú x'óow! *Draw a Beaver and whale design on the leather blanket!*
·Tsaa geení aankadushxit át teen akawshixít. *She took a picture of the seal tail flippers with a camera.*

- **kawjixít | kashxeet | kashxítx̲**
*s/he wrote | s/he writes; s/he is writing | s/he writes (regularly).*
THEME: ka-S-d-sh-xeet~ (ø act)
*for S to write, draw,or paint; for S to take a photograph*
·Lingít x̲'éinák̲ kashxeet áwé ashigóok. *He knows how to write in the Tlingit language.*

XEET' verb root

- **t'aa ká aawaxéet' | t'aa ká axít'kw | t'aa ká yei axéet'ch**
*s/he swept the floor | s/he is sweeping the floor | s/he sweeps the floor (regularly).*
THEME: O-S-ø-xéet'~ (g̲a act)
*for S to sweep O (esp. floor)*
·Xít'aa een du neilí axít'gi nooch. *He always sweeps his house with a broom.*

- **wudixéet' | daxít'kw | yei daxít'ch**
*s/he swept | s/he is sweeping | s/he sweeps (regularly).*
THEME: S-d-xéet'~ (g̲a act)
*for S to sweep*
NOTES: Tlél udaxít'k which literally translates as "s/he doesn't sweep" is an expression commonly used to insinuate that the person is slovenly, lazy.

XEEX verb root

- **aadé wjixeex | aadé yaa nashíx | aadé yoo jixíxk**
*he/she/it ran there | he/she/it is running there | he/she/it runs there (regularly).*
THEME: P-dé S-j-xeex~ (na motion)
*for (singular) S to run toward P*
NOTES: Note that the classifier sh- combined with the verb stem -xeex becomes -sheex.
·Wé xóots awusnéex'i a yinaadé wjixeex haa keidlí. *Our dog is running toward the brown bear it smelled.*
·Yóode wujixeexi dzísk'w a ítde woogoot ax̲ éek'. *My brother went after the moose that ran off that way.*

- **anax̲ kaawaxeex | --- | anax̲ yei kaxíxch**
*it fell through it | --- | it falls through it (regularly).*
THEME: P-náx̲ ka-ø-xeex~ (g̲a motion)
*for something (usually a round object) to fall, drop through P*
·Du waak̲náx̲ kaawaxeex. *He's staring at it. (Lit: It fell through his eye.)*

- **át kaawaxíx | --- | áx̲ kaxeex**
*it fell into it | --- | it falls into it (regularly).*

THEME: P-t~ ka-ø-xeex~ (ø motion)
*for something (usually a round object) to fall, drop into P*
·Kei kawduwag̲ix'i té du káak't kaawaxíx. *The rock that was thrown hit him on the forehead.*
·Du kwéiyi k̲ínt kaawaxíx wé at katé. *The bullet fell short of his mark.*

• **át uwaxíx | --- | áx̲ xeex**
*it fell on it | --- | it falls on it (regularly).*
THEME: P-t~ ø-xeex~ (ø motion)
*for something to fall or drop on P; for a bullet to hit P; for a rumor, news to spread, go around at P*
·Óoxjaa héen x̲'akát uwaxíx. *Wind has hit the surface of the water.*
·Kagán shaa kát uwaxíx. *Light fell on the mountain.*

• **át wooxeex | --- | ---**
*it's falling around; it's wobbly | --- | ---.*
THEME: P-t ø-xeex~ (na motion)
*for something to fall around at P (esp. inside a container)*
·Du wak̲ltáaknáx̲ át wooxeex. *Something fell in her eye.*

• **át wujixeex | --- | át yoo jixíxk**
*he/she/it is running around; he/she/it ran around | --- | he/she/it runs around (regularly).*
THEME: P-t S-j-xeex~ (na motion)
*for (singular) S to run around at P*
NOTES: Note that the classifier sh- combined with the verb stem -xeex becomes -sheex.
·X̲'al'daayéeji éek̲t wujixeex. *The sandpiper is running around the beach.*
·K̲'asigóo kaltéelk̲ l'éiw kát át wusheex. *It's fun running around barefoot in the sand.*

• **át wujixíx | aadé nashíx | áx̲ sheex**
*he/she/it ran to it | he/she/it is running to it | he/she/it runs to it (regularly).*
THEME: P-t~ S-j-xeex~ (ø motion)
*for (singular) S to run to P, arrive at P by running*
NOTES: Note that the classifier sh- combined with the verb stem -xeex becomes -sheex.
·Wé aas seiyít wujixíx séew tóodáx̲. *She ran to the shelter of the tree to get out of the rain.*
·Eesháank' kaltéelk̲ áwé haat wujixíx ax̲ dachx̲ánk'. *Poor thing, my grandchild ran over here shoeless.*

• **daak uwaxíx | --- | daak xíxch**
*it fell | --- | it falls (regularly).*
THEME: daak ø-xeex~ (ø motion)
*for the sun, moon to move through the sky into the open; for something (esp. a small, compact object) to fall, drop*
NOTES: This verb can also be used in expressions such as: Déix̲ yagiyee káx' áwé daak uxeexch "It falls on a Tuesday".
·G̲agaan daak uwaxíx wé séew ítdáx̲. *The sun came out after the rain.*

- **g̱unéi wjixíx | --- | g̱unéi shíxx̱**
*he/she/it started running | --- | he/she/it starts running (regularly).*
THEME: g̱unéi S-j-xeex~ (ø motion)
*for (singular) S to begin running*
NOTES: Note that the classifier sh- combined with the verb stem -xeex becomes -sheex.
·Du gawdáani aadé woo.aadi yé, a niyaadé g̱unéi wjixíx. *He started running in the direction his horses went.*
- **du jeet shuwaxíx | du jeedé yaa shunaxíx | du jeex̱ shuxeex**
*s/he ran out of it | s/he is running out of it | s/he runs out of it (regularly).*
THEME: N jeet~ shu-ø-xeex~ (ø event)
*for N to run out of something*
- **a káa wooxeex | --- | a káa yei xíxch**
*it fell on it | --- | it falls on it (regularly).*
THEME: N káa ø-xeex~ (g̱a motion)
*for an object (usually small, compact) to fall on N*
- **kei uwaxíx | kei naxíx | kei xíxch**
*it rose | it's rising | it rises (regularly).*
THEME: kei ø-xeex~ (ø motion)
*for the sun, moon to rise*
NOTES: This verb can also be used in expressions that don't pertain to the sun or moon, as in: Neekw kei uwaxíx "News/gossip went around".
- **ḵut wujixeex | --- | ḵut kei shíxch**
*he/she/it ran away | --- | he/she/it runs away (regularly).*
THEME: ḵut S-j-xeex~ (ga motion)
*for (singular) S to run away*
NOTES: Note that the classifier sh- combined with the verb stem -xeex becomes -sheex.
·Du kooḵénayi ḵut wujixeex. *His messenger ran away.*
·Ax̱ jináḵ ḵut wujixeex. *He ran away from me.*
- **shuwaxeex | yaa shunaxíx | yoo shuyaxíxk**
*it came to an end | it's coming to an end | it comes to an end (quickly, regularly).*
THEME: shu-ø-xeex~ (na event)
*for something to end, come to an end, pass; for something to be used up (of supplies, etc.)*
- **du tóot wooxeex | --- | du tóot yoo yaxíxk**
*s/he is worried about him/her/it | --- | s/he worries about him/her/it (regularly).*
THEME: N tóot O-ø-xeex~ (na motion)
*for O to worry N; for N to have O constantly on the mind*
NOTES: Note that literally translated, du tóot wooxeex means "it's rolling around inside him/her".
- **yaawaxeex | yaa yanaxíx | yoo yaxíxk**
*it happened | it's happening | it happens (regularly).*

THEME: ya-ø-xeex~ (na event)
*for something to take place, occur, happen*
·G̲aax̲ shí teen áwé yaawaxeex wé k̲u.éex'. *A cry song took place at the potlatch.*

• **yínde wooxeex | yínde yaa naxíx | yínde yoo yaxíxk**
*it set | it is setting | it sets (regularly).*
THEME: yínde ø-xeex~ (na motion)
*for the sun, moon to set*

**xéidu** noun *comb*
VARIANTS: shaxéidu
·Shaxéidu x̲waa.oo. *I bought a comb.*

**xein** noun *spawned-out salmon with white scabs, ready to die*
·Xein nageich k̲utaan eetíx'. *After the summer there are a lot of spawned-out salmon.*

du **xeitká** noun *his/her thorax; flat upper surface of his/her chest*

**Xeitl** noun *Thunderbird*
·Xeitl naax̲ has sitee Shangukeidí. *The Shangukeidí are Thunderbird.*
·Xeitl a káa kawduwach'ák'w yá kées. *A Thunderbird is carved on this bracelet.*

**xeitl l'íkws'i (At)** noun *lightning*
VARIANTS: xeitl l'úkx̲u, xeitl l'óokx̲u (T)

**xeitl l'úkx̲u** noun *lightning*
VARIANTS: xeitl l'óokx̲u (T), xeitl l'íkws'i (At)
·Xeitl l'úkx̲u yóo tliyaawú. *The lightnting is way over there.*

**xeitl táax'aa** noun *horsefly*
·Xeitl táax'aa x̲at wusitáax'. *A horsefly bit me.*

**xén** noun *plastic*
·Yéi x̲waa.áx̲ xén hél ushk'é wé microwave tóox' yéi du.oowú. *I heard that it's not good to put plastic in the microwave.*
·Tléix' k̲'ateil yáx̲ áwé liyék wéi xén. *That plastic container can hold one gallon.*

**xídlaa** noun *herring rake*
·Yaaw xídlaa yéi wdu.oowú, tlél uldzée nooch. *Using a herring rake is not difficult.*

**xít'aa** noun *broom; brush*
·Xít'aa een du neilí axít'gi nooch. *He always sweeps his house with a broom.*

**xíxch'** noun *frog*
·Xíxch' a yáax' kax̲waach'ák'w. *I carved a frog on it's face.*
·Xíxch' at óowu woosh jeedé duhéin nooch. *The frog crest is claimed by more than one clan.*

**xi.áat** noun *dusk; twilight*
·Xi.átt k̲uwaháa. *It is dusk.*

**xoodzí** noun *comet; falling star*

**xoodzí** noun *burnt or charred wood*

XOOK verb root

- **awsixúk | asxook | asxúkx̲**
  *s/he dried it | s/he is drying it | s/he dries it (regularly).*
  THEME: O-S-s-xook~ (ø act)
  *for S to dry O (by any method)*
- **uwaxúk | yaa naxúk | xúkx̲**
  *it dried | it's drying | it dries (regularly).*
  THEME: ø-xook~ (ø event)
  *for something to be dry, dried*
  ·Wé x̲áat a kajeig̲í a kát uwaxúk. *The scales of the fish dried on it.*
  ·Yaa naxúk ax̲ naa.ádi. *My clothes are drying.*

**xóon** noun *north wind*
·X̲eil neech káa yéi nateech xóon wudunoogú. *Foam is on the beach when the north wind blows.*
·Haa kát ayawashát wé xóon. *The north wind hit us in gusts.*

**xóosht'** noun *singed, burnt, or charred matter*
·Xóosht' has du yáa yéi has ana.eich yaa (ha)s jinda.ádi. *The dark burnt ashes would be put on their faces when going to war.*

**xóots** noun *grizzly bear*
·Xóots tlein áwé aawaják̲ wé k̲áa. *That man killed a big brown bear.*
·Has du yáa daak uwagút wé xóots tlein kanat'á has a.éeni. *While they were picking blueberries, the brown bear came face to face with them.*

**xóow** noun *memorial pile of rocks*
·Xóow héen wátx' yéi wdudzinei. *They put a memorial pile of rocks at the mouth of the water.*

**Xudzidaa K̲wáan** noun *people of Admiralty Island*
·Xudzidaa K̲wáan áwé Aangóon k̲u.oo. *The people of Angoon are known as Xudzidaa Ñwáan.*

**Xunaa** noun *Hoonah*
·Ax̲ dlaak' tín Xunaadé k̲ugax̲tootéen kanat'á k̲uk'éet' yís. *We are going to travel to Hoonah to pick blueberries with my sister.*
·Xunaa K̲áawu áwé k̲únáx̲ has litseen. *Hoonah people are very strong.*

du **xux̲aawú** noun *pubic hair*

# « Xw »

XWAACH verb root

- **awlixwách | alxwácht | alxwáchx̲**
  *s/he scraped it | s/he's scraping it | s/he scrapes it (regularly).*
  THEME: O-S-l-xwaach~ (ø act)
  *for S to soften, make O flexible; for S to scrape O (hide) to soften it*
  ·Wé watsíx doogú awlixwách. *She scraped the caribou skin.*
  ·G̲ooch doogú awlixwách. *She softened a wolf hide.*

**xwaasdáa** noun *canvas; tarp; tent*
·Du gáni a kaháadi yís áwé xwaasdáa aawa.oo. *He bought a tarp to cover his firewood.*
·Wé yées xwaasdáa g̲ákw yáx̲ yatee. *The new tent is stiff.*

du **xwáayi** noun *his/her clan brother*

**xwájaa** noun *skin scraper*

**xweitl** noun *fatigue*

XWEITL verb root

- **ash wulixwétl | yaa ash nalxwétl | ash laxwétlx̲**
  *he/she/it made him/her tired | he/she/it is making him/her tired | he/she/it makes him/her tired (regularly).*
  THEME: O-S-l-xweitl~ (ø event)
  *for S to tire O, make O tired (either physically or emotionally)*
  ·X̲at wulixwétl wé séew. *I'm tired of the rain.*
- **kawlixwétl | yaa kanalxwétl | kalaxwétlx̲**
  *it's itchy | it's starting to itch | it gets itchy (regularly).*
  THEME: ka-S-l-xweitl~ (ø event)
  *for S to itch, tickle*
  ·Ax̲ lú tukawlixwétl. *My nose tickled (inside).*
- **wudixwétl | yaa ndaxwétl | daxwétlx̲**
  *s/he's tired; s/he was tired | s/he's getting tired | s/he gets tired (regularly).*
  THEME: O-d-xweitl~ (ø event)
  *for O to be tired, weary*
  ·Aatlein wudixwétl a ítdáx̲. *She was really tired after that.*

# « X’ »

**-x’** postpos. *at (the scene of); at (the time of)*
VARIANTS: -ø
NOTES: The postposition -x’ has the alternate form -ø (unmarked) when attaching to a noun ending in a long vowel.
·Atx̱á daakahídix’ gishoo taayí k̲a k’wát’ awdzig̱áax̱. *She ordered bacon and eggs at the restaurant.*
·Kawóot teen k̲’eikaxwéin a káa kak̲á! *Embroider a flower on it with beads!*

**x’aa** noun *point (of land)*
·X’aa daax̱ yaawak̲úx̱ wé yaakw. *The boat motored around the point.*
·Wé x’aa g̱ei xóon tléil aan utí. *The North Wind does not bother the shelter of the point.*

**X’AAK** verb root

- **át uwax’ák | --- | áx̱ x’aak**
*it swam underwater to it | --- | it swims underwater to it (regularly).*
THEME: P-t~ S-ø-x’aak~ (ø motion)
*for S to swim under water to P*
·Héen wátt uwax’ák wé t’ási. *The grayling swam to the mouth of the river.*

a **x’aakeidí** noun *its seeds*
·Tléik̲w x’aakeidí áwé ts’ítskw gánde nagoodí tóox’ yéi nateech. *Berry seeds are found in bird poop.*
·Wé at x’aakeidí ín x’eesháa tóox’ yéi na.oo! *Put the seeds in a bottle!*

**X’AAK̲W** verb root

- **a kát seiwax’ák̲w | --- | a káx̱ sax’aak̲w**
*s/he forgot | --- | s/he forgets (regularly).*
THEME: N kát~ O-sa-ø-x’aak̲w~ (ø state)
*for O to forget N*
·Tlél a káx̱ yiseix’aag̱úk̲ wé yaakw kakúxaa! *Don’t you all forget the bailer for the boat!*
·A kát tsé iseix’áak̲w haa hít katíx̱’aayi! *Don’t forget our house key!*

**x’aa luká** noun *on the ridge or elevated part of the point (of land)*
·X’aa luká áwé áx’ yéi nateech wé tsaa. *The seal is always on the point.*

**x’aalx’éi** noun *dwarf maple*

a **x’aan** RelationalNoun *its tip (of pointed object); top, tips of its branches (of tree, bush)*
·Tléi a x’aant áwé daak̲ wudig̱wát’ wé yadák’w. *The young boy crawled*

*out the limb.*
·K'idéin yax'át wé lítaa x'aan! *Sharpen the tip of the knife good!*

**x'áan** noun *anger*
·X'áan át iwax̱óot'i tlél ushk'é. *Anger pulling you around is not good.*

**x'áan kanáayi** noun *general; leader of war, battle*

**x'áan yinaa.át** noun *war clothes (of moosehide)*

**X'AAS** verb root

- **kawlix'áas | yaa kanalx'áas | ---**
*it's leaking | it's beginning to leak | ---.*
THEME: ka-l-x'áas (ø event)
*for something to drip, leak (at fairly fast rate)*
·Awdagaaních áwé, dleit kaax̱ kalóox̱jaa koolx'áasch hít kaadáx̱. *Because the sun is shining, the snow drips fast off the house.*
·Awdagaaní yáa yagiyee, ldakát át kaadáx̱ kagux̱lax'áas. *When it sunshines today everything will be dripping off.*

**x'áas** noun *waterfall*
·X'áas tóot áwé át woohaan. *She is standing around in the waterfall.*

du **x'aash** noun *cheek of his/her buttocks*

**X'AAT** verb root

- **ayaawax'át | ayax'áat | ayax'átx̱**
*s/he sharpened it | s/he's sharpening it | s/he sharpens it (regularly).*
THEME: O-ya-S-ø-x'áat~ (ø act)
*for S to sharpen O (an edge) with a file*
·At x̱éidi yax'aat a shóox' g̱anú! *Sit down and do some arrow-head sharpening!*
·Kax'ás'aa yax'áat áwé ashigóok. *He really knows how to sharpen the rip saw.*

**x'áat'** noun *island*
·X'áat' káx' áwé yéi wootee Naatsilanéi. *Naatsilanéi stayed on an island.*
·K'wát' X'áadidé gax̱took̲óox̱ kéidladi k'wádig̱áa. *We are going to Egg Island for seagull eggs.*

**x'áax'** noun *apple; crabapple*
·X'áax' yak'éi g̱uwakaan dleeyí een. *Apple is good with deer meat.*
·X'áax' tlax̱ k̲únáx̱ si.áax'w. *Crabapples are very sour.*

**x'áax' kahéeni** noun *apple juice*
·X'áax' kahéeni yéi wtusinei. *We made apple juice.*

**x'ádaa** noun *file*
·X'ádaa yéi ndu.eich lítaa yís. *A file is used to make a knife.*

**x'akaskéin** noun *unfinished basket*
·Wé x'akaskéin daax' áwé yéi jiné. *She is working on the unfinished basket.*

**x'átgu** noun *dogfish; mudshark*
·X'átgu áwé Shangukeidí has du at óowux̲ sitee. *The dogfish is an artifact of the Thunderbiird people.*

**x'at'daayéejayi** noun *black turnstone*
·X'at'daayéejayi héenák'w át nagútch. *The black turnstone walks around in shallow water.*

**x'éedadi** noun *uprooted tree or stump (with roots protruding)*
VARIANTS: x'éededi (C)
·X'éedadi kaanáx̲ yéi ax̲ wudzigít at gutóox'. *I fell over a stump in the woods.*
·X'éedadi tóox' awdlisín. *She hid in a tree stump.*

**x'ees** noun *boil; inflammation and swelling*
·Wé x'ees du kaanáx̲ yatee. *The boil is too much for him.*

X'EES' verb root

• **wudix'ís' | yaa ndax'ís' | dax'ís'x̲**
*it's swollen | it's beginning to swell | it swells (regularly).*
THEME: d-x'ees'~ (ø event)
*for something to swell, be swollen locally; for something to be matted, tangled in lumps*
·Wudix'ís' du goosh. *His thumb is swollen.*
·Du káak' wudix'ís' k̲a kawdiyés'. *His forehead is swollen and bruised.*

du **x'ées'i** noun *lock of his/her hair; his/her matted hair*
VARIANTS: du shax'ées'i
·Du shax'ées'i kulijée. *His matted hair is unattractive.*

**x'eesháa** noun *bucket; pail*
·X'eesháa yaa anatán. *She is carrying a bucket.*

**x'éig̲aa** Adverb *truly, really; in truth, for sure*
·X'éig̲aa Lingít áwé wa.é. *You are a true Lingít.*

**x'éig̲aa át** noun *truth*
VARIANTS: x'éig̲aa ét (C)
·X'éig̲aa átx̲ sitee k̲usax̲án. *Love is true.*

**x'éitaa** noun *cutthroat trout*
·X'éitaa nageich Jilk̲óotx'. *There are a lot of cutthroat trout at Chilkoot.*

a **x'éix'u** noun *its gill (of fish)*
·A x'éix'u áwé yoo dudlik'útsk wé x̲áat. *One breaks the gills of the fish.*
·Wé káast kaadéi lít wé a x'éix'u! *Throw the gills in the barrel!*

**x'éix̲** noun *crab (king, spider)*
·X'éix̲ k̲aa x̲'é yak'éi. *King crab is a delight to the mouth.*

**x'ig̲aak̲áa** noun *brave, fearless man; temperamental, quick-tempered, hot-headed or domineering man*

VARIANTS: x'éeg̱aa ḵáa (T)
·Ḵúnáx̱ x'ig̱aaḵáa áwé wé ḵáa. *That man is a real warrior.*

**X'OO** verb root

- **át akawsix'óo | aadé yaa akanasx'wéin | áx̱ aksax'oo**
  *s/he nailed it on it | s/he is nailing it on it | s/he nails it on it (regularly).*
  THEME: O-ka-S-s-x'oo~ (ø event)
  *for S to nail O*
  NOTES: Note that the postpositional phrase át/aadé/áx̱ "on it" is not required with this verb, and therefore is not given in the Leer-Edwards theme. It is given in the forms above however, to show how the postposition changes with each mode. Without the át, one could say: akawsix'óo "s/he drove nails in it".
  ·Tuháayi teen áwé át kawtusix'óo. *We nailed it on it with a nail.*
  ·G̱ayéis' du hídi kát akawsix'óo. *He nailed tin on his roof.*

**x'óol'** noun *whirlpool; boiling tide; chaos*
·X'óol' áa litseen Aangóon yadá. *The boiling tide is strong in Angoon.*

**x'oon sá** Pronoun *how many; some number (of)*
·X'oon gaawx' sá? *At what time?*

**x'óow** noun *blanket; robe*
·Yéil x'óow aawaḵáa du x̱án aa jeeyís. *She sewed a Raven blanket for her husband.*
·Yáat hán du x'óowu teen. *Here he stands with his robe.*

**x'úkjaa** noun *steam (visible, in the air); mist, fog (rising from a body of standing water)*
·X'úkjaa héen káa yéi wootee. *Steam was on top of the water.*

**x'ús'** noun *club*
·X'ús' teen shawduwax̱ích. *He was hit with a club.*

**x'úx'** noun *paper; book, magazine, newspaper; letter, mail*
·Yáa a daat x'úx' yáx̱ áwé a daax' yéi jix̱waanei. *I worked on it according to the book.*
·Ax̱ éesh kak'dakwéiy s'aatíx̱ sitee, x'úx' awux̱áax'un. *As a captain, my father used to haul mail.*

**x'úx' daakahídi** noun *post office*
·Tléix' dáanaa yéi x̱'alitseen katíx̱'aa x'úx' daakahídix'. *A key costs one dollar at the post office.*

**x'úx' daakax'úx'u** noun *envelope*

# « Xw’ »

**x’wán** noun *boot(s)*

**x’wán** particle *be sure to*
NOTES: This particle is used with the Imperative and Hortative verb modes.

X’WÁS’K̲ verb root

- **wulix’wás’k̲ | yaa nax’wás’k̲ | yoo lix’wás’k̲k**
  *it's numb | it's beginning to get numb | it gets numb (regularly).*
  THEME: l-x’wás’k̲ (na event)
  *for something to be numb, have no feeling*
  VARIANTS: -x’ús’k̲
  ·Ax̲ k’í wulix’wás’k̲. *My rump is numb.*

# « X̱ »

**-x̱** postpos. *(in prolonged contact) at; (repeatedly arriving) at; being, in the form of*
·Du gúk káx̱ ayaawayeesh du sadaat'aayí. *She pulled her scarf down over her ears.*
·Yeedát ḵuyak'éi g̱aatáa yéi daané yís yá kaxwaan káx̱ yaa nagúdi. *Today the weather is good for walking out on the frost to check the traps.*

**x̱a-** Pronoun *I [subject]*
·X̱áay een áwé x̱waliyéx̱ wé kanéist. *I built that cross out of yellow cedar.*

**x̱á** particle *you see*
VARIANTS: x̱áa
NOTES: This particle softens an assertion.

**X̱AA**[1] verb root

- **aawax̱áa | ax̱á | ax̱éix̱**
*s/he ate it | s/he is eating it | s/he eats it (regularly).*
THEME: O-S-ø-x̱aa~ (ø act)
*for S to eat O*
·Atx̱a átch áwé uwax̱áa ax̱ kinaak.ádi. *A moth ate my coat.*
·Ch'áakw dux̱áa noojín wé kals'áak. *They used to eat squirrels long ago.*

- **at uwax̱áa | at x̱á | at x̱éix̱**
*s/he ate | s/he eats; s/he is eating | s/he eats (regularly).*
THEME: at S-ø-x̱aa~ (ø act)
*for S to eat*

- **yax̱ ayawsix̱áa | yax̱ yaa ayanasx̱éin | yax̱ ayasax̱éix̱**
*s/he ate it all up | s/he is eating it all up | s/he eats it all up (regularly).*
THEME: yax̱ O-ya-S-s-x̱aa~ (ø event)
*for S to eat up, finish, consume O (eating lots of pieces)*
·Ḵ'alkátsk yáxwch'ich yax̱ yawsix̱áa haa aaní kaadáx̱. *The sea otter has devoured the yellowneck clams on our land.*

**X̱AA**[2] verb root

- **aawax̱áa | ax̱áa | ---**
*s/he rowed | s/he is rowing | ---.*
THEME: a-S-ø-x̱áa (ø act)
*for S to paddle, row*
·Tláakw ax̱áa du aandaayaagú. *He is rowing his rowboat quickly.*

- **át ayaawax̱aa | --- | át yoo ayax̱éik**
*s/he is transporting him/her/it around; s/he transported him/her/it around | --- | s/he transports him/her/it around (regularly).*
THEME: P-t O-ya-S-ø-x̱aa~ (na motion)

*for S to transport O around P by boat or car*
·Káa tlein yíkt át yawduwax̲aa wé aank̲áawu. *The rich person is being driven around in a limosine.*

- **át ayaawax̲áa | --- | áx̲ ayax̲aa**
  *s/he transported him/her/it there | --- | s/he transports him/her/it there (regularly).*
  THEME: P-t~ O-ya-S-ø-x̲aa~ (ø motion)
  *for S to transport O by boat or car to P; for S to bring, take or fetch O by boat or car to P*
  ·Atx̲á tlein áyá k̲u.éex'de yakk̲wax̲áa. *I am going to haul a lot of food to the potlatch.*
  ·K̲aanaawú tl'átgi kaadéi yakk̲wax̲áa k̲'eikaxwéin. *I will transport flowers to the graveyard.*
- **ayaawax̲áax'w | ayax̲áax'w | ---**
  *s/he hauled it | s/he is hauling it | ---.*
  THEME: O-ya-S-ø-x̲áax'w (na act)
  *for S to regularly transport, haul O (mail, newspaper, e.g.) by boat or car*
  ·Ax̲ éesh kak'dakwéiy s'aatíx̲ sitee, x'úx' awux̲áax'un. *As a captain, my father used to haul mail.*

**x̲áa** noun *war party, attacking force of warriors or soldiers; army*

X̲AACH verb root

- **aawax̲aach | yaa anax̲ách | yoo ayax̲áchk**
  *s/he towed it | s/he is towing it | s/he tows it (regularly).*
  THEME: O-S-ø-x̲aach~ (na motion)
  *for S to tow O (usually by boat)*
  ·Dax̲áchx'i yaakw tlénx' át has anax̲áchch.. *Tugboats tow large vessels.*

a **x̲aagú** noun *its claw*
·Nóosk x̲aagú k̲únáx̲ yalik'áts'. *Wolverine claws are really sharp.*

**x̲aaheiwú** noun *black currant*
·X̲aaheiwú tléik̲wx̲ sitee. *Black currant is a fruit.*

du **x̲aakw** noun *his/her nail (of finger or toe)*
·Du x̲aakw áx̲ ayawlixásh. *He cut his fingernails.*

du **x̲aakw eetí** noun *his/her fingernail markings*
·Du x̲aakw eetí áwé wé l'éiw káwu. *His fingernail markings are in the sand.*

**x̲aanás'** noun *rafter*
VARIANTS: x̲aanés' (C)
·X̲aanás' awliyéx̲ wé k̲áa. *That man built rafters.*

**x̲aanás' éinaa** noun *rack for drying fish*

**a x̲aani** noun *its prongs (of spear)*
VARIANTS: a x̲aaní
·A x̲aaní k'idéin yax'át! *Sharpen its prongs well!*

**x̲aat** noun *root; especially spruce root*
·X̲aat áyá gax̲tulas'éil'. *We're going to dig spruce roots.*
·Wé x̲aat kanat'á kahéeni káa yéi gax̲too.oo. *We will put the roots in the blueberry juice.*

**x̲áat** noun *fish; salmon*
·S'eik̲ x̲áat xáas'i áwé yak'éi g̲altóot idateení latseen sákw at eel'óoni. *When you're out hunting a piece of smoked fish skin in your pocket is good for energy.*
·I léelk'u keekándei aneelg̲ein - x̲áat yéi adaané! *Go check on your grandpa - he's working on fish!*

**x̲áat daakahídi** noun *cannery*
·Cháanwaanch áwé wuliyéx̲ yá x̲áat daakahídi. *The Chinese built this cannery.*

**x̲áat g̲íjaa** noun *fish pitchfork*

**x̲áat héeni** noun *salmon creek*

**x̲áat k'áax̲'i** noun *bloodline inside fish, along the backbone*

**x̲aat s'áaxw** noun *woven root hat*

**x̲áat yádi** noun *whitefish; baby fish; tiny fish*
·X̲áat yádi héen sháakdáx̲ asg̲eiwú. *She nets whitefish from the head of the river.*
·X̲áat yádi g̲ík̲s yís akaawaxaash. *She cut the whitefish to barbeque over the fire.*

**x̲aatl'** noun *algae found on rocks*
·X̲aatl' áwé yagéi Jilk̲áatx'. *There is a lot of algae in the Chilkat.*

X̲AAW verb root

• **--- | daadzix̲áaw | kei isx̲áawch**
--- | *it's hairy* | *it gets hairy (regularly).*
THEME: N daa-d-s-x̲áaw (ga state)
*for N to have a hairy body*
NOTES: Note that the posessive pronoun is used with this verb when talking about a person. For example: du daadzix̲áaw "s/he is hairy"; ax̲ daadzix̲áaw "I am hairy".
·Gantutl'úk'x̲u tléil daa.usx̲áaw. *Woodworms are not furry.*

**x̲áaw** noun *log (fallen tree)*
·X̲áaw yan x̲út'! *Pull the log to shore!*
·Ax̲ k̲atlyát wujix̲ín wé x̲áaw tlein. *That big log fell on my side.*

**x̱aawaag̱éi** noun *window*
VARIANTS: x̱aawaag̱í
·A tóonáx̱ áwé at duwatéen wé x̱aawaag̱éi. *You can see through the window.*

**x̱aawaag̱éi kas'ísayi** noun *window curtain*
VARIANTS: x̱aawaag̱í kas'ísaa (T), x̱aawaag̱í kes'íseyi (C)

**x̱aawaag̱í** noun *window*
VARIANTS: x̱aawaag̱éi

a **x̱aawú** noun *its hair, fur; its quill(s) (of porcupine)*
·Ḵúnáx̱ x̱'alitseen a x̱aawú. *It's fur is very expensive.*
·Wé x̱alak'ách' x̱aawú ax̱ keidlí x̱'éit yawdlig̱ích. *The porcupine quills stuck in my dogs mouth.*

du **x̱aawú** noun *his/her body hair, fuzz*

**x̱aay** noun *steambath*
·X̱aaydé nax̱too.aat. *Let's go into the steambath.*

**x̱áay** noun *yellow cedar, Alaska cedar*
·Kootéeyaa gax̱dulyeix̱í x̱áay yéi ndu.eich. *When a totem is made it is yellow cedar that is used.*
·X̱áay kayeix̱tág̱u a takáx' yéi na.oo! *Put yellow cedar shavings in the bottom of it!*

**x̱alak'ách'** noun *porcupine*
VARIANTS: x̱alek'ách' (C)
·X̱alak'ách' katéix̱i ax̱ x̱'é yak'éi. *Porcupine soup is delightful to my mouth.*
·Wé x̱alak'ách' x̱aawú ax̱ keidlí x̱'éit yawdlig̱ích. *The porcupine quills stuck in my dogs mouth.*

**x̱aldleit** noun *white fox*
·X̱aldleit kinaa.át yéi aya.óo wé G̱unanaa ḵáa. *That Athabaskan man is wearing a white fox overcoat.*

**x̱alt'ooch' naag̱as'éi** noun *black fox*
·X̱'alitseen wé x̱alt'ooch' naag̱as'éi doogú. *The skin of a black fox is expensive.*

du **x̱án** RelationalNoun *near him/her, by him/her*
·Wé gáal' g̱eiyí aan nagú i léelk'w x̱ánde! *Go with the clams to your grandparent!*
·Du séek' du x̱ánt uwagút. *Her daughter came to her.*

**X̱ÁN** verb root

- **awsix̱án | asix̱án | ---**
  *s/he loved him/her/it | s/he loves him/her/it | ---.*
  THEME: O-S-s-x̱án (ga state)
  *for S to love O*

·Asix̲án áwé du kéilk'. *He loves his nephew.*
·"Ix̲six̲án," yoo ayawsik̲aa du yadák'u. *She told her boyfriend, "I love you."*

**du x̲án aa** noun *his/her mate, his "old lady"; her "old man"*
·Yéil x'óow aawak̲áa du x̲án aa jeeyís. *She sewed a Raven blanket for her husband.*

**x̲at** Pronoun *me [object]*
VARIANTS: ax̲ (An)
·Katíx̲'aa s'aatíx̲ x̲at gux̲satée yá keijín yagiyeedáx̲. *After Friday I will be the jailer.*
·Áx' k̲aa ée at dultóow yé áa yéi x̲at gug̲watée seig̲án. *I will be in school tomorrow.*

**x̲át** Pronoun *I [independent]*

**x̲át'aa** noun *whip*
·X̲át'aa yéi awsinei ax̲ éesh. *My father made a whip.*

**X̲EECH** verb root

- **ashaawax̲ích | --- | ashax̲íchx̲**
*s/he clubbed it | --- | s/he clubs it (regularly).*
THEME: O-sha-S-ø-x̲eech~ (ø event)
*for S to club, hit O on the head*
·X'ús' teen shawduwax̲ích. *He was hit with a club.*
- **át akaawax̲ích | --- | áx̲ akax̲eech**
*s/he threw it to it | --- | s/he throws it to it (regularly).*
THEME: P-t~ O-ka-S-ø-x̲eech~ (ø motion)
*for S to throw O (esp. liquid) to P*
NOTES: To give the meaning "throw out", use: yóo-t~ "over there". For example: Yóot akaawax̲ích. "S/he threw it (liquid) out."
·Ax̲ x̲'éit aa kax̲ích tléik̲w kahéeni! *Give me some juice! (Lit: Throw some juice at my mouth!)*
- **yax̲ akaawax̲ích | --- | yax̲ akax̲íchx̲**
*s/he spilled it | --- | s/he spills it (regularly).*
THEME: yax̲ O-ka-S-ø-x̲eech~ (ø event)
*for S to spill, upset O*
·Yaa ntoo.ádi áwé, daak wudzigít yax̲ akaawax̲ích wutuwa.ini kaneilts'ákw. *When we were walking along, she fell down and spilled all the swamp currants we picked.*

**du x̲eek** noun *his/her upper arm*
VARIANTS: du x̲eik (C)
·Du x̲eek áwé wool'éex'. *His upper arm is broken.*
·Wéi kashóok' gwéil ax̲ x̲eek káa yan satí! *Set the heating pad on my upper arm!*

**x̲eel** noun *foam; whitecaps*
VARIANTS: x̲eil

·X̱eil neech káa yéi nateech xóon wudunoogú. *Foam is on the beach when the north wind blows.*

**x̱éel** noun *granite*
·X̱éel yéi ndu.eich hítx̱ dulyeix̱í. *Granite is used to build a house.*

**x̱éel'** noun *slime; thick mucus*
·Wé x̱éel' wuls'eexí lichán. *When the slime rots it stinks.*
·Wé x̱éel' du jíndáx̱ awlig̱oo. *She wiped the slime off her hands.*

**X̱EEN** verb root

• **a kát wujix̱ín | --- | a káx̱ ishx̱een**
*it fell on it | --- | it falls on it (regularly).*
THEME: N-t~ j-x̱een~ (ø motion)
*for a hard, solid object to fall, drop on N*
·Ax̱ ḵatlyát wujix̱ín wé x̱áaw tlein. *That big log fell on my side.*

**x̱éet'** noun *giant clam*
VARIANTS: x̱éit'
·X̱éet' a daat shkalneek ḵudzitee. *There is a story about a giant clam.*

**x̱éex̱** noun *small owl*
·X̱éex̱ wuduwa.áx̱. *A small owl was heard.*

**x̱éey** noun *pack; backpack; pack sack*

**X̱EI** verb root

• **(áa) uwax̱éi | --- | (áa) x̱eix̱**
*s/he stayed overnight (there) | --- | s/he stays overnight (there) (regularly).*
THEME: O-ø-x̱ei~ (ø event)
*for O to stay overnight, spend the night, camp out overnight*
VARIANTS: -x̱ee~ (An)
·Áak'wx' uwax̱éi wé shaawát. *That woman camped at Auke Bay.*
·Ḵaa t'áak áwé áa uwax̱ée. *She camped behind everyone.*

at **x̱éidi** noun *arrowhead*
·Yei googénk'i at x̱éidi teen áwé x̱waat'úk wé t'aawáḵ. *I shot the Canada goose with a small arrow.*
·At x̱éidi yax'aat a shóox' g̱anú! *Sit down and do some arrow-head sharpening!*

**X̱EIḴ** verb root

• **ash wusix̱éḵ | --- | ash sax̱éḵx̱**
*he/she/it kept him/her awake | --- | he/she/it keeps him/her awake (regularly).*
THEME: O-S-s-x̱eiḵ~ (ø event)
*for S to keep O awake*
VARIANTS: -x̱eeḵ~ (An)
·Taat kanax̱ x̱at wusix̱éḵ wé katl'úḵjaa. *All night I was kept awake by that slow drip.*

**x̲eil** noun *foam*
VARIANTS: x̲eel
·X̲eil yáx̲ x̲'ayatee. *It's foaming at the mouth.*

X̲EIT² verb root

- **awsix̲eit | kei anasx̲ét | kei asx̲étch**
*s/he bred them | s/he is breeding them | s/he breeds them (regularly).*
THEME: O-S-s-x̲eit~ (ga event)
*for S to breed O*
VARIANTS: -x̲eet~ (An)
·Kanóox' áwé kéi anasx̲ít. *He is breeding turtles.*

- **has wudzix̲eit | kei (ha)s nasx̲ét | kei (ha)s isx̲étch**
*they multiplied | they are multiplying | they multiply (regularly).*
THEME: d-s-x̲eit~ (ga event)
*for something to multiply, increase in numbers; for animals to produce young, breed*
VARIANTS: -x̲eet~ (An)

X̲EITL verb root

- **wulix̲éitl | lix̲éitl | kei lax̲éitlch**
*s/he got lucky | s/he's lucky | s/he gets lucky (regularly).*
THEME: O-li-x̲éitl (ga state)
*for O to be blessed, be lucky*
·Gu.aal kwshé iwulx̲éidlik̲. *Bless you. (Lit: I hope you get lucky.)*

X̲EITL' verb root

- **áa akawdlix̲éitl' | áa akwdlix̲éitl' | ---**
*s/he was afraid of it | s/he is afraid of it | ---.*
THEME: P-x' a-ka-u-S-d-l-x̲éitl' (ga state)
*for S to be afraid of, fear P*
VARIANTS: -x̲éetl' (An)
·Náakw yís kayaaní ashigóok, áx' k̲u.aa akwdlix̲éitl' k̲aa x̲'éix̲ aa wuteeyí. *He knows medicinal plants but he is afraid to give them to anyone.*
·Áa akwdlix̲éitl' wé kag̲ít tú. *He is afraid of the dark.*

X̲ÉITL'SHÁN verb root

- **kawlix̲éitl'shán | kulix̲éitl'shán | kei klax̲éitl'shánch**
*it was scary | it's scary | it gets to be scary (regularly).*
THEME: O-ka-u-l-x̲éitl'shán (ga state)
*for O to be scary, dangerous*
VARIANTS: -x̲éetl'shán (An)
·Héen yík héen kanadaayí wáa yateeyi yéix' kulix̲éitl'shán nooch. *Sometimes currents in a river are dangerous.*
·Tláakw naadaayi héen kulix̲éitl'shán. *A fast river is dangerous.*

X̲EIX'W verb root

- **has woox̲éix'w | has x̲éx'w | has x̲éx'wx̲**
*they slept | they're sleeping | they sleep (regularly).*

THEME: S-ø-x̲éix'w~ (na act)
*for (plural) S to sleep, sleep in company with others, go to bed*

**a x̲íji** noun *its mane (esp. the hair on the neck hump of a moose)*

**x̲ík** noun *puffin*

**du x̲ikshá** noun *his/her shoulder*
·Du x̲ikshá káx̲ yaa anayéin wé jánwu. *He is carrying the moutain goat on his shoulder.*

**a x̲oo** RelationalNoun *(in) the midst of it; among it*
·Kanat'á a x̲oo yéi nateech kaxwéix̲. *Blueberries are usually in the midst of cranberries.*
·Ldakát wooch x̲oot has yawdiháa. *Everybody came together.*

**a x̲oo aa** noun *some of them*
·A x̲oo aa k̲u.oo woolnáx̲ wooshk̲ák̲ has al'óon. *Some people hunt the wren.*

**du x̲ooní** noun *his/her relative, friend; his/her tribesman*
·Du naax̲ sitee áwé du x̲ooní. *His tribesman are those of his clan.*
·Haa x̲ooní Anóoshi aaní kaadé k̲uwuteenín. *Our friend had traveled to Russia.*

**a x̲ooní** noun *one that matches it; an amount that matches it; equivalent to it; one like it*
·A x̲oonéet kax̲wdig̲íx'. *I added to it.*
·Wáa sá yax̲wak̲aayí a x̲oonéet kashaxít! *Write what I am saying in addition to it!*

**X̲OOT'[1]** verb root

- **aadé aawax̲óot' | aadé yaa nax̲út' | aadé yoo ayax̲út'k**
*he/she/it dragged him/her/it there | he/she/it is dragging him/her/it there | he/she/it drags him/her/it there (regularly).*
THEME: P-dé O-S-ø-x̲oot'~ (na motion)
*for S to drag, pull O (esp. light object or solid, stiff object) to P; for S to pull O in quick movements to P*
·Du g̲eiwú yaakwdé yaa anax̲út'. *He is pulling his seine in.*
- **aadé awsix̲óot' | aadé yaa anasx̲út' | aadé yoo asix̲út'k**
*s/he drug it there | s/he is dragging it there | s/he drags it there (regularly).*
THEME: P-dé O-S-s-x̲oot'~ (na motion)
*for S to drag, pull O to P; for S to haul, transport O (by motor power) to P*
·K̲u.éex'dei nasx̲óot' yá kak̲áshx̲i! *Pack the steamed berries to the potlatch!*
- **át aawax̲óot' | --- | át yoo ayax̲út'k**
*he/she/it is dragging him/her/it around; he/she/it dragged him/her/it around | --- | s/he drags it around (regularly).*
THEME: P-t O-S-ø-x̲oot'~ (na motion)
*for S to drag, pull O (esp. person) around at P; for S to pull O in quick movement*

*around at P*
·X'áan át iwax̱óot'i tlél ushk'é. *Anger pulling you around is not good.*

- **shawdlix̱óot' | shalx̱óot' | yoo shadlix̱út'k**
*s/he sportfished | s/he's sportfishing | s/he sportfishes (regularly).*
THEME: sha-S-d-l-x̱óot' (na act)
*for S to fish with rod, sportfish*
·Ísh yíkde shalx̱óot'. *She is casting into the deep water hole.*

- **yan aawax̱út' | yánde yaa anax̱út' | ---**
*s/he pulled it in | s/he is pulling it in | ---.*
THEME: yan~ O-S-ø-x̱oot'~ (ø motion)
*for S to drag, pull O (esp. light object or solid, stiff object) in, to shore; for S to pull O in to shore in quick movement*
·X̱áaw yan x̱út'! *Pull the log to shore!*

**X̱OOT'[2]** verb root

- **aawax̱út' | ax̱út't | ---**
*s/he chopped it | s/he is chopping it | ---.*
THEME: O-S-ø-x̱óot'~ (ø act)
*for S to chop O (wood); for S to chip O out (with adze)*
·Yá kas'úwaa teen a yíkdáx̱ x̱út'! *Chip the inside out with this chopper!*

- **akawlix̱óot' | aklax̱út't | yei aklax̱óot'ch**
*s/he chopped it up | s/he's chopping it up | s/he chops it up (regularly).*
THEME: O-ka-S-l-x̱óot' (g̱a act)
*for S to chop up O; for S to split O (wood)*
·Gán kaḵás'ti akawlix̱óot' wé x̱'aan yís. *He chopped kindling for the fire.*

**X̱OOX̱** verb root

- **aawax̱oox̱ | ax̱oox̱ | yei ax̱oox̱ch**
*s/he summoned him/her | s/he summons him/her; s/he is summoning him/her | s/he summons him/her (regularly).*
THEME: O-S-ø-x̱oox̱ (g̱a act)
*for S to call, summon O*
·Tlék'g̱aanáx̱ áwé has wuduwax̱oox̱. *They called them one by one.*
·G̱uwakaan x̱ax̱oox̱ nooch ḵ'eikaxétl'k kayaaní teen. *I always use a bunchberry leaf to call deer.*

- **shukawlix̱oox̱ | --- | ---**
*s/he composed a song | --- | ---.*
THEME: shu-ka-S-l-x̱oox̱~ (na event)
*for S to call forth a response (from opposite clan, by means of a song); for S to compose a song*
·Shí áwé shukḵwalax̱óox̱. *I'm going to compose a song.*

**x̱út'aa** noun *adze*

du **x̱úx̱** noun *her husband*
·Tóos' hítdáx̱ áwé du x̱úx̱. *Her husband is from the Shark house.*
·Ch'a tlákw áwé yéi nateech ax̱ x̱úx̱, ch'u atk'átsk'ux̱ sateeyídáx̱. *My husband is like this often, and has been even since he was a child.*

# « X̲w »

*(None.)*

# « X̱' »

a **x̱'áak** RelationalNoun *between them*

NOTES: When followed by the -t postposition (which is required by positional verbs), the final -k optionally falls out, as in one of the examples given here.

·Has du x̱'áakt wuhaan du káak. *His maternal uncle stood between them.*
·Has du léelk'w du x̱'áat .áa. *Their grandmother is sitting between them.*

**x̱'áakw** noun *sockeye or coho salmon that has entered fresh water*

·X̱'áakw x̱'úx̱u haa x̱'eis sa.í stoox kaanáx̱! *Cook us red sockeye soup on the stove!*
·X̱'áakw hél a kajeig̱í ḵoostí. *The freshwater sockeye doesn't have any scales.*

**x̱'áal'** noun *skunk cabbage*

·X̱'áal' tóox' wutusi.ée. *We cooked it in skunk cabbage.*

**x̱'aan** noun *fire*

·X̱'aan yeenayát'ch wé yées stoox tóox'. *The fire lasts in the new stove.*
·X̱'aan wusit'áax̱'. *The fire is burning hot.*

**x̱'aan** noun *red*

·X̱'aan yáx̱ wutuwanéegwál' a yá. *We painted the side of it red.*
·X̱'aan kakéin haat yéi x̱wsiné kasné yís. *I brought some red yarn for knitting.*

**X̱'AAN** verb root

• **at uwax̱'án | at x̱'áan | at x̱'ánx̱**

*s/he dried fish | s/he is drying fish | s/he dries fish (regularly).*

THEME: at S-ø-x̱'aan~ (ø act)

*for S to dry (fish, meat) over fire, smoke lightly*

·At toox̱'áan áyá táakwni yís, kaldáanaaḵx̱ haa nasteech. *We are smoking fish for the winter because we are usually without money.*

**x̱'aan gook** noun *fireside; by the fire, facing the fire*

·X̱'aan gookx' áwé yéi aḵéech. *Around the fire is where people sit.*

**x̱'aan káx̱ túlaa** noun *fire drill, hand drill used to start fires by friction*

·X̱'aan káx̱ túlaa tín x̱'aan yilayéx̱! *Build a fire with the fire drill!*

**X̱'AAT'** verb root

• **--- | kadlix̱'át' | ---**

*--- | they're green (unripe) | ---.*

THEME: ka-d-l-x̱'át' (state)

*for berries to be unripe, green and hard*

NOTES: This verb only occurs in the imperfective. Here's an example

sentence: Hél ushk'é duxaayí ch'a yeisú kalx̱'ádi - ikg̱wasdéek. "It's not good to eat them when they're still green - you'll get constipated."
·Yeisú kadlix̱'át' wé tléik̲w. *The berries are still green.*

**x̱'áax'w** noun *ling cod*
·X̱'áax'w útlx̱i áwé yak'éi. *Boiled ling cod is good.*

du **x̱'adaa** noun *his/her lips; area around his/her mouth*

du **x̱'adaadzaayí** noun *his/her whiskers*
·Tlél x̱'adaadzaayí du jee. *He doesn't have whiskers.*
·Sindi Claus yáx̱ áwé dleit yáx̱ yatee du x̱'adaadzaayí. *His whiskers are white like Santa Clause.*

a **x̱'adéex'i** noun *cork, plug*

**x̱'agáax'** noun *prayer*
·X̱'agáax' áwé litseen yéi yaawak̲aa ax̱ léelk'w. *My grandparent said that prayer is powerful.*
·X̱'agáax' has du g̱aneix̱íx̱ sitee. *Prayer is their salvation.*

**x̱'agáax' daakahídi** noun *house of prayer; church*
·X̱'agáax' daakahídix' ali.áx̱ch wé g̱íx̱'jaa k̲óok. *He plays the organ at the Church.*
·X̱'agáax' daakahídix' áwé at kashéex̱' shí áa dushí. *Songs of praise are sung in church.*

**x̱'aháat** noun *door*
·Wé x̱'aháatde nagú! *Go to the door!*
·X̱'aháat kináak áwé át akawsix'óo, du saayí. *He nailed his name above the door.*

du **x̱'ahéeni** noun *his/her saliva*
·Du x̱'ahéeni kaawadaa. *His saliva is flowing.*
·X̱'ahéeni du x̱'éit uwadáa. *He is drooling.*

**x̱'akakeix̱í** noun *chain*
·X̱'akakeix̱í aan wuduwa.áx̱w. *He was bound with a chain.*

**x̱'akasék̲'waa** noun *lipstick*
VARIANTS: x̱'akaséik̲'u, x̱'adaaséik̲'u (T), x̱'akaséik̲'waa
·X̱'aan x̱'akasék̲'waa yéi aya.óo. *She is wearing red lipstick.*

du **x̱'akooká** noun *in response, reply to him/her; answering him/her; following his/her train of speech*

**x̱'al'daakeit** noun *small covered box*
·X̱'al'daakeit awliyéx̱. *She built a small covered box.*

**x̱'al'daayéeji** noun *sandpiper (shore bird)*
·X̱'al'daayéeji éek̲t wujixeex. *The sandpiper is running around the beach.*

a **x̲'anaa** RelationalNoun *in its way; keeping it away; protecting, shielding, screening from it; blocking it*
·A x̲'anaa áwé át eehán. *You are standing in its way.*
·Haa x̲'anaatx̲ wuhán, yak'éiyi k̲áa! *Move out of our way, good man!*

**x̲'aséikw** noun *life; breath*
·Du x̲'aséigu yaa shunaxíx. *He is running out of breath.*

**x̲'astóox̲** noun *spit*
·Shé a x̲oodé ayatéen du x̲'astóox̲u. *He sees blood in his sputum.*

du **x̲'astus'aag̲í** noun *his/her jawbone; jaws*

**x̲'asúnjaa** noun *small bubbles (in water)*

du **x̲'ás'** noun *his/her lower jaw, mandible*
·Du x̲'ás' aawagwál wé k̲áa. *That man socked him on the jaw.*
·Kaxées' teen wóoshdei kdudzixát du x̲'ás'. *His jaw is held together with a wire.*

du **x̲'as'guwéis'i** noun *his/her tonsils*
·Du x̲'as'guwéis'i wuduwaxaash. *His tonsils were taken out.*

du **x̲'asheeyí** noun *his/her song*
·Anóoshi x̲'asheeyí at shí k̲óok tóode too.áx̲jin. *We used to hear Russian songs on the radio.*

**X̲'atas'aak̲** noun *Eskimo*
·Yá X̲'atas'aak̲ k̲únáx̲ k̲usi.áat'i yéix' áwé yéi has yatee. *Eskimos live in a very cold place.*

**x̲'atl'ook̲** noun *cold sore*
·X̲'atl'ook̲ du jeewú. *She has an ulcer inside her mouth.*

**x̲'awool** noun *doorway*
·Wé x̲'awool yinaat hán. *She is standing in the doorway.*

**x̲'awool kayáashi** noun *porch; patio*
·X̲'awool kayáashi ká áwé át .áa wé shaawát. *The woman is sitting around on the porch.*

du **x̲'ax̲án** noun *at hand (for him/her to eat or drink)*
VARIANTS: du x̲'ax̲áni
·Du x̲'ax̲áni yéi awsinei wé atx̲á. *The food that was made for him was placed close at hand.*

a **x̲'ax̲éedli** noun *its trim, trimming*
·K'idéin aax̲ xásh wé t'áa at x̲'ax̲éedli! *Cut the trimming off the board good!*
·Wé g̲uwakaan dleeyí at x̲'ax̲éedli k'idéin aax̲ xásh, téix̲ sákw! *Cut the trimming off the deer meat well for the broth!*

**du x̲'ayáx̲** noun *according to his/her words, instructions*
·Du x̲'ayáx̲ awliyéx̲ wé kootéeyaa. *He made the totem according to his instructions.*

**du x̲'ayee** noun *ready, waiting for him/her to eat, drink; waiting for him/her to speak or finish speaking*
·Du x̲'ayee yan yéi wdudzinéi. *They set a place for him to eat.*

**x̲'ayeit** noun *food container; pot or pan; dish, large bowl*
·Yak'éiyi x̲'ayeit áwé du jeewú ax̲ aat. *My paternal aunt has nice dishes.*

**du x̲'a.eetí** noun *his/her food scraps, left-over food; crumbs of food left or scattered where s/he has eaten*

**du x̲'é** noun *his/her mouth*
·G̲áx̲ dleeyí gé i x̲'é yak'éi? *Does rabbit meat taste good to you?*
·Yat'aayi héen du k̲áawu x̲'éit awsi.ín. *She gave her husband's clan brother coffee.*

**a x̲'é** RelationalNoun *its mouth, opening*
·A x̲'éináx̲ áwé kadul.eesh wé k̲áas' kaadéi wé saak. *Those hooligan are strung through the mouth on the stick.*

**X̲'EEL'** verb root

- **át wushix̲'éel' | --- | át yoo shix̲'íl'k**
  *he/she/it is sliding around; he/she/it slid around | --- | he/she/it slides around (regularly).*
  THEME: P-t O-sh-x̲'éel'~ (na motion)
  *for O to slip, slide around at P*
  ·Du keey shakanóox'u áwé tlei át nashx̲'íl'ch. *His kneecap slides around.*
- **át wushix̲'íl' | aadé yaa nashx̲'íl' | ---**
  *he/she/it slid there | he/she/it is sliding there | ---.*
  THEME: P-t~ O-sh-x̲'éel'~ (ø motion)
  *for O to slip, slide to P*
  ·Héent wushix̲'íl'. *He slipped into the water.*
- **kawshix̲'íl'k | kashix̲'íl'k | ---**
  *it was slippery | it's slippery | ---.*
  THEME: ka-sh-x̲'íl'k (state)
  *for something to be slippery (oil, ice, wet rocks, etc.)*
  ·Tlél tlax̲ kooshx̲'íl'k yá kaxwaan. *It's not very slippery with this frost.*
- **wushix̲'éel' | yei nashx̲'íl' | yei ishx̲'éel'ch**
  *s/he slipped | s/he is slipping | s/he slips (regularly).*
  THEME: O-sh-x̲'éel' (g̲a event)
  *for O to slip, slide*
  NOTES: Note a couple of common metaphorical uses of this verb. Wushix̲'éel' can be used to mean "S/he fell off the wagon" (as in started drinking again). Another common expression is: Átk'

aheení wushix̲éel' which means "s/he stopped believing, lost faith".

**x̲'éen** noun *wall crest; wall screen*

a **x̲'éeshi** noun *its dried flesh, strips (of fish)*
·L'ook at x̲'éeshi áwé yak'éi. *Coho salmon dryfish is good.*
·Tsaa eex̲í teen yak'éi at x̲'éeshi. *Seal oil is good with dryfish.*

at **x̲'éeshi** noun *dry fish*

**X̲'EEX'** verb root

- **áx̲ kawlix̲'éex' | --- | áx̲ yoo kalix̲'íx'k**
*he/she/it is stuck there* | --- | *he/she/it gets stuck there (regularly).*
THEME: P-x̲ O-ka-l-x̲'éex'~ (na motion)
*for O to get stuck, be squeezed at P*
NOTES: Note that this verb gives a literal meaning only. It would be used to indicate that someone is stuck in a tight space, but not in the non-literal sense used in phrases such as "stuck at home" or "stuck there (due to weather)", etc.
·A x̲'áakx' tsé ikanalx̲'éex'! *Don't get stuck between it now!*

**x̲'éex'w** noun *wedge, shim*

**x̲'éex'wál'** noun *safety pin*
VARIANTS: x̲'éigwál'

**x̲'éigwál'** noun *safety pin*
VARIANTS: x̲'éex'wál'

a **x̲'éináx̲** Adverb *through its mouth*
·Lingít x̲'éináx̲ kashxeet áwé ashigóok. *He knows how to write in the Tlingit language.*

**x̲'eint'áax'aa** noun *labret, lip plug*
·Ch'áakw x̲'eint'áax'aa shaawát x̲'é yéi ndu.eich. *Long ago women would wear a labret.*

du **x̲'eis** noun *for him/her to eat or drink*
·Dei káx' yéi jinéiyi x̲'eis has at gawdzi.ée wé aantk̲eení. *The townspeople cooked food for the people working on the road.*
·Du kéilk' du x̲'eis at wusi.ée. *His niece cooked for him.*

**x̲'eis'awáa** noun *willow ptarmigan; pigeon*
·X̲'eis'awáa l'eix̲í kulitées'shan nooch. *The dance of the ptarmigan is always a wonder to behold.*

**x̲'éi shadagutx̲i lítaa** noun *knife with fold-in blade*
·Dleit k̲áach áwé awliyéx̲ wé x̲'éi shadagutx̲i lítaa. *The white man invented the pocket knife.*

**x̲'éishx'w** noun *bluejay, Stellar's jay*
VARIANTS: x̲'éishk'w (C)
·X̲'éishx'w áwé nageich k̲utaan ítdáx̲. *After the summer is over there are a lot of bluejays*
·A kaséik̲'u x̲'éishx'w kayaax̲ sitee. *The color is in the likeness of a bluejay.*

**x̲'éishx'w** noun *dark blue*

du **x̲'eitákw** noun *his/her heel*
·Du x̲'eitákw yanéekw. *His heel hurts.*

**X̲'EIX̲'** verb root

• **awlix̲'éx̲' | --- | ---**
*he/she/it burned him/her/it | --- | ---.*
THEME: O-S-l-x̲'éix̲'~ (ø event)
*for S to burn O (flesh, skin); for S to scald O*
VARIANTS: -x̲'éex̲'~ (An)
·Du tl'ek̲shá áwé awlix̲'éx̲' wé stoox káx'. *He burned his fingertip on the stove.*

• **wudix̲'éx̲' | --- | dax̲'éx̲'x̲**
*s/he got burned | --- | s/he gets burned (regularly).*
THEME: O-d-x̲'éix̲'~ (ø event)
*for O to be burned (of flesh, skin), become shriveled and brittle through burning*
VARIANTS: -x̲'éex̲'~ (An)
·Du jikóol wudix̲'íx̲'. *The back of his hand was burned.*
·Du jiwán wudix̲'íx̲'. *The outside edge of her hand was burned.*

**x̲'íx'** noun *eggs (of eels, etc.)*

du **x̲'óol'** noun *his/her belly, paunch*
·Du x̲'óol' néekw nooch. *His belly always hurts.*

**x̲'oon** noun *soft brown wood for tanning dye*
·X̲'oon yéi ndu.eich wé at doogú kaséik̲'w yís. *Soft brown wood is used for coloring the skin.*

**x̲'óon** noun *fur seal*

du **x̲'oos** noun *his/her foot, leg*
·G̲agaan át x̲'oos uwatsóow. *Sun rays are shining on it. (Lit: The sun is poking its feet out.)*
·Wooshdakádin x̲'oosdé awdiyik̲ du téeli. *He put his shoes on the wrong feet.*

a **x̲'oosí** RelationalNoun *its leg*
·A x̲'oosí aax̲ aawaxásh wé shaawátch. *The woman cut the legs off.*
·A x̲'oosí k'idéin át kalatéx̲'! *Screw the leg on it good!*

du **x̲'usgoosh** noun *his/her big toe*
·Du x̲'usgoosh áwé wudlix'ís. *His big toe is swollen.*

**x̲'uskeit** noun *dancing leggings; leggings for climbing*

du **x̲'ustáak** noun *sole of his/her foot*

du **x̲'ust'ákl'i** noun *knob on outer side of his/her ankle*

du **x̲'ustl'eek̲** noun *his/her toe*
VARIANTS: du x̲'ustl'eik̲

du **x̲'ustl'eik̲** noun *his/her toe*
VARIANTS: du x̲'ustl'eek̲

du **x̲'usyee** noun *under his/her feet*
·I yádi ax̲ x̲'usyeet wudig̲wáat'. *Your child is crawling around under my feet.*

a **x̲'usyee** RelationalNoun *at the foot of it*
·I téeli yee.át x̲'usyeex' yéi na.oo! *Put your shoes at the foot of the bed!*

du **x̲'us.eetí** noun *his/her footprint*

a **x̲'us.eetí** noun *its tracks*
·Aasgutóot wugoodí, dzísk'w x̲'us.eetí awsiteen. *He saw moose tracks when he was walking in the woods.*
·Xóots x̲'us.eetí áwé awsiteen wé kík'i aa. *The younger one saw the bear tracks.*

a **x̲'úx̲u** noun *its flesh (of fish)*
·X̲'áakw x̲'úx̲u haa x̲'eis sa.í stoox kaanáx̲! *Cook us red sockeye soup on the stove!*

# « X̲'w »

**x̲'wáal'** noun *down (feathers)*

**x̲'waash** noun *sea urchin*

**x̲'wáat'** noun *Dolly Varden trout*
·X̲'wáat' héen táakde has ayatéen. *They see trout in the river.*
·X̲'wáat tlénx' dust'eix̲ G̲aat Héenidáx̲. *People catch big trout at Garteeni.*

**x̲'wéinaa** noun *roasting stick (split so that the meat can be inserted; the end is then bound)*

# « Y »

**yá** Demonstrative *this (right here)*
VARIANTS: yáa
·Ḵúnáx̱ woo.aat gis'óoḵ yá xáanaa. *The Northern Lights are really moving about this evening.*
·Kaldaag̱éináx̱ yaa gax̱tooḵóox̱, tlél g̱wadlaan yá éix̱' yík. *We will travel along slowly, it's not deep in this slough.*

**du yá** noun *his/her face*
NOTES: When the postposition -x' is added to du yá, the vowel becomes long and the -x' optionally falls out, producing: du yáa. This accounts for the forms seen in the examples given here.
·Xóosht' has du yáa yéi has ana.eich yaa (ha)s jinda.ádi. *The dark burnt ashes would be put on their faces when going to war.*
·Ḵaa yáx̱ kei jisatánch wáadishgaa. *The priest blesses people.*

**a yá** RelationalNoun *face, (vertical) side, (vertical) surface of it*
·X̱'aan yáx̱ wutuwanéegwál' a yá. *We painted the side of it red.*
·G̱íl' yáx̱ kei naltl'ét' wé yadák'w. *The young boy is climbing the cliff face.*

**yaa** Adverb *along; down*
·Yaa ntoo.ádi áwé, daak wudzigít yax̱ akaawax̱ích wutuwa.ini kaneilts'ákw. *When we were walking along, she fell down and spilled all the swamp currants we picked.*
·Kaldaag̱éináx̱ yaa gax̱tooḵóox̱, tlél g̱wadlaan yá éix̱' yík. *We will travel along slowly, it's not deep in this slough.*

**yaa** noun *trout (sea)*

YAA[1] verb root

- **aadáx̱ kawdiyaa | --- | ---**
*he/she/it disappeared from there | --- | ---.*
THEME: P-dáx̱ O-ka-di-yaa~ (na motion)
*for O to disappear from P; for O to move (often almost imperceptably) from P; for O to travel (indefinite as to method) from P*
·Tle yeedát yáatx̱ haa kagux̱dayáa. *We need to leave from here right now.*
- **--- | oowayáa | ---**
*--- | it looks like it | ---.*
THEME: O-S-u-ø-yaa~ (g̱a state)
*for S to resemble, look like O; for S to be almost identical with O*
NOTES: This verb can be a little confusing because of the thematic prefix u-, which contracts with the object prefix a- (and the classifier ya-), producing the prefix oowa- in the imperfective. Note that this only happens when the subject and object are both third person (and in this case, non-human). For third person

human objects, the object pronoun ash is preferred. For example: ash uwayáa "s/he looks like him/her." Since there's no object prefix a- here (which is used for non-human objects), the prefix is uwa- in the imperfective. Here's another example: Ax̲ kéek' x̲at uwayáa "My little sister looks like me." Here's an example sentence with a first person subject: Ax̲ tláa x̲waayáa "I look like my mother." Note that the thematic prefix u- contracts with the first person subject prefix (and the classifier ya-), producing x̲waa-. To say "they look like each other", the pronoun wooch is used along with the d- classifier: wooch has wudiyáa. In the negative, this verb can take on the meaning "improper". For example: tlél oowaa "it's not right; it's not proper" OR "it doesn't look like it."

·Tínx kaxwéix̲ oowayáa tl'átgi káx' k̲u.aa ka.éix̲. *Bearberries look like cranberries but they grow on the ground.*

·Tléil oowaa wé aan káa k̲ududziteeyi yoo x̲'atánk géide k̲udunoogú. *It is wrong to act against the law of the land.*

- **yan kawdiyáa | --- | yax̲ kadayaa**

*it happened | --- | it happens (regularly).*

THEME: yan~ ka-di-yaa~ (ø motion)

*for an event to happen, take place*

·Hú k̲u.aa áyá ch'a g̲óot yéide yan kawdiyáa ax̲ tláa, du éeshch áyá du yát saa uwatí Shaaxeidi Tláa. *But with my mother it happened differently, because her father named her Shaaxeidi Tláa.*

YAA[2] verb root

- **aawayaa | yaa anayáan / yaa anayéin | kei ayeich**

*he/she/it carried it on his/her/its back | he/she/it is carrying in on his/her/its back | he/she/it carries it on his/her/its back (regularly).*

THEME: O-S-ø-yaa~ (ga event)

*for S to carry O on back; for S to pack O*

NOTES: In the progressive aspect, there is dialect variation between yaa anayáan and yaa anayéin and in the perfective habitual there is dialect variation between agayáach and agayéich.

·Du x̲ikshá káx̲ yaa anayéin wé jánwu. *He is carrying the moutain goat on his shoulder.*

·Dák̲de k̲ákw aawayaa i léelk'w. *Your grandmother died. (Lit: Your grandmother took her basket into the woods).*

- **ashawsiyaa | --- | yoo ashasiyéik**

*s/he anchored the boat | --- | s/he anchors the boat (regularly).*

THEME: O-sha-S-s-yaa~ (na event)

*for S to anchor O*

- **áx̲ akaawayaa | áx̲ yei akanayéin | áx̲ yei akayéich**
  *s/he spread it out | s/he's spreading it out | s/he spreads it out (regularly).*
  THEME: P-x̲ O-ka-S-ø-yaa~ (g̲a motion)
  *for S to spread out, unfold, lay out (singular) O along P*
  ·Kinguchwáan x'óowu du káx̲ kawduwayaa. *He was covered with a Hudson Bay blanket.*
- **shawdziyaa | --- | shasyéix̲**
  *s/he anchored | --- | s/he anchors (regularly).*
  THEME: sha-S-d-s-yaa~ (na event)
  *for S to anchor, lower anchor*
  ·Déili áa has shawdziyaa. *They anchored in a harbor.*
- **at wooyaa | yaa at nayáan / yaa at nayéin | kei at yeich**
  *he/she/it carried things on his/her/its back | he/she/it is carrying things on his/her/its back | he/she/it carries things on his/her/its back (regularly).*
  THEME: at S-ø-yaa~ (ga event)
  *for S to carry things on back; for S to pack things*
  NOTES: In the progressive aspect, there is dialect variation between yaa at nayáan and yaa at nayéin. Both are correct.
  ·Yaa at nayáan wé gukkudayáat'. *The donkey is packing things.*

**yaa at naskwéini** noun *student; learner*

**yáa at wooné** noun *respect*

**yaadachóon** noun *straight ahead; directly ahead*
VARIANTS: yaadechóon (C)

**yaak** noun *mussel*

**yaakw** noun *boat, canoe*
·Wé yéi kuwoox̲'u yaakw yá yéil a káa gax̲toonéegwál'. *We will paint a raven on the widest side of the skiff.*
·Yax̲ kei kg̲wadláax̲'w wé yaakw. *The boat will get stuck on the beach.*

**Yaakwdáat** noun *Yakutat*
·Sgóonwaan atyátx'i has shayadihéin Yaakwdáatx'. *There are a lot of school children in Yakutat.*
·Tleidahéen áwé Yaakwdáatt aa wlihásh wé kanóox'. *One time a turtle floated to Yakutat.*

**yaakw x̲uká** noun *deck of a boat*
·Anóoshi aan kwéiyi áwé át wududziyík̲ wé s'ísaa yaakw x̲uká. *They raised a Russian flag on the deck of that sailboat.*

**yaakw x̲ukahídi** noun *cabin (of boat); pilot house*

**yaakw yasatáni** noun *captain (of a boat)*

**yaakw yík** noun *in the boat*

**yaakw yiks'ísayi** noun *sail*

**yaa k̲udzigéiyi ts'ats'ée** noun *pigeon*
·Neek ash atláx'w yaa k̲udzigéiyi ts'ats'ée. *Pigeons carry messages.*

**yaan** noun *hunger*

du **yaanaayí** noun *his/her enemy, adversary*

**yáanadi** noun *backpack; pack sack*

a **yáanáx̲** RelationalPostposition *beyond it, more than it; too much; excessively*
·A yáanáx̲ áwé kaylisék̲'w yá néegwál'. *You tinted this paint too much.*
·A yáanáx̲ yaawatáa. *She slept in.*

**yaana.eit** noun *wild celery*
NOTES: Warning: contains furanocoumarins which can cause rash and edema

**yaash ká** noun *smokehouse shelf*

YAAT' verb root

- **--- | dliyát'x' | ---**
  --- | *they're long* | ---.
  THEME: d-l-yát'x' (ga state)
  *for (plural, general) objects to be long*
  ·Dliyát'x' du wax̲'ax̲éix̲'u. *Her eyelashes are long.*
- **wooyáat' | yayát' | yát'x̲**
  *it became long* | *it is long* | *it becomes long (regularly).*
  THEME: ø-yáat'~ (na state)
  *for an object (usually stick-like) to be long*
  ·Dagwatgiyáa lú yayát' k̲a yéi kwlisáa. *A hummingbird's beak is long and skinny.*
- **wuliyát' | liyát' | ---**
  *it became long* | *it's long* | ---.
  THEME: l-yát' (na state)
  *for something to be long (of time or physical objects)*
  NOTES: Speakers accept this verb with either a short, high stem -yát' (as given here) or a long, high stem -yáat' throughout the paradigm.
  ·S'eek l'eedí tléil ulyát'. *A black bear's tail is short.*
- **yeeywooyáat' | yeeyayát' | yeeyát'x̲**
  *it was long (time)* | *it's long (time)* | *it's long (time) (regularly).*
  THEME: yee-ø-yáat'~ (na state)
  *for something to be long (of time)*
  ·I tuwáx' yeewooyáat' yóo k̲u.éex'. *You thought the potlach was long.*
  ·X̲'aan yeenayát'ch wé yées stoox tóox'. *The fire lasts in the new stove.*
- **yéi kaawayáat' | yéi koowáat' | yéi kuwát'x̲**
  *it got that long* | *it is that long* | *it gets that long (regularly).*

THEME: (yéi) ka-u-ø-yáat'~ (na state)
*for an object (usually stick-like) to be (so) long*
·Jinkaat ḵa gooshúḵ ḵaa x̱'oos yéi koowáat' du yaagú. *Her boat is nineteen feet long.*

• --- | **yéi kwliyáat'** | ---
--- | *it's that long* | ---.
THEME: (yéi) ka-u-l-yáat' (na state)
*for a general object to be (so) long*
·Tléix' ḵaa x̱'oos yéi kwliyáat' wé tíx'. *That rope is one foot long.*
·Tleidooshú ḵaa x̱'oos yéi kwliyáat' wé kaay. *That measuring stick is six feet long.*

**yaaw** noun *herring*
·Yaaw xídlaa yéi wdu.oowú, tlél uldzée nooch. *Using a herring rake is not difficult.*

**yaax̱** Adverb *into a boat, vehicle*

**yáay** noun *whale*
·S'igeidí ḵa yáay a káa kashax̱ít wé at doogú x'óow! *Draw a Beaver and whale design on the leather blanket!*
·Wé yáay yax̱ woodláax̱'w. *The whale is stuck on the beach.*

a **yaayí** RelationalNoun *one of them (a pair)*
·Hél gé a yaayí ḵoostí? *Is the matching pair missing?*
·Du guk.ádi yaayí ḵut akaawagéex'. *She lost one of her earrings.*

**yáay x̱'axéni** noun *baleen; whalebone*

**yaa.aanuné** noun *oldsquaw duck*

du **yadák'u** noun *his/her boyfriend*
·"Ix̱six̱án," yoo ayawsiḵaa du yadák'u. *She told her boyfriend, "I love you."*

**yadák'w** noun *young man (not married)*
·Tléi a x'aant áwé daaḵ wudigwát' wé yadák'w. *The young boy crawled out the limb.*
·Gíl' yáx̱ kei naltl'ét' wé yadák'w. *The young boy is climbing the cliff face.*

**yadak'wátsk'u** noun *boy*
·Wé yadak'wátsk'u chooneit tín áwé aawat'úk wé ts'ítskw. *The young boy shot the bird with a barbed arrow.*

du **yádi** noun *his/her child*
·I yádi ax̱ x̱'usyeet wudigwáat'. *Your child is crawling around under my feet.*
·Kast'áat' tlein áwé wóoshde aḵéis' ax̱ yádi jeeyís. *She is sewing together a big quilt for my child.*

**yagee (T)** noun *day, afternoon*
VARIANTS: yakyee (AtT), yagiyee

·Du séek' yageeyí kayís áwé gáaxw awsi.ée. *She cooked a duck for her daughter's birthday.*

**yagiyee** noun *day, afternoon*
VARIANTS: yakyee, yagee (T)
·Tleidooshú g̲uwakaan wutusiteen tléix' yagiyee. *We saw six deer one day.*
·Dax̲adooshú yagiyee shunaaxéex aag̲áa daak wusitani yé. *It has been raining for seven days.*

**yagootl** noun *young deer*

**yagúnl'** noun *growth on the face*

du **yahaayí** noun *his/her soul (of departed person)*
·Yéi sh kadulneek a yahaayí k̲udzitee dáanaa. *They say money has a spirit.*

du **yahaayí** noun *his/her shadow; image*
·Wé tóonáx̲ k̲aateen kaadé awsiteen du yahaayí. *He saw his image in the mirror.*
·Du eetí a kax̲yeet akawlis'íx'w k̲aa yahaayí wé shaatk'átsk'u. *The young girl pasted a photo on the ceiling of her room.*

**yaka.óot'** noun *button*
VARIANTS: yuka.óot', waka.óot'
·Gunx̲aa yaka.óot' aawa.oo. *She bought abalone buttons.*
·Gunx̲aa yaka.óot' du l.uljíni kát akaawak̲áa. *She sewed the abalone buttons on her vest.*

**yaka.óot' x'óow** noun *button blanket*
VARIANTS: yuka.óot' x'óow
·Yaka.óot' x'óow aawak̲áa du séek' jeeyís. *She sewed a button blanket for her daughter.*
·T'ooch' k̲a x̲'aan yáx̲ yatee wé yaka.óot' x'óow. *That button blanket is black and red.*

du **yakg̲wahéiyagu** noun *his/her spirit*

**yakyee** noun *day, afternoon*
VARIANTS: yagiyee, yagee (T)

**yakw daa.ideidí** noun *shell of a boat*

**yakwteiyí** noun *tricks, sleight of hand; juggling*

**yakwtlénx'** noun *cruise ship; large ship*

**yakwyádi** noun *skiff; small boat; flat-bottom canoe*
·Yaakwdáatx' áwé yakwyádi kát át k̲uyaawagoowún héen kát. *People used to travel around in flat-bottomed canoes in the rivers in Yakutat.*

du **yak̲áawu** noun *his/her partner*

**yalooleit** noun *cockle*

**yan~** Adverb *ashore, onto ground; to rest*
·Wé té tlein a kaháadi káa yan tán! *Put that large rock on top of its cover!*
·K̲aa oox̲ yéi daanéiyi yís sgóon yan ashawlihík *She finished dentistry school.*

**yán** noun *hemlock*
·Yán aas daadáx̲ kayeix̲ áwé átx̲ gag̲ilayéix̲ s'agwáat kasék̲'x̲u sákw. *Shavings from a hemlock tree is what you will use for the brown dye.*

**yán** noun *shore; land*

a **yanáa** RelationalNoun *over it, covering it (a container or something with an opening)*
·Ax̲ k̲'wádli yanáak aa tsé k̲ut gaytáan! *Don't misplace my pot cover!*
·Wé kóok̲ kax'ás'ti a yanáa yan aawatán. *He put plywood over the pit in the ground.*

**yanax̲** Adverb *underground*
VARIANTS: yaanax̲

a **yana.áat'ani** noun *its lid, cover (of pot, etc.)*
VARIANTS: a yana.áat'i (T)
·Goosú á yana.áat'ani wé s'áaw a kát isa.eeyi k̲'wátl? *Where is the cover for the pot you're cooking the crab in?*
·Wé k̲'wátl yana.áat'ani k̲ut x̲waataan. *I misplaced the lid for the pot.*

**yánde át** noun *west wind; wind blowing ashore*

**yaneis'í (T)** noun *face cream; cold cream*
VARIANTS: yaneis'

**yanshuká** noun *campsite; (out in) camp; (out in) the bush, wilderness*
·Yanshukáx' áwé k'idéin wutuliyéx̲ yá k̲'anáax̲án. *We built the fence really well out here in the wilderness.*

**yanwáat** noun *adult; elder*

**yanxoon** noun *pile of driftwood, driftlogs; snag pile*

**Yanyeidí** noun *Yanyeidí, locally known as "Bear"; a clan of the Eagle moiety whose principal crest is the Brown Bear*
·G̲ooch Yanyeidí k̲aa at oohéini áwé. *The Wolf crest is the property of the Yanyeidí Clan.*

YÁT verb root

- **ash kawdliyát | ash koolyát | yóo ash koodliyátk**
*s/he played | s/he is playing | s/he plays (regularly).*
THEME: ash ka-u-S-d-l-yát (na act)
*for S to play (esp. active games)*
·Kooch'éit'aa áwé aan has ash koolyát wé atyátx'i. *The children are*

*playing with a ball.*
·Tlél ux̱ganḵáas' teen ash kayeelyádiḵ! *Don't play with matches!*

du **yátx'i** noun *his/her children*

**yat'aayi héen** noun *coffee; hot water*
·Yat'aayi héen a káa yéi nay.oo wéi a kát yadu.us'ku át! *You all put hot water in the wash basin!*
·Yat'aayi héen du ḵáawu x̱'éit awsi.ín. *She gave her husband's clan brother coffee.*

du **yat'ákw** noun *his/her temple; upper side of his/her face (from the cheekbones to the top of the head)*

du **yat'éik** noun *behind his/her back, where s/he can't see*

du **yat'éinától** noun *in secret (where nobody can see); away from people's view*

**yawéinaa** noun *face powder*

**yáxwch'** noun *sea otter*
VARIANTS: yúxch' (C)
·Yáxwch'i doogú x̱'alitseen. *Sea otter fur is valuable.*
·Ḵ'alkátsk yáxwch'ich yax̱ yawsix̱áa haa aaní kaadáx̱. *The sea otter has devoured the yellowneck clams on our land.*

**yáxwch'i yaakw** noun *small canoe with high carved prow*
VARIANTS: yáxch' yaakw

**yax̱** Adverb *to completion*

a **yáx̱** RelationalPostposition *like it, in accordance with it, as much as it*
·Yáa a daat x'úx' yáx̱ áwé a daax' yéi jix̱waanei. *I worked on it according to the book.*
·L át yáx̱ ḵoonook. *He doesn't act normal.*

**yax̱ak'áaw** noun *its crosspiece (of boat, snowshoe); thwart (of boat)*
·Wéi yaakw yax̱ak'áaw kas'éet áa yéi du.oowú, k'idéin yéi agux̱lasháat. *If a screw is put in the thwart of the boat, it will hold pretty well.*

**yax̱ at g̱wakú** noun *saying, proverb; event that is so common it has become a saying or proverb*
VARIANTS: yax̱ et g̱wakú (C)

**yax̱té** noun *Big Dipper; Ursa Major*

**yayéinaa** noun *whetstone*

a **yayík** noun *sound, noise of it (something whose identity is unknown)*
·A yayík gé iya.áx̱ch wé xóots héen yaax̱ dé. *Do you hear the brown bears by the water?*
·Sagú yáx̱ ḵaa yayík du.ax̱ji nooch héendei yaa ana.ádi. *Men's voices would always sound happy when they went to the sea.*

a **yayís** noun *getting ready for it; in anticipation of it*

a **ya.áak** noun *room, space, place for it; time for it; chance, opportunity for it*
·Haadéi at kagax̱dujéil, a ya.áak x'wán yéi nasné! *Make sure you make room, they will be bringing it all!*
·Dáx̱náx̱ ḵáa ya.áak áwé. *It's wide enough for two people.*

**yé** noun *place; way*
NOTES: This noun is unique in that it is very limited in its use and occurs mostly in attributive clauses.
·Kag̱akl'eedí ldakát yéix' kanas.éich. *Yarrow grows all over.*
·A géide yoo x̱'ayatánk wé aadé át kadu.aaḵw yé. *He is speaking out against the proposed decision.*

**yee** Pronoun *your (plural) [possessive]*
·Yá ḵut'aayg̱áa gági ugootch yee éesh. *During the warm season your father would come out.*
·Ḵúnáx̱ wé yee woo.éex'i aa tsú yee x̱oo yéi kg̱watée toowú k'é teen. *Your hostess will welcome you all as well. (Lit: Your hostess will be among you all with good feelings.)*

**yee** Pronoun *you (plural) [object]*
·Wooch teenx̱ yee nastí! *Stay together!*

**yee-** Pronoun *you (plural) [subject]*
VARIANTS: yi-
·Yeeytéen has du téix̱' tóotx̱ áyá toodé has yee uwaxích haa ḵu.éex'i. *You all can see that our hosts thank you from their hearts.*

a **yee** RelationalNoun *inside it (a building)*
·Ḵuwduwa.éex' ANB hall yeedéi. *People were invited to the ANB hall.*
·Jikaḵáas' káx̱ ashayaawatée wé g̱aat atx'aan hídi yeex'. *She hung the sockeye salmon on the stick in the smokehouse.*

YEECH verb root

- **anáḵ kawdliyeech | anáḵ yaa kanalyích | anáḵ yoo kadliyíchk**
  *they flew away from it | they are flying away from it | they fly away from it (regularly).*
  THEME: P-náḵ ka-d-l-yeech~ (na motion)
  *for creatures (that flap wings visibly) to fly away from P*
  ·Dunáḵ kawdliyeech wé káax'. *The grouse flew away from him.*
- **át kawdliyeech | --- | at yoo kadliyíchk**
  *they're flying around; they flew around | --- | they fly around (regularly).*
  THEME: P-t ka-d-l-yeech~ (na motion)
  *for creatures (that flap wings visibly) to fly around at P*
  ·Ts'axweil át kawdliyeech. *Crows are flying around.*
  ·Gijook wéit kawdliyeech. *Hawks are flying around there.*

• **át kawdliyích | aadé yaa kanalyích | áx̲ kalyeech**
*they flew there | they are flying there | they fly there (regularly).*
THEME: P-t~ ka-d-l-yeech~ (ø motion)
*for creatures (that flap wings visibly) to fly to P*
·Gus'yadóoli taakw.eetíx' haax̲ kalyeech. *Sandpipers fly here in the early summer.*
·K̲aashashx̲áaw taakw.eetíx' haax̲ kalyeech. *The dragonflies come in the summer time.*

**yeedát** Adverb *now*
VARIANTS: yeedét (C)
·G̲unayéide a daat sh tudinook yeedát. *He feels differently about it now.*
·Tle yeedát yáatx̲ haa kagux̲dayáa. *We need to leave from here right now.*

a **yeeg̲áa** noun *waiting for it*
VARIANTS: a yig̲áa
·X'úx' wux̲áax'u yeeg̲áa áyá took̲éen. *We are waiting in anticipation of the mail delivery.*
·Gáanu hás, i yeeg̲áax̲ has sitee. *They are outside waiting for you.*

**yeek̲** Adverb *down to beach, shore*
VARIANTS: yeik̲, eek̲

YEEK̲[1] verb root

• **át awsiyík̲ | aadé yaa anasyík̲ | áx̲ asyeek̲**
*s/he pulled it up there | s/he is pulling it up there | s/he pulls it up there (regularly).*
THEME: P-t~ O-S-s-yeek̲~ (ø motion)
*for S to pull, hoist O up to P*
·Anóoshi aan kwéiyi áwé át wududziyík̲ wé s'ísaa yaakw x̲uká. *They raised a Russian flag on the deck of that sailboat.*

• **kei awsiyík̲ | kei anasyík̲ | kei asyík̲ch**
*s/he pulled it up | s/he is pulling it up | s/he pulls it up (regularly).*
THEME: kei O-S-s-yeek̲~ (ø motion)
*for S to pull, haul O (esp. of line) up; for S to hoist O up*

• **x̲'oosdé awdiyík̲ | x̲'oosdé adayeek̲ | x̲'oosx̲ adayík̲x̲**
*s/he put them on | s/he's putting them on | s/he puts them on (regularly).*
THEME: x̲'oos-dé a-S-d-yeek̲~ (ø act)
*for S to put on, pull on O (shoes, trousers)*
NOTES: Note that the postposition -dé changes to -x̲ in the imperative and repetitive imperfective forms.
·Tuk̲'atáal x̲'oosdé awdiyík̲. *He put on his pants.*
·Wooshdakádin x̲'oosdé awdiyik̲ du téeli. *He put his shoes on the wrong feet.*

YEEK̲[2] verb root

• **aawayeek̲ | --- | kei ayík̲ch**
*he/she/it bit him/her/it | --- | he/she/it bites him/her/it (regularly).*

THEME: O-S-ø-yeek~ (ga event)
*for S to bite O; for S to carry O in mouth (of animal)*
·Igayeik tsá wé keitl! *Don't let the dog bite you!*

a **yeen** noun *(sometime) during it (period of time)*

**yees** noun *stone axe*

**yées** adj. *new; young; fresh*
·X'aan yeenayát'ch wé yées stoox tóox'. *The fire lasts in the new stove.*
·Wé yées shaawát du shaatk'ix sitee. *That young woman is his girlfriend.*

**yées ku.oo** noun *young adult(s); young people*

**yées wáat** noun *young adult*

**yees'** noun *scraper for hemlock bark*

**yées'** noun *mussel (large mussel on stormy coast, used for scraping)*

YEESH verb root

- **aax kei aawayísh | --- | ---**
*s/he pulled it out of there | --- | ---.*
THEME: P-dáx kei O-S-ø-yeesh~ (ø motion)
*for S to pull O (a fairly light object) out of P*
NOTES: This verb would be used to talk about such things as pulling out a sliver, opening a window (by pushing it up), pulling a tooth, or pulling the sheets off a bed.
·Sheey kakáas'i du jíndáx kei aawayísh. *She pulled a splinter out of her hand.*

- **a káx aawayeesh | a káx yei anayísh | a káx yei ayíshch**
*s/he pulled it over him/her/it | s/he is pulling it over him/her/it | s/he pulls it over him/her/it (regularly).*
THEME: N káx O-S-ø-yeesh~ (ga motion)
*for S to pull O (fairly light object) over N; for S to cover N with O*
NOTES: Note that the verb in the example sentence below has the ya- thematic prefix, meaning "face".
·Du gúk káx ayaawayeesh du sadaat'aayí. *She pulled her scarf down over her ears.*

**yéesh** noun *leech; bloodsucker*

du **yéet** noun *his/her son, cousin*
·Du kíkt hán wé du yéet. *His son is standing beside him.*
·Kashxeedíx sitee haa yéet. *Our son is a scribe.*

**yeewháan** Pronoun *you (plural) [independent]*

a **yee.ádi** noun *receptacle for it*
·A yee.ádi gataan sháchgi tléigu yís! *Carry a container for swamp berries!*

**yee.át** noun *mattress; bedding*

·I téeli yee.át x̱'usyeex' yéi na.oo! *Put your shoes at the foot of the bed!*
·I yee.ádi ká yís áyá yá x'óow. *This blanket is to put on top of your bed.*

**yei** Adverb *down; out of boat, vehicle*

VARIANTS: yéi

**yéi** Adverb *thus, specifically*

VARIANTS: yóo
·Ḵa x̱át tsú ax̱ toowú yak'éi yaa a káa yéi x̱at gug̱wateeyí yaa Lingítx̱ x̱at sateeyí. *And I too am thankful that I'm part of this being that I'm Lingít.*
·Téil yéi aya.óo at doogú aklas'éḵx̱i yís. *She is using dry wood for smoking that hide.*

a **yeidí** noun *its price, value; the money from the sale of it*

·A ḵín ax̱ jee koogéi wé k'oodás' yeidí. *I have less than the price of that shirt.*

**yéi jiné** noun *work, job*

·G̱alsaayít áwé du yéi jineiyí a náḵ woogoot. *She went away from her work so that she could rest.*
·Ax̱ yéi jineiyí áwé kaxíl'aa k'idéin daané. *My job is to clean erasers.*

**yéi jinéiyi** noun *worker*

YEIK[2] verb root

• **--- | liyék | ---**

--- | *it holds more* | ---.
THEME: l-yék (ga state)
*for something to hold more, contain more; for something to hold a lot*
NOTES: This verb only occurs in the imperfective. To specify the amount that something holds, state the amount followed by yáx̱, as in: tléix' gúx'aa yáx̱ liyék "it holds one cup". Two more examples of this verb in context are: yáat'aa yáanáx̱ liyék wéit'aa "this one holds more than that one" and: wooch yáx̱ liyék "they hold the same amount".
·Tléix' ḵ'ateil yáx̱ áwé liyék wéi xén. *That plastic container can hold one gallon.*

**yéik** noun *Indian doctor's spirit*

YEIL verb root

• **sh ḵ'awdliyél | --- | sh ḵ'alyélx̱**

*s/he lied* | --- | *s/he lies (regularly).*
THEME: sh ḵ'a-S-d-l-yéil~ (ø event)
*for S to lie, decieve*
NOTES: To specify who one is lying to, use: N een "to N". For example: Du een sh ḵ'awdliyél "s/he lied to him/her".

**yéil** noun *raven*

·Yaa uháan haa naax̲ sitee, Yéil áyá haa shukáx̲ sitee. *For our clan, Raven is our main crest.*

·X̲áat yís áwé has akawliník Yéilch, wé kéidladi k̲a kag̲eet. *Raven talked the seagull and loon out of the salmon.*

**yéil kawóodi** noun *petrified coral*

**yéil koox̲étl'aa** noun *scarecrow*

**yéil ts'áaxu** noun *limpet*

YEIL' verb root

- **kawduwayél' | yaa kanduyél' | kaduyél'x̲**
  *it's calm | it's calming down | it calms down (regularly).*
  THEME: ka-du-ø-yéil'~ (ø event)
  *for something (esp. bodies of water) to be calm, peaceful*
  ·Áa Tlein káa kawduwayél'. *It is calm on Atlin Lake.*
- **k̲ukawduwayél' | yaa k̲ukanduyél' | k̲ukaduyél'x̲**
  *the weather is calm | the weather is calming down | the weather calms down (regularly).*
  THEME: k̲u-ka-du-yéil'~ (ø event)
  *for the weather to be calm, peaceful, without storm*
  ·K̲ukawduwayél' áyá - naakéede nax̲took̲oox̲. *It's calm out - let's go up the bay.*
  ·K̲ukawduyéil'i áwé Galyéx̲dei g̲unayéi uk̲oox̲ch wéi yaakw tlein. *The big boat would start traveling to the Kahliyet River when the weather was calm.*

**yéil'** noun *elderberry*

YEIN verb root

- **ashakawliyén | --- | ashaklayénx̲**
  *s/he's waving it | --- | s/he waves it (regularly).*
  THEME: O-sha-ka-S-l-yéin~ (ø event)
  *for S to wag O (tail); for S to wave O (hand, etc.); for S to twirl, spin O around above one's head*
  ·Aan kwéiyi shakawdudliyén. *Someone is waving a flag.*
  ·Du tl'eek̲ áwé ax̲ yáa ash akaawliyén. *He's shaking his finger at me.*

**yéin** noun *sea cucumber*

**yeis** noun *fall; autumn*

·Kalag̲éi nooch aasgutú yeist k̲uwuhaayí. *The forest is brilliant when fall comes.*

**yeisú** Adverb *just now; just then; still; yet*

·X̲'éidei kakg̲ilatix̲' yé ch'a yeisú lingít áwu. *There are still people in the place you are locking.*

·Yeisú kadlix̲'át' wé tléik̲w. *The berries are still green.*

**YEIS’** verb root

- **kawdiyés’ | --- | kadayés’x̱**
  *he/she/it is bruised | --- | he/she/it buises easily.*
  THEME: O-ka-d-yéis’~ (ø event)
  *for O to be colored, discolored, bruised*
  ·X̱’aan yáx̱ kawdiyés’ wé g̱áach. *The rug is colored red.*
  ·Du káak’ wudix’ís’ ḵa kawdiyés’. *His forehead is swollen and bruised.*

**YEIX̱[1]** verb root

- **akaawayéx̱ | akayéix̱ | akayéx̱x̱**
  *s/he whittled it | s/he is whittling it | s/he whittles it (regularly).*
  THEME: O-ka-S-ø-yeix̱~ (ø act)
  *for S to whittle, plane O; for S to make O (kindling)*
  ·Aankayéx̱aa tín akaawayéx̱. *He planed it with a plane.*
  ·Du tséegi a lú akaawayéx̱. *He sharpened the point of his barbecue stick.*
- **átx̱ awliyéx̱ | átx̱ alyéix̱ | átx̱ alyéx̱x̱**
  *s/he used it for it | s/he is using it for it | s/he uses it for it (regularly).*
  THEME: P-x̱ O-S-l-yeix̱~ (ø act)
  *for S to use O for P; for S to make O into P*
  ·X̱éel yéi ndu.eich hítx̱ dulyeix̱í. *Granite is used to build a house.*
  ·Kag̱akl’eedí náakwx̱ dulyéix̱. *Yarrow is used for medicine.*
- **awliyéx̱ | alyéix̱ | ---**
  *s/he built it | s/he is building it | ---.*
  THEME: O-S-l-yeix̱~ (ø act)
  *for S to build O; for S to make, construct O*
  VARIANTS: -yeex̱~
  ·Ax̱ léelk’u hás jeeyís áwé wududliyéx̱ wé atx’aan hídi tlein. *That big smoke house was built for my grandparents.*
  ·Tle a tuwán áwé atx̱á daakahídi áa wdudliyéx̱. *They built a restaurant next to it.*

**yéix̱** noun *deadfall trap for large animals*

**yetx̱** Adverb *starting off taking off*
VARIANTS: yedax̱

**yéts’ shál** noun *black horn spoon*

a **yig̱áa** noun *waiting for it*
VARIANTS: a yeeg̱áa
·Wé bus yig̱áa x̱a.áa. *I am sitting waiting for the bus.*

a **yík** RelationalNoun *inside it (a river, road, boat, or other shallow concave landform or object)*
·Káa tlein yíkt át yawduwax̱aa wé aanḵáawu. *The rich person is being driven around in a limosine.*
·Kaldaag̱éináx̱ yaa gax̱tooḵóox̱, tlél g̱wadlaan yá éix̱’ yík. *We will travel along slowly, it's not deep in this slough.*

a **yik.ádi** noun *its internal organs, viscera; its guts*
VARIANTS: a yik.édi (C)
·Naaliyéidei kanasxá wé x̲áat yik.ádi! *Dump the fish guts far away!*
·Yak'éi k'ínk' x̲oox' x̲áat yik.ádi. *The fish guts are good in fermenting stink heads.*

**yík̲dlaa** noun *spark*

a **yinaa** RelationalNoun *in its way; blocking its way; acting as a shield for it*
·Wé x̲'awool yinaat hán. *She is standing in the doorway.*

a **yinaadé** Adverb *in the direction or general area of it; (headed) toward it*
VARIANTS: a yinaadéi, a niyaadé, a niyaadéi
·Áa agax̲tool'oon yé yinaadé yaa gagú! *Walk toward the place we will hunt!*
·Wé xóots awusnéex'i a yinaadé wjixeex haa keidlí. *Our dog is running toward the brown bear it smelled.*

**yinaaháat** noun *body armor, breastplate*

du **yinaanáx̲** noun *his/her family line of descent, side*
·Yaa ax̲ léelk'w ax̲ tláa yinaanáx̲ K̲éin yóo dusáagun yaa Xutsnoowúdáx̲. *My grandmother on my mother's side was called Ñéin, from Angoon.*
·John Soboleff yóo duwasáa - yaa ax̲ éesh yinaanáx̲, ax̲ éesh du éesh. *John Soboleff was his name - on my father's side, my father's father.*

a **yís** RelationalPostposition *for it; to that end*
·Yan eewanéi gé a yís? *Are you ready for it?*
·Du ée yan at wududlitóow k̲aa oox̲ yéi daanéiyi yís. *She completed dentistry school.*

**yoo** Adverb *back and forth; to and fro; up and down*

**yoo aan ka.á** noun *earthquake*
VARIANTS: yoo aan ke.á (C)

**yoo at koojeek** noun *curiosity*

**yoo katan lítaa** noun *curved carving knife*

**yook̲** noun *cormorant*

**yóot~** Adverb *away, off (to someplace indefinite)*
·G̲ítg̲aa ayax̲saháa yóode woogoot. *She went over there to gather spruce needles.*

**yoo tutánk** noun *consciousness, thought process, thinking*

du **yoowá** noun *his/her abdomen; surface of his/her belly; front of his/her body*

du **yoowú** noun *his/her stomach; gizzard (of bird)*
·Sh tóog̲áa wditee ax̲ yoowú. *My stomach was satisfied.*

**yoo x̲'ala.átk** noun *conversation, dialog; talk, discourse (between more than one person)*
VARIANTS: yoo x̲'ale.étk (C)

**yoo x̲'atánk** noun *speech, talk; language; word, phrase, sentence, or discourse*
VARIANTS: yoo x̲'aténk (C)
·I yoo x̲'atángi káa yan hán! *Stand on your words!*
·Wáang̲aneensx' yanax̲ kei shak'íx̲'ch ax̲ yoo x̲'atángi. *Sometimes my words get hung up.*

**yú** Demonstrative *that (distant), yonder*
VARIANTS: yóo
·Yóo diyáanax̲.aadáx̲ áwé haat yax̲waax̲áa wéi kax'ás'ti haa hídi sákw. *I hauled the lumber from across the other side for our house.*
·Yóo tliyaa aasdéi ksaxát wéi kaxées' ax̲ at shí k̲óok gúgu yís! *Attach the wire to that tree over there for my radio antenna!*

**yuka.óot'** noun *button*
VARIANTS: yaka.óot', waka.óot'
·Dleit yáx̲ kaatee wé yuka.óot'. *The button is white.*

**yuka.óot' x'óow** noun *button blanket*
VARIANTS: yaka.óot' x'óow

**yúxch' (C)** noun *sea otter*
VARIANTS: yáxwch'

**yux̲** Adverb *outside*

## « . »

.AA[1] verb root

- **--- | át as.áa | ---**

  *--- | s/he has him/her seated there | ---.*
  THEME: P-t O-S-s-.aa~ (position)
  *for S to have O (live creature) seated at P*
  NOTES: This verb only occurs in the imperfective.
  ·T'ook kát as.áa du yádi. *He has his child seated on the papoose board.*

- **--- | át la.áa | ---**

  *--- | it's situated there | ---.*
  THEME: P-t l-.áa (position)
  *for a building to be situated at P*
  NOTES: This verb only occurs in the imperfective.
  ·Yaa Aangóont áyá la.áa haa hídi Aanx'aagi Hít yóo duwasáakw. *Our clan house standing in Angoon is called Aanx'aagi Hít.*
  ·Héen t'iká át la.áa du hídi. *His house sits beside the river.*

- **--- | .áa | ---**

  *--- | s/he sits; s/he is sitting | ---.*
  THEME: S-ø-.aa~ (position)
  *for (singlular) S to be seated*
  NOTES: This verb only occurs in the imperfective. Note that a noun phrase with (-t) postposition is used to indicate where one is sitting, but this noun phrase is not required by the verb. For example, one could say: .áa "s/he is sitting", or: át .áa "s/he is sitting there".
  ·Ch'a tlákw .áa áwé yanéekw du k'í. *His rump hurts from sitting all the time.*
  ·Has du léelk'w du x̱'áat .áa. *Their grandmother is sitting between them.*

.AA[2] verb root

- **ax̱ x̱'éit yawdzi.áa | ax̱ x̱'éide yaa yanas.éin | ax̱ x̱'éix̱ yas.aa**

  *s/he kissed me | s/he is kissing me | s/he kisses me (regularly).*
  THEME: N x̱'éit~ ya-S-d-s-.aa~ (ø motion)
  *for S to kiss N*

- **a daa yawdzi.aa | a daa yas.éix̱ | a daa yas.éix̱**

  *s/he examined it | s/he is examining it | s/he examines it (regularly).*
  THEME: N daa ya-S-d-s-.aa~ (na act)
  *for S to examine, inspect, look into, judge, assess N*
  NOTES: The form: a daa yas.éix̱ gives both a basic imperfective meaning "s/he is examining it" and a repetitive imperfective meaning "s/he examines it (reguarly)".

·Du kalóox'sháni néegooch áwé du daa yawdudzi.aa. *He is being examined because of his bladder pain.*

.AA[3] verb root

- **akawsi.aa | aksa.éix̱ | yoo aksi.éik**
  *s/he grew it | s/he grows it; s/he's growing it | s/he grows it (regularly).*
  THEME: O-ka-S-s-.aa~ (na act)
  *for S to cause O (plant) to grow; for S to turn on O (hose), cause O to flow*
  NOTES: The form: aksa.éix̱ gives both a basic imperfective meaning "s/he grows it; s/he is growing it" and a repetitive imperfective meaning "s/he grows it (regularly)".
- **kaawa.aa | ka.éix̱ | yoo kaya.éik**
  *it grew | it grows; it's growing | it grows (regularly).*
  THEME: ka-ø-.aa~ (na act)
  *for a plant to grow; for a stream of water to flow, pour forth*
  ·Aas tlénx' áa kaawa.aa. *Big trees grew there.*
  ·Tlél kalchaneit áa koo.éix̱ Yaakwdáat. *Mountain ash doesn't grow in Yakutat.*
- **kawsi.aa | kasa.éix̱ | yoo ksi.éik**
  *it grew | it grows; it's growing | it grows (regularly).*
  THEME: ka-s-.aa~ (na act)
  *for a plant to grow*
  NOTES: In classical Tlingit, this verb meant specifically for a plant with a long stalk to grow (the length of the plant indicated by the s- classifier), however this meaning has been lost for most current speakers, and now just means for a plant in general to grow.
  ·Kag̱akl'eedí ldakát yéix' kanas.éich. *Yarrow grows all over*

.AAK[1] verb root

- **shóot awdi.ák | --- | shóox̱ ada.aak**
  *s/he built a fire | --- | s/he builds a fire (regularly).*
  THEME: shóot~ a-S-d-.aak~ (ø event)
  *for S to build a fire (using wood)*
  ·Wé gán aan nagú wé ḵáa shaan du shóot ag̱ida.aagít! *Go with the wood to build a fire for the elderly man!*
  ·Aan áwé shóot ax̱wdi.ák wé kayeix̱tág̱u. *I built a fire with the wood shavings.*

.AAḴW verb root

- **át akaawa.aaḵw | --- | át yoo akaya.áḵwk**
  *s/he gave him/her orders | --- | s/he gives him/her orders (regularly).*
  THEME: át O-ka-S-ø-.aaḵw~ (na event)
  *for S to give orders to, command, instruct O*
  ·A géide yoo x̱'ayatánk wé aadé át kadu.aaḵw yé. *He is speaking out against the proposed decision.*
- **yan akaawa.áḵw | yánde yaa akana.áḵw | ---**
  *s/he made a decision | s/he's making a decision | ---.*

THEME: yan~ O-ka-S-ø-.aak̲w~ (ø motion)
*for S to make a decision about O; for S to finish planning O*

.AAN[1] verb root

- **--- | tuli.aan | ---**

--- | *s/he is kind* | ---.
THEME: O-tu-l-.aan (ga state)
*for O to be kind, gentle*
·Haa k̲oon sh kalneegí áwé k̲únáx̲ tuli.aan. *Our preacher is very kind.*

.AAT[1] verb root

- **aadé has woo.aat | aadé yaa (ha)s na.át | aadé yoo (ha)s ya.átk**

*they walked there* | *they are walking there* | *they walk there (regularly).*
THEME: P-dé S-ø-.aat~ (na motion)
*for (plural) S to walk, go (by walking or as a general term) to P*
·Gáande yaa nay.ádi wooch yáx̲ x'wán anayl'eix̲! *Be sure to all dance alike when you walk out!*
·Dleeyg̲áa áwé aadéi aawa.aat. *People went there for meat.*

- **aag̲áa has woo.aat | aag̲áa yaa (ha)s na.át | aag̲áa yoo ya.átk**

*they went to get it* | *they are going to get it* | *they go get it (regularly).*
THEME: P-g̲aa S-ø-.aat~ (na motion)
*for (plural) S to go after P, go seeking P (on foot)*
NOTES: Note that -g̲aa takes the opposite tone of the final syllable of the noun that it attaches to. Hence: kanat'ág̲aa "(going) after blueberries", but shaawg̲áa "(going) after gumboots".
·K̲uk'éet' áwé gax̲too.áat kalchaneit tléig̲ug̲áa. *We are going to pick mountain ash berries.*

- **áa kei (ha)s uwa.át | áa kei (ha)s na.át | áa kei (ha)s .átch**

*they walked up there* | *they are walking up there* | *they walk up there (regularly).*
THEME: kei S-ø-.aat~ (ø motion)
*for (plural) S to walk up, go up (by walking or as a general term)*

- **anax̲ has yaawa.át | anax̲ yaa (ha)s wuna.át | anax̲ yaa (ha)s .átch**

*they walked through it* | *they are walking through it* | *they walk through it (regularly).*
THEME: P-náx̲ ya-u-S-ø-.aat~ (ø motion)
*for (plural) S to walk, go (by walking or as a general term) through, by way of P*
·Nás'k yagiyee a kaanáx̲ has yaawa.át. *They walked for three days.*

- **át has uwa.át | aadé yaa (ha)s na.át | áx̲ has .aat**

*they walked there* | *they are walking there* | *they walk there (regularly).*
THEME: P-t~ S-ø-.aat~ (ø motion)
*for (plural) S to walk, go (by walking or as a general term) to P*

·Ana.óot ḵu.oo haa x̱ánt has uwa.át. *Aleut people came to see us.*
·Wéis' du shaktóot uwa.át. *She got lice in her hair.*

- **át has woo.aat | --- | át yoo (ha)s ya.átk**

*they are walking around; they walked around | --- | they walk around (regularly).*
THEME: P-t S-ø-.aat~ (na motion)
*for (plural) S to walk, go (by walking or as a general term) around at P*
·Dei át has woo.aat wéi yées kéidladi. *The young seagulls are already walking around.*
·A daat aawa.aat. *People are walking around on it.*

- **áx̱ has woo.aat | áx̱ yei (ha)s na.át | áx̱ yei (ha)s .átch**

*they walked down along it | they are walking down along it | they walk down along it (regularly).*
THEME: P-x̱ S-ø-.aat~ (g̱a motion)
*for (plural) S to walk, go (by walking or as a general term) down along P*
·Gántiyaakw Séedix' yaakw tlein yíx̱ aawa.aat. *People boarded the big boat at Petersburg.*

- **--- | áx̱ yaa (ha)s na.át | ---**

*--- | they are walking along there | ---.*
THEME: P-x̱ yaa S-ø-.aat~ (ga motion)
*for (plural) S to be walking, going (by foot or as general term) along P*
NOTES: This is an example of a progressive epiaspectual paradigm (Leer, 91), which basically means that all forms are based on the progressive aspect. The progressive epiaspect is characterized by: 1)having the yaa preverb in all forms, 2)having no perfective form, and 3)denotes semantically a continuous transition from one location or state to another.
·Wé kag̱ít tóox̱ yaa ntoo.ádi awdlidées. *As we walked along in the darkness, the moon shined bright.*
·Wé dzísk'u tlein ítx̱ yaa na.át wé g̱ooch. *The wolves are following behind the big moose.*

- **gági (ha)s uwa.át | gági yaa (ha)s na.át | gági (ha)s .átx̱**

*they emerged | they are emerging | they emerge (regularly).*
THEME: gági S-ø-.aat~ (ø motion)
*for (plural) S to emerge, walk out into the open*

- **has ashoowa.aat | yaa (ha)s ashuna.át | kei (ha)s ashu.átch**

*s/he led them | s/he is leading them | s/he leads them (regularly).*
THEME: yaa O-shu-S-ø-.aat~ (ga event)
*for S to lead (plural) O (especially by walking ahead)*
NOTES: Note that yaa occurs in every form except the perfective. This verb has a plural stem, meaning that multiple people or animals are being led. In the paradigm given here, the plural object pronoun has "them" is used. One could also use ḵaa "people", as in: ḵaa shoowa.aat "s/he led people". Another option is the object prefix ḵu- "people", as in: ḵushoowa.aat "s/he led

people". For both of these, note that the third person object pronoun a- on the verb is dropped. If you want to indicate that animals are being led, omit the has/k̲aa/k̲u- and use: ashoowa.aat "s/he led them (animals)".
·K'idéin yaa k̲aa shuna.át wé k̲aa sháade háni. *The leader is leading the people well.*

- **has ayawdi.át | yaa (ha)s ayanda.át | has ayada.átx̲**
*they turned back | they are turning back | they turn back (regularly).*
THEME: a-ya-u-S-d-.aat~ (ø motion)
*for (plural) S to turn back, go back (by walking or as general term)*

- **has woo.aat | yaa (ha)s na.át | yoo (ha)s ya.átk**
*they walked | they are walking | they walk (regularly).*
THEME: S-ø-.aat~ (na motion)
*for (plural) S to walk, go (by walking or as a general term)*
·K̲aa daakeidí een yaa ana.át. *People are walking along with a casket.*
·Yan yéi jiwtooneiyí a ítnáx̲ tsá gax̲too.áat. *After we have finished work, then we will go.*

- **héide has yaawa.át | héide yaa (ha)s wuna.át | héide yaa (ha)s .átch**
*they moved over that way | they are moving over that way | they move over that way (regularly).*
THEME: héide ya-u-S-ø-.aat~ (ø motion)
*for (plural) S to move over (away from speaker)*

- **k̲aa éet has jiwdi.át | --- | k̲aa ée yoo has jidi.átk**
*they attacked someone | --- | they attack people (regularly).*
THEME: ji-S-d-.aat~ (ø event)
*for (plural) S to attack, assault, fall upon*
NOTES: To indicate who is being attacked, use: N éet~ "they attacked N". For example: Haa éet has jiwdi.át. "They attacked us". It is also acceptable to use this verb without specifying who was attacked. For example: Has jiwdi.át "They attacked". Therefore, the N éet~ is not required and is not given in the Leer-Edwards theme.
·Xóosht' has du yáa yéi has ana.eich yaa (ha)s jinda.ádi. *The dark burnt ashes would be put on their faces when going to war.*

- **k̲ut has woo.aat | k̲ut kei (ha)s na.át | k̲ut kei (ha)s .átch**
*they got lost | they are getting lost | they get lost (regularly).*
THEME: k̲ut S-ø-.aat~ (ga motion)
*for (plural) S to get lost (on foot)*

- **woosh kaanáx̲ has wudi.aat | woosh kaanáx̲ kei (ha)s nada.át | woosh kaanáx̲ kei (ha)s da.átch**
*they gathered together | they are beginning to gather together | they gather together (regularly).*
THEME: woosh kaanáx̲ S-d-.aat~ (ga motion)
*for (plural) S to assemble, congregate, gather together (for meetings)*

·Wé naa sháadi nák̲x'i áwé woosh kaanáx̲ has wudi.aat. *The clan leaders gathered there.*

- **woosh x̲oot has wudi.át | woosh x̲oodé yaa (ha)s nada.át | woosh x̲oox̲ has da.aat**

*they gathered together | they are gathering together | they gather together (regularly).*
THEME: woosh x̲oot~ S-d-.aat~ (ø motion)
*for (plural) S to assemble, congregate, gather together (for meetings)*
NOTES: Woosh and wooch seem to be interchangeable here.
·Wé aank̲áax'u wéix' woosh x̲oot has wudi.át. *The chiefs gathered there.*
·Wooch x̲oot wuduwa.át. *People came together.*

.AAT[2] verb root

- **aadé awli.aat | aadé yaa anal.át | aadé yoo ali.átk**

*s/he carried them there | s/he is carrying them there | s/he carries them there (regularly).*
THEME: P-dé O-S-l-.aat~ (na motion)
*for S to carry, take (plural) O (esp. baggage and personal belongings) to P*
·Haaw héende awli.aat g̲áax'w káx̲. *She put branches in the water for herring eggs.*

- **--- | át akla.át | ---**

*--- | s/he has them lying there | ---.*
THEME: P-t O-ka-S-l-.át (position)
*for S to have O (small, round or hoop-like objects) lying at P*
NOTES: This verb only occurs in the imperfective. Note that in the example sentence below, the classifier in the verb: waak̲t akal.át is l- and NOT la- . For some common nouns such as waak̲ "eye", it is possible to leave off the overt possessor du "his/her". The D-element of the classifier (in this case l-) replaces the overt possessor. Therefore, in the sentence below there is no overt possessor of waak̲, and the verb has the D- component of the classifier (l-), producing the phrase: waak̲t akal.át.
·Wak̲dáanaa waak̲t akal.át. *She has eyeglasses on. (Lit: She has glasses lying on her eyes.)*

- **--- | át kala.át | ---**

*--- | they are lying there | ---.*
THEME: P-t ka-l-.át (position)
*for small, round or hoop-like objects to lie at P*
NOTES: This verb only occurs in the imperfective.

- **--- | át la.át | ---**

*--- | they're lying there | ---.*
THEME: P-t l-.át (position)
*for several things to lie at P; for several persons or animals to lie dead, unconscious, or incapacitated at P*
NOTES: This verb only occurs in the imperfective.
·Dei kát la.ádi g̲éechadi aax̲ yéi awsinei. *He removed the windfall lying*

*in the road.*

·Téil dei yaax̲t la.át. *Scraps of pitchwood are lying along the road.*

- **a daa yoo (ha)s tuwli.át | a daa yoo (ha)s tuli.átk | a daa yoo (ha)s tuli.átk**

*they thought about it | they think about it; they are thinking about it | they think about it (regularly).*

THEME: N daa yoo tu-S-l-.aat~ (ø act)

*or (plural) S to think over, consider, make up one's mind about N*

- **du jeet akawli.át | --- | du jeex̲ akla.aat**

*s/he gave them to him/her | --- | s/he gives them to him/her (regularly); s/he is trying to give them to him/her.*

THEME: N jeet~ O-ka-S-l-.aat~ (ø motion)

*for S to give, take, hand O (small, round or hoop-like objects) to N*

·Guk.át ax̲ jeet kawdudli.át. *I was given earrings.*

- **du jeet awli.át | --- | du jeex̲ al.aat**

*s/he gave them to him/her | --- | s/he gives them to him/her (regularly); s/he is trying to give them to him/her.*

THEME: N jeet~ O-S-l-.aat~ (ø motion)

*for S to give, take, hand (plural) O (esp. baggage and personal belongings) to N*

- **kei ayawli.át | --- | kei ayala.átch**

*s/he turned the boat | --- | s/he turns the boat (regularly); s/he is trying to turn the boat.*

THEME: kei O-ya-S-l-.aat~ (ø event)

*for S to turn O (boat)*

·X'aa g̲eiyí niyaadé kei ayawli.át. *He steered (his boat) toward the inside of the point.*

- **yan awli.át | --- | yax̲ al.aat**

*s/he put them down | --- | s/he puts them down (regularly).*

THEME: yan~ O-S-l-.aat~ (ø motion)

*for S to put down, lay down, leave (plural) O (esp. baggage and personal belongings)*

·Ch'a áa yan awli.át wé gán láx̲'i. *He just left the wet outer part of firewood there.*

·Du jiyeex' yan awli.át du dak̲éis'i. *She placed her sewing nearby for her.*

- **yoo (ha)s x̲'awli.át | yoo (ha)s x̲'ali.átk | yoo (ha)s x̲'ali.átk**

*they conversed | they are conversing | they converse (regularly).*

THEME: yoo x̲'a-S-l-.aat~ (ø act)

*for (plural) S to speak, talk, converse*

NOTES: The form: yoo (ha)s x̲'ali.átk gives both a basic imperfective meaning "they are conversing" and a repetitive imperfective meaning "they coverse (regularly)".

·Wé naakéedáx̲ lingít g̲unayáade yóo has x̲'ali.átk. *The people from the north speak differently.*

·Wé hoon s'aatí een yóo x̱'ali.átk ax̱ aat. *My paternal aunt is talking with the storekeeper.*

.AAT' verb root

- **awsi.át' | as.áat' | as.át'x̱**
  *s/he chilled it | s/he is chilling it | s/he chills it (regularly).*
  THEME: O-S-s-.áat'~ (ø act)
  *for S to make O cold, cool*
  NOTES: The form: as.át'x̱ has both a basic imperfective meaning "s/he is chilling it" and a repetitive imperfective meaning "s/he chills it (regularly)".
- **ḵuwsi.áat' | ḵusi.áat' | kei ḵusa.áat'ch**
  *the weather was cold | the weather is cold | the weather gets cold (regularly).*
  THEME: ḵu-s-.áat' (ga state)
  *for the weather to be cold*
  ·Yá X̱'atas'aaḵ ḵúnáx̱ ḵusi.áat'i yéix' áwé yéi has yatee. *Eskimos live in a very cold place.*
  ·Ḵusi.áat' gáan - kakéin k'oodás' yéi na.oo! *It's cold out - wear a sweater!*

.AAX'W[1] verb root

- **wusi.áax'w | si.áax'w | kei sa.áax'wch**
  *it was sour | it's sour | it gets sour (regularly).*
  THEME: O-s-.áax'w (ga state)
  *for O to be bitter, sour (of taste); for O to be spicy hot*
  ·X'áax' tlax̱ ḵúnáx̱ si.áax'w. *Crabapples are very sour.*
  ·Wusi.áax'w du yoo x̱'atángi, ch'a aan áwé du x̱'éide ḵuwdudzi.aax̱. *His words were biting, yet people listened to him.*

.AAX̱[1] verb root

- **aawa.áx̱ | --- | ---**
  *s/he heard it | --- | ---.*
  THEME: O-S-ø-.aax̱~ (ø event)
  *for S to hear O*
  ·Yéi x̱waa.áx̱ xén hél ushk'é wé microwave tóox' yéi du.oowú. *I heard that it's not good to put plastic in the microwave.*
  ·Yaa ḵaa lunagúg̱u a kayéik has aawa.áx̱. *They heard the sound of people running.*
- **--- | ali.áx̱ch | ali.áx̱ch**
  *--- | s/he is playing it | s/he plays it (regularly).*
  THEME: O-S-l-.áx̱ch (ga state)
  *for S to play O (musical instrument)*
  NOTES: The form: ali.áx̱ch gives both a basic imperfective meaning "s/he is playing it" and a repetitive imperfective meaning "s/he plays it (regularly)".
- **--- | asaya.áx̱ch | ---**
  *--- | s/he hears a voice | ---.*

THEME: O-sa-S-ø-.áx̱ch (ga state)
*for S to hear O (voice)*
·Gus'yadóoli wéide sax̱aa.áx̱ch. *I hear the sandpiper over there.*

- **aseiwa.áx̱ | --- | ---**
*s/he heard a voice | --- | ---.*
THEME: O-sa-S-ø-.aax̱~ (ø event)
*for S to hear O (a voice, esp. singing)*
·Tusconx' áwé aa sax̱waa.áx̱ gus'yé kindachooneidí. *I heard some doves in Tuscon.*

- **át wusi.áx̱ | --- | áx̱ sa.aax̱**
*s/he's listening to it; s/he listened to it | --- | s/he listens to it (regularly).*
THEME: P-t~ S-s-.aax̱~ (ø motion)
*for S to listen to P*

- **awli.áx̱ | --- | ali.áx̱ch**
*s/he played it | --- | s/he plays it (regularly).*
THEME: O-S-l-.áax̱~ (ø event)
*for S to play O (musical instrument)*
·X̱'agáax' daakahídix' ali.áx̱ch wé g̱íx̱'jaa ḵóok. *He plays the organ at the Church.*
·Sh tóo awdlitóow g̱íx̱'jaa ḵóok al.áx̱ji. *He taught himself to play the piano.*

- **--- | ax̱'aya.áx̱ch | ---**
*--- | s/he understands him/her | ---.*
THEME: O-x̱'a-S-ø-.áx̱ch (ga state)
*for S to hear O with understanding; for S to understand, comprehend O*
·Tlél k'idéin ix̱'eix̱a.áx̱ch. *I don't understand you well.*

- **ax̱'eiwa.áx̱ | --- | ---**
*s/he understood him/her | --- | ---.*
THEME: O-x̱'a-S-ø-.aax̱~ (ø event)
*for S to hear O with understanding; for S to understand, comprehend O*

- **--- | aya.áx̱ch | ---**
*--- | s/he can hear it | ---.*
THEME: O-S-ø-.áx̱ch (ga state)
*for S to be able to hear O*
·Yéi x̱a.áx̱jin yáa chíl xook Jilḵáatx' áwé yéi daadunéiyin. *I used to hear of smoked salmon being prepared on the Chilkat.*
·G̱unayéide at x̱aa.áx̱ch. *I'm hearing strange sounds.*

- **a kayéikg̱aa ḵoowdzi.aax̱ | --- | a kayéikg̱aa yoo ḵudzi.áx̱k**
*s/he listened for the sound of it | --- | s/he listens for the sound of it (regularly).*
THEME: P-g̱aa ḵu-S-d-s-.aax̱~ (na motion)
*for S to listen for P*
·A kayéikg̱aa áwé ḵuntoos.áx̱ch shtéen káa haadé yaa naḵúx̱u. *We always listen for the sound of the steam engine when it's coming.*

- **du x̲'éide k̲uwdzi.aax̲ | --- | du x̲'éide yoo k̲udzi.áx̲k**

  *s/he listened to him/her | --- | s/he listens to him/her (regularly).*
  THEME: N x̲'éide k̲u-S-d-s-.aax̲~ (na motion)
  *for S to listen to N*
  ·Wusi.áax'w du yoo x̲'atángi, ch'a aan áwé du x̲'éide k̲uwdudzi.aax̲.
  *His words were biting, yet people listened to him.*

- **du x̲'éit wusi.áx̲ | --- | du x̲'éix̲ sa.aax̲**

  *s/he's listening to him/her; s/he listens to him/her | --- | s/he listens to him/her (regularly).*
  THEME: N x̲'éit~ S-s-.aax̲~ (ø motion)
  *for S to listen to, obey, give heed to N*
  ·Gunalchéesh ax̲ x̲'éit yeeysa.aax̲í. *Thank you all for listening to me.*

.AAX̲[2] verb root

- **át aawa.aax̲ | --- | át yoo aya.áx̲k**

  *s/he is carrying it around; s/he carried it around | --- | s/he carries it around (regularly).*
  THEME: P-t O-S-ø-.aax̲~ (na motion)
  *for S to carry, take O (textile-like object) around at P*

- **--- | át .áx̲ | ---**

  *--- | it's lying there | ---.*
  THEME: P-t ø-.áx̲ (position)
  *for a textile-like object to lie at P*
  NOTES: This verb only occurs in the imperfective.
  ·Wéit .ax̲ kinaak.át a káx' áwé x̲wsiteen i gwéili. *On top of that coat lying there is where I saw your bag.*

- **du jeet aawa.áx̲ | du jeedé yaa ana.áx̲ | du jeex̲ a.aax̲**

  *s/he gave it to him/her | s/he is giving it to him/her | s/he gives it to him/her (regularly).*
  THEME: N jeet~ O-S-ø-.aax̲~ (ø motion)
  *for S to give, take, hand O (textile-like object) to N*
  ·K̲óok yígu ax̲ kast'áat'i - ax̲ jeet .áx̲. *My quilt is in the box - give it to me.*

.AAX̲W verb root

- **adaawsi.áx̲w | adaasa.áax̲w | adaasa.áx̲wx̲**

  *s/he wrapped it up | s/he's wrapping it up | s/he wraps it up (regularly).*
  THEME: O-daa-S-s-.aax̲w~ (ø act)
  *for S to tie O together in a bundle; for S to wrap O up*
  ·K̲aa yat'éináx̲ x'wán daasa.áx̲w wé k̲óok! *Wrap that box when no one is looking now!*

- **yánde aawa.áx̲w | yánde a.aax̲w | ---**

  *s/he tied it up | s/he's tying it up | ---.*
  THEME: yánde O-S-ø-.aax̲w~ (ø act)
  *for S to tie up, secure O (esp. a boat to shore)*

.EE verb root

• **awsi.ée | as.ée | as.éex̱**
*s/he cooked it | s/he cooks it; s/he is cooking it | s/he cooks it (regularly).*
THEME: O-S-s-.ee~ (ø act)
*for S to cook O*
·X̱'áakw x̱'úx̱u haa x̱'eis sa.í stoox kaanáx̱! *Cook us red sockeye soup on the stove!*
·Wé ḵáa dzísk'u shaayí gangooknáx̱ as.eeyín. *He used to cook moose head next to the campfire.*

• **at wusi.ée | at sa.ée | at is.éex̱**
*s/he cooked | s/he is cooking | s/he cooks (regularly).*
THEME: at S-s-.ee~ (ø act)
*for S to cook*
·Du léelk'w du x̱'eis at wusi.ée. *Her grandmother cooked for her.*
·Du kéilk' du x̱'eis at wusi.ée. *His niece cooked for him.*

• **yan uwa.ée | yánde yaa na.éen | yax̱ .ee**
*it's cooked | it's cooking | it cooks (regularly, quickly).*
THEME: yan~ ø-.ee~ (ø motion)
*for food to be cooked, done cooking*
·Wé sakwnéin éewu yan g̱a.eet eeg̱áa áwé x̱a.áa. *I am sitting, waiting for the bread to finish cooking.*

.EEN[1] verb root

• **aawa.ín | a.éen | a.ínx̱**
*s/he picked them | s/he's picking them | s/he picks them (regularly).*
THEME: O-S-ø-.een~ (ø act)
*for S to pick O (esp. berries) into a container*
·Aatlein dáxw aawa.ín. *She picked lots of lowbush cranberries.*
·Shaax̱ a.éen haa hídi daatx̱ kanéegwál' sákw. *She is picking gray currants from around our house for a berry and salmon egg dish.*

• **át awsi.ín | --- | áx̱ as.een**
*s/he carried it there | --- | s/he carries it there (regularly).*
THEME: P-t~ O-S-s-.een~ (ø motion)
*for S to carry O (container full of liquid or small objects) to P*
·Yaawat'aayi káaxwei ín x'eesháa tóot haat awsi.ín. *She brought hot coffee in a bottle.*
·Yat'aayi héen du ḵáawu x̱'éit awsi.ín. *She gave her husband's clan brother coffee.*

• **du jeet awsi.ín | --- | du jeex̱ as.een**
*s/he gave it to him/her | --- | s/he gives it to him/her (regularly).*
THEME: N jeet~ O-S-s-.een~ (ø motion)
*for S to give, take, hand O (container full of liquid or small objects) to N*
·Wé shaatk' gúx'aa kát cháayoo ax̱ jeet awsi.ín. *The young girl gave me tea in a cup.*

• **neil awsi.ín | --- | neilx̱ as.een**
*s/he brought it inside | --- | s/he brings it inside (regularly).*

THEME: neil O-S-s-.een~ (ø motion)
*for S to bring O (container full of liquid or small objects) inside*
·Gán kaḵás'ti ḵóok tóox' neil awsi.ín. *He brought the kindling inside in a box.*

- **yan awsi.ín | --- | yax̱ as.een**
*s/he put it down | --- | s/he puts it down (regularly).*
THEME: yan~ O-S-s-.een~ (ø motion)
*for S to put down, lay down, leave, place O (a container full of liquid or small objects)*
·Wé shaawát du g̱ushkáa yan awsi.ín du s'íx'i. *The woman put her plate on her lap.*
·Stoox káa yan sa.ín wé at téix̱i! *Set the broth on top of the stove!*

### .EESH verb root

- **akawli.ísh | akla.eesh | akla.íshx̱**
*s/he strung them together | s/he is stringing them together | s/he strings them together (regularly).*
THEME: O-ka-S-l-.eesh~ (ø act)
*for S to thread, string together O (esp. beads)*
·A x̱'éináx̱ áwé kadul.eesh wé ḵáas' kaadéi wé saak. *Those hooligan are strung through the mouth on the stick.*

### .EEX' verb root

- **aawa.éex' | --- | yei a.éex'ch**
*s/he invited him/her | --- | s/he invites him/her (regularly).*
THEME: O-S-ø-.éex' (g̱a event)
*for S to invite O, ask O to a party*
·Haa k'ínk' yan wuneeyí a yís áyá ḵoox̱waa.éex'. *I invited everyone for when our stink heads are done.*
·Ḵúnáx̱ wé yee woo.éex'i aa tsú yee x̱oo yéi kg̱watée toowú k'é teen. *Your hostess will welcome you all as well. (Lit: Your hostess will be among you all with good feelings.)*

- **aawa.éex' | --- | yoo aya.éex'k**
*s/he called out to him/her | --- | s/he calls out to him/her (regularly).*
THEME: O-S-ø-.éex' (na event)
*for S to call out to, shout to, holler at O*

### .ÍT'CH verb root

- **kawdli.ít'ch | kadli.ít'ch | yoo kadli.ít'ch**
*it's sparkling; it sparkled | it's sparkling; it sparkles | it sparkles (regularly).*
THEME: ka-d-l-ít'ch (na state)
*for something to sparkle, reflect light*
·Dís x̱'usyee kawdli.it'ch wé dleit káx̱. *Moonbeams are sparkling on the snow.*
·Kadli.ít'ch éedaa xáanax'. *The phosphoresence glows at night.*

.oo[1] verb root

**• áa k̲oowa.oo | áa k̲uya.óo / áa k̲uwa.óo | ---**

*s/he lived there | s/he lives there | ---.*

THEME: k̲u-S-ø-.oo~ (na act)

*for S to live, live at, dwell permanently*

NOTES: To specify where one lives, use: P-x' "at P". For example: Sheet'káx' k̲uya.óo. "S/he lives in Sitka". Note that áa and áx' are synonymous, both meaning "there". Often when occuring directly before the verb, the preferred form is áa.

·Shayadihéin Áankichx' k̲uwa.oowu Lingít. *There are a lot of Tlingit people living in Anchorage.*

·Du káak x̲áni k̲uya.óo. *He is living with his maternal uncle.*

**• áa yéi aawa.oo | --- | áa yéi a.úx̲x'**

*s/he put them there | --- | s/he puts them there (regularly).*

THEME: P-x' yéi O-S-ø-.oo (na event)

*for S to put, leave (plural) O at P*

·Wé at x'aakeidí ín x'eesháa tóox' yéi na.oo! *Put the seeds in a bottle!*

·Wéi yaakw yax̲ak'áaw kas'éet áa yéi du.oowú, k'idéin yéi agux̲lasháat. *If a screw is put in the thwart of the boat, it will hold pretty well.*

**• yéi aawa.oo | yéi aya.óo | ---**

*s/he wore it | s/he's wearing it | ---.*

THEME: yéi O-S-ø-.oo~ (na state)

*for S to wear, put on, dress in O; for S to use O*

·Ch'áakw x̲'eint'áax'aa shaawát x̲'é yéi ndu.eich. *Long ago women would wear a labret.*

·Téil yéi aya.óo at doogú aklas'ék̲x̲i yís. *She is using dry wood for smoking that hide.*

.oo[2] verb root

**• aawa.oo | --- | yoo aya.eik**

*s/he bought it | --- | s/he buys it (regularly).*

THEME: O-S-ø-.oo (na event)

*for S to buy O*

·Aank̲áawuch áwé woo.oo, wé tlagu hít tlein. *A rich person bought the big old house.*

·Hoon daakahídidáx̲ g̲ánch has aawa.oo. *They bought tobacco from the store.*

**• akaawa.oo | --- | yoo akaya.eik**

*s/he bought it | --- | s/he buys it (regularly).*

THEME: O-ka-S-ø-.oo (na event)

*for S to buy O (usually round, spherical object)*

NOTES: While the ka- prefix once referred specifically to something round or spherical in shape, this distinction may be falling out of use, as some modern speakers consider akaawa.oo and aawa.oo to mean exactly the same thing.

·Ax̲ léelk'w jeeyís áyá kax̲waa.oo yá kanéist guk.át. *I bought these cross earrings for my grandmother.*

### .OOK verb root

- **awli.úk | --- | al.úkx̲**

  *s/he boiled it | --- | s/he boils it (regularly).*
  THEME: O-S-l-.ook~ (ø event)
  *for S to boil O (esp. water)*

- **wudli.úk | yaa nal.úk | il.úkx̲**

  *it's boiling; it boiled | it's starting to boil | it comes to a boil (regularly).*
  THEME: d-l-.óok~ (ø event)
  *for something to boil*
  ·Wudli.úk gé wé yat'aayi héen? *Did the coffee boil?*

### .OON verb root

- **aawa.ún | --- | ---**

  *s/he shot it | --- | ---.*
  THEME: O-S-ø-.óon~ (ø event)
  *for S to shoot O (with firearms)*
  ·Cháash a kaadéi kawtuwachák wé wutuwa.uni dzísk'w. *We packed branches on the moose that we shot.*
  ·A kageidéex' áwé x̲waa.ún wé g̲uwakaan tlein. *I shot the big deer in its side*

- **--- | a.únt | ---**

  *--- | s/he is shooting at it | ---.*
  THEME: O-S-ø-.únt (na act)
  *for S to shoot at O (with firearms)*

### .OOS verb root

- **wuli.oos | li.oos | ---**

  *s/he was noisy | s/he's being noisy | ---.*
  THEME: O-l-.oos (ga state)
  *for O to be crazy, lively, noisy, never still*
  ·Yá atk'átsk'u li.oos ch'ak'yéis' yáx̲. *This child is as playful as a young eagle.*

### .OOS' verb root

- **aawa.óos' | a.ús'k | yoo aya.ús'k**

  *s/he washed it | s/he is washing it | s/he washes it (regularly).*
  THEME: O-S-ø-.óos'~ (na act)
  *for S to wash O*
  ·Wé i wak̲dlóog̲u aax̲ na.óos'! *Clean the sleep from your eyes!*
  ·Aawa.óos'i jig̲wéinaa gáanx̲ ashayaawatée. *She hung the towel that she washed outside.*

- **akaawa.óos' | aka.ús'k | yoo akaa.ús'k**

  *s/he washed it | s/he's washing it | s/he washes it (regularly).*
  THEME: O-ka-S-ø-.óos'~ (na act)
  *for S to wash O (usually surface of pot, table, etc.)*
  ·S'íx' kawtoo.óos'i ítnáx̲ agax̲toolk̲áa. *After we have washed the dishes we will play cards.*

**.OOW** verb root

- **aawa.óow | a.óow | ---**

  *s/he bought them | s/he buys them | ---.*

  THEME: O-S-ø-.óow

  *for S to buy lots of O*

  NOTES: This verb only seems to occur in the perfective and imperfective. More research is needed.

  ·Yak'éiyi naa.át aax̲ du.óow wé hoon daakahídi. *Good clothing can be bought from that store.*

  ·Costcodáx̲ aawa.óow atx̲á. *He bought food from Costco.*

~

# English to Tlingit

# English to Tlingit

**abalone**

*abalone:* gunx̱aa.

**abdomen**

*his/her abdomen; surface of his/her belly; front of his/her body:* du yoowá.

**aboard**

*s/he carried it aboard; s/he took it aboard (container or hollow object):* TAAN yaax̱ aawataan. *s/he went aboard:* GOOT[1] yaax̱ woogoot.

**about**

*around it; about it; concerning it:* a daa. *(resting) at; coming to, arriving at; moving about:* -t. *(telling) about it:* a daat.

**above**

*above it:* a kináak. *top of it (something with a rounded top, as a mountain); above it; (elevated) over it:* a shakée.

**acceptably**

*enough, acceptably:* g̱aa.

**accident**

*accident; unfortunate mistake or mishap:* ḵaaḵx̱wdaagané (A). *s/he had an accident; s/he got hurt; something bad happened to him/her:* NEI ḵáakwt uwanéi.

**accidentally**

*accidentally, wrongly:* ḵáakwt~.

**accomplish**

*s/he won it; s/he got it; s/he accomplished it; s/he defeated him/her:* DLAAḴ ayaawadlaaḵ.

**according to**

*according to his/her words, instructions:* du x̱'ayáx̱. *according to the way s/he does it:* du jiyáx̱.

**accustomed to**

*s/he got used to it; s/he became accustomed to it (the flavor, pronunciation of something):* DAA[2] du x̱'éix̱ woodaa.

**acknowledge**

*s/he said that; s/he confessed that; s/he acknowledged that:* ḴAA[1] yéi yaawaḵaa.

**across**

*area across, on the other side (especially of body of water):* diyáanax̱.á.

**actually**

*actually; in fact; contrary to what was thought:* ḵachoo.

**add**
*s/he contributed to it; s/he donated to it; s/he added to it:* G̱EEX' át kawdiG̱íx'.

**adequate**
*(big) enough for him/her to have or use; adequate for him/her:* du jeeG̱áa. *enough; adequate:* tl'aG̱áa.

**Admiralty Island**
*people of Admiralty Island:* Xudzidaa K̲wáan.

**adult**
*adult; elder:* yanwáat. *young adult:* yées wáat.

**advise**
*s/he instructed him/her; s/he advised him/her:* JAA ashukaawajáa.

**adze**
*adze:* x̱út'aa. *stone adze:* s'oow x̱út'aa.

**afraid**
*s/he was afraid of it:* X̱EITL' áa akawdlix̱éitl'.

**African-American**
*Black (man or person); African-American:* t'ooch' k̲áa.

**after**
*after it:* a ít. *(distributed) in the area of; (going) after, (waiting) for; about the time of:* -G̱aa. *then, around, after, for:* aaG̱áa.

**afterlife**
*afterlife, "happy hunting ground":* daG̱ank̲ú.

**afternoon**
*day, afternoon:* yakyee, yagiyee, yagee (T).

**again**
*again; still; some more:* tsu.

**against**
*against it; wrongly, improperly:* a géit~. *against it, wrong (so as to foul up what s/he had done):* du jiyagéix̱.

**age**
*his/her age:* du katáagu. *it aged; it spoiled:* S'EEX wulis'íx. *s/he is old:* SHAAN wudishán.

**aground**
*aground, into shallow water:* kux.

**ahead**
*front of it; ahead of it:* a shuká. *straight ahead; directly ahead:* yaadachóon.

**Ahtna**
*Ahtna, Copper River Athabascan:* Ik̲kaa.

**Alaska**
*Alaska:* Anáaski.

**alcohol**
*liquor; booze; alcoholic beverage:* kasiyaayi héen.

**alcoholic**
*alcoholic:* náaw éesh.

**alder**
*alnus alder (beach or mountain alder):* keishísh. *red alder:* shéix̲'w.

**Aleut**
*Aleut:* Ana.óot, Giyak̲w.

**algae**
*algae found on rocks:* x̲aatl'. *ocean algae:* káas'.

**all**
*all; every:* ldakát.

**along**
*along; down:* yaa. *along, via; including the time of:* -náx̲.

**alongside**
*alongside it; catching up with it:* a kík.

**already**
*already, (by) now:* de.

**also**
*also, too, as well:* tsú.

**although**
*although, even though, however, nonetheless, yet:* ch'a aan.

**aluminum**
*aluminum:* géxtl'.

**always**
*always, all the time, constantly:* tlákw, ch'a tlákw. *always; [auxiliary]:* nooch.

**American**
*American:* Waashdan K̲wáan.

**American Indian**
*American Indian:* T'aawyáat.

**among**
*(in) the midst of it; among it:* a x̲oo.

**ancestor**
*ancestor(s) of his/her clan or nation; his/her background, heredity:* du shagóon. *in front of him/her; his/her geneology, history; his/her ancestors:* du shuká.

**anchor**

*anchor:* shayéinaa. *s/he anchored:* YAA$^{2}$ shawdziyaa. *s/he anchored the boat:* YAA$^{2}$ ashawsiyaa.

**Anchorage**

*Anchorage:* Áankich.

**and**

*and:* k̲a.

**anemic**

*he/she/it was weak; s/he is anemic; it is mild (of weather):* TSEEN tlél wultseen.

**angel**

*messenger; angel:* kook̲énaa.

**anger**

*anger:* x'áan.

**Angoon**

*Angoon:* Aangóon.

**angry**

*s/he's angry:* NOOK$^{2}$ x'áant uwanúk.

**ankle**

*knob on outer side of his/her ankle:* du x̲'ust'ákl'i. *outer side of his/her foot up to the anklebone:* du shutóox̲'.

**answer**

*in response, reply to him/her; answering him/her; following his/her train of speech:* du x̲'akooká.

**ant**

*ant:* wanatóox, wanatíx.

**antenna**

*its antenna (of radio):* a gúgu.

**anticipate**

*getting ready for it; in anticipation of it:* a yayís. *s/he anticipated it; s/he foresaw it; s/he expected him/her/it:* TEE$^{2}$ ashoowsitee.

**anus**

*his/her anus:* du tuk̲.woolí.

**anxiety**

*anxiety; wracked nerves; preoccupation; something weighing on one's mind:* tux'andaxeech.

**anybody**

*anyone, anybody; whoever:* ch'a aadóo sá, ch'a aa sá.

**anything**

*anything; whatever:* ch'a daa sá.

**any time**
*any time (in the future); whenever (in the future):* ch'a gwátgeen sá.

**anywhere**
*anywhere, anyplace; wherever:* ch'a goot'á sá.

**apparent**
*he/she/it appeared before him/her; it was apparent to him/her:* TEE[1] du wa<u>k</u>shiyeex' yéi wootee.

**appealing**
*it was fun; it was enjoyable; it was appealing:* GOO[1] <u>k</u>'awsigóo.

**appear**
*he/she/it appeared before him/her; it was apparent to him/her:* TEE[1] du wa<u>k</u>shiyeex' yéi wootee.

**apple**
*apple; crabapple:* x'áax'. *apple juice:* x'áax' kahéeni. *crabapple:* lingít x'áax'i.

**approve**
*s/he praised him/her; s/he approved it:* SHEI<u>X</u>' akaawashé<u>x</u>'.

**area**
*the foot of it; below it (raised place); flat area at the end of it (lake); down from the crest of it (slope); the end of it (dock):* a shuyee.

**aristocrat**
*high class person, aristocrat:* aanyádi.

**arm**
*crook of his/her arm; in his/her embrace:* du ji<u>g</u>ei. *his/her upper arm:* du <u>x</u>eek.

**armor**
*armor made of tough hide or wooden rods:* sankeit. *body armor, breastplate:* niyaháat, yinaaháat.

**armpit**
*his/her armpit:* du éenee. *his/her armpit hair:* du éenee <u>x</u>aawú.

**armspan**
*armspan; fathom:* waat.

**army**
*war party, attacking force of warriors or soldiers; army:* <u>x</u>áa.

**arnica**
*large-leaved avens (Geum macrophyllum) or possibly arnica species-- Arnica species, especially A. amplexicaulus, A. latifolia, A. gracilis:* aankanáagu.

**around**
*around it; about it; concerning it:* a daa. *around it (bypassing it, avoiding it); around the end of it:* a shuwadaa. *around the outside surface of it:* a daaká. *(in) the area of it or around it, (in) its vicinity:* a déin.

**arrest**

*s/he caught it; s/he grabbed him/her/it; s/he arrested him/her; s/he trapped him/her/it:* SHAAT aawasháat.

**arrive**

*he/she/it arrived there; he/she/it went there:* GOOT[1] át uwagút. *they walked there; they arrived there; they went there:* .AAT[1] át has uwa.át.

**arrow**

*arrow:* chooneit. *arrowhead:* at x̱éidi. *blunt arrow for stunning:* gútl. *sharp arrow for killing:* tláaḵ.

**arthritis**

*arthritis:* daa.ittunéekw.

**artifact**

*his/her handiwork, artifact:* du ji.eetí.

**ash**

*ash; ashes:* kél't'. *ashes:* gan eetí.

**ashore**

*ashore, onto ground; to rest:* yan~.

**ask**

*s/he asked for it; s/he cried for it:* G̱AAX̱ awdzig̱áax̱. *s/he asked him/her:* WOOS'[1] ax̱'eiwawóos'. *s/he told him/her that; s/he said that to him/her; s/he asked him/her to do that:* ḴAA[1] yoo ayawsiḵaa.

**asleep**

*s/he fell on his/her face; s/he fell asleep while sitting up:* GAAS' yan yaawagás'.

**assault**

*s/he beat him/her up; s/he assaulted him/her; s/he violently attacked him/her:* JAAḴW[1] aawajáaḵw.

**assist**

*he/she/it is helping me; s/he helped me:* SHEE[1] ax̱ éet wudishée.

**as soon as**

*(along) with, by means of; as soon as:* een, teen.

**astray**

*astray, getting lost:* ḵut.

**at**

*at (the scene of); at (the time of):* -x'. *(in prolonged contact) at; (repeatedly arriving) at; being, in the form of:* -x̱. *is/are at:* -u. *(resting) at; coming to, arriving at; moving about:* -t.

**Athabaskan**

*Athabaskan (Indian):* G̱unanaa.

**at least**

*at least, once in a while:* ch'a k'ikát.

**Atlin**

*Atlin:* Áa Tlein. *people of Atlin:* Áa Tlein Ḵwáan.

**attack**

*s/he beat him/her up; s/he assaulted him/her; s/he violently attacked him/her:* JAAḴW[1] aawajáaḵw. *they attacked someone:* .AAT[1] ḵaa éet has jiwdi.át.

**attic**

*upstairs; attic:* hít shantú.

**Auke Bay**

*Auke Bay:* Áak'w. *people of Auke Bay, southern Lynn Canal, Juneau area, and northern Admiralty Island:* Áak'w Ḵwáan.

**auklet**

*auklet or murrelet:* ch'eet, kéel. *Was'eeneidí; a clan of the Eagle moiety whose principal crests are the Wolf and Auklet:* Was'eeneidí.

**aunt**

*his/her maternal aunt:* du tláak'w. *his/her paternal aunt:* du aat.

**aurora borealis**

*northern lights; aurora borealis:* gis'óoḵ.

**autumn**

*fall; autumn:* yeis.

**avalanche**

*snowslide; snow avalanche:* dleit ḵaadí.

**aven**

*large-leaved avens (Geum macrophyllum) or possibly arnica species-- Arnica species, especially A. amplexicaulus, A. latifolia, A. gracilis:* aankanáagu.

**awake**

*he/she/it kept him/her awake:* X̱EIK ash wusix̱éḵ.

**away**

*away from it, leaving it behind (taking something away from him/her):* du jináḵ. *away, off (to someplace indefinite):* yóot~. *beside it; out past it; out away from it; (on) the outskirts of it (town):* a t'iká. *(going, taking something) away from it:* a náḵ. *in its way; keeping it away; protecting, shielding, screening from it; blocking it:* a niyaa, a x̱'anaa. *in secret (where nobody can see); away from people's view:* ḵaa yat'éinách, du yat'éinách.

**awful**

*it looked terrible; it looked awful; it was eerie; it was unattractive:* JEE[2] kawlijée.

**awl**

*awl; chopping block:* s'úwaa.

**axe**

*axe:* shanax̱wáayi, shunax̱wáayi. *stone axe:* tayees, yees.

**babiche**

*babiche, string, leather thonging:* dzaas.

**baby**

*baby:* t'ukanéiyi.

**babysitter**

*babysitter:* atyátx'i latíni.

**back**

*at his/her back; right behind him/her:* du dzúk. *behind him/her; back of him/her; at his/her back:* du t'áak. *behind his/her back, where s/he can't see:* du yat'éik. *his/her back:* du díx̲'. *near the base of it; at the foot of it; the back, rear or it (house); behind it (house); under the shelter of it (a standing object or structure):* a k'iyee. *(on) the back of it (fish); on the crest, ridge, backbone of it (hill, ridge, point):* a litká.

**back and forth**

*back and forth; to and fro; up and down:* yoo.

**back end**

*its back end; stern (of boat):* a k'óol'.

**backpack**

*backpack; pack sack:* yáanadi. *pack; backpack; pack sack:* x̲éey.

**backwards**

*backwards:* k̲ux̲ dak'óol'een.

**bacon**

*bacon:* gishoo taayí.

**bad**

*he/she/it was bad; he/she/it was evil:* K'EI tlél wushk'é.

**bag**

*bag; sack:* gwéil.

**baggage**

*baggage, luggage; things, stuff packed up for carrying:* at la.át.

**baggy**

*its wrinkled, baggy skin, hide:* a daaleilí.

**bailer**

*bailer:* kakúxaa. *wooden bailer (for boat):* sheen.

**bait hooks**

*s/he baited hooks:* NAAK̲W[1] yawdinák̲w.

**bald**

*bald spot; bald head:* shax̲'wáas' (T).

**baleen**

*baleen; whalebone:* yáay x̲'axéni.

**ball**
*ball:* kooch'éit'aa.

**balloon**
*balloon:* kadu.uxx̱u át.

**bandage**
*s/he bandaged it; s/he bound it up; s/he wrapped it:* S'EET akaawas'ít.

**bangs**
*his/her bangs:* du kak'x̱aawú.

**banister**
*banister; railing:* a daax̱ yaa dulsheech át.

**baptize**
*s/he baptized him/her:* TEE² héent ayaawatée.

**barbecue**
*s/he barbecued it:* TSEEK awlitsík.

**bare**
*bare; naked:* kaldaag̱ákw.

**barefoot**
*barefoot; shoeless:* kaltéelḵ.

**bark**
*dry woody outer bark:* loon. *flaky surface of the outer bark of conifers, especially hemlock:* s'agwáat. *its bark:* a daayí. *yellow cedar bark (for weaving):* teey woodí.

**barnacle**
*barnacle:* s'ook.

**barrel**
*barrel:* káast.

**base**
*its base (of tree or other plant); the lower part of its trunk or stem:* a k'eeyí. *near the base of it; at the foot of it; the back, rear or it (house); behind it (house); under the shelter of it (a standing object or structure):* a k'iyee. *the base or foot of it (a standing object):* a k'í.

**basket**
*basket:* ḵákw. *basket of woven red cedar bark:* néil'. *basket or pan used to collect berries by knocking them off the bush:* kadádzaa yeit. *basket with a rattle in the lid:* tudaxákw. *basket with rattle in the lid:* tuḵdaadaxákw. *berrying basket:* kaltásk. *berrying basket or can hung around the neck, resting on the chest:* seig̱atáanaa. *birch bark basket:* at daayí ḵákw. *flat open basket woven from wide strips of bark (for carrying fish, etc.); large platter:* táal. *long, flat loosely woven basket for pressing out herring oil:* kaat. *roots or vines used in basket decoration:* léet'. *round basket made of split red cedar branches:* ts'anéi. *unfinished basket:* x'akaskéin.

**bastard**

*fatherless child; bastard:* neechkayádi.

**bathe**

*s/he bathed:* SHOOCH wudishúch.

**bay**

*bay:* g̱eey, g̱eiy (TC), eey. *head of the bay:* g̱eey tá.

**be**

*he/she/it was that way:* TEE[1] yéi wootee. *it existed; s/he was born:* TEE[1] ḵoowdzitee. *it's situated there:* .AA[1] át la.áa. *s/he became a (noun):* TEE[1] (noun)-x̱ wusitee. *s/he was with him/her; s/he stayed with him/her; s/he lived with him/her:* TEE[1] du x̱ánx' yéi wootee. *the building was situated there (suddenly as if overnight):* NOOK[1] áa wdinook. *the weather was that way:* TEE[1] yéi ḵoowatee.

**beach**

*beach; waterside; down on the beach, shore:* éeḵ. *down to beach, shore:* yeeḵ. *from the woods onto the beach, shore:* éeg̱i. *out of the water onto the beach, shore:* dáag̱i. *shoreline; beach:* neech. *the beach, shore below it (a town):* a eeg̱ayáak.

**beached**

*it got stuck on the beach:* DLAAX̱'W yax̱ woodláax̱'w.

**bead**

*bead:* kawóot. *light bluish-gray trade bead(s):* s'eeḵ kawóot.

**beak**

*dark yellow; eagle's beak:* ch'áak' loowú. *its beak:* a loowú.

**bear**

*Chookaneidí; a clan of the Eagle moiety whose principal crests are the Porpoise and Brown Bear:* Chookaneidí. *grizzly bear:* xóots. *Teiḵweidí, locally called "Brown Bear"; a clan of the Eagle moiety whose principal crest is the Brown Bear:* Teiḵweidí. *Yanyeidí, locally known as "Bear"; a clan of the Eagle moiety whose principal crest is the Brown Bear:* Yanyeidí.

**bearberry**

*alpine bearberry, kinnikinnick:* tínx.

**beard**

*its whiskers, beard (of fish):* a ḵ'anoox̱ú.

**bear root**

*bear root, Indian potato:* tsáats.

**beat**

*s/he beat it; s/he rang it; s/he stabbed it:* GWAAL aawagwaal.

**beat up**

*s/he beat him/her up; s/he assaulted him/her; s/he violently attacked him/her:* JAAḴW[1] aawajáaḵw.

**beaver**

*beaver:* s'igeidí. *beaver dam:* s'igeidí áayi. *beaver's den:* s'igeidí x̱aayí. *Deisheetaan, locally called "Beaver"; a clan of the Raven moiety whose principal crest is the Beaver:* Deisheetaan.

**because**

*because of; by means of:* -ch. *because of it; due to it; by virtue of it; on the strength of it; encouraged by it:* a tuwáadáx̱.

**become**

*s/he became a (noun):* TEE[1] (noun)-x̱ wusitee.

**bed**

*bed:* káa x̱ex̱x'u yeit. *mattress; bedding:* yee.át.

**bee**

*bee's nest:* gandaas'aají kúdi. *bee; wasp:* gandaas'aají.

**beer**

*beer:* géewaa.

**beetle**

*beetle:* k'ul'kaskéxkw.

**before**

*before his/her eyes; where he/she can see (it):* du waḵshiyee.

**begin**

*beginning:* g̱unayéi. *start, begin:* g̱unéi.

**behave**

*s/he did it; s/he behaved that way:* NOOK[2] yéi ḵoowanook.

**behind**

*at his/her back; right behind him/her:* du dzúk. *behind him/her; back of him/her; at his/her back:* du t'áak. *behind his/her back, where s/he can't see:* du yat'éik. *behind it:* a t'éik. *behind it; back inland from it; on the landward side of it (something on the water):* a t'áak. *near the base of it; at the foot of it; the back, rear or it (house); behind it (house); under the shelter of it (a standing object or structure):* a k'iyee.

**believe**

*s/he believed him/her; s/he trusted him/her:* HEEN[1] du éek' aawaheen.

**believer**

*believer:* átk' aheení.

**bell**

*bell:* gaaw.

**belly**

*his/her abdomen; surface of his/her belly; front of his/her body:* du yoowá. *his/her belly, paunch:* du x̱'óol'. *his/her flank, side of his/her belly:* du ḵaatl.

**bellybutton**
    *his/her navel, bellybutton:* du kool.
**below**
    *the foot of it; below it (raised place); flat area at the end of it (lake); down from the crest of it (slope); the end of it (dock):* a shuyee, a shuwee. *underneath it; beneath it; below it:* a tayee.
**belt**
    *belt:* séek.
**bend**
    *s/he bent it:* TAAN akaawataan.
**bent**
    *it's bent:* TAAN yóo katán.
**berries**
    *half-dried, compressed food, esp. berries or seaweed:* kat'ákx̱i. *swamp berries:* sháchgi tléig̱u. *various odd looking, tasteless, or otherwise undesirable berries, some poisonous; meaning varies locally, incl. twistedstalk (Streptopus species), snowberry (Symphoricarpos albus), fool's huckleberry (Menziesia ferruginea), etc.:* s'ig̱eeḵáawu tléig̱u.
**berry**
    *berry, berries:* tléiḵw. *berry juice:* tléiḵw kahéeni. *dish made with berries and salmon eggs:* kanéegwál'. *green, unripe berry:* kax̱'át'. *mashed berries:* kag̱útlx̱i. *s/he picked berries:* K'EET' ḵoowak'it'. *steamed berries:* kanálx̱i. *steamed berries put up in soft grease:* kaḵáshx̱i.
**berry bush**
    *berry bush:* tléiḵw wás'i.
**beside**
    *beside, alongside, next to him/her:* du t'aḵká. *beside, alongside, next to it:* a t'aḵká. *beside it, at its side:* a t'aaḵ. *beside it, next to it:* a tuwán. *beside it; out past it; out away from it; (on) the outskirts of it (town):* a t'iká.
**between**
    *between them:* a x̱'áak. *enclosed within (the folds of) it, between the folds, covers, walls of it:* a g̱ei.
**beyond**
    *beyond it, more than it; too much; excessively:* a yáanáx̱.
**bicycle**
    *bicycle:* a kát sh kadultsex̱t át.
**big**
    *big:* tlein. *he/she/it is big, tall (live creature or building):* GEI[1] ligéi. *it got this big; there were this many:* GEI[1] yéi kaawagéi. *it's big (round, spherical object):* GEI[1] kayagéi. *it's that big around:* TLAA yéi kwditláa. *it was big; there were many; there was plenty:* GEI[1] woogéi. *they're big:* GEI[1] digéix', GEI[1] kadigéix'. *they're that big:* GEI[1] yéi kwdigéi.

**Big Dipper**
*Big Dipper; Ursa Major:* ya<u>x</u>té.

**bight**
*cove; bight:* kuna<u>g</u>eey.

**bile**
*his/her bile:* du teiyí.

**bind**
*s/he bandaged it; s/he bound it up; s/he wrapped it:* S'EET akaawas'ít.

**birch**
*birch:* at daayí. *birch bark basket:* at daayí <u>k</u>ákw.

**bird**
*green bird (sparrow or finch):* asx'aan sháach'i. *grey singing bird (sparrow or finch):* tlagu ts'ats'éeyee. *robin-like bird:* shoo<u>x</u>'. *songbird; bird:* ts'ats'ée, ts'ítskw.

**bison**
*bison, buffalo; ox, muskox; cow; horse:* xaas.

**bite**
*he/she/it bit him/her/it:* YEE<u>K</u>[2] aawayee<u>k</u>. *it bit him/her/it:* TAAX' ash wusitáax'. *it pierced it; it bit him/her/it:* <u>G</u>EECH át yawdi<u>g</u>ích, <u>G</u>EECH aadé yawdi<u>g</u>eech.

**bitter**
*it was sour; it was bitter; it was spicy:* .AAX'W[1] wusi.áax'w.

**black**
*black:* t'ooch'. *Black (man or person); African-American:* t'ooch' <u>k</u>áa. *black with dirt, filth, stain:* ts'á<u>k</u>l.

**black bass**
*black bass:* lit.isdúk.

**black bear**
*black bear:* s'eek.

**blackboard**
*blackboard, chalkboard:* kadushxit t'aa yá.

**black cod**
*black cod:* ish<u>k</u>een.

**black currant**
*black currant:* <u>x</u>aaheiwú.

**blacksmith**
*blacksmith:* <u>g</u>ayéis' layei<u>x</u>í, <u>g</u>ayéis' t'éi<u>x</u>'i.

**bladder**
*his/her bladder:* du kalóox'shani.

**blame**

*s/he brought it onto him/her (esp. shame, blame, joy):* TEE[2] du kát ashuwatée.

**blanket**

*blanket; robe:* x'óow. *blanket sewn from scraps of hide:* at xáshdi x'óow. *cotton; cotton blanket, quilt:* kast'áat'. *Hudson Bay blanket:* kinguchwáan x'óowu. *quilt; cotton blanket:* kast'áat' x'óow. *wool blanket (used as potlatch gift or for dancing):* l'ée.

**blessed**

*s/he got lucky; s/he was blessed:* X̲EITL wulix̲éitl.

**blind**

*blind person:* l k̲ooshtéeni. *s/he is blind:* TEEN tlél k̲ooshtéen.

**blindfold**

*blindfold:* wak̲kadóox'.

**block**

*in its way; keeping it away; protecting, shielding, screening from it; blocking it:* a niyaa.

**blond**

*grayish; blond (hair):* l'áax̲'.

**blood**

*blood:* shé. *bloodline inside fish, along the backbone:* x̲áat k'áax̲'i.

**bloodsucker**

*leech; bloodsucker:* yéesh.

**blossom**

*flower; blossom:* k̲'eikaxwéin.

**blow**

*it blew; it's blowing:* NOOK[2] wuduwanúk. *it's blowing around; it blew around; s/he is sailing around; s/he sailed around:* S'EES át wulis'ees. *it's blowing in the wind there:* S'EES aadé kawdlis'ées. *spray of air exhaled through its blowhole (of sea mammal):* a óoxu.

**blowfish**

*moonfish, suckerfish, blowfish:* tl'éitl'.

**blubber**

*fat; blubber:* taay.

**blue**

*dark blue:* x̲'éishx'w. *green, light blue:* s'oow. *sky blue:* xáats'.

**blueberry**

*alpine blueberry:* ts'éekáx̲k'w. *blueberry; huckleberry:* kanat'á. *blueberry juice; purple:* kanat'á kahéeni. *huckleberry; blueberry:* naanyaa kanat'aayí. *swamp blueberry:* láx̲' loowú.

**bluejay**
*bluejay, Stellar's jay:* x̱'éishx'w.

**blunt**
*it's dull; it's blunt:* G̱EEL yaawdig̱íl.

**board**
*board:* t'áa.

**boat**
*boat, canoe:* yaakw. *gas-powered boat:* s'eenáa yaakw. *in the boat:* yaakw yík. *old, worn-out boat:* l'áaḵw. *shell of a boat:* yakw daa.ideidí. *skiff; small boat; flat-bottom canoe:* yakwyádi. *steamboat; riverboat:* gántiyaakw. *stern (of a boat):* a géek.

**body**
*his/her body parts:* du daashagóon. *his/her/its body:* du daa.it.

**boil[1]**
*it's boiling; it boiled:* .OOK wudli.úk. *s/he boiled it:* .OOK awli.úk. *s/he steamed it; s/he boiled it:* TAA[3] awsitáa.

**boil[2]**
*boil; inflammation and swelling:* x'ees.

**boiled**
*boiled food; broth:* téix̱, a téix̱i.

**bone**
*bone:* s'aaḵ. *his/her bone marrow:* s'aḵtu.eex̱í. *his/her skeleton, bare bones:* du xaagú.

**book**
*paper; book, magazine, newspaper; letter, mail:* x'úx'.

**boot**
*boot(s):* x'wán.

**boredom**
*loneliness; boredom:* tuteesh.

**born**
*it existed; s/he was born:* TEE[1] ḵoowdzitee.

**borrow**
*s/he borrowed it:* HEES' aawahées'. *s/he borrowed it (round, spherical object):* HEES' akaawahées'.

**boss**
*boss:* ḵaa s'aatí. *his/her boss, master:* du s'aatí.

**both**
*both:* ch'u déix̱.

**bother**
*he/she/it bothered him/her; he/she/it is bothering him/her:* XEEL' akaawaxíl'.

**bottle**

*bottle; jug:* t'ooch'ineit, ín x'eesháa.

**bottom**

*(around) the bottom of it:* a tuḵdaa. *the bottom of it (a cavity):* a táak. *the inside surface of its bottom (of container, vessel):* a taká.

**bough**

*bough, branch with needles on it, especially of hemlock:* haaw. *bough, branch with needles on it, especially of spruce:* cháash.

**boulder**

*underwater reef; large rock or boulder lying under the water:* hintu.eejí.

**bow**[1]

*its cutwater; the curved part of a bow or stern (of boat):* a xées'i.

**bow**[2]

*bow (ribbon tied into a bow):* lag̱wán.

**bow and arrow**

*bow:* sáḵs. *close quarter bow and arrow:* sheixw, sheexw.

**bowl**

*food container; pot or pan; dish, large bowl:* x̱'ayeit.

**bowstay**

*its bowstay:* a lukatíx'i.

**box**

*bentwood box:* láḵt. *box:* ḵóok. *large box for storing grease, oil:* daneit. *small covered box:* x̱'al'daakeit.

**boy**

*boy:* yadak'wátsk'u. *boys, young men:* k'isáani.

**boyfriend**

*his/her boyfriend:* du yadák'u. *his/her husband's clan brother; his/her man, boyfriend, husband:* du ḵáawu.

**bracelet**

*bracelet:* kées.

**brailer bag**

*dipper, scoop, ladle; brailer bag:* kaxwénaa.

**brain**

*his/her brain:* du tlag̱eiyí.

**branch**

*bough, branch with needles on it, especially of hemlock:* haaw. *bough, branch with needles on it, especially of spruce:* cháash. *its secondary branch:* a t'áni. *limb, primary branch; limb knot:* sheey. *old, dead branch:* tl'áxch'.

**brant**

*brant (small goose):* ḵín.

**brass**

*brass:* ik̲náach'.

**brave**

*brave, fearless man; temperamental, quick-tempered, hot-headed or domineering man:* x'ig̲aak̲áa.

**bread**

*bread crumbs:* sakwnéin kax̲'eiltí. *Easter bread; communion bread:* léikwaa. *flour; bread:* sakwnéin. *(loaf of) bread:* sakwnéin éewu.

**break**

*it broke (general, solid object):* L'EEX' wool'éex'. *it broke (long object):* L'EEX' wulil'éex'. *s/he broke it (general, solid object):* L'EEX' aawal'éex'. *s/he broke it (long object):* L'EEX' awlil'éex'. *s/he broke it (rope-like object):* K'OOTS awlik'oots. *s/he did something wrong; s/he broke the law:* GEET[2] at géit wudzigít.

**breast**

*his/her breast:* du l'aa.

**breastplate**

*body armor, breastplate:* niyaháat.

**breath**

*life; breath:* x̲'aséikw, daséikw.

**breed**

*s/he bred them:* X̲EIT[2] awsix̲eit. *they multiplied; they bred:* X̲EIT[2] has wudzix̲eit.

**bright**

*it's bright; it's shining:* GAAN[1] kawdigán.

**bring**

*hand it here, bring it here:* haandé. *s/he brought it onto him/her (esp. shame, blame, joy):* TEE[2] du kát ashuwatée. *s/he brought it out; s/he picked it up (general, often compact object):* TEE[2] kei aawatée. *s/he brought it out; s/he picked it up (long, complex object):* TAAN kei awsitán.

**British**

*Canadian, British:* Ginjoochwáan, Ginjichwáan.

**broke**

*broke; penniless; without money:* kaldáanaak̲.

**broom**

*broom; brush:* xít'aa.

**broth**

*boiled food; broth:* téix̲, a téix̲i. *soup broth; soup:* tax̲héeni.

**brother**

*her brother, cousin:* du éek'. *her younger sister; his younger brother; cousin:* du kéek'. *his/her clan brother:* du xwáayi. *his/her clan brother or sister, distant relative, comrade:* du t'aag̲í. *his older brother, cousin:* du húnx̲w.

**brother-in-law**

*his/her brother-in-law, sister-in-law:* du káani.

**brown**

*brown:* s'agwáat.

**brown bear**

*solid-ribbed brown bear:* s'uk̲kasdúk.

**bruise**

*s/he injured it; s/he wounded it; s/he bruised it:* CHOON awlichún.

**bruised**

*he/she/it is bruised; it's colored; it's discolored:* YEIS' kawdiyés'. *he/she/it is injured; he/she/it is wounded; he/she/it is bruised; s/he is hurting (emotionally):* CHOON wudichún.

**brush**[1]

*broom; brush:* xít'aa. *clothes brush:* naa.át kaxít'aa. *pencil; pen; brush:* kooxéedaa.

**brush**[2]

*windfall; dead tree(s) or brush that has fallen:* g̲éejadi. *woods; bush; brush, underbrush:* at gutú.

**bubble**

*bubbles, esp. from whale:* kúk̲dlaa. *fast drip with bubbles:* kúk̲jaa. *small bubbles (in water):* x̲'asúnjaa.

**bucket**

*bucket; pail:* x'eesháa.

**buckshot**

*buckshot; moccasin lining:* at tux̲'wáns'i.

**buffalo**

*bison, buffalo; ox, muskox; cow; horse:* xaas.

**build**

*s/he built it; s/he made it; s/he constructed it:* YEIX̲[1] awliyéx̲.

**building**

*house; building:* hít.

**bullet**

*bullet:* at katé.

**bullhead**

*bullhead:* éetkatlóox̲u. *bullhead, sculpin:* wéix̲'. *little bullhead (found under beach rocks):* té tayee tlóox̲u. *mud bullhead:* tlóox̲.

**bump**
*bump, lump, hump, mound:* gootl.

**bunchberry**
*bunchberry:* k̲'eikaxétl'k.

**buoy**
*fixed buoy:* eech kakwéiyi. *floating buoy:* eech kwéiyi.

**burden**
*under the burden, weight of it; belabored or suffering from it (a burden, hardship):* a jiyeet.

**burl**
*growth on the trunk of a tree, burl:* gúnl'.

**burn**
*he/she/it burned him/her/it; s/he scalded him/her/it:* X̲'EIX̲' awlix̲'éx̲'. *it's on (light); it's burning (fire):* GAAN[1] át akaawagán. *s/he burned it up:* GAAN[1] kei awsigán.

**burned**
*s/he got burned:* X̲'EIX̲' wudix̲'éx̲'.

**burnt**
*burnt or charred wood:* xoodzí. *singed, burnt, or charred matter:* xóosht'.

**bush**
*bush:* wás'. *false azalea (fruitless bush):* k'éets'an. *wilderness; the bush:* katk̲aak̲ú, g̲alg̲aak̲u. *woods; bush; brush, underbrush:* at gutú.

**buttock**
*cheek of his/her buttocks:* du x'aash. *crack of his/her buttocks; his/her butt crack:* du tux̲'ax'aayí. *his/her buttocks, butt:* du tóok̲. *his/her buttocks, thighs:* du g̲áts.

**button**
*button:* k̲aayaku.óot'i (At), yuka.óot', yaka.óot'.

**button blanket**
*button blanket:* k̲aayuka.óot'i x'óow (T), yaka.óot' x'óow, yuka.óot' x'óow.

**buy**
*s/he bought it:* .OO[2] aawa.oo. *s/he bought it (round, spherical object):* .OO[2] akaawa.oo. *s/he bought them (lots of something):* .OOW aawa.óow.

**by**
*near him/her, by him/her:* du x̲án. *near him/her, by him/her (at hand, for him/her to work with):* du jix̲án.

**cabin**
*cabin (of boat); pilot house:* yaakw x̲ukahídi.

**cable**
*cable:* g̲ayéis' tíx'.

**cache**

*platform cache; house cache; shed:* chál.

**cairn**

*cairn; rock pile:* té xóow.

**calendar**

*calendar:* dís woox̱éiyi.

**call**

*s/he called him/her/it that (name):* SAA$^{2}$ yéi aawasáakw. *s/he called him/her on the phone:* TAAN du jeet x̱'awditán, TAAN du jeedé x̱'awditaan. *s/he called out to him/her; s/he shouted to him/her:* .EEX' aawa.éex'. *s/he composed a song; s/he called forth a response (from opposite clan by means of a song):* X̱OOX̱ shukawlix̱oox̱. *s/he summoned him/her; s/he called him/her:* X̱OOX̱ aawax̱oox̱.

**calm**

*it's calm; it's peaceful:* YEIL' kawduwayél'. *peace, calm:* kayéil'. *the weather is calm:* YEIL' ḵukawduwayél'.

**cambium**

*cambium, sap scraped from inner bark:* sáx'.

**camera**

*camera:* aankadushxit át.

**camp**

*campsite; (out in) camp; (out in) the bush, wilderness:* yanshuká. *s/he stayed overnight; s/he camped out:* X̱EI uwax̱éi.

**can**

*berrying basket or can hung around the neck, resting on the chest:* seig̱atáanaa. *cup; can:* gúx'aa.

**Canadian**

*Canadian, British:* Ginjoochwáan, Ginjichwáan.

**canary**

*goldfinch, canary:* s'áas'.

**cancer**

*rotting sore; gangrene; cancer:* tl'ooḵ.

**candle**

*candle:* toow s'eenáa.

**candlefish**

*eulachon; candlefish; hooligan:* saak.

**cane**

*cane; walking stick; staff:* wootsaag̱áa.

**cannery**

*cannery:* x̱áat daakahídi.

**cannibal**

*tribe of cannibals, man-eaters:* k̲usax̲ak̲wáan.

**cannister**

*large cannister:* naasa.áa.

**canoe**

*boat, canoe:* yaakw. *canoe made of cottonwood:* dúk̲. *canoe of caribou skins:* jaak̲úx̲. *canoe under construction:* dáax̲. *dug-out canoe designed to go through shallow waters:* seet. *sea otter hunting canoe with an angular prow for breaking the waves:* ch'iyáash. *skiff; small boat; flat-bottom canoe:* yakwyádi. *small canoe with high carved prow:* yáxwch'i yaakw.

**canvas**

*canvas; tarp; tent:* xwaasdáa.

**canyon**

*draw, gully, box canyon:* séet.

**cape**

*shawl; cape; poncho:* teik̲.

**Cape Fox**

*people of Cape Fox, Saxman:* Sanyaa K̲wáan.

**captain**

*captain (in the navy):* kak'kakwéiy s'aatí (At). *captain (of a boat):* yaakw yasatáni. *captain; person in charge:* kak'dakwéiy s'aatí.

**captive**

*captive:* g̲alsháatadi.

**capture**

*s/he held it; s/he captured it:* SHAAT awlisháat.

**car**

*car, automobile:* káa.

**caribou**

*caribou:* watsíx.

**carpenter**

*carpenter:* at layeix̲ s'aatí.

**carrot**

*carrot:* s'ín.

**carry**

*he/she/it carried it on his/her/its back; he/she/it packed it on his/her/its back:* YAA$^{2}$ aawayaa. *he/she/it carried things on his/her/its back; he/she/it packed things on his/her/its back:* YAA$^{2}$ at wooyaa. *s/he carried him/her/it (live creature):* NOOK$^{1}$ awsinook. *s/he carried it aboard; s/he took it aboard (container or hollow object):* TAAN yaax̲ aawataan. *s/he carried it all there; s/he took it all there:* JEIL aadé akaawajeil. *s/he carried it inside; s/he took it inside (container full of liquid or small objects):* .EEN$^{1}$ neil awsi.ín. *s/he carried it inside; s/he took it inside (general, compact object):* TEE[2] neil aawatée. *s/he carried it; s/he took it (container or hollow object):* TAAN aawataan. *s/he carried it (solid, complex object):* TEE[2] awsitee. *s/he carried it there; s/he took it there (container full of liquid or small objects):* .EEN[1] át awsi.ín. *s/he carried it there; s/he took it there (container or hollow object):* TAAN át aawatán. *s/he carried it there; s/he took it there (general, compact object):* TEE[2] aadé aawatee. *s/he carried it there; s/he took it there (solid, often complex object):* TEE[2] aadé awsitee. *s/he carried stuff there; s/he took stuff there:* JEIL aadé at kaawajeil. *s/he carried them there; s/he took them there (esp. baggage or personal belongings):* .AAT[2] aadé awli.aat. *s/he is carrying him/her/it around; s/he carried him/her/it around (live creature):* NOOK[1] át awsinook. *s/he is carrying it around; s/he carried it around (container or hollow object):* TAAN át aawataan. *s/he is carrying it around; s/he carried it aroundj (textile-like object):* .AAX̲[2] át aawa.aax̲.

**cartilage**

*cartilage, gristle:* a túk̲l'i. *cartilage, gristle at the end of its bones:* a s'ak̲shutúk̲l'i. *cartilage, gristle between its bones:* a s'ak̲x̲'áak túk̲l'i.

**carve**

*s/he carved it:* CH'AAK'W akaawach'ák'w. *s/he cut it up; s/he carved it; s/he sliced it:* XAASH akaawaxaash.

**carver**

*carver:* at kach'áak'u.

**casket**

*coffin; casket:* k̲aa daakeidí.

**cast**

*s/he sportfished; s/he casted:* X̲OOT'[1] shawdlix̲óot'.

**cat**

*cat:* dóosh.

**cataract**

*cataract:* gáal'.

**catch**

*s/he caught it; s/he grabbed him/her/it; s/he arrested him/her; s/he trapped him/her/it:* SHAAT aawasháat.

**caterpillar**

*worm; larva; grub; caterpillar; snake:* tl'úk'x̲.

**Caucasian**

*White, European, Caucasian (man or person):* Gus'k'iyee k̲wáan, dleit k̲áa.

**cave**

*cave:* tatóok, katóok.

**cedar**

*red cedar:* laax̲. *yellow cedar, Alaska cedar:* x̲áay.

**ceiling**

*its ceiling:* a kax̱yee.

**cellar**

*pit; hole dug in the ground; cellar:* kóoḵ.

**centipede**

*centipede:* atxaayí.

**chain**

*chain:* wóoshnáx̱ x̱'akakéix̱i, x̱'akakeix̱í.

**chainsaw**

*chainsaw:* sh daxash washéen.

**chair**

*chair:* káayag̱ijeit.

**chalkboard**

*blackboard, chalkboard:* kadushxit t'aa yá.

**chance**

*room, space, place for it; time for it; chance, opportunity for it:* a ya.áak.

**chaos**

*whirlpool; boiling tide; chaos:* x'óol'.

**charcoal**

*charcoal:* t'ooch'.

**charm**

*sympathetic magic, charm:* héix̱waa.

**charred**

*singed, burnt, or charred matter:* xóosht'.

**chase**

*he/she/it chased it into the open:* KEIL'[1] daak awlikél'.

**cheek**

*his/her cheek:* du wásh. *inside of his/her cheek:* du washtú. *(outside of) his/her cheek:* du washká.

**chest**

*chest pain; tuberculosis:* wuwtunéekw. *his/her chest:* du wóow. *his/her thorax; flat upper surface of his/her chest:* du xeitká. *(on) his/her chest:* du woowká.

**chickadee**

*chickadee:* ḵaatoowú.

**chicken**

*spruce grouse, spruce hen; chicken:* káax'.

**chief**

*rich man; man of wealth; chief:* aanḵáawu.

**child**

*child:* atk’átsk’u. *fatherless child; bastard:* neechkayádi. *his/her child:* du yádi.

**children**

*children:* atyátx’i, adátx’i. *his/her children:* du yátx’i.

**Chilkat blanket**

*Chilkat blanket:* naaxein.

**chill**

*s/he chilled it:* .AAT’ awsi.át’.

**chin**

*his/her chin:* du téey.

**Chinese**

*Chinese:* Cháanwaan.

**chinook salmon**

*king salmon; chinook salmon; spring salmon:* t’á.

**chip**

*s/he chopped it (wood); s/he chipped it out (with adze):* X̲OOT’[2] aawax̲út’.

**chisel**

*chisel:* tíyaa. *rounded carving chisel:* kach’ák’waa.

**chiton**

*gumboots; chiton:* shaaw.

**choir**

*singers, choir:* at shéex’i.

**Chookaneidí**

*Chookaneidí; a clan of the Eagle moiety whose principal crests are the Porpoise and Brown Bear:* Chookaneidí.

**chop**

*s/he chopped it (esp. tree, branch):* S’OOW aawas’úw. *s/he chopped it up; s/he split it (wood):* X̲OOT’[2] akawlix̲óot’. *s/he chopped it (wood); s/he chipped it out (with adze):* X̲OOT’[2] aawax̲út’.

**chopper**

*chopper:* kas’úwaa.

**chopping block**

*awl; chopping block:* s’úwaa.

**Chugach**

*Chugach Eskimo:* Gutéix̲’.

**chum salmon**

*dog salmon; chum salmon:* téel’.

**church**

*house of prayer; church:* x̲’agáax’ daakahídi.

**circle**

*s/he drove around it; s/he went around it; s/he circled it (by boat, car):* K̲OOX̲[1] a daax̲ yaawak̲úx̲.

**claim**

*possession; that which is claimed:* k̲aa at oohéini. *s/he claimed it; s/he owns it:* HEIN aawahéin.

**clam**

*baby clams:* dzéex'w. *clam:* gáal'. *giant clam:* x̲éet'. *its edible part (of clam):* a g̲eiyí. *littleneck clams:* tl'ildaaskeit. *razor clam:* k̲'alkátsk. *slime (inside clamshell):* átl'áni. *tiny clams (too small to eat):* dzóox'.

**clan**

*nation; moiety; clan; band of people:* naa.

**clan house**

*head of a clan house; master of the house:* hít s'aatí.

**claw**

*its claw:* a x̲aagú.

**clay**

*clay; alluvial silt:* s'é.

**clerk**

*salesman; clerk; storekeeper:* dahooní.

**cliff**

*cliff:* g̲íl'.

**climb**

*he/she/it climbed the face of it:* TL'EIT' a yáx̲ wudlitl'éit'. *he/she/it climbed up it:* TL'EIT' a daax̲ kei wdlitl'ét'.

**clock**

*clock:* gaaw.

**cloth**

*cheesecloth, loose-woven cloth; netting, screen:* kag̲ádaa. *cloth; sailcloth:* s'ísaa.

**clothes**

*clothes, clothing; garment:* naa.át. *under or inside his/her clothes; next to his/her skin:* du doonyaa.

**cloud**

*cloud cover; sky, cloudy sky:* góos'. *cloud(s):* k̲ugóos'.

**cloudberry**

*yellow cloudberry:* néx̲'w.

**cloudy**

*it was cloudy:* GÓOS' k̲oowligóos'.

**club**

*club:* x'ús'. *s/he clubbed it; s/he hit it on the head:* X̲EECH ashaawax̲ích.

**coal**

*coal:* t'ooch' té.

**coal oil**

*kerosene; coal oil:* ux̲ganhéen.

**coat**

*coat, overcoat:* kinaa.át, kinaak.át.

**cobbler**

*shoemaker, cobbler:* téel layeix̲í.

**cockle**

*cockle:* yalooleit.

**cod**

*ling cod:* s'áax̲'. *tomcod:* chudéi.

**coffee**

*coffee:* káaxwei. *coffee; hot water:* yat'aayi héen.

**coffin**

*coffin; casket:* k̲aa daakeidí.

**coho**

*L'uknax̲.ádi, locally called "Coho"; a clan of the Raven moiety whose principal crest is the Coho:* L'uknax̲.ádi.

**coho salmon**

*coho salmon; silver salmon:* l'ook. *sockeye or coho salmon that has entered fresh water:* x̲'áakw.

**coin**

*money, coin, dollar:* dáanaa.

**cold**

*chest cold:* k̲usa.áat' néekw. *cold weather:* k̲usa.áat'. *the weather was cold:* .AAT' k̲uwsi.áat'.

**cold sore**

*cold sore:* x̲'atl'ook̲.

**cold water**

*cold water:* si.áat'i héen.

**color**

*its color:* a kaséik̲'u.

**colored**

*he/she/it is bruised; it's colored; it's discolored:* YEIS' kawdiyés'.

**colt**

*colt:* gawdáan yádi.

**comb**

*comb:* xéidu, k̲aa shaksayéigu.

**come out**

*it fell (small, compact object); it came out (sun, moon):* XEEX daak uwaxíx.

**comet**

*comet; falling star:* xoodzí.

**comfort**

*comfort:* k̲aa toowú lat'aa. *he/she/it comforted him/her:* T'AA du toowú awlit'áa.

**commander**

*director, planner; commander:* át k̲ukawu.aag̲ú.

**community**

*people; community:* k̲u.oo.

**complete**

*s/he finished it; s/he completed it:* NEI yan awsinéi, HEEK yan ashawlihík. *to completion:* yax̲.

**complexion**

*his/her skin, complexion:* du dook.

**component**

*its what it is (to be) made of; its parts, components, materials:* a shagóon.

**compose**

*s/he composed a song; s/he called forth a response (from opposite clan by means of a song):* X̲OOX̲ shukawlix̲oox̲.

**comrade**

*his/her clan brother or sister, distant relative, comrade:* du t'aag̲í.

**conceited**

*s/he is proud; s/he is conceited; s/he is particular; s/he is picky:* G̲EI sh tukdlig̲éi.

**concentrate**

*s/he exerted his/her full strength on it; s/he concentrated on it; s/he strove for it:* XEECH aawaxích.

**confess**

*s/he said that; s/he confessed that; s/he acknowledged that:* K̲AA[1] yéi yaawak̲aa.

**conflict**

*trouble; conflict:* kaxéel'.

**connect**

*s/he connected it there:* XAAT[1] aadé akawsixát.

**connected**

*it's connected there; it's tied there:* XAAT[1] aadé ksixát.

**conscious**

*consciousness, thought process, thinking:* yoo tutánk.

**consider**

*s/he thought about it; s/he considered it; s/he made up his/her mind about it:* TAAN a daa yoo toowatán. *they thought about it; they considered it; they made up their minds about it:* .AAT$^{2}$ a daa yoo (ha)s tuwli.át.

**conspicuous**

*he/she/it was fancy; he/she/it was conspicuous; he/she/it was prominent:* G̱EI kawlig̱éi.

**construct**

*s/he built it; s/he made it; s/he constructed it:* YEIX̱$^{1}$ awliyéx̱.

**container**

*container for it:* daakeit. *container for traveling provisions; lunch basket, lunch container:* wóow daakeit.

**contribute**

*s/he contributed; s/he donated:* G̱EEX' kawdig̱éex'. *s/he contributed to it; s/he donated to it; s/he added to it:* G̱EEX' át kawdig̱íx'.

**control**

*out of control; blindly:* ux̱ kei.

**conversation**

*conversation, dialog; talk, discourse (between more than one person):* yoo x̱'ala.átk.

**converse**

*they conversed; they spoke; they talked:* .AAT$^{2}$ yoo (ha)s x̱'awli.át.

**cook**

*s/he cooked:* .EE at wusi.ée. *s/he cooked it:* .EE awsi.ée.

**cooked**

*it's cooked:* .EE yan uwa.ée.

**copper**

*copper:* eeḵ.

**copper shield**

*copper shield:* tináa.

**coral**

*coral:* hintakx'úxi, hintaak x'óosi. *petrified coral:* yéil kawóodi.

**cord**

*cord (of wood):* at kaayí.

**cork**

*cork, plug:* a x̱'adéex'i.

**cork up**

*s/he corked it up; s/he covered his/her mouth:* DEEX' ax̱'eiwadíx'.

**cormorant**
*cormorant:* yook̲.

**corner**
*corner:* gúkshi. *(in) the corner of it:* a gukshatú, a gukshitú (An). *(in) the corner, (on or along) the edge, end of it:* a shutú.

**correctional facility**
*correctional facility:* áa k̲uyadujee yé.

**corset**
*corset:* kasanka.át.

**cotton**
*cotton; cotton blanket, quilt:* kast'áat'. *cottongrass, Alaska cotton, swamp cotton:* sháchk kax̲'wáal'i.

**cottonwood**
*cottonwood:* dúk̲.

**country**
*earth; land, country; soil:* tl'átk.

**courage**
*strength of mind or heart; courage; resolve:* toowú latseen.

**cousin**
*her brother, cousin:* du éek'. *her fraternal niece, nephew, cousin:* du káalk'w. *her older sister, cousin:* du shátx̲. *her younger sister; his younger brother; cousin:* du kéek'. *his/her daughter, cousin:* du sée. *his/her paternal uncle, cousin:* du sáni. *his/her son, cousin:* du yéet.

**cove**
*cove; bight:* kunag̲eey. *in a fort, shelter, cove:* noow g̲ei.

**cover**
*(draped) over it, covering it:* a náa. *its covering; cover (over a large opening or something without an opening):* a kaháadi. *its lid, cover (of pot, etc.):* a yana.áat'ani. *over it, covering it (a container or something with an opening):* a yanáa. *s/he corked it up; s/he covered his/her mouth:* DEEX' ax̲'eiwadíx'. *s/he covered it:* TAAN a yanáax̲ at wootaan. *s/he pulled it over him/her/it; s/he covered him/her/it with it:* YEESH a káx̲ aawayeesh. *smokehole cover:* gaan x̲'aháadi.

**cow**
*bison, buffalo; ox, muskox; cow; horse:* xaas. *cow:* wasóos.

**coward**
*coward:* k̲'atx̲áan.

**crab**
*crab (king, spider):* x'éix̲. *dungeness crab:* s'áaw.

**cradleboard**
*cradleboard; papoose carrier:* t'ook.

**cramp**

*it cramped; it's cramping; he/she/it got shocked (by electricity):* SHOOK' kawdlishúk'.

**cranberry**

*bog cranberry; low bush cranberry:* k̲'eishkaháagu. *high bush cranberry:* kaxwéix̲. *lowbush cranberry, bog cranberry:* dáxw.

**crane**

*heron; Canada crane:* láx̲'. *sandhill crane:* dóol.

**cranky**

*crankiness; irritation; petulance:* k̲ukahín.

**crawl**

*he/she/it crawled there on his/her/its belly; he/she/it crept there on his/her/its belly:* TLOOX' aadé wootlóox'. *he/she/it is crawling around on his/her/its belly; he/she/it crawled around on his/her/its belly; he/she/it is creeping around on his/her/its belly; he/she/it crept around on his/her/its belly; he/she/it is squirming around; he/she/it squirmed around:* TLOOX' át wootlóox'. *s/he crawled away (from the open):* G̲WAAT'[1] daak̲ wudig̲wát'. *s/he is crawling around there; s/he crawled around there:* G̲WAAT'[1] át wudig̲wáat'.

**crazy**

*crazy; insane; disturbed; mentally unbalanced:* sh kahaadí. *person who acts crazy or possesssed:* lookanáa. *s/he was noisy; s/he was crazy; s/he was lively:* .OOS wuli.oos.

**cream**

*face cream; cold cream:* yaneis'í (T).

**creek**

*creek; small stream:* héenák'w. *fishing hole; hole in stream, river, creek:* ísh. *mouth of it (a river, creek):* a wát. *river, stream, creek:* héen. *river; stream; creek:* kanaadaayi héen, naadaayi héen. *salmon creek:* x̲áat héeni.

**creep**

*he/she/it crawled there on his/her/its belly; he/she/it crept there on his/her/its belly:* TLOOX' aadé wootlóox'. *he/she/it is crawling around on his/her/its belly; he/she/it crawled around on his/her/its belly; he/she/it is creeping around on his/her/its belly; he/she/it crept around on his/her/its belly; he/she/it is squirming around; he/she/it squirmed around:* TLOOX' át wootlóox'.

**crest**

*(on) the back of it (fish); on the crest, ridge, backbone of it (hill, ridge, point):* a litká. *wall crest; wall screen:* x̲'éen.

**crevice**

*rock crevice; fissure in rock:* té k̲áas'.

**crew**

*worker; crew:* ganaswáan.

**crochet**
*knitting, crocheting:* kasné. *s/he knitted; s/he crocheted; s/he wove:* NEI kawdzinéi. *s/he made it (by weaving, knitting, crocheting); s/he mended it (net):* NEI akawsinei.

**crooked**
*it's crooked; s/he is crooked, wicked:* TEEX̱' kawdzitíx̱'.

**cross**
*cross:* kanéist.

**crosspiece**
*its crosspiece (of boat, snowshoe); thwart (of boat):* yax̱ak'áaw.

**crotch**
*his/her crotch; between his/her legs:* du g̱atsx̱'áak.

**crow**
*crow:* ts'axweil.

**crowbar**
*pry; stick or tool for prying; crowbar:* kít'aa.

**crowd**
*they crowded the place; they all went there:* HAA át has yawdiháa. *townspeople; crowd or large group of people:* aantḵeení.

**cry**
*crying, weeping:* g̱aax̱. *he/she/it cried out:* G̱AAX̱ kawdig̱aax̱. *person who cries easily:* ánk'w. *s/he asked for it; s/he cried for it:* G̱AAX̱ awdzig̱áax̱. *s/he cried:* G̱AAX̱ woog̱aax̱.

**cup**
*cup; can:* gúx'aa.

**cure**
*s/he saved him/her/it; s/he healed him/her/it; s/he cured him/her/it:* NEIX̱ awsineix̱. *s/he was saved; s/he was healed; s/he was cured; s/he recovered; s/he was satisfied:* NEIX̱ wooneix̱.

**curious**
*curiosity:* yoo at koojeek.

**curlew**
*curlew:* ayaheeyáa.

**curly**
*his/her curly hair:* du shakakóoch'i.

**currant**
*black currants or swamp currants:* kaneilts'íkw (At). *gray currant, stink currant:* shaax̱.

**currants**
*black currants or swamp currants:* kaneilts'ákw. *currants:* kadooheix̱.aa.

**current**
*current; tidal action:* héen kanadaayí. *current, tide:* haat.

**curtain**
*window curtain:* x̲aawaag̲éi kas'ísayi.

**cut**
*cut; knife wound:* k̲'éik̲'w. *s/he cut him/her/it (accidentally); s/he wounded him/her/it:* K̲'EIK'W[1] aawak̲'ék'w. *s/he cut himself/herself; s/he wounded himself/herself (with a sharp instrument):* K̲'EIK'W[1] sh wudik̲'ék'w. *s/he cut it off; s/he sawed it off:* XAASH aax̲ aawaxásh. *s/he cut it (rope-like object):* XAASH awlixaash. *s/he cut it up; s/he carved it; s/he sliced it:* XAASH akaawaxaash. *s/he cut it (with a knife); s/he sawed it:* XAASH aawaxaash. *s/he cut; s/he did some cutting:* XAASH wudixaash.

**cute**
*Cute!:* Óos'k'!. *she is pretty; it is cute:* G̲EI shakligéi.

**daddy long legs**
*daddy long legs; mosquito eater:* táax'aa x̲'uskudayáat'.

**dagger**
*dagger; machete, long knife:* gwálaa. *double-ended dagger:* shak'áts'.

**Dak̲l'aweidí**
*Dak̲l'aweidí, locally called "Killer Whale"; a clan of the Eagle moiety whose principal crest is the Killer Whale:* Dak̲l'aweidí.

**dam**
*beaver dam:* s'igeidí áayi.

**dance**
*dance:* al'eix̲. *neck cord worn for dance:* kaséik̲'w. *s/he danced:* L'EIX̲ aawal'eix̲. *s/he danced out:* L'EIX̲ daak aawal'éx̲. *s/he started dancing:* L'EIX̲ g̲unéi aawal'éx̲.

**dandruff**
*dandruff:* shakéil'.

**dangerous**
*it was scary; it was dangerous:* X̲ÉITL'SHÁN kawlix̲éitl'shán.

**dark**
*it's dark:* G̲EET k̲ukawjig̲ít.

**darkness**
*darkness:* kag̲ít.

**daughter**
*his/her daughter, cousin:* du sée.

**dawn**
*dawn, daybreak:* k̲ee.á, k̲eex̲'é, k̲eix̲'é (An), k̲ei.á.

**day**
*dawn, daybreak:* k̲ee.á, k̲ei.á. *day, afternoon:* yakyee, yagiyee, yagee (T). *the other day; a few days ago:* tliyaatgé.

**deaf**
*deaf person:* l k̲ool.áx̲ji.

**death**
*death:* naná.

**decide**
*s/he made a decision about it:* TAAN a daa toowditaan. *s/he made a decision; s/he planned it:* .AAK̲W yan akaawa.ák̲w.

**deck**
*deck of a boat:* yaakw x̲uká.

**deep**
*it became deep:* DLAAN woodlaan. *it got that deep:* DLAAN yéi kaawadláan. *it's piled up; it's deep:* DLAAN yan kaawadlán.

**deer**
*deer:* g̲uwakaan, k̲uwakaan (TC). *deer or other ruminant having a horn with only one point:* shataag̲áa. *deer or other ruminant with full-grown horns:* shals'áaw. *deer sprouting horns:* shak'únts'. *deer with full-grown antlers:* shalas'áaw. *young deer:* yagootl.

**deer cabbage**
*deer cabbage, lily-of-the-valley:* k'uwaaní.

**defeat**
*s/he won it; s/he got it; s/he accomplished it; s/he defeated him/her:* DLAAK̲ ayaawadlaak̲.

**Deisheetaan**
*Deisheetaan, locally called "Beaver"; a clan of the Raven moiety whose principal crest is the Beaver:* Deisheetaan.

**delayed**
*he/she/it got hung up; s/he got delayed; s/he got stuck:* K'EEX̲' yanax̲ wushik'éex̲'. *s/he is delayed:* SEEK[1] yaawasík.

**deliver**
*s/he let him/her/it go; s/he released him/her/it; s/he left him/her/it; s/he delivered it:* NAAK̲[2] ajeewanák̲.

**demonstrate**
*s/he demonstrated it to him/her; s/he showed him/her how to do it; s/he performed it for him/her:* NEI du wak̲shiyeex' yéi awsinei.

**den**
*beaver's den:* s'igeidí x̲aayí. *its den, lair (of animal, undergound):* a k̲oowú.

**dentist**

*dentist:* k̲aa oox̲ layeix̲í, k̲aa oox̲ yei daanéiyi.

**devilfish**

*octopus; devilfish:* náak̲w.

**devil's club**

*devil's club:* s'áxt'.

**diaper**

*diaper:* tuk̲daa.át.

**different**

*different:* g̲unayéide. *different directions:* wooshdakádin. *differently:* woosh g̲unayáade, woosh g̲unayáade, woosh g̲uwanyáade. *differently from it:* a g̲unayáade, a g̲uwanyáade (An). *different ones; variety:* woosh g̲unayáade aa. *different, other:* ch'a g̲óot.

**difficult**

*it was difficult:* DZEE wulidzée, T'EEX' woot'éex'.

**dig**

*s/he dug it:* HAA akaawaháa. *s/he dug it up:* HAA kei akaawaháa. *s/he gardened; s/he did some digging:* HAA akaawahaa.

**dime**

*dime:* gút.

**<diminutive>**

*little; precious; [diminutive suffix]:* -k'.

**dipnet**

*dipnet (for eulachon):* deegáa.

**dipper**

*dipper (for dipping water):* sheen x̲'ayee. *dipper, scoop, ladle; brailer bag:* kaxwénaa. *dipper; water ouzel:* hinyikl'eix̲í. *water dipper; ladle:* héen gúx'aa.

**direction**

*different directions:* wooshdakádin.

**director**

*director, planner; commander:* át k̲ukawu.aag̲ú.

**dirt**

*black with dirt, filth, stain:* ts'ák̲l. *dirt, dust:* ch'éix̲'w. *dirt; scrap(s); rubbish, trash, clutter; lint:* s'eex. *soil; dirt:* l'éx̲'kw.

**dirty**

*he/she/it is dirty:* CH'EIX̲'W wulich'éx̲'w. *s/he got it dirty:* CH'EIX̲'W awlich'éx̲'w.

**disappear**

*he/she/it disappeared from there:* YAA[1] aadáx̲ kawdiyaa.

**discharge**

*pus; discharge (from a sore, wound); sore, wound that discharges pus:* k̲éet'.

**disciple**

*his/her follower, disciple:* du ítx̲ nagoodí. *his/her followers, disciples:* du ítx̲ na.aadí.

**discolored**

*he/she/it is bruised; it's colored; it's discolored:* YEIS' kawdiyés'.

**disease**

*sickness; illness; disease:* néekw.

**dish**

*dish; plate:* s'íx'. *dish; platter:* kélaa, kílaa. *food container; pot or pan; dish, large bowl:* x̲'ayeit.

**dissolve**

*it melted; it dissolved; it thawed:* LAA[1] wuliláa.

**distribute**

*s/he put up food; s/he stored up food (for the winter); s/he preserved food; s/he finished distributing things (at party):* GAA yan akawligáa.

**dive**

*it dove into the water; it slapped its tail down into the water:* T'AAKW héende awjit'ákw.

**do**

*s/he did it; s/he behaved that way:* NOOK[2] yéi k̲oowanook. *s/he does it; s/he is doing it; s/he works on it; s/he is working on it:* NEI yéi adaanéi. *s/he fixed it; s/he did that to it:* NEI yéi awsinei. *s/he's in the habit of doing it:* TAAN akwshitán. *s/he worked; s/he did that:* NEI yéi jeewanei.

**dock**

*at the landing of a dock:* dzeit shuyee. *dock, pier:* dzeit.

**doctor**

*doctor:* k̲aa daa yaséix̲i. *healer; doctor; nurse:* k̲unáagu.

**dog**

*dog:* keitl.

**dogfish**

*dogfish; mudshark:* x'átgu.

**dog salmon**

*dog salmon; chum salmon:* téel'. *L'eeneidí, locally called "Dog Salmon"; a clan of the Raven moiety whose principal crest is the Dog Salmon:* L'eeneidí. *Suk̲teeneidí, locally called "Dog Salmon"; a clan of the Raven moiety whose principal crest is the Dog Salmon:* Suk̲teeneidí.

**doll**

*doll:* sée.

**dollar**
*half dollar; fifty cents:* dáanaa shoowú. *money, coin, dollar:* dáanaa.

**dolly**
*wheelbarrow; hand truck, dolly:* koojúxwaa (An), koojúxaa (TC).

**dolphin**
*dolphin:* k̲’aan.

**domineering**
*brave, fearless man; temperamental, quick-tempered, hot-headed or domineering man:* x’ig̲aak̲áa.

**donate**
*s/he contributed; s/he donated:* G̲EEX’ kawdig̲éex’. *s/he contributed to it; s/he donated to it; s/he added to it:* G̲EEX’ át kawdig̲íx’. *s/he donated it; s/he loaded it (gun); s/he shot it (basketball):* G̲EEX’ akaawag̲éex’.

**donkey**
*donkey:* gukkudayáat’.

**door**
*door:* x̲’aháat.

**doorway**
*doorway:* x̲’awool.

**dove**
*pigeon or dove:* gus’yé kindachooneidí.

**down**
*down; out of boat, vehicle:* yei.

**downstream**
*downstream; south:* éex. *downstream; south; lower 48 states, (locally: down south):* ixkée. *(toward) downstream:* íxde.

**drag**
*he/she/it dragged it there; s/he pulled it there (esp. light object or solid, stiff object):* X̲OOT’[1] aadé aawax̲óot’. *he/she/it is dragging him/her/it around; he/she/it dragged him/her/it around:* X̲OOT’[1] át aawax̲óot’. *s/he dragged it away; s/he pulled it away; s/he hauled it away; (heavy object or limp object such as dead animal):* XAAT’ aadáx̲ awsixáat’. *s/he dragged it; s/he pulled it; s/he hauled it (esp. heavy object or limp object such as dead animal):* XAAT’ awsixáat’. *s/he dragged it there; s/he pulled it there; s/he hauled it there (by motor power):* X̲OOT’[1] aadé awsix̲óot’. *s/he dragged it there; s/he pulled it there; s/he hauled it there; (heavy object or limp object such as dead animal):* XAAT’ aadé awsixáat’. *s/he pulled it in; s/he dragged it in (esp. light object or solid, stiff object):* X̲OOT’[1] yan aawax̲út’.

**dragonfly**
*dragonfly:* k̲aashashx̲áaw.

**drain**

*it drained out; it went dry:* KOOX kawlikoox. *s/he strained it; s/he filtered it; s/he drained it off:* CHAA akawlicháa.

**draw**

*s/he wrote:* XEET kawshixít.

**draw$^{1}$**

*s/he wrote it; s/he drew it; s/he painted it; s/he photographed it; s/he took X-rays of it:* XEET akawshixít.

**draw$^{2}$**

*draw, gully, box canyon:* séet.

**dress**

*dress:* l'aak.

**dress up**

*s/he is dressed up:* NEI yan sh wudzinéi.

**dried**

*dried thing, esp. food:* at kaawaxúkw.

**drift**

*he/she/it drifted out to sea; he/she/it is drifting out to sea; he/she/it floated out to sea; he/she/it is floating out to sea:* HAASH daak wulihásh. *he/she/it drifted to it; he/she/it floated to it:* HAASH át wulihásh. *it's floating around; it floated around; it's drifting around; it drifted around:* HAASH át wulihaash.

**driftwood**

*driftwood:* nalháashadi. *pile of driftwood, driftlogs; snag pile:* yanxoon. *snag; driftlog, driftwood:* shaaḵ.

**drill**

*drill:* túlaa. *drill bit:* túlx'u.

**drink**

*at hand (for him/her to eat or drink):* du x̱'ax̱án. *for him/her to eat or drink:* du x̱'eis. *s/he drank:* NAA$^{2}$ at wudináa. *s/he drank it:* NAA$^{2}$ awdináa.

**drip**

*drip, leak with dripping:* katl'úḵjaa. *fast drip, leak:* kalóox'jaa, kalóox̱jaa. *fast drip with bubbles:* kúḵjaa. *it's leaking; it's dripping:* X'AAS kawlix'áas. *trickle of water; steady drip or leak:* kax'áasjaa.

**drive**

*s/he drove around it; s/he went around it; s/he circled it (by boat, car):* ḴOOX̱$^{1}$ a daax̱ yaawaḵúx̱. *s/he drove it:* ḴOOX̱$^{1}$ awsiḵoox̱. *s/he drove it there:* ḴOOX̱$^{1}$ aadé awsiḵoox̱. *s/he drove it to it:* ḴOOX̱$^{1}$ át awsiḵúx̱. *s/he drove there; s/he went there (by boat, car):* ḴOOX̱$^{1}$ aadé wooḵoox̱. *s/he drove through it; s/he went through it (by boat, car):* ḴOOX̱$^{1}$ a tóonáx̱ yaawaḵúx̱. *s/he drove to it; s/he went to it (by boat, car):* ḴOOX̱$^{1}$ át uwaḵúx̱. *s/he is driving along; s/he is going along (by boat, car):* ḴOOX̱$^{1}$

yaa nak̲úx̲. *s/he is driving around; s/he drove around:* K̲OOX̲[1] át wook̲oox̲. *s/he started driving; s/he started going:* K̲OOX̲[1] g̲unéi uwak̲úx̲.

**drum**

*drum:* gaaw.

**drunk**

*drunk; drunkard:* at danáayi, náaw s'aatí. *drunkenness; inebriation; giddiness:* kanashú.

**dry**

*dried and hard; stiff (as canvas, dry fish):* g̲ákw. *it drained out; it went dry:* KOOX kawlikoox. *it dried; it's dry:* XOOK uwaxúk. *s/he dried fish; s/he smoked fish:* X̲'AAN at uwax̲'án. *s/he dried it:* XOOK awsixúk. *s/he is thirsty; it is dry:* KOOX shaawakúx.

**Dry Bay**

*people of Dry Bay:* G̲unaax̲oo K̲wáan.

**duck**

*bufflehead (duck):* hintakx'wás'g̲i. *duck:* gáaxw. *flathead duck:* s'élasheesh. *harlequin duck:* s'ús'. *kind of duck:* hinyikgáaxu. *mallard duck:* kindachooneit. *merganser:* k̲aax̲. *oldsquaw duck:* yaa.aanuné. *scooter duck:* wak̲kals'oox̲' gáaxw, lak'eech'wú.

**due to**

*because of it; due to it; by virtue of it; on the strength of it; encouraged by it:* a tuwáadáx̲.

**dull**

*it's dull; it's blunt:* G̲EEL yaawdig̲íl.

**during**

*along, via; including the time of:* -náx̲. *(sometime) during it (period of time):* a yeen.

**dusk**

*dusk; twilight:* xi.áat.

**dust**

*dirt, dust:* ch'éix̲'w. *dust cloud; snow cloud:* kals'éesjaa. *dust; pollen:* kadánjaa.

**dye**

*dye:* kasék̲'x̲u. *s/he dyed it; s/he stained it:* SEIK̲'W akawlisék̲'w.

**dyed**

*it's dyed; it's stained:* SEIK̲'W kawdisék̲'w.

**eagle**

*bald eagle:* ch'áak'. *immature eagle:* ch'ak'yéis'.

**ear**

*his/her ear:* du gúk.

**earlier**

*just now; a while ago, earlier:* dziyáak.

**earring**

*earring:* guk.át, guk kajaash. *earring; yarn dangling from the ears that sways during dancing:* guk tl'éinx̱w.

**earth**

*earth; land, country; soil:* tl'átk.

**earthquake**

*earthquake:* yoo aan ka.á.

**earwax**

*his/her earwax:* du gukyikk'óox̱'u.

**eat**

*at hand (for him/her to eat or drink):* du x̱'ax̱án. *for him/her to eat or drink:* du x̱'eis. *ready, waiting for him/her to eat, drink; waiting for him/her to speak or finish speaking:* du x̱'ayee. *s/he ate:* X̱AA[1] at uwax̱áa. *s/he ate it:* X̱AA[1] aawax̱áa. *s/he ate it all up:* X̱AA[1] yax̱ ayawsix̱áa.

**ebb**

*the tide went out from under it; the tide ebbed out from under it:* LAA[1] áx̱ woolaa.

**edge**

*edge of it; (to the) side of it:* a wán. *(in) the corner, (on or along) the edge, end of it:* a shutú. *its hem, bottom edge (of coat, dress, shirt); rim (of hat):* a kóon. *on the edge, side of it (as a trail); on the shoulder of it:* a wanká. *separate from it; on the edge, side of it; missing its mark:* a wanáak.

**eel**

*eel:* lóot'.

**eerie**

*it looked terrible; it looked awful; it was eerie; it was unattractive:* JEE[2] kawlijée.

**egg**

*egg (of bird):* k'wát'. *eggs (of eels, etc.):* x̱'íx'. *herring eggs:* g̱áax'w. *it laid an egg:* K'WÁT' awdlik'wát'. *roe, eggs (of fish):* kaháakw.

**eggshell**

*eggshell:* nóox'.

**eight**

*eight:* nas'gadooshú. *eight (people):* nas'gadooshóonáx̱.

**elbow**

*his/her elbow:* du t'eey. *tip of his/her elbow:* du t'iyshú.

**elder**

*adult; elder:* yanwáat.

**elderberry**

*elderberry:* yéil'.

**electricity**

*electricity:* kashóok'.

**eleven**

*eleven:* jinkaat k̲a tléix'. *eleven (people):* jinkaat k̲a tléináx̲.

**email**

*email:* kashóok' yoo x̲'atánk.

**embarassment**

*shame, embarrassment:* kadéix'.

**embrace**

*crook of his/her arm; in his/her embrace:* du jig̲ei.

**embroider**

*s/he embroidered it on it; s/he sewed beads on it:* K̲AA[2] a káa akaawak̲áa.

**emerge**

*he/she/it emerged:* GOOT[1] gági uwagút. *they emerged:* .AAT[1] gági has uwa.át.

**empty**

*its empty shell (of house); empty container:* a xákwti. *s/he poured it out there; s/he emptied it there:* XAA aadé akawsixaa. *s/he poured it there; s/he emptied it there:* XAA át akawsixáa.

**encounter**

*meeting, encountering, intercepting it; (arriving) at the same place or time as it:* du kagé.

**end**

*(in) the corner, (on or along) the edge, end of it:* a shutú. *it came to an end; it was used up:* XEEX shuwaxeex. *it ended there:* TAAN áa yan shukaawatán. *it extends to it; it ends at it:* TAAN át shukatán. *the end of it:* a shú. *the foot of it; below it (raised place); flat area at the end of it (lake); down from the crest of it (slope); the end of it (dock):* a shuwee.

**enemy**

*his/her enemy, adversary:* du yaanaayí.

**engine**

*engine, motor:* washéen.

**enjoyable**

*it was fun; it was enjoyable; it was appealing:* GOO[1] k̲'awsigóo.

**enough**

*(big) enough for him/her to have or use; adequate for him/her:* du jeeg̲áa. *enough, acceptably:* g̲aa. *enough; adequate:* tl'ag̲áa. *less than it; (reaching, falling) short of it; not (big or far) enough for it:* a k̲ín.

**envelope**
*envelope:* x'úx' daakax'úx'u.

**equivalent**
*one that matches it; an amount that matches it; equivalent to it; one like it:* a x̲ooní.

**Eskimo**
*Chugach Eskimo:* Gutéix̲'. *Eskimo:* X̲'atas'aak̲.

**eulachon**
*eulachon; candlefish; hooligan:* saak.

**European**
*White, European, Caucasian (man or person):* Gus'k'iyee k̲wáan, dleit k̲áa.

**even**
*still, even:* ch'u.

**evening**
*evening:* xáanaa.

**every**
*all; every:* ldakát.

**everybody**
*everyone, everybody:* ch'a ldakát k̲áa.

**everything**
*everything:* ch'a ldakát át, ldakát át.

**everywhere**
*everywhere:* ch'a ldakát yé, ldakát yé.

**evil**
*evil, sin:* l ushk'é. *he/she/it was bad; he/she/it was evil:* K'EI tlél wushk'é.

**examine**
*s/he examined it:* .AA[2] a daa yawdzi.aa.

**excess**
*beyond it, more than it; too much; excessively:* a yáanáx̲.

**<exclamation>**
*Check it out!; Wow!:* É!. *Cool it!; Calm down!:* Ch'a keetáanáx̲!. *Cute!:* Óos'k'!. *Don't!; Stop it!:* Ilí!. *[exclamation toward someone who is putting on airs in order to impress others]:* Ha.é!. *Good grief!:* Hadláa!. *Oh no!; Yikes!:* Aganáa!. *Oops!:* Tláp!. *Ouch!:* Hú!. *Poor baby!:* Haa yátx'u ée!. *Poor thing!:* Eesháan!. *See how you are!; Look what you did!:* Doó!. *Shame on you! [reprimand]:* Húsh!. *Shut up!; Be quiet!:* Sh eelk'átl'!. *Stop it!; That's enough!:* Déi áwé!. *That's all!; All gone!; No more!; All done!:* Hóoch!. *Wait!:* Ilí s'é!. *Yikes!; Scary!:* Atskanée!. *Yuck!; Eeeew!:* Ée!. *Yum!:* Éits'k'!.

**exert**
*s/he exerted his/her full strength on it; s/he concentrated on it; s/he strove for it:* XEECH aawaxích.

**exist**
*it existed; s/he was born:* TEE[1] k̲oowdzitee.

**expect**
*s/he anticipated it; s/he foresaw it; s/he expected him/her/it:* TEE[2] ashoowsitee.

**expensive**
*it was expensive; it was precious:* TSEEN x̲'awlitseen.

**explode**
*it exploded:* TOOK[2] kei wjitúk.

**extend**
*it extends around it:* SHOO[1] áx̲ yaawashóo. *it extends to it; it ends at it:* TAAN át shukatán. *it extends up there:* SHOO[1] áx̲ kei wlishóo.

**eye**
*before his/her eyes; where he/she can see (it):* du wak̲shiyee. *corner of his/her eye:* du wak̲shú. *his/her eye:* du waak̲. *inside of his/her eye:* du wak̲latáak, du wak̲ltáak.

**eyebrow**
*his/her eyebrow:* du s'ee, du s'ei.

**eyeglasses**
*eyeglasses:* wak̲dáanaa.

**eyelash**
*his/her eyelash:* du wax̲'ax̲éix̲'u.

**eyelid**
*his/her eyelid:* du wak̲kadoogú.

**face**
*face, (vertical) side, (vertical) surface of it:* a yá. *growth on the face:* yagúnl'. *his/her face:* du yá.

**facing**
*facing it:* a dayéen.

**fact**
*it; that place, time, reason, fact:* á.

**faith**
*faith:* átk' aheen.

**fall[1]**
*he/she/it fell against it (of live creature):* GEET[1] át wudzigít. *he/she/it fell (of live creature):* GEET[1] daak wudzigít. *he/she/it fell there (of live creature):* GEET[1] aadé wdzigeet. *it fell into it (round, spherical object):* XEEX át kaawaxíx. *it fell on it (hard, solid object):* X̲EEN a kát wujix̲ín. *it fell on*

*it; it hit it (of bullet); it spread around (rumor, news):* XEEX át uwaxíx. *it fell on it (of small, compact object):* XEEX a káa wooxeex. *it fell (small, compact object); it came out (sun, moon):* XEEX daak uwaxíx. *it fell through it (round, spherical object):* XEEX anax̲ kaawaxeex. *it's falling around; it's wobbly:* XEEX át wooxeex. *s/he fell on his/her face; s/he fell asleep while sitting up:* GAAS' yan yaawagás'. *s/he fell over it; s/he tripped over it (of live creature):* GEET[1] anax̲ yei wdzigít.

**fall[2]**

*fall; autumn:* yeis.

**false hellebore**

*false hellebore:* s'íksh.

**family**

*his/her family line of descent, side:* du yinaanáx̲.

**famine**

*famine; starvation:* laaxw.

**fancy**

*he/she/it was fancy; he/she/it was conspicuous; he/she/it was prominent:* G̲EI kawlig̲éi.

**far**

*it became that far:* LEI yéi kaawalei.

**farmer**

*farmer:* akahéix̲i.

**fart**

*fart:* g̲wáal'. *noiseless fart:* kóoch'.

**farther over**

*farther over; way over:* tliyaa.

**fascinating**

*it was a sight to behold; it was fascinating to watch:* TÉES'SHÁN kawlitées'shán.

**fast**

*fast:* tláakw. *he/she/it was fast:* SÁTK woosátk.

**fat**

*cracklings of rendered fat, grease unfit for consumption:* dákwtasi. *fat; blubber:* taay. *tallow, hard fat:* toow.

**fate**

*fate; bad luck:* jinaháa. *his/her fate:* du daakashú.

**father**

*his/her father:* du éesh.

**father-in-law**

*his/her father-in-law:* du wóo.

**fathom**
*armspan; fathom:* waat.

**fatigue**
*fatigue:* xweitl.

**fawn**
*fawn:* g̱uwakaan yádi.

**fear**
*fear:* akoolx̱éitl'.

**feast**
*feast, potlatch; party:* ḵu.éex'.

**feather**
*down (feathers):* x̱'wáal'. *feather:* t'aaw. *long feather; quill (of bird):* ḵínaa, ḵénaa.

**feces**
*feces:* gánde nagoodí. *feces; dung:* háatl'.

**feed**
*s/he fed him/her/it; s/he gave him/her/it something to eat:* TEE[2] du x̱'éix̱ at wootee. *s/he fed it to him/her/it; s/he gave it to him/her/it to eat:* TEE[2] du x̱'éix̱ aawatee.

**feel**
*s/he feels that way; s/he wants to do it; s/he feels like doing it:* TEE[1] yéi tuwatee. *s/he felt it:* NOOK[2] jée awdinúk. *s/he felt that way:* NOOK[2] yéi sh tuwdinook.

**feelings**
*his/her inner being; mind; soul; feelings; intention:* du toowú.

**feline**
*man-eating feline; mountain lion; tiger, leopard:* haadaadóoshi.

**female**
*female (animal):* sheech, shich.

**fence**
*fence:* ḵ'anáax̱án.

**fern**
*fiddlehead fern (with edible rhizome):* k'wálx̱. *shield fern:* s'aach.

**fetus**
*her fetus, unborn child:* du kayádi.

**fever**
*fever:* t'aay néekw (AtT).

**field**
*garden; field:* táay.

**fighting**

*fighting; war, conflict:* k̲ulagaaw.

**file**

*file:* x'ádaa.

**fill**

*s/he filled it (with liquid):* TL'EET' ashawlitl'ít'. *s/he filled it (with solids or abstracts):* HEEK ashawlihík.

**filter**

*s/he strained it; s/he filtered it; s/he drained it off:* CHAA akawlicháa.

**filth**

*black with dirt, filth, stain:* ts'ák̲l. *filth, mess; trash, rubbish, garbage:* tl'eex.

**fin**

*its dorsal fin (of killerwhale):* a gooshí.

**find**

*s/he found it:* T'EI[1] aawat'ei. *s/he found it (round, spherical object):* T'EI[1] akaawat'ei.

**fine**

*he/she/it was good; he/she/it got better; he/she/it was fine; he/she/it was pretty:* K'EI wook'éi.

**finger**

*between his/her fingers:* du tl'ek̲x̲'áak. *his/her finger:* du tl'eek̲, du tl'eik̲. *his/her first finger:* du ch'éex̲'i. *his/her little finger:* du wankach'eek̲. *his/her middle finger:* du tl'ik̲tlein, du tl'ek̲tlein. *his/her ring finger:* du laaylg̲águ.

**fingernail**

*his/her fingernail markings:* du x̲aakw eetí. *his/her nail (of finger or toe):* du x̲aakw.

**fingertip**

*his/her fingertip:* du tl'ek̲shá, du tl'ik̲shá.

**finish**

*s/he finished it; s/he completed it:* NEI yan awsinéi, HEEK yan ashawlihík.

**finished**

*he/she/it is ready; he/she/it is finished; he/she/it is prepared; he/she/it is permanent:* NEI yan uwanéi.

**fir**

*fir:* leiyís.

**fire**

*around the fire:* gandaa. *fire:* x̲'aan. *fireside; by the fire, facing the fire:* x̲'aan gook, gangook. *in the fire:* ganaltáak. *s/he built a fire:* .AAK[1] shóot awdi.ák. *s/he lit it (fire); s/he turned it on (light):* GAAN[1] át akawligán.

**fire drill**

*fire drill, hand drill used to start fires by friction:* x̱'aan káx̱ túlaa.

**firestone**

*firestone; iron pyrite:* dáadzi.

**fireweed**

*fireweed:* lóol.

**firewood**

*dry inner part of firewood:* gantuxoogú. *firewood:* gán. *small pieces of firewood; kindling:* gán yátx'i. *wet firewood:* gán tl'áak'.

**first**

*(at) first, originally:* shux'áanáx̱. *(at) first; originally; in the beginning:* shóogunáx̱. *first:* s'é.

**fish**

*aged fish head:* k'ínk'. *bloodline inside fish, along the backbone:* x̱áat k'áax̱'i. *boiled fish:* útlx̱i. *dried fish strips, dried necktie style:* ts'ak'áawásh. *dry fish:* at x̱'éeshi. *fish air-dried in cold weather and allowed to freeze:* chíl xook. *fish cleaned and hung to dry:* kadútlx̱i. *fish heads cooked on ground around fire:* gangukg̱áx̱i. *fish hung over the fire to cook:* g̱íḵs. *fishing hole; hole in stream, river, creek:* ísh. *fish pitchfork:* x̱áat g̱íjaa. *fish roasted whole, strung up by its tail over the fire and twirled periodically:* g̱íḵsaa (T). *fish; salmon:* x̱áat. *fish smoked for a short time with the backbone taken out:* kadúkli. *fish trap:* sháal. *half-dried salmon (smoked):* náayadi. *its dried flesh, strips (of fish):* a x̱'éeshi. *its flesh (of fish):* a x̱'úx̱u. *its skin (of fish):* a xáas'i. *rack for drying fish:* x̱aanás' éinaa. *s/he fished (with a hook); s/he trolled:* T'EIX̱ awdzit'eix̱. *s/he seined; s/he fished (with a net):* G̱EIWOO awdzig̱eiwú. *s/he sportfished; s/he casted:* X̱OOT'[1] shawdlix̱óot'. *soaked dried fish:* téeyí. *whitefish; baby fish; tiny fish:* x̱áat yádi.

**fisherman**

*fisherman (troller):* ast'eix̱í. *halibut fisherman:* cháatl ast'eix̱í. *seine fisherman; seine boat:* asg̱eiwú. *sport fisherman:* ashalx̱óot'i. *troller:* shukalx̱aají.

**fishing rod**

*fishing rod:* shax̱'út'aa.

**fissure**

*rock crevice; fissure in rock:* té ḵáas'.

**five**

*five:* keijín. *five (people):* keijínin憎x̱.

**fix**

*s/he fixed it; s/he did that to it:* NEI yéi awsinei.

**flag**

*flag:* aan kwéiyi.

**flagpole**
*flagpole:* aan kwéiyi tugáas'i.

**flame**
*flame:* ganyal'óot'.

**flank**
*his/her flank, side of his/her belly:* du k̲aatl. *his/her flank, side of his/her body between the ribs and the hip:* du k̲atlyá.

**flashlight**
*flashlight:* kadulg̲úkx̲ s'eenáa, kadulg̲óok s'eenáa.

**flea**
*flea:* tíx.

**flesh**
*his/her flesh:* du daadleeyí. *meat, flesh:* dleey. *the quick (the flesh under the outer skin):* séik̲'w.

**flicker**
*northern flicker:* kóon.

**flint**
*flint:* ín.

**flipper**
*its tail flippers:* a geení.

**float**
*he/she/it drifted out to sea; he/she/it is drifting out to sea; he/she/it floated out to sea; he/she/it is floating out to sea:* HAASH daak wulihásh. *he/she/it drifted to it; he/she/it floated to it:* HAASH át wulihásh. *it's floating around; it floated around; it's drifting around; it drifted around:* HAASH át wulihaash.

**flood**
*flood:* aan galak̲ú. *flood; tide:* k̲ées'. *it flowed through it; it flooded it:* DAA$^{1}$ anax̲ yaawadáa.

**floor**
*floor:* t'áa ká.

**flounder**
*flounder:* dzánti. *starry flounder:* wankashxéet.

**flour**
*flour; bread:* sakwnéin.

**flow**
*it flowed along it:* DAA$^{1}$ áx̲ kaawadaa. *it flowed; it's flowing; it's running (of nose):* DAA$^{1}$ kaawadaa. *it flowed through it; it flooded it:* DAA$^{1}$ anax̲ yaawadáa. *it flowed to it:* DAA$^{1}$ át uwadáa. *it grew; it flowed (stream of water):* .AA$^{3}$ kaawa.aa. *s/he grew it; s/he turned it on (hose); s/he caused it to flow (water):* .AA$^{3}$ akawsi.aa. *the (water) level rose to there; it flowed to there:* DAA$^{1}$ át kaawadáa.

**flower**

*flower; blossom:* k̲'eikaxwéin.

**fly**

*housefly; bluebottle fly:* xéen. *s/he is flying around; s/he flew around:* K̲EEN át wudik̲een. *they flew away from it:* YEECH anák̲ kawdliyeech. *they flew there:* YEECH át kawdliyích. *they're flying around; they flew around:* YEECH át kawdliyeech.

**foam**

*foam:* x̲eil. *foam (on waves); sponge:* teet x̲'achálx̲i. *foam; whitecaps:* x̲eel.

**[focus]**

*[focus + interrogative]:* ágé. *[puts focus on preceding phrase]:* á.

**fog**

*gray; fog:* k̲ugáas'. *steam (visible, in the air); mist, fog (rising from a body of standing water):* x'úkjaa.

**foggy**

*it's foggy; it was foggy:* GWAAS' k̲oowdigwás'.

**follow**

*(following) him, her, it:* du ít. *he/she/it followed it:* GOOT[1] a ítx̲ woogoot. *his/her follower, disciple:* du ítx̲ nagoodí. *his/her followers, disciples:* du ítx̲ na.aadí. *the next one, the following one:* a ít aa.

**food**

*food, a meal:* atx̲á. *food taken home from a feast or dinner to which one was invited:* éenwu. *his/her food scraps, left-over food; crumbs of food left or scattered where s/he has eaten:* du x̲'a.eetí. *leftovers, food scraps:* k̲aa x̲'a.eetí.

**foolishness**

*foolishness; recklessness:* l yaa k̲ooshgé.

**foot**

*at the foot of it:* a x̲'usyee. *foot (measurement):* k̲aa x̲'oos. *his/her foot, leg:* du x̲'oos. *outer side of his/her foot up to the anklebone:* du shutóox̲'. *sole of his/her foot:* du x̲'ustáak. *the base or foot of it (a standing object):* a k'í. *the foot of it; below it (raised place); flat area at the end of it (lake); down from the crest of it (slope); the end of it (dock):* a shuyee, a shuwee. *top of his/her foot:* du ik̲ká. *under his/her feet:* du x̲'usyee.

**foot path**

*foot path:* k̲aa x̲'oos deiyí.

**footprint**

*his/her footprint:* du x̲'us.eetí.

**for**

*(distributed) in the area of; (going) after, (waiting) for; about the time of:* -g̲aa. *for him/her:* du jís, du jeeyís. *for it (a day, week; a dish):* a kayís. *for it; to that end:* a yís. *future (noun), (noun) to be, for (noun):* sákw.

**forehead**

*his/her forehead:* du káak'.

**foresee**

*s/he anticipated it; s/he foresaw it; s/he expected him/her/it:* TEE[2] ashoowsitee.

**forest**

*forest; timbered area:* aasgutú.

**forever**

*forever:* ch'u tleix̲.

**forget**

*s/he forgot:* X'AAK̲W a kát seiwax'ák̲w.

**fork**

*fork:* ách at dusx̲a át. *sharpened stick (for digging up clams, roots, etc.); gardening fork:* káat'.

**form**

*stretcher, form for shaping:* kanágaa.

**for nothing**

*in vain; for nothing; without success:* ch'a g̲ég̲aa.

**fort**

*fort:* noow. *in a fort, shelter, cove:* noow g̲ei.

**four**

*four:* daax'oon. *four (people):* daax'ooninráx̲. *four times:* daax'oondahéen.

**fox**

*black fox:* x̲alt'ooch' naag̲as'éi. *fox; red fox:* naag̲as'éi. *white fox:* x̲aldleit.

**fragrant**

*he/she/it was fragrant; he/she/it smelled sweet:* TS'AA wulits'áa.

**frame**

*tanning frame; frame for stretching skin:* t'éesh.

**freeze**

*it's frozen; it froze; it solidified; it hardened:* T'EEX' wudlit'íx'.

**freezer**

*freezer:* a tóo at dult'ix'x̲i át.

**fresh**

*new; young; fresh:* yées.

**Friday**

*Friday:* keijín yagiyee.

**fried**

*fried food:* a kas'úkx̲u.

**friend**

*his/her relative, friend; his/her tribesman:* du x̲ooní.

**frog**

*G̲aanax̲teidí, locally called "Frog"; a clan of the Raven moiety whose principal crest is the Frog:* G̲aanax̲teidí. *frog:* xíxch'. *Kiks.ádi, locally called "Frog"; a clan of the Raven moiety whose principal crest is the Frog:* Kiks.ádi.

**from**

*from, out of; since:* -dáx̲.

**front**

*front of it; ahead of it:* a shuká.

**frost**

*frost:* kaxwaan.

**frustrating**

*it was difficult:* DZEE wulidzée.

**fry**

*s/he fried it; s/he toasted it:* S'OOK akawlis'úk.

**fry bread**

*fry bread, bannock:* eex̲ kát sakwnein.

**full**

*he/she/it is full:* HEEK shaawahík.

**fun**

*it was fun; it was enjoyable; it was appealing:* GOO[1] k̲'awsigóo.

**fungus**

*bracket fungus:* aasdaag̲áadli.

**fur**

*its hair, fur; its quill(s) (of porcupine):* a x̲aawú.

**future**

*future (noun), (noun) to be, for (noun):* sákw.

**G̲aanax̲teidí**

*G̲aanax̲teidí, locally called "Frog"; a clan of the Raven moiety whose principal crest is the Frog:* G̲aanax̲teidí.

**gaff**

*fish spear with a long pole and detachable gaff hook:* kooxídaa (At). *gaff hook; grappling hook:* k'íx̲'aa.

**gamble**

*s/he gambled; s/he played cards:* K̲AA[3] awdlik̲áa. *s/he shot it (with bow and arrow); s/he chose it (in gambling with sticks):* T'OOK aawat'úk.

**gambling**

*gambling; game of chance:* alk̲áa.

**game**

*checkers; games played using string in the hands:* aldaawáa.

**gangrene**

*rotting sore; gangrene; cancer:* tl'ook̲.

**garbage**

*filth, mess; trash, rubbish, garbage:* tl'eex.

**garden**

*garden; field:* táay. *s/he gardened; s/he did some digging:* HAA akaawahaa.

**gardener**

*gardener:* táay kahéix̲i.

**gather**

*s/he gathered it:* HAA ayawsiháa. *they gathered together:* .AAT[1] woosh kaanáx̲ has wudi.aat, .AAT[1] woosh x̲oot has wudi.át.

**general**

*general; leader of war, battle:* x'áan kanáayi.

**generosity**

*kindness; generosity of heart:* tula.aan.

**gentle**

*s/he is kind; s/he is gentle:* .AAN[1] tuli.aan.

**gentleman**

*respected person; gentleman; lady:* sh yáa awudanéiyi.

**get**

*s/he went to get it:* GOOT[1] aag̲áa woogoot. *s/he won it; s/he got it; s/he accomplished it; s/he defeated him/her:* DLAAK̲ ayaawadlaak̲. *they went to get it:* .AAT[1] aag̲áa has woo.aat.

**get up**

*s/he got up:* NOOK[1] shawdinúk.

**ghost**

*ghost:* s'ig̲eek̲áawu.

**giddy**

*drunkenness; inebriation; giddiness:* kanashú.

**gill**

*its gill (of fish):* a x'éix'u.

**girl**

*girl:* shaatk'iyátsk'u, shaatk'átsk'u. *girls, young women:* shaax'wsáani.

**girlfriend**

*his/her girlfriend:* du shaatk'í.

**give**

*s/he fed him/her/it; s/he gave him/her/it something to eat:* TEE[2] du x̱'éix̱ at wootee. *s/he fed it to him/her/it; s/he gave it to him/her/it to eat:* TEE[2] du x̱'éix̱ aawatee. *s/he gave it to him/her; s/he took it to him/her (container full of liquid or small objects):* .EEN[1] du jeet awsi.ín. *s/he gave it to him/her; s/he took it to him/her (container or hollow object):* TAAN du jeet aawatán. *s/he gave it to him/her; s/he took it to him/her (general, esp. abstract object):* TEE[2] du jeet aawatée. *s/he gave it to him/her; s/he took it to him/her (long, complex object):* TAAN du jeet awsitán. *s/he gave it to him/her; s/he took it to him/her (round object):* TEE[2] du jeet akaawatée. *s/he gave it to him/her; s/he took it to him/her (textile-like object):* .AAX̱[2] du jeet aawa.áx̱. *s/he gave them to him/her; s/he took them to him/her:* NEI du jeet yéi awsinei. *s/he gave them to him/her; s/he took them to him/her (esp. baggage or personal belongings):* .AAT[2] du jeet awli.át. *s/he gave them to him/her; s/he took them to him/her (small, round or hoop-like objects):* .AAT[2] du jeet akawli.át. *s/he sent him/her there; s/he ordered him/her to go there; s/he gave it (in accordance with clan relationship):* NAA[3] aadé akaawanáa.

**gizzard**

*his/her stomach; gizzard (of bird):* du yoowú.

**glacier**

*glacier:* sít'.

**glacier bear**

*glacier bear:* sít' tuxóodzi.

**gland**

*his/her gland:* du daa.itwéis'i.

**glass**

*glass (the substance):* ít'ch.

**glorify**

*praise, glorification:* kashéex̱'.

**gloves**

*rubber gloves:* s'éil' tsáax'.

**go**

*he/she/it arrived there; he/she/it went there:* GOOT[1] át uwagút. *he/she/it went there; he/she/it walked there:* GOOT[1] aadé woogoot. *s/he drove around it; s/he went around it; s/he circled it (by boat, car):* K̲OOX̱[1] a daax̱ yaawak̲úx̱. *s/he drove there; s/he went there (by boat, car):* K̲OOX̱[1] aadé wook̲oox̱. *s/he drove through it; s/he went through it (by boat, car):* K̲OOX̱[1] a tóonáx̱ yaawak̲úx̱. *s/he drove to it; s/he went to it (by boat, car):* K̲OOX̱[1] át uwak̲úx̲. *s/he is driving along; s/he is going along (by boat, car):* K̲OOX̲[1] yaa nak̲úx̲. *s/he is walking along; s/he is going along:* GOOT[1] yaa nagút. *s/he started driving; s/he started going:* K̲OOX̲[1] g̲unéi uwak̲úx̲. *s/he turned back; s/he went back; s/he walked back:* GOOT[1] ayawdigút. *s/he went ashore; s/he came to a stop:* K̲OOX̲[1] yan uwak̲úx̲. *s/he went (by motorized vehicle):* K̲OOX̲[1] wook̲oox̲. *s/he went out to sea:* K̲OOX̲[1] daak uwak̲úx̲. *s/he went to get it:* GOOT[1] aag̲áa woogoot. *the group went there:* K'EET' aadé (ha)s kawdik'éet'. *the group went to it:* K'EET' át has kawdik'ít'. *they are walking along there; they are going along there:* .AAT[1] áx̲ yaa (ha)s na.át. *they crowded the place; they all went there:* HAA át has yawdiháa. *they turned back; they went back; they walked back:* .AAT[1] has ayawdi.át. *they walked there; they arrived there; they went there:* .AAT[1] át has uwa.át. *they walked there; they went there:* .AAT[1] aadé has woo.aat. *they walked through it; they went through it:* .AAT[1] anax̲ has yaawa.át. *they walked up there; they went up there:* .AAT[1] áa kei (ha)s uwa.át. *they went to get it:* .AAT[1] aag̲áa has woo.aat.

**goat**

*mountain goat:* jánwu.

**God**

*God:* Dikáank̲áawu, Dikée aank̲áawu. *God, Lord:* Aank̲áawu.

**gold**

*gold:* góon. *gold-rust; flecked with gold or rust:* katl'áak'.

**goldfinch**

*goldfinch, canary:* s'áas'.

**good**

*he/she/it was good; he/she/it got better; he/she/it was fine; he/she/it was pretty:* K'EI wook'éi. *the weather became good:* K'EI k̲oowak'ei.

**goose**

*brant (small goose):* k̲ín. *Canada goose:* t'aawák̲.

**goose tongue**

*goose tongue:* suk̲téitl'.

**go out**

*it went out (light, fire):* KEES' yakawlikís'.

**gossip**

*gossip, rumormonger:* niks'aatí. *gossip; rumormonger:* neek shatl'ék̲x'u, neek s'aatí (T). *news; gossip, rumor:* neek.

**grab**

*s/he caught it; s/he grabbed him/her/it; s/he arrested him/her; s/he trapped him/her/it:* SHAAT aawasháat.

**grandchild**

*his/her grandchild:* du dachx̲án.

**grandfather**
*Grandmother!; Grandfather!:* Léelk'w!.

**grandmother**
*Grandmother!; Grandfather!:* Léelk'w!.

**grandparent**
*his/her grandparent:* du áali, du léelk'w. *his/her grandparent (term of respect):* du daakanóox'u.

**granite**
*granite:* x̱éel.

**grass**
*grass:* chookán. *hairy grass, seaweed on which herring spawn:* né. *timothy grass (used for basket decoration):* sháak.

**grateful**
*s/he was grateful; s/he was thankful; s/he was satisfied:* TEE[1] sh tóog̱áa wditee.

**gravel**
*fine sand or gravel:* l'éiw yátx'i. *sandbar; gravel bar; sand beach; gravel beach:* xákw. *sand; gravel:* l'éiw.

**graveyard**
*graveyard:* ḵaanaawú tl'átgi.

**gray**
*gray:* lawúx̱. *gray; fog:* ḵugáas'. *gray hair:* du shashaaní. *grayish; blond (hair):* l'áax̱'.

**grayling**
*grayling:* t'ási.

**grease**
*cracklings of rendered fat, grease unfit for consumption:* dákwtasi. *large box for storing grease, oil:* daneit. *oil, grease:* eex̱, eix̱ (C). *oil, grease (for coating skin or rubbing); lotion; liniment:* neis'.

**grebe**
*horned grebe or red-necked grebe:* cháax̱.

**green**
*green, light blue:* s'oow. *green, unripe berry:* kax̱'át'. *they're unripe; they're green (of berries):* X̱'AAT' kadlix̱'át'.

**greenstone**
*greenstone:* s'oow.

**grin**
*s/he is grinning; s/he is smiling:* NOOTS[1] at kaawanúts.

**grindstone**
*grindstone:* g̱íl'aa.

**grip**
*his/her grip:* du jintú.

**groan**
*mourning, wailing, loud weeping or crying; wail, groan, moan:* kasG̱aax̱.

**groundhog**
*hoary marmot; groundhog, whistler:* s'aax̱.

**group**
*townspeople; crowd or large group of people:* aantḵeení.

**grouse**
*blue grouse:* núkt. *spruce grouse, spruce hen; chicken:* káax'.

**grow**
*it grew:* .AA$^{3}$ kawsi.aa. *it grew; it flowed (stream of water):* .AA$^{3}$ kaawa.aa. *s/he grew it; s/he turned it on (hose); s/he caused it to flow (water):* .AA$^{3}$ akawsi.aa. *s/he grew up:* WAAT kei uwawát. *s/he raised him/her/it; s/he grew it:* WAAT awsiwát.

**growl**
*his/her stomach growled:* TOOX̱' du x̱'óol' kawditóox̱'. *his/her stomach is growling:* TOOX̱' du x̱'óol' kastóox̱'.

**growth**
*growth on the face:* yagúnl'. *growth on the trunk of a tree, burl:* gúnl'.

**grub**
*worm; larva; grub; caterpillar; snake:* tl'úk'x̱.

**guard**
*guard, watchman:* at káx̱ adéli.

**gull**
*gull, seagull:* kéidladi.

**gully**
*draw, gully, box canyon:* séet.

**gum**
*gum; lead:* k'óox̱'.

**gumboots**
*gumboots; chiton:* shaaw.

**gums**
*his/her gums:* du ux̱k'idleeyí.

**gun**
*gun, rifle:* óonaa. *gunshot wound:* óonaa eetí.

**gunpowder**
*gunpowder:* at tugáni.

**gurgle**
*his/her stomach is growling:* TOOX̱' du x̱'óol' kastóox̱'.

**gust**

*the wind hit it in gusts:* SHAAT át ayawashát.

**guts**

*his/her intestines, guts:* du naasí. *its internal organs, viscera; its guts:* a yik.ádi.

**habit**

*s/he's in the habit of doing it:* TAAN akwshitán.

**Haida**

*Haida:* Deikeenaa.

**hail**

*hail:* kadás'. *it's pouring rain; it's hailing; it's snowing:* G̱EET aawag̱éet.

**Haines**

*Haines:* Deishú.

**hair**

*gray hair:* du shashaaní. *his/her body hair, fuzz:* du x̱aawú. *his/her curly hair:* du shakakóoch'i. *his/her hair:* du shax̱aawú. *its hair, fur; its quill(s) (of porcupine):* a x̱aawú. *lock of his/her hair; his/her matted hair:* du x'ées'i. *pubic hair:* du xux̱aawú.

**hair pendant**

*hair pendant:* ḵaa shaksayíḵs'i.

**hair pin**

*hair pin:* shax̱'ée x'wál'.

**hairy**

*it's hairy:* X̱AAW daadzix̱áaw.

**half**

*half of it (something cut or broken in half); one side of it (a symmetrical object):* a kígi. *part of it; half of it:* a shoowú.

**halibut**

*halibut:* cháatl. *halibut fisherman:* cháatl ast'eix̱í.

**hammer**

*hammer:* táḵl. *mallet, wooden hammer:* l'oowú táḵl.

**hammock**

*swing, hammock:* g̱eig̱ách'. *swing; hammock:* g̱eeg̱ách'.

**hand**

*back of his/her hand:* du jikóol. *his/her hand:* du jín. *near him/her, by him/her (at hand, for him/her to work with):* du jix̱án. *outer edge of his/her hand:* du jiwán.

**handiwork**

*handiwork, handmade crafts:* ḵaa ji.eetí. *his/her handiwork, artifact:* du ji.eetí.

**handkerchief**

*handkerchief:* lug̲wéinaa.

**handle**

*its handle (stick-like); its shaft (of spear, etc.):* a sáxwdi, a sákwti.

**hang**

*it's hanging there:* SHOO$^1$ áx̲ g̲aashóo. *s/he hung it there (esp. to dry):* TEE$^2$ áx̲ ashayaawatée. *s/he put it there; s/he hung it there; s/he installed it there (general, compact object):* TEE$^2$ áx̲ aawatee.

**happen**

*it happened:* XEEX yaawaxeex. *it happened (of event):* YAA$^1$ yan kawdiyáa. *that happened to him/her/it; that occurred to him/her/it:* NEI yéi woonei. *that's what happened:* NEI yéi at woonei.

**happiness**

*good thoughts; felicity; happiness:* toowú k'é. *joy; happiness:* sagú.

**happy**

*s/he was happy:* K'EI du toowú wook'éi, GOO$^1$ du toowú wsigóo.

**harbor**

*shelter (from wind or weather), harbor:* déili.

**hard**

*dried and hard; stiff (as canvas, dry fish):* g̲ákw. *it's hard:* T'EEX' kasit'éex'.

**harden**

*it hardened:* T'EEX' kaawat'íx'. *it's frozen; it froze; it solidified; it hardened:* T'EEX' wudlit'íx'.

**harpoon**

*fish spear; harpoon for spearing salmon:* dlagwáa.

**hat**

*ceremonial woven root hat with a stack of basket-like cylinders on top:* shadakóox̲'. *hat:* s'áaxw. *headdress, dance hat:* shakee.át. *woven root hat:* x̲aat s'áaxw.

**hatchet**

*hatchet:* shanax̲wáayi yádi.

**hate**

*s/he hated him/her/it:* K'AAN awshik'aan.

**haul**

*s/he dragged it away; s/he pulled it away; s/he hauled it away; (heavy object or limp object such as dead animal):* XAAT' aadáx̲ awsixáat'. *s/he dragged it; s/he pulled it; s/he hauled it (esp. heavy object or limp object such as dead animal):* XAAT' awsixáat'. *s/he dragged it there; s/he pulled it there; s/he hauled it there (by motor power):* X̲OOT'$^1$ aadé awsix̲óot'. *s/he dragged it there; s/he pulled it there; s/he hauled it there; (heavy object or limp object such as dead animal):* XAAT' aadé awsixáat'. *s/he hauled it:* X̲AA$^2$ ayaawax̲áax'w.

**hawk**
*kind of hawk:* gijook, kijook, shaayáal.

**he**
*he, she [independent]:* hú.

**head**
*back of his/her head at the base:* du shaláx̲'. *head of a clan house; master of the house:* hít s'aatí. *head of river, stream:* héen sháak. *head of the bay:* g̲eey tá. *his/her head:* du shá. *his/her occiput; nape of neck; back of head:* du lak'éech'. *its head:* a shá. *over his/her head; covering his/her head:* du shanáa.

**headdress**
*headdress, dance hat:* shakee.át.

**heal**
*healer; doctor; nurse:* k̲unáagu. *s/he saved him/her/it; s/he healed him/her/it; s/he cured him/her/it:* NEIX̲ awsineix̲. *s/he was saved; s/he was healed; s/he was cured; s/he recovered; s/he was satisfied:* NEIX̲ wooneix̲.

**hear**
*hearing:* k̲u.áx̲ch. *s/he can hear it:* .AAX̲[1] aya.áx̲ch. *s/he heard a voice:* .AAX̲[1] aseiwa.áx̲. *s/he heard it:* .AAX̲[1] aawa.áx̲. *s/he hears a voice:* .AAX̲[1] asaya.áx̲ch. *s/he understands him/her; s/he hears (and understands) him/her:* .AAX̲[1] ax̲'aya.áx̲ch.

**hearing aid**
*hearing aid:* k̲u.áx̲ji.

**heart**
*his/her heart:* du téix̲'.

**heating pad**
*heating pad:* kashéek'w gwéil, kashóok' gwéil.

**heavy**
*it got heavy; it was weighty (of abstracts):* DAAL woodál. *something compact and very heavy:* éech'.

**heel**
*his/her heel:* du x̲'eitákw.

**help**
*he/she/it is helping me; s/he helped me:* SHEE[1] ax̲ éet wudishée.

**hem**
*hem of his/her coat, shirt, dress:* du kóon. *its hem, bottom edge (of coat, dress, shirt); rim (of hat):* a kóon.

**hemlock**
*hemlock:* yán. *swamp hemlock:* s'éx̲. *water hemlock:* lingít k'únts'i. *young spruce or hemlock:* dúk̲l'.

**hen**

*spruce grouse, spruce hen; chicken:* káax'.

**her**

*him, her:* du ee~. *him, her, it [object]:* a-. *his/her [possessive]:* du.

**herb**

*leaf, leaves; vegetation, plants, herbs, herbiage:* kayaaní.

**here**

*hand it here, bring it here:* haandé.

**heredity**

*ancestor(s) of his/her clan or nation; his/her background, heredity:* du shagóon.

**heron**

*heron; Canada crane:* láx̱'.

**herring**

*herring:* yaaw. *herring eggs:* g̱áax'w. *herring rake:* xídlaa. *young herring:* sháach'.

**hide[1]**

*he/she/it hid; s/he's hiding:* SEEN awdlisín. *s/he hid it; s/he's hiding it:* SEEN awlisín.

**hide[2]**

*its skin (of animal); hide:* a doogú. *its wrinkled, baggy skin, hide:* a daaleilí.

**hill**

*small hill; mound, knoll:* gooch.

**him**

*him, her:* du ee~. *him, her, it [object]:* a-.

**hindquarter**

*its hindquarters; thigh:* a g̱ádzi.

**hip**

*his/her pelvis, hip:* du ḵáash.

**his**

*his/her [possessive]:* du.

**hit**

*it fell on it; it hit it (of bullet); it spread around (rumor, news):* XEEX át uwaxíx. *s/he clubbed it; s/he hit it on the head:* X̱EECH ashaawax̱ích. *s/he hit him/her in the face; s/he punched him/her:* GWAAL ayaawagwál.

**hither**

*hither, toward speaker:* haat~.

**hold**

*it holds more:* YEIK[2] liyék. *s/he held it open; s/he tore it away (from the hook):* S'EIL' ax̲'eiwas'él'. *s/he held it; s/he captured it:* SHAAT awlisháat.

**hole**

*hole:* wool. *it has a hole in it:* WOOL yawóol.

**Holy Spirit**

*Holy Spirit:* l ulitoogu K̲aa Yakg̲wahéiyagu.

**home**

*home:* neil. *inside, into the house, home:* neil~.

**honey**

*honey:* gandaas'aají háatl'i (T). *honey!:* jáa.

**hoof**

*its hoof:* a gwéinli.

**hook**

*fish hook:* t'eix̲, t'eix̲áa (T). *gaff hook; grappling hook:* k'íx̲'aa. *halibut hook (made of wood):* náxw. *s/he hooked it in the head:* K'EIX̲' ashaawak'éx̲'.

**hooligan**

*eulachon; candlefish; hooligan:* saak. *hooligan oil:* saak eex̲í.

**Hoonah**

*Hoonah:* Xunaa, Gaawt'ak̲.aan.

**hope**

*hope; intention; focus of hopes or thoughts:* tután. *I hope; would that:* gu.aal. *s/he hopes for it:* SHEE[1] át awdishée.

**horizon**

*horizon:* goos' shú.

**horn**

*its horn:* a sheidí.

**horse**

*bison, buffalo; ox, muskox; cow; horse:* xaas. *horse:* gawdáan.

**horsefly**

*horsefly:* xeitl táax'aa.

**horsetail**

*horsetail:* taan x̲'adaadzaayí.

**hot**

*it's burning hot:* T'AAX̲' wusit'áax̲'. *it's hot:* T'AA yaawat'áa. *it's hot; it's warm:* T'AA uwat'áa. *the weather got hot; the weather got warm:* T'AA k̲oowat'áa.

**hot springs**

*hot springs:* t'aay.

**hour**

*hour:* gaaw x̲'áak.

**house**

*house; building:* hít. *house post:* gáas'.

**housefly**

*housefly:* neil yee táax'ayi.

**how**

*how:* wáa sá.

**however**

*although, even though, however, nonetheless, yet:* ch'a aan. *however:* k̲u.aa. *however, any which way:* ch'a koogéiyi.

**how many**

*how many; some number (of):* x'oon sá.

**huckleberry**

*blueberry; huckleberry:* kanat'á. *huckleberry; blueberry:* naanyaa kanat'aayí. *red huckleberry:* tleikatánk.

**Hudson Bay tea**

*Hudson Bay tea:* s'ikshaldéen.

**hummingbird**

*hummingbird:* dagatgiyáa, digitgiyáa.

**hump**

*bump, lump, hump, mound:* gootl.

**humpback salmon**

*Kwaashk'i K̲wáan, locally called "Humpback Salmon"; a clan of the Raven moiety whose principal crest is the Humpback Salmon:* Kwaashk'i K̲wáan. *pink salmon; humpy, humpback salmon:* cháas'.

**hunger**

*hunger:* yaan.

**hungry**

*s/he is hungry:* HAA du éet yaan uwaháa.

**hung up**

*he/she/it got hung up; s/he got delayed; s/he got stuck:* K'EEX̲' yanax̲ wushik'éex̲'.

**hunt**

*hunt:* al'óon. *s/he hunted:* L'OON aawal'óon. *s/he hunted it:* L'OON aawal'óon.

**hunter**

*hunter:* al'óoni.

**hurry**

*war; trouble; rush, hurry:* adawóotl.

**hurt**

*he/she/it is injured; he/she/it is wounded; he/she/it is bruised; s/he is hurting (emotionally):* CHOON wudichún. *s/he got sick; he/she/it hurt; s/he was in pain:* NEEKW woonéekw. *s/he had an accident; s/he got hurt; something bad happened to him/her:* NEI ḵáakwt uwanéi.

**husband**

*her husband:* du x̱úx̱. *his/her husband's clan brother; his/her man, boyfriend, husband:* du ḵáawu.

**I**

*I [independent]:* x̱át. *I [subject]:* x̱a-.

**ice**

*ice:* t'éex'.

**iceberg**

*iceberg:* xáatl.

**if only**

*as if; if only; even if:* óosh.

**illness**

*sickness; illness; disease:* néekw.

**image**

*his/her shadow; image:* du yahaayí.

**imitate**

*s/he imitated him/her; s/he quoted him/her:* TEE[3] ax̱'eiwatee.

**immediately**

*suddenly, immediately, right away:* ch'a yák'w.

**improve**

*s/he improved it; s/he made peace with him/her/it:* K'EI awlik'éi.

**in**

*enclosed within (the folds of) it, between the folds, covers, walls of it:* a g̱ei. *(in) the area of it or around it, (in) its vicinity:* a déin. *in the boat:* yaakw yík. *in the midst of it (a crowd, an activity or event involving several people); in the hubbub:* a ḵóox'.

**indeed**

*indeed, for sure:* dágáa.

**Indian potato**

*bear root, Indian potato:* tsáats.

**infected**

*it's infected:* ḴEET' wudliḵít'.

**in front**

*in front of him/her; his/her geneology, history; his/her ancestors:* du shuká.

**inheritance**

*his/her inheritance; possessions of deceased given to him/her at a feast:* du néix'i.

**injure**

*s/he injured it; s/he wounded it; s/he bruised it:* CHOON awlichún.

**injured**

*he/she/it is injured; he/she/it is wounded; he/she/it is bruised; s/he is hurting (emotionally):* CHOON wudichún.

**inland**

*toward the inland, interior; up to the woods; back (away from the open):* dáḵde. *up in the woods; inland; back (away from the open, away from the water's edge, inside):* daaḵ. *up in the woods; inland; back (away from the open, away from the water's edge, inside); inland; interior:* daḵká.

**insane**

*crazy; insane; disturbed; mentally unbalanced:* sh kahaadí.

**insect**

*crawling insect; spider:* kanas.aadí.

**inside**

*inside, into the house, home:* neil~. *inside it:* a tú. *inside it (a building):* a yee. *inside it (a river, road, boat, or other shallow concave landform or object):* a yík. *the inside of it (clothing, bedding); lining it:* a t'einyaa. *the inside surface of its bottom (of container, vessel):* a taká.

**install**

*s/he put it there; s/he hung it there; s/he installed it there (general, compact object):* TEE[2] áx̱ aawatee.

**instruct**

*s/he gave him/her orders; s/he instructed him/her:* ḴAA[1] áa ajikaawaḵaa, .AAḴW át akaawa.aaḵw. *s/he instructed him/her; s/he advised him/her:* JAA ashukaawajáa.

**instructions**

*according to his/her words, instructions:* du x̱'ayáx̱.

**intention**

*his/her inner being; mind; soul; feelings; intention:* du toowú. *hope; intention; focus of hopes or thoughts:* tután.

**interior**

*toward the inland, interior; up to the woods; back (away from the open):* dáḵde. *up in the woods; inland; back (away from the open, away from the water's edge, inside); inland; interior:* daḵká.

**[interrogative]**

*[focus + interrogative]:* ágé. *[interrogative - marks WH-questions]:* sá. *[interrogative marks yes-no questions]:* gé.

**intestine**
*his/her intestines, guts:* du naasí.

**in the way**
*in its way; blocking its way; acting as a shield for it:* a yinaa.

**into**
*into a boat, vehicle:* yaax̱.

**in vain**
*in vain; for nothing; without success:* ch'a g̱ég̱aa.

**investigate**
*s/he investigated it; s/he researched it:* TLAAKW akaawatlaakw.

**invite**
*s/he invited him/her:* .EEX' aawa.éex'.

**iron**
*iron (for ironing):* kax̱'íl'aa. *iron, tin:* g̱ayéis', iḵyéis'.

**island**
*flat-topped island with steep sides; low flat island or hill:* noow. *island:* x'áat'. *nucleus of emerging river island; reef above high tide level:* shaltláax̱.

**isthmus**
*portage, passage across it; its isthmus:* a góon.

**it**
*him, her, it [object]:* a-. *it; that place, time, reason, fact:* á.

**itch**
*itch; rash:* kaxweitl. *it's itchy; it tickles:* XWEITL kawlixwétl.

**its**
*its [possessive]:* a.

**jab**
*s/he poked it; s/he jabbed at it; s/he speared it:* TAAḴ[1] aawatáḵ.

**jail**
*jail:* g̱ayéis' hít.

**jailer**
*keeper of the key; jailer; night watchman:* katíx̱'aa s'aatí.

**jaw**
*his/her jawbone; jaws:* du x̱'astus'aag̱í. *his/her lower jaw, mandible:* du x̱'ás'.

**jellyfish**
*jellyfish:* taakw aanási.

**job**
*work, job:* yéi jiné.

**joint**

*his/her joints:* du daa.eit x̱'áak.

**joist**

*piling, foundation post; floor joist:* hít tayeegáas'i.

**joy**

*joy; happiness:* sagú. *s/he brought it onto him/her (esp. shame, blame, joy):* TEE$^{2}$ du kát ashuwatée.

**jug**

*bottle; jug:* t'ooch'ineit, ín x'eesháa. *pitcher; jug:* ḵ'ateil.

**juice**

*apple juice:* x'áax' kahéeni. *juice:* at kahéeni. *orange juice:* áanjís kahéeni.

**jump**

*he/she/it is jumping around; he/she/it jumped around:* K'EIN át wujik'éin. *they jumped:* K'EIN kei has kawduwak'én.

**Juneau**

*Juneau; Gold Creek (in Juneau):* Dzántik'i Héeni.

**just**

*just, simply; just then:* tle. *only, just:* ch'as. *the very, just:* ch'a.

**just now**

*just now; a while ago, earlier:* dziyáak. *just now; just then; still; yet:* yeisú.

**Ḵaach.ádi**

*Ḵaach.ádi, locally called "Sockeye"; a clan of the Raven moiety whose principal crest is the Sockeye:* Ḵaach.ádi.

**Kaagwaantaan**

*Kaagwaantaan, locally called "Wolf"; a clan of the Eagle moiety whose principal crest is the Wolf:* Kaagwaantaan.

**Kake**

*Kake:* Ḵéex̱', Ḵéix̱'. *people of Kake:* Ḵéex̱' Ḵwáan.

**Kaliakh River**

*people of Kaliakh River (Cape Yakataga to Controller Bay):* G̱alyáx̱ Ḵwáan.

**kelp**

*bull kelp:* sú. *kelp:* geesh. *seaweed, kelp on which herring spawn:* daaw.

**kerchief**

*headscarf, kerchief covering the head:* shadaa.át.

**kerosene**

*kerosene; coal oil:* ux̱ganhéen.

**Ketchikan**

*Ketchikan:* Kichx̱áan.

**key**

*keeper of the key; jailer; night watchman:* katíx̲'aa s'aatí. *key:* katíx̲'aa.

**kick**

*s/he kicked it; s/he stamped on it:* TSEIX̲ aawatséx̲.

**Kiks.ádi**

*Kiks.ádi, locally called "Frog"; a clan of the Raven moiety whose principal crest is the Frog:* Kiks.ádi.

**kill**

*s/he killed him/her/it; s/he let it go:* JAAK̲ aawaják̲.

**killer whale**

*Dak̲l'aweidí, locally called "Killer Whale"; a clan of the Eagle moiety whose principal crest is the Killer Whale:* Dak̲l'aweidí. *Tsaagweidí; a clan of the Eagle moiety whose principal crests are the Seal and Killerwhale:* Tsaagweidí.

**killerwhale**

*killerwhale:* kéet.

**Killisnoo**

*Killisnoo:* Kenasnoow.

**kind**

*s/he is kind; s/he is gentle:* .AAN[1] tuli.aan.

**kindling**

*kindling:* gán kak̲ás'ti.

**kindness**

*kindness; generosity of heart:* tula.aan.

**kingfisher**

*kingfisher:* tlax̲aneis'.

**king salmon**

*king salmon; chinook salmon; spring salmon:* t'á.

**kinnikinnick**

*alpine bearberry, kinnikinnick:* tínx.

**kinsman**

*his/her kinsman, moiety mate:* du een aa.

**kiss**

*s/he kissed me:* .AA[2] ax̲ x̲'éit yawdzi.áa.

**kitten**

*kitten:* dóosh yádi.

**Klawock**

*Klawock:* Lawáak. *people of Klawock:* Hinyaa K̲wáan.

**Klukwan**

*Klukwan:* Tlákw Aan.

**knead**

*s/he kneaded it:* CHOOX akaawachúx.

**knee**

*end of his/her knee:* du kiyshá. *his/her knee:* du keey. *underside of his/her knee; (inside of) his/her lower leg:* du saayee.

**kneecap**

*his/her kneecap:* du kiyshakanóox'u, du keey shakanóox'u.

**knife**

*curved carving knife:* yoo katan lítaa. *dagger; machete, long knife:* gwálaa. *knife:* lítaa. *knife with fold-in blade:* x̱'éi shadagutx̱i lítaa. *knife wound:* lítaa eetí. *pocket knife:* g̱altulítaa. *woman's curved knife:* wéiksh.

**knit**

*knitting, crocheting:* kasné. *s/he knitted; s/he crocheted; s/he wove:* NEI kawdzinéi. *s/he made it (by weaving, knitting, crocheting); s/he mended it (net):* NEI akawsinei.

**knoll**

*small hill; mound, knoll:* gooch.

**knot**

*knot hole:* sheey woolí. *limb knot:* sheey tukagoodlí.

**know**

*s/he knows it; s/he learned it:* KOO[2] awsikóo. *s/he learned how to do it; s/he knows how to do it:* GOOK awshigóok.

**knowledgeable**

*knowledgeable person:* at wuskóowu.

**Kuiu Island**

*Kuiu Island people:* Kooya Ḵwáan.

**Kwaashk'i Ḵwáan**

*Kwaashk'i Ḵwáan, locally called "Humpback Salmon"; a clan of the Raven moiety whose principal crest is the Humpback Salmon:* Kwaashk'i Ḵwáan.

**labret**

*labret hole:* ḵ'anoox̱ eetí. *labret, lip plug:* x̱'eint'áax'aa. *labret, small lip plug:* ḵ'anoox̱.

**lack**

*he/she/it needed it; he/she/it lacked it:* TEE[1] a eetéenáx̱ wootee.

**lacking**

*lacking it; without it:* a eetéenáx̱. *without it; lacking it:* a g̱óot.

**ladder**

*ladder; stairs:* dzeit.

**ladle**

*dipper, scoop, ladle; brailer bag:* kaxwénaa. *handmade ladle:* tseeneidi shál. *water dipper; ladle:* héen gúx'aa.

**lady**

*respected person; gentleman; lady:* sh yáa awudanéiyi.

**lair**

*its den, lair (of animal, undergound):* a k̲oowú.

**lake**

*lake:* áa. *little lake; pond:* áak'w.

**lamb**

*lamb:* wanadóo yádi.

**lamp**

*lamp:* s'eenáa.

**lancet**

*lancet:* tág̲aa.

**land1**

*earth; land, country; soil:* tl'átk. *on the ridge or elevated part of the point (of land):* x'aa luká. *point (of land):* x'aa. *shore; land:* yán. *town; village; settlement; inhabited or owned land:* aan.

**land2**

*he/she/it squatted; he/she it sat down low; he/she/it landed (of waterfowl, plane):* K̲AAK̲ wujik̲aak̲.

**landing**

*at the landing of a dock:* dzeit shuyee.

**language**

*speech, talk; language; word, phrase, sentence, or discourse:* yoo x̲'atánk.

**lap**

*(on) his/her lap:* du g̲ushká.

**larva**

*worm; larva; grub; caterpillar; snake:* tl'úk'x̲.

**late**

*late; after the appointed time:* gaaw ítx'.

**later**

*after a while; later on:* dziyáagin.

**laugh**

*s/he laughed:* SHOOK̲ at wooshook̲.

**laughter**

*laughter:* at shook̲.

**laundry**

*laundry:* óos'i.

**law**

*law, words one lives by:* a káa k̲ududziteeyi yoo x̲'atánk.

**lazy**

*s/he is lazy:* KAA[1] oodzikaa.

**lead1**

*gum; lead:* k'óox̲'. *soft lead:* k'óox̲' létl'k.

**lead2**

*s/he led them:* .AAT[1] has ashoowa.aat.

**leader**

*leader:* k̲aa sháade háni. *leaders:* k̲aa sháade nák̲x'i.

**leadline**

*leadline (of net):* k'óox̲' tíx'i.

**leaf**

*its sprouts, fleshy leaves growing toward the top of the stem (e.g. of bear root):* a shaadí. *leaf, leaves; vegetation, plants, herbs, herbiage:* kayaaní.

**leak**

*drip, leak with dripping:* katl'úk̲jaa. *fast drip, leak:* kalóox'jaa, kalóox̲jaa. *it's leaking; it's dripping:* X'AAS kawlix'áas. *trickle of water; steady drip or leak:* kax'áasjaa.

**leap**

*he/she/it leapt on it; s/he pounced on it:* GAAS' a kát sh wudligás'.

**learn**

*s/he knows it; s/he learned it:* KOO[2] awsikóo. *s/he learned how to do it; s/he knows how to do it:* GOOK awshigóok. *s/he studied it; s/he learned it; s/he practiced it:* TOOW sh tóo awdlitóow.

**learner**

*student; learner:* yaa at naskwéini.

**leather**

*babiche, string, leather thonging:* dzaas.

**leave**

*he/she/it left there:* GOOT[1] aadáx̲ woogoot. *s/he left it behind:* GOOT[1] a nák̲ woogoot. *s/he let him/her/it go; s/he released him/her/it; s/he left him/her/it; s/he delivered it:* NAAK̲[2] ajeewanák̲. *s/he put it down; s/he left it (container full of liquid or small objects):* .EEN[1] yan awsi.ín. *s/he put it down; s/he left it (container or hollow object):* TAAN yan aawatán. *s/he put it down; s/he left it (general, compact object):* TEE[2] yan aawatée. *s/he put it down; s/he left it (long, complex object):* TAAN yan awsitán. *s/he put it down; s/he left it (round, spherical object):* TEE[2] yan akaawatée. *s/he put it down; s/he left it (small, stick-like object):* TAAN yan akawsitán. *s/he put it down; s/he left it (solid, complex object):* TEE[2] yan awsitée. *s/he put them down; s/he left them (esp. baggage or personal belongings):* .AAT[2] yan awli.át. *s/he put them down; s/he left them (round objects):* NEI yan yéi akawsinéi. *s/he put them there; s/he left them there:* .OO[1] áa yéi aawa.oo.

**lee**

*the shelter of it; the lee of it; the (beach) area below it (a mountain, hill, etc.):* a seiyí.

**leech**

*leech; bloodsucker:* yéesh.

**L'eeneidí**

*L'eeneidí, locally called "Dog Salmon"; a clan of the Raven moiety whose principal crest is the Dog Salmon:* L'eeneidí.

**leftovers**

*his/her food scraps, left-over food; crumbs of food left or scattered where s/he has eaten:* du x̱'a.eetí. *leftovers, food scraps:* ḵaa x̱'a.eetí.

**leg**

*his/her foot, leg:* du x̱'oos. *its leg:* a x̱'oosí. *underside of his/her knee; (inside of) his/her lower leg:* du saayee.

**legend**

*myth; legend; children's tale:* tlaagú.

**leggings**

*dancing leggings; leggings for climbing:* x̱'uskeit.

**lend**

*s/he lent it to him/her:* HEES' du éet aawahís'.

**leopard**

*man-eating feline; mountain lion; tiger, leopard:* haadaadóoshi.

**less**

*less than it; (reaching, falling) short of it; not (big or far) enough for it:* a ḵín.

**let go**

*s/he killed him/her/it; s/he let it go:* JAAḴ aawajáḵ. *s/he let him/her/it go; s/he released him/her/it; s/he left him/her/it; s/he delivered it:* NAAḴ[2] ajeewanáḵ.

**letter**

*paper; book, magazine, newspaper; letter, mail:* x'úx'.

**lichen**

*lichen that hangs down from trees:* s'éix̱wani.

**lid**

*its lid, cover (of pot, etc.):* a yana.áat'ani.

**lie[1]**

*s/he lied:* YEIL sh ḵ'awdliyél.

**lie[2]**

*it's lying there (textile-like object):* .AAX̱[2] át .áx̱. *s/he has it lying there:* TEE[2] át akatéen, TAAN át astán. *s/he has them lying there (small, round or hoop-like objects):* .AAT[2] át akla.át. *they are lying there (small, round or hoop-like objects):* .AAT[2] át kala.át. *they're lying there (things, unconscious creatures):* .AAT[2] át la.át.

**life**

*life; breath:* x̱'aséikw, daséikw. *life; way of living:* ḵustí.

**lift up**

*s/he lifted him/her/it up:* NOOK[1] kei awsinúk.

**light**

*it's on (light); it's burning (fire):* GAAN[1] át akaawagán. *light:* kagán. *s/he lit it (fire); s/he turned it on (light):* GAAN[1] át akawligán.

**lightning**

*lightning:* xeitl l'úkx̱u, xeitl l'íkws'i (At).

**like[1]**

*s/he liked the taste of it:* K'EI du x̱'é wook'éi. *s/he wanted it; s/he liked it; it was pleasing to him/her:* GOO[1] du tuwáa wsigóo.

**like[2]**

*he/she/it was like it; he/she/it was similar to it:* TEE[1] a yáx̱ wootee. *like it, in accordance with it, as much as it:* a yáx̱. *one that matches it; an amount that matches it; equivalent to it; one like it:* a x̱ooní. *something sort of like it; something not measuring up to it; where one expects it to be:* a kayaa.

**limb**

*limb, primary branch; limb knot:* sheey.

**limpet**

*limpet:* yéil ts'áaxu.

**ling cod**

*ling cod:* x̱'áax'w.

**liniment**

*liniment:* kóoshdaa náagu. *oil, grease (for coating skin or rubbing); lotion; liniment:* neis'.

**lining**

*its lining:* a t'einyaakawoowú (At).

**lint**

*dirt; scrap(s); rubbish, trash, clutter; lint:* s'eex.

**lion**

*man-eating animal; lion; tiger; man-eating wolf:* haadaag̱oojí. *man-eating feline; mountain lion; tiger, leopard:* haadaadóoshi.

**lip**

*his/her lips; area around his/her mouth:* du x̱'adaa.

**lip plug**

*labret, lip plug:* x̱'eint'áax'aa. *labret, small lip plug:* ḵ'anoox̱.

**lipstick**
*lipstick:* x̱'akaséḵ'waa.

**liquor**
*liquor; booze; alcoholic beverage:* náaw.

**listen**
*s/he listened for the sound of it:* .AAX̱[1] a kayéikg̱aa ḵoowdzi.aax̱. *s/he listened to him/her:* .AAX̱[1] du x̱'éide ḵuwdzi.aax̱. *s/he's listening to him/her; s/he listens to him/her; s/he obeys him/her:* .AAX̱[1] du x̱'éit wusi.áx̱. *s/he's listening to it; s/he listened to it:* .AAX̱[1] át wusi.áx̱.

**little**
*little; precious; [diminutive suffix]:* -k'.

**Lituya Bay**
*Lituya Bay:* Ltu.aa.

**live**
*s/he lived there:* .OO[1] áa ḵoowa.oo. *s/he was with him/her; s/he stayed with him/her; s/he lived with him/her:* TEE[1] du x̱ánx' yéi wootee.

**lively**
*s/he was noisy; s/he was crazy; s/he was lively:* .OOS wuli.oos.

**liver**
*his/her liver:* du tl'óog̱u.

**lizard**
*lizard, newt:* tseenx̱'é.

**load**
*s/he donated it; s/he loaded it (gun); s/he shot it (basketball):* G̱EEX' akaawag̱éex'.

**lock**
*s/he locked it:* TEIX̱' x̱'éit akawlitíx̱'.

**log**
*log (fallen tree):* x̱áaw.

**loneliness**
*loneliness; boredom:* tuteesh.

**long**
*it became long (of stick-like object):* YAAT' wooyáat'. *it became long (of time or physical objects):* YAAT' wuliyát'. *it got that long (of stick-like object):* YAAT' yéi kaawayáat'. *it's that long (of general object):* YAAT' yéi kwliyáat'. *it was long (time):* YAAT' yeeywooyáat'. *long:* kuwáat'. *they're long (of plural, general objects):* YAAT' dliyát'x'.

**long ago**
*long ago; back then; in the old days:* ch'ákw, ch'áakw.

**look**

*he/she/it looked there:* GEIN aadé awdligein. *s/he looked for it; s/he searched for it:* SHEE[1] aagáa koowashee. *s/he searched there; s/he looked there:* SHEE[1] át kuwashée.

**look after**

*s/he watched him/her/it; s/he looked after him/her/it; s/he took care of him/her/it:* TEEN awlitín.

**look like**

*it looks like it; it resembles it:* XAAT[2] a yáx kaaxát, YAA[1] oowayáa.

**loon**

*common loon:* kageet.

**lose**

*s/he lost it:* GEEX' kut aawagéex'. *s/he lost it (round, spherical object):* GEEX' kut akaawagéex'. *s/he lost it; s/he misplaced it (container or hollow object):* TAAN kut aawataan. *s/he lost them (of plural objects):* SOOS[1] kut akaawlisóos.

**lost**

*astray, getting lost:* kut. *s/he got lost:* GEET[1] kut wudzigeet. *s/he got lost (by boat, car):* KOOX[1] kut wookoox. *s/he got lost (on foot):* GOOT[1] kut woogoot. *they are lost; they got lost:* SOOS[1] kut has kaawasóos. *they got lost (on foot):* .AAT[1] kut has woo.aat.

**lotion**

*oil, grease (for coating skin or rubbing); lotion; liniment:* neis'.

**loud**

*he/she/it was loud-voiced:* GAAW sawligaaw.

**louse**

*louse, lice:* wéis'.

**love**

*love (of people):* kusaxán. *love (of things, of everything):* at saxán. *s/he loved him/her/it:* XÁN awsixán.

**luck**

*fate; bad luck:* jinaháa.

**lucky**

*s/he got lucky; s/he was blessed:* XEITL wulixéitl.

**luggage**

*baggage, luggage; things, stuff packed up for carrying:* at la.át.

**L'ukaax.ádi**

*L'ukaax.ádi, locally called "Sockeye"; a clan of the Raven moiety whose principal crest is the Sockeye:* L'ukaax.ádi.

**L'uknax̱.ádi**

*L'uknax̱.ádi, locally called "Coho"; a clan of the Raven moiety whose principal crest is the Coho:* L'uknax̱.ádi.

**lumber**

*lumber:* kax'ás'ti.

**luminescence**

*phosphorescence (sparks of light in ocean water); luminescence (on rotten wood):* éedaa.

**lump**

*bump, lump, hump, mound:* gootl. *lump in the flesh; tumor:* kawáat.

**lunch**

*container for traveling provisions; lunch basket, lunch container:* wóow daakeit. *food, lunch, provisions taken along (on a trip, to work or school):* wóow.

**lung**

*his/her lungs:* du keigú.

**lupine**

*lupine:* kantáḵw.

**lynx**

*lynx:* g̱aaḵ.

**machete**

*dagger; machete, long knife:* gwálaa.

**mackerel**

*mackerel:* dákdesak'aak.

**magazine**

*paper; book, magazine, newspaper; letter, mail:* x'úx'.

**maggot**

*maggot:* woon.

**magic**

*s/he performed rites; s/he made magic:* HÉIX̱WAA aawahéix̱waa. *sympathetic magic, charm:* héix̱waa.

**magpie**

*magpie:* ts'eeg̱éeni, ts'eig̱éeni (T).

**mail**

*paper; book, magazine, newspaper; letter, mail:* x'úx'.

**make**

*s/he built it; s/he made it; s/he constructed it:* YEIX̱[1] awliyéx̱. *s/he made it (by weaving, knitting, crocheting); s/he mended it (net):* NEI akawsinei. *s/he used it for it; s/he made it into it:* YEIX̱[1] átx̱ awliyéx̱.

**make up mind**

*s/he thought about it; s/he considered it; s/he made up his/her mind about it:* TAAN a daa yoo toowatán. *they thought about it; they considered it; they made up their minds about it:* .AAT[2] a daa yoo (ha)s tuwli.át.

**male**

*man; male; person, people:* k̲áa.

**mallet**

*mallet, wooden hammer:* l'oowú ták̲l.

**man**

*Black (man or person); African-American:* t'ooch' k̲áa. *boys, young men:* k'isáani. *his/her husband's clan brother; his/her man, boyfriend, husband:* du k̲áawu. *man; male; person, people:* k̲áa. *men:* k̲áax'w. *old man:* k̲áa shaan. *rich man; man of wealth; chief:* aank̲áawu. *shaman; medicine man:* íx̲t'. *young man (not married):* yadák'w.

**mandible**

*his/her lower jaw, mandible:* du x̲'ás'.

**mane**

*its mane (esp. the hair on the neck hump of a moose):* a x̲íji.

**many**

*it got this big; there were this many:* GEI[1] yéi kaawagéi. *it was big; there were many; there was plenty:* GEI[1] woogéi. *there got to be many; there got to be plenty:* HAA shayawdihaa.

**maple**

*dwarf maple:* x'aalx'éi.

**marble**

*marble:* néex̲', koot'áax'aa.

**marijuana**

*marijuana:* kasiyéiyi s'eik̲.

**marker**

*marker; mark, sign:* kwéiy.

**marmot**

*hoary marmot; groundhog, whistler:* s'aax̲.

**married**

*s/he got married:* SHAA[1] wuduwasháa.

**marrow**

*his/her bone marrow:* s'ak̲tu.eex̲í. *its bone marrow:* a s'ak̲tu.eex̲í.

**marry**

*s/he married him/her; s/he is married:* SHAA[1] aawasháa. *they married each other:* SHAA[1] wooch has wudisháa.

**marten**

*marten:* k'óox.

**mash**

*s/he mashed it; s/he squeezed it:* G̱OOTL akaawaG̱útl.

**mast**

*its mast (of boat):* a ka.aasí.

**master**

*head of a clan house; master of the house:* hít s'aatí. *his/her boss, master:* du s'aatí.

**master of ceremonies**

*master of ceremonies, elder of the opposite clan consulted conducting a ceremony:* naa káani.

**mat**

*mat, doormat; rug:* g̱áach.

**match**

*match:* ux̱gank̲áas'. *match; stick:* k̲áas'.

**mate**

*his/her mate, his "old lady"; her "old man":* du x̱án aa.

**material**

*its what it is (to be) made of; its parts, components, materials:* a shagóon.

**math**

*math:* wooch yáx̱ yaa datóowch.

**mattress**

*mattress; bedding:* yee.át.

**maybe**

*maybe; I'm not sure; [expression of uncertainly]:* kwshéi.

**mayor**

*mayor:* aan s'aatí.

**me**

*me [object]:* x̱at.

**meal**

*food, a meal:* atx̱á.

**measure**

*measure; mile:* kaay. *pattern, model, template for it; measure of it; measurement for it:* a kaayí.

**measuring stick**

*measuring stick:* kaay.

**meat**

*its raw (flesh or meat); rare (meat):* a shís'k̲. *meat, flesh:* dleey.

**medicine**

*medicine:* náakw. *shaman; medicine man:* íx̱t'.

**meet**
*meeting, encountering, intercepting it; (arriving) at the same place or time as it:* du kagé.

**melt**
*it melted; it dissolved; it thawed:* LAA[1] wuliláa.

**memorial**
*memorial pile of rocks:* xóow.

**mend**
*s/he made it (by weaving, knitting, crocheting); s/he mended it (net):* NEI akawsinei.

**menstruation**
*menstrual discharge; period:* gáan.

**merchant**
*merchant; seller:* hoon s'aatí.

**merganser**
*merganser:* k̲aax̲.

**mess**
*filth, mess; trash, rubbish, garbage:* tl'eex.

**messenger**
*messenger; angel:* kook̲énaa.

**mica**
*mica:* katl'áak'.

**middle**
*middle of it:* a dagiygé.

**midnight**
*midnight:* taat sitgawsáani.

**midst**
*in the midst of it (a crowd, an activity or event involving several people); in the hubbub:* a k̲óox'.

**migrate**
*s/he migrated; s/he moved:* DAAK̲[2] kei wusidák̲.

**mild**
*he/she/it was weak; s/he is anemic; it is mild (of weather):* TSEEN tlél wultseen.

**mile**
*measure; mile:* kaay.

**milk**
*cow's milk:* wasóos l'aayí.

**Milky Way**
*Milky Way:* lk̲'ayáak'w x̲'us.eetí.

**milt**
*its semen; its milt (of fish):* a tl'éili.

**mind**
*his/her inner being; mind; soul; feelings; intention:* du toowú. *s/he is worried about him/her/it; s/he has him/her/it on her mind:* XEEX du tóot wooxeex.

**minister**
*priest; pastor; minister:* nakwnéit.

**mink**
*mink:* nukshiyáan, lukshiyáan.

**mirror**
*mirror:* tóonáx̱ ḵaateen.

**misplace**
*s/he lost it; s/he misplaced it (container or hollow object):* TAAN ḵut aawataan.

**mist**
*steam (visible, in the air); mist, fog (rising from a body of standing water):* x'úkjaa.

**mistake**
*accident; unfortunate mistake or mishap:* ḵaaḵx̱wdaagané (A). *by mistake, wrongly:* ḵwaaḵx̱ daaḵ.

**moan**
*mourning, wailing, loud weeping or crying; wail, groan, moan:* kasg̱aax̱.

**moccasin**
*buckshot; moccasin lining:* at tux̱'wáns'i. *moccasins:* at xáshdi téel. *moccasin top:* téel iḵkeidí. *wooden form for shaping/stretching moccasins:* téel tukanágaa.

**model**
*pattern, model, template for it; measure of it; measurement for it:* a kaayí.

**moiety**
*his/her kinsman, moiety mate:* du een aa. *nation; moiety; clan; band of people:* naa.

**mold**
*mold:* tlaax̱.

**moldy**
*it's moldy; it got moldy:* TLAAX̱ wuditláx̱.

**money**
*broke; penniless; without money:* kaldáanaaḵ. *its price, value; the money from the sale of it:* a yeidí. *money, coin, dollar:* dáanaa.

**monkey**
*monkey:* aandaat kanahík.

**month**
*month:* dís.

**moon**
*moon:* dís. *moonbeam:* dís x̲'usyee.

**moonfish**
*moonfish, suckerfish, blowfish:* tl'éitl'.

**moose**
*moose:* dzísk'w.

**mop**
*s/he wiped it; s/he mopped it:* G̲OO awlig̲oo.

**more**
*beyond it, more than it; too much; excessively:* a yáanáx̲.

**morning**
*morning:* ts'ootaat.

**mortar**
*mortar for grinding:* kaxágwaa yeit. *mortar for pounding:* kat'éx̲'aa yeit.

**mosquito**
*mosquito:* táax'aa.

**mosquito eater**
*daddy long legs; mosquito eater:* táax'aa x̲'uskudayáat'.

**moss**
*moss:* s'íx'g̲aa. *peat moss:* sook̲.

**mossberry**
*mossberry:* xéel'i.

**moth**
*moth:* atx̲a át.

**mother**
*his/her mother:* du tláa.

**mother-in-law**
*his/her mother-in-law:* du chaan.

**motor**
*engine, motor:* washéen.

**mound**
*bump, lump, hump, mound:* gootl. *small hill; mound, knoll:* gooch.

**mountain**
*mountain:* shaa. *mountainside; around the mountain:* shaa yadaa. *mountaintop; on top of the mountain:* shaa shakée. *the shelter of a mountain, area on the beach below a mountain:* shaa seiyí.

**mountain ash**
*mountain ash:* kalchaneit.

**mountain ash berry**
*mountain ash berry:* kalchaneit tléig̱u.

**mourn**
*mourning, wailing, loud weeping or crying; wail, groan, moan:* kasg̱aax̱.

**mouse**
*mouse:* kag̱ák. *mouse, deer mouse; vole:* kag̱áak. *mouse; rat:* kuts'een.

**mouth**
*his/her mouth:* du x̱'é. *inside of his/her mouth:* du laká. *its mouth, opening:* a x̱'é. *mouth of it (a river, creek):* a wát. *mouth ulcer; soreness of the mouth (as of a baby teething):* xáatl'ákw. *through its mouth:* a x̱'éináx̱.

**move**
*s/he migrated; s/he moved:* DAAḴ[2] kei wusidáḵ. *s/he moved it out of his/her way:* TAAN du jikaadáx̱ ayaawatán. *s/he moved there:* GAAS' át wuligás', GAAS' aadé wligáas'.

**move over**
*s/he moved over that way:* GOOT[1] héide yaawagút. *they moved over that way:* .AAT[1] héide has yaawa.át.

**much**
*much, lots of, really:* aatlein.

**mucus**
*slime; thick mucus:* x̱éel'. *thick mucus, phlegm:* g̱eitl'.

**mud**
*mud:* ḵútl'kw.

**muddy**
*it got muddy:* ḴOOTL' kawshiḵútl'.

**mudflats**
*river flats; tidelands; mudflats:* taashuká.

**mudshark**
*dogfish; mudshark:* x'átgu.

**multiply**
*they multiplied; they bred:* X̱EIT[2] has wudzix̱eit.

**murder**
*murderer:* ḵu.eení.

**murderer**
*murderer:* ḵoowajag̱i aa.

**murky**
*silty, murky water:* l'óox̱.

**murrelet**
*auklet or murrelet:* ch'eet, kéel.
**muscle**
*its muscles (of shell creature):* a ts'éek'u. *muscles of a shell creature; pincher; thing that pinches:* at ts'ík'wti.
**mush**
*mush, oatmeal, porridge:* wásh.
**music**
*music, singing, song:* at shí.
**music box**
*radio, phonograph, stereo, music box, ipod; any device that plays music:* at shí ḵóok.
**muskox**
*bison, buffalo; ox, muskox; cow; horse:* xaas.
**muskrat**
*muskrat:* tsín.
**mussel**
*mussel:* yaak. *mussel (large mussel on stormy coast, used for scraping):* yées'. *red mussel:* s'igeeḵáawu yaagí.
**mute**
*mute; person who cannot speak:* l yoo ḵ'eishtángi.
**my**
*my [possessive]:* aḵ.
**myth**
*myth; legend; children's tale:* tlaagú.
**nagoonberry**
*nagoonberry, lagoonberry, dwarf nagoonberry:* neigóon.
**nail**
*nail:* tuháayi, shayéen. *s/he nailed it on it:* X'OO át akawsix'óo.
**naked**
*bare; naked:* kaldaagákw.
**name**
*his/her name; his/her namesake:* du saayí. *name:* saa. *s/he called him/her/it that (name):* SAA² yéi aawasáakw. *s/he named him/her/it that; s/he nominated him/her:* SAA² yéi aawasáa.
**namesake**
*his/her name; his/her namesake:* du saayí. *his/her namesake:* du tlagooḵwansaayí.
**narrate**
*s/he told a story; s/he preached; s/he narrated:* NEEK sh kawdlineek.

**narrow**

*it's narrow:* SAA[1] yéi kwlisáa.

**nation**

*nation; moiety; clan; band of people:* naa.

**navel**

*his/her navel, bellybutton:* du kool.

**near**

*near him/her, by him/her:* du x̱án. *near him/her, by him/her (at hand, for him/her to work with):* du jix̱án.

**neck**

*back of his/her neck:* du ludíx̱', du lidíx̱'. *his/her occiput; nape of neck; back of head:* du lak'éech'.

**necklace**

*necklace:* seit.

**necktie**

*necktie:* saka.át.

**need**

*he/she/it needed it; he/she/it lacked it:* TEE[1] a eetéenáx̱ wootee.

**needle**

*fine needle for stringing beads:* kawóot ka.íshaa. *leather needle:* lukat'íshaa. *needle:* táax'ál'. *three-cornered needle for sewing skin or leather:* kat'íshaa.

**needlefish**

*needlefish:* tooḵ.

**neighbor**

*neighbor:* k'idaaká aa. *neighbors:* k'idaaḵwáani.

**nephew**

*her fraternal niece, nephew, cousin:* du káalk'w. *his sororal niece, nephew:* du kéilk'.

**nest**

*bee's nest:* gandaas'aají kúdi. *it laid an egg:* K'WÁT' awdlik'wát'. *nest:* kút. *nest (of animal):* a kúdi.

**net**

*cheesecloth, loose-woven cloth; netting, screen:* kag̱ádaa. *dipnet (for eulachon):* deegáa. *fish net; seine net:* g̱eiwú.

**nettle**

*nettle:* t'óok'.

**new**

*new; young; fresh:* yées.

**news**

*news; gossip, rumor:* neek.

**newspaper**

*paper; book, magazine, newspaper; letter, mail:* x'úx'.

**newt**

*lizard, newt:* tseenx̲'é.

**next**

*the next one, the following one:* a ít aa.

**next to**

*beside, alongside, next to him/her:* du t'ak̲ká. *beside, alongside, next to it:* a t'ak̲ká. *beside it, next to it:* a tuwán. *next door to him/her/it:* du k'idaaká.

**niece**

*her fraternal niece, nephew, cousin:* du káalk'w. *his sororal niece, nephew:* du kéilk'.

**night**

*during the night; in the middle of the night:* taat yeen. *last night:* nisdaat. *night:* taat.

**nine**

*nine:* gooshúk̲. *nine (people):* gooshúg̲unáx̲.

**no**

*no:* tléik'. *no, none, not:* tléil.

**noise**

*noise:* lagaaw. *sound, noise of it:* a kayéik. *sound, noise of it (something whose identity is unknown):* a yayík. *sound of stamping, pounding fists, clapping; sound of running quickly:* tíxwjaa (At), túxjaa.

**noisy**

*s/he was noisy; s/he was crazy; s/he was lively:* .OOS wuli.oos.

**nominate**

*s/he named him/her/it that; s/he nominated him/her:* SAA² yéi aawasáa.

**none**

*no, none, not:* tléil.

**noon**

*noon:* sitgawsáan.

**north**

*upstream; north:* naakée.

**northern lights**

*northern lights; aurora borealis:* gis'óok̲.

**nose**
*his/her nose:* du lú. *his/her nose cartilage:* a lututúḵl'i. *inside of his/her nose:* du lutú. *lobe of his/her nostril:* du lugóoch'. *side of his/her nose:* du lut'aaḵ.

**nose ring**
*nose ring:* lunás.

**not**
*no, none, not:* tléil.

**nothing**
*nothing:* tlél daa sá.

**now**
*already, (by) now:* de. *now:* yeedát. *now, this time:* déi.

**numb**
*it's numb:* X'WÁS'Ḵ wulix'wás'ḵ.

**nurse**
*healer; doctor; nurse:* ḵunáagu.

**oak**
*oak:* gus'k'iḵwáan l'oowú.

**oatmeal**
*mush, oatmeal, porridge:* wásh.

**obey**
*s/he's listening to him/her; s/he listens to him/her; s/he obeys him/her:* .AAX̱[1] du x̱'éit wusi.áx̱.

**obvious**
*it's obvious; it's clearly visible:* HAA tlél gooháa.

**occur**
*that happened to him/her/it; that occurred to him/her/it:* NEI yéi woonei.

**ocean**
*ocean; salt water:* éil'.

**octopus**
*octopus; devilfish:* náaḵw.

**offshore**
*thing heading offshore, esp. wind:* dákde át.

**oil**
*hooligan oil:* saak eex̱í. *large box for storing grease, oil:* daneit. *oil, grease:* eex̱, eix̱ (C). *oil, grease (for coating skin or rubbing); lotion; liniment:* neis'. *petroleum, oil:* t'ooch' eex̱í.

**old**
*(little) old person:* shaanák'w. *old:* ch'áagu. *old age:* shaan. *old; from the past:* tlagu. *old man:* ḵáa shaan. *old person:* shaan.

**on**

*the (horizontal) surface of it; on it; on top of it; in it ( a dish; a path):* a ká.

**once**

*once, one time:* tleidahéen, tlex'dahéen.

**one**

*one:* tléix'. *one at a time, one by one:* tlék'g̲aa. *one hundred:* tléix' hándit. *one kind, type; one way, direction:* tleiyeekaadé. *one, one of [object]:* aa. *one (person):* tléiná̲x̲. *one (person) at a time:* tlék'g̲aaná̲x̲.

**only**

*only, just:* ch'as.

**open**

*from hiding into open:* gági.

**opening**

*its mouth, opening:* a x̲'é.

**opinion**

*in his/her opinion; to his/her way of thinking, feeling:* du tuwáx'.

**opportunity**

*room, space, place for it; time for it; chance, opportunity for it:* a ya.áak.

**orange**

*bright red or orange:* shex̲'wtáax'i. *orange:* áanjís. *orange (in color):* shéix̲'w. *orange juice:* áanjís kahéeni.

**order**

*s/he gave him/her orders; s/he instructed him/her:* K̲AA[1] áa ajikaawak̲aa, .AAK̲W át akaawa.aak̲w. *s/he ordered it:* WOO[1] aag̲áa aawawóo. *s/he sent him/her there; s/he ordered him/her to go there; s/he gave it (in accordance with clan relationship):* NAA[3] aadé akaawanáa.

**ordinary**

*ordinary, usual:* ch'a yéi.

**organ**

*organ, piano:* g̲íx̲'jaa k̲óok.

**organs**

*its internal organs, viscera; its guts:* a yik.ádi.

**originally**

*(at) first, originally:* shux'áaná̲x̲. *(at) first; originally; in the beginning:* shóoguná̲x̲.

**orphan**

*orphan:* kuhaankée.

**other**

*different, other:* ch'a g̲óot. *this/that (over here), the other:* hé.

**otter**

*land otter; river otter:* kóoshdaa.

**our**

*our [possessive]:* haa.

**out**

*down; out of boat, vehicle:* yei. *out to sea; out into the open; (falling) down:* daak.

**outdoors**

*outdoors; outside:* gáan.

**outside**

*around the outside surface of it:* a daaká. *outdoors; outside:* gáan. *outside:* yux̱.

**outskirts**

*beside it; out past it; out away from it; (on) the outskirts of it (town):* a t'iká.

**ouzel**

*dipper; water ouzel:* hinyikl'eix̱í.

**over**

*(draped) over it, covering it:* a náa. *over it, covering it (a container or something with an opening):* a yanáa.

**owl**

*owl; great horned owl:* dzísk'w (AtT). *owl with ear tufts:* tsísk'w. *owl without ear tufts:* k'ákw. *small owl:* x̱éex̱.

**own**

*possession(s); that which is owned (by them):* ḵaa at óowu. *s/he claimed it; s/he owns it:* HEIN aawahéin.

**ox**

*bison, buffalo; ox, muskox; cow; horse:* xaas.

**pack**

*he/she/it carried it on his/her/its back; he/she/it packed it on his/her/its back:* YAA$^2$ aawayaa. *he/she/it carried things on his/her/its back; he/she/it packed things on his/her/its back:* YAA$^2$ at wooyaa. *s/he packed it; s/he stacked it:* CHAAK akaawachák.

**paddle**

*paddle:* ax̱áa. *s/he rowed; s/he paddled:* X̱AA$^2$ aawax̱áa.

**pail**

*bucket; pail:* x'eesháa.

**pain**

*s/he got sick; he/she/it hurt; s/he was in pain:* NEEKW woonéekw.

**paint**

*crimson red; face paint:* léix̱'w. *paint:* néegwál'. *s/he painted it:* NÉEGWÁL' aawanéegwál'. *s/he wrote:* XEET kawshixít. *s/he wrote it;*

*s/he drew it; s/he painted it; s/he photographed it; s/he took X-rays of it:* XEET akawshixít.

**pair**

*one of them (a pair):* a yaayí. *pair:* woosh yaayí.

**palate**

*his/her palate:* du k'ik̲l'án.

**pale**

*pale; pastel:* tl'áak'.

**palm**

*his/her palm (center):* du jintakyádi. *his/her palm (of hand):* du jintáak.

**pan**

*basket or pan used to collect berries by knocking them off the bush:* kadádzaa yeit. *cast-iron skillet:* té kas'úgwaa yeit (T). *food container; pot or pan; dish, large bowl:* x̲'ayeit. *frying pan, skillet:* kax̲gáani yeit, kas'ígwaa yeit (A).

**pants**

*pants, trousers:* tuk̲'atáal.

**paper**

*paper; book, magazine, newspaper; letter, mail:* x'úx'.

**parable**

*parable:* at kookeidí.

**paralysis**

*paralysis; polio:* l uwaxwachgi néekw.

**part**

*its what it is (to be) made of; its parts, components, materials:* a shagóon. *part of it; half of it:* a shoowú.

**particular**

*s/he is proud; s/he is conceited; s/he is particular; s/he is picky:* G̲EI sh tukdlig̲éi.

**partner**

*his/her partner:* du yak̲áawu.

**party**

*feast, potlatch; party:* k̲u.éex'. *the life of the party:* naa shuklag̲eeyí.

**passage**

*portage, passage across it; its isthmus:* a góon.

**past**

*beside it; out past it; out away from it; (on) the outskirts of it (town):* a t'iká.

**pastel**

*pale; pastel:* tl'áak'.

**pastor**

*priest; pastor; minister:* nakwnéit.

**patch**

*patch:* téey.

**path**

*on the path, trail, road; bed of the path, trail, road:* dei yík. *path, trail; road, street:* dei.

**patio**

*porch; patio:* x̲'awool kayáashi.

**pattern**

*pattern, model, template for it; measure of it; measurement for it:* a kaayí.

**paw**

*its paw:* a jíni.

**pay**

*s/he paid him/her; s/he paid for it:* K̲EI[1] ajeewak̲éi.

**peace**

*peace, calm:* kayéil'. *s/he improved it; s/he made peace with him/her/it:* K'EI awlik'éi.

**peaceful**

*it's calm; it's peaceful:* YEIL' kawduwayél'.

**peavy**

*peavy:* dlágwaa.

**peddle**

*s/he went peddling it; s/he went selling it:* HOON awlihóon.

**peel**

*s/he tore it; s/he peeled it off; s/he ripped it off:* S'EIL' akaawas'éil'.

**pelvis**

*his/her pelvis, hip:* du k̲áash.

**pen**

*pencil; pen; brush:* kooxéedaa.

**pencil**

*pencil; pen; brush:* kooxéedaa.

**penis**

*his penis:* du l'íli. *privates (of male); penis and testicles:* du láaw.

**people**

*people; community:* k̲u.oo. *people of long ago:* tlagu k̲wáanx'i. *person or people from that place:* a k̲wáan.

**pepper**

*pepper:* si.áax'u át, tux̲'wáns'i náakw.

**perceive**

*s/he can see it; s/he perceives it:* TEEN ayatéen.

**perform**

*s/he demonstrated it to him/her; s/he showed him/her how to do it; s/he performed it for him/her:* NEI du wak̲shiyeex' yéi awsinei.

**perhaps**

*perhaps:* gwál. *perhaps; I guess, it would seem:* gí. *perhaps, probably:* shákdéi.

**permanent**

*he/she/it is ready; he/she/it is finished; he/she/it is prepared; he/she/it is permanent:* NEI yan uwanéi.

**person**

*high class person, aristocrat:* aanyádi. *man; male; person, people:* k̲áa. *person:* lingít. *person or people from that place:* a k̲wáan.

**Petersburg**

*Petersburg:* Gántiyaakw Séedi.

**petrel**

*petrel:* g̲anook.

**petroleum**

*petroleum, oil:* t'ooch' eex̲í.

**petticoat**

*petticoat; slip:* doonyaax̲l'aak.

**pharynx**

*his/her windpipe; pharynx:* du leikachoox̲'u.

**phlegm**

*thick mucus, phlegm:* g̲eitl'.

**phonograph**

*radio, phonograph, stereo, music box, ipod; any device that plays music:* at shí k̲óok.

**phosphorescence**

*phosphorescence (sparks of light in ocean water); luminescence (on rotten wood):* éedaa.

**photograph**

*s/he wrote:* XEET kawshixít. *s/he wrote it; s/he drew it; s/he painted it; s/he photographed it; s/he took X-rays of it:* XEET akawshixít.

**piano**

*organ, piano:* g̲íx̲'jaa k̲óok.

**pick**[1]

*pick, pickaxe:* kéit'u.

**pick[2]**

*s/he picked berries:* K'EET' k̲oowak'ít'. *s/he picked them:* .EEN[1] aawa.ín.

**pick up**

*s/he brought it out; s/he picked it up (general, often compact object):* TEE[2] kei aawatée. *s/he brought it out; s/he picked it up (long, complex object):* TAAN kei awsitán. *s/he picked it up off of it (general, compact object):* TEE[2] aax̲ aawatée. *s/he picked them up off of it:* NEI aax̲ yéi awsinei. *s/he touched it; s/he picked it up; s/he took it:* SHEE[1] át uwashée.

**picky**

*s/he is proud; s/he is conceited; s/he is particular; s/he is picky:* G̲EI sh tukdlig̲éi.

**pier**

*dock, pier:* dzeit.

**pierce**

*it pierced it; it bit him/her/it:* G̲EECH át yawdig̲ích, G̲EECH aadé yawdig̲eech. *they peirced it:* G̲EECH át yawdlig̲ích.

**pig**

*pig:* gishoo.

**pigeon**

*pigeon:* yaa k̲udzigéiyi ts'ats'ée. *pigeon or dove:* gus'yé kindachooneidí. *willow ptarmigan; pigeon:* x̲'eis'awáa.

**pile up**

*it's piled up; it's deep:* DLAAN yan kaawadlán.

**piling**

*piling, foundation post; floor joist:* hít tayeegáas'i.

**pillow**

*pillow:* shayeit.

**pilot bread**

*pilot bread:* g̲áatl.

**pilot house**

*cabin (of boat); pilot house:* yaakw x̲ukahídi.

**pin**

*safety pin:* x̲'éex'wál', x̲'éigwál'.

**pincher**

*muscles of a shell creature; pincher; thing that pinches:* at ts'ík'wti.

**pine**

*pine needles, spruce needles:* g̲ítg̲aa.

**pine cone**

*pine cone, spruce cone:* s'óos'ani.

**pink**

*pink:* lóol.

**pink salmon**

*pink salmon; humpy, humpback salmon:* cháas'.

**pipe**

*pipe (for carrying water):* tunax̱hinnadaa. *pipe (for tobacco):* s'eiḵdaakeit. *tobacco pipe:* s'iḵdaakeit.

**pit**

*pit; hole dug in the ground; cellar:* kóoḵ.

**pitch**

*pitch scab (where bark has been removed); pitchwood:* téil. *tree pitch:* aasdaak'óox̱'u.

**pitcher**

*pitcher; jug:* ḵ'ateil.

**pitchfork**

*fish pitchfork:* x̱áat g̱íjaa.

**pith**

*its stem (of plant); pith (of tree):* a kadíx'i.

**place**

*(in) place of it; place where it was; its imprint or aftermath:* a eetí. *it; that place, time, reason, fact:* á. *place; way:* yé.

**plan**

*s/he made a decision; s/he planned it:* .AAḴW yan akaawa.áḵw.

**plane**

*plane for scraping wood:* aankayéx̱aa, t'áa kayéx̱aa.

**planner**

*director, planner; commander:* át ḵukawu.aag̱ú.

**plant**

*leaf, leaves; vegetation, plants, herbs, herbiage:* kayaaní. *s/he planted it:* HAA akaawahaa.

**plastic**

*plastic:* xén.

**plate**

*dish; plate:* s'íx'. *plate:* s'íx' ḵ'áatl'.

**platform**

*platform; porch:* kayáash.

**platter**

*dish; platter:* kélaa, kílaa. *flat open basket woven from wide strips of bark (for carrying fish, etc.); large platter:* táal.

**play**

*s/he gambled; s/he played cards:* K̲AA[3] awdlik̲áa. *s/he played:* YÁT ash kawdliyát. *s/he played it (musical instrument):* .AAX̲[1] awli.áx̲. *s/he plays it (musical instrument):* .AAX̲[1] ali.áx̲ch.

**plaything**

*plaything:* k̲us.ook'.

**please**

*s/he wanted it; s/he liked it; it was pleasing to him/her:* GOO[1] du tuwáa wsigóo.

**pleased**

*s/he became proud; s/he became pleased:* G̲EI du toowú kawlig̲éi.

**plenty**

*it was big; there were many; there was plenty:* GEI[1] woogéi. *there got to be many; there got to be plenty:* HAA shayawdihaa.

**pliers**

*pliers:* at katáx'aa, kakatáx'aa.

**<plural>**

*[pluralizer]:* dag̲a-. *[plural marker for kinship terms]:* hás.

**pneumonia**

*pneumonia:* k'inashóo.

**pocket**

*pocket:* g̲altú. *pocket knife:* g̲altulítaa.

**point**

*its point (of a long thin pointed object):* a lú. *its tip, point:* a lux'aa. *on the ridge or elevated part of the point (of land):* x'aa luká. *point (of land):* x'aa. *rock point:* tax'aayí. *sand point:* l'éiw x'aayí.

**poke**

*s/he poked it; s/he jabbed at it; s/he speared it:* TAAK̲[1] aawaták̲.

**polar bear**

*polar bear:* hintaak xóodzi.

**pole**

*long smokehouse pole(s):* jikak̲áas'. *pole (for boating, for pushing skin toboggan):* tság̲aa. *pole; sapling:* tlag̲anís. *pole(s) on which fish are hung for drying in smokehouse:* s'óos'. *poles used to push aside ice (from a boat):* xáatl kaltság̲aa. *sapling; pole made from sapling:* tag̲anís. *s/he pushed the boat out (with a pole):* TAAK̲[1] yaakw daak ayawliták̲.

**police**

*policeman; policewoman:* wáachwaan.

**polio**

*paralysis; polio:* l uwaxwachgi néekw.

**pollen**
*dust; pollen:* kadánjaa.

**polliwog**
*tadpole; polliwog:* dúsh.

**poncho**
*shawl; cape; poncho:* teik̲.

**pond**
*little lake; pond:* áak'w.

**poor**
*poor man:* k̲'anashgidéi k̲áa.

**porch**
*platform; porch:* kayáash. *porch; patio:* x̲'awool kayáashi.

**porcupine**
*porcupine:* x̲alak'ách'.

**porpoise**
*Chookaneidí; a clan of the Eagle moiety whose principal crests are the Porpoise and Brown Bear:* Chookaneidí. *porpoise:* cheech.

**porridge**
*mush, oatmeal, porridge:* wásh. *porridge:* sakwnéin katéix̲i. *soup, porridge:* katéix̲.

**portage**
*portage, passage across it; its isthmus:* a góon.

**possessed**
*person who acts crazy or possesssed:* lookanáa.

**possession**
*his/her inheritance; possessions of deceased given to him/her at a feast:* du néix'i. *in his/her possession:* du jee. *possession(s); that which is owned (by them):* k̲aa at óowu. *possession; that which is claimed:* k̲aa at oohéini.

**post**
*piling, foundation post; floor joist:* hít tayeegáas'i.

**post office**
*post office:* x'úx' daakahídi.

**pot**
*food container; pot or pan; dish, large bowl:* x̲'ayeit. *pot, cooking pot:* k̲'wátl.

**potato**
*potato:* k'únts'.

**potlatch**
*feast, potlatch; party:* k̲u.éex'. *in public; at a potlatch, feast:* k̲aankak.eetx' (T).

**pounce**
*he/she/it leapt on it; s/he pounced on it:* GAAS' a kát sh wudligás'.

**pound**
*pounder (for meat or grease):* kat'éx̱'aa. *s/he pounded it:* T'EEX̱' akaawat'éx̱'.

**pour**
*s/he poured it on there:* XAA a kaadé ayawsixaa. *s/he poured it out there; s/he emptied it there:* XAA aadé akawsixaa. *s/he poured it there; s/he emptied it there:* XAA át akawsixáa.

**powder**
*face powder:* yawéinaa.

**power**
*strength, power:* latseen.

**powerful**
*he/she/it became strong; he/she/it became powerful:* TSEEN wulitseen.

**practice**
*s/he studied it; s/he learned it; s/he practiced it:* TOOW sh tóo awdlitóow.

**praise**
*praise, glorification:* kashéex̱'. *s/he praised him/her; s/he approved it:* SHEIX̱' akaawashéx̱'.

**pray**
*s/he prayed:* GAAX' sh káa x̱'awdigáx'.

**prayer**
*prayer:* x̱'agáax'. *wish; prayer:* oolxéis'.

**preach**
*s/he told a story; s/he preached; s/he narrated:* NEEK sh kawdlineek.

**preacher**
*preacher:* sh kalneegí. *storyteller; preacher:* ḵoon sh kalneegí.

**precious**
*it was expensive; it was precious:* TSEEN x̱'awlitseen. *little; precious; [diminutive suffix]:* -k'.

**prepared**
*he/she/it is ready; he/she/it is finished; he/she/it is prepared; he/she/it is permanent:* NEI yan uwanéi.

**preserve**
*s/he put up food; s/he stored up food (for the winter); s/he preserved food; s/he finished distributing things (at party):* GAA yan akawligáa.

**pretending**
*pretending; make-believe:* ḵ'eildaháak'u.

**pretty**

*he/she/it was good; he/she/it got better; he/she/it was fine; he/she/it was pretty:* K'EI wook'éi. *she is pretty; it is cute:* G̲EI shakliG̲éi.

**price**

*its price, value; the money from the sale of it:* a yeidí.

**pride**

*pride; self-esteem, feeling good about oneself:* toowú klaG̲é.

**priest**

*priest:* wáadishgaa. *priest; pastor; minister:* nakwnéit.

**probably**

*perhaps, probably:* shákdéi.

**profitable**

*s/he got rich; s/he got wealthy; it became profitable:* NÁALX̲ wulináalx̲.

**prominent**

*he/she/it was fancy; he/she/it was conspicuous; he/she/it was prominent:* G̲EI kawliG̲éi.

**prosperity**

*wealth; prosperity; riches:* lanáalx̲.

**prostitute**

*prostitute:* sh kalyéiyi.

**protect**

*in its way; keeping it away; protecting, shielding, screening from it; blocking it:* a niyaa.

**proud**

*s/he became proud; s/he became pleased:* G̲EI du toowú kawliG̲éi. *s/he is proud; s/he is conceited; s/he is particular; s/he is picky:* G̲EI sh tukdliG̲éi.

**proverb**

*saying, proverb; event that is so common it has become a saying or proverb:* yax̲ at G̲wakú.

**ptarmigan**

*willow ptarmigan; pigeon:* x̲'eis'awáa.

**public**

*in public; at a potlatch, feast:* k̲aankak.eetx' (T).

**puffin**

*puffin:* x̲ík. *tufted puffin:* lugán.

**pull**

*he/she/it dragged it there; s/he pulled it there (esp. light object or solid, stiff object):* X̲OOT'[1] aadé aawax̲óot'. *he/she/it is dragging him/her/it around; he/she/it dragged him/her/it around:* X̲OOT'[1] át aawax̲óot'. *s/he dragged it away; s/he pulled it away; s/he hauled it away; (heavy object or limp object such as dead animal):* XAAT' aadáx̲ awsixáat'. *s/he dragged it; s/he pulled it;*

*s/he hauled it (esp. heavy object or limp object such as dead animal):* XAAT’ awsixáat’. *s/he dragged it there; s/he pulled it there; s/he hauled it there (by motor power):* X̲OOT’[1] aadé awsix̲óot’. *s/he dragged it there; s/he pulled it there; s/he hauled it there; (heavy object or limp object such as dead animal):* XAAT’ aadé awsixáat’. *s/he pulled it in; s/he dragged it in (esp. light object or solid, stiff object):* X̲OOT’[1] yan aawax̲út’. *s/he pulled it out of there:* YEESH aax̲ kei aawayísh. *s/he pulled it over him/her/it; s/he covered him/her/it with it:* YEESH a káx̲ aawayeesh. *s/he pulled it tight:* XAAT[1] k’idéin akawsixát. *s/he pulled it up (esp. line):* YEEK̲[1] kei awsiyík̲. *s/he pulled it up there:* YEEK̲[1] át awsiyík̲. *s/he pulled up spruce roots:* S’EIL’ x̲aat awlis’él’.

**punch**

*s/he hit him/her in the face; s/he punched him/her:* GWAAL ayaawagwál.

**pupil**

*student; pupil; scholar:* sgóonwaan.

**purple**

*blueberry juice; purple:* kanat’á kahéeni.

**pus**

*it's infected:* K̲EET’ wudlik̲ít’. *pus; discharge (from a sore, wound); sore, wound that discharges pus:* k̲éet’.

**push**

*s/he pushed the boat out (with a pole):* TAAK̲[1] yaakw daak ayawliták̲.

**put**

*s/he put it there; s/he hung it there; s/he installed it there (general, compact object):* TEE[2] áx̲ aawatee. *s/he put them there; s/he left them there:* .OO[1] áa yéi aawa.oo.

**put down**

*s/he put him/her/it down (live creature):* NOOK[1] yan awsinúk. *s/he put his/her hand down:* TAAN yan jiwsitán. *s/he put it down; s/he left it (container full of liquid or small objects):* .EEN[1] yan awsi.ín. *s/he put it down; s/he left it (container or hollow object):* TAAN yan aawatán. *s/he put it down; s/he left it (general, compact object):* TEE[2] yan aawatée. *s/he put it down; s/he left it (long, complex object):* TAAN yan awsitán. *s/he put it down; s/he left it (round, spherical object):* TEE[2] yan akaawatée. *s/he put it down; s/he left it (small, stick-like object):* TAAN yan akawsitán. *s/he put it down; s/he left it (solid, complex object):* TEE[2] yan awsitée. *s/he put them down; s/he left them (esp. baggage or personal belongings):* .AAT[2] yan awli.át. *s/he put them down; s/he left them (round objects):* NEI yan yéi akawsinéi.

**put on**

*s/he put it on:* TEE[2] káx̲ awditee. *s/he put them on:* YEEK̲[1] x̲’oosdé awdiyík̲. *s/he wore it; s/he put it on; s/he used it:* .OO[1] yéi aawa.oo.

**put out**

*s/he put it out (fire); s/he turned it off (light):* KEES’ ayakawlikís’.

**put up**

*s/he put up food; s/he stored up food (for the winter); s/he preserved food; s/he finished distributing things (at party):* GAA yan akawligáa.

**pyrite**

*firestone; iron pyrite:* dáadzi.

**quick**

*the quick (the flesh under the outer skin):* séiḵ'w.

**quill**

*its hair, fur; its quill(s) (of porcupine):* a x̱aawú. *long feather; quill (of bird):* ḵínaa, ḵénaa. *quills on rear end of it (porcupine):* a k'ishataag̱aní.

**quilt**

*cotton; cotton blanket, quilt:* kast'áat'. *quilt; cotton blanket:* kast'áat' x'óow.

**quote**

*s/he imitated him/her; s/he quoted him/her:* TEE$^{3}$ ax̱'eiwatee.

**rabbit**

*rabbit:* g̱áx̱.

**rack**

*rack for drying fish:* x̱aanás' éinaa.

**radio**

*radio, phonograph, stereo, music box, ipod; any device that plays music:* at shí ḵóok.

**rafter**

*rafter:* x̱aanás'.

**rafters**

*rafters (large roof beams):* hít kaságu. *rafters (modern):* hít kagaadí.

**railing**

*banister; railing:* a daax̱ yaa dulsheech át.

**rain**

*it's pouring rain; it's hailing; it's snowing:* G̱EET aawag̱éet. *it's raining:* TAAN séew daak wusitán. *rain:* séew, sóow (C).

**rainbow**

*rainbow:* kichx̱.anagaat.

**raise**

*s/he raised a hand:* TSAAḴ kei jiwlitsáḵ. *s/he raised him/her/it; s/he grew it:* WAAT awsiwát. *s/he raised his/her hand:* TAAN kei jiwsitán.

**rake**

*herring rake:* xídlaa.

**rare**

*its raw (flesh or meat); rare (meat):* a shís'ḵ.

**rash**

*itch; rash:* kaxweitl. *rash:* xéesh.

**raspberry**

*raspberry:* tléḵw yádi.

**rat**

*mouse; rat:* kuts'een.

**ratfish**

*ratfish:* g̱eey kanax̱ ḵutées'.

**rattle**

*rattle (of shaman):* sheishóox̱.

**raven**

*raven:* yéil.

**raw**

*its raw (flesh or meat); rare (meat):* a shís'ḵ.

**razor**

*razor:* aan yaduxas' át.

**reach**

*s/he reached his/her hand through it:* JEIL anax̱ yaawajél.

**read**

*s/he read:* TOOW wuditóow. *s/he read it:* TOOW aawatóow.

**ready**

*getting ready for it; in anticipation of it:* a yayís. *he/she/it is ready; he/she/it is finished; he/she/it is prepared; he/she/it is permanent:* NEI yan uwanéi. *ready, waiting for him/her to eat, drink; waiting for him/her to speak or finish speaking:* du x̱'ayee. *ready, waiting for him/her to use:* du jiyee.

**really**

*much, lots of, really:* aatlein. *truly, really; in truth, for sure:* x'éig̱aa.

**reason**

*it; that place, time, reason, fact:* á.

**receptacle**

*receptacle for it:* a yee.ádi.

**recklessness**

*foolishness; recklessness:* l yaa ḵooshgé.

**recover**

*s/he was saved; s/he was healed; s/he was cured; s/he recovered; s/he was satisfied:* NEIX̱ wooneix̱.

**recovery**

*recovery; salvation:* g̱aneix̱.

**red**

*bright red or orange:* shex̱'wtáax'i. *crimson red; face paint:* léix̱'w. *red:* x̱'aan.

**red salmon**

*sockeye salmon; red salmon:* g̱aat.

**red snapper**

*red rockfish; red snapper:* léik̲'w.

**reef**

*nucleus of emerging river island; reef above high tide level:* shaltláax̱. *reef; large rock or boulder lying on the ocean floor:* eech. *underwater reef; large rock or boulder lying under the water:* hintu.eejí.

**reflect light**

*it's sparkling; it's reflecting light:* .ÍT'CH kawdli.ít'ch.

**regalia**

*dance regalia:* l'ax̱keit.

**relative**

*his/her clan brother or sister, distant relative, comrade:* du t'aag̱í. *his/her relative, friend; his/her tribesman:* du x̱ooní.

**release**

*s/he let him/her/it go; s/he released him/her/it; s/he left him/her/it; s/he delivered it:* NAAK̲[2] ajeewanák̲.

**reply**

*in response, reply to him/her; answering him/her; following his/her train of speech:* du x̱'akooká.

**report**

*s/he told about it; s/he reported about it; s/he witnessed it; s/he testified about it:* NEEK akaawaneek.

**research**

*s/he investigated it; s/he researched it:* TLAAKW akaawatlaakw.

**resemble**

*it looks like it; it resembles it:* XAAT[2] a yáx̱ kaaxát, YAA[1] oowayáa.

**resolve**

*strength of mind or heart; courage; resolve:* toowú latseen.

**respect**

*respect:* yáa at wooné. *respected person; gentleman; lady:* sh yáa awudanéiyi. *s/he respects him/her:* NEI du yáa ayaawanéi / du yáa awuwanéi.

**response**

*in response, reply to him/her; answering him/her; following his/her train of speech:* du x̱'akooká.

**rest**
*ashore, onto ground; to rest:* yan~. *s/he rested; s/he's resting:* SAA[3] wudlisáa. *the rest of it:* a déinde aa.

**restaurant**
*restaurant; tavern:* atx̲á daakahídi.

**return**
*(returning) back:* k̲ux̲. *s/he returned it:* TAAN k̲ux̲ aawatán.

**rheumatism**
*rheumatism:* s'aag̲itunéekw (AtT).

**rib**
*his/her rib:* du s'óog̲u.

**ribbon**
*hair ribbon:* shach'éen. *ribbon:* ch'éen.

**rice**
*rice; Kamchatka lily root:* kóox.

**rich**
*rich man:* dáanaa s'aatí. *rich man; man of wealth; chief:* aank̲áawu. *s/he got rich; s/he got wealthy; it became profitable:* NÁALX̲ wulináalx̲.

**ridge**
*(on) the back of it (fish); on the crest, ridge, backbone of it (hill, ridge, point):* a litká. *on the ridge or elevated part of the point (of land):* x'aa luká.

**rifle**
*gun, rifle:* óonaa.

**right away**
*suddenly, immediately, right away:* ch'a yák'w.

**rim**
*its hem, bottom edge (of coat, dress, shirt); rim (of hat):* a kóon.

**ring[1]**
*ring:* tl'ik̲kakées.

**ring[2]**
*it rang:* GWAAL sh wudigwál. *s/he beat it; s/he rang it; s/he stabbed it:* GWAAL aawagwaal.

**rip**
*s/he tore it; s/he peeled it off; s/he ripped it off:* S'EIL' akaawas'éil'.

**rise**
*it rose:* XEEX kei uwaxíx. *the water level rose; the tide came up:* DAA[1] kei uwadáa. *the (water) level rose to there; it flowed to there:* DAA[1] át kaawadáa.

**rites**
*s/he performed rites; s/he made magic:* HÉIX̲WAA aawahéix̲waa.

**river**

*edge of river channel:* héen wantú. *fishing hole; hole in stream, river, creek:* ísh. *head of river, stream:* héen sháak. *(in the) river valley:* héen yík. *in the water; in the river:* héen táak. *mouth of it (a river, creek):* a wát. *mouth of river, stream:* héen wát. *on (top of) the water, river:* héen x̱'aká. *river, stream, creek:* héen. *river; stream; creek:* kanaadaayi héen, naadaayi héen.

**river flats**

*river flats; tidelands; mudflats:* taashuká.

**riverside**

*riverside:* héen x̱'ayaax̱.

**road**

*on the path, trail, road; bed of the path, trail, road:* dei yík. *path, trail; road, street:* dei. *side of the path, trail, road, street:* dei yaax̱.

**robe**

*blanket; robe:* x'óow.

**robin**

*robin-like bird:* shoox̱'.

**rock**

*cairn; rock pile:* té xóow. *memorial pile of rocks:* xóow. *reef; large rock or boulder lying on the ocean floor:* eech. *stone; rock:* té. *underwater reef; large rock or boulder lying under the water:* hintu.eejí.

**rockfish**

*red rockfish; red snapper:* léiḵ'w.

**rockslide**

*rockslide:* taḵaadí.

**rod**

*engine cylinder connecting rod:* washéen katág̱ayi.

**roe**

*roe, eggs (of fish):* kaháakw.

**roll**

*it rolled to it:* GWAATL át kaawagwátl. *it's running (of engine); it started (of engine); it's rolling (of wheel); it's spinning (of wheel):* JOOX kaawajóox.

**roof**

*roof:* hít ká.

**room**

*(in) his/her room, bedroom:* du eetí ká. *room:* eet. *room, space, place for it; time for it; chance, opportunity for it:* a ya.áak.

**root**

*rice; Kamchatka lily root:* kóox. *root; especially spruce root:* x̱aat. *roots or vines used in basket decoration:* léet'.

**rope**
*rope:* tíx'.

**rose**
*rose:* k'inchéiyi.

**rosehip**
*rosehip:* k'inchéiyi tléig̲u.

**rough**
*it's rough (of ocean):* TAAN jiwsitaan. *it's stormy; it's rough (of weather):* TEE[2] ayawditee.

**row**
*s/he rowed; s/he paddled:* X̲AA[2] aawax̲áa.

**rowboat**
*rowboat:* aandaayaagú.

**rubber**
*rubber:* s'él'.

**rug**
*mat, doormat; rug:* g̲áach.

**rumen**
*its rumen, main stomach (of ruminant):* a dáali.

**rumor**
*gossip, rumormonger:* niks'aatí. *gossip; rumormonger:* neek shatl'ék̲x'u, neek s'aatí (T). *news; gossip, rumor:* neek.

**rump**
*his/her rump; the flesh around his/her hips:* du k'í.

**run**
*he/she/it is running around; he/she/it ran around:* XEEX át wujixeex. *he/she/it ran away:* XEEX k̲ut wujixeex. *he/she/it ran there:* XEEX aadé wjixeex. *he/she/it ran to it:* XEEX át wujixíx. *he/she/it started running:* XEEX g̲unéi wjixíx. *it flowed; it's flowing; it's running (of nose):* DAA[1] kaawadaa. *it's running (of engine); it started (of engine); it's rolling (of wheel); it's spinning (of wheel):* JOOX kaawajóox. *they ran:* GOOK̲ has loowagook̲. *they ran after it:* GOOK̲ a ítx̲ has loowagook̲. *they ran there:* GOOK̲ aadé (ha)s loowagook̲. *they ran to it:* GOOK̲ át has luwagúk̲.

**run out**
*s/he ran out of it:* XEEX du jeet shuwaxíx.

**rush**
*war; trouble; rush, hurry:* adawóotl.

**Russia**
*Russia:* Anóoshi aaní.

**Russian**
*Russian:* Anóoshi.

**rust**
*rust:* g̲ayéis' háatl'i.

**rutabaga**
*rutabaga; turnip:* anahoo.

**sack**
*bag; sack:* gwéil.

**sadness**
*sorrow; sadness:* toowú néekw, toowú nóok.

**sail**
*it's blowing around; it blew around; s/he is sailing around; s/he sailed around:* S'EES át wulis'ees. *sail:* yaakw yiks'ísayi.

**sailboat**
*sailboat:* s'ísaa yaakw.

**sale**
*sale:* hoon.

**salesman**
*salesman; clerk; storekeeper:* dahooní.

**saliva**
*his/her saliva:* du x̲'ahéeni.

**salmon**
*coho salmon; silver salmon:* l'ook. *dead salmon (after spawning):* nóosh. *dog salmon; chum salmon:* téel'. *fish; salmon:* x̲áat. *half-dried salmon (smoked):* náayadi. *king salmon; chinook salmon; spring salmon:* t'á. *pink salmon; humpy, humpback salmon:* cháas'. *salmon creek:* x̲áat héeni. *sockeye or coho salmon that has entered fresh water:* x̲'áakw. *sockeye salmon; red salmon:* g̲aat. *spawned-out salmon with white scabs, ready to die:* xein.

**salmonberry**
*salmonberry:* was'x'aan tléig̲u. *young salmonberry bush shoots (edible):* k'eit.

**salmon eggs**
*dish made with berries and salmon eggs:* kanéegwál'.

**salt**
*salt:* éil'.

**saltwater brine**
*saltwater brine:* éil' kahéeni.

**salvation**
*recovery; salvation:* g̲aneix̲.

**same**
*the same:* ch'u shóogu.

**sand**
*fine sand or gravel:* l'éiw yátx'i. *sandbar; gravel bar; sand beach; gravel beach:* xákw. *sand; gravel:* l'éiw. *sand point:* l'éiw x'aayí.

**sandhopper**
*sandhopper:* kook'énaa.

**sandpiper**
*sandpiper:* gus'yadóoli. *sandpiper (shore bird):* x̲'al'daayéeji.

**sap**
*cambium, sap scraped from inner bark:* sáx'. *its sap, phloem:* a káx̲i. *its sapwood; its sappy inner bark (of a tree):* a láx̲'i.

**sapling**
*pole; sapling:* tlag̲anís. *sapling:* aas yádi. *sapling; pole made from sapling:* tag̲anís.

**sapwood**
*its sapwood; its sappy inner bark (of a tree):* a láx̲'i.

**sash**
*sash (worn over shoulder):* koogéinaa.

**Satan**
*Satan:* Diyée aank̲áawu.

**satisfied**
*s/he was grateful; s/he was thankful; s/he was satisfied:* TEE[1] sh tóog̲áa wditee.

**satisfy**
*s/he was saved; s/he was healed; s/he was cured; s/he recovered; s/he was satisfied:* NEIX̲ wooneix̲.

**save**
*s/he saved him/her/it; s/he healed him/her/it; s/he cured him/her/it:* NEIX̲ awsineix̲. *s/he was saved; s/he was healed; s/he was cured; s/he recovered; s/he was satisfied:* NEIX̲ wooneix̲.

**saw**
*narrow saw used to cut corners off lumber; bevel saw:* t'áa shuxáshaa. *rip saw; double-handled saw for sawing lumber:* kax'ás'aa. *saw:* xáshaa. *s/he cut it (with a knife); s/he sawed it:* XAASH aawaxaash.

**sawmill**
*sawmill:* kax'ás'ti daakahídi, sh kadax'áshti hít.

**Saxman**
*people of Cape Fox, Saxman:* Sanyaa K̲wáan.

**say**

*s/he said that; s/he confessed that; s/he acknowledged that:* K̲AA[1] yéi yaawak̲aa. *s/he told him/her that; s/he said that to him/her; s/he asked him/her to do that:* K̲AA[1] yoo ayawsik̲aa.

**saying**

*saying, proverb; event that is so common it has become a saying or proverb:* yax̲ at g̲wakú.

**scab**

*scab:* k̲éech'.

**scald**

*he/she/it burned him/her/it; s/he scalded him/her/it:* X̲'EIX̲' awlix̲'éx̲'.

**scale**

*its scale (of fish):* a jeig̲í.

**scales**

*its scales (of fish):* a kajeig̲í.

**scalp**

*his/her scalp:* du shadaadoogú.

**scar**

*scar:* teel.

**scarecrow**

*scarecrow:* yéil koox̲étl'aa.

**scarf**

*headscarf, kerchief covering the head:* shadaa.át. *neck scarf; kerchief:* sadaat'aay.

**scary**

*it was scary; it was dangerous:* X̲ÉITL'SHÁN kawlix̲éitl'shán.

**scholar**

*student; pupil; scholar:* sgóonwaan.

**school**

*school:* áx' k̲aa ée at dultóow yé, at wuskú daakahídi, sgóon.

**scissors**

*scissors:* k̲aashaxáshaa.

**scrap**

*dirt; scrap(s); rubbish, trash, clutter; lint:* s'eex.

**scrape**

*s/he scraped it:* XAAS' aawaxás'. *s/he scraped it; s/he softened it:* XWAACH awlixwách.

**scraper**

*scraper, as for scraping off bark from roots:* éenaa. *scraper for hemlock bark:* yees'. *skin scraper:* xwájaa.

**screen**
*cheesecloth, loose-woven cloth; netting, screen:* kag̱ádaa. *wall crest; wall screen:* x̱'éen.

**screw**
*screw:* kas'éet. *s/he screwed it on it:* TEIX̱' át akawlitíx̱'.

**screwdriver**
*screwdriver:* kas'éet katíx̱'aa.

**scribe**
*writer; scribe; secretary:* kashxeedí.

**scrubber**
*scrubber:* kaxíl'aa.

**sculpin**
*bullhead, sculpin:* wéix̱'.

**sea anemone**
*sea anemone:* tayataayí. *small red sea anemone:* tayashagoo.

**sea cucumber**
*sea cucumber:* yéin.

**seagull**
*gull, seagull:* kéidladi. *T'aḵdeintaan, locally called "Seagull"; a clan of the Raven moiety whose principal crest is the Seagull:* T'aḵdeintaan. *young seagull:* lawúx̱.

**seal**
*fur seal:* x̱'óon. *hair seal:* tsaa. *Tsaagweidí; a clan of the Eagle moiety whose principal crests are the Seal and Killerwhale:* Tsaagweidí.

**sea lion**
*sea lion:* taan.

**seam**
*seam:* ḵéich'ál'.

**sea monster**
*legendary sea monster:* g̱unakadeit.

**sea otter**
*sea otter:* yáxwch', yúxch' (C).

**search**
*s/he looked for it; s/he searched for it:* SHEE[1] aag̱áa ḵoowashee. *s/he searched there; s/he looked there:* SHEE[1] át ḵuwashée.

**seat**
*s/he has him/her seated there:* .AA[1] át as.áa. *s/he seated him/her:* NOOK[1] awsinook.

**sea urchin**
*sea urchin:* nées', x̱'waash.

**seaweed**

*bladder rack; rock weed; yellow seaweed:* tayeidí. *dulse (type of seaweed):* laak̲'ásk. *hairy grass, seaweed on which herring spawn:* né. *half-dried, compressed food, esp. berries or seaweed:* kat'ákx̲i. *ribbon seaweed:* k̲'áach'. *seaweed, kelp on which herring spawn:* daaw.

**secret**

*in secret (where nobody can see); away from people's view:* k̲aa yat'éinák̲, du yat'éinák̲.

**secretary**

*secretary (stenographer):* k̲aa x̲'éidák̲ kashxeedí. *writer; scribe; secretary:* kashxeedí.

**see**

*blocking his/her view; in his/her way (so that he/she can't see):* du wak̲ká. *coming to see him/her:* du keekán. *s/he can see it; s/he perceives it:* TEEN ayatéen. *s/he sees it; s/he saw it:* TEEN awsiteen. *you see:* x̲á.

**seed**

*its seeds:* a x'aakeidí. *its seeds (inside it, as inside a berry):* a tukayátx'i.

**seesaw**

*seesaw:* kookíts'aa.

**seine**

*seine fisherman; seine boat:* asg̲eiwú. *s/he seined; s/he fished (with a net):* G̲EIWOO awdzig̲eiwú.

**sell**

*s/he sold it:* HOON aawahoon. *s/he went peddling it; s/he went selling it:* HOON awlihoon.

**seller**

*merchant; seller:* hoon s'aatí.

**semen**

*its semen; its milt (of fish):* a tl'éili.

**send**

*s/he sent him/her on a mission:* K̲AA[1] akaawak̲aa. *s/he sent him/her there; s/he ordered him/her to go there; s/he gave it (in accordance with clan relationship):* NAA[3] aadé akaawanáa.

**separate**

*separate from it; on the edge, side of it; missing its mark:* a wanáak.

**serviceberry**

*serviceberry; saskatoonberry:* gaawák̲.

**set**

*it set (sun, moon):* XEEX yínde wooxeex.

**settlement**

*town; village; settlement; inhabited or owned land:* aan.

**seven**

*seven:* dax̱adooshú. *seven (people):* dax̱adooshóonáx̱.

**sew**

*s/he embroidered it on it; s/he sewed beads on it:* ḴAA[2] a káa akaawaḵáa. *s/he sewed:* ḴAA[2] wudiḵáa. *s/he sewed it:* ḴAA[2] aawaḵáa. *s/he sewed it on it:* ḴAA[2] a kát akawliḵáa.

**sewing**

*sewing:* daḵéis'.

**shade**

*shade, shadow(s) cast by landforms, etc.:* chéx̱'i (C).

**shadow**

*his/her shadow; image:* du yahaayí. *shade, shadow(s) cast by landforms, etc.:* chéx̱'i (C).

**shaft**

*its handle (stick-like); its shaft (of spear, etc.):* a sáxwdi, a sákwti.

**shaman**

*shaman; medicine man:* íx̱t'.

**shame**

*shame, embarrassment:* kadéix'. *Shame on you! [reprimand]:* Húsh!. *s/he brought it onto him/her (esp. shame, blame, joy):* TEE[2] du kát ashuwatée.

**Shangukeidí**

*Shangukeidí, locally known as "Thunderbird"; a clan of the Eagle moiety whose principal crest is the Thunderbird:* Shangukeidí.

**shark**

*man-eating shark (legendary):* shax̱dáḵw. *shark:* tóos'. *shark (porpoise-like):* chichuyaa.

**sharp**

*it got sharp:* K'ÁTS' yawlik'áts'.

**sharpen**

*s/he sharpened it:* X'AAT ayaawax'át, G̱EEL' ayaawag̱íl'.

**shawl**

*shawl; cape; poncho:* teiḵ.

**she**

*he, she [independent]:* hú.

**shed**

*platform cache; house cache; shed:* chál.

**sheep**

*mountain sheep, bighorn sheep:* tawéi. *sheep:* wanadóo.

**shell**

*dentalia shells:* t'áx'x̲i. *empty bivalve shell:* xáak. *pounded shell powder:* káts. *shell; shell-like chip or flake; china; carapace:* nóox'.

**shelter**

*in a fort, shelter, cove:* noow g̲ei. *shelter (from wind or weather), harbor:* déili. *shelter of it (especially a tree):* a jiseiyí. *the shelter of a mountain, area on the beach below a mountain:* shaa seiyí. *the shelter of a tree:* aas jiseiyí. *the shelter of it; the lee of it; the (beach) area below it (a mountain, hill, etc.):* a seiyí.

**shepherd**

*shepherd:* wanadóo latíni.

**shield**

*in its way; blocking its way; acting as a shield for it:* a yinaa. *in its way; keeping it away; protecting, shielding, screening from it; blocking it:* a niyaa.

**shim**

*wedge, shim:* x̲'éex'w.

**shin**

*his/her shin:* du xées' (C).

**shine**

*it's bright; it's shining:* GAAN[1] kawdigán. *it's shining on it:* GAAN[1] a kát kawdigán. *it's sunny; the sun is shining:* GAAN[1] awdigaan. *sun rays are shining on it:* TSOOW g̲agaan át x̲'oos uwatsóow. *the moon is shining:* DEES awdlidées.

**shingle**

*shingle(s):* hít kat'áayi. *shingles:* t'aa yátx'i.

**ship**

*cruise ship; large ship:* yakwtlénx'.

**shirt**

*shirt:* k'oodás'.

**shock**

*it cramped; it's cramping; he/she/it got shocked (by electricity):* SHOOK' kawdlishúk'.

**shoe**

*shoe(s):* téel. *slipper(s); house shoe(s):* neilyeetéeli.

**shoelace**

*shoelace(s):* téel x̲'agudzaasí, téel x̲'akadzaazí, téel x̲'adzaasí.

**shoemaker**

*shoemaker, cobbler:* téel layeix̲í.

**shoe polish**

*shoe polish:* téel daakeyéis'i (C).

**shoot**

*s/he donated it; s/he loaded it (gun); s/he shot it (basketball):* G̲EEX' akaawag̲éex'. *s/he is shooting at it:* .OON a.únt. *s/he shot it:* .OON aawa.ún. *s/he shot it (with bow and arrow); s/he chose it (in gambling with sticks):* T'OOK aawat'úk.

**shopping**

*s/he went shopping:* HOON wudlihoon.

**shore**

*beach; waterside; down on the beach, shore:* éek̲. *down to beach, shore:* yeek̲. *shore; land:* yán. *the beach, shore below it (a town):* a eeg̲ayáak.

**shoreline**

*shoreline:* tleiyán. *shoreline; beach:* neech.

**short**

*less than it; (reaching, falling) short of it; not (big or far) enough for it:* a k̲ín. *short:* guwáatl'.

**shoulder**

*his/her shoulder:* du x̲ikshá.

**shoulderblade**

*his/her shoulderblade; scapula:* du óox'u.

**shout**

*s/he called out to him/her; s/he shouted to him/her:* .EEX' aawa.éex'.

**shovel**

*shovel:* k̲utl'ídaa.

**show**

*s/he demonstrated it to him/her; s/he showed him/her how to do it; s/he performed it for him/her:* NEI du wak̲shiyeex' yéi awsinei.

**shrimp**

*shrimp:* s'éex'át.

**sick**

*s/he got sick; he/she/it hurt; s/he was in pain:* NEEKW woonéekw.

**sickness**

*sickness; illness; disease:* néekw.

**side**

*face, (vertical) side, (vertical) surface of it:* a yá. *his/her family line of descent, side:* du yinaanáx̲. *his/her flank, side of his/her belly:* du k̲aatl. *his/her flank, side of his/her body between the ribs and the hip:* du k̲atlyá. *in addition to it; along with it; to the side of it; besides that:* a kíknáx̲. *one side of his/her torso:* du kík. *on the edge, side of it (as a trail); on the shoulder of it:* a wanká. *separate from it; on the edge, side of it; missing its mark:* a wanáak. *side of it (house, building, animal); slab of meat covering its ribcage:* a kageidí. *side of the path, trail, road, street:* dei yaax̲.

**sideways**
*sideways:* tl'aadéin.

**sight**
*it was a sight to behold; it was fascinating to watch:* TÉES'SHÁN kawlitées'shán. *s/he has sight:* TEEN k̲uwatéen / k̲uyatéen.

**sign**
*marker; mark, sign:* kwéiy.

**silt**
*clay; alluvial silt:* s'é.

**silty**
*silty, murky water:* l'óox̲.

**silver**
*silver:* dáanaa.

**silver salmon**
*coho salmon; silver salmon:* l'ook.

**silversmith**
*silversmith:* dáanaa kat'éex̲'i, dáanaa t'éex̲'i.

**similar**
*he/she/it was like it; he/she/it was similar to it:* TEE[1] a yáx̲ wootee.

**simply**
*just, simply; just then:* tle.

**sin**
*evil, sin:* l ushk'é.

**since**
*from, out of; since:* -dáx̲.

**sinew**
*its sinew:* a tási. *thread; sinew:* tás.

**sing**
*s/he sang:* SHEE[2] at wooshee. *s/he sang it:* SHEE[2] aawashee.

**singed**
*singed, burnt, or charred matter:* xóosht'.

**singer**
*singer:* at shéeyi. *singers, choir:* at shéex'i.

**singing**
*music, singing, song:* at shí.

**sink**
*it sank:* TAAX̲'W wootáax̲'w.

**sister**

*her older sister, cousin:* du shátx̲. *her younger sister; his younger brother; cousin:* du kéek'. *his/her clan brother or sister, distant relative, comrade:* du t'aag̲í. *his/her clan sister:* du sháawu. *his sister:* du dlaak'.

**sister-in-law**

*his/her brother-in-law, sister-in-law:* du káani.

**sit**

*it's sitting there:* TEE$^{2}$ át satéen, TAAN át tán. *s/he sits; s/he is sitting:* .AA$^{1}$ .áa. *they are sitting:* K̲EE has k̲éen.

**sit down**

*he/she/it squatted; he/she it sat down low; he/she/it landed (of waterfowl, plane):* K̲AAK̲ wujik̲aak̲. *s/he sat down:* NOOK$^{1}$ woonook. *they sat down:* K̲EE has wook̲ee.

**Sitka**

*people of Sitka:* Shee At'iká K̲wáan. *Sitka:* Sheet'ká.

**situated**

*it's situated there:* .AA$^{1}$ át la.áa. *the building was situated there (suddenly as if overnight):* NOOK$^{1}$ áa wdinook.

**six**

*six:* tleidooshú. *six (people):* tleidooshóonáx̲.

**Skagway**

*Skagway:* Shg̲agwei.

**skate**

*skate (ocean creature related to the shark and the ray):* ch'éetg̲aa.

**skeleton**

*his/her skeleton, bare bones:* du xaagú.

**skewer**

*spit, skewer, roasting stick, barbecue stick:* tséek.

**ski**

*ski(s):* t'áa jáaji.

**skiff**

*skiff; small boat; flat-bottom canoe:* yakwyádi.

**skillet**

*cast-iron skillet:* té kas'úgwaa yeit (T). *frying pan, skillet:* kax̲gáani yeit, kas'ígwaa yeit (A).

**skin**

*his/her skin, complexion:* du dook. *his/her skin (surface):* du ch'áatwu. *its skin (of animal); hide:* a doogú. *its skin (of fish):* a xáas'i. *its wrinkled, baggy skin, hide:* a daaleilí. *under or inside his/her clothes; next to his/her skin:* du doonyaa.

**ski pole**
*ski pole(s):* t'áa jáaji wootsaag̱ayí.

**skull**
*pit at base of his/her skull:* du lak'eech'kóog̱u.

**skunk cabbage**
*skunk cabbage:* x̱'áal'.

**sky**
*clear sky, blue sky:* xáats'.

**slap**
*it dove into the water; it slapped its tail down into the water:* T'AAKW héende awjit'ákw. *s/he slapped him/her/it; s/he tagged him/her/it:* T'AACH aawat'ách.

**slave**
*slave:* goox̱.

**sled**
*sled:* xát'aa. *sled (for recreational sledding):* ach kooshx̱'íl'aa yeit.

**sledgehammer**
*sledgehammer:* té shanax̱wáayi.

**sleep**
*s/he overslept:* TAA[1] a yáanáx̱ yaawatáa. *s/he slept:* TAA[1] wootaa. *sleep:* tá. *sleep in his/her eyes:* waḵdlóoḵ. *they slept:* X̱EIX'W has woox̱éix'w.

**sleeve**
*it's sleeve (of shirt, coat):* a jíni.

**slice**
*s/he cut it up; s/he carved it; s/he sliced it:* XAASH akaawaxaash.

**slide**
*he/she/it is sliding around; he/she/it slid around:* X̱'EEL' át wushix̱'éel'. *he/she/it slid there:* X̱'EEL' át wushix̱'íl'. *s/he slipped; s/he slid:* X̱'EEL' wushix̱'éel'.

**slime**
*slime (inside clamshell):* átl'áni. *slime; thick mucus:* x̱éel'.

**sling**
*sling:* júx̱'aa.

**slip[1]**
*petticoat; slip:* doonyaax̱l'aak.

**slip[2]**
*s/he slipped; s/he slid:* X̱'EEL' wushix̱'éel'.

**slipper**
*slipper(s); house shoe(s):* neilyeetéeli.

**slippers**
*slippers (shell creature):* koow.

**slippery**
*it's slippery:* X̲'EEL' kashix̲'íl'k.

**slough**
*slough:* éix̲'.

**slowly**
*slowly:* kaldaaG̲éinák̲.

**slug**
*slug, snail:* táax̲'.

**slush**
*wet snow; slush:* kaklahéen.

**small**
*they're small:* GEI[1] yéi kwdzigéi.

**smallpox**
*smallpox:* kwaan.

**smell**
*he/she/it stank; he/she/it smelled:* CHAAN wulichán. *he/she/it was fragrant; he/she/it smelled sweet:* TS'AA wulits'áa. *s/he smelled it:* NEEX' awsiníx' / awdziníx'.

**smile**
*s/he is grinning; s/he is smiling:* NOOTS[1] at kaawanúts.

**smoke**
*s/he dried fish; s/he smoked fish:* X̲'AAN at uwax̲'án. *s/he smoked:* S'EIK̲ sh x̲'awdis'eik̲. *s/he tanned it; s/he smoked it:* S'EIK̲ áx̲ akawlis'eik̲. *smoke:* s'eik̲, s'eek̲. *smoke spreaders (board suspended horizontally above smokehouse fire):* ganigeidí.

**smokehole**
*opening of smokehole:* gaan woolí. *smokehole:* gaan, gaan ká. *smokehole cover:* gaan x̲'aháadi.

**smokehouse**
*long smokehouse pole(s):* jikak̲áas'. *smokehouse:* atx'aan hídi. *smokehouse shelf:* yaash ká. *smokehouse (with smoke piped in from outside):* s'eik̲ daakahídi.

**snag**
*pile of driftwood, driftlogs; snag pile:* yanxoon. *snag; driftlog, driftwood:* shaak̲.

**snail**
*slug, snail:* táax̲'. *snail with shell:* ts'ésx̲'w.

**snake**
*snake:* l'ut'tláak̲. *worm; larva; grub; caterpillar; snake:* tl'úk'x̲.

**snare**

*s/he snared it:* DAAS' awdlidás'. *snare:* dáas'aa.

**snob**

*snob; person who considers himself/herself better than others:* ḵaa kanax̱ḵáa.

**snot**

*snot:* lug̱eitl'.

**snow**

*dry snow:* dleit kakétsk. *dust cloud; snow cloud:* kals'éesjaa. *it's pouring rain; it's hailing; it's snowing:* G̱EET aawag̱éet. *it's raining:* TAAN séew daak wusitán. *snow:* dleit. *wet snow; slush:* kaklahéen.

**snowberry**

*snowberry:* dleit tléig̱u.

**snowshoe**

*snowshoe:* jáaji.

**snowslide**

*snowslide; snow avalanche:* dleit ḵaadí.

**snowstorm**

*snowstorm, snow shower:* dleit g̱éedi.

**soak**

*s/he soaked it:* KEIL akawlikél.

**soap**

*soap:* ús'aa.

**soapberry**

*soapberry:* xákwl'i.

**sock**

*sock(s):* l'ée x'wán.

**sockeye**

*Ḵaach.ádi, locally called "Sockeye"; a clan of the Raven moiety whose principal crest is the Sockeye:* Ḵaach.ádi. *L'ukaax̱.ádi, locally called "Sockeye"; a clan of the Raven moiety whose principal crest is the Sockeye:* L'ukaax̱.ádi.

**sockeye salmon**

*sockeye or coho salmon that has entered fresh water:* x̱'áakw. *sockeye salmon; red salmon:* g̱aat.

**soften**

*s/he scraped it; s/he softened it:* XWAACH awlixwách.

**soil**

*earth; land, country; soil:* tl'átk. *soil; dirt:* l'éx̱'kw.

**solidify**

*it's frozen; it froze; it solidified; it hardened:* T'EEX' wudlit'íx'.

**some**

*some of them:* a x̱oo aa. *which (one); some (certain one):* daaḵw.aa sá.

**sometimes**

*sometimes:* wáa yateeyi yéix'. *sometimes, once in a while:* wáang̱aneens.

**son**

*his/her son, cousin:* du yéet.

**song**

*his/her song:* du x̱'asheeyí. *music, singing, song:* at shí. *song:* shí.

**songbird**

*songbird; bird:* ts'ats'ée, ts'ítskw.

**soon**

*(along) with, by means of; as soon as:* tin.

**soot**

*soot:* dús'.

**sore**

*pus; discharge (from a sore, wound); sore, wound that discharges pus:* ḵéet'. *rotting sore; gangrene; cancer:* tl'ooḵ.

**sorrow**

*sorrow; sadness:* toowú néekw, toowú nóok.

**soul**

*his/her inner being; mind; soul; feelings; intention:* du toowú. *his/her soul (of departed person):* du yahaayí.

**sound**

*sound, noise of it:* a kayéik. *sound, noise of it (something whose identity is unknown):* a yayík. *sound of stamping, pounding fists, clapping; sound of running quickly:* tíxwjaa (At), túxjaa.

**soup**

*soup broth; soup:* tax̱héeni. *soup, porridge:* katéix̱.

**sour**

*it was sour; it was bitter; it was spicy:* .AAX'W[1] wusi.áax'w.

**sourdock**

*sourdock; wild rhubarb:* tl'aaḵ'wách'.

**south**

*downstream; south:* éex. *downstream; south; lower 48 states, (locally: down south):* ixkée.

**space**

*room, space, place for it; time for it; chance, opportunity for it:* a ya.áak.

**spark**

*spark:* yíḵdlaa.

**sparkle**

*it's sparkling; it's reflecting light:* .ÍT'CH kawdli.ít'ch.

**speak**

*ready, waiting for him/her to eat, drink; waiting for him/her to speak or finish speaking:* du x̱'ayee. *s/he spoke; s/he talked; s/he made a speech:* TAAN x̱'awditaan. *s/he spoke to him/her; s/he talked to him/her:* TAAN du éet x̱'eiwatán. *s/he talked; they spoke:* TAAN yoo x̱'eiwatán. *they conversed; they spoke; they talked:* .AAT$^{2}$ yoo (ha)s x̱'awli.át.

**spear**

*fish spear; harpoon for spearing salmon:* dlagwáa. *fish spear with a long pole and detachable gaff hook:* kooxídaa (At). *its head (of spear):* a kádi. *its prongs (of spear):* a x̱aani. *s/he poked it; s/he jabbed at it; s/he speared it:* TAAḴ$^{1}$ aawatáḵ. *spear:* tsaaǥál'. *spear for clubbing:* at shax̱ishdi dzáas. *spear (for devilfish):* táanaa. *spear (for fish and seal):* áadaa. *spear for hunting:* woosáani. *spear which binds rope around seal:* at s'aan.ax̱w dzáas.

**speech**

*s/he spoke; s/he talked; s/he made a speech:* TAAN x̱'awditaan. *speech, talk; language; word, phrase, sentence, or discourse:* yoo x̱'atánk.

**spicy**

*it was sour; it was bitter; it was spicy:* .AAX'W$^{1}$ wusi.áax'w.

**spider**

*crawling insect; spider:* kanas.aadí. *spider:* asgutuyikshúa.

**spill**

*s/he spilled it:* X̱EECH yax̱ akaawax̱ích.

**spin**

*it's running (of engine); it started (of engine); it's rolling (of wheel); it's spinning (of wheel):* JOOX kaawajóox.

**spirit**

*fighting spirit:* lékwaa. *his/her spirit:* du yakǥwahéiyagu. *Indian doctor's spirit:* yéik. *spirit:* ḵaa yakǥwahéiyagu.

**spit**

*s/he spat:* TOOX̱ yóot ḵ'awdzitúx̱. *spit:* x̱'astóox̱.

**splinter**

*splinter, sliver:* sheey kaḵáas'i.

**split**

*s/he chopped it up; s/he split it (wood):* X̱OOT'$^{2}$ akawlix̱óot'.

**spoil**

*it aged; it spoiled:* S'EEX wulis'íx.

**sponge**

*foam (on waves); sponge:* teet x̱'achálx̱i.

**spoon**

*black horn spoon:* yéts' shál. *large wooden spoon:* shéen. *sheep or goat horn spoon:* leineit shál. *spoon:* shál.

**sport**

*sport fisherman:* ashalx̲óot'i.

**spotted**

*it's spotted:* KÁX'X̲ kajikáx'x̲, CH'ÁCH'X̲ kadlich'ách'x̲.

**spray**

*spray of air exhaled through its blowhole (of sea mammal):* a óoxu.

**spread**

*it fell on it; it hit it (of bullet); it spread around (rumor, news):* XEEX át uwaxíx. *s/he spread it out; s/he unfolded it:* YAA² áx̲ akaawayaa.

**spring**

*spring (AT):* k̲ukalt'éex' ká. *spring (of water):* goon.

**sprout**

*its sprouts, fleshy leaves growing toward the top of the stem (e.g. of bear root):* a shaadí.

**spruce**

*pine needles, spruce needles:* g̲ítg̲aa. *Sitka spruce:* shéiyi. *young spruce or hemlock:* dúk̲l', túk̲l'.

**square**

*square:* t'éesh kaayí. *square (for marking boards):* t'áa shukaayí.

**squat**

*he/she/it squatted; he/she it sat down low; he/she/it landed (of waterfowl, plane):* K̲AAK̲ wujik̲aak̲.

**squeeze**

*s/he mashed it; s/he squeezed it:* G̲OOTL akaawag̲útl.

**squeezed**

*he/she/it is stuck there; he/she/it is squeezed (in) there:* X̲'EEX' áx̲ kawlix̲'éex'.

**squid**

*squid:* dag̲asaa.

**squirm**

*he/she/it is crawling around on his/her/its belly; he/she/it crawled around on his/her/its belly; he/she/it is creeping around on his/her/its belly; he/she/it crept around on his/her/its belly; he/she/it is squirming around; he/she/it squirmed around:* TLOOX' át wootlóox'.

**squirrel**

*arctic ground squirrel:* tsálk. *red squirrel:* kanals'áak. *squirrel:* kals'áak (T).

**stab**

*s/he beat it; s/he rang it; s/he stabbed it:* GWAAL aawagwaal.

**stack**
*s/he packed it; s/he stacked it:* CHAAK akaawachák.

**stain**
*black with dirt, filth, stain:* ts'ák̲l. *s/he dyed it; s/he stained it:* SEIK̲'W akawlisék̲'w.

**stained**
*it's dyed; it's stained:* SEIK̲'W kawdisék̲'w.

**stairs**
*ladder; stairs:* dzeit.

**stamp**
*s/he kicked it; s/he stamped on it:* TSEIX̲ aawatséx̲.

**stand**
*s/he is standing:* HAAN[1] hán. *s/he remained standing:* HAAN[1] yan uwahán. *they are standing:* NAAK̲[1] has nák̲. *they kept standing; they stood:* NAAK̲[1] yan has uwanák̲.

**stand up**
*s/he stood up:* HAAN[1] wudihaan.

**star**
*comet; falling star:* xoodzí. *star:* k̲utx̲.ayanahá.

**starfish**
*starfish:* s'áx.

**start**
*it's running (of engine); it started (of engine); it's rolling (of wheel); it's spinning (of wheel):* JOOX kaawajòox. *start, begin:* g̲unei. *starting off taking off:* yetx̲.

**starvation**
*famine; starvation:* laaxw.

**starving**
*he/she/it starved:* LAAXW uwaláxw.

**stay**
*s/he stayed overnight; s/he camped out:* X̲EI uwax̲éi. *s/he was with him/her; s/he stayed with him/her; s/he lived with him/her:* TEE[1] du x̲ánx' yéi wootee.

**steal**
*s/he stole it:* TAAW aawatáw.

**steam**
*s/he steamed it; s/he boiled it:* TAA[3] awsitáa. *steam (visible, in the air); mist, fog (rising from a body of standing water):* x'úkjaa.

**steambath**
*steambath:* x̲aay.

**steam engine**

*steam engine, train:* shtéen káa.

**stem**

*its stem (of plant); pith (of tree):* a kadíx'i.

**stereo**

*radio, phonograph, stereo, music box, ipod; any device that plays music:* at shí k̲óok.

**stern**

*its back end; stern (of boat):* a k'óol'. *its cutwater; the curved part of a bow or stern (of boat):* a xées'i. *stern (of a boat):* a géek.

**stick[1]**

*match; stick:* k̲áas'. *planting stick:* katsóowaa. *pry; stick or tool for prying; crowbar:* kít'aa. *roasting stick (split so that the meat can be inserted; the end is then bound):* x̲'wéinaa. *sharpened stick (for digging up clams, roots, etc.); gardening fork:* káat'. *spit, skewer, roasting stick, barbecue stick:* tséek. *stick:* sheey. *sticks woven through the fish lengthwise after it has been filleted for barbecuing:* tl'éek'at.

**stick[2]**

*s/he stuck it to it:* S'EEX'W át akawlis'íx'w.

**stickleback**

*stickleback:* k'aagán.

**stiff**

*dried and hard; stiff (as canvas, dry fish):* g̲ákw.

**Stikine**

*Stikine River:* Shtax'héen.

**still1**

*again; still; some more:* tsu. *just now; just then; still; yet:* yeisú. *still, even:* ch'u.

**still2**

*he/she/it became still:* TEE[1] tleiyéi yéi wootee.

**stink**

*he/she/it stank; he/she/it smelled:* CHAAN wulichán.

**stomach**

*his/her stomach; gizzard (of bird):* du yoowú. *its rumen, main stomach (of ruminant):* a dáali.

**stone**

*stone; rock:* té. *wide, flat stone (used for cooking):* té k̲'áatl'.

**stop**

*Don't!; Stop it!:* Ilí!. *he/she/it became still:* TEE[1] tleiyéi yéi wootee. *s/he went ashore; s/he came to a stop:* K̲OOX̲[1] yan uwak̲úx̲. *Stop it!; That's enough!:* Déi áwé!.

**store**
*store:* hoon daakahídi.

**storekeeper**
*salesman; clerk; storekeeper:* dahooní.

**store up**
*s/he put up food; s/he stored up food (for the winter); s/he preserved food; s/he finished distributing things (at party):* GAA yan akawligáa.

**stormy**
*it's stormy; it's rough (of weather):* TEE$^2$ ayawditee.

**story**
*s/he told the story of it; s/he talked into it:* NEEK akawlineek. *story:* shkalneek.

**storyteller**
*storyteller; preacher:* k̲oon sh kalneegí.

**stout**
*stout:* kutlá.

**stove**
*stove:* stoox.

**straight**
*straight ahead; directly ahead:* yaadachóon.

**straighten out**
*s/he straightened it out:* NEI wooch yáx̲ awsinei.

**strain**
*s/he strained it; s/he filtered it; s/he drained it off:* CHAA akawlicháa.

**straw**
*straw (for drinking):* a tóonáx kadus'ík̲s' át.

**strawberry**
*strawberry:* shákw. *wild strawberry:* lingít shákw.

**stream**
*creek; small stream:* héenák'w. *fishing hole; hole in stream, river, creek:* ísh. *head of river, stream:* héen sháak. *mouth of river, stream:* héen wát. *river, stream, creek:* héen. *river; stream; creek:* kanaadaayi héen, naadaayi héen.

**strength**
*strength of mind or heart; courage; resolve:* toowú latseen. *strength, power:* latseen.

**stretcher**
*stretcher, form for shaping:* kanágaa.

**string**

*babiche, string, leather thonging:* dzaas. *s/he strung them together; s/he threaded it:* .EESH akawli.ísh. *string:* tíx' yádi.

**striped**

*it's striped:* G̱AAS' kadliG̱áas'.

**strive**

*s/he exerted his/her full strength on it; s/he concentrated on it; s/he strove for it:* XEECH aawaxích.

**strong**

*he/she/it became strong; he/she/it became powerful:* TSEEN wulitseen.

**stuck**

*he/she/it got hung up; s/he got delayed; s/he got stuck:* K'EEX̱' yanax̱ wushik'éex̱'. *he/she/it is stuck there; he/she/it is squeezed (in) there:* X̱'EEX' áx̱ kawlix̱'éex'. *it got stuck on the beach:* DLAAX̱'W yax̱ woodláax̱'w.

**student**

*student; learner:* yaa at naskwéini. *student; pupil; scholar:* sgóonwaan.

**study**

*s/he studied it; s/he learned it; s/he practiced it:* TOOW sh tóo awdlitóow. *s/he studied; s/he taught himself/herself:* TOOW sh tóo at wudlitóow.

**stump**

*its stump, butt end (of tree or other plant):* a goowú. *uprooted tree or stump (with roots protruding):* x'éedadi.

**sucker**

*its sucker (devilfish):* a óot'i.

**suckerfish**

*moonfish, suckerfish, blowfish:* tl'éitl'.

**suddenly**

*suddenly, immediately, right away:* ch'a yóok'.

**suffer**

*under the burden, weight of it; belabored or suffering from it (a burden, hardship):* a jiyeet.

**Suḵteeneidí**

*Suḵteeneidí, locally called "Dog Salmon"; a clan of the Raven moiety whose principal crest is the Dog Salmon:* Suḵteeneidí.

**summer**

*summer:* ḵutaan. *summer; early summer:* taakw.eetí.

**summon**

*s/he summoned him/her; s/he called him/her:* X̱OOX̱ aawax̱oox̱.

**sun**

*sun:* g̱agaan.

**sunbeam**

*sunbeam; ray of sunlight:* g̱agaan x̱'usyee.

**sun-dried**

*sun-dried:* g̱agaan kas'úkwx̱u.

**sunlight**

*sunbeam; ray of sunlight:* g̱agaan x̱'usyee.

**sunny**

*it's sunny; the sun is shining:* GAAN[1] awdigaan.

**sure**

*be sure not to:* tsé. *be sure to:* x'wán. *indeed, for sure:* dágáa.

**surface**

*face, (vertical) side, (vertical) surface of it:* a yá. *the (horizontal) surface of it; on it; on top of it; in it ( a dish; a path):* a ká.

**surgeon**

*surgeon:* ḵaadaaxaashí.

**surprise**

*[expression of mild surprise]:* shé. *[expression of strong surprise]:* gwáa.

**swallow[1]**

*swallow:* séew kooshdaneit.

**swallow[2]**

*s/he swallowed it:* NOOT' akaawanóot'.

**swamp**

*stunted tree in swamp; jackpine, swamp spruce:* sháchk ka.aasí. *swamp:* sháchk.

**swan**

*swan:* gúḵl'.

**sweater**

*sweater:* kakéin k'oodás'.

**sweep**

*s/he swept:* XEET' wudixéet'. *s/he swept the floor:* XEET' t'aa ká aawaxéet'.

**sweet**

*he/she/it was fragrant; he/she/it smelled sweet:* TS'AA wulits'áa. *it was sweet:* NÚKTS wulinúkts.

**sweetheart**

*his/her sweetheart:* du tseiyí, du kacháwli.

**swell**

*wave; swell:* teet.

**swelling**

*boil; inflammation and swelling:* x'ees.

**swim**

*it is swimming around there; it swam around there:* KWAAN át jiwsikwaan. *it swam ashore:* HEEN² yan uwahín. *it swam underwater to it:* X'AAK át uwax'ák. *they are swimming around there; they swam around there:* KWAAN át has wusikwaan. *they are traveling around (of a group of cars or fleet of boats); they are swimming around (of a school of sea mammals):* GOO² át has yaawagoo. *they swam to it:* GOO² át yawsigóo.

**swing**

*swing, hammock:* g̱eig̱ách'. *swing; hammock:* g̱eeg̱ách'.

**swollen**

*it's swollen; it's tangled:* X'EES' wudix'ís'.

**table**

*table:* nadáakw.

**tadpole**

*tadpole; polliwog:* dúsh.

**tag**

*s/he slapped him/her/it; s/he tagged him/her/it:* T'AACH aawat'ách.

**tail**

*its tail flippers:* a geení. *its tail (of animal):* a l'eedí. *its tail (of bird or fish):* a koowú.

**tailbone**

*his/her tailbone; bottom of his/her spine:* du k'óol'.

**T'ak̲deintaan**

*T'ak̲deintaan, locally called "Seagull"; a clan of the Raven moiety whose principal crest is the Seagull:* T'ak̲deintaan.

**take**

*s/he carried it aboard; s/he took it aboard (container or hollow object):* TAAN yaax̲ aawataan. *s/he carried it all there; s/he took it all there:* JEIL aadé akaawajeil. *s/he carried it inside; s/he took it inside (container full of liquid or small objects):* .EEN¹ neil awsi.ín. *s/he carried it inside; s/he took it inside (general, compact object):* TEE² neil aawatée. *s/he carried it; s/he took it (container or hollow object):* TAAN aawataan. *s/he carried it there; s/he took it there (container full of liquid or small objects):* .EEN¹ át awsi.ín. *s/he carried it there; s/he took it there (container or hollow object):* TAAN át aawatán. *s/he carried it there; s/he took it there (general, compact object):* TEE² aadé aawatee. *s/he carried it there; s/he took it there (solid, often complex object):* TEE² aadé awsitee. *s/he carried stuff there; s/he took stuff there:* JEIL aadé at kaawajeil. *s/he carried them there; s/he took them there (esp. baggage or personal belongings):* .AAT² aadé awli.aat. *s/he gave it to him/her; s/he took it to him/her (container full of liquid or small objects):* .EEN¹ du jeet awsi.ín. *s/he gave it to him/her; s/he took it to him/her (container or hollow object):* TAAN du jeet aawatán. *s/he gave it to him/her; s/he took it to him/her (general, esp. abstract object):* TEE² du jeet aawatée. *s/he gave it to him/her; s/he took it to him/her (long, complex object):* TAAN du jeet awsitán. *s/he gave it to him/her; s/he took it to him/her (round object):* TEE[2] du jeet akaawatée. *s/he gave it to him/her; s/he took it to him/her (textile-like object):* .AAX̲[2] du jeet aawa.áx̲. *s/he gave them to him/her; s/he took them to him/her:* NEI du jeet yéi awsinei. *s/he gave them to him/her; s/he took them to him/her (esp. baggage or personal belongings):* .AAT[2] du jeet awli.át. *s/he gave them to him/her; s/he took them to him/her (small, round or hoop-like objects):* .AAT[2] du jeet akawli.át. *s/he touched it; s/he picked it up; s/he took it:* SHEE[1] át uwashée.

**take care**

*s/he watched him/her/it; s/he looked after him/her/it; s/he took care of him/her/it:* TEEN awlitín.

**take off**

*starting off taking off:* yetx̲.

**Takhini**

*Takhini hot springs (north of Whitehorse, Yukon Territory):* Tax̲héeni.

**Taku**

*Taku:* T'aak̲ú.

**tale**

*myth; legend; children's tale:* tlaagú.

**talk**

*conversation, dialog; talk, discourse (between more than one person):* yoo x̲'ala.átk. *s/he spoke; s/he talked; s/he made a speech:* TAAN x̲'awditaan. *s/he spoke to him/her; s/he talked to him/her:* TAAN du éet x̲'eiwatán. *s/he talked; they spoke:* TAAN yoo x̲'eiwatán. *s/he told the story of it; s/he talked into it:* NEEK akawlineek. *speech, talk; language; word, phrase, sentence, or discourse:* yoo x̲'atánk. *they conversed; they spoke; they talked:* .AAT[2] yoo (ha)s x̲'awli.át.

**talk out of**

*s/he talked him/her out of it:* NEEK a káx̲ akawliník.

**tall**

*he/she/it is big, tall (live creature or building):* GEI[1] ligéi.

**tallow**

*tallow, hard fat:* toow.

**tan**

*s/he tanned it; s/he smoked it:* S'EIK̲ áx̲ akawlis'eik̲.

**tangled**

*it's swollen; it's tangled:* X'EES' wudix'ís'.

**tarp**

*canvas; tarp; tent:* xwaasdáa.

**tarpaper**

*bark roofing material; tarpaper:* hít kax'úx'u.

**taste**

*s/he liked the taste of it:* K'EI du x̱'é wook'éi. *s/he tasted it:* NOOK[2] x̱'éi awdinúk.

**tavern**

*restaurant; tavern:* atx̱á daakahídi.

**tea**

*tea:* cháayoo.

**teach**

*s/he studied; s/he taught himself/herself:* TOOW sh tóo at wudlitóow. *s/he taught him/her:* TOOW du éex' at wulitóow. *s/he taught it to him/her:* TOOW du éex' awlitóow.

**teacher**

*teacher:* ḵóo at latóowu (T).

**tea kettle**

*tea kettle (originally with long curved spout):* t'aawáḵ x'eesháa.

**tear**

*s/he held it open; s/he tore it away (from the hook):* S'EIL' ax̱'eiwas'él'. *s/he tore it:* S'EIL' aawas'éil'. *s/he tore it; s/he peeled it off; s/he ripped it off:* S'EIL' akaawas'éil'.

**tears**

*his/her tears:* du wax̱'ahéeni.

**Teiḵweidí**

*Teiḵweidí, locally called "Brown Bear"; a clan of the Eagle moiety whose principal crest is the Brown Bear:* Teiḵweidí.

**telephone**

*s/he called him/her on the phone:* TAAN du jeet x̱'awditán, TAAN du jeedé x̱'awditaan.

**tell**

*s/he tells him/her that:* ḴAA[1] yéi adaayaḵá. *s/he told about it; s/he reported about it; s/he witnessed it; s/he testified about it:* NEEK akaawaneek. *s/he told a story; s/he preached; s/he narrated:* NEEK sh kawdlineek. *s/he told him/her that; s/he said that to him/her; s/he asked him/her to do that:* ḴAA[1] yoo ayawsiḵaa. *s/he told people a legend:* TLAAKW ḵoon aawatlákw.

**temple**

*his/her temple; upper side of his/her face (from the cheekbones to the top of the head):* du yat'ákw.

**tempt**

*he/she/it tempted him/her; he/she tried it out; he/she tested it:* DLÉNX̱AA akaawadlénx̱aa.

**temptation**

*temptation, trial:* ḵukadlénx̱aa.

**ten**

*ten:* jinkaat. *ten (people):* jinkaadináx̱.

**tendon**

*vein; tendon (inside body):* téet'.

**tent**

*canvas; tarp; tent:* xwaasdáa. *tent:* s'ísaa hít.

**tentacle**

*its tentacle (of octopus):* a tl'eig̱í (C), a tl'eeg̱í.

**tern**

*tern:* ḵ'eiḵ'w, kichyát, kootl'éit'aa.

**terrible**

*it looked terrible; it looked awful; it was eerie; it was unattractive:* JEE[2] kawlijée.

**Teslin**

*Teslin:* Deisleen. *Teslin Lake people:* Deisleen Ḵwáan.

**test**

*he/she/it tempted him/her; he/she tried it out; he/she tested it:* DLÉNX̱AA akaawadlénx̱aa.

**testicles**

*his testicles:* du k'wát'. *its testicles (of moose, caribou):* a k'únts'i.

**testify**

*s/he told about it; s/he reported about it; s/he witnessed it; s/he testified about it:* NEEK akaawaneek.

**thankful**

*s/he was grateful; s/he was thankful; s/he was satisfied:* TEE[1] sh tóog̱áa wditee.

**thank you**

*Thank you!:* Gunalchéesh!.

**that**

*that (at hand):* wé. *that (at hand) [focus]:* áwé. *that (at hand) [interrogative]:* ák.wé. *that (distant), yonder:* yú. *that (distant), yonder [focus]:* áyú. *that (distant), yonder [interrogative]:* ákyú. *this/that (over here), the other:* hé. *this/that (over here), the other [focus]:* áhé. *this/that (over here), the other [interrogative]:* ák.hé.

**that's how**

*thus, that's how:* ayáx̱.

**thaw**

*it melted; it dissolved; it thawed:* LAA[1] wuliláa.

**their**

*their [possessive]:* has du.

**them**

*them [object]:* has.

**then**

*only then:* tsá. *then, around, after, for:* aag̱áa.

**they**

*they [independent]:* hás. *they [subject]:* has.

**thick**

*it became thick:* KAAK wusikaak. *it got that thick; it thickened:* KAAK yéi kawsikaak. *thick:* kusakaak.

**thief**

*thief:* táaw s'aatí.

**thigh**

*its hindquarters; thigh:* a g̱ádzi.

**thighs**

*his/her buttocks, thighs:* du g̱áts.

**thimble**

*thimble:* tl'ik̲naa.át.

**thimbleberry**

*thimbleberry:* ch'eex̲'.

**thin**

*thin (flat object):* k̲'áatl'.

**thing**

*thing:* át.

**things**

*baggage, luggage; things, stuff packed up for carrying:* at la.át.

**think**

*in his/her opinion; to his/her way of thinking, feeling:* du tuwáx'. *s/he thought about it; s/he considered it; s/he made up his/her mind about it:* TAAN a daa yoo toowatán. *they thought about it; they considered it; they made up their minds about it:* .AAT[2] a daa yoo (ha)s tuwli.át.

**thirsty**

*s/he is thirsty; it is dry:* KOOX shaawakúx.

**thirty**

*thirty:* nás'k jinkaat.

**thirty one**

*thirty one:* nás'k jinkaat k̲a tléix'.

**this**

*this (right here):* yá. *this (right here) [focus]:* áyá. *this (right here) [interrogative]:* ákyá. *this/that (over here), the other:* hé. *this/that (over here), the other [focus]:* áhé. *this/that (over here), the other [interrogative]:* ák.hé.

**thought**

*consciousness, thought process, thinking:* yoo tutánk. *I thought:* k̲ashde. *thought:* tundatáan.

**thread**

*s/he strung them together; s/he threaded it:* .EESH akawli.ísh. *thread; sinew:* tás.

**three**

*three:* nás'k. *three at a time, three by three:* nás'gig̲áa. *three (people):* nás'gináx̲.

**three times**

*three times:* nas'gidahéen.

**throat**

*his/her throat:* du leitóox̲.

**throw**

*s/he threw it:* G̲EEX' kei akaawag̲íx'. *s/he threw it to it:* X̲EECH át akaawax̲ích, LEET át aawalít.

**throw up**

*s/he vomited; s/he threw up:* K̲OO wudlik̲oo.

**thumb**

*his/her thumb:* du goosh.

**thunderbird**

*Shangukeidí, locally known as "Thunderbird"; a clan of the Eagle moiety whose principal crest is the Thunderbird:* Shangukeidí.

**Thunderbird**

*Thunderbird:* Xeitl.

**thus**

*thus, specifically:* yéi.

**thwart**

*its crosspiece (of boat, snowshoe); thwart (of boat):* yax̲ak'áaw.

**tickle**

*it's itchy; it tickles:* XWEITL kawlixwétl.

**tide**

*current; tidal action:* héen kanadaayí. *current, tide:* haat. *flood; tide:* k̲ées'. *high tide line:* k̲ées' shuwee. *low tide (point at which the tide will begin coming in):* éek̲ lukak̲ées'i. *the tide is in:* DAA[1] daak̲ uwadáa. *the tide is low:* LAA[1] yan uwaláa. *the tide went out from under it; the tide ebbed out from under it:* LAA[1] áx̲ woolaa. *the water level rose; the tide came up:* DAA[1] kei uwadáa. *whirlpool; boiling tide; chaos:* x'óol'.

**tide flats**

*tide flats:* léin.

**tidelands**

*river flats; tidelands; mudflats:* taashuká.

**tie**

*s/he tied it:* DOOX' akaawadúx'. *s/he tied it up:* .AAX̲W yánde aawa.áx̲w. *s/he wrapped it up; s/he tied it in a bundle:* .AAX̲W adaawsi.áx̲w.

**tied**

*it's connected there; it's tied there:* XAAT[1] aadé ksixát.

**tiger**

*man-eating animal; lion; tiger; man-eating wolf:* haadaag̲ooji. *man-eating feline; mountain lion; tiger, leopard:* haadaadóoshi.

**tighten**

*s/he pulled it tight:* XAAT[1] k'idéin akawsixát.

**timbers**

*house timbers:* hít da.ideidí.

**time**

*(distributed) in the area of; (going) after, (waiting) for; about the time of:* -g̲aa. *it's time for it:* HAA át k̲uwaháa. *it; that place, time, reason, fact:* á. *it was long (time):* YAAT' yeeywooyáat'. *late; after the appointed time:* gaaw ítx'. *on time; in time:* gaaw yáx̲. *room, space, place for it; time for it; chance, opportunity for it:* a ya.áak. *time:* gaaw.

**tin**

*iron, tin:* g̲ayéis', ik̲yéis'.

**tip**

*its tip (of pointed object); top, tips of its branches (of tree, bush):* a x'aan. *its tip, point:* a lux'aa.

**tired**

*he/she/it made him/her tired:* XWEITL awlixwétl. *s/he's tired; s/he's weary:* XWEITL wudixwétl.

**Tlingit**

*Tlingit:* Lingít.

**to**

*(resting) at; coming to, arriving at; moving about:* -t. *to, toward; until; in the manner of:* -dé(i) ~ -de(i).

**toast**

*s/he fried it; s/he toasted it:* S'OOK akawlis'úk.

**tobacco**

*(plug of) chewing tobacco:* kat'éex'. *tobacco:* g̲ánch, tuwaakú.

**toe**

*his/her big toe:* du x̲'usgoosh. *his/her toe:* du x̲'ustl'eik̲, du x̲'ustl'eek̲.

**toenail**
*his/her nail (of finger or toe):* du x̱aakw.

**together**
*together [object]:* woosh, wooch.

**tomorrow**
*tomorrow:* seig̱án, seig̱ánin.

**tongs**
*tongs:* l'át'aa.

**tongue**
*his/her tongue:* du l'óot'.

**tonsils**
*his/her tonsils:* du x̱'as'guwéis'i.

**too**
*also, too, as well:* tsú.

**tool**
*tool, tools:* jishagóon.

**too much**
*too much:* ḵútx̱.

**tooth**
*his/her missing tooth:* du oox̱k'i.eetí. *his/her tooth:* du oox̱. *its tooth:* a oox̱ú.

**toothpick**
*toothpick:* oox̱ katság̱aa.

**top**
*around the top of it (object with rounded top):* a shadaa. *its tip (of pointed object); top, tips of its branches (of tree, bush):* a x'aan. *top of it (something with a rounded top, as a mountain); above it; (elevated) over it:* a shakée. *top (spinning toy):* toolch'án.

**torn**
*it's torn:* S'EIL' kawdis'éil'.

**totem pole**
*totem pole:* kootéeyaa.

**touch**
*s/he felt it:* NOOK[2] jée awdinúk. *s/he touched it; s/he picked it up; s/he took it:* SHEE[1] át uwashée.

**tourist**
*tourist:* sh tuwáa kasyéiyi.

**tow**
*s/he towed it:* X̱AACH aawax̱aach.

**toward**

*in the direction or general area of it; (headed) toward it:* a yinaadé, a niyaadé. *straight towards it; directly towards it:* a dachóon. *to, toward; until; in the manner of:* -dé(i) ~ -de(i).

**towel**

*towel, hand towel:* jig̲wéinaa.

**town**

*in a town, on the streets of a town:* aan x̲'ayee. *town; village; settlement; inhabited or owned land:* aan.

**townspeople**

*townspeople; crowd or large group of people:* aantk̲eení.

**tracks**

*its tracks:* a x̲'us.eetí.

**trail**[1]

*on the path, trail, road; bed of the path, trail, road:* dei yík. *path, trail; road, street:* dei.

**trail**[2]

*s/he untangled it; s/he trailed him/her/it; s/he undid it:* KEI akawsikei.

**transport**

*s/he is transporting him/her/it around; s/he transported him/her/it around:* X̲AA[2] át ayaawax̲aa. *s/he transported him/her/it there:* X̲AA[2] át ayaawax̲áa.

**trap**

*deadfall trap for large animals:* yéix̲. *fish trap:* sháal. *rock pile fish trap:* óot'. *s/he caught it; s/he grabbed him/her/it; s/he arrested him/her; s/he trapped him/her/it:* SHAAT aawasháat. *trap (esp. steel trap):* g̲aatáa.

**trapper**

*trapper:* g̲aatáa yéi daanéiyi.

**trash**

*dirt; scrap(s); rubbish, trash, clutter; lint:* s'eex. *filth, mess; trash, rubbish, garbage:* tl'eex.

**travel**

*s/he traveled there:* TEEN át k̲uwatín, TEEN aadé k̲oowateen. *they are traveling around (of a group of cars or fleet of boats); they are swimming around (of a school of sea mammals):* GOO[2] át has yaawagoo. *they traveled through it:* GOO[2] anax̲ has yaawagóo.

**tree**

*dead dry tree, still standing:* láax̲. *fallen tree:* l'ákwti. *growth on the trunk of a tree, burl:* gúnl'. *its stump, butt end (of tree or other plant):* a goowú. *stunted tree in swamp; jackpine, swamp spruce:* sháchk ka.aasí. *the shelter of a tree:* aas jiseiyí. *tree (esp. conifer):* aas. *tree pitch:* aasdaak'óox̲'u. *tumor in a tree, with branches growing from it:* aasdaax'ées'i. *uprooted tree or stump (with roots protruding):* x'éedadi. *windfall; dead tree(s) or brush that has fallen:* g̱éejadi. *windfall; tree lying in the woods:* g̱éechadi.

**trial**

*temptation, trial:* ḵukadlénx̱aa.

**tribesman**

*his/her relative, friend; his/her tribesman:* du x̱ooní.

**trickle**

*trickle of water; steady drip or leak:* kax'áasjaa.

**tricks**

*tricks, sleight of hand; juggling:* yakwteiyí.

**trim**

*its trim, trimming:* a x̱'ax̱éedli.

**trip**

*s/he fell over it; s/he tripped over it (of live creature):* GEET[1] anax̱ yei wdzigít.

**troll**

*s/he fished (with a hook); s/he trolled:* T'EIX̱ awdzit'eix̱.

**troller**

*fisherman (troller):* ast'eix̱í. *troller:* shukalx̱aají.

**trouble**

*he/she/it bothered him/her; he/she/it is bothering him/her:* XEEL' akaawaxíl'. *trouble; conflict:* kaxéel'. *war; trouble; rush, hurry:* adawóotl.

**troublemaker**

*troublemaker:* at lux'aaḵáawu.

**trout**

*cutthroat trout:* x'éitaa. *Dolly Varden trout:* x̱'wáat'. *lake trout:* daleiyí. *steelhead trout:* aashát. *trout (sea):* yaa.

**truly**

*truly, really; in truth, for sure:* x'éig̱aa.

**trunk**

*its base (of tree or other plant); the lower part of its trunk or stem:* a k'eeyí.

**trust**

*s/he believed him/her; s/he trusted him/her:* HEEN[1] du éek' aawaheen.

**truth**

*truth:* x'éig̱aa át.

**try**

*he/she/it tempted him/her; he/she tried it out; he/she tested it:* DLÉNX̱AA akaawadlénx̱aa.

**Tsaagweidí**

*Tsaagweidí; a clan of the Eagle moiety whose principal crests are the Seal and Killerwhale:* Tsaagweidí.

**Tsimshian**

*Tsimshian:* Ts'ootsxán.

**tub**

*large rectangular tub for soaking skins while tanning them:* k̲'aakanéi.

**tuberculosis**

*chest pain; tuberculosis:* wuwtunéekw.

**tugboat**

*tugboat:* dax̲áchx'i.

**tumor**

*lump in the flesh; tumor:* kawáat. *tumor in a tree, with branches growing from it:* aasdaax'ées'i.

**turn**

*it's his/her turn:* HAA du éet k̲uwaháa. *s/he turned the boat:* .AAT[2] kei ayawli.át.

**turn back**

*s/he turned back:* K̲OOX̲[1] ayawdik̲úx̲. *s/he turned back; s/he went back; s/he walked back:* GOOT[1] ayawdigút. *they turned back; they went back; they walked back:* .AAT[1] has ayawdi.át.

**turnip**

*rutabaga; turnip:* anahoo. *turnip:* tl'aadéin.aa.

**turn off**

*s/he put it out (fire); s/he turned it off (light):* KEES' ayakawlikís'.

**turn on**

*s/he grew it; s/he turned it on (hose); s/he caused it to flow (water):* .AA[3] akawsi.aa. *s/he lit it (fire); s/he turned it on (light):* GAAN[1] át akawligán.

**turn over**

*s/he turned it over:* TAAN áa yax̲ aawatán. *turning over:* áa yax̲. *turning over endwise:* shóo yax̲.

**turnstone**

*black turnstone:* x'at'daayéejayi.

**turtle**

*turtle:* tadanóox', kanóox'.

**twenty**

*twenty:* tleik̲áa. *twenty (people):* tleik̲áanáx̲.

**twenty one**

*twenty one:* tleik̲áa k̲a tléix'. *twenty one (people):* tleik̲áa k̲a tléináx̲.

**twilight**

*dusk; twilight:* xi.áat.

**twin**

*his/her twin:* du kikyádi.

**twirl**

*s/he's waving it (hand, etc.); it's wagging it (tail); s/he is twirling it around above his/her head:* YEIN ashakawliyén.

**two**

*both:* ch'u déix̱. *twice, two times:* dax̱dahéen. *two:* déix̱. *two at a time, two by two:* dáx̱G̱aa. *two different kinds, types; two different ways, directions:* dax̱yeekaadé. *two (people):* dáx̱náx̱. *two (people) at a time:* dáx̱G̱aanáx̱.

**type**

*one kind, type; one way, direction:* tleiyeekaadé. *s/he typed it:* DAAL' akawlidál'. *two different kinds, types; two different ways, directions:* dax̱yeekaadé.

**typist**

*typist:* kaldáal'i.

**ulcer**

*mouth ulcer; soreness of the mouth (as of a baby teething):* xáatl'ákw.

**umbilical cord**

*his/her umbilical cord:* du taaní (TC), du taanú (AtT).

**umbrella**

*umbrella:* kéi daḵinji s'áaxw.

**unattractive**

*it looked terrible; it looked awful; it was eerie; it was unattractive:* JEE[2] kawlijée.

**uncle**

*his/her maternal uncle:* du káak. *his/her paternal uncle, cousin:* du sáni.

**under**

*near the base of it; at the foot of it; the back, rear or it (house); behind it (house); under the shelter of it (a standing object or structure):* a k'iyee. *under his/her feet:* du x̱'usyee. *underneath it; beneath it; below it:* a tayee. *under or inside his/her clothes; next to his/her skin:* du doonyaa.

**underground**

*underground:* yanax̱.

**undershirt**

*undershirt:* doonyaax̱ k'oodás'.

**understand**

*s/he understands him/her; s/he hears (and understands) him/her:* .AAX̱[1] ax̱'aya.áx̱ch. *s/he understood:* GEI[2] du daa yaa ḵushuwsigéi. *s/he understood him/her; s/he heard (and understood) him/her:* .AAX̱[1] ax̱'eiwa.áx̱.

**undo**

*s/he untangled it; s/he trailed him/her/it; s/he undid it:* KEI akawsikei.

**unfold**

*s/he spread it out; s/he unfolded it:* YAA[2] áx̱ akaawayaa.

**unripe**

*green, unripe berry:* kax̱'át'. *they're unripe; they're green (of berries):* X̱'AAT' kadlix̱'át'.

**untangle**

*s/he untangled it; s/he trailed him/her/it; s/he undid it:* KEI akawsikei.

**until**

*to, toward; until; in the manner of:* -dé(i) ~ -de(i).

**up**

*partway up it; halfway up it (the inside of a vessel or container):* a kat'óot. *up:* kei.

**upstairs**

*upstairs; attic:* hít shantú.

**upstream**

*upstream; north:* naakée.

**upward**

*upward:* kíndei.

**urine**

*his/her urine:* du lóox'u. *strong urine smell:* kax̱'ees.

**us**

*us [object]:* haa.

**use**

*ready, waiting for him/her to use:* du jiyee. *s/he used it for it; s/he made it into it:* YEIX̱[1] átx̱ awliyéx̱. *s/he wore it; s/he put it on; s/he used it:* .OO[1] yéi aawa.oo.

**used to**

*s/he got used to it; s/he became accustomed to it (the flavor, pronunciation of something):* DAA[2] du x̱'éix̱ woodaa.

**used up**

*it came to an end; it was used up:* XEEX shuwaxeex.

**utensil**

*kitchen utensil:* atx̱á jishagóon.

**vagina**
*privates (of female); vulva; vagina:* du góos.

**valley**
*mountain valley; valley:* shaanáx̱.

**value**
*its price, value; the money from the sale of it:* a yeidí.

**variety**
*different ones; variety:* woosh g̱unayáade aa.

**vegetation**
*leaf, leaves; vegetation, plants, herbs, herbiage:* kayaaní.

**vein**
*vein; tendon (inside body):* téet'.

**Venus**
*Venus:* k'óox dísi.

**verdigris**
*verdigris:* eeḵ háatl'i.

**very**
*very:* ḵúnáx̱, tlax̱.

**vest**
*vest; sleeveless top:* l.uljíni.

**via**
*along, via; including the time of:* -náx̱.

**view**
*blocking his/her view; in his/her way (so that he/she can't see):* du waḵkas'óox', du waḵká.

**village**
*town; village; settlement; inhabited or owned land:* aan.

**vine**
*roots or vines used in basket decoration:* léet'.

**visible**
*it's obvious; it's clearly visible:* HAA tlél goohá.

**voice**
*his/her voice:* du satú, du sé.

**vole**
*mouse, deer mouse; vole:* kag̱áak.

**vomit**
*s/he is vomiting; s/he vomited:* HAAS' uwahás'. *s/he vomited; s/he threw up:* ḴOO wudliḵoo. *vomit; urge to vomit:* háas'.

**wade**

*he/she/it waded ashore:* HOO yan uwahóo.

**wag**

*s/he's waving it (hand, etc.); it's wagging it (tail); s/he is twirling it around above his/her head:* YEIN ashakawliyén.

**wagon**

*flywheel; wheelbarrow; wagon; hand truck:* kajúxaa.

**wail**

*mourning, wailing, loud weeping or crying; wail, groan, moan:* kasg̲aax̲.

**waist**

*his/her waist:* du kasán.

**wait**

*ready, waiting for him/her to eat, drink; waiting for him/her to speak or finish speaking:* du x̲'ayee. *Wait!:* Ilí s'é!. *waiting for it:* a eeg̲áa, a yeeg̲áa, a yig̲áa.

**wake up**

*s/he woke him/her up:* GEET[1] kei awsigít. *s/he woke up:* GEET[1] kei wdzigít.

**walk**

*he/she/it is walking around there; he/she/it walked around there:* GOOT[1] át woogoot. *he/she/it walked along it:* GOOT[1] áx̲ woogoot. *he/she/it walked into the open;:* GOOT[1] daak uwagút. *he/she/it walked through it:* GOOT[1] anax̲ yaawagút. *he/she/it went there; he/she/it walked there:* GOOT[1] aadé woogoot. *s/he is walking along; s/he is going along:* GOOT[1] yaa nagút. *s/he turned back; s/he went back; s/he walked back:* GOOT[1] ayawdigút. *they are walking along there; they are going along there:* .AAT[1] áx̲ yaa (ha)s na.át. *they are walking around:* .AAT[1] át has woo.aat. *they turned back; they went back; they walked back:* .AAT[1] has ayawdi.át. *they walked:* .AAT[1] has woo.aat. *they walked down along it:* .AAT[1] áx̲ has woo.aat. *they walked there; they arrived there; they went there:* .AAT[1] át has uwa.át. *they walked there; they went there:* .AAT[1] aadé has woo.aat. *they walked through it; they went through it:* .AAT[1] anax̲ has yaawa.át. *they walked up there; they went up there:* .AAT[1] áa kei (ha)s uwa.át.

**wall**

*wall:* t'áa yá.

**walrus**

*walrus:* kooléix̲'waa.

**want**

*s/he feels that way; s/he wants to do it; s/he feels like doing it:* TEE[1] yéi tuwatee. *s/he wanted it; s/he liked it; it was pleasing to him/her:* GOO[1] du tuwáa wsigóo.

**war**

*fighting; war, conflict:* k̲ulagaaw. *war; trouble; rush, hurry:* adawóotl.

**war clothes**
*war clothes (of moosehide):* x'áan yinaa.át.

**warm**
*it's hot; it's warm:* T'AA uwat'áa. *s/he warmed it up:* T'AA awsit'áa. *the weather got hot; the weather got warm:* T'AA k̲oowat'áa.

**warrior**
*war party, attacking force of warriors or soldiers; army:* x̲áa.

**wart**
*wart:* t'áax̲'w.

**Was'eeneidí**
*Was'eeneidí; a clan of the Eagle moiety whose principal crests are the Wolf and Auklet:* Was'eeneidí.

**wash**
*s/he washed it:* .OOS' aawa.óos', .OOS' akaawa.óos'.

**wash basin**
*wash basin:* kát yadu.us'ku át.

**washboard**
*washboard:* kát dul.us'ku át, a káa dul.us'ku át.

**wash over**
*waves washed over it:* TAAN a kanax̲ jiyawsitán.

**wasp**
*bee; wasp:* gandaas'aají.

**watch1**
*wristwatch:* jikawáach.

**watch2**
*s/he watched him/her/it; s/he looked after him/her/it; s/he took care of him/her/it:* TEEN awlitín.

**watchman**
*guard, watchman:* at káx̲ adéli. *keeper of the key; jailer; night watchman:* katíx̲'aa s'aatí. *night watchman:* taat aayí adéli.

**water**
*coffee; hot water:* yat'aayi héen. *edge of body of water:* héen shú. *end of body of standing water:* hinshú (At). *in the water; in the river:* héen táak. *into water:* héenx̲, héeni. *on (top of) the water, river:* héen x̲'aká, hinx̲uká. *out of the water onto the beach, shore:* dáag̲i. *water:* héen.

**waterfall**
*waterfall:* x'áas.

**watermelon berry**
*watermelon berry, twisted stalk, wild cucumber:* tleik̲w kahínti.

**wave**[1]

*waves washed over it:* TAAN a kanax̱ jiyawsitán. *wave; swell:* teet.

**wave**[2]

*s/he's waving it (hand, etc.); it's wagging it (tail); s/he is twirling it around above his/her head:* YEIN ashakawliyén.

**waves1**

*waves reached the beach:* TAAN yan jiwsitán.

**way**

*place; way:* yé.

**we**

*we [independent]:* uháan. *we [subject]:* too-.

**weak**

*he/she/it was weak; s/he is anemic; it is mild (of weather):* TSEEN tlél wultseen.

**wealth**

*wealth; prosperity; riches:* lanáalx̱.

**wealthy**

*rich man; man of wealth; chief:* aanḵáawu. *s/he got rich; s/he got wealthy; it became profitable:* NÁALX̱ wulináalx̱.

**wear**

*s/he is wearing it:* TEE[2] kát adatéen. *s/he wore it; s/he put it on; s/he used it:* .OO[1] yéi aawa.oo.

**wear out**

*it wore out:* SHAASH woosháash.

**weary**

*s/he's tired; s/he's weary:* XWEITL wudixwétl.

**weasel**

*weasel:* dáa.

**weather**

*dry weather; clear day:* ḵuxaak. *the weather was that way:* TEE[1] yéi ḵoowatee. *weather:* ḵutí.

**weave**

*s/he knitted; s/he crocheted; s/he wove:* NEI kawdzinéi. *s/he made it (by weaving, knitting, crocheting); s/he mended it (net):* NEI akawsinei.

**web**

*its web (of spider):* a g̱eiwú.

**wedge**

*wedge, shim:* x̱'éex'w.

**weep**

*crying, weeping:* g̱aax̱.

**weighty**
*it got heavy; it was weighty (of abstracts):* DAAL woodál.

**well**
*well:* k'idéin.

**wet**
*he/she/it is wet:* TL'AAK' wuditl'ák'.

**whale**
*whale:* yáay.

**whatever**
*anything; whatever:* ch'a daa sá.

**wheel**
*s/he wheeled it there:* JOOX aadé akawlijoox. *s/he wheeled it to it:* JOOX át akawlijúx.

**wheelbarrow**
*flywheel; wheelbarrow; wagon; hand truck:* kajúxaa. *wheelbarrow; hand truck, dolly:* koojúxwaa (An), koojúxaa (TC).

**when**
*when, while:* ch'u tlei.

**whenever**
*any time (in the future); whenever (in the future):* ch'a gwátgeen sá.

**wherever**
*anywhere, anyplace; wherever:* ch'a goot'á sá.

**whetstone**
*whetstone:* yayéinaa.

**which**
*which (one); some (certain one):* daaḵw.aa sá.

**while**
*when, while:* ch'u tlei.

**whip**
*whip:* x̱át'aa.

**whirlpool**
*whirlpool:* haat kool. *whirlpool; boiling tide; chaos:* x'óol'.

**whisker**
*his/her whiskers:* du x̱'adaadzaayí. *its whiskers, beard (of fish):* a ḵ'anoox̱ú.

**white**
*white:* dleit. *White, European, Caucasian (man or person):* Gus'k'iyee ḵwáan, dleit ḵáa.

**whitecap**
*foam; whitecaps:* x̱eel.

**whittle**
*s/he whittled it:* YEIX̲[1] akaawayéx̲.

**whoever**
*anyone, anybody; whoever:* ch'a aadóo sá, ch'a aa sá.

**wide**
*it's wide:* WOOX̲' yawúx̲'.

**widow**
*widow:* l s'aatí shaawát.

**wife**
*his old lady (wife):* du shaawádi. *his wife:* du shát.

**wild celery**
*wild celery:* yaana.eit.

**wilderness**
*wilderness; the bush:* katk̲aak̲ú, g̲alg̲aak̲u.

**wild rhubarb**
*sourdock; wild rhubarb:* tl'aak̲'wách'.

**will**
*will; wish(es):* at sag̲ahaayí.

**willow**
*willow:* ch'áal'.

**win**
*s/he won it; s/he got it; s/he accomplished it; s/he defeated him/her:* DLAAK̲ ayaawadlaak̲.

**wind**
*chinook wind; south wind:* k'eeljáa, k'eiljáa. *north wind:* xóon. *thing heading offshore, esp. wind:* dákde át. *west wind:* l'ag̲akáx̲. *west wind; wind blowing ashore:* yánde át. *wind:* óoxjaa. *wind (blowing) from the south:* sáanáx̲.

**window**
*window:* x̲aawaag̲éi, x̲aawaag̲í.

**windpipe**
*his/her windpipe; pharynx:* du leikachóox̲'u.

**wing**
*its wing:* a kíji.

**winter**
*(in preparation) for winter:* táakw niyís. *winter; year:* táakw.

**wipe**
*s/he wiped it; s/he mopped it:* G̲OO awlig̲oo.

**wire**
*wire:* kaxées'.

**wish**
*will; wish(es):* at sag̲ahaayí. *wish; prayer:* oolxéis'.

**witch**
*witch:* nakws'aatí.

**with**
*(along) with, by means of; as soon as:* een, tin, teen. *in addition to it; along with it; to the side of it; besides that:* a kíknáx̲. *with it:* aan. *working with him/her; helping him/her work or do something:* du ji.een.

**without**
*lacking it; without it:* a eetéenáx̲. *without it; lacking it:* a g̲óot.

**witness**
*s/he told about it; s/he reported about it; s/he witnessed it; s/he testified about it:* NEEK akaawaneek.

**wolf**
*Kaagwaantaan, locally called "Wolf"; a clan of the Eagle moiety whose principal crest is the Wolf:* Kaagwaantaan. *man-eating animal; lion; tiger; man-eating wolf:* haadaag̲oojí. *Was'eeneidí; a clan of the Eagle moiety whose principal crests are the Wolf and Auklet:* Was'eeneidí. *wolf:* g̲ooch.

**wolverine**
*wolverine:* nóoskw, nóosk.

**woman**
*girls, young women:* shaax'wsáani. *woman:* shaawát. *young woman (not married):* shaatk'.

**women**
*women:* sháa.

**[wonder]**
*Eh?; I wonder:* kwshé.

**wonder**
*s/he wondered about it:* JEE[1] yoo akaawajeek.

**wood**
*burnt or charred wood:* xoodzí. *cord (of wood):* at kaayí. *dead wood that's wet on the outside:* gán láx̲'i. *its green wood (of tree):* a shís'k̲. *punk wood, decayed dry wood:* g̲unanaa tetl. *rotten wood:* naak̲w. *soft brown wood for tanning dye:* x̲'oon. *very rotton wood:* k̲úlk. *wood chips; wood shavings:* kayeix̲tág̲u (C). *wood, piece of wood; wood chip:* l'eiwú, l'oowú. *wood shavings:* kayeix̲.

**woodpecker**
*woodpecker:* gandaadagóogu.

**woods**
*from the woods onto the beach, shore:* éeg̲i. *thing of the woods:* at gutu.ádi. *woods; bush; brush, underbrush:* at gutú.

**woodworm**

*woodworm:* gantutl'úk'x̲u.

**wool**

*yarn; wool:* kakéin.

**work**

*s/he worked; s/he did that:* NEI yéi jeewanei. *working with him/her; helping him/her work or do something:* du ji.een. *work, job:* yéi jiné.

**worker**

*worker:* yéi jinéiyi. *worker; crew:* ganaswáan.

**work on**

*s/he does it; s/he is doing it; s/he works on it; s/he is working on it:* NEI yéi adaanéi.

**world**

*world:* lingít aaní.

**worm**

*worm; larva; grub; caterpillar; snake:* tl'úk'x̲.

**worry**

*s/he is worried about him/her/it; s/he has him/her/it on her mind:* XEEX du tóot wooxeex.

**wound**

*cut; knife wound:* k̲'éik̲'w. *gunshot wound:* óonaa eetí. *knife wound:* lítaa eetí. *pus; discharge (from a sore, wound); sore, wound that discharges pus:* k̲éet'. *s/he cut him/her/it (accidentally); s/he wounded him/her/it:* K̲'EIK'W[1] aawak̲'ék'w. *s/he cut himself/herself; s/he wounded himself/herself (with a sharp instrument):* K̲'EIK'W[1] sh wudik̲'ék'w. *s/he injured it; s/he wounded it; s/he bruised it:* CHOON awlichún. *wound:* s'éil'.

**wounded**

*he/she/it is injured; he/she/it is wounded; he/she/it is bruised; s/he is hurting (emotionally):* CHOON wudichún.

**Wrangell**

*Wrangell:* K̲aachx̲ana.áak'w.

**wrap**

*s/he bandaged it; s/he bound it up; s/he wrapped it:* S'EET akaawas'ít. *s/he wrapped it up; s/he tied it in a bundle:* .AAX̲W adaawsi.áx̲w.

**wren**

*wren:* woolnáx̲ wooshk̲ák̲.

**wrench**

*wrench:* kas'éet kag̲úkwaa, kas'éet kagwádlaa.

**wrist**

*back of his/her wrist:* du jiká. *his/her wrist:* du jiklix'ées', du jigúnl'i.

**wrist gaurd**

*wrist guard:* jiG̲ei.át.

**wrist guard**

*wrist guard:* jika.át.

**write**

*s/he wrote:* XEET kawjixít. *s/he wrote it; s/he drew it; s/he painted it; s/he photographed it; s/he took X-rays of it:* XEET akawshixít.

**writer**

*writer; scribe; secretary:* kashxeedí.

**wrong**

*against it; wrongly, improperly:* a géit~. *against it, wrong (so as to foul up what s/he had done):* du jiyagéix̲. *s/he did something wrong; s/he broke the law:* GEET$^2$ at géit wudzigít.

**X-ray**

*s/he wrote it; s/he drew it; s/he painted it; s/he photographed it; s/he took X-rays of it:* XEET akawshixít.

**Yakutat**

*Yakutat:* Yaakwdáat.

**Yanyeidí**

*Yanyeidí, locally known as "Bear"; a clan of the Eagle moiety whose principal crest is the Brown Bear:* Yanyeidí.

**yarn**

*yarn; wool:* kakéin.

**yarrow**

*yarrow; (locally) rat's tail:* kaG̲akl'eedí.

**year**

*winter; year:* táakw.

**yellow**

*dark yellow; eagle's beak:* ch'áak' loowú. *yellow:* ketllóox'u, s'éix̲wani, tl'áatl'.

**yes**

*yes:* aáa.

**yesterday**

*yesterday:* tatgé.

**yet**

*just now; just then; still; yet:* yeisú.

**yonder**

*that (distant), yonder:* yú. *that (distant), yonder [focus]:* áyú. *that (distant), yonder [interrogative]:* ákyú.

**you**

*you (plural) [independent]:* yeewháan. *you (plural) [object]:* yee. *you (plural) [subject]:* yee-. *you (singular) [independent]:* wa.é. *you (singular) [object]:* i-. *you (singular) [subject]:* i-.

**young**

*new; young; fresh:* yées. *young adult:* yées wáat. *young adult(s); young people:* yées <u>k</u>u.oo. *younger one:* kík'i aa.

**your**

*your (plural) [possessive]:* yee. *your (singular) [possessive]:* i.

~

# Tlingit Thematic Lexicon

*1- The physical universe*

- 1.1 Sky
  - 1.1.1 Objects in the sky
  - 1.1.3 Weather
    - 1.1.3.1 Natural Disaster
    - 1.1.3.2 Wind
  - 1.2.1 Land
  - 1.2.2 Matter
- 1.3 Water
  - 1.3.1 Bodies of water
  - 1.3.2 Movement of water
  - 1.3.4 Be in water
- 1.5 Plant
  - 1.5.1 Tree
  - 1.5.2 Bush, shrub
  - 1.5.3 Grass, herb, vine
  - 1.5.4 Moss, fungus, algae
  - 1.5.5 Parts of a plant
  - 1.5.6 Growth of plants
  - 1.5.7 Plant diseases
- 1.6 Animal
  - 1.6.1 Types of animals
    - 1.6.1.1 Mammal
    - 1.6.1.2 Bird
    - 1.6.1.3 Reptile
    - 1.6.1.4 Amphibian
    - 1.6.1.5 Fish
    - 1.6.1.6 Shark, ray
    - 1.6.1.7 Insect
    - 1.6.1.9 Sea creatures
  - 1.6.2 Parts of an animal
  - 1.6.3 Animal life cycle
  - 1.6.4 Animal actions
  - 1.6.5 Animal homes
  - 1.6.7 Male and female animals

*2- Person*

- 2.1 Types of people
- 2.2 Body
  - 2.2.1 Head
  - 2.2.2 Torso
  - 2.2.3 Arm, leg
  - 2.2.4 Skin
  - 2.2.5 Hair
  - 2.2.6 Bone, joint
  - 2.2.8 Internal organs
- 2.3 Body functions
- 2.4 The senses
  - 2.4.1 See
  - 2.4.2 Hear
  - 2.4.3 Taste
  - 2.4.4 Smell
  - 2.4.5 Sense of touch
- 2.5 Body condition
- 2.6 Health
  - 2.6.1 Sick
- 2.7 Life
  - 2.7.1 Marriage
  - 2.7.3 Birth
  - 2.7.4 Stage of life
  - 2.7.5 Male, female
  - 2.7.6 Die

*3- Language and thought*

- 3.1 Soul, spirit
  - 3.1.1 Personality
- 3.2 Mind
  - 3.2.1 Think
- 3.3 Want
- 3.4 Emotion
- 3.5 Communication
  - 3.5.4 Verbal tradition
  - 3.5.5 Reading and writing
- 3.6 Teach
  - 3.6.2 School

*4- Social behavior*

- 4.1 Relationships
  - 4.1.8 Show affection
  - 4.1.9 Related by kinship
- 4.2 Social activity
  - 4.2.3 Music
  - 4.2.4 Dance
  - 4.2.6 Entertainment, recreation
  - 4.2.7 Play, fun
- 4.3 Behavior
  - 4.3.4 Do good/evil to
  - 4.3.9 Culture
- 4.5 Authority
  - 4.5.1 Person in authority
- 4.7 Law
  - 4.7.3 Break the law
  - 4.7.7 Punish
- 4.8 Strife
  - 4.8.3 Peace
  - 4.8.4 War
- 4.9 Religion

*5- Home*

- 5.1 Rooms of a house
  - 5.1.3 Furniture
  - 5.1.4 Household tools
- 5.2 Food
  - 5.2.1 Food preparation
  - 5.2.2 Eat
  - 5.2.3 Types of food
    - 5.2.3.1 Food from plants
    - 5.2.3.2 Food from animals
    - 5.2.3.4 Prepared food
    - 5.2.3.6 Beverages
    - 5.2.3.7 Alcoholic beverages
  - 5.2.4 Tobacco
- 5.3 Clothing
  - 5.3.3 Traditional clothing
  - 5.3.6 Parts of clothing
  - 5.3.7 Wear clothing
  - 5.3.8 Naked
- 5.4 Adornment
  - 5.4.1 Jewelry
  - 5.4.2 Cosmetics
  - 5.4.3 Caring for hair
- 5.5 Fire
- 5.6 Cleaning
  - 5.6.1 Clean, dirty
- 5.7 Sleep

*6- Work and occupation*

- 6.1 Work
  - 6.1.3 Difficult, impossible
- 6.2 Agriculture
  - 6.2.1 Growing crops
- 6.4 Hunt and fish
  - 6.4.1 Hunt
  - 6.4.2 Trap

- 6.4.5 Fishing
- 6.5 Working with buildings
  - 6.5.1 Building
  - 6.5.2 Parts of a building
  - 6.5.3 Building materials
- 6.6 Occupations
  - 6.6.1 Working with cloth
  - 6.6.2 Working with minerals
  - 6.6.3 Working with wood
  - 6.6.5 Art
- 6.7 Tool
  - 6.7.7 Container
  - 6.7.9 Machine
- 6.8 Finance
  - 6.8.4 Financial transactions
  - 6.8.5 Borrow

*7- Physical actions*

- 7.1 Posture
  - 7.1.1 Stand
  - 7.1.2 Sit
  - 7.1.3 Lie down
  - 7.1.8 Bend down
  - 7.1.9 Move a part of the body
- 7.2 Move
  - 7.2.1 Manner of movement
  - 7.2.2 Move in a direction
  - 7.2.6 Travel
- 7.3 Move something
  - 7.3.1 Carry
  - 7.3.2 Move something in a direction
  - 7.3.4 Handle something
  - 7.3.5 Turn something
  - 7.3.6 Open/Shut
  - 7.3.7 Cover/Uncover
  - 7.3.8 Transportation
  - 7.3.9 Keep/Leave something
- 7.4 Arrange
  - 7.4.1 Gather
  - 7.4.2 Join, attach
- 7.5 Hide
  - 7.5.1 Search
  - 7.5.2 Find
  - 7.5.3 Lose, misplace
- 7.6 Physical impact
  - 7.6.1 Hit
- 7.7 Divide into pieces
  - 7.7.6 Dig

*8- States*

- 8.1 Quantity
  - 8.1.2 Number
  - 8.1.5 All/Some
- 8.2 Measure
  - 8.2.2 Long/Short
  - 8.2.4 Size
  - 8.2.5 Volume
- 8.3 Quality
  - 8.3.1 Shape
  - 8.3.2 Texture
  - 8.3.3 Light
  - 8.3.4 Temperature
  - 8.3.5 Decay
  - 8.3.6 Type, kind
  - 8.3.8 Good/Bad
  - 8.3.9 Appearance
- 8.4 Time
  - 8.4.1 Period of time
  - 8.4.2 Time of the day
  - 8.4.7 Take time
  - 8.4.8 Speed

8.5 Location
8.5.1 Here, there
8.5.2 Direction
8.5.3 Be at a place
8.5.5 Spatial relations
8.6 Parts of things

*9- Grammar*
9.1 General words
9.1.1 Be
9.1.2 Do
9.1.3 Thing
9.2 Part of speech
9.2.1 Adjectives
9.2.2 Adverbs
9.2.3 Pronouns
9.2.4 Prepositions, postpositions
9.2.6 Particles
9.2.7 Interjections
9.3 Propositions
9.3.4 Plurality
9.7 Name
9.7.2 Name of a place

## 1.1 Sky

*clear sky, blue sky* - xáats'
*darkness* - kag̲ít
*dusk; twilight* - xi.áat
*horizon* - goos' shú
*it's dark* - k̲ukawjig̲ít
*light* - kagán

## 1.1.1 Objects in the sky

*Big Dipper; Ursa Major* - yax̲té
*cloud cover; sky, cloudy sky* - góos'
*comet; falling star* - xoodzí
*it fell (small, compact object); it came out (sun, moon)* - daak uwaxíx
*it rose* - kei uwaxíx
*it set (sun, moon)* - yínde wooxeex
*Milky Way* - lk̲'ayáak'w x̲'us.eetí
*moon* - dís
*moonbeam* - dís x̲'usyee
*northern lights; aurora borealis* - gis'óok̲
*the moon is shining* - awdlidées
*rainbow* - kichx̲.anagaat
*star* - k̲utx̲.ayanahá
*sun* - g̲agaan
*sunbeam; ray of sunlight* - g̲agaan x̲'usyee
*Venus* - k'óox dísi

## 1.1.3 Weather

*cloud(s)* - k̲ugóos'
*cold weather* - k̲usa.áat'
*dry snow* - dleit kakétsk
*dry weather; clear day* - k̲uxaak
*dust cloud; snow cloud* - kals'éesjaa

*the weather became good* - k̲oowak’ei

*the weather got hot; the weather got warm* - k̲oowat’áa

*the weather is calm* - k̲ukawduwayél’

*the weather was cold* - k̲uwsi.áat’

*the weather was that way* - yéi k̲oowatee

*fall; autumn* - yeis

*flood; tide* - k̲ées’

*frost* - kaxwaan

*gray; fog* - k̲ugáas’

*hail* - kadás’

*it's foggy; it was foggy* - k̲oowdigwás’

*it's piled up; it's deep* - yan kaawadlán

*it's pouring rain; it's hailing; it's snowing* - aawag̲éet

*it's raining* - séew daak wusitán

*it's rough (of ocean)* - jiwsitaan

*it's stormy; it's rough (of weather)* - ayawditee

*it's sunny; the sun is shining* - awdigaan

*it was cloudy* - k̲oowligóos’

*lightning* - xeitl l’úkx̲u; xeitl l’íkws’i (At)

*phosphorescence (sparks of light in ocean water); luminescence (on rotten wood)* - éedaa

*rain* - séew; sóow (C)

*shade, shadow(s) cast by landforms, etc.* - chéx̲’i (C)

*snow* - dleit

*snowstorm, snow shower* - dleit g̲éedi

*spring (AT)* - k̲ukalt’éex’ ká

*summer* - k̲utaan

*summer; early summer* - taakw.eetí

*sun-dried* - g̲agaan kas’úkwx̲u

*sun rays are shining on it* - g̲agaan át x̲’oos uwatsóow

*weather* - k̲utí

*wet snow; slush* - kaklahéen

*winter; year* - táakw

### 1.1.3.1 Natural Disaster

*earthquake* - yoo aan ka.á

*flood* - aan galak̲ú

*rockslide* - tak̲aadí

*snowslide; snow avalanche* - dleit k̲aadí

### 1.1.3.2 Wind

*chinook wind; south wind* - k'eeljáa; k'eiljáa

*the wind hit it in gusts* - át ayawashát

*it blew; it's blowing* - wuduwanúk

*it's blowing around; it blew around; s/he is sailing around; s/he sailed around* - át wulis'ees

*it's blowing in the wind there* - aadé kawdlis'ées

*north wind* - xóon

*thing heading offshore, esp. wind* - dákde át

*west wind* - l'ag̲akáx̲

*west wind; wind blowing ashore* - yánde át

*wind* - óoxjaa

*wind (blowing) from the south* - sáanáx̲

### 1.2.1 Land

*beach; waterside; down on the beach, shore* - éek̲

*bump, lump, hump, mound* - gootl

*campsite; (out in) camp; (out in) the bush, wilderness* - yanshuká

*cave* - katóok; tatóok

*clay; alluvial silt* - s'é

*cliff* - g̲íl'

*dirt, dust* - ch'éix̲'w

*draw, gully, box canyon* - séet

*earth; land, country; soil* - tl'átk

*fine sand or gravel* - l'éiw yátx'i

*flat-topped island with steep sides; low flat island or hill* - noow

*foot path* - k̲aa x̲'oos deiyí

*forest; timbered area* - aasgutú

*garden; field* - táay

*glacier* - sít'

*the shelter of a mountain, area on the beach below a mountain* - shaa seiyí

*island* - x'áat'

*mountain* - shaa

*mountainside; around the mountain* - shaa yadaa

*mountaintop; on top of the mountain* - shaa shakée

*mountain valley; valley* - shaanáx̱

*mud* - ḵútl'kw

*nucleus of emerging river island; reef above high tide level* - shaltláax̱

*(on) the back of it (fish); on the crest, ridge, backbone of it (hill, ridge, point)* - a litká

*on the ridge or elevated part of the point (of land)* - x'aa luká

*outdoors; outside* - gáan

*path, trail; road, street* - dei

*point (of land)* - x'aa

*portage, passage across it; its isthmus* - a góon

*reef; large rock or boulder lying on the ocean floor* - eech

*river flats; tidelands; mudflats* - taashuká

*rock crevice; fissure in rock* - té ḵáas'

*rock point* - tax'aayí

*sandbar; gravel bar; sand beach; gravel beach* - xákw

*sand; gravel* - l'éiw

*sand point* - l'éiw x'aayí

*shore; land* - yán

*shoreline* - tleiyán

*shoreline; beach* - neech

*small hill; mound, knoll* - gooch

*soil; dirt* - l'éx̱'kw

*stone; rock* - té

*town; village; settlement; inhabited or owned land* - aan

*underground* - yanax̱

*wide, flat stone (used for cooking)* - té ḵ'áatl'

*wilderness; the bush* - katḵaaḵú; g̱alg̱aaḵu

*woods; bush; brush, underbrush* - at gutú
*world* - lingít aaní

### 1.2.2 Matter

*aluminum* - géxtl'
*brass* - ik̲náach'
*charcoal* - t'ooch'
*coal* - t'ooch' té
*copper* - eek̲
*flint* - ín
*gold-rust; flecked with gold or rust* - katl'áak'
*granite* - x̲éel
*greenstone* - s'oow
*gum; lead* - k'óox̲'
*iron, tin* - ik̲yéis'; g̲ayéis'
*marble* - néex̲'
*mica* - katl'áak'
*petroleum, oil* - t'ooch' eex̲í
*pounded shell powder* - káts
*silver* - dáanaa
*soft lead* - k'óox̲' létl'k
*something compact and very heavy* - éech'
*thing* - át
*verdigris* - eek̲ háatl'i

### 1.3 Water

*cold water* - si.áat'i héen
*foam* - x̲eil
*foam (on waves); sponge* - teet x̲'achálx̲i
*foam; whitecaps* - x̲eel
*ice* - t'éex'
*(in the) river valley* - héen yík
*on (top of) the water, river* - héen x̲'aká

*silty, murky water* - l'óox̱
*small bubbles (in water)* - x̱'asúnjaa
*water* - héen

## 1.3.1 Bodies of water

*bay* - eey; g̱eey; g̱eiy (TC)
*cove; bight* - kunag̱eey
*creek; small stream* - héenák'w
*edge of body of water* - héen shú
*edge of river channel* - héen wantú
*end of body of standing water* - hinshú (At)
*fishing hole; hole in stream, river, creek* - ísh
*head of river, stream* - héen sháak
*head of the bay* - g̱eey tá
*hot springs* - t'aay
*lake* - áa
*little lake; pond* - áak'w
*mouth of it (a river, creek)* - a wát
*mouth of river, stream* - héen wát
*ocean; salt water* - éil'
*riverside* - héen x̱'ayaax̱
*river, stream, creek* - héen; kanaadaayi héen; naadaayi héen
*salmon creek* - x̱áat héeni
*shelter (from wind or weather), harbor* - déili
*slough* - éix̱'
*spring (of water)* - goon
*swamp* - sháchk
*Takhini hot springs (north of Whitehorse, Yukon Territory)* - Tax̱héeni
*waterfall* - x'áas

## 1.3.2 Movement of water

*the water level rose; the tide came up* - kei uwadáa
*bubbles, esp. from whale* - kúḵdlaa

*current; tidal action* - héen kanadaayí

*current, tide* - haat

*drip, leak with dripping* - katl'úk̲jaa

*fast drip, leak* - kalóox̲jaa

*fast drip with bubbles* - kúk̲jaa

*high tide line* - k̲ées' shuwee

*the tide is in* - daak̲ uwadáa

*the tide is low* - yan uwaláa

*the tide went out from under it; the tide ebbed out from under it* - áx̲ woolaa

*it drained out; it went dry* - kawlikoox

*it flowed along it* - áx̲ kaawadaa

*it flowed; it's flowing; it's running (of nose)* - kaawadaa

*it flowed through it; it flooded it* - anax̲ yaawadáa

*it flowed to it* - át uwadáa

*it melted; it dissolved; it thawed* - wuliláa

*it's leaking; it's dripping* - kawlix'áas

*low tide (point at which the tide will begin coming in)* - éek̲ lukak̲ées'i

*steam (visible, in the air); mist, fog (rising from a body of standing water)* - x'úkjaa

*tide flats* - léin

*trickle of water; steady drip or leak* - kax'áasjaa

*the (water) level rose to there; it flowed to there* - át kaawadáa

*waves reached the beach* - yan jiwsitán

*waves washed over it* - a kanax̲ jiyawsitán

*wave; swell* - teet

*whirlpool* - haat kool

*whirlpool; boiling tide; chaos* - x'óol'

## 1.3.4 Be in water

*fixed buoy* - eech kakwéiyi

*floating buoy* - eech kwéiyi

*he/she/it drifted out to sea; he/she/it is drifting out to sea; he/she/it floated out to sea; he/she/it is floating out to sea* - daak wulihásh

*he/she/it drifted to it; he/she/it floated to it* - át wulihásh

*he/she/it is wet* - wuditl'ák'

*he/she/it waded ashore* - yan uwahóo

*iceberg* - xáatl

*in the water; in the river* - héen táak

*into water* - héeni; héenx̱

*it is swimming around there; it swam around there* - át jiwsikwaan

*it sank* - wootáax̱'w

*it's floating around; it floated around; it's drifting around; it drifted around* - át wulihaash

*it swam underwater to it* - át uwax'ák

*s/he anchored the boat* - ashawsiyaa

*s/he soaked it* - akawlikél

*underwater reef; large rock or boulder lying under the water* - hintu.eejí

## 1.5 Plant

*bear root, Indian potato* - tsáats

*bladder rack; rock weed; yellow seaweed* - tayeidí

*bull kelp* - sú

*coral* - hintaak x'óosi

*coral* - hintakx'úxi

*deer cabbage, lily-of-the-valley* - k'uwaaní

*devil's club* - s'áxt'

*dulse (type of seaweed)* - laaḵ'ásk

*false hellebore* - s'íksh

*fiddlehead fern (with edible rhizome)* - k'wálx̱

*fireweed* - lóol

*goose tongue* - suḵtéitl'

*horsetail* - taan x̱'adaadzaayí

*Hudson Bay tea* - s'ikshaldéen

*kelp* - geesh

*large-leaved avens (Geum macrophyllum) or possibly arnica species-- Arnica species, especially A. amplexicaulus, A. latifolia, A. gracilis* - aankanáagu

*leaf, leaves; vegetation, plants, herbs, herbiage* - kayaaní

*lupine* - kantáḵw

*nettle* - t'óok'

*petrified coral* - yéil kawóodi

*ribbon seaweed* - k̲'áach'

*seaweed, kelp on which herring spawn* - daaw

*shield fern* - s'aach

*skunk cabbage* - x̲'áal'

*sourdock; wild rhubarb* - tl'aak̲'wách'

*wild celery* - yaana.eit

*yarrow; (locally) rat's tail* - kag̲akl'eedí

## 1.5.1 Tree

*alnus alder (beach or mountain alder)* - keishísh

*birch* - at daayí

*cottonwood* - dúk̲

*driftwood* - nalháashadi

*dwarf maple* - x'aalx'éi

*fallen tree* - l'ákwti

*fir* - leiyís

*flaky surface of the outer bark of conifers, especially hemlock* - s'agwáat

*the shelter of a tree* - aas jiseiyí

*hemlock* - yán

*its bark* - a daayí

*its green wood (of tree)* - a shís'k̲

*limb, primary branch; limb knot* - sheey

*mountain ash* - kalchaneit

*oak* - gus'k'ik̲wáan l'oowú

*punk wood, decayed dry wood* - g̲unanaa tetl

*red alder* - shéix̲'w

*red cedar* - laax̲

*sapling* - aas yádi

*Sitka spruce* - shéiyi

*stunted tree in swamp; jackpine, swamp spruce* - sháchk ka.aasí

*swamp hemlock* - s'éx̲

*tree (esp. conifer)* - aas

*tumor in a tree, with branches growing from it* - aasdaax'ées'i

*water hemlock* - lingít k'únts'i

*willow* - ch'áal'

*windfall; dead tree(s) or brush that has fallen* - G̱éejadi; G̱éechadi

*wood shavings* - kayeix̱

*yellow cedar, Alaska cedar* - x̱áay

*young spruce or hemlock* - dúḵl’; túḵl’

## 1.5.2 Bush, shrub

*berry bush* - tléiḵw wás’i

*bush* - wás’

*false azalea (fruitless bush)* - k’éets’an

## 1.5.3 Grass, herb, vine

*cottongrass, Alaska cotton, swamp cotton* - sháchk kax̱’wáal’i

*grass* - chookán

*hairy grass, seaweed on which herring spawn* - né

*timothy grass (used for basket decoration)* - sháak

## 1.5.4 Moss, fungus, algae

*algae found on rocks* - x̱aatl’

*bracket fungus* - aasdaaG̱áadli

*it's moldy; it got moldy* - wuditláx̱

*lichen that hangs down from trees* - s’éix̱wani

*mold* - tlaax̱

*moss* - s’íx’G̱aa

*ocean algae* - káas’

*peat moss* - sooḵ

## 1.5.5 Parts of a plant

*alpine bearberry, kinnikinnick* - tínx

*berry, berries* - tléiḵw

*bough, branch with needles on it, especially of hemlock* - haaw *bough, branch with needles on it, especially of spruce* - cháash

*cambium, sap scraped from inner bark* - sáx'

*dead wood that's wet on the outside* - gán láx̱'i

*dry woody outer bark* - loon

*dust; pollen* - kadánjaa

*flower; blossom* - ḵ'eikaxwéin

*green, unripe berry* - kax̱'át'

*its sap, phloem* - a káx̱i

*its sapwood; its sappy inner bark (of a tree)* - a láx̱'i

*its secondary branch* - a t'áni

*its seeds* - a x'aakeidí

*its seeds (inside it, as inside a berry)* - a tukayátx'i

*its sprouts, fleshy leaves growing toward the top of the stem (e.g. of bear root)* - a shaadí

*its stem (of plant); pith (of tree)* - a kadíx'i

*knot hole* - sheey woolí

*limb knot* - sheey tukagoodlí

*log (fallen tree)* - x̱áaw

*match; stick* - ḵáas'

*old, dead branch* - tl'áxch'

*pile of driftwood, driftlogs; snag pile* - yanxoon

*pine cone, spruce cone* - s'óos'ani

*pine needles, spruce needles* - g̱ítg̱aa

*pitch scab (where bark has been removed); pitchwood* - téil

*pole; sapling* - tlag̱anís

*rice; Kamchatka lily root* - kóox

*root; especially spruce root* - x̱aat

*roots or vines used in basket decoration* - léet'

*rose* - k'inchéiyi

*rosehip* - k'inchéiyi tléig̱u

*sapling; pole made from sapling* - tag̱anís

*snag; driftlog, driftwood* - shaaḵ

*soft brown wood for tanning dye* - x̱'oon

*splinter, sliver* - sheey kaḵáas'i

*stick* - sheey

*swamp berries* - sháchgi tléig̱u

*they're unripe; they're green (of berries)* - kadlix̱'át'

*uprooted tree or stump (with roots protruding)* - x'éedadi

*various odd looking, tasteless, or otherwise undesirable berries, some poisonous; meaning varies locally, incl. twistedstalk (Streptopus species), snowberry (Symphoricarpos albus), fool's huckleberry (Menziesia ferruginea), etc.* - s'ig̱eeḵáawu tléig̱u

*wood chips; wood shavings* - kayeix̱tág̱u (C)

*wood, piece of wood; wood chip* - l'eiwú; l'oowú

*yellow cedar bark (for weaving)* - teey woodí

*young salmonberry bush shoots (edible)* - k'eit

## 1.5.6 Growth of plants

*it grew* - kawsi.aa

*it grew; it flowed (stream of water)* - kaawa.aa

## 1.5.7 Plant diseases

*dead dry tree, still standing* - láax̱

*growth on the trunk of a tree, burl* - gúnl'

*rotten wood* - naaḵw

*very rotton wood* - ḵúlk

## 1.6.1.1 Mammal

*arctic ground squirrel* - tsálk

*beaver* - s'igeidí

*bison, buffalo; ox, muskox; cow; horse* - xaas

*black bear* - s'eek

*black fox* - x̱alt'ooch' naag̱as'éi

*caribou* - watsíx

*cat* - dóosh

*colt* - gawdáan yádi

*cow* - wasóos

*deer* - g̱uwakaan; ḵuwakaan (TC)

*deer or other ruminant having a horn with only one point* - shataag̱áa *deer or other ruminant with full-grown horns* - shals'áaw

*deer sprouting horns* - shak'únts'

*deer with full-grown antlers* - shalas'áaw

*dog* - keitl

*dolphin* - k̲'aan

*donkey* - gukkudayáat'

*fawn* - g̲uwakaan yádi

*fox; red fox* - naag̲as'éi

*fur seal* - x̲'óon

*glacier bear* - sít' tuxóodzi

*grizzly bear* - xóots

*hair seal* - tsaa

*hoary marmot; groundhog, whistler* - s'aax̲

*horse* - gawdáan

*killerwhale* - kéet

*kitten* - dóosh yádi

*lamb* - wanadóo yádi

*land otter; river otter* - kóoshdaa

*lynx* - g̲aak̲

*man-eating animal; lion; tiger; man-eating wolf* - haadaag̲oojí

*man-eating feline; mountain lion; tiger, leopard* - haadaadóoshi

*marten* - k'óox

*mink* - lukshiyáan; nukshiyáan

*moose* - dzísk'w

*mountain goat* - jánwu

*mountain sheep, bighorn sheep* - tawéi

*mouse, deer mouse; vole* - kag̲ák; kag̲áak

*mouse; rat* - kuts'een

*muskrat* - tsín

*pig* - gishoo

*polar bear* - hintaak xóodzi

*porcupine* - x̲alak'ách'

*porpoise* - cheech

*rabbit* - g̲áx̲

*red squirrel* - kanals'áak

*sea lion* - taan

*sea otter* - yáxwch'; yúxch' (C)
*sheep* - wanadóo
*solid-ribbed brown bear* - s'uk̲kasdúk
*squirrel* - kals'áak (T)
*thing of the woods* - at gutu.ádi
*walrus* - kooléix̲'waa
*weasel* - dáa
*whale* - yáay
*white fox* - x̲aldleit
*wolf* - g̲ooch
*wolverine* - nóosk; nóoskw
*young deer* - yagootl

### 1.6.1.2 Bird

*auklet or murrelet* - ch'eet; kéel
*bald eagle* - ch'áak'
*black turnstone* - x'at'daayéejayi
*blue grouse* - núkt
*bluejay, Stellar's jay* - x̲'éishx'w
*brant (small goose)* - k̲ín
*bufflehead (duck)* - hintakx'wás'g̲i
*Canada goose* - t'aawák̲
*chickadee* - k̲aatoowú
*common loon* - kag̲eet
*cormorant* - yook̲
*crow* - ts'axweil
*curlew* - ayaheeyáa
*dipper; water ouzel* - hinyikl'eix̲í
*duck* - gáaxw
*egg (of bird)* - k'wát'
*flathead duck* - s'élasheesh
*goldfinch, canary* - s'áas'
*green bird (sparrow or finch)* - asx'aan sháach'i
*grey singing bird (sparrow or finch)* - tlagu ts'ats'éeyee
*gull, seagull* - kéidladi

*harlequin duck* - s'ús'
*heron; Canada crane* - láx̱'
*horned grebe or red-necked grebe* - cháax̱
*hummingbird* - dagatgiyáa; digitgiyáa
*immature eagle* - ch'ak'yéis'
*kind of duck* - hinyikgáaxu
*kind of hawk* - gijook; kijook
*kind of hawk* - shaayáal
*kingfisher* - tlax̱aneis'
*magpie* - ts'eeg̱éeni; ts'eig̱éeni (T)
*mallard duck* - kindachooneit
*merganser* - ḵaax̱
*northern flicker* - kóon
*oldsquaw duck* - yaa.aanuné
*owl; great horned owl* - dzísk'w (AtT)
*owl with ear tufts* - tsísk'w
*owl without ear tufts* - k'ákw
*petrel* - g̱anook
*pigeon* - yaa ḵudzigéiyi ts'ats'ée
*pigeon or dove* - gus'yé kindachooneidí
*puffin* - x̱ík
*raven* - yéil
*robin-like bird* - shoox̱'
*sandhill crane* - dóol
*sandpiper* - gus'yadóoli
*sandpiper (shore bird)* - x̱'al'daayéeji
*scooter duck* - lak'eech'wú; waḵkals'oox̱' gáaxw
*small owl* - x̱éex̱
*songbird; bird* - ts'ats'ée; ts'ítskw
*spruce grouse, spruce hen; chicken* - káax'
*swallow* - séew kooshdaneit
*swan* - gúḵl'
*tern* - kichyát; kootl'éit'aa; ḵ'eiḵ'w
*Thunderbird* - Xeitl
*tufted puffin* - lugán
*willow ptarmigan; pigeon* - x̱'eis'awáa

*woodpecker* - gandaadagóogu
*wren* - woolnáx̱ wooshḵáḵ
*young seagull* - lawúx̱

### 1.6.1.3 Reptile

*lizard, newt* - tseenx̱'é
*snake* - l'ut'tláaḵ
*turtle* - kanóox'; tadanóox'

### 1.6.1.4 Amphibian

*frog* - xíxch'
*tadpole; polliwog* - dụsh

### 1.6.1.5 Fish

*black bass* - lit.isdúk
*black cod* - ishḵeen
*bullhead* - éetkatlóox̱u
*bullhead, sculpin* - wéix̱'
*coho salmon; silver salmon* - l'ook
*cutthroat trout* - x'éitaa
*dead salmon (after spawning)* - nóosh
*dog salmon; chum salmon* - téel'
*Dolly Varden trout* - x̱'wáat'
*eel* - lóot'
*eulachon; candlefish; hooligan* - saak
*fish; salmon* - x̱áat
*flounder* - dzánti
*grayling* - t'ási
*halibut* - cháatl
*herring* - yaaw
*king salmon; chinook salmon; spring salmon* - t'á
*lake trout* - daleiyí

*ling cod* - s'áax̱'; x̱'áax'w

*little bullhead (found under beach rocks)* - té tayee tlóox̱u

*mackerel* - dákdesak'aak

*moonfish, suckerfish, blowfish* - tl'éitl'

*mud bullhead* - tlóox̱

*needlefish* - tooḵ

*octopus; devilfish* - náaḵw

*pink salmon; humpy, humpback salmon* - cháas'

*ratfish* - g̱eey kanax̱ ḵutées'

*red rockfish; red snapper* - léiḵ'w

*sockeye or coho salmon that has entered fresh water* - x̱'áakw

*sockeye salmon; red salmon* - g̱aat

*spawned-out salmon with white scabs, ready to die* - xein

*starry flounder* - wankashxéet

*stickleback* - k'aagán

*tomcod* - chudéi

*trout (sea)* - yaa

*whitefish; baby fish; tiny fish* - x̱áat yádi

*young herring* - sháach'

## 1.6.1.6 Shark, ray

*dogfish; mudshark* - x'átgu

*man-eating shark (legendary)* - shax̱dáḵw

*shark* - tóos'

*shark (porpoise-like)* - chichuyaa

*skate (ocean creature related to the shark and the ray)* - ch'éetg̱aa

## 1.6.1.7 Insect

*ant* - wanatíx; wanatóox

*beetle* - k'ul'kaskéxkw

*bee; wasp* - gandaas'aají

*centipede* - atxaayí

*crawling insect; spider* - kanas.aadí

*daddy long legs; mosquito eater* - táax'aa x̲'uskudayáat'
*dragonfly* - k̲aashashx̲áaw
*flea* - tíx
*horsefly* - xeitl táax'aa
*housefly* - neil yee táax'ayi
*housefly; bluebottle fly* - xéen
*it bit him/her/it* - ash wusitáax'
*louse, lice* - wéis'
*maggot* - woon
*mosquito* - táax'aa
*moth* - atx̲a át
*sandhopper* - kook'énaa
*slug, snail* - táax̲'
*spider* - asgutuyiksháa
*woodworm* - gantutl'úk'x̲u
*worm; larva; grub; caterpillar; snake* - tl'úk'x̲

## 1.6.1.9 Sea creatures

*abalone* - gunx̲aa
*baby clams* - dzéex'w
*barnacle* - s'ook
*clam* - gáal'
*cockle* - yalooleit
*crab (king, spider)* - x'éix̲
*dungeness crab* - s'áaw
*giant clam* - x̲éet'
*gumboots; chiton* - shaaw
*jellyfish* - taakw aanási
*leech; bloodsucker* - yéesh
*limpet* - yéil ts'áaxu
*littleneck clams* - tl'ildaaskeit
*mussel* - yaak
*mussel (large mussel on stormy coast, used for scraping)* - yées'
*razor clam* - k̲'alkátsk
*red mussel* - s'igeek̲áawu yaagí

*sea anemone* - tayataayí

*sea cucumber* - yéin

*sea urchin* - nées'; x̱'waash

*shrimp* - s'éex'át

*slippers (shell creature)* - koow

*small red sea anemone* - tayashagoo

*snail with shell* - ts'ésx̱'w

*squid* - dag̱asaa

*starfish* - s'áx

*tiny clams (too small to eat)* - dzóox'

## 1.6.2 Parts of an animal

*baleen; whalebone* - yáay x̱'axéni

*bloodline inside fish, along the backbone* - x̱áat k'áax̱'i

*cartilage, gristle* - a túḵl'i

*cartilage, gristle at the end of its bones* - a s'aḵshutúḵl'i

*cartilage, gristle between its bones* - a s'aḵx̱'áak túḵl'i

*dark yellow; eagle's beak* - ch'áak' loowú

*down (feathers)* - x̱'wáal'

*feather* - t'aaw

*his/her bone marrow* - s'aḵtu.eex̱í

*his/her stomach; gizzard (of bird)* - du yoowú

*his/her whiskers* - du x̱'adaadzaayí

*its beak* - a loowú

*its bone marrow* - a s'aḵtu.eex̱í

*its claw* - a x̱aagú

*its dorsal fin (of killerwhale)* - a gooshí

*its flesh (of fish)* - a x̱'úx̱u

*its gill (of fish)* - a x'éix'u

*its hair, fur; its quill(s) (of porcupine)* - a x̱aawú

*its head* - a shá

*its hindquarters; thigh* - a g̱ádzi

*its hoof* - a gwéinli

*its horn* - a sheidí

*its internal organs, viscera; its guts* - a yik.ádi

*its leg* - a x̱'oosí

*its mane (esp. the hair on the neck hump of a moose)* - a x̱íji

*its mouth, opening* - a x̱'é

*its muscles (of shell creature)* - a ts'éek'u

*its paw* - a jíni

*its rumen, main stomach (of ruminant)* - a dáali

*its scale (of fish)* - a jeig̱í

*its scales (of fish)* - a kajeig̱í

*its sinew* - a tási

*its skin (of animal); hide* - a doogú

*its skin (of fish)* - a xáas'i

*its sucker (devilfish)* - a óot'i

*its tail flippers* - a geení

*its tail (of animal)* - a l'eedí

*its tail (of bird or fish)* - a koowú

*its tentacle (of octopus)* - a tl'eeg̱í; a tl'eig̱í (C)

*its testicles (of moose, caribou)* - a k'únts'i

*its tooth* - a oox̱ú

*its tracks* - a x̱'us.eetí

*its whiskers, beard (of fish)* - a ḵ'anoox̱ú

*its wing* - a kíji

*long feather; quill (of bird)* - ḵénaa

*long feather; quill (of bird)* - ḵínaa

*muscles of a shell creature; pincher; thing that pinches* - at ts'ík'wti

*quills on rear end of it (porcupine)* - a k'ishataag̱aní

*side of it (house, building, animal); slab of meat covering its ribcage* - a kageidí

*slime (inside clamshell)* - átl'áni

*slime; thick mucus* - x̱éel'

*tallow, hard fat* - toow

*the quick (the flesh under the outer skin)* - séiḵ'w

### 1.6.3 Animal life cycle

*eggshell* - nóox'

*eggs (of eels, etc.)* - x̱'íx'

*it laid an egg* - awdlik'wát'

*its semen; its milt (of fish)* - a tl'éili
*s/he bred them* - awsix̱eit
*they multiplied; they bred* - has wudzix̱eit

## 1.6.4 Animal actions

*he/she/it bit him/her/it* - aawayeeḵ
*spray of air exhaled through its blowhole (of sea mammal)* - a óoxu
*they are swimming around there; they swam around there* - át has wusikwaan
*they swam to it* - át yawsigóo

## 1.6.5 Animal homes

*beaver dam* - s'igeidí áayi
*beaver's den* - s'igeidí x̱aayí
*bee's nest* - gandaas'aají kúdi
*dentalia shells* - t'áx'x̱i
*empty bivalve shell* - xáak
*its den, lair (of animal, undergound)* - a ḵoowú
*its web (of spider)* - a g̱eiwú
*nest* - kút
*nest (of animal)* - a kúdi
*shell; shell-like chip or flake; china; carapace* - nóox'

## 1.6.7 Male and female animals

*female (animal)* - sheech
*female (animal)* - shich

## 2 Person

*alcoholic* - náaw éesh
*drunk; drunkard* - at danáayi
*drunk; drunkard* - náaw s'aatí

*orphan* - kuhaankée
*people; community* - k̲u.oo
*people of long ago* - tlagu k̲wáanx'i
*person* - lingít
*person or people from that place* - a k̲wáan
*respected person; gentleman; lady* - sh yáa awudanéiyi
*slave* - goox̲
*townspeople; crowd or large group of people* - aantk̲eení

## 2.1 Types of people

*Ahtna, Copper River Athabascan* - Ik̲kaa
*Aleut* - Ana.óot
*Aleut* - Giyak̲w
*American* - Waashdan K̲wáan
*American Indian* - T'aawyáat
*Athabaskan (Indian)* - G̲unanaa
*Black (man or person); African-American* - t'ooch' k̲áa
*Canadian, British* - Ginjichwáan; Ginjoochwáan
*Chinese* - Cháanwaan
*Chugach Eskimo* - Gutéix̲'
*Eskimo* - X̲'atas'aak̲
*Haida* - Deikeenaa
*Russian* - Anóoshi
*Tlingit* - Lingít
*tribe of cannibals, man-eaters* - k̲usax̲ak̲wáan
*Tsimshian* - Ts'ootsxán
*White, European, Caucasian (man or person)* - Gus'k'iyee k̲wáan; dleit k̲áa

## 2.2 Body

*his/her body parts* - du daashagóon
*his/her flesh* - du daadleeyí
*his/her/its body* - du daa.it
*his/her shadow; image* - du yahaayí

## 2.2.1 Head

*back of his/her head at the base* - du shaláx̱'

*back of his/her neck* - du lidíx̱'

*back of his/her neck* - du ludíx̱'

*corner of his/her eye* - du waḵshú

*his/her cheek* - du wásh

*his/her chin* - du téey

*his/her ear* - du gúk

*his/her eye* - du waaḵ

*his/her eyebrow* - du s'ee; du s'ei

*his/her eyelash* - du wax̱'ax̱éix̱'u

*his/her eyelid* - du waḵkadoogú

*his/her face* - du yá

*his/her forehead* - du káak'

*his/her gums* - du ux̱k'idleeyí

*his/her head* - du shá

*his/her jawbone; jaws* - du x̱'astus'aag̱í

*his/her lips; area around his/her mouth* - du x̱'adaa

*his/her lower jaw, mandible* - du x̱'ás'

*his/her missing tooth* - du oox̱k'i.eetí

*his/her mouth* - du x̱'é

*his/her nose* - du lú

*his/her nose cartilage* - a lututúḵl'i

*his/her occiput; nape of neck; back of head* - du lak'éech'

*his/her palate* - du k'iḵl'án

*his/her scalp* - du shadaadoogú

*his/her temple; upper side of his/her face (from the cheekbones to the top of the head)* - du yat'ákw

*his/her throat* - du leitóox̱

*his/her tongue* - du l'óot'

*his/her tonsils* - du x̱'as'guwéis'i

*his/her tooth* - du oox̱

*his/her whiskers* - du x̱'adaadzaayí

*inside of his/her cheek* - du washtú

*inside of his/her eye* - du waḵlatáak; du waḵltáak

*inside of his/her mouth* - du laká

*inside of his/her nose* - du lutú
*lobe of his/her nostril* - du lugóoch'
*(outside of) his/her cheek* - du washká
*pit at base of his/her skull* - du lak'eech'kóoG̱u
*side of his/her nose* - du lut'aaḵ

### 2.2.2 Torso

*cheek of his/her buttocks* - du x'aash
*crack of his/her buttocks; his/her butt crack* - du tux̱'ax'aayí
*his/her abdomen; surface of his/her belly; front of his/her body* - du yoowá
*his/her anus* - du tuḵ.woolí
*his/her back* - du díx̱'
*his/her belly, paunch* - du x̱'óol'
*his/her breast* - du l'aa
*his/her buttocks, butt* - du tóoḵ
*his/her chest* - du wóow
*his/her crotch; between his/her legs* - du g̱atsx̱'áak
*his/her flank, side of his/her belly* - du ḵaatl
*his/her flank, side of his/her body between the ribs and the hip* - du ḵatlyá
*his/her navel, bellybutton* - du kool
*his/her rib* - du s'óog̱u
*his/her shoulderblade; scapula* - du óox'u
*his/her stomach; gizzard (of bird)* - du yoowú
*his/her tailbone; bottom of his/her spine* - du k'óol'
*his/her thorax; flat upper surface of his/her chest* - du xeitká
*his/her waist* - du kasán
*his penis* - du l'íli
*his testicles* - du k'wát'
*(on) his/her chest* - du woowká
*privates (of female); vulva; vagina* - du góos
*privates (of male); penis and testicles* - du láaw

## 2.2.3 Arm, leg

*back of his/her hand* - du jikóol

*back of his/her wrist* - du jiká

*between his/her fingers* - du tl'eḵx̱'áak

*crook of his/her arm; in his/her embrace* - du jig̱ei

*end of his/her knee* - du kiyshá

*his/her armpit* - du éenee

*his/her armpit hair* - du éenee x̱aawú

*his/her big toe* - du x̱'usgoosh

*his/her buttocks, thighs* - du g̱áts

*his/her elbow* - du t'eey

*his/her finger* - du tl'eeḵ; du tl'eiḵ

*his/her fingernail markings* - du x̱aakw eetí

*his/her fingertip* - du tl'eḵshá; du tl'iḵshá

*his/her first finger* - du ch'éex̱'i

*his/her foot, leg* - du x̱'oos

*his/her footprint* - du x̱'us.eetí

*his/her grip* - du jintú

*his/her hand* - du jín

*his/her heel* - du x̱'eitákw

*his/her knee* - du keey

*his/her kneecap* - du keey shakanóox'u; du kiyshakanóox'u

*his/her little finger* - du wankach'eeḵ

*his/her middle finger* - du tl'eḵtlein; du tl'iḵtlein

*his/her nail (of finger or toe)* - du x̱aakw

*his/her palm (center)* - du jintakyádi

*his/her palm (of hand)* - du jintáak

*his/her ring finger* - du laayig̱águ

*his/her rump; the flesh around his/her hips* - du k'í

*his/her shin* - du xées' (C)

*his/her thumb* - du goosh

*his/her toe* - du x̱'ustl'eeḵ; du x̱'ustl'eiḵ

*his/her upper arm* - du x̱eek

*his/her wrist* - du jigúnl'i; du jiklix'ées'

*knob on outer side of his/her ankle* - du x̱'ust'ákl'i

*(on) his/her lap* - du gushká
*outer edge of his/her hand* - du jiwán
*outer side of his/her foot up to the anklebone* - du shutóox̱'
*s/he raised a hand* - kei jiwlitsák̲
*sole of his/her foot* - du x̲'ustáak
*top of his/her foot* - du ik̲ká
*under his/her feet* - du x̲'usyee
*underside of his/her knee; (inside of) his/her lower leg* - du saayee

## 2.2.4 Skin

*his/her skin, complexion* - du dook
*his/her skin (surface)* - du ch'áatwu
*its wrinkled, baggy skin, hide* - a daaleilí

## 2.2.5 Hair

*bald spot; bald head* - shax̲'wáas' (T)
*dandruff* - shakéil'
*gray hair* - du shashaaní
*his/her bangs* - du kak'x̲aawú
*his/her body hair, fuzz* - du x̲aawú
*his/her curly hair* - du shakakóoch'i
*his/her hair* - du shax̲aawú
*it's hairy* - daadzix̱áaw
*lock of his/her hair; his/her matted hair* - du x'ées'i
*pubic hair* - du xux̲aawú

## 2.2.6 Bone, joint

*bone* - s'aak̲
*his/her joints* - du daa.eit x̲'áak
*his/her pelvis, hip* - du k̲áash
*his/her shoulder* - du x̲ikshá

*his/her skeleton, bare bones* - du xaagú
*tip of his/her elbow* - du t'iyshú

### 2.2.8 Internal organs

*blood* - shé
*his/her bile* - du teiyí
*his/her bladder* - du kalóox'shani
*his/her brain* - du tlag̱eiyí
*his/her gland* - du daa.itwéis'i
*his/her heart* - du téix̱'
*his/her intestines, guts* - du naasí
*his/her liver* - du tl'óog̱u;  du keigú
*his/her windpipe; pharynx* - du leikachóox̱'u
*vein; tendon (inside body)* - téet'

### 2.3 Body functions

*crying, weeping* - g̱aax̱
*fart* - G̱wáal'
*feces* - gánde nagoodí
*feces; dung* - háatl'
*his/her earwax* - du gukyikk'óox̱'u
*his/her saliva* - du x̱'ahéeni
*his/her stomach growled* - du x̱'óol' kawditóox̱'
*his/her stomach is growling* - du x̱'óol' kastóox̱'
*his/her tears* - du wax̱'ahéeni
*his/her urine* - du lóox'u
*life; breath* - daséikw; x̱'aséikw
*menstrual discharge; period* - gáan
*noiseless fart* - kóoch'
*s/he cried* - woog̱aax̱
*s/he is grinning; s/he is smiling* - at kaawanúts
*s/he spat* - yóot ḵ'awdzitúx̱
*s/he swallowed it* - akaawanóot'

*sleep in his/her eyes* - wak̲dlóok̲

*snot* - lug̲eitl'

*spit* - x̲'astóox̲

*strong urine smell* - kax̲'ees

## 2.4.1 See

*before his/her eyes; where he/she can see (it)* - du wak̲shiyee

*blindfold* - wak̲kadóox'

*blocking his/her view; in his/her way (so that he/she can't see)* - du wak̲kas'óox'

*blocking his/her view; in his/her way (so that he/she can't see)* - du wak̲ká

*eyeglasses* - wak̲dáanaa

*he/she/it looked there* - aadé awdlig̲ein

*it's obvious; it's clearly visible* - tlél gooháa

*it was a sight to behold; it was fascinating to watch* - kawlitées'shán

*s/he can see it; s/he perceives it* - ayatéen

*s/he has sight* - k̲uwatéen / k̲uyatéen

*s/he is blind* - tlél k̲ooshtéen

*s/he sees it; s/he saw it* - awsiteen

*s/he watched him/her/it; s/he looked after him/her/it; s/he took care of him/her/it* - awlitín

## 2.4.2 Hear

*hearing* - k̲u.áx̲ch

*he/she/it was loud-voiced* - sawligaaw

*it rang* - sh wudigwál

*noise* - lagaaw

*s/he can hear it* - aya.áx̲ch

*s/he heard a voice* - aseiwa.áx̲

*s/he heard it* - aawa.áx̲

*s/he hears a voice* - asaya.áx̲ch

*s/he listened for the sound of it* - a kayéikg̲aa k̲oowdzi.aax̲

*s/he listened to him/her* - du x̲'éide k̲uwdzi.aax̲

*s/he's listening to him/her; s/he listens to him/her; s/he obeys him/her* - du x̲'éit wusi.áx̲ *s/he's listening to it; s/he listened to it* - át wusi.áx̱

*s/he understands him/her; s/he hears (and understands) him/her* - ax̱'aya.áx̱ch

*s/he understood him/her; s/he heard (and understood) him/her* - ax̱'eiwa.áx̱

*sound, noise of it* - a kayéik

*sound, noise of it (something whose identity is unknown)* - a yayík

### 2.4.3 Taste

*it was sour; it was bitter; it was spicy* - wusi.áax'w

*it was sweet* - wulinúkts

*s/he got used to it; s/he became accustomed to it (the flavor, pronunciation of something)* - du x̱'éix̱ woodaa

*s/he liked the taste of it* - du x̱'é wook'éi

*s/he tasted it* - x̱'éi awdinúk

### 2.4.4 Smell

*he/she/it stank; he/she/it smelled* - wulichán

*he/she/it was fragrant; he/she/it smelled sweet* - wulits'áa

*s/he smelled it* - awsiníx' / awdziníx'

### 2.4.5 Sense of touch

*it's itchy; it tickles* - kawlixwétl

*it's numb* - wulix'wás'ḵ

*s/he felt it* - jée awdinúk

*s/he felt that way* - yéi sh tuwdinook

### 2.5 Body condition

*fatigue* - xweitl

*he/she/it became strong; he/she/it became powerful* - wulitseen

*he/she/it made him/her tired* - awlixwétl

*he/she/it was weak; s/he is anemic; it is mild (of weather)* - tlél wultseen

*hunger* - yaan

*itch; rash* - kaxweitl

*s/he is hungry* - du éet yaan uwaháa

*s/he is thirsty; it is dry* - shaawakúx

*s/he rested; s/he's resting* - wudlisáa

*s/he's tired; s/he's weary* - wudixwétl

*strength, power* - latseen

## 2.6 Health

*arthritis* - daa.ittunéekw

*blind person* - l k̲ooshtéeni

*boil; inflammation and swelling* - x'ees

*cataract* - g̲áal'

*chest cold* - k̲usa.áat' néekw

*chest pain; tuberculosis* - wuwtunéekw

*cold sore* - x̲'atl'ook̲

*cut; knife wound* - k̲'éik̲'w

*deaf person* - l k̲ool.áx̲ji

*face cream; cold cream* - yaneis'í (T)

*fever* - t'aay néekw (AtT)

*growth on the face* - yagúnl'

*gunshot wound* - óonaa eetí

*hearing aid* - k̲u.áx̲ji

*he/she/it burned him/her/it; s/he scalded him/her/it* - awlix̲'éx̲'

*he/she/it is injured; he/she/it is wounded; he/she/it is bruised; s/he is hurting (emotionally)* - wudichún

*it cramped; it's cramping; he/she/it got shocked (by electricity)* - kawdlishúk'

*it's infected* - wudlik̲ít'

*it's swollen; it's tangled* - wudix'ís'

*knife wound* - lítaa eetí

*lancet* - tág̲aa

*liniment* - kóoshdaa náagu

*lump in the flesh; tumor* - kawáat

*medicine* - náakw

*mouth ulcer; soreness of the mouth (as of a baby teething)* - xáatl'ákw

*oil, grease (for coating skin or rubbing); lotion; liniment* - neis'

*Ouch!* - Hú!

*paralysis; polio* - l uwaxwachgi néekw

*pneumonia* - k'inashóo

*pus; discharge (from a sore, wound); sore, wound that discharges pus* - ḵéet'

*rash* - xéesh

*rheumatism* - s'aagitunéekw (AtT)

*rotting sore; gangrene; cancer* - tl'ooḵ

*scab* - ḵéech'

*scar* - teel

*shaman; medicine man* - íxt'

*s/he bandaged it; s/he bound it up; s/he wrapped it* - akaawas'ít

*s/he cut him/her/it (accidentally); s/he wounded him/her/it* - aawaḵ'ék'w

*s/he cut himself/herself; s/he wounded himself/herself (with a sharp instrument)* - sh wudiḵ'ék'w

*s/he got sick; he/she/it hurt; s/he was in pain* - woonéekw

*s/he had an accident; s/he got hurt; something bad happened to him/her* - ḵáakwt uwanéi

*s/he injured it; s/he wounded it; s/he bruised it* - awlichún

*s/he saved him/her/it; s/he healed him/her/it; s/he cured him/her/it* - awsineix̱

*s/he was saved; s/he was healed; s/he was cured; s/he recovered; s/he was satisfied* - wooneix̱

*sickness; illness; disease* - néekw

*sling* - júx̱'aa

*smallpox* - kwaan

*thick mucus, phlegm* - geitl'

*vomit; urge to vomit* - háas'

*wart* - t'áax̱'w

*wound* - s'éil'

*wrist guard* - jika.át; jigei.át

## 2.6.1 Sick

*s/he vomited; s/he threw up* - wudliḵoo

## 2.7 Life

*life; way of living* - k̲ustí

### 2.7.1 Marriage

*her husband* - du x̲úx̲
*his/her mate, his "old lady"; her "old man"* - du x̲án aa
*his old lady (wife)* - du shaawádi
*his wife* - du shát
*s/he got married* - wuduwasháa
*s/he married him/her; s/he is married* - aawasháa
*they married each other* - wooch has wudisháa
*widow* - l s'aatí shaawát

### 2.7.3 Birth

*her fetus, unborn child* - du kayádi
*his/her umbilical cord* - du taaní (TC); du taanú (AtT)
*it existed; s/he was born* - k̲oowdzitee

### 2.7.4 Stage of life

*adult; elder* - yanwáat
*baby* - t'ukanéiyi
*child* - atk'átsk'u
*children* - adátx'i
*children* - atyátx'i
*his/her age* - du katáagu
*(little) old person* - shaanák'w
*new; young; fresh* - yées
*old age* - shaan
*old man* - k̲áa shaan
*old person* - shaan
*s/he grew up* - kei uwawát

*s/he is old* - wudishán
*young adult* - yées wáat
*young adult(s); young people* - yées ḵu.oo
*younger one* - kík'i aa

## 2.7.5 Male, female

*boy* - yadak'wátsk'u
*boys, young men* - k'isáani
*girl* - shaatk'iyátsk'u; shaatk'átsk'u
*girls, young women* - shaax'wsáani
*man; male; person, people* - ḵáa
*men* - ḵáax'w
*woman* - shaawát
*women* - sháa
*young man (not married)* - yadák'w
*young woman (not married)* - shaatk'

## 2.7.6 Die

*afterlife, "happy hunting ground"* - dag̲anḵú
*cairn; rock pile* - té xóow
*coffin; casket* - ḵaa daakeidí
*death* - naná
*graveyard* - ḵaanaawú tl'átgi
*his/her inheritance; possessions of deceased given to him/her at a feast* - du néix'i
*memorial pile of rocks* - xóow

## 3.1 Soul, spirit

*fighting spirit* - lékwaa
*ghost* - s'ig̲eeḵáawu
*his/her inner being; mind; soul; feelings; intention* - du toowú
*his/her soul (of departed person)* - du yahaayí
*his/her spirit* - du yakg̲wahéiyagu

## 3.1.1 Personality

*brave, fearless man; temperamental, quick-tempered, hot-headed or domineering man* - x'ig̲aak̲áa

*coward* - k̲'atx̲áan

*crazy; insane; disturbed; mentally unbalanced* - sh kahaadí

*foolishness; recklessness* - l yaa k̲ooshgé

*the life of the party* - naa shuklag̲eeyí

*person who acts crazy or possesssed* - lookanáa

*person who cries easily* - ánk'w

*s/he is kind; s/he is gentle* - tuli.aan

*s/he is lazy* - oodzikaa

*s/he was noisy; s/he was crazy; s/he was lively* - wuli.oos

*snob; person who considers himself/herself better than others* - k̲aa kanax̲k̲áa

*troublemaker* - at lux'aak̲áawu

## 3.2 Mind

*consciousness, thought process, thinking* - yoo tutánk

*curiosity* - yoo at koojeek

*faith* - átk' aheen

*in his/her opinion; to his/her way of thinking, feeling* - du tuwáx'

*knowledgeable person* - at wuskóowu

*respect* - yáa at wooné

*s/he anticipated it; s/he foresaw it; s/he expected him/her/it* - ashoowsitee

*s/he believed him/her; s/he trusted him/her* - du éek' aawaheen

*s/he forgot* - a kát seiwax'ák̲w

*s/he knows it; s/he learned it* - awsikóo

*s/he learned how to do it; s/he knows how to do it* - awshigóok

*s/he made a decision about it* - a daa toowditaan

*s/he made a decision; s/he planned it* - yan akaawa.ák̲w

*s/he respects him/her* - du yáa ayaawanéi / du yáa awuwanéi

*s/he studied it; s/he learned it; s/he practiced it* - sh tóo awdlitóow

*s/he studied; s/he taught himself/herself* - sh tóo at wudlitóow

*s/he understands him/her; s/he hears (and understands) him/her* - ax̲'aya.áx̲ch

*s/he understood* - du daa yaa k̲ushuwsigéi

*s/he understood him/her; s/he heard (and understood) him/her* - ax̱'eiwa.áx̱

*s/he wondered about it* - yoo akaawajeek

*thought* - tundatáan

*truth* - x'éig̱aa át

*under the burden, weight of it; belabored or suffering from it (a burden, hardship)* - a jiyeet

## 3.2.1 Think

*s/he thought about it; s/he considered it; s/he made up his/her mind about it* - a daa yoo toowatán

*they thought about it; they considered it; they made up their minds about it* - a daa yoo (ha)s tuwli.át

## 3.3 Want

*he/she/it needed it; he/she/it lacked it* - a eetéenáx̱ wootee

*he/she/it tempted him/her; he/she tried it out; he/she tested it* - akaawadlénx̱aa

*s/he feels that way; s/he wants to do it; s/he feels like doing it* - yéi tuwatee

*s/he hopes for it* - át awdishée

*s/he ordered it* - aag̱áa aawawóo

*s/he wanted it; s/he liked it; it was pleasing to him/her* - du tuwáa wsigóo

*temptation, trial* - ḵukadlénx̱aa

*will; wish(es)* - at sag̱ahaayí

## 3.4 Emotion

*anger* - x'áan

*anxiety; wracked nerves; preoccupation; something weighing on one's mind* - tux'andaxeech

*comfort* - ḵaa toowú lat'aa

*crankiness; irritation; petulance* - ḵukahín

*crying, weeping* - g̱aax̱

*drunkenness; inebriation; giddiness* - kanashú

*fear* - akoolx̱éitl'

*good thoughts; felicity; happiness* - toowú k'é

*hope; intention; focus of hopes or thoughts* - tután

*it was scary; it was dangerous* - kawlix̲éitl'shán

*joy; happiness* - sagú

*kindness; generosity of heart* - tula.aan

*laughter* - at shook̲

*loneliness; boredom* - tuteesh

*love (of people)* - k̲usax̲án

*love (of things, of everything)* - at sax̲án

*mourning, wailing, loud weeping or crying; wail, groan, moan* - kasg̲aax̲

*pride; self-esteem, feeling good about oneself* - toowú klag̲é

*shame, embarrassment* - kadéix'

*s/he became proud; s/he became pleased* - du toowú kawlig̲éi

*s/he cried* - woog̲aax̲

*s/he felt that way* - yéi sh tuwdinook

*s/he hated him/her/it* - awshik'aan

*s/he is proud; s/he is conceited; s/he is particular; s/he is picky* - sh tukdlig̲éi

*s/he is worried about him/her/it; s/he has him/her/it on her mind* - du tóot wooxeex

*s/he laughed* - at wooshook̲

*s/he loved him/her/it* - awsix̲án

*s/he's angry* - x'áant uwanúk

*s/he was afraid of it* - áa akawdlix̲éitl'

*s/he was grateful; s/he was thankful; s/he was satisfied* - sh tóog̲áa wditee

*s/he was happy* - du toowú wook'éi; du toowú wsigóo

*sorrow; sadness* - toowú néekw; toowú nóok

*strength of mind or heart; courage; resolve* - toowú latseen

## 3.5 Communication

*conversation, dialog; talk, discourse (between more than one person)* - yoo x̲'ala.átk

*email* - kashóok' yoo x̲'atánk

*gossip, rumormonger* - niks'aatí; neek shatl'ék̲x'u; neek s'aatí (T)

*he/she/it cried out* - kawdig̲aax̲

*his/her voice* - du satú; du sé

*in response, reply to him/her; answering him/her; following his/her train of speech* - du x̲'akooká

*messenger; angel* - kook̲énaa

*mute; person who cannot speak* - l yoo k̲'eishtángi

*news; gossip, rumor* - neek

*s/he asked for it; s/he cried for it* - awdzig̲áax̲

*s/he asked him/her* - ax̲'eiwawóos'

*s/he brought it onto him/her (esp. shame, blame, joy)* - du kát ashuwatée

*s/he called him/her on the phone* - du jeedé x̲'awditaan

*s/he called him/her on the phone* - du jeet x̲'awditán

*s/he called out to him/her; s/he shouted to him/her* - aawa.éex'

*s/he gave him/her orders; s/he instructed him/her* - áa ajikaawak̲aa

*s/he gave him/her orders; s/he instructed him/her* - át akaawa.aak̲w

*s/he got used to it; s/he became accustomed to it (the flavor, pronunciation of something)* - du x̲'éix̲ woodaa

*s/he imitated him/her; s/he quoted him/her* - ax̲'eiwatee

*s/he invited him/her* - aawa.éex'

*s/he lied* - sh k̲'awdliyél

*s/he praised him/her; s/he approved it* - akaawashéx̲'

*s/he said that; s/he confessed that; s/he acknowledged that* - yéi yaawak̲aa

*s/he sent him/her on a mission* - akaawak̲aa

*s/he sent him/her there; s/he ordered him/her to go there; s/he gave it (in accordance with clan relationship)* - aadé akaawanáa

*s/he spoke; s/he talked; s/he made a speech* - x̲'awditaan

*s/he spoke to him/her; s/he talked to him/her* - du éet x̲'eiwatán

*s/he summoned him/her; s/he called him/her* - aawax̲oox̲

*s/he talked him/her out of it* - a káx̲ akawliník

*s/he talked; they spoke* - yoo x̲'eiwatán

*s/he tells him/her that* - yéi adaayak̲á

*s/he told about it; s/he reported about it; s/he witnessed it; s/he testified about it* - akaawaneek

*s/he told him/her that; s/he said that to him/her; s/he asked him/her to do that* - yoo ayawsik̲aa

*speech, talk; language; word, phrase, sentence, or discourse* - yoo x̲'atánk

*they conversed; they spoke; they talked* - yoo (ha)s x̲'awli.át

### 3.5.4 Verbal tradition

*master of ceremonies, elder of the opposite clan consulted conducting a ceremony* - naa káani

*myth; legend; children's tale* - tlaagú

*saying, proverb; event that is so common it has become a saying or proverb* - yax̱ at g̱wakú

*s/he told a story; s/he preached; s/he narrated* - sh kawdlineek

*s/he told people a legend* - k̲oon aawatlákw

*s/he told the story of it; s/he talked into it* - akawlineek

*story* - shkalneek

*storyteller; preacher* - k̲oon sh kalneegí

### 3.5.5 Reading and writing

*s/he read* - wuditóow

*s/he read it* - aawatóow

*s/he typed it* - akawlidál’

*s/he wrote* - kawjixít

*s/he wrote it; s/he drew it; s/he painted it; s/he photographed it; s/he took X-rays of it* - akawshixít

### 3.6 Teach

*according to his/her words, instructions* - du x̱’ayáx̱

*s/he demonstrated it to him/her; s/he showed him/her how to do it; s/he performed it for him/her* - du wak̲shiyeex’ yéi awsinei

*s/he instructed him/her; s/he advised him/her* - ashukaawajáa

*s/he taught him/her* - du éex’ at wulitóow

*s/he taught it to him/her* - du éex’ awlitóow

### 3.6.2 School

*math* - wooch yáx̱ yaa datóowch

*pack; backpack; pack sack* - x̱éey

*paper; book, magazine, newspaper; letter, mail* - x’úx’

*pencil; pen; brush* - kooxéedaa

*school* - at wuskú daakahídi; sgóon; áx' k̲aa ée at dultóow yé

*s/he investigated it; s/he researched it* - akaawatlaakw

*student; learner* - yaa at naskwéini

*student; pupil; scholar* - sgóonwaan

*table* - nadáakw

## 4.1 Relationships

*his/her boyfriend* - du yadák'u

*his/her girlfriend* - du shaatk'í

*his/her sweetheart* - du kacháwli; du tseiyí

*love (of people)* - k̲usax̲án

*nation; moiety; clan; band of people* - naa

*neighbor* - k'idaaká aa

*neighbors* - k'idaak̲wáani

*s/he kissed me* - ax̲ x̲'éit yawdzi.áa

*s/he loved him/her/it* - awsix̲án

*s/he raised him/her/it; s/he grew it* - awsiwát

## 4.1.8 Show affection

*honey!* - jáa

## 4.1.9 Related by kinship

*ancestor(s) of his/her clan or nation; his/her background, heredity* - du shagóon

*Chookaneidí; a clan of the Eagle moiety whose principal crests are the Porpoise and Brown Bear* - Chookaneidí

*Dak̲l'aweidí, locally called "Killer Whale"; a clan of the Eagle moiety whose principal crest is the Killer Whale* - Dak̲l'aweidí

*Deisheetaan, locally called "Beaver"; a clan of the Raven moiety whose principal crest is the Beaver* - Deisheetaan

*fatherless child; bastard* - neechkayádi

*G̲aanax̲teidí, locally called "Frog"; a clan of the Raven moiety whose principal crest is the Frog* - G̲aanax̲teidí

*Grandmother!; Grandfather!* - Léelk'w!

*her brother, cousin* - du éek'

*her fraternal niece, nephew, cousin* - du káalk'w

*her husband* - du x̱úx̱

*her older sister, cousin* - du shátx̱

*her younger sister; his younger brother; cousin* - du kéek'

*his/her brother-in-law, sister-in-law* - du káani

*his/her child* - du yádi

*his/her children* - du yátx'i

*his/her clan brother* - du xwáayi

*his/her clan brother or sister, distant relative, comrade* - du t'aag̱í

*his/her clan sister* - du sháawu

*his/her daughter, cousin* - du sée

*his/her family line of descent, side* - du yinaanáx̱

*his/her father* - du éesh

*his/her father-in-law* - du wóo

*his/her grandchild* - du dachx̱án

*his/her grandparent* - du áali

*his/her grandparent (term of respect)* - du daakanóox'u

*his/her husband's clan brother; his/her man, boyfriend, husband* - du ḵáawu

*his/her kinsman, moiety mate* - du een aa

*his/her mate, his "old lady"; her "old man"* - du x̱án aa

*his/her maternal aunt* - du tláak'w

*his/her maternal uncle* - du káak

*his/her mother* - du tláa

*his/her mother-in-law* - du chaan

*his/her partner* - du yaḵáawu

*his/her paternal aunt* - du aat

*his/her paternal uncle, cousin* - du sáni

*his/her relative, friend; his/her tribesman* - du x̱ooní

*his/her son, cousin* - du yéet

*his/her twin* - du kikyádi

*his older brother, cousin* - du húnx̱w

*his old lady (wife)* - du shaawádi

*his sister* - du dlaak'

*his sororal niece, nephew* - du kéilk'

*his wife* - du shát

*in front of him/her; his/her geneology, history; his/her ancestors* - du shuká

*K̲aach.ádi, locally called "Sockeye"; a clan of the Raven moiety whose principal crest is the Sockeye* - K̲aach.ádi

*Kaagwaantaan, locally called "Wolf"; a clan of the Eagle moiety whose principal crest is the Wolf* - Kaagwaantaan

*Kiks.ádi, locally called "Frog"; a clan of the Raven moiety whose principal crest is the Frog* - Kiks.ádi

*Kwaashk'i K̲wáan, locally called "Humpback Salmon"; a clan of the Raven moiety whose principal crest is the Humpback Salmon* - Kwaashk'i K̲wáan

*L'eeneidí, locally called "Dog Salmon"; a clan of the Raven moiety whose principal crest is the Dog Salmon* - L'eeneidí

*L'ukaax̲.ádi, locally called "Sockeye"; a clan of the Raven moiety whose principal crest is the Sockeye* - L'ukaax̲.ádi

*L'uknax̲.ádi, locally called "Coho"; a clan of the Raven moiety whose principal crest is the Coho* - L'uknax̲.ádi

*Shangukeidí, locally known as "Thunderbird"; a clan of the Eagle moiety whose principal crest is the Thunderbird* - Shangukeidí

*Suk̲teeneidí, locally called "Dog Salmon"; a clan of the Raven moiety whose principal crest is the Dog Salmon* - Suk̲teeneidí

*T'ak̲deintaan, locally called "Seagull"; a clan of the Raven moiety whose principal crest is the Seagull* - T'ak̲deintaan

*Teik̲weidí, locally called "Brown Bear"; a clan of the Eagle moiety whose principal crest is the Brown Bear* - Teik̲weidí

*Tsaagweidí; a clan of the Eagle moiety whose principal crests are the Seal and Killerwhale* - Tsaagweidí

*Was'eeneidí; a clan of the Eagle moiety whose principal crests are the Wolf and Auklet* - Was'eeneidí

*Yanyeidí, locally known as "Bear"; a clan of the Eagle moiety whose principal crest is the Brown Bear* - Yanyeidí

## 4.2 Social activity

*coming to see him/her* - du keekán

*feast, potlatch; party* - k̲u.éex'

*in public; at a potlatch, feast* - k̲aankak.eetx' (T)

*master of ceremonies, elder of the opposite clan consulted conducting a ceremony* - naa káani

*s/he invited him/her* - aawa.éex'

*sound of stamping, pounding fists, clapping; sound of running quickly* - tíxwjaa (At)

*sound of stamping, pounding fists, clapping; sound of running quickly* - túxjaa

*they crowded the place; they all went there* - át has yawdiháa

*they gathered together* - woosh kaanáx̱ has wudi.aat

*they gathered together* - woosh x̱oot has wudi.át

*townspeople; crowd or large group of people* - aantḵeení

## 4.2.3 Music

*bell* - gaaw

*drum* - gaaw

*his/her song* - du x̱'asheeyí

*music, singing, song* - at shí

*organ, piano* - g̱íx̱'jaa ḵóok

*radio, phonograph, stereo, music box, ipod; any device that plays music* - at shí ḵóok

*s/he composed a song; s/he called forth a response (from opposite clan by means of a song)* - shukawlix̱oox̱

*s/he played it (musical instrument)* - awli.áx̱

*s/he plays it (musical instrument)* - ali.áx̱ch

*s/he sang* - at wooshee

*s/he sang it* - aawashee

*singer* - at shéeyi

*singers, choir* - at shéex'i

*song* - shí

## 4.2.4 Dance

*button blanket* - ḵaayuka.óot'i x'óow (T)

*dance* - al'eix̱

*headdress, dance hat* - shakee.át

*s/he danced* - aawal'eix̱

*s/he danced out* - daak aawal'éx̱

*s/he started dancing* - g̱unéi aawal'éx̱

## 4.2.6 Entertainment, recreation

*ball* - kooch'éit'aa

*checkers; games played using string in the hands* - aldaawáa

*gambling; game of chance* - alk̲áa

*marble* - koot'áax'aa

*seesaw* - kookíts'aa

*s/he gambled; s/he played cards* - awdlik̲áa

*sled* - xát'aa

*sled (for recreational sledding)* - ach kooshx̲'íl'aa yeit

*tricks, sleight of hand; juggling* - yakwteiyí

## 4.2.7 Play, fun

*doll* - sée

*it's his/her turn* - du éet k̲uwaháa

*it was fun; it was enjoyable; it was appealing* - k̲'awsigóo

*plaything* - k̲us.ook'

*pretending; make-believe* - k̲'eildaháak'u

*s/he played* - ash kawdliyát

*s/he won it; s/he got it; s/he accomplished it; s/he defeated him/her* - ayaawadlaak̲

*top (spinning toy)* - toolch'án

## 4.3.4 Do good/evil to

*against it, wrong (so as to foul up what s/he had done)* - du jiyagéix̲

*evil, sin* - l ushk'é

*he/she/it bothered him/her; he/she/it is bothering him/her* - akaawaxíl'

*he/she/it comforted him/her* - du toowú awlit'áa

*he/she/it is helping me; s/he helped me* - ax̲ éet wudishée

*murderer* - k̲oowajag̲i aa; k̲u.eení

*they attacked someone* - k̲aa éet has jiwdi.át

*thief* - táaw s'aatí

*trouble; conflict* - kaxéel'

### 4.3.9 Culture

*armor made of tough hide or wooden rods* - sankeit

*bentwood box* - láḵt

*black horn spoon* - yéts' shál

*blanket; robe* - x'óow

*button blanket* - yaka.óot' x'óow

*cairn; rock pile* - té xóow

*ceremonial woven root hat with a stack of basket-like cylinders on top* - shadakóox̱'

*Chilkat blanket* - naaxein

*copper shield* - tináa

*dance regalia* - l'ax̱keit

*dancing leggings; leggings for climbing* - x̱'uskeit

*his/her inheritance; possessions of deceased given to him/her at a feast* - du néix'i

*labret, lip plug* - x̱'eint'áax'aa

*memorial pile of rocks* - xóow

*rattle (of shaman)* - sheishóox̱

*s/he claimed it; s/he owns it* - aawahéin

*sheep or goat horn spoon* - leineit shál

*s/he performed rites; s/he made magic* - aawahéix̱waa

*totem pole* - kootéeyaa

*wall crest; wall screen* - x̱'éen

*wool blanket (used as potlatch gift or for dancing)* - l'ée

*woven root hat* - x̱aat s'áaxw

### 4.5.1 Person in authority

*boss* - ḵaa s'aatí

*head of a clan house; master of the house* - hít s'aatí

*his/her boss, master* - du s'aatí

*leader* - ḵaa sháade háni

*leaders* - ḵaa sháade náḵx'i

## 4.7 Law

*law, words one lives by* - a káa k̲ududziteeyi yoo x̲'atánk

## 4.7.3 Break the law

*s/he did something wrong; s/he broke the law* - at géit wudzigít
*s/he stole it* - aawatáw

## 4.7.7 Punish

*correctional facility* - áa k̲uyadujee yé
*jail* - g̲ayéis' hít

## 4.8.3 Peace

*it's calm; it's peaceful* - kawduwayél'
*peace, calm* - kayéil'
*s/he improved it; s/he made peace with him/her/it* - awlik'éi

## 4.8.4 War

*body armor, breastplate* - niyaháat
*body armor, breastplate* - yinaaháat
*bullet* - at katé
*captive* - g̲alsháatadi
*club* - x'ús'
*double-ended dagger* - shak'áts'
*fighting; war, conflict* - k̲ulagaaw
*fort* - noow
*general; leader of war, battle* - x'áan kanáayi
*gunpowder* - at tugáni
*gun, rifle* - óonaa
*his/her enemy, adversary* - du yaanaayí

*s/he killed him/her/it; s/he let it go* - aawajáḵ

*war clothes (of moosehide)* - x'áan yinaa.át

*war party, attacking force of warriors or soldiers; army* - x̱áa

*war; trouble; rush, hurry* - adawóotl

*whip* - x̱át'aa

## 4.9 Religion

*believer* - átk' aheení

*cross* - kanéist

*Easter bread; communion bread* - léikwaa

*faith* - átk' aheen

*fate; bad luck* - jinaháa

*fighting spirit* - lékwaa

*ghost* - s'iǥeeḵáawu

*God* - Dikáanḵáawu; Dikée aanḵáawu

*God, Lord* - Aanḵáawu

*his/her fate* - du daakashú

*his/her follower, disciple* - du ítx̱ nagoodí

*his/her followers, disciples* - du ítx̱ na.aadí

*his/her spirit* - du yakǥwahéiyagu

*Holy Spirit* - l ulitoogu Ḵaa Yakǥwahéiyagu

*house of prayer; church* - x̱'agáax' daakahídi

*Indian doctor's spirit* - yéik

*messenger; angel* - kooḵénaa

*parable* - at kookeidí

*possession(s); that which is owned (by them)* - ḵaa at óowu

*praise, glorification* - kashéex̱'

*prayer* - x̱'agáax'

*preacher* - sh kalneegí

*priest* - wáadishgaa

*priest; pastor; minister* - nakwnéit

*recovery; salvation* - ǥaneix̱

*Satan* - Diyée aanḵáawu

*shaman; medicine man* - íx̱t'

*s/he baptized him/her* - héent ayaawatée

*s/he got lucky; s/he was blessed* - wulix̱éitl

*s/he prayed* - sh káa x̱'awdigáx'

*s/he was saved; s/he was healed; s/he was cured; s/he recovered; s/he was satisfied* - wooneix̱

*spirit* - ḵaa yakg̱wahéiyagu

*storyteller; preacher* - ḵoon sh kalneegí

*wish; prayer* - oolxéis'

*witch* - nakws'aatí

## 5 Home

*banister; railing* - a daax̱ yaa dulsheech át

*door* - x̱'aháat

*doorway* - x̱'awool

*electricity* - kashóok'

*fence* - ḵ'anáax̱án

*floor* - t'áa ká

*gardener* - táay kahéix̱i

*home* - neil

*house; building* - hít

*house post* - gáas'

*(in) his/her room, bedroom* - du eetí ká

*platform cache; house cache; shed* - chál

*porch; patio* - x̱'awool kayáashi

*possession; that which is claimed* - ḵaa at oohéini

*rafter* - x̱aanás'

*rafters (large roof beams)* - hít kaságu

*rafters (modern)* - hít kagaadí

*roof* - hít ká

*room* - eet

*shingle(s)* - hít kat'áayi

*shingles* - t'aa yátx'i

*smokehole* - gaan; gaan ká

*smokehouse (with smoke piped in from outside)* - s'eiḵ daakahídi

*steambath* - x̱aay

*tent* - s'ísaa hít

*upstairs; attic* - hít shantú
*wall* - t’áa yá
*window* - x̲aawaag̲éi; x̲aawaag̲í

### 5.1.3 Furnishings

*blanket sewn from scraps of hide* - at xáshdi x’óow
*flag* - aan kwéiyi
*freezer* - a tóo at dult’ix’x̲i át
*mat, doormat; rug* - g̲áach
*mattress; bedding* - yee.át
*quilt; cotton blanket* - kast’áat’ x’óow
*stove* - stoox
*window curtain* - x̲aawaag̲éi kas’ísayi

### 5.1.3 Furniture

*bed* - káa x̲ex̲x’u yeit
*chair* - káayag̲ijeit
*organ, piano* - g̲íx̲’jaa k̲óok
*swing, hammock* - g̲eig̲ách’
*table* - nadáakw

### 5.1.4 Household tools

*adze* - x̲út’aa
*axe* - shanax̲wáayi; shunax̲wáayi
*babiche, string, leather thonging* - dzaas
*backpack; pack sack* - yáanadi
*baggage, luggage; things, stuff packed up for carrying* - at la.át
*bag; sack* - gwéil
*balloon* - kadu.uxx̲u át
*barrel* - káast
*basket* - k̲ákw
*basket of woven red cedar bark* - néil’

*basket or pan used to collect berries by knocking them off the bush* - kadádzaa yeit

*basket with a rattle in the lid* - tudaxákw; tu<u>k</u>daadaxákw

*bentwood box* - lá<u>k</u>t

*berrying basket* - kaltásk

*berrying basket or can hung around the neck, resting on the chest* - sei<u>g</u>atáanaa

*birch bark basket* - at daayí <u>k</u>ákw

*blackboard, chalkboard* - kadushxit t'aa yá

*black horn spoon* - yéts' shál

*bottle; jug* - t'ooch'ineit; ín x'eesháa

*box* - <u>k</u>óok

*bucket; pail* - x'eesháa

*calendar* - dís woo<u>x</u>éiyi

*camera* - aankadushxit át

*candle* - toow s'eenáa

*cane; walking stick; staff* - wootsaa<u>g</u>áa

*canvas; tarp; tent* - xwaasdáa

*cast-iron skillet* - té kas'úgwaa yeit (T)

*chain* - <u>x</u>'akakei<u>x</u>í; wóoshná<u>x</u> <u>x</u>'akakéi<u>x</u>i

*cheesecloth, loose-woven cloth; netting, screen* - ka<u>g</u>ádaa

*clock* - <u>g</u>aaw

*clothes brush* - naa.át kaxít'aa

*cloth; sailcloth* - s'ísaa

*container for it* - daakeit

*container for traveling provisions; lunch basket, lunch container* - wóow daakeit

*cork, plug* - a <u>x</u>'adéex'i

*cotton; cotton blanket, quilt* - kast'áat'

*cradleboard; papoose carrier* - t'ook

*cup; can* - <u>g</u>úx'aa

*curved carving knife* - yoo katan lítaa

*dagger; machete, long knife* - gwálaa

*dipper (for dipping water)* - sheen <u>x</u>'ayee

*dipper, scoop, ladle; brailer bag* - kaxwénaa

*dish; plate* - s'íx'

*dish; platter* - kélaa; kílaa

*drill* - túlaa

*envelope* - x'úx' daakax'úx'u

*file* - x'ádaa

*flagpole* - aan kwéiyi tugáas'i

*flashlight* - kadulg̱óok s'eenáa; kadulg̱úkx̱ s'eenáa

*flat open basket woven from wide strips of bark (for carrying fish, etc.); large platter* - táal

*flywheel; wheelbarrow; wagon; hand truck* - kajúxaa

*foam (on waves); sponge* - teet x̱'achálx̱i

*food container; pot or pan; dish, large bowl* - x̱'ayeit

*fork* - ách at dusx̱a át

*frying pan, skillet* - kax̱gáani yeit; kas'ígwaa yeit (A)

*glass (the substance)* - ít'ch

*grindstone* - g̱íl'aa

*handkerchief* - lug̱wéinaa

*handmade ladle* - tseeneidi shál

*hatchet* - shanax̱wáayi yádi

*heating pad* - kashéek'w gwéil; kashóok' gwéil

*Hudson Bay blanket* - kinguchwáan x'óowu

*iron (for ironing)* - kax̱'íl'aa

*its antenna (of radio)* - a gúgu

*its covering; cover (over a large opening or something without an opening)* - a kaháadi

*its handle (stick-like); its shaft (of spear, etc.)* - a sákwti

*its handle (stick-like); its shaft (of spear, etc.)* - a sáxwdi

*its lid, cover (of pot, etc.)* - a yana.áat'ani

*kerosene; coal oil* - ux̱ganhéen

*key* - katíx̱'aa

*kitchen utensil* - atx̱á jishagóon

*knife* - lítaa

*knife with fold-in blade* - x̱'éi shadagutx̱i lítaa

*lamp* - s'eenáa

*large box for storing grease, oil* - daneit

*large cannister* - naasa.áa

*large rectangular tub for soaking skins while tanning them* - ḵ'aakanéi

*large wooden spoon* - shéen

*leather needle* - lukat'íshaa

*mallet, wooden hammer* - l'oowú táḵl

*mirror* - tóonáx̲ k̲aateen

*mortar for grinding* - kaxágwaa yeit

*mortar for pounding* - kat'éx̲'aa yeit

*needle* - táax'ál'

*paper; book, magazine, newspaper; letter, mail* - x'úx'

*pencil; pen; brush* - kooxéedaa

*pick, pickaxe* - kéit'u

*pillow* - shayeit

*pipe (for carrying water)* - tunax̲hinnadaa

*pipe (for tobacco)* - s'eik̲daakeit

*pitcher; jug* - k̲'ateil

*plastic* - xén

*plate* - s'íx' k̲'áatl'

*pliers* - at katáx'aa; kakatáx'aa

*pocket knife* - g̲altulítaa

*pot, cooking pot* - k̲'wátl

*pounder (for meat or grease)* - kat'éx̲'aa

*rack for drying fish* - x̲aanás' éinaa

*radio, phonograph, stereo, music box, ipod; any device that plays music* - at shí k̲óok

*receptacle for it* - a yee.ádi

*roasting stick (split so that the meat can be inserted; the end is then bound)* - x̲'wéinaa

*rope* - tíx'

*round basket made of split red cedar branches* - ts'anéi

*rubber* - s'él'

*safety pin* - x̲'éigwál'

*saw* - xáshaa

*scissors* - k̲aashaxáshaa

*scraper, as for scraping off bark from roots* - éenaa

*scraper for hemlock bark* - yees'

*screwdriver* - kas'éet katíx̲'aa

*scrubber* - kaxíl'aa

*sharpened stick (for digging up clams, roots, etc.); gardening fork* - káat'

*sheep or goat horn spoon* - leineit shál

*shell; shell-like chip or flake; china; carapace* - nóox'

*shoe polish* - téel daakeyéis'i (C)

*shovel* - ḵutl'ídaa

*skin scraper* - xwájaa

*sled* - xát'aa

*small covered box* - x̱'al'daakeit

*smokehole cover* - gaan x̱'aháadi

*spoon* - shál

*straw (for drinking)* - a tóonáx kadus'íḵs' át

*string* - tíx' yádi

*swing; hammock* - g̱eeg̱ách'

*tanning frame; frame for stretching skin* - t'éesh

*tea kettle (originally with long curved spout)* - t'aawáḵ x'eesháa

*thimble* - tl'iḵnaa.át

*thread; sinew* - tás

*three-cornered needle for sewing skin or leather* - kat'íshaa

*tongs* - l'át'aa

*tool, tools* - jishagóon

*toothpick* - oox̱ katság̱aa

*towel, hand towel* - jig̱wéinaa

*umbrella* - kéi daḵinji s'áaxw

*wash basin* - kát yadu.us'ku át

*washboard* - a káa dul.us'ku át; kát dul.us'ku át

*water dipper; ladle* - héen gúx'aa

*wheelbarrow; hand truck, dolly* - koojúxaa (TC); koojúxwaa (An)

*whetstone* - yayéinaa

*wire* - kaxées'

*woman's curved knife* - wéiksh

*wooden bailer (for boat)* - sheen

*wool blanket (used as potlatch gift or for dancing)* - l'ée

*wrench* - kas'éet kagwádlaa

## 5.2 Food

*at hand (for him/her to eat or drink)* - du x̱'ax̱án

*bread crumbs* - sakwnéin kax̱'eiltí

*famine; starvation* - laaxw

*food, a meal* - atx̱á

*food, lunch, provisions taken along (on a trip, to work or school)* - wóow

*food taken home from a feast or dinner to which one was invited* - éenwu

*for him/her to eat or drink* - du x̱'eis

*half-dried, compressed food, esp. berries or seaweed* - kat'ákx̱i

*he/she/it starved* - uwaláxw

*his/her food scraps, left-over food; crumbs of food left or scattered where s/he has eaten* - du x̱'a.eetí

*leftovers, food scraps* - ḵaa x̱'a.eetí

*(loaf of) bread* - sakwnéin éewu

*pilot bread* - g̱áatl

*restaurant; tavern* - atx̱á daakahídi

## 5.2.1 Food preparation

*fish cleaned and hung to dry* - kadútlx̱i

*flour; bread* - sakwnéin

*it's boiling; it boiled* - wudli.úk

*long, flat loosely woven basket for pressing out herring oil* - kaat

*long smokehouse pole(s)* - jikaḵáas'

*pepper* - si.áax'u át

*pepper* - tux̱'wáns'i náakw

*pole(s) on which fish are hung for drying in smokehouse* - s'óos'

*salt* - éil'

*saltwater brine* - éil' kahéeni

*s/he barbecued it* - awlitsík

*s/he boiled it* - awli.úk

*s/he cooked* - at wusi.ée

*s/he cooked it* - awsi.ée

*s/he dried it* - awsixúk

*s/he fried it; s/he toasted it* - akawlis'úk

*s/he put up food; s/he stored up food (for the winter); s/he preserved food; s/he finished distributing things (at party)* - yan akawligáa

*s/he steamed it; s/he boiled it* - awsitáa

*s/he tanned it; s/he smoked it* - áx̱ akawlis'eiḵ

*s/he warmed it up* - awsit'áa

*smokehouse* - atx'aan hídi

*smokehouse shelf* - yaash ká

*spit, skewer, roasting stick, barbecue stick* - tséek

*sticks woven through the fish lengthwise after it has been filleted for barbecuing* - tl'éek'at

*sun-dried* - g̲agaan kas'úkwx̲u

*wide, flat stone (used for cooking)* - té k̲'áatl'

## 5.2.2 Eat

*s/he ate* - at uwax̲áa

*s/he ate it* - aawax̲áa

*s/he ate it all up* - yax̲ ayawsix̲áa

*s/he fed him/her/it; s/he gave him/her/it something to eat* - du x̲'éix̲ at wootee

*s/he fed it to him/her/it; s/he gave it to him/her/it to eat* - du x̲'éix̲ aawatee

*s/he liked the taste of it* - du x̲'é wook'éi

## 5.2.3.1 Food from plants

*alpine blueberry* - ts'éekáx̲k'w

*apple; crabapple* - x'áax'

*berry, berries* - tléik̲w

*black currant* - x̲aaheiwú

*black currants or swamp currants* - kaneilts'ákw; kaneilts'íkw (At)

*blueberry; huckleberry* - kanat'á

*blueberry juice; purple* - kanat'á kahéeni

*bog cranberry; low bush cranberry* - k̲'eishkaháagu

*bunchberry* - k̲'eikaxétl'k

*carrot* - s'ín

*crabapple* - lingít x'áax'i

*currants* - kadooheix̲.aa

*dulse (type of seaweed)* - laak̲'ásk

*elderberry* - yéil'

*fiddlehead fern (with edible rhizome)* - k'wálx̲

*gray currant, stink currant* - shaax̲

*high bush cranberry* - kaxwéix̲

*huckleberry; blueberry* - naanyaa kanat'aayí
*lowbush cranberry, bog cranberry* - dáxw
*mossberry* - xéel'i
*mountain ash berry* - kalchaneit tléiǥu
*nagoonberry, lagoonberry, dwarf nagoonberry* - neigóon
*potato* - k'únts'
*raspberry* - tlékw yádi
*red huckleberry* - tleikatánk
*ribbon seaweed* - ḵ'áach'
*rice; Kamchatka lily root* - kóox
*rutabaga; turnip* - anahoo
*salmonberry* - was'x'aan tléiǥu
*serviceberry; saskatoonberry* - gaawáḵ
*snowberry* - dleit tléiǥu
*soapberry* - xákwl'i
*sourdock; wild rhubarb* - tl'aaḵ'wách'
*strawberry* - shákw
*swamp blueberry* - láx̱' loowú
*thimbleberry* - ch'eex̱'
*turnip* - tl'aadéin.aa
*watermelon berry, twisted stalk, wild cucumber* - tleiḵw kahínti
*wild strawberry* - lingít shákw
*yellow cloudberry* - néx̱'w
*young salmonberry bush shoots (edible)* - k'eit

## 5.2.3.2 Food from animals

*bacon* - gishoo taayí
*cracklings of rendered fat, grease unfit for consumption* - dákwtasi
*dry fish* - at x̱'éeshi
*egg (of bird)* - k'wát'
*fat; blubber* - taay
*fish; salmon* - x̱áat
*herring eggs* - ǥáax'w
*honey* - gandaas'aaji háatl'i (T)
*hooligan oil* - saak eex̱í

*its edible part (of clam)* - a g̱eiyí

*its flesh (of fish)* - a x̱'úx̱u

*its raw (flesh or meat); rare (meat)* - a shís'ḵ

*meat, flesh* - dleey

*oil, grease* - eex̱; eix̱ (C)

*roe, eggs (of fish)* - kaháakw

*seaweed, kelp on which herring spawn* - daaw

*tallow, hard fat* - toow

### 5.2.3.4 Prepared food

*aged fish head* - k'ínk'

*boiled fish* - útlx̱i

*boiled food; broth* - a téix̱i

*boiled food; broth* - téix̱

*dish made with berries and salmon eggs* - kanéegwál'

*dried fish strips, dried necktie style* - ts'ak'áawásh

*dried thing, esp. food* - at kaawaxúkw

*fish air-dried in cold weather and allowed to freeze* - chíl xook

*fish heads cooked on ground around fire* - gangukg̱áx̱i

*fish hung over the fire to cook* - g̱íḵs

*fish roasted whole, strung up by its tail over the fire and twirled periodically* - g̱íḵsaa (T)

*fish smoked for a short time with the backbone taken out* - kadúkli

*fried food* - a kas'úkx̱u

*fry bread, bannock* - eex̱ kát sakwnein

*half-dried salmon (smoked)* - náayadi

*it's cooked* - yan uwa.ée

*its dried flesh, strips (of fish)* - a x̱'éeshi

*mashed berries* - kag̱útlx̱i

*mush, oatmeal, porridge* - wásh

*porridge* - sakwnéin katéix̱i

*s/he dried fish; s/he smoked fish* - at uwax̱'án

*soaked dried fish* - téeyí

*soup broth; soup* - tax̱héeni

*soup, porridge* - katéix̱

*steamed berries* - kanálx̱i

*steamed berries put up in soft grease* - kaḵáshx̱i

## 5.2.3.6 Beverages

*apple juice* - x'áax' kahéeni

*berry juice* - tléiḵw kahéeni

*coffee* - káaxwei

*coffee; hot water* - yat'aayi héen

*cow's milk* - wasóos l'aayí

*Hudson Bay tea* - s'ikshaldéen

*juice* - at kahéeni

*liquor; booze; alcoholic beverage* - náaw

*s/he drank* - at wudináa

*tea* - cháayoo

## 5.2.3.7 Alcoholic beverages

*beer* - géewaa

*drunkenness; inebriation; giddiness* - kanashú

*liquor; booze; alcoholic beverage* - kasiyaayi héen

## 5.2.4 Tobacco

*marijuana* - kasiyéiyi s'eiḵ

*(plug of) chewing tobacco* - kat'éex'

*s/he smoked* - sh x̱'awdis'eiḵ

*tobacco* - tuwaakú

*tobacco* - g̱ánch

*tobacco pipe* - s'iḵdaakeit

## 5.3 Clothing

*belt* - séek

*blindfold* - wak̲kadóox'

*boot(s)* - x'wán

*bow (ribbon tied into a bow)* - lag̲wán

*clothes, clothing; garment* - naa.át

*coat, overcoat* - kinaa.át; kinaak.át

*corset* - kasanka.át

*diaper* - tuk̲daa.át

*dress* - l'aak

*hat* - s'áaxw

*headscarf, kerchief covering the head* - shadaa.át

*moccasins* - at xáshdi téel

*neck scarf; kerchief* - sadaat'aay

*necktie* - saka.át

*pants, trousers* - tuk̲'atáal

*petticoat; slip* - doonyaax̲l'aak

*rubber gloves* - s'éil' tsáax'

*shawl; cape; poncho* - teik̲

*shirt* - k'oodás'

*shoe(s)* - téel

*slipper(s); house shoe(s)* - neilyeetéeli

*snowshoe* - jáaji

*sock(s)* - l'ée x'wán

*sweater* - kakéin k'oodás'

*undershirt* - doonyaax̲ k'oodás'

*vest; sleeveless top* - l.uljíni

### 5.3.3 Traditional clothing

*armor made of tough hide or wooden rods* - sankeit

*blanket; robe* - x'óow

*body armor, breastplate* - yinaaháat

*button blanket* - yaka.óot' x'óow; yuka.óot' x'óow; k̲aayuka.óot'i x'óow (T) *ceremonial woven root hat with a stack of basket-like cylinders on top* - shadakóox̱'

*Chilkat blanket* - naaxein

*dance regalia* - l'ax̱keit

*dancing leggings; leggings for climbing* - x̱'uskeit

*neck cord worn for dance* - kaséik̲'w

*sash (worn over shoulder)* - koogéinaa

*war clothes (of moosehide)* - x'áan yinaa.át

*woven root hat* - x̱aat s'áaxw

### 5.3.6 Parts of clothing

*buckshot; moccasin lining* - at tux̱'wáns'i

*button* - yaka.óot'; yuka.óot'

*button* - k̲aayaku.óot'i (At)

*hem of his/her coat, shirt, dress* - du kóon

*its hem, bottom edge (of coat, dress, shirt); rim (of hat)* - a kóon

*it's sleeve (of shirt, coat)* - a jíni

*pocket* - g̲altú

*shoelace(s)* - téel x̱'adzaasí; téel x̱'agudzaasí; téel x̱'akadzaazí

### 5.3.7 Wear clothing

*barefoot; shoeless* - kaltéelk̲

*s/he is dressed up* - yan sh wudzinéi

*s/he is wearing it* - kát adatéen

*s/he put it on* - káx̱ awditee

*s/he put them on* - x̱'oosdé awdiyík̲

*s/he wore it; s/he put it on; s/he used it* - yéi aawa.oo

### 5.3.8 Naked

*bare; naked* - kaldaag̲ákw

### 5.4.1 Jewelry

*bracelet* - kées
*earring* - guk kajaash
*earring* - guk.át
*earring; yarn dangling from the ears that sways during dancing* - guk tl'éinx̱w
*labret hole* - ḵ'anoox̱ eetí
*labret, lip plug* - x̱'eint'áax'aa
*labret, small lip plug* - ḵ'anoox̱
*necklace* - seit
*nose ring* - lunás
*ring* - tl'iḵkakées
*wristwatch* - jikawáach

### 5.4.2 Cosmetics

*crimson red; face paint* - léix̱'w
*face cream; cold cream* - yaneis'í (T)
*face powder* - yawéinaa
*lipstick* - x̱'akaséḵ'waa

### 5.4.3 Caring for hair

*comb* - xéidu
*comb* - ḵaa shaksayéigu
*hair pendant* - ḵaa shaksayíḵs'i
*hair pin* - shax̱'ée x'wál'
*hair ribbon* - shach'éen
*razor* - aan yaduxas' át
*ribbon* - ch'éen

### 5.5 Fire

*around the fire* - gandaa
*ash; ashes* - kél't'

*ashes* - gan eetí

*burnt or charred wood* - xoodzí

*coal* - t'ooch' té

*cord (of wood)* - at kaayí

*dry inner part of firewood* - gantuxoogú

*fire* - x̱'aan

*fire drill, hand drill used to start fires by friction* - x̱'aan káx̱ túlaa

*fireside; by the fire, facing the fire* - gangook

*firestone; iron pyrite* - dáadzi

*firewood* - gán

*flame* - ganyal'óot'

*he/she/it burned him/her/it; s/he scalded him/her/it* - awlix̱'éx̱'

*in the fire* - ganaltáak

*it exploded* - kei wjitúk

*it went out (light, fire)* - yakawlikís'

*kindling* - gán kaḵás'ti

*match* - ux̱ganḵáas'

*match; stick* - ḵáas'

*opening of smokehole* - gaan woolí

*punk wood, decayed dry wood* - g̱unanaa tetl

*s/he built a fire* - shóot awdi.ák

*s/he burned it up* - kei awsigán

*s/he got burned* - wudix̱'éx̱'

*s/he lit it (fire); s/he turned it on (light)* - át akawligán

*s/he put it out (fire); s/he turned it off (light)* - ayakawlikís'

*singed, burnt, or charred matter* - xóosht'

*small pieces of firewood; kindling* - gán yátx'i

*smoke* - s'eeḵ

*smoke* - s'eiḵ

*smoke spreaders (board suspended horizontally above smokehouse fire)* - ganigeidí

*soot* - dús'

*spark* - yíḵdlaa

*wet firewood* - gán tl'áak'

*wood, piece of wood; wood chip* - l'eiwú; l'oowú

## 5.6 Cleaning

*broom; brush* - xít'aa
*laundry* - óos'i
*s/he bathed* - wudishúch
*s/he swept* - wudixéet'
*s/he swept the floor* - t'aa ká aawaxéet'
*s/he washed it* - aawa.óos'
*s/he washed it* - akaawa.óos'
*s/he wiped it; s/he mopped it* - awlig̱oo
*soap* - ús'aa

## 5.6.1 Clean, dirty

*black with dirt, filth, stain* - ts'áḵl
*dirt, dust* - ch'éix̱'w
*dirt; scrap(s); rubbish, trash, clutter; lint* - s'eex
*filth, mess; trash, rubbish, garbage* - tl'eex
*he/she/it is dirty* - wulich'éx̱'w
*it got muddy* - kawshiḵútl'
*s/he got it dirty* - awlich'éx̱'w

## 5.7 Sleep

*he/she/it kept him/her awake* - ash wusix̱éḵ
*s/he got up* - shawdinúk
*s/he overslept* - a yáanáx̱ yaawatáa
*s/he slept* - wootaa
*s/he woke him/her up* - kei awsigít
*s/he woke up* - kei wdzigít
*sleep* - tá
*they slept* - has woox̱éix'w

## 6.1 Work

*in vain; for nothing; without success* - ch'a g̲ég̲aa
*s/he raised him/her/it; s/he grew it* - awsiwát
*s/he used it for it; s/he made it into it* - átx̲ awliyéx̲
*s/he worked; s/he did that* - yéi jeewanei
*worker* - yéi jinéiyi
*worker; crew* - ganaswáan
*working with him/her; helping him/her work or do something* - du ji.een
*work, job* - yéi jiné

## 6.1.3 Difficult, impossible

*it was difficult* - wulidzée

## 6.2.1 Growing crops

*gardener* - táay kahéix̲i
*planting stick* - katsóowaa
*scarecrow* - yéil koox̲étl'aa
*s/he grew it; s/he turned it on (hose); s/he caused it to flow (water)* - akawsi.aa
*s/he planted it* - akaawahaa

## 6.4.1 Hunt

*arrow* - chooneit
*arrowhead* - at x̲éidi
*blunt arrow for stunning* - gútl
*bow* - sák̲s
*buckshot; moccasin lining* - at tux̲'wáns'i
*close quarter bow and arrow* - sheexw; sheixw
*gunpowder* - at tugáni
*gun, rifle* - óonaa
*hunt* - al'óon
*hunter* - al'óoni

*its head (of spear)* - a kádi

*sea otter hunting canoe with an angular prow for breaking the waves* - ch'iyáash

*sharp arrow for killing* - tláak̲

*s/he hunted* - aawal'óon

*s/he hunted it* - aawal'óon

*s/he is shooting at it* - a.únt

*s/he killed him/her/it; s/he let it go* - aawajják̲

*s/he shot it* - aawa.ún

*s/he shot it (with bow and arrow); s/he chose it (in gambling with sticks)* - aawat'úk

*spear for clubbing* - at shax̲ishdi dzáas

*spear for hunting* - woosáani

*spear which binds rope around seal* - at s'aan.ax̲w dzáas

## 6.4.2 Trap

*deadfall trap for large animals* - yéix̲

*s/he snared it* - awdlidás'

*snare* - dáas'aa

*trap (esp. steel trap)* - g̲aatáa

*trapper* - g̲aatáa yéi daanéiyi

## 6.4.5 Fishing

*dipnet (for eulachon)* - deegáa

*fisherman (troller)* - ast'eix̲í

*fish hook* - t'eix̲; t'eix̲áa (T)

*fishing rod* - shax̲'út'aa

*fish net; seine net* - g̲eiwú

*fish pitchfork* - x̲áat g̲íjaa

*fish spear; harpoon for spearing salmon* - dlagwáa

*fish spear with a long pole and detachable gaff hook* - kooxídaa (At)

*fish trap* - sháal

*gaff hook; grappling hook* - k'íx̲'aa

*halibut fisherman* - cháatl ast'eix̲í

*halibut hook (made of wood)* - náxw

*herring rake* - xídlaa

*its prongs (of spear)* - a x̱aani

*leadline (of net)* - k'óox̱' tíx'i

*pole (for boating, for pushing skin toboggan)* - tság̱aa

*rock pile fish trap* - óot'

*seine fisherman; seine boat* - asg̱eiwú

*s/he anchored* - shawdziyaa

*s/he anchored the boat* - ashawsiyaa

*s/he baited hooks* - yawdináḵw

*s/he caught it; s/he grabbed him/her/it; s/he arrested him/her; s/he trapped him/her/it* - aawasháat

*s/he fished (with a hook); s/he trolled* - awdzit'eix̱

*s/he hooked it in the head* - ashaawak'éx̱'

*s/he pulled it up (esp. line)* - kei awsiyíḵ

*s/he seined; s/he fished (with a net)* - awdzig̱eiwú

*s/he sportfished; s/he casted* - shawdlix̱óot'

*spear* - tsaag̱ál'

*spear (for devilfish)* - táanaa

*spear (for fish and seal)* - áadaa

*sport fisherman* - ashalx̱óot'i

*troller* - shukalx̱aají

## 6.5.1 Building

*cannery* - x̱áat daakahídi

*house; building* - hít

*jail* - g̱ayéis' hít

*platform cache; house cache; shed* - chál

*post office* - x'úx' daakahídi

*restaurant; tavern* - atx̱á daakahídi

*sawmill* - sh kadax'áshti hít

*s/he built it; s/he made it; s/he constructed it* - awliyéx̱

*smokehouse* - atx'aan hídi

*smokehouse (with smoke piped in from outside)* - s'eiḵ daakahídi

*steambath* - x̱aay

*store* - hoon daakahídi

*tent* - s'ísaa hít

### 6.5.2 Parts of a building

*door* - x̱'aháat

*doorway* - x̱'awool

*house post* - gáas'

*its ceiling* - a kax̱yee

*ladder; stairs* - dzeit

*piling, foundation post; floor joist* - hít tayeegáas'i

*pit; hole dug in the ground; cellar* - kóoḵ

*platform; porch* - kayáash

*rafter* - x̱aanás'

*rafters (large roof beams)* - hít kaságu

*rafters (modern)* - hít kagaadí

*roof* - hít ká

*shingle(s)* - hít kat'áayi

*shingles* - t'aa yátx'i

*smokehouse shelf* - yaash ká

*wall* - t'áa yá

*window* - x̱aawaag̱éi; x̱aawaag̱í

### 6.5.3 Building materials

*bark roofing material; tarpaper* - hít kax'úx'u

*board* - t'áa

*house timbers* - hít da.ideidí

*lumber* - kax'ás'ti

*nail* - shayéen; tuháayi

### 6.6 Occupations

*babysitter* - atyátx'i latíni

*blacksmith* - g̱ayéis' layeix̱í

*captain (in the navy)* - kak'kakwéiy s'aatí (At)

*captain (of a boat)* - yaakw yasatáni

*captain; person in charge* - kak'dakwéiy s'aatí

*carpenter* - at layeix̲ s'aatí

*dentist* - k̲aa oox̲ layeix̲í; k̲aa oox̲ yei daanéiyi

*director, planner; commander* - át k̲ukawu.aag̲ú

*doctor* - k̲aa daa yaséix̲i

*farmer* - akahéix̲i

*general; leader of war, battle* - x'áan kanáayi

*guard, watchman* - at káx̲ adéli

*healer; doctor; nurse* - k̲unáagu

*keeper of the key; jailer; night watchman* - katíx̲'aa s'aatí

*mayor* - aan s'aatí

*merchant; seller* - hoon s'aatí

*night watchman* - taat aayí adéli

*policeman; policewoman* - wáachwaan

*preacher* - sh kalneegí

*priest* - wáadishgaa

*priest; pastor; minister* - nakwnéit

*prostitute* - sh kalyéiyi

*salesman; clerk; storekeeper* - dahooní

*secretary (stenographer)* - k̲aa x̲'éidáx̲ kashxeedí

*shepherd* - wanadóo latíni

*shoemaker, cobbler* - téel layeix̲í

*silversmith* - dáanaa t'éex̲'i

*storyteller; preacher* - k̲oon sh kalneegí

*student; learner* - yaa at naskwéini

*student; pupil; scholar* - sgóonwaan

*surgeon* - k̲aadaaxaashí

*teacher* - k̲óo at latóowu (T)

*typist* - kaldáal'i

*writer; scribe; secretary* - kashxeedí

### 6.6.1 Working with cloth

*cloth; sailcloth* - s'ísaa
*hem of his/her coat, shirt, dress* - du kóon
*its hem, bottom edge (of coat, dress, shirt); rim (of hat)* - a kóon
*its lining* - a t'einyaakawoowú (At)
*knitting, crocheting* - kasné
*needle* - táax'ál'
*patch* - téey
*safety pin* - x̲'éex'wál'; x̲'éigwál'
*seam* - k̲éich'ál'
*sewing* - dak̲éis'
*s/he embroidered it on it; s/he sewed beads on it* - a káa akaawak̲áa
*s/he knitted; s/he crocheted; s/he wove* - kawdzinéi
*s/he made it (by weaving, knitting, crocheting); s/he mended it (net)* - akawsinei
*s/he sewed* - wudik̲áa
*s/he sewed it* - aawak̲áa
*s/he sewed it on it* - a kát akawlik̲áa
*s/he tanned it; s/he smoked it* - áx̲ akawlis'eik̲
*s/he untangled it; s/he trailed him/her/it; s/he undid it* - akawsikei
*thimble* - tl'ik̲naa.át
*thread; sinew* - tás
*yarn; wool* - kakéin

### 6.6.2 Working with minerals

*blacksmith* - g̲ayéis' t'éix̲'i
*silversmith* - dáanaa kat'éex̲'i

### 6.6.3 Working with wood

*carver* - at kach'áak'u
*sawmill* - kax'ás'ti daakahídi
*scraper for hemlock bark* - yees'
*s/he carved it* - akaawach'ák'w

*s/he chopped it (esp. tree, branch)* - aawas'úw
*s/he whittled it* - akaawayéx̲

## 6.6.5 Art

*bead* - kawóot
*button* - yuka.óot'; k̲aayaku.óot'i (At)
*Chilkat blanket* - naaxein
*dye* - kasék̲'x̲u
*fine needle for stringing beads* - kawóot ka.íshaa
*handiwork, handmade crafts* - k̲aa ji.eetí
*his/her handiwork, artifact* - du ji.eetí
*it's dyed; it's stained* - kawdisék̲'w
*leather needle* - lukat'íshaa
*light bluish-gray trade bead(s)* - s'eek̲ kawóot
*moccasin top* - téel ik̲keidí
*paint* - néegwál'
*root; especially spruce root* - x̲aat
*roots or vines used in basket decoration* - léet'
*s/he dyed it; s/he stained it* - akawlisék̲'w
*s/he painted it* - aawanéegwál'
*s/he pulled up spruce roots* - x̲aat awlis'él'
*soft brown wood for tanning dye* - x̲'oon
*stretcher, form for shaping* - kanágaa
*three-cornered needle for sewing skin or leather* - kat'íshaa
*timothy grass (used for basket decoration)* - sháak
*totem pole* - kootéeyaa
*unfinished basket* - x'akaskéin
*wooden form for shaping/stretching moccasins* - téel tukanágaa
*yellow cedar bark (for weaving)* - teey woodí

## 6.7 Tool

*adze* - x̲út'aa
*awl; chopping block* - s'úwaa

*axe* - shanax̱wáayi; shunax̱wáayi

*cable* - g̱ayéis' tíx'

*chain* - x̱'akakeix̱í ; wóoshnáx̱ x̱'akakéix̱i

*chainsaw* - sh daxash washéen

*chisel* - tíyaa

*chopper* - kas'úwaa

*curved carving knife* - yoo katan lítaa

*drill* - túlaa

*drill bit* - túlx'u

*file* - x'ádaa

*hammer* - táḵl

*hatchet* - shanax̱wáayi yádi

*knife with fold-in blade* - x̱'éi shadagutx̱i lítaa

*mallet, wooden hammer* - l'oowú táḵl

*marker; mark, sign* - kwéiy

*measuring stick* - kaay

*narrow saw used to cut corners off lumber; bevel saw* - t'áa shuxáshaa

*pack; backpack; pack sack* - x̱éey

*peavy* - dlágwaa

*plane for scraping wood* - aankayéx̱aa; t'áa kayéx̱aa

*pliers* - at katáx'aa

*poles used to push aside ice (from a boat)* - xáatl kaltság̱aa

*pry; stick or tool for prying; crowbar* - kít'aa

*rip saw; double-handled saw for sawing lumber* - kax'ás'aa

*rope* - tíx'

*rounded carving chisel* - kach'ák'waa

*saw* - xáshaa

*screw* - kas'éet

*screwdriver* - kas'éet katíx̱'aa

*sharpened stick (for digging up clams, roots, etc.); gardening fork* - káat'

*shovel* - ḵutl'ídaa

*sledgehammer* - té shanax̱wáayi

*square* - t'éesh kaayí

*square (for marking boards)* - t'áa shukaayí

*stone adze* - s'oow x̱út'aa

*stone axe* - tayees; yees

*string* - tíx' yádi
*tongs* - l'át'aa
*tool, tools* - jishagóon
*wedge, shim* - x̱'éex'w
*wheelbarrow; hand truck, dolly* - koojúxaa (TC)
*wheelbarrow; hand truck, dolly* - koojúxwaa (An)
*whetstone* - yayéinaa
*wire* - kaxées'
*woman's curved knife* - wéiksh
*wrench* - kas'éet kag̱úkwaa

## 6.7.7 Container

*baggage, luggage; things, stuff packed up for carrying* - at la.át
*basket* - ḵákw
*basket of woven red cedar bark* - néil'
*basket or pan used to collect berries by knocking them off the bush* - kadádzaa yeit
*basket with a rattle in the lid* - tudaxákw
*basket with rattle in the lid* - tuḵdaadaxákw
*bentwood box* - láḵt
*birch bark basket* - at daayí ḵákw
*box* - ḵóok
*bucket; pail* - x'eesháa
*container for it* - daakeit
*container for traveling provisions; lunch basket, lunch container* - wóow daakeit
*flat open basket woven from wide strips of bark (for carrying fish, etc.); large platter* - táal
*its empty shell (of house); empty container* - a xákwti
*large box for storing grease, oil* - daneit
*large cannister* - naasa.áa
*long, flat loosely woven basket for pressing out herring oil* - kaat
*over it, covering it (a container or something with an opening)* - a yanáa
*receptacle for it* - a yee.ádi
*round basket made of split red cedar branches* - ts'anéi
*small covered box* - x̱'al'daakeit

## 6.7.9 Machine

*engine cylinder connecting rod* - washéen katág̲ayi
*engine, motor* - washéen

## 6.8 Finance

*broke; penniless; without money* - kaldáanaak̲
*dime* - gút
*half dollar; fifty cents* - dáanaa shoowú
*its price, value; the money from the sale of it* - a yeidí
*it was expensive; it was precious* - x̲'awlitseen
*money, coin, dollar* - dáanaa
*poor man* - k̲'anashgidéi k̲áa
*rich man* - dáanaa s'aatí
*rich man; man of wealth; chief* - aank̲áawu
*s/he contributed; s/he donated* - kawdig̲éex'
*s/he contributed to it; s/he donated to it; s/he added to it* - át kawdig̲íx'
*s/he donated it; s/he loaded it (gun); s/he shot it (basketball)* - akaawag̲éex'
*s/he got rich; s/he got wealthy; it became profitable* - wulináalx̲
*wealth; prosperity; riches* - lanáalx̲

## 6.8.4 Financial transactions

*sale* - hoon
*s/he bought it* - aawa.oo
*s/he bought it (round, spherical object)* - akaawa.oo
*s/he bought them (lots of something)* - aawa.óow
*s/he gambled; s/he played cards* - awdlik̲áa
*s/he paid him/her; s/he paid for it* - ajeewak̲éi
*s/he sold it* - aawahoon
*s/he went peddling it; s/he went selling it* - awlihóon
*s/he went shopping* - wudlihoon

## 6.8.5 Borrow

*s/he borrowed it* - aawahées'

*s/he borrowed it (round, spherical object)* - akaawahées'

*s/he lent it to him/her* - du éet aawahís'

## 7.1.1 Stand

*s/he is standing* - hán

*s/he remained standing* - yan uwahán

*s/he stood up* - wudihaan

*they are standing* - has náḵ

*they kept standing; they stood* - yan has uwanáḵ

## 7.1.2 Sit

*he/she/it squatted; he/she it sat down low; he/she/it landed (of waterfowl, plane)* - wujiḵaaḵ

*it's sitting there* - át tán

*s/he has him/her seated there* - át as.áa

*s/he sat down* - woonook

*s/he seated him/her* - awsinook

*s/he sits; s/he is sitting* - .áa

*they are sitting* - has ḵéen

*they sat down* - has wooḵee

## 7.1.3 Lie down

*it's lying there (textile-like object)* - át .áx̱

*it's sitting there* - át satéen

*s/he has it lying there* - át akatéen; át astán

*s/he has them lying there (small, round or hoop-like objects)* - át akla.át

*they are lying there (small, round or hoop-like objects)* - át kala.át

*they're lying there (things, unconscious creatures)* - át la.át

### 7.1.8 Bend down

*it's bent* - yóo katán

*s/he bent it* - akaawataan

### 7.1.9 Move a part of the body

*he/she/it bit him/her/it* - aawayeek̲

*s/he exerted his/her full strength on it; s/he concentrated on it; s/he strove for it* - aawaxích

*s/he put his/her hand down* - yan jiwsitán

*s/he raised a hand* - kei jiwlitsák̲

*s/he raised his/her hand* - kei jiwsitán

*s/he reached his/her hand through it* - anax̲ yaawajél

### 7.2.1 Manner of movement

*he/she/it climbed the face of it* - a yáx̲ wudlitl'éit'

*he/she/it climbed up it* - a daax̲ kei wdlitl'ét'

*he/she/it crawled there on his/her/its belly; he/she/it crept there on his/her/its belly* - aadé wootlóox'

*he/she/it disappeared from there* - aadáx̲ kawdiyaa

*he/she/it fell against it (of live creature)* - át wudzigít

*he/she/it fell (of live creature)* - daak wudzigít

*he/she/it fell there (of live creature)* - aadé wdzigeet

*he/she/it is crawling around on his/her/its belly; he/she/it crawled around on his/her/its belly; he/she/it is creeping around on his/her/its belly; he/she/it crept around on his/her/its belly; he/she/it is squirming around; he/she/it squirmed around* - át wootlóox'

*he/she/it is jumping around; he/she/it jumped around* - át wujik'éin

*he/she/it is running around; he/she/it ran around* - át wujixeex

*he/she/it is sliding around; he/she/it slid around* - át wushix̲'éel'

*he/she/it is stuck there; he/she/it is squeezed (in) there* - áx̲ kawlix̲'éex'

*he/she/it leapt on it; s/he pounced on it* - a kát sh wudligás'

*he/she/it slid there* - át wushix̲'íl'

*he/she/it started running* - g̲unéi wjixíx

*it dove into the water; it slapped its tail down into the water* - héende awjit'ákw *it fell into it (round, spherical object)* - át kaawaxíx

*it fell on it (hard, solid object)* - a kát wujix̲ín

*it fell on it; it hit it (of bullet); it spread around (rumor, news)* - át uwaxíx

*it fell on it (of small, compact object)* - a káa wooxeex

*it fell (small, compact object); it came out (sun, moon)* - daak uwaxíx

*it fell through it (round, spherical object)* - anax̲ kaawaxeex

*it is swimming around there; it swam around there* - át jiwsikwaan

*it rolled to it* - át kaawagwátl

*it's falling around; it's wobbly* - át wooxeex

*it's running (of engine); it started (of engine); it's rolling (of wheel); it's spinning (of wheel)* - kaawajóox

*it swam ashore* - yan uwahín

*it swam underwater to it* - át uwax'ák

*out of control; blindly* - ux̲ kei

*s/he crawled away (from the open)* - daak̲ wudig̲wát'

*s/he fell on his/her face; s/he fell asleep while sitting up* - yan yaawagás'

*s/he fell over it; s/he tripped over it (of live creature)* - anax̲ yei wdzigít

*s/he is crawling around there; s/he crawled around there* - át wudig̲wáat'

*s/he is driving along; s/he is going along (by boat, car)* - yaa nak̲úx̲

*s/he is flying around; s/he flew around* - át wudik̲een

*s/he is walking along; s/he is going along* - yaa nagút

*s/he rowed; s/he paddled* - aawax̲áa

*s/he slipped; s/he slid* - wushix̲'éel'

*s/he started driving; s/he started going* - g̲unéi uwak̲úx̲

*s/he went (by motorized vehicle)* - wook̲oox̲

*they are swimming around there; they swam around there* - át has wusikwaan

*they flew there* - át kawdliyích

*they jumped* - kei has kawduwak'én

*they ran* - has loowagook̲

*they're flying around; they flew around* - át kawdliyeech

*they swam to it* - át yawsigóo

*they walked* - has woo.aat

## 7.2.2 Move in a direction

*aground, into shallow water* - kux

*along; down* - yaa

*ashore, onto ground; to rest* - yan~

*back and forth; to and fro; up and down* - yoo

*coming to see him/her* - du keekán

*down; out of boat, vehicle* - yei

*down to beach, shore* - yeeḵ

*(following) him, her, it* - du ít

*from hiding into open* - gági

*he/she/it arrived there; he/she/it went there* - át uwagút

*he/she/it chased it into the open* - daak awlikél'

*he/she/it emerged* - gági uwagút

*he/she/it followed it* - a ítx̱ woogoot

*he/she/it is walking around there; he/she/it walked around there* - át woogoot

*he/she/it left there* - aadáx̱ woogoot

*he/she/it ran away* - ḵut wujixeex

*he/she/it ran there* - aadé wjixeex

*he/she/it ran to it* - át wujixíx

*he/she/it waded ashore* - yan uwahóo

*he/she/it walked along it* - áx̱ woogoot

*he/she/it walked into the open;* - daak uwagút

*he/she/it walked through it* - anax̱ yaawagút

*he/she/it went there; he/she/it walked there* - aadé woogoot

*hither, toward speaker* - haat~

*inside, into the house, home* - neil~

*into a boat, vehicle* - yaax̱

*out of the water onto the beach, shore* - dáag̱i

*out to sea; out into the open; (falling) down* - daak

*(returning) back* - ḵux̱

*the group went there* - aadé (ha)s kawdik'éet'

*the group went to it* - át has kawdik'ít'

*s/he drove around it; s/he went around it; s/he circled it (by boat, car)* - a daax̱ yaawaḵúx̱

*s/he drove there; s/he went there (by boat, car)* - aadé wooḵoox̱

*s/he drove through it; s/he went through it (by boat, car)* - a tóonáx̱ yaawaḵúx̱

*s/he drove to it; s/he went to it (by boat, car)* - át uwaḵúx̱

*s/he is driving around; s/he drove around* - át wooḵoox̱

*s/he led them* - has ashoowa.aat

*s/he left it behind* - a nák̲ woogoot

*s/he migrated; s/he moved* - kei wusidák̲

*s/he moved over that way* - héide yaawagút

*s/he moved there* - aadé wligáas'z; át wuligás'

*s/he turned back* - ayawdik̲úx̲

*s/he turned back; s/he went back; s/he walked back* - ayawdigút

*s/he untangled it; s/he trailed him/her/it; s/he undid it* - akawsikei

*s/he went aboard* - yaax̲ woogoot

*s/he went ashore; s/he came to a stop* - yan uwak̲úx̲

*s/he went out to sea* - daak uwak̲úx̲

*s/he went to get it* - aag̲áa woogoot

*starting off taking off* - yetx̲

*they are walking along there; they are going along there* - áx̲ yaa (ha)s na.át

*they are walking around* - át has woo.aat

*they emerged* - gági has uwa.át

*they flew away from it* - anák̲ kawdliyeech

*they moved over that way* - héide has yaawa.át

*they ran after it* - a ítx̲ has loowagook̲

*they ran there* - aadé (ha)s loowagook̲

*they ran to it* - át has luwagúk̲

*they turned back; they went back; they walked back* - has ayawdi.át

*they walked down along it* - áx̲ has woo.aat

*they walked there; they arrived there; they went there* - át has uwa.át

*they walked there; they went there* - aadé has woo.aat

*they walked through it; they went through it* - anax̲ has yaawa.át

*they walked up there; they went up there* - áa kei (ha)s uwa.át

*they went to get it* - aag̲áa has woo.aat

*up* - kei

*up in the woods; inland; back (away from the open, away from the water's edge, inside)* - daak̲

## 7.2.6 Travel

*s/he traveled there* - aadé k̲oowateen

*s/he traveled there* - át k̲uwatín

*they are traveling around (of a group of cars or fleet of boats); they are swimming around (of a school of sea mammals)* - át has yaawagoo

*they traveled through it* - ana<u>x</u> has yaawagóo

*tourist* - sh tuwáa kasyéiyi

## 7.3.1 Carry

*he/she/it carried it on his/her/its back; he/she/it packed it on his/her/its back* - aawayaa

*he/she/it carried things on his/her/its back; he/she/it packed things on his/her/its back* - at wooyaa

*s/he carried him/her/it (live creature)* - awsinook

*s/he carried it aboard; s/he took it aboard (container or hollow object)* - yaa<u>x</u> aawataan

*s/he carried it all there; s/he took it all there* - aadé akaawajeil

*s/he carried it inside; s/he took it inside (container full of liquid or small objects)* - neil awsi.ín

*s/he carried it inside; s/he took it inside (general, compact object)* - neil aawatée

*s/he carried it; s/he took it (container or hollow object)* - aawataan

*s/he carried it (solid, complex object)* - awsitee

*s/he carried it there; s/he took it there (container full of liquid or small objects)* - át awsi.ín

*s/he carried it there; s/he took it there (container or hollow object)* - át aawatán

*s/he carried it there; s/he took it there (general, compact object)* - aadé aawatee

*s/he carried it there; s/he took it there (solid, often complex object)* - aadé awsitee

*s/he carried stuff there; s/he took stuff there* - aadé at kaawajeil

*s/he carried them there; s/he took them there (esp. baggage or personal belongings)* - aadé awli.aat

*s/he is carrying him/her/it around; s/he carried him/her/it around (live creature)* - át awsinook

*s/he is carrying it around; s/he carried it around (container or hollow object)* - át aawataan

*s/he is carrying it around; s/he carried it aroundj (textile-like object)* - át aawa.aa<u>x</u>

## 7.3.2 Move something in a direction

*he/she/it dragged it there; s/he pulled it there (esp. light object or solid, stiff object)* - aadé aawax̲óot'

*he/she/it is dragging him/her/it around; he/she/it dragged him/her/it around* - át aawax̲óot'

*s/he brought it out; s/he picked it up (long, complex object)* - kei awsitán

*s/he dragged it away; s/he pulled it away; s/he hauled it away; (heavy object or limp object such as dead animal)* - aadáx̲ awsixáat'

*s/he dragged it; s/he pulled it; s/he hauled it (esp. heavy object or limp object such as dead animal)* - awsixáat'

*s/he dragged it there; s/he pulled it there; s/he hauled it there (by motor power)* - aadé awsix̲óot'

*s/he dragged it there; s/he pulled it there; s/he hauled it there; (heavy object or limp object such as dead animal)* - aadé awsixáat'

*s/he drove it* - awsik̲oox̲

*s/he drove it there* - aadé awsik̲oox̲

*s/he drove it to it* - át awsik̲úx̲

*s/he filled it (with liquid)* - ashawlitl'ít'

*s/he filled it (with solids or abstracts)* - ashawlihík

*s/he gave it to him/her; s/he took it to him/her (container full of liquid or small objects)* - du jeet awsi.ín

*s/he gave it to him/her; s/he took it to him/her (container or hollow object)* - du jeet aawatán

*s/he gave it to him/her; s/he took it to him/her (general, esp. abstract object)* - du jeet aawatée

*s/he gave it to him/her; s/he took it to him/her (long, complex object)* - du jeet awsitán

*s/he gave it to him/her; s/he took it to him/her (round object)* - du jeet akaawatée

*s/he gave it to him/her; s/he took it to him/her (textile-like object)* - du jeet aawa.áx̲

*s/he gave them to him/her; s/he took them to him/her* - du jeet yéi awsinei

*s/he gave them to him/her; s/he took them to him/her (esp. baggage or personal belongings)* - du jeet awli.át

*s/he gave them to him/her; s/he took them to him/her (small, round or hoop-like objects)* - du jeet akawli.át

*s/he hauled it* - ayaawax̲áax'w

*s/he hung it there (esp. to dry)* - áx̲ ashayaawatée

*s/he is transporting him/her/it around; s/he transported him/her/it around* - át ayaawax̱aa

*s/he lifted him/her/it up* - kei awsinúk

*s/he moved it out of his/her way* - du jikaadáx̱ ayaawatán

*s/he packed it; s/he stacked it* - akaawachák

*s/he poured it on there* - a kaadé ayawsixaa

*s/he poured it out there; s/he emptied it there* - aadé akawsixaa

*s/he poured it there; s/he emptied it there* - át akawsixáa

*s/he pulled it in; s/he dragged it in (esp. light object or solid, stiff object)* - yan aawax̱út'

*s/he pulled it out of there* - aax̱ kei aawayísh

*s/he pulled it up (esp. line)* - kei awsiyíḵ

*s/he pulled it up there* - át awsiyíḵ

*s/he pushed the boat out (with a pole)* - yaakw daak ayawlitáḵ

*s/he put him/her/it down (live creature)* - yan awsinúk

*s/he put it there; s/he hung it there; s/he installed it there (general, compact object)* - áx̱ aawatee

*s/he put them there; s/he left them there* - áa yéi aawa.oo

*s/he returned it* - ḵux̱ aawatán

*s/he spread it out; s/he unfolded it* - áx̱ akaawayaa

*s/he straightened it out* - wooch yáx̱ awsinei

*s/he's waving it (hand, etc.); it's wagging it (tail); s/he is twirling it around above his/her head* - ashakawliyén

*s/he threw it* - kei akaawag̱íx'

*s/he threw it to it* - át aawalít

*s/he threw it to it* - át akaawax̱ích

*s/he towed it* - aawax̱aach

*s/he transported him/her/it there* - át ayaawax̱áa

*s/he turned the boat* - kei ayawli.át

*s/he wheeled it there* - aadé akawlijoox

*s/he wheeled it to it* - át akawlijúx

### 7.3.4 Handle something

*s/he brought it out; s/he picked it up (general, often compact object)* - kei aawatée

*s/he held it; s/he captured it* - awlisháat

*s/he picked it up off of it (general, compact object)* - aax̱ aawatée *s/he picked them up off of it* - aax̱ yéi awsinei

*s/he spilled it* - yax̱ akaawax̱ích

*s/he touched it; s/he picked it up; s/he took it* - át uwashée

*s/he wrapped it up; s/he tied it in a bundle* - adaawsi.áx̱w

## 7.3.5 Turn something

*s/he screwed it on it* - át akawlitíx̱'

*s/he turned it over* - áa yax̱ aawatán

*turning over* - áa yax̱

*turning over endwise* - shóo yax̱

## 7.3.6 Open/Shut

*s/he held it open; s/he tore it away (from the hook)* - ax̱'eiwas'él'

*s/he locked it* - x̱'éit akawlitíx̱'

## 7.3.7 Cover/Uncover

*(draped) over it, covering it* - a náa

*its covering; cover (over a large opening or something without an opening)* - a kaháadi

*its lid, cover (of pot, etc.)* - a yana.áat'ani

*over it, covering it (a container or something with an opening)* - a yanáa

*s/he corked it up; s/he covered his/her mouth* - ax̱'eiwadíx'

*s/he covered it* - a yanáax̱ at wootaan

*s/he pulled it over him/her/it; s/he covered him/her/it with it* - a káx̱ aawayeesh

## 7.3.8 Transportation

*anchor* - shayéinaa

*bicycle* - a kát sh kadultsex̱t át

*boat, canoe* - yaakw

*cabin (of boat); pilot house* - yaakw x̱ukahídi

*canoe made of cottonwood* - dúḵ

*canoe of caribou skins* - jaak̲úx̲

*canoe under construction* - dáax̲

*cruise ship; large ship* - yakwtlénx'

*deck of a boat* - yaakw x̲uká

*dug-out canoe designed to go through shallow waters* - seet

*gas-powered boat* - s'eenáa yaakw

*its crosspiece (of boat, snowshoe); thwart (of boat)* - yax̲ak'áaw

*its cutwater; the curved part of a bow or stern (of boat)* - a xées'i

*its mast (of boat)* - a ka.aasí

*old, worn-out boat* - l'áak̲w

*paddle* - ax̲áa

*poles used to push aside ice (from a boat)* - xáatl kaltság̲aa

*rowboat* - aandaayaagú

*sail* - yaakw yiks'ísayi

*sailboat* - s'ísaa yaakw

*s/he anchored* - shawdziyaa

*shell of a boat* - yakw daa.ideidí

*skiff; small boat; flat-bottom canoe* - yakwyádi

*ski pole(s)* - t'áa jáaji wootsaag̲ayí

*ski(s)* - t'áa jáaji

*sled* - xát'aa

*small canoe with high carved prow* - yáxwch'i yaakw

*steam engine, train* - shtéen káa

## 7.3.9 Keep/Leave something

*s/he let him/her/it go; s/he released him/her/it; s/he left him/her/it; s/he delivered it* - ajeewanák̲

*s/he put it down; s/he left it (container full of liquid or small objects)* - yan awsi.ín

*s/he put it down; s/he left it (container or hollow object)* - yan aawatán

*s/he put it down; s/he left it (general, compact object)* - yan aawatée

*s/he put it down; s/he left it (long, complex object)* - yan awsitán

*s/he put it down; s/he left it (round, spherical object)* - yan akaawatée

*s/he put it down; s/he left it (small, stick-like object)* - yan akawsitán

*s/he put it down; s/he left it (solid, complex object)* - yan awsitée *s/he put them down; s/he left them (esp. baggage or personal belongings)* - yan awli.át

*s/he put them down; s/he left them (round objects)* - yan yéi akawsinéi

### 7.4.1 Gather

*s/he gathered it* - ayawsiháa

*s/he picked berries* - k̲oowak'ít'

*s/he picked them* - aawa.ín

### 7.4.2 Join, attach

*it's connected there; it's tied there* - aadé ksixát

*s/he connected it there* - aadé akawsixát

*s/he nailed it on it* - át akawsix'óo

*s/he pulled it tight* - k'idéin akawsixát

*s/he sewed it on it* - a kát akawlik̲áa

*s/he strung them together; s/he threaded it* - akawli.ísh

*s/he stuck it to it* - át akawlis'íx'w

*s/he tied it* - akaawadúx'

*s/he tied it up* - yánde aawa.áx̲w

### 7.5 Hide

*he/she/it hid; s/he's hiding* - awdlisín

*s/he hid it; s/he's hiding it* - awlisín

### 7.5.1 Search

*s/he looked for it; s/he searched for it* - aag̲áa k̲oowashee

*s/he searched there; s/he looked there* - át k̲uwashée

### 7.5.2 Find

*s/he found it* - aawat'ei

*s/he found it (round, spherical object)* - akaawat'ei

### 7.5.3 Lose, misplace

*astray, getting lost* - k̲ut

*s/he got lost* - k̲ut wudzigeet

*s/he got lost (by boat, car)* - k̲ut wook̲oox̲

*s/he got lost (on foot)* - k̲ut woogoot

*s/he lost it* - k̲ut aawag̲éex'

*s/he lost it (round, spherical object)* - k̲ut akaawag̲éex'

*s/he lost it; s/he misplaced it (container or hollow object)* - k̲ut aawataan

*s/he lost them (of plural objects)* - k̲ut akaawlisóos

*they are lost; they got lost* - k̲ut has kaawasóos

*they got lost (on foot)* - k̲ut has woo.aat

### 7.6 Physical impact

*it pierced it; it bit him/her/it* - aadé yawdig̲eech

*it pierced it; it bit him/her/it* - át yawdig̲ích

*s/he beat it; s/he rang it; s/he stabbed it* - aawagwaal

*s/he clubbed it; s/he hit it on the head* - ashaawax̲ích

*s/he hit him/her in the face; s/he punched him/her* - ayaawagwál

*s/he kicked it; s/he stamped on it* - aawatséx̲

*s/he kneaded it* - akaawachúx

*s/he mashed it; s/he squeezed it* - akaawag̲útl

*s/he poked it; s/he jabbed at it; s/he speared it* - aawaták̲

*s/he pounded it* - akaawat'éx̲'

*s/he scraped it* - aawaxás'

*s/he scraped it; s/he softened it* - awlixwách

*s/he sharpened it* - ayaawax'át; ayaawag̲íl'

*s/he shot it* - aawa.ún

*s/he shot it (with bow and arrow); s/he chose it (in gambling with sticks)* - aawat'úk

*s/he slapped him/her/it; s/he tagged him/her/it* - aawat'ách
*they peirced it* - át yawdlig̱ích

### 7.6.1 Hit

*s/he beat him/her up; s/he assaulted him/her; s/he violently attacked him/her* - aawajáaḵw

## 7.7 Divide into pieces

*it broke (general, solid object)* - wool'éex'
*it broke (long object)* - wulil'éex'
*it's torn* - kawdis'éil'
*s/he broke it (general, solid object)* - aawal'éex'
*s/he broke it (long object)* - awlil'éex'
*s/he broke it (rope-like object)* - awlik'oots
*s/he chopped it (esp. tree, branch)* - aawas'úw
*s/he chopped it up; s/he split it (wood)* - akawlix̱óot'
*s/he chopped it (wood); s/he chipped it out (with adze)* - aawax̱út'
*s/he cut it off; s/he sawed it off* - aax̱ aawaxásh
*s/he cut it (rope-like object)* - awlixaash
*s/he cut it up; s/he carved it; s/he sliced it* - akaawaxaash
*s/he cut it (with a knife); s/he sawed it* - aawaxaash
*s/he cut; s/he did some cutting* - wudixaash
*s/he strained it; s/he filtered it; s/he drained it off* - akawlicháa
*s/he tore it* - aawas'éil'
*s/he tore it; s/he peeled it off; s/he ripped it off* - akaawas'éil'
*s/he whittled it* - akaawayéx̱

### 7.7.6 Dig

*s/he dug it* - akaawaháa
*s/he dug it up* - kei akaawaháa
*s/he gardened; s/he did some digging* - akaawahaa

*s/he planted it* - akaawahaa

*s/he pulled up spruce roots* - x̱aat awlis'él'

## 8.1 Quantity

*enough, acceptably* - G̱aa

*he/she/it is full* - shaawahík

*how many; some number (of)* - x'oon sá

*it came to an end; it was used up* - shuwaxeex

*it's piled up; it's deep* - yan kaawadlán

*less than it; (reaching, falling) short of it; not (big or far) enough for it* - a ḵín

*much, lots of, really* - aatlein

*one that matches it; an amount that matches it; equivalent to it; one like it* - a x̱ooní

*s/he ran out of it* - du jeet shuwaxíx

*there got to be many; there got to be plenty* - shayawdihaa

### 8.1.2 Number

*one* - tléix'

*one (person)* - tléináx̱

*one at a time, one by one* - tlék'G̱aa

*one (person) at a time* - tlék'G̱aanáx̱

*once, one time* - tleidahéen

*once, one time* - tlex'dahéen

*two* - déix̱

*two (people)* - dáx̱náx̱

*two at a time, two by two* - dáx̱G̱aa

*two (people) at a time* - dáx̱G̱aanáx̱

*twice, two times* - dax̱dahéen

*both* - ch'u déix̱

*three* - nás'k

*three (people)* - nás'gináx̱

*three at a time, three by three* - nás'giG̱áa

*three times* - nas'gidahéen

*four* - daax'oon

*four (people)* - daax'ooníná<u>x</u>

*four times* - daax'oondahéen

*five* - keijín

*five (people)* - keijíniná<u>x</u>

*six* - tleidooshú

*six (people)* - tleidooshóoná<u>x</u>

*seven* - da<u>x</u>adooshú

*seven (people)* - da<u>x</u>adooshóoná<u>x</u>

*eight* - nas'gadooshú

*eight (people)* - nas'gadooshóoná<u>x</u>

*nine* - gooshú<u>k</u>

*nine (people)* - gooshú<u>g</u>uná<u>x</u>

*ten* - jinkaat

*ten (people)* - jinkaadiná<u>x</u>

*eleven* - jinkaat <u>k</u>a tléix'

*eleven (people)* - jinkaat <u>k</u>a tléiná<u>x</u>

*twenty* - tlei<u>k</u>áa

*twenty (people)* - tlei<u>k</u>áaná<u>x</u>

*twenty-one* - tlei<u>k</u>áa <u>k</u>a tléix'

*twenty-one (people)* - tlei<u>k</u>áa <u>k</u>a tléiná<u>x</u>

*thirty* - nás'k jinkaat

*thirty one* - nás'k jinkaat <u>k</u>a tléix'

*one hundred* - tléix' hándit

*they multiplied; they bred* - has wudzi<u>x</u>eit

## 8.1.5 All/Some

*all; every* - ldakát

*everyone, everybody* - ch'a ldakát <u>k</u>áa

*everything* - ch'a ldakát át

*everything* - ldakát át

*some of them* - a <u>x</u>oo aa

*which (one); some (certain one)* - daa<u>k</u>w.aa sá

## 8.2 Measure

*armspan; fathom* - waat

*foot (measurement)* - k̲aa x̲'oos

*it became that far* - yéi kaawalei

*it ended there* - áa yan shukaawatán

*it extends to it; it ends at it* - át shukatán

*it got heavy; it was weighty (of abstracts)* - woodál

*measure; mile* - kaay

*measuring stick* - kaay

*pattern, model, template for it; measure of it; measurement for it* - a kaayí

## 8.2.2 Long/Short

*it became long (of stick-like object)* - wooyáat'

*it became long (of time or physical objects)* - wuliyát'

*it got that long (of stick-like object)* - yéi kaawayáat'

*it's that long (of general object)* - yéi kwliyáat'

*long* - kuwáat'

*short* - guwáatl'

*they're long (of plural, general objects)* - dliyát'x'

## 8.2.4 Size

*big* - tlein

*he/she/it is big, tall (live creature or building)* - ligéi

*it became thick* - wusikaak

*it got that thick; it thickened* - yéi kawsikaak

*it got this big; there were this many* - yéi kaawagéi

*it's big (round, spherical object)* - kayagéi

*it's narrow* - yéi kwlisáa

*it's that big around* - yéi kwditláa

*it's wide* - yawúx̲'

*it was big; there were many; there was plenty* - woogéi

*little; precious; [diminutive suffix]* - -k'

*they're big* - digéix'; kadigéix'
*they're small* - yéi kwdzigéi
*they're that big* - yéi kwdigéi
*thick* - kusakaak
*thin (flat object)* - ḵ'áatl'

### 8.2.5 Volume

*it became deep* - woodlaan
*it got that deep* - yéi kaawadláan
*it holds more* - liyék

## 8.3 Quality

*black* - t'ooch'
*blueberry juice; purple* - kanat'á kahéeni
*bright red or orange* - sheḵ'wtáax'i
*brown* - s'agwáat
*crimson red; face paint* - léiḵ'w
*dark blue* - x̱'éishx'w
*dark yellow; eagle's beak* - ch'áak' loowú
*different* - g̱unayéide
*differently* - woosh g̱unayáade; woosh g̱uwanyáade
*differently from it* - a g̱unayáade; a g̱uwanyáade (An)
*different ones; variety* - woosh g̱unayáade aa
*gold* - góon
*gray* - lawúx̱
*gray; fog* - ḵugáas'
*grayish; blond (hair)* - l'áax̱'
*green, light blue* - s'oow
*he/she/it is bruised; it's colored; it's discolored* - kawdiyés'
*it dried; it's dry* - uwaxúk
*it got sharp* - yawlik'áts'
*its color* - a kaséiḵ'u
*it's dull; it's blunt* - yaawdig̱íl

*it's dyed; it's stained* - kawdiséḵ'w

*it wore out* - wooshháash

*like it, in accordance with it, as much as it* - a yáx̱

*new; young; fresh* - yées

*old* - ch'áagu

*old; from the past* - tlagu

*orange (in color)* - shéix̱'w

*pale; pastel* - tl'áak'

*pink* - lóol

*red* - x̱'aan

*sky blue* - xáats'

*something sort of like it; something not measuring up to it; where one expects it to be* - a kayaa

*water* - héen

*yellow* - ketllóox'u

*yellow* - s'éix̱wani

*yellow* - tl'áatl'

## 8.3.1 Shape

*it looks like it; it resembles it* - a yáx̱ kaaxát

*it's crooked; s/he is crooked, wicked* - kawdzitíx̱'

*stout* - kutlá

## 8.3.2 Texture

*dried and hard; stiff (as canvas, dry fish)* - g̱ákw

*it hardened* - kaawat'íx'

*it's hard* - kasit'éex'

*it's slippery* - kashix̱'íl'k

## 8.3.3 Light

*it's bright; it's shining* - kawdigán

*it's on (light); it's burning (fire)* - át akaawagán

*it's shining on it* - a kát kawdigán
*it's sparkling; it's reflecting light* - kawdli.ít’ch
*shade, shadow(s) cast by landforms, etc.* - chéx̱’i (C)

### 8.3.4 Temperature

*cold water* - si.áat’i héen
*it's burning hot* - wusit’áax̱’
*it's frozen; it froze; it solidified; it hardened* - wudlit’íx’
*it's hot* - yaawat’áa
*it's hot; it's warm* - uwat’áa
*s/he chilled it* - awsi.át’
*s/he warmed it up* - awsit’áa

### 8.3.5 Decay

*it aged; it spoiled* - wulis’íx
*it has a hole in it* - yawóol
*rotten wood* - naaḵw
*rust* - g̱ayéis’ háatl’i

### 8.3.6 Type, kind

*he/she/it was like it; he/she/it was similar to it* - a yáx̱ wootee
*one kind, type; one way, direction* - tleiyeekaadé
*two different kinds, types; two different ways, directions* - dax̱yeekaadé

### 8.3.8 Good/Bad

*accidentally, wrongly* - ḵáakwt~
*accident; unfortunate mistake or mishap* - ḵaaḵx̱wdaagané (A)
*against it; wrongly, improperly* - a géit~
*the weather became good* - ḵoowak’ei
*he/she/it was bad; he/she/it was evil* - tlél wushk’é

*he/she/it was good; he/she/it got better; he/she/it was fine; he/she/it was pretty* - wook'éi

*it was scary; it was dangerous* - kawlix̲éitl'shán

*s/he had an accident; s/he got hurt; something bad happened to him/her* - k̲áakwt uwanéi

### 8.3.9 Appearance

*he/she/it was fancy; he/she/it was conspicuous; he/she/it was prominent* - kawlig̲éi

*it looked terrible; it looked awful; it was eerie; it was unattractive* - kawlijée

*it looks like it; it resembles it* - oowayáa

*it's spotted* - kadlich'ách'x̲; kajikáx'x̲

*it's striped* - kadlig̲áas'

*she is pretty; it is cute* - shaklig̲éi

## 8.4 Time

*after a while; later on* - dziyáagin

*any time (in the future); whenever (in the future)* - ch'a gwátgeen sá

*calendar* - dís woox̲éiyi

*the next one, the following one* - a ít aa

*Friday* - keijín yagiyee

*he/she/it got hung up; s/he got delayed; s/he got stuck* - yanax̲ wushik'éex̲'

*(in preparation) for winter* - táakw niyís

*it's his/her turn* - du éet k̲uwaháa

*it's time for it* - át k̲uwaháa

*just now; a while ago, earlier* - dziyáak

*just now; just then; still; yet* - yeisú

*late; after the appointed time* - gaaw ítx'

*now* - yeedát

*now, this time* - déi

*on time; in time* - gaaw yáx̲

*s/he is delayed* - yaawasík

*start, begin* - g̲unéi

*suddenly, immediately, right away* - ch'a yák'w; ch'a yóok'

*then, around, after, for* - aag̲áa

*time* - gaaw

*tomorrow* - seiG̲án; seiG̲ánin

*wristwatch* - jikawáach

*yesterday* - tatgé

## 8.4.1 Period of time

*day, afternoon* - yagee (T)

*day, afternoon* - yakyee

*fall; autumn* - yeis

*hour* - gaaw x̲'áak

*long ago; back then; in the old days* - ch'áakw; ch'ákw

*month* - dís

*(sometime) during it (period of time)* - a yeen

*summer; early summer* - taakw.eetí

*the other day; a few days ago* - tliyaatgé

*winter; year* - táakw

## 8.4.2 Time of the day

*dawn, daybreak* - k̲ee.á; k̲eex̲'é; k̲ei.á

*dawn, daybreak* - k̲eix̲'é (An)

*day, afternoon* - yagiyee

*during the night; in the middle of the night* - taat yeen

*dusk; twilight* - xi.áat

*evening* - xáanaa

*last night* - nisdaat

*midnight* - taat sitgawsáani

*morning* - ts'ootaat

*night* - taat

*noon* - sitgawsáan

## 8.4.7 Take time

*it was long (time)* - yeeywooyáat'
*ready, waiting for him/her to eat, drink; waiting for him/her to speak or finish speaking* - du x̱'ayee
*waiting for it* - a yeegáa; a yigáa


## 8.4.8 Speed

*fast* - tláakw
*he/she/it was fast* - woosátk


## 8.5 Location

*anywhere, anyplace; wherever* - ch'a goot'á sá
*area across, on the other side (especially of body of water)* - diyáanax̱.á
*at hand (for him/her to eat or drink)* - du x̱'ax̱án
*at the landing of a dock* - dzeit shuyee
*before his/her eyes; where he/she can see (it)* - du wak̲shiyee
*blocking his/her view; in his/her way (so that he/she can't see)* - du wak̲kas'óox'
*blocking his/her view; in his/her way (so that he/she can't see)* - du wak̲ká
*downstream; south; lower 48 states, (locally: down south)* - ixkée
*enclosed within (the folds of) it, between the folds, covers, walls of it* - a gei
*everywhere* - ch'a ldakát yé
*everywhere* - ldakát yé
*farther over; way over* - tliyaa
*the (horizontal) surface of it; on it; on top of it; in it ( a dish; a path)* - a ká
*in addition to it; along with it; to the side of it; besides that* - a kíknáx̱
*in a fort, shelter, cove* - noow gei
*in a town, on the streets of a town* - aan x̱'ayee
*in his/her possession* - du jee
*in its way; blocking its way; acting as a shield for it* - a yinaa
*in its way; keeping it away; protecting, shielding, screening from it; blocking it* - a x̱'anaa
*in public; at a potlatch, feast* - k̲aankak.eetx' (T)
*in secret (where nobody can see); away from people's view* - du yat'éináx̱

*in secret (where nobody can see); away from people's view* - ḵaa yat'éináx̱
*inside it* - a tú
*inside it (a river, road, boat, or other shallow concave landform or object)* - a yík
*in the boat* - yaakw yík
*(in) the corner of it* - a gukshatú; a gukshitú (An)
*(in) the corner, (on or along) the edge, end of it* - a shutú
*in the fire* - ganaltáak
*(in) the midst of it; among it* - a x̱oo
*(in the) river valley* - héen yík
*in the water; in the river* - héen táak
*it; that place, time, reason, fact* - á
*mountainside; around the mountain* - shaa yadaa
*mouth of river, stream* - héen wát
*on the path, trail, road; bed of the path, trail, road* - dei yík
*on the ridge or elevated part of the point (of land)* - x'aa luká
*on (top of) the water, river* - hinx̱uká
*on (top of) the water, river* - héen x'aká
*outdoors; outside* - gáan
*partway up it; halfway up it (the inside of a vessel or container)* - a kat'óot
*room, space, place for it; time for it; chance, opportunity for it* - a ya.áak
*under or inside his/her clothes; next to his/her skin* - du doonyaa
*up in the woods; inland; back (away from the open, away from the water's edge, inside); inland; interior* - daḵká
*with it* - aan


## 8.5.1 Here, there

*that (at hand)* - wé
*that (at hand) [focus]* - áwé
*that (at hand) [interrogative]* - ák.wé
*that (distant), yonder* - yú
*that (distant), yonder [focus]* - áyú
*that (distant), yonder [interrogative]* - ákyú
*this (right here)* - yá
*this (right here) [focus]* - áyá
*this/that (over here), the other* - hé

*this/that (over here), the other [focus]* - áhé
*this/that (over here), the other [interrogative]* - ák.hé

## 8.5.2 Direction

*away, off (to someplace indefinite)* - yóot~
*backwards* - k̲ux̲ dak'óol'een
*different directions* - wooshdakádin
*downstream; south* - éex
*(going, taking something) away from it* - a nák̲
*in the direction or general area of it; (headed) toward it* - a niyaadé; a yinaadé
*meeting, encountering, intercepting it; (arriving) at the same place or time as it* - du kagé
*straight ahead; directly ahead* - yaadachóon
*straight towards it; directly towards it* - a dachóon
*upstream; north* - naakée

## 8.5.3 Be at a place

*he/she/it appeared before him/her; it was apparent to him/her* - du wak̲shiyeex' yéi wootee
*he/she/it became still* - tleiyéi yéi wootee
*it got stuck on the beach* - yax̲ woodláax̲'w
*it's situated there* - át la.áa
*place; way* - yé
*s/he lived there* - áa k̲oowa.oo
*s/he stayed overnight; s/he camped out* - uwax̲éi
*s/he was with him/her; s/he stayed with him/her; s/he lived with him/her* - du x̲ánx' yéi wootee
*the building was situated there (suddenly as if overnight)* - áa wdinook

## 8.5.5 Spatial relations

*above it* - a kináak
*after it* - a ít
*alongside it; catching up with it* - a kík

*around it; about it; concerning it* - a daa

*around it (bypassing it, avoiding it); around the end of it* - a shuwadaa

*(around) the bottom of it* - a tuk̲daa

*around the fire* - gandaa

*around the outside surface of it* - a daaká

*around the top of it (object with rounded top)* - a shadaa

*at his/her back; right behind him/her* - du dzúk

*at the foot of it* - a x̲'usyee

*behind him/her; back of him/her; at his/her back* - du t'áak

*behind his/her back, where s/he can't see* - du yat'éik

*behind it* - a t'éik

*behind it; back inland from it; on the landward side of it (something on the water)* - a t'áak

*beside, alongside, next to him/her* - du t'ak̲ká

*beside, alongside, next to it* - a t'ak̲ká

*beside it, at its side* - a t'aak̲

*beside it, next to it* - a tuwán

*beside it; out past it; out away from it; (on) the outskirts of it (town)* - a t'iká

*between them* - a x̲'áak

*the beach, shore below it (a town)* - a eeg̲ayáak

*edge of it; (to the) side of it* - a wán

*facing it* - a dayéen

*fireside; by the fire, facing the fire* - gangook

*fireside; by the fire, facing the fire* - x̲'aan gook

*front of it; ahead of it* - a shuká

*in front of him/her; his/her geneology, history; his/her ancestors* - du shuká

*(in) place of it; place where it was; its imprint or aftermath* - a eetí

*inside it (a building)* - a yee

*(in) the area of it or around it, (in) its vicinity* - a déin

*middle of it* - a dagiygé

*near him/her, by him/her* - du x̲án

*near him/her, by him/her (at hand, for him/her to work with)* - du jix̲án

*near the base of it; at the foot of it; the back, rear or it (house); behind it (house); under the shelter of it (a standing object or structure)* - a k'iyee

*next door to him/her/it* - du k'idaaká

*(on) the back of it (fish); on the crest, ridge, backbone of it (hill, ridge, point)* - a litká

*on the edge, side of it (as a trail); on the shoulder of it* - a wanká

*the foot of it; below it (raised place); flat area at the end of it (lake); down from the crest of it (slope); the end of it (dock)* - a shuwee

*over his/her head; covering his/her head* - du shanáa

*separate from it; on the edge, side of it; missing its mark* - a wanáak

*shelter of it (especially a tree)* - a jiseiyí

*through its mouth* - a x̲'éináx̲

*top of it (something with a rounded top, as a mountain); above it; (elevated) over it* - a shakée

*under his/her feet* - du x̲'usyee

*underneath it; beneath it; below it* - a tayee

## 8.6 Parts of things

*the base or foot of it (a standing object)* - a k'í

*corner* - g̱úkshi

*deck of a boat* - yaakw x̲uká

*the rest of it* - a déinde aa

*face, (vertical) side, (vertical) surface of it* - a yá

*its back end; stern (of boat)* - a k'óol'

*its bowstay* - a lukatíx'i

*its cutwater; the curved part of a bow or stern (of boat)* - a xées'i

*its lining* - a t'einyaakawoowú (At)

*its mouth, opening* - a x̲'é

*its point (of a long thin pointed object)* - a lú

*its tip (of pointed object); top, tips of its branches (of tree, bush)* - a x'aan

*its tip, point* - a lux'aa

*its trim, trimming* - a x̲'ax̲éedli

*its what it is (to be) made of; its parts, components, materials* - a shagóon

*mouth of it (a river, creek)* - a wát

*the end of it* - a shú

*the inside of it (clothing, bedding); lining it* - a t'einyaa

*the inside surface of its bottom (of container, vessel)* - a taká

*one of them (a pair)* - a yaayí

*the foot of it; below it (raised place); flat area at the end of it (lake); down from the crest of it (slope); the end of it (dock)* - a shuyee *the bottom of it (a cavity)* - a táak

*pair* - woosh yaayí

*part of it; half of it* - a shoowú

## 9.1 General words

*and* - k̲a

*anyone, anybody; whoever* - ch'a aa sá

*anyone, anybody; whoever* - ch'a aadóo sá

*anything; whatever* - ch'a daa sá

*any time (in the future); whenever (in the future)* - ch'a gwátgeen sá

*anywhere, anyplace; wherever* - ch'a goot'á sá

*everyone, everybody* - ch'a ldakát k̲áa

*everything* - ch'a ldakát át

*everywhere* - ch'a ldakát yé

*it; that place, time, reason, fact* - á

*no, none, not* - tléil

*thing* - át

### 9.1.1 Be

*he/she/it was that way* - yéi wootee

*it existed; s/he was born* - k̲oowdzitee

*it's hanging there* - áx̲ g̲aashóo

*s/he became a (noun)* - (noun)-x̲ wusitee

### 9.1.2 Do

*s/he demonstrated it to him/her; s/he showed him/her how to do it; s/he performed it for him/her* - du wak̲shiyeex' yéi awsinei

*s/he did it; s/he behaved that way* - yéi k̲oowanook

*s/he does it; s/he is doing it; s/he works on it; s/he is working on it* - yéi adaanéi

*s/he finished it; s/he completed it* - yan ashawlihík

*s/he finished it; s/he completed it* - yan awsinéi

*s/he fixed it; s/he did that to it* - yéi awsinei

*s/he's in the habit of doing it* - akwshitán
*s/he worked; s/he did that* - yéi jeewanei

### 9.1.3 Thing

*nothing* - tlél daa sá

### 9.2.1 Adjectives

*big* - tlein
*female (animal)* - sheech
*female (animal)* - shich
*future (noun), (noun) to be, for (noun)* - sákw
*little; precious; [diminutive suffix]* - -k'
*long* - kuwáat'
*new; young; fresh* - yées
*old* - ch'áagu
*old; from the past* - tlagu
*short* - guwáatl'
*stout* - kutlá
*thick* - kusakaak
*thin (flat object)* - ḵ'áatl'

### 9.2.2 Adverbs

*accidentally, wrongly* - ḵáakwt~
*against it; wrongly, improperly* - a géit~
*(at) first, originally* - shux'áanáx̱
*(at) first; originally; in the beginning* - shóogunáx̱
*away, off (to someplace indefinite)* - yóot~
*beginning* - g̱unayéi
*broke; penniless; without money* - kaldáanaaḵ
*by mistake, wrongly* - ḵwaaḵx̱ daaḵ
*different* - g̱unayéide
*different directions* - wooshdakádin

*differently* - woosh g̱unayáade; woosh g̱uwanyáade

*differently from it* - a g̱unayáade

*downstream; south* - éex

*enough, acceptably* - g̱aa

*enough; adequate* - tl'ag̱áa

*from hiding into open* - gági

*from the woods onto the beach, shore* - éeg̱i

*hand it here, bring it here* - haandé

*how* - wáa sá

*however, any which way* - ch'a koogéiyi

*in the direction or general area of it; (headed) toward it* - a yinaadé

*into a boat, vehicle* - yaax̱

*into water* - héeni; héenx̱

*in vain; for nothing; without success* - ch'a g̱ég̱aa

*just now; a while ago, earlier* - dziyáak

*just now; just then; still; yet* - yeisú

*lacking it; without it* - a eetéenáx̱

*one kind, type; one way, direction* - tleiyeekaadé

*out of control; blindly* - ux̱ kei

*out of the water onto the beach, shore* - dáag̱i

*outside* - yux̱

*sideways* - tl'aadéin

*slowly* - kaldaag̱éináx̱

*sometimes* - wáa yateeyi yéix'

*sometimes, once in a while* - wáang̱aneens

*start, begin* - g̱unéi

*then, around, after, for* - aag̱áa

*through its mouth* - a x̱'éináx̱

*thus, specifically* - yéi

*to completion* - yax̱

*too much* - ḵútx̱

*(toward) downstream* - íxde

*toward the inland, interior; up to the woods; back (away from the open)* - dáḵde

*truly, really; in truth, for sure* - x'éig̱aa

*turning over* - áa yax̱

*turning over endwise* - shóo yax̱

*two different kinds, types; two different ways, directions* - dax̱yeekaadé

*underground* - yanax̱

*very* - ḵúnáx̱

*well* - k'idéin

### 9.2.3 Pronouns

*he, she [independent]* - hú

*him, her* - du ee~

*him, her, it [object]* - a-

*his/her [possessive]* - du

*how many; some number (of)* - x'oon sá

*I [independent]* - x̱át

*I [subject]* - x̱a-

*its [possessive]* - a

*me [object]* - x̱at

*my [possessive]* - ax̱

*one, one of [object]* - aa

*our [possessive]* - haa

*their [possessive]* - has du

*them [object]* - has

*they [independent]* - hás

*they [subject]* - has

*together [object]* - wooch; woosh

*us [object]* - haa

*we [independent]* - uháan

*we [subject]* - too-

*you (plural) [independent]* - yeewháan

*you (plural) [object]* - yee

*you (plural) [subject]* - yee-

*your (plural) [possessive]* - yee

*your (singular) [possessive]* - i

*you (singular) [independent]* - wa.é

*you (singular) [object]* - i-

*you (singular) [subject]* - i-

## 9.2.4 Prepositions, postpositions

*along, via; including the time of* - -náx̱
*(along) with, by means of; as soon as* - een
*(along) with, by means of; as soon as* - teen
*(along) with, by means of; as soon as* - tin
*at (the scene of); at (the time of)* - -x'
*because of; by means of* - -ch
*beyond it, more than it; too much; excessively* - a yáanáx̱
*(distributed) in the area of; (going) after, (waiting) for; about the time of* - -g̱aa
*for him/her* - du jeeyís
*for it; to that end* - a yís
*from, out of; since* - -dáx̱
*(going, taking something) away from it* - a náḵ
*(in prolonged contact) at; (repeatedly arriving) at; being, in the form of* - -x̱
*is/are at* - -u
*less than it; (reaching, falling) short of it; not (big or far) enough for it* - a ḵín
*like it, in accordance with it, as much as it* - a yáx̱
*(resting) at; coming to, arriving at; moving about* - -t
*to, toward; until; in the manner of* - -dé(i) ~ -de(i)
*with it* - aan
*without it; lacking it* - a g̱óot

## 9.2.6 Particles

*[expression of mild surprise]* - shé
*[expression of strong surprise]* - gwáa
*[focus + interrogative]* - ágé
*[interrogative - marks WH-questions]* - sá
*[interrogative marks yes-no questions]* - gé
*[puts focus on preceding phrase]* - á
*actually; in fact; contrary to what was thought* - ḵachoo
*again; still; some more* - tsu
*already, (by) now* - de
*also, too, as well* - tsú
*although, even though, however, nonetheless, yet* - ch'a aan

*always; [auxiliary]* - nooch

*always, all the time, constantly* - ch'a tlákw; tlákw

*the same* - ch'u shóogu

*as if; if only; even if* - óosh

*at least, once in a while* - ch'a k'ikát

*be sure not to* - tsé

*different, other* - ch'a g̱óot

*Eh?; I wonder* - kwshé

*the very, just* - ch'a

*first* - s'é

*forever* - ch'u tleix̱

*however* - ḵu.aa

*I hope; would that* - gu.aal

*indeed, for sure* - dágáa

*I thought* - ḵashde

*just, simply; just then* - tle

*no* - tléik'

*now, this time* - déi

*only, just* - ch'as

*only then* - tsá

*ordinary, usual* - ch'a yéi

*perhaps* - gwál

*perhaps; I guess, it would seem* - gí

*perhaps, probably* - shákdéi

*still, even* - ch'u

*suddenly, immediately, right away* - ch'a yák'w

*suddenly, immediately, right away* - ch'a yóok'

*that (at hand) [focus]* - áwé

*that (at hand) [interrogative]* - ák.wé

*that (distant), yonder [focus]* - áyú

*that (distant), yonder [interrogative]* - ákyú

*this (right here) [focus]* - áyá

*this (right here) [interrogative]* - ákyá

*this/that (over here), the other [focus]* - áhé

*this/that (over here), the other [interrogative]* - ák.hé

*thus, that's how* - ayáx̱

*very* - tlax̱

*when, while* - ch'u tlei

*yes* - aáa

*you see* - x̱á

## 9.2.7 Interjections

*[exclamation toward someone who is putting on airs in order to impress others]* - Ha.é!

*Check it out!; Wow!* - É!

*Cool it!; Calm down!* - Ch'a keetáanáx̱!

*Cute!* - Óos'k'!

*Don't!; Stop it!* - Ilí!

*Good grief!* - Hadláa!

*maybe; I'm not sure; [expression of uncertainly]* - kwshéi

*Oh no!; Yikes!* - Aganáa!

*Oops!* - Tláp!

*Ouch!* - Hú!

*Poor baby!* - Haa yátx'u ée!

*Poor thing!* - Eesháan!

*See how you are!; Look what you did!* - Doó!

*Shame on you! [reprimand]* - Húsh!

*Shut up!; Be quiet!* - Sh eelk'átl'!

*Stop it!; That's enough!* - Déi áwé!

*Thank you!* - Gunalchéesh!

*That's all!; All gone!; No more!; All done!* - Hóoch!

*Wait!* - Ilí s'é!

*Yikes!; Scary!* - Atskanée!

*Yuck!; Eeeew!* - Ée!

*Yum!* - Éits'k'!

## 9.3.4 Plurality

*[plural marker for kinship terms]* - hás

*[pluralizer]* - dag̱a-

## 9.7 Name

*Chookaneidí; a clan of the Eagle moiety whose principal crests are the Porpoise and Brown Bear* - Chookaneidí

*Daḵl'aweidí, locally called "Killer Whale"; a clan of the Eagle moiety whose principal crest is the Killer Whale* - Daḵl'aweidí

*Deisheetaan, locally called "Beaver"; a clan of the Raven moiety whose principal crest is the Beaver* - Deisheetaan

*G̱aanax̱teidí, locally called "Frog"; a clan of the Raven moiety whose principal crest is the Frog* - G̱aanax̱teidí

*his/her name; his/her namesake* - du saayí

*his/her namesake* - du tlagooḵwansaayí

*Ḵaach.ádi, locally called "Sockeye"; a clan of the Raven moiety whose principal crest is the Sockeye* - Ḵaach.ádi

*Kaagwaantaan, locally called "Wolf"; a clan of the Eagle moiety whose principal crest is the Wolf* - Kaagwaantaan

*Kiks.ádi, locally called "Frog"; a clan of the Raven moiety whose principal crest is the Frog* - Kiks.ádi

*Kwaashk'i Ḵwáan, locally called "Humpback Salmon"; a clan of the Raven moiety whose principal crest is the Humpback Salmon* - Kwaashk'i Ḵwáan

*L'eeneidí, locally called "Dog Salmon"; a clan of the Raven moiety whose principal crest is the Dog Salmon* - L'eeneidí

*L'ukaax̱.ádi, locally called "Sockeye"; a clan of the Raven moiety whose principal crest is the Sockeye* - L'ukaax̱.ádi

*L'uknax̱.ádi, locally called "Coho"; a clan of the Raven moiety whose principal crest is the Coho* - L'uknax̱.ádi

*name* - saa

*Shangukeidí, locally known as "Thunderbird"; a clan of the Eagle moiety whose principal crest is the Thunderbird* - Shangukeidí

*s/he called him/her/it that (name)* - yéi aawasáakw

*s/he named him/her/it that; s/he nominated him/her* - yéi aawasáa

*Suḵteeneidí, locally called "Dog Salmon"; a clan of the Raven moiety whose principal crest is the Dog Salmon* - Suḵteeneidí

*T'aḵdeintaan, locally called "Seagull"; a clan of the Raven moiety whose principal crest is the Seagull* - T'aḵdeintaan

*Teiḵweidí, locally called "Brown Bear"; a clan of the Eagle moiety whose principal crest is the Brown Bear* - Teiḵweidí

*Tsaagweidí; a clan of the Eagle moiety whose principal crests are the Seal and Killerwhale* - Tsaagweidí

*Was'eedeidí; a clan of the Eagle moiety whose principal crests are the Wolf and Auklet* - Was'eeneidí

*Yanyeidí, locally known as "Bear"; a clan of the Eagle moiety whose principal crest is the Brown Bear* - Yanyeidí

## 9.7.2 Name of a place

*Alaska* - Anáaski

*Anchorage* - Áankich

*Angoon* - Aangóon

*Atlin* - Áa Tlein

*Auke Bay* - Áak'w

*Haines* - Deishú

*Hoonah* - Gaawt'ak̲.aan; Xunaa

*Juneau; Gold Creek (in Juneau)* - Dzántik'i Héeni

*Kake* - K̲éex̲'; K̲éix̲'

*Ketchikan* - Kichx̲áan

*Killisnoo* - Kenasnoow

*Klawock* - Lawáak

*Klukwan* - Tlákw Aan

*Kuiu Island people* - Kooya K̲wáan

*Lituya Bay* - Ltu.aa

*people of Admiralty Island* - Xudzidaa K̲wáan

*people of Atlin* - Áa Tlein K̲wáan

*people of Auke Bay, southern Lynn Canal, Juneau area, and northern Admiralty Island* - Áak'w K̲wáan

*people of Cape Fox, Saxman* - Sanyaa K̲wáan

*people of Dry Bay* - G̲unaax̲oo K̲wáan

*people of Kake* - K̲éex̲' K̲wáan

*people of Kaliakh River (Cape Yakataga to Controller Bay)* - G̲alyáx̲ K̲wáan

*people of Klawock* - Hinyaa K̲wáan

*people of Sitka* - Shee At'iká K̲wáan

*Petersburg* - Gántiyaakw Séedi

*Russia* - Anóoshi aaní

*Sitka* - Sheet'ká

*Skagway* - Shg̲agwei

*Stikine River* - Shtax'héen

*Takhini hot springs (north of Whitehorse, Yukon Territory)* - Tax̱héeni

*Taku* - T'aaḵú

*Teslin* - Deisleen

*Teslin Lake people* - Deisleen Ḵwáan

*Wrangell* - Ḵaachx̱ana.áak'w

*Yakutat* - Yaakwdáat

~

# Appendix:
# *Derivational Strings for Motion Verbs*

*Adapted from Leer, 1991*

The groups of derivational strings outlined here pertain to motion verbs. Any motion verb can be paired with any of these groups of direction words as long as the combination makes sense. Each group of derivational strings below is characterized by belonging to one of the four conjugation prefix groups: *ø-, na-, ga-,* or *g̲a* and by having a unique repetitive imperfective form.

Four verb stems are used throughout this document to illustrate the verb stem plus direction word combinations in the imperative, perfective, and repetitive imperfective forms. The verbs stems are: *-goot* 'for (singular) subject to walk, go on foot'; *-.aat* 'for (plural) subject to walk, go on foot'; *-k̲oox̲* 'for subject to go by motorized vehicle'; and *-taan* 'for subject to carry, take object (usually container or hollow object)'.

Note how the verb stem length and tone changes from group to group in each of the given forms for a particular verb. For a more thorough description of motion verbs, see the section titled VERB TYPES in the introduction.

—

**Ø- conjugation Derivational Strings**

Group I. Repetitive forms have -ch suffix.
Group II. Repetitive forms use the -x̲ form of the postposition and have long low verb stem.
Group III. Repetitive forms have -x̲ suffix.
Group IV. Repetitive forms have yoo preverb + I form of the classifier + -k suffix.
Group V. Repetitive forms have yaa preverb + -ch suffix.
Group VI. Repetitive forms have ya-u- prefixes and -x̲ suffix.

**Na- conjugation Derivational Strings**

Group VII. Repetitive forms have yoo preverb + I form of the classifier + -k suffix.

**Ga- conjugation Derivational Strings**

Group VIII. Repetitive forms have kei preverb + -ch suffix.

**G̲a- conjugation Derivational Strings**

Group IX. Repetitive forms have *yei* preverb + *-ch* suffix.

—

# Ø- conjugation Derivational Strings

**Group I. Repetitive forms have -*ch* suffix.**
*(motion toward an area)*

| | |
|---|---|
| 1. kei | moving up |
| 2. ux̲ kei | moving out of control, blindly, amiss |
| 3. N x̲'éi kei | catching up with N |
| 4. yei | getting out of a canoe, boat, vehicle |
| 5a. yeek̲ / yeik̲ / eek̲ | moving down to beach, shore |
| 5b. héeni yeek̲ | moving down into the water |
| 6. daak̲ | moving up from beach, away from open |
| 7. k̲wáak̲x̲ daak̲ | doing by mistake, erroneously |
| 8. daak | moving out to sea, into open, onto fire |
| 9a. k̲ux̲ / k̲úx̲dei | returning, going/coming back |
| 9b. P-x' k̲ux̲ | returning to P |

Examples:

| Direction word + verb stem | Imperative | Perfective | Repetitive Imperfective |
|---|---|---|---|
| *kei + -goot* | *Kei gú!*<br>Go up! | *kei uwagút*<br>s/he went up | *kei gútch*<br>s/he goes up |
| *daak̲ + -.aat* | *Daak̲ yi.á!*<br>You all go inland! | *daak̲ has uwa.át*<br>they went inland | *daak̲ has .átch*<br>they go inland |
| *daak + -k̲oox̲* | *Daak k̲úx̲!*<br>Go out to sea! | *daak uwak̲úx̲*<br>s/he went out to sea | *daak k̲úx̲ch*<br>s/he goes out to sea |
| *k̲ux̲ + -taan* | *K̲ux̲ tán!*<br>Bring it back! | *k̲ux̲ aawatán*<br>s/he brought it back | *k̲ux̲ atánch*<br>s/he brings it back |

**Group II. Repetitive forms use the -x̱ form of the postposition and have long low verb stem.**
*(motion toward terminus)*

| | |
|---|---|
| 1. P-t (~-x̱ ~-dei) | arriving at P, coming to P |
| 2a. yan (~yax̱~yándei) | moving ashore, coming to rest, to a stop |
| 2b. P-x' yan (~yax̱~yándei) | coming to rest, to a stop at P |
| 3. P-náx̱ yan (~yax̱~yándei) | moving across P, to the other side of P |
| 4. kux (~kuxx̱~kúxdei) | moving around, into shallow water |
| 5a. neil (~neilx̱~neildéi) | moving inside, coming home |
| 5b. P-x' neil (~neilx̱~neildéi) | moving inside house at P |
| 6. haat (~haax̱~haa(n)déi) | moving toward speaker |
| 7. yóot (~yóox̱~yóodei) | going away |

Examples:

| Direction word + verb stem | Imperative | Perfective | Repetitive Imperfective |
|---|---|---|---|
| *P-t~ + -goot* | *Át gú!*<br>Go there! | *át uwagút*<br>s/he went there | *áx̱ goot*<br>s/he goes there |
| *haat~ + -.aat* | *Haat yi.á!*<br>You all come here! | *haat has uwa.át*<br>they came here | *haax̱ has .aat*<br>they go inland |
| *yan~ + -k̲oox* | *Yan k̲úx̱!*<br>Go ashore! | *yan uwak̲úx̱*<br>s/he went ashore | *yax̱ k̲oox̱*<br>s/he goes ashore |
| *P-t~ + -taan* | *Du jeet tán!*<br>Give it to him/her! | *du jeet aawatán*<br>s/he gave it to him/her | *du jeex̱ ataan*<br>s/he gives it to him/her |

**Group III. Repetitive forms have -x̲ suffix.**
*(motion originating from or confined to a location)*

| | |
|---|---|
| 1. P-x' | coming/heading into the area of P |
| 2. N yáa | coming up to N |
| 3. N g̲unayáa | separating from N |
| 4. N jisháa(x') | getting ahead of N |
| 5. gági | emerging, coming out into the open |
| 6. dáag̲i | coming out of the water |
| 7. héeni | going into the water |
| 8. g̲unayéi/g̲unéi | starting off, beginning to V |
| 9. P-x̲ | moving in place at P |
| 10. P-x' yax̲ | turning over by P |
| 11. áa yax̲ | turning over |
| 12. shóo yax̲ | turning over by the end |
| 13. yetx̲/yatx̲/yedax̲ | starting off, taking off |

Examples:

| Direction word + verb stem | Imperative | Perfective | Repetitive Imperfective |
|---|---|---|---|
| *gági + -goot* | *Gági gú!*<br>Emerge! | *gági uwagút*<br>s/he emerged | *gági gútx̲*<br>s/he emerges |
| *gági + -.aat* | *Gági yi.á!*<br>You all emerge! | *gági has uwa.át*<br>they emerged | *gági has .átx̲*<br>they emerge |
| *g̲unéi + -k̲oox̲* | *G̲unéi k̲úx̲!*<br>Get going! | *g̲unéi uwak̲úx̲*<br>s/he got going | *g̲unéi k̲úx̲x̲*<br>s/he goes ashore |
| *áa yax̲ + -taan* | *Áa yax̲ taan!*<br>Turn it over! | *áa yax̲ aawatán*<br>s/he turned it over | *áa yax̲ atánx̲*<br>s/he turns it over |

**Group IV. Repetitive forms have *yoo* preverb + I form of the classifier + *-k* suffix.** *(oscillatory motion)*

| | |
|---|---|
| 1. yoo | moving back and forth; to and fro |
| 2. yan yoo | moving up and down (from rest, from the ground) |

Note:
These forms were documented in Leer (1991) however, speakers consulted for this project are not familiar with them. For examples, see Leer (1991).

**Group V. Repetitive forms have *yaa* preverb + *-ch* suffix.**
All non-repetitive forms have *ya-u-* prefixes on the verb. This derivational string is always preceded by a postpositional phrase. *(moving obliquely, circuitously)*

| | |
|---|---|
| 1. P-x̱ | moving circuitously, obliquely along P |
| 2. N daax̱ | circling around N |
| 3. P-dei | moving circuitously, obliquely toward P |
| 4. haandéi | moving over this way (toward speaker) |
| 5. héidei | moving over that way (away from speaker) |
| 6. P-dáx̱ | moving circuitously, obliquely away from P |
| 7. N jikaadáx̱ | getting out of N's way |
| 8. P-náx̱ | moving circuitously, obliquely through N |
| 9. P-x' | moving circuitously at P; making the round of P |
| 10. N daséi(x') | trading places with N |

Examples:

| Direction word + verb stem | Imperative | Perfective | Repetitive Imperfective |
|---|---|---|---|
| *héide + -goot* | *Héide woogú!*<br>Move over! | *héide yaawagút*<br>s/he moved over | *héide yaa gútch*<br>s/he moves over |
| *P-náx̱ + -.aat* | *Anax̱ yay.á!*<br>You all walk through it! | *anax̱ has yaawa.át*<br>they walked through it | *anax̱ yaa has .átch*<br>they walk through it |
| *N daax̱ + -ḵoox̱* | *A daax̱ wooḵúx̱!*<br>Drive around it! | *a daax̱ yaawaḵúx̱*<br>s/he drove around it | *a daax̱ yaa ḵúx̱ch*<br>s/he drives around it |
| *N jikaadáx̱ + -taan* | *Du jikaadáx̱ wootán!*<br>Move it out of his/her way! | *du jikaadáx̱ ayaawatán*<br>s/he moved it out of his/her way | *du jikaadáx̱ yaa atánch*<br>s/he moves it out of his/her way |

**Group VI. Repetitive forms have *ya-u-* prefixes and *–x̲* suffix.**
All verb forms use the *a-ya-u-* prefixes and D-component of the classifier.

a-ya-(u-)-D + verb stem turning back

Examples:

| Direction word + verb stem | Imperative | Perfective | Repetitive Imperfective |
|---|---|---|---|
| *a-ya-u-d-g̲oot* | *Ayeedag̲ú!* | *ayawdig̲út* | *awudag̲útx̲* |
| | Turn back! | s/he turned back | s/he turns back |
| *a-ya-u-d-.aat* | *Ayeeda.á!* | *has ayawdi.át* | *has awuda.átx̲* |
| | You all turn back! | they turned back | they turn back |
| *a-ya-u-d-k̲oox̲* | *Ayidak̲úx̲!* | *ayawdik̲úx̲* | *awudak̲úx̲x̲* |
| | Turn back! | s/he turned back | s/he turns back |

# Na- conjugation Derivational Strings

**Group VII. Repetitive forms have *yoo* preverb + I form of the classifier + *-k* suffix.**
*(unbounded motion proceeding directly)*

| | |
|---|---|
| 1. ---* | moving (along) |
| 2. P-t** | moving about P (often no repetitive form) |
| 3. P-x̲ | moving along P |
| 4. P-dei | moving toward P |
| 5. P-dáx̲ | moving away from P |
| 6. P-náx̲ | moving by way of P |
| 7a. yux̲ | moving out of house |
| 7b. P-x' yux̲ | moving out of house at P |
| 8. P-nák̲ | leaving P behind |
| 9. P-g̲aa | going to get P |

*Note: String (1) above indicates no postpositional phrase. Na- conjugation motion verbs with no preceding postpositional phrase give the meaning "moving along."

**Note: Regarding (2) P-t "moving about P" above, this string is unique in that it has no progressive imperfective form and the perfective form conveys a present tense meaning as well as a past tense meaning.

Examples:

| Direction word + verb stem | Imperative | Perfective | Repetitive Imperfective |
|---|---|---|---|
| *P-dáx̲ + -goot* | *Aadáx̲ nagú!*<br>Leave there! | *aadáx̲ woogoot*<br>s/he left there | *aadáx̲ yoo yagútk*<br>s/he leaves there |
| *P-g̲aa + -.aat* | *Aag̲áa nay.á!*<br>You all go get it! | *aag̲áa (ha)s woo.aat*<br>they went to get it | *aag̲áa yoo (ha)s ya.átk*<br>they go get it |
| *P-de(i) + -k̲oox̲* | *Aadé nak̲oox̲!*<br>Drive there! | *aadé wook̲oox̲*<br>s/he drove there | *aadé yoo yak̲úx̲k*<br>s/he drives around it |
| *P-t + -taan* | *Át nataan!*<br>Carry it around! | *át aawataan*<br>s/he is carrying it around; s/he carried it around | *[does not occur]* |

# Ga- conjugation Derivational Strings

**Group VIII. Repetitive forms have *kei* preverb + *-ch* suffix.**
Preverb *kei* is used in repetitive, progressive, and future forms *(inceptive motion)*

1. ---* taking off, starting off, picking up
2. P-dáx̱ taking off from P, starting off from P, picking up from P
3. ḵut going astray, getting lost

*Note: String (1) above indicates no postpositional phrase. Ga-conjugation motion verbs with no preceding postpositional phrase give the meaning "taking off, starting off, or picking up" depending on the verb.

Examples:

| Direction word + verb stem | Imperative | Perfective | Repetitive Imperfective |
|---|---|---|---|
| *ḵut + -goot* | *[does not occur]* | *ḵut woogoot*<br>s/he got lost | *ḵut kei gútch*<br>s/he gets lost |
| *ḵut + -.aat* | *[does not occur]* | *ḵut has woo.aat*<br>they got lost | *ḵut kei (ha)s .átch*<br>they get lost |
| *ḵut + -ḵoox̱* | *[does not occur]* | *ḵut wooḵoox̱*<br>s/he got lost | *ḵut kei ḵúx̱ch*<br>s/he gets lost |
| *--- + -taan* | *Gataan!*<br>Carry it! | *aawataan*<br>s/he carried it | *kei atánch*<br>s/he carries it |

# G̱a- conjugation Derivational Strings

**Group IX. Repetitive forms have *yei* preverb + *-ch* suffix.**
Preverb *yei* is used in repetitive, progressive, and future forms
*(motion downward)*

| | |
|---|---|
| 1. ---* | falling (only w/ nontransitives) |
| 2. yaa | moving down (no yaa before aspect marker yei) |
| 3. yaax̱ | getting into canoe, boat, or other vehicle |
| 4. yanax̱ | moving into the earth |
| 5. P-x̱ | moving down along P |
| 6. héenx̱ | moving into the water |
| 7. P-náx̱ | moving down by way of P, through P |

*Note: String (1) above indicates no postpositional phrase. G̱a-conjugation motion verbs with no preceding postpositional phrase give the meaning "falling" and only occur with non-transitive verbs.

Examples:

| Direction word + verb stem | Imperative | Perfective | Repetitive Imperfective |
|---|---|---|---|
| *yaax̱ + -goot* | *Yaax̱ g̱agú!*<br>Go aboard! | *yaax̱ woogoot*<br>s/he went aboard | *yaax̱ yei gútch*<br>s/he goes aboard |
| *P-x̱ + -.aat* | *Áx̱ g̱ay.á!*<br>You all walk down along it! | *áx̱ (ha)s woo.aat*<br>they walked down along it | *áx̱ yei (ha)s .átch*<br>they walk down along it |
| *yaax̱ + -taan* | *Yaax̱ g̱ataan!*<br>Carry it aboard! | *yaax̱ aawataan*<br>s/he carried it aboard | *yaax̱ yei atánch*<br>s/he carries it aboard |

www.ingramcontent.com/pod-product-compliance
Lightning Source LLC
Chambersburg PA
CBHW060102170426
43198CB00010B/733
*9780982578667*